GRANT APPLICATION WRITER'S HANDBOOK

The woodcut print by Damon Lehrer pictured here illustrates the passage in the book of Genesis in which Jacob wrestles with an angel. I hope this book will help my readers wrestle with the process of writing grant applications—and that my readers, like Jacob, will prevail.

GRANT APPLICATION WRITER'S HANDBOOK

Liane Reif-Lehrer, Ph.D.

Tech-Write Consultants/Erimon Associates

JONES AND BARTLETT PUBLISHERS

Boston   London

Editorial, Sales, and Customer Service Offices
Jones and Bartlett Publishers
One Exeter Plaza
Boston, MA 02116
1-617-859-3900
1-800-832-0034

Jones and Bartlett Publishers International
7 Melrose Terrace
London W6 7RL
England

Portions of this book first appeared in *Writing a Successful Grant Application* © 1989, 1982.

Library of Congress Cataloging-in-Publication Data
Reif-Lehrer, Liane, 1934–
    Grant application writer's handbook/ by Liane Reif-Lehrer.
      p. cm. — (The Jones and Bartlett series in biology)
    Includes bibliographical references and index.
    ISBN 0-86720-874-0
    1. Proposal writing in medicine.   2. Proposal writing for grants.
    3. Medicine—Research grants.   I. Title.   II. Series.
    R853.P75R439   1995
    808' .06661—dc20

94-28487
CIP

Acquisitions Editor: Clayton Jones
Editorial Assistant: Deborah L. Haffner
Production Editor: Nadine Fitzwilliam
Manufacturing Buyer: Dana L. Cerrito
Typesetting: LeGwin Associates
Cover Design: Hannus Design Associates
Printing and Binding: Hamilton Printing Company
Cover Printing: New England Book Components

The detail on the cover of this book is an electronically scanned and manipulated image of the leaves from the woodcut pictured on the frontispiece. The woodcuts and etchings on the Part Openers of this book are by Damon Lehrer. The woodcuts for Parts I and VII are from the book *Aphorisms* by William Cole, illustrated by Damon Lehrer. All the plates are reproduced with permission of the artist.

Printed in the United States of America
98 97 96 95   10 9 8 7 6 5 4 3 2

Dedication

To my husband, Dr. Sherwin (Sam) Lehrer, and my children, Damon and Erica, for all I have learned from them and for always "bearing with me;"

To my mother, Clara Reif, who, at great sacrifice to herself, made it possible for me to have the luxury of a lengthy education;

To my brother, Dr. Fred Reif, for all that he taught me and for taking it for granted that I would have a career;

To all those who taught me and encouraged me;

To Cho Cho San, Pete, and Kitty for sharing their lives with us;

And, as always,

To "The Little Prince" (A. de St. Exupéry).

CONTENTS

INTRODUCTION

Please use the material conveyed in this book as a guide—not as a set of rules. Every Study Section is different, every granting agency is different, every Reviewer is different, every principal investigator is different! *You* are responsible for your proposal. You must feel comfortable with what you submit.

Please do not use this book in place of reading the instructions provided by the National Institutes of Health (NIH) or other granting agency. This book is intended as an aid. It is your responsibility to read the instructions of the granting agency carefully and to follow them meticulously. If you (1) have a good project idea that interests the funding agency, (2) respond to the needs and instructions of the granting agency to which you are applying, and (3) practice the principles of good proposal writing set forth in this book, you will be in a good position to compete for funding.

Note that this book was written in the spring, summer, and fall of 1993. The material presented is, to the best of my knowledge, correct at the time of writing. Some corrections and additions were made at press time in August 1994 and for the second printing January 1995 to make you aware of recent changes. Although the principles presented are unlikely to change for some time, the specifics *do* change frequently. With new directors at both NIH and NSF, the rate of change at both agencies is likely to accelerate in the next few years. Always check with your potential granting agency about changes in policy and procedures—and about whether it is interested in your proposal objectives—before investing time in preparing an application.

It would be unwise for a grant applicant to permit redundancies to creep into her/his proposal and thereby squander precious space in a document with stringent page limits. However, this book has no page limits. Therefore, I have intentionally introduced redundancies on occasion for reasons of emphasis or convenience to readers, especially those who use this book as a reference, rather than reading it from cover to cover. I hope readers will find these repetitions helpful rather than annoying.

Although grant-seekers often make statements such as "My grant is due," or "I have to write a grant," they are actually referring to the application. The grant is the award they get if their application is successful. Also, you should be aware that NIH and some other agencies have very specific definitions of words such as "agency," "institution," "applicant," "investigator," and "grantee." "Agency" technically refers to the funding agency, that is, the organization that awards the funding; the "institution" generally refers to the organization that applies for the funding. The word "applicant" refers to the institution of the principal investigator (PI); "grantee" refers to this institution after it has been awarded funding. These terms are often used more casually in the scientific community, and I have also taken this liberty, referring sometimes, for example, to a PI who has received an award as a "grantee," and to her/his institution as the "grantee's institution." Likewise, strictly speaking, at NIH, an application that is funded results in a grant for the PI, whereas a proposal that is funded results in a contract for the PI. However, as is common in the scientific community, I have used the terms "application" and "proposal" more or less interchangeably—though in common usage in the community, the "proposal" often refers primarily to the Research Plan, whereas the "application" tends to refer to the completed packet of information submitted to the funding agency.

In some parts of my book I have included direct quotes from government documents without specific attribution. Thus, when I have wanted to convey information from the NIH instructions (PHS-398 or PHS-2590) that was clear as stated in the NIH instructions, and for which I did not think I could improve on the clarity by rewording the text, I have inserted in my book, verbatim, the text in the instructions (or other NIH publications) without quotation marks. I have used quotation marks only when I specifically wanted to emphasize that the wording was unchanged from that of NIH. Because government documents are not copyrighted, because my major goal is to inform the reader, and because this book is not an exercise in creative writing, I trust that no one will be offended by my taking this liberty.

Note added at second printing

Many changes in NIH peer review occurred during 1994. Some of these were indicated in the page proofs for this book in August 1994. Others, such as adoption of triage (a procedure whereby applications deemed by reviewers to be unlikely to be funded—up to fifty percent of applications received by a study section—are reviewed, as usual, by the primary and secondary reviewers but are not discussed by the full study section), and associated changes in the summary statements, occurred after the book had gone to press. I have tried to incorporate some of these changes into the second printing but was limited by pagination issues. The result is a somewhat uneven writing style and less than optimal logical flow—but I considered it most important to provide the most up-to-date information possible. For more information see:

- "Triage and Streamlined Summary Statement Format to be Used by the Division of Research Grants." *NIH Guide for Grants and Contracts*. Vol. 23, No. 34, Sept. 23, 1994, page 2.
- Liane Reif-Lehrer, "Science Community Gives Mixed Review To Triage." *The Scientist*, 1994, November 28, pages 1, 8–9. It may interest the reader that Dr. Gregory Milman, Chief, Pathogenesis and Basic Research Branch, National Institute of Allergy and Infectious Diseases, requested permission to use this article as a handout to applicants for grants in his branch.
- Liane Reif-Lehrer, "Peer Review Changes at NIH: Too Many Applications, Too Little Funding Drives Streamlining Efforts," *Journal of the National Grantseekers Institute*, 1995, Vol. 2, No. 1, published by Capitol Publications (1-800-655-5597). Covers triage and other procedures which NIH adopted, or was considering, studying, or testing as of 1994: Modification and expedited release of summary statements, changes in post-council notification of actions taken on grant applications, modifications in post-award management of grants, possible use of modular or "chunk" grants, "Just-in-time" submission of certain administrative data for grant applications, identification of high risk/high impact research, possible use of retrospective instead of prospective reviews of research by investigators requesting funding, increased use of electronic media for administration of grant applications and dissemination of information about extramural programs, and a restructuring of NIH Division of Research Grants (DRG) review groups.

More changes are likely at NIH in 1995. Trying to keep up with them is, in the words of one high-level NIH administrator, "like shooting at a moving target." Readers should watch the news from NIH and other funding agencies.

PREFACE

This book is based on an earlier book, *Writing a Successful Grant Application, Second Edition* (Jones and Bartlett Publishers, Boston, MA 1989). The first edition was originally written as a monograph, in response to a request by an administrator at the Eye Research Institute of Retina Foundation [now the Schepens Eye Research Institute (SERI)] that I put together a document to help my colleagues improve their proposal-writing skills.

The suggestions in the first book were based largely on my own experience serving on an NIH Vision Study Section, Vis. A (later Vis. A ad hoc), from 1976 to 1978. Some information was also obtained from the various publications put out by the U.S. Department of Health and Human Services and from seminars presented by NIH administrators. Starting in 1984, I began to give workshops on grant proposal writing throughout the United States. The second edition of the book encompassed what was in the first edition but also incorporated much from a handout I had developed for my workshops.

Since that second edition was written, I have given many more seminars and workshops at universities and professional meetings, including two 2-day workshops in the former Soviet Union (in April 1994) sponsored by the American Association for the Advancement of Science, and have continued to learn more about the needs of the people who attend. On occasion, over the years, NIH Study Section members, Scientific Review Administrators (called Executive Secretaries prior to 1991), and other grant administrators as well as well-funded senior faculty members' have attended my workshops. It has been gratifying to have them almost always concur with what I said and to get additional useful information from them. Officers in charge of grants offices at the many universities where I have lectured have also been generous in sharing information—and in some cases cartoons—with me. I also learned much from grants I have critiqued for clients, from researching answers to questions that have come up in the course of the workshops and from discussions with scientists at universities and at the NIH and NSF who have been involved, more recently than I, in the grant process as grantees, reviewers, or administrators. I try to stay current with what is happening at NIH and NSF by reading their various publications, by keeping in touch with scientists who serve on Study Sections/Review Boards, and by maintaining contact with the agencies. I have added much recently acquired information to this book. The new book also serves to bring the reader up to date with respect to (1) the PHS-398 forms as revised 9/91[1] (and issued by NIH in March 1992), (2) the changes in NIH Study Section voting procedures that were instituted in Fall 1991 and those under study at DRG in 1994, and (3) the new NSF forms released in January 1994 (*Grant Proposal Guide (GPG)* NSF 94-2; revised 1/94). In the course of doing research for the present book, I found myself making multiple telephone calls to

---

[1] The application form for a noncompetitive grant continuation (PHS-2590) was also revised 9/91. Both forms are being revised again 9/94. Apparently, changes to the Research Plan are minimal. However, the order of presentation will be different and there will be new material about assurances and certifications.

NIH, NSF, and other agencies to obtain definitions of terms I thought would be helpful to my readers. I was surprised to find that NIH did not have a unified glossary of all terms and acronyms used by the agency. Thus, I decided to create an extensive glossary for the book. I have also indexed the new book.

NIH revises the PHS-398 packet approximately every 3 years. Recent revisions have been dated 9/86 (major revisions), 10/88 (minor revisions), and 9/91 (moderate revisions). The 9/91 revision was approved through 6/30/94. The next revision, which is likely to be dated 9/94, is expected to be in circulation by early 1995. Thus, it is impossible for the specifics in my book to remain current for very long. However, the basic advice will probably be valid for many years. You, the reader, must try to keep abreast of changes. In particular, it is likely that grants will be submitted and managed electronically within the next several years (see Appendix I-A about the NIH Project EGAD).

The basic principles in this book are useful for writing many types of grant applications and proposals (to both government agencies and private foundations)—as well as research papers, business plans, and other similar documents. However, a National Institutes of Health (NIH) investigator-initiated research grant application (R01) is used as the primary example for discussion throughout this book. An appendix by Dr. Bruce Trumbo[2] addresses some of the similarities and differences in grant application and review at the National Science Foundation (NSF). There is also some information in Appendix IX about applying to private foundations. Although the review process may be different at the various funding agencies, the sorts of things that Reviewers look for in a grant application are not very different in essence. Therefore, the information given in this book can easily be extrapolated for use with applications to many other agencies.

Some of the information in this book is intentionally presented in outline form—and in some cases in both narrative and outline form. In addition, at the excellent suggestion of Dr. Janet Rasey, one of the readers for my book (see below), I have added a "Recap" section at the end of each part of the book. I hope in this way to satisfy the variety of readers who may require or prefer more or less information.

This book has been reviewed, prior to submission to the publisher, by five readers, listed in the "Acknowledgments" section, who were in some way associated with the grants process in 1993. I have learned a great deal from their comments and have incorporated most of their suggestions into the book.

Note added in June 1994: New directors were appointed at both NIH and NSF in 1993. Dr. Harold Varmus, a molecular biologist and Nobel Prize winner became the director of NIH; Dr. Neal F. Lane, a physicist, and previously Provost at Rice University became the director of NSF. A new PHS-398 kit will be released in early 1995. It contains substantial policy changes, a reorganization of the order of the parts of the instructions, as well as minor changes to the Research Plan. A new *Grant Proposal Guide* with more forms, many of which look similar to NIH application forms, was released by NSF in January 1994. New leadership, increasing costs in an era of tight funding, and a general sense in the community that the grants process needs streamlining all indicate that there are likely to be some significant changes at both agencies in the near future. Watch for them. It's important to be aware of what's happening in the funding arena.

---

[2] This appendix was revised for the second edition of *Writing A Successful Grant Application* by Dr. Sherwin S. Lehrer, who served on a National Science Foundation review panel from 1985 to 1988, and was further revised for this book by Dr. Trumbo and Dr. Hartmut Wohlrab, a member of an NSF grant review panel in 1993.

ACKNOWLEDGMENTS

My sincere thanks go to many colleagues, friends, and associates who helped in various ways with the preparation of the book.

For critical reading of Parts I-VIII of the manuscript:

- Donna J. Dean, Ph.D., Chief, Biological and Physiological Sciences Review Section, Division of Research Grants, National Institutes of Health, Bethesda, MD. I am doubly indebted to Dr. Dean not only for reading and critiquing the manuscript sent to all my readers (listed here), but also for rereading the parts of the manuscript that I changed in response to all the readers' comments. Despite her own heavy schedule, she also tirelessly and promptly responded to my many queries and provided me with various forms and documents that I needed for the book.
- Jane F. Koretz, Ph.D., Director, Center for Biophysics, and Professor, Department of Biology, Science Center, Rensselaer Polytechnic Institute, Troy, NY. Dr. Koretz served as a member of the NIH Visual Science–A Study Section from 1989 to 1993.
- Richard Pharo, Ph.D., Associate Director for Research Affairs, Massachusetts General Hospital (MGH), Boston, MA. Before his affiliation with MGH, Dr. Pharo was the Director of Research Administration at the Eye Research Institute of Retina Foundation (now the Schepens Eye Research Institute) for over 20 years and had a primary responsibility as the major grants administrator at the Institute.
- Janet S. Rasey, Ph.D., Professor of Radiation Oncology and Director of the Research Funding Service, University of Washington Medical Center, Seattle, WA. Dr. Rasey has served 2 terms on NIH Study Sections. I am especially grateful to Dr. Rasey for suggesting that I add a "Recap" section at the end of each part of the book.
- A member of an NIH Study Section in 1993 who wished to remain anonymous.

I told the five aforementioned readers that I was not afraid of red ink or harsh criticism. I am pleased to say that they took me at my word, for which I am most grateful. They have all helped to make this a much better book.

For critical reading of Appendix VII (about the review process for NSF grant applications):

- Bruce Trumbo, Ph.D., Professor of Statistics and Mathematics, California State University, Hayward, who wrote Appendix VII about the review process for NSF grant applications for the first edition of my earlier book and rerevised that section for this book.
- Hartmut Wohlrab, Ph.D., Senior Staff Scientist, Boston Biomedical Research Institute, Research Associate, Department of Biological Chemistry and Molecular Pharmacology, Harvard Medical School, and, beginning in 1992, Member of Metabolic Biochemistry Review Panel at NSF.
- A current NSF Program Director who wished to remain anonymous.

For other help and support:

- Philip R. Conley, Director of Library Services, Associated Grantmakers of Massachusetts, Inc., who has graciously helped me find information—especially about foundation grants—over the years.
- John J. Elsbree, Product Development Specialist, Office of Business and Product Development, NTIS, for information about the services of NTIS.
- Jean Feldman, Grant and Contract Policy Specialist, Division of Contracts, Policy, and Oversight, Policy Office, NSF, for sending me the pre-final forms of the new NSF grant application instructions so that I could get the information about NSF in this book updated at "zero hour" before the book was due at the publishers.
- Sam Joseloff, Ph.D., Director of the Grants Information Office, Division of Research Grants, NIH, who has throughout the years generously provided me with information about NIH about changes in NIH policy, personnel, and telephone number; and about other matters relevant to my workshops, articles, and book revisions. He has been especially helpful to me in responding rapidly to a multitude of queries I put to him during the preparation of this book.
- Sonny Kreitman, PHS and NIH SBIR/STTR Program Coordinator, Office of Extramural Research, Office of the Director, NIH, for an extensive and enlightening discussion about certain aspects of the SBIR and STTR programs.
- William E. McGarvey, Acting Head, and Robert Moore, Program Analyst, both of the Statistical Analysis Unit, Statistical Analysis and Evaluation Section, Information Systems Branch, Division of Research Grants, NIH, who provided data about grant applications and awards.
- Charles A. Miller, U.S. Army Corps of Engineers, Special Staff Assistant, Strategic Environmental Research Defense Program (SERDP) for discussions about the SERDP.
- Vincent Raso, CPA, Assistant Director/Controller, Boston Biomedical Research Institute, for a helpful discussion about "overhead deficits."
- Clifford Scharke, DMD, MPH, Chief, Assurance Branch, Division of Human Subject Protection, OPRR, NIH, for discussions about human subjects studies.
- The principal investigators who graciously gave permission to publish, anonymously, their Summary Statements ("Pink Sheets"—which are no longer pink as of 1992!) and, in some cases, parts of their grant applications.
- The many investigators and grant administrators with whom I have had helpful discussions over the years about grants and the peer review process. I am especially indebted to the institutional grants officers who have recommended my workshops and other services to their colleagues and to those who have sent me interesting materials to use in subsequent workshops.
- The many people who have been to my workshops, especially those who have taken time to give me thoughtful, constructive feedback about how to improve the workshops.
- The many people not specifically mentioned above, at NIH, NSF, other granting agencies, book publishing and software companies, and various libraries, who were helpful in my efforts to gather up-to-date information for the book—especially for the Glossary and the Resource Appendix.
- Don Jones, Sr., Clayton Jones, Deborah Haffner, Nadine Fitzwilliam, Judy Songdahl, Paula Carroll and the many other people at Jones and Bartlett Publishers who have supported my efforts in the preparation of this book and the two editions of my earlier book about writing grant applications.

ABOUT THE AUTHOR

Dr. Liane Reif-Lehrer was born in Vienna, Austria, and after two and a half years in France, where she had her first year of schooling, came to New York in November 1941 at the age of seven. She graduated from Erasmus Hall High School in Brooklyn, New York, in 1952, received a B.A. degree in chemistry from Barnard College, Columbia University, in 1956, and a Ph.D. in physical organic chemistry from the University of California at Berkeley in 1960 under the tutelage of Professor Andrew Streitwieser. From 1963 to 1966 she was a postdoctoral fellow with Dr. Harold Amos in the then Department of Microbiology and Immunology at Harvard Medical School, where she became interested in control mechanisms in animal cells, especially in the retina. In 1966 she was appointed an instructor at the Howe Laboratory of Ophthalmology of Harvard Medical School at the Massachusetts Eye and Ear Infirmary and was later promoted to assistant professor. In 1972 she moved her laboratory to Boston Biomedical Research Institute and in 1975 to the Eye Research Institute of Retina Foundation (now called the Schepens Eye Research Institute), where she held an appointment as Senior Scientist. In 1977 she attained the rank of associate professor at Harvard Medical School.

From 1976 to 1978, Dr. Reif-Lehrer was a member of a National Institutes of Health Initial Review Group ("Study Section"). In 1978–1979, she was a Senior Visiting Fellow at the Institute of Ophthalmology, University of London, England.

It was her experience as a member of the NIH Study Section—and a request from the Eye Research Institute administration that she write a monograph to help her fellow faculty members write better grant proposals—that prompted her to write the first, abbreviated (82 pages), edition of *Writing a Successful Grant Application,* published in 1982. The book was published as a 282-page second edition in 1989.

In October 1985, Dr. Reif-Lehrer left the Eye Research Institute and Harvard Medical School to start Tech-Write Consultants/Erimon Associates (TWC/EA), a consulting firm.

A veteran lecturer and writer of grant proposals, and the author of some 40 publications in the scientific literature, Dr. Reif-Lehrer has also written for *The Scientist, Journal of Science Education and Technology, Boston Magazine,* the *Boston Globe,* and the *Christian Science Monitor,* among other publications.

Dr. Reif-Lehrer now gives workshops and seminars and does private consulting in a number of areas, including proposal writing, business writing, and time management. She has given workshops and seminars on proposal writing at universities and professional meetings throughout the United States and more recently in the former Soviet Union. TWC/EA helps companies and individuals write grant proposals, software documentation, instruction manuals for science/engineering equipment as well as consumer products, and other technical and business documents. TWC/EA also provides help with product development, problem solving, and project management and helps companies, universities, and individuals find consultants who will help them solve specific problems.

SERVICES OF TWC/EA

- Workshops and seminars about "How to write a better grant application"
- Individual help with all stages of writing proposals and journal manuscripts (planning and outlining, writing, critiquing the final manuscript) or other technical writing
- Coaching in oral presentations for professional meetings, seminars, and other public speaking
- Coaching in expository writing for academics and business executives
- Consultation/writing of software documentation, instruction manuals, etc.
- Help with product development; small laboratory equipment, consumer products, software, etc.

For information about workshops and other services of TWC/EA call 617-863-1117, Fax 617-674-0436, or write: TWC/EA, Box 645, Belmont, MA 02178.

The outlines for NIH and NSF grant applications provided in the Appendices of this book are available on disk from TWC/EA for $35 + $3 (P&H). These are available only on 3.5-inch disks. They can be formatted for Microsoft Word for the Macintosh, MS-DOS, or text-only. Please specify desired format and whether for NIH or NSF outline. Allow 6 to 8 weeks for delivery.

Grants Info Letter: By subscription, for researchers/grant-seekers.

A *quarterly digest newsletter* intended to inform researchers/grant-seekers *quickly* about new developments in funding and peer review at NIH, NSF and, as appropriate, other funding agencies.

Grants Info Letter will consist of about 3–5 photocopied pages of brief summaries of information that researchers/grant-seekers should know about and, if appropriate, will provide references so additional information about a topic can be obtained if desired. The first issue will be mailed approximately at the end of March 1995, and is planned to coincide with the distribution by NIH of the newly revised PHS-398 grant application forms.

To subscribe to the quarterly newsletter, please send to the address below:

- A check for $25 (payable to TWC/EA)
- Four (4) self-addressed #10 business envelopes with $0.55 (fifty-five cents) postage stamps affixed (SASE). (**PLEASE DO NOT USE A POSTAGE METER.**)

Newsletters will be mailed only to those who enclose both the check and the SASEs with proper postage. Reminders to renew subscriptions will be published in the year-end newsletter.

Tech-Write Consultants/Erimon Associates (TWC/EA), Box 645, Belmont, MA 02178; (617) 863-1117; Fax: (617) 674-0436 (If no fax-tone, press *)

PART I

GETTING STARTED

INTRODUCTION

Success in obtaining grant funding depends on many factors; the major ones are a good research idea (project), a good match between the proposed project and the mandate (mission) of the funding agency, a carefully thought-out approach to the project, and a well-written, focused proposal. No matter how good your idea is and how well-written your proposal is, if the agency to which you are applying is not interested in your project, you will not be funded. Thus, you should understand, for example, that the scientific mission of NIH is not to fund good research but rather to improve the health of the people in the United States.[1] This understanding should have a great impact on how you present your project and may, other things being equal, enhance your chances of success. Granting agencies change their missions from time to time—as problems get resolved, more pressing problems arise, or the administrators and/or trustees of the agency change. Sometimes the changes are major, sometimes they are subtle. An idea rejected one year may have a high priority at a later time. Likewise, an agency may, over time, lose interest in projects it had previously given high priority. The cost of a long-distance phone call is a small price to pay compared to time spent "barking up the wrong tree." Before you spend any time on a grant application, call the program officer(s) at the agency to which you intend to submit the proposal, and be sure they are interested in your research idea. Also try to find out what aspects of the project are of greatest interest to the agency so that you can make the best match between your research plans and the agency's funding priorities.

SOME TRAITS OF A SUCCESSFUL GRANT GETTER

Successful grant getters need:

- Good research skills
- Salesmanship skills (to convince the granting agency that your idea is worth funding)
- Good communication skills (writing and speaking effectively)
    Writing skills are necessary to write a good grant proposal and to write high-quality publications that will build your reputation.
    Good speaking skills are necessary to:
        —Give good talks that will help bring your work to the attention of the scientific community
        —Make a convincing presentation if your laboratory is site visited
        —Successfully negotiate the interactive process that is often involved in foundation grant applications.
- Ingenuity and flexibility (to take advantage of current program relevance and funding priorities)
- Administrative skills (from leadership to accounting). Know where, how, and when to get information about available funding. If in doubt about any aspect of the grants process, don't guess, call the program officer or other grants personnel at the potential funding agency. Periodically evaluate your progress. Keep close tabs on your grant budget once you are funded.

---

[1] The mission of NIH, as stated in the NIH publication, *Orientation Handbook for Members of Scientific Review Groups* (interim revision, March 1992) is "to improve the health of the people of the US by increasing our understanding of the process underlying human health and by acquiring new knowledge to help prevent, detect, diagnose, and treat disease."

- Good human relations (the ability to motivate and gain the cooperation and confidence of your immediate staff, people in other departments, and granting agency officials)
- Persistence, dedication, patience, and the ability to work hard. Don't give up. Keep revising wisely until you get funded, but know when it is time to change to a different project.
- Political awareness and action. Be aware of funding sources and funding levels. Scientists must get more involved in lobbying for their own cause. Write and/or call your congressional representatives when your professional associations request that you do so. Make your voice heard: Vote for officials who support research.
- Integrity. Guard against poor judgment that may impair your credibility and/or reputation.

Successful grant getters understand:

- The essentials of grantsmanship (psychology)
- The mission of the potential funding agency (keeping in touch, staying informed and up to date)
- The nature of the review process (psychology)
- The concept (psychology) of writing for the reader (the Reviewer) and for the wider audience (the potential funding agency)
- The art of responding to a set of instructions
- The basic elements of good expository writing (to expose). A grant proposal should never sound like a novel or mystery story. The Reviewer wants to get the maximum information in the minimum number of words. S/he wants accuracy and clarity. The Reviewer should never have to guess what you mean.

SOME GENERAL INFORMATION FOR BEGINNING GRANT APPLICATION WRITERS

What is a grant?

A grant is a form of sponsorship for a project, the ideas for which generally originate with and are designed and carried out by the applicant. Grants can be classified according to:

- Type of activity or activities supported (research, training, service, etc.)
- Degree of discretion allowed the awarding office (mandatory or discretionary)
- Method of determining amounts of awards (negotiated or formula)

The project may be education, research, a performance, creation of a work of art, construction of a housing development or other community improvement, organizing a conference, travel with a purpose, acquisition of equipment, etc. (Although the examples used in this book focus on grants awarded in response to applications or proposals for biomedical research projects, the general principles put forth in the book are applicable to many fields of endeavor.)

The grant may cover part or all of the expenses associated with the project. It may cover only direct operating costs, or it may also cover indirect (overhead) costs.

Direct costs   Costs readily identified as necessary for carrying out the project (e.g., salaries, fringe benefits, equipment, supplies, project-related travel, publication costs). Direct costs are requested by the grantee and are subject to approval by the grantor.

Indirect costs (overhead)   Costs incurred by the grantee institution to provide support services shared by other projects, such as administrative expenses, plant operation and maintenance (library, restrooms, cafeteria, electricity and other utilities, security, institutional store, parking facility, etc.). Indirect costs are negotiated between the grantee institution and the grantor. The "negotiated indirect cost rate" is generally a percent of salaries and wages or a percent of total direct costs.

Grants from agencies that do not provide overhead may be considered unacceptable by grantee institutions. But it is sometimes possible to charge certain items, normally considered overhead, as direct costs, for example, "administrative costs." This must be cleared with the grantee institution and must be consistent with its normal accounting practices.

Be aware that many granting agencies will award a grant only to an institution, not to an unaffiliated individual. For example, when you apply for funding to NIH, strictly speaking, it is not you but your institution that is applying for the award. If the award is granted, it is granted not to you but to your institution. Your institution sets up an account for you upon which you draw for funds to carry out your project. A few agencies do give funds to unaffiliated individuals. The National Science Foundation (NSF) is one example.

Categories of awards

Fellowships support continuing or advanced education of researchers or other scholars. *Grants, cooperative agreements,* and *contracts* provide recipients with the means to carry on their work in the sense that the grantee has a commitment to perform some work that fulfills the expectation of the grantor. Grants and cooperative agreements come out of assistance programs; contracts result from acquisition programs.

The characteristics of these three types of awards are as follows:

Grant

- An agreement to support research.
- Ideas originate with and are defined by the applicant.
- Generally for basic research.
- Allows the recipient a reasonable amount of freedom. No programmatic involvement by the sponsoring agency.

Contract

- An instrument to procure research.
- The work required is spelled out by the funding agency.
- Generally for applied research.
- The funding agency exercises more control over the recipient than with a grant.
- Involves stricter financial accountability than with a grant.

Cooperative Agreement

- Identical to a grant except that there is substantial programmatic involvement by the sponsoring agency.[2]

---

[2] According to the Federal Grant and Cooperative Agreement Act, Public Law 95-224 (Feb. 3, 1978), the only difference between a "Grant" and a "Cooperative Agreement" is the amount of programmatic involvement by the sponsoring agency. At NIH, grant applications are reviewed by Division of Research Grants (DRG) Study Sections, whereas cooperative agreements are generally reviewed by Institute review groups.

Types of granting agencies

Government

- Most abundant source.
- Lots of materials and information available.
- Trendy (e.g., may change with federal administration), but must be responsive to voters and the democratic process, so response to external changes is slow.
- Information about review procedures is readily available.

Private Foundations

- Funding depends on matching specific interests.
- Some materials and information are available.
- The mandate may remain the same over a long period or may change frequently. (For example, the focus of the March of Dimes has changed from polio to birth defects.)
- Can respond quickly to new ideas/unique needs.
- Information about review procedures may not be readily available.

Business and Industry

- The least abundant source of funding for academic institutions.
- No good central source of information.
- Identifying a corporation that will sponsor an activity or a research project is difficult.
- Finding a funding source takes time, initiative, energy, imagination, and persistence.
- Information about review procedures may not be readily available.

Building relationships with the appropriate staff members (before there is any mention of money) is an important aspect of getting funding from the business community. A good resource is *Get Funded! A Practical Guide for Scholars Seeking Research Support from Business*, by Dorin Schumacher, Ph.D., Sage Publications, 1992.

Some NIH awards for beginning grant seekers

The programs listed below are described briefly in Appendix I-G.[3]

NIH FIRST Award (R29)
NIH Pilot Projects or Feasibility Studies (R21)
NIH Small Grants Programs (R-03)
NIH Academic Research Enhancement (AREA) Award (R-15)
Small Business Innovation Research (SBIR) Grant (At NIH: R43, R44)
Small Business Technology Transfer Program (STTR)
NIH Physician Scientist Award (PSA) (K11, K12)
NIH Research Career Re-Entry Program (K17)

Where to get information about available grants

See also Appendix XI.

- Libraries: There are some libraries dedicated entirely to information about fund-

---

[3] See also Samuel M. Schwartz and Mischa E. Friedman, *A Guide to NIH Grant Programs* (Oxford University Press, New York, 1992, 296 pages, $39.95) and the review by Daniel E. Atkinson, in *Science*, Vol. 261, July 23, 1993, pages 498–499).

ing sources, such as The Associated Grantmakers of Massachusetts, in Boston. (See the list of resources in Appendix XI.)

General libraries also usually have many listings of grants and sources of grants, such as *The Foundation Directory and The Foundation Grant Index.* (See the list of resources in Appendix XI.)

- Computerized lists (databases) of available funding, such as SPIN (Sponsored Programs Information Network); see Appendix XI.
- On-line sources such as
  (A) NIH Gopher Server, access available over Internet. For information, send e-mail to Gopher@Gopher.NIH.Gov.[4] For other information about NIH Gopher Server, call Ms. Charlene Osborn, (301) 496-4823. The NIH Gopher Server provides:
      (1) The NIH Guide to Grants and Contracts in a searchable form and generally has the Guide available about a week or more earlier than the printed version.
      (2) Access to CRISP, a database of information about all NIH-funded grants. For information, call Ms. Seu Lain Chen, (301) 594-7267.
      (3) Access to the Johns Hopkins University Gopher Server, which has additional information about grants.
  (B) NIH Grant Line, an electronic bulletin board information system. The Grant Line also carries the NIH Guide to Grants and Contracts, as well as NIH extramural program guidelines[5] and the organizational section of the NIH telephone directory (the NIH extramural green pages).[6] For information, call Dr. John C. James, (301) 594-7270.
- Institutional grant offices (Office of Grants and Contracts, Office for Sponsored Research)
- Direct communication with agencies that have a specific interest in the area of the proposed application
- Newsletters from granting agencies and professional organizations, including private foundations
- Commercial newsletters such as
  (A) ARIS Funding Reports; publishes three different reports, including *Biomedical Sciences Report, Social and Natural Sciences Report,* and *Creative Arts and Humanities Report.* Lists a combination of federal and non-federal funding opportunities. Tel: 415-558-8133; Fax: 415-558-8135.
  (B) Medical Research Funding Bulletin, Science Support Center, PO Box 7507, FDR Station, New York, NY 10150.
  (C) Health Grants and Contracts Weekly/Federal Grants and Contracts Weekly, Capitol Publications, 1-800-327-7203.
- Annual reports of foundations; these reports usually provide a good overview of areas of interest to the foundation.
- Professional and society journals:
  —Announcements section

---

[4] This period is to end the sentence and is *not* part of the e-mail address.
[5] Note that guidelines for complex multi-faceted, unsolicited grant applications such as program project grants are not uniform across NIH. Contact the specific Institute for information. (See *NIH Guide for Grants and Contracts*: Vol. 19, No. 4, Jan. 26, 1990, page 1, and Vol. 20, No. 12, Mar. 22, 1991, page 2.)
[6] Note that this feature may be especially useful because many NIH telephone numbers were changed in 1992. Moreover, the Division of Research Grants is scheduled to move to a new location in 1995, which may once again entail changes in telephone numbers.

—Acknowledgments in journal articles that cite sources of funding for the work described.
- News media
- Private workshops and seminars
- Colleagues
- Requests for proposals (RFPs), Requests for applications (RFAs). These are sent to institutions and organizations that are known to be interested. They are also published in the NIH Guide for Grants and Contracts and other newsletters.

For specific sources, see the list of resources in Appendix XI. (Some of the source materials are expensive; you can probably find them at the library or in your institutional grants office.)

Information to gather before you apply for a grant

From yourself

Do you have a very clear concept of what your project entails?
Have you clearly defined what your project is intended to accomplish?
Have you determined that there are funding agencies that are interested in your project?
Do you know what methods you will use to achieve your goals?
Do you have a clear understanding of what the personnel, equipment, supplies, and space requirements are for your project?
Do you have a clear understanding of how long your project will take?
Do you have a clear understanding of how much it will cost to carry out your project? Have you done some preliminary realistic budget calculations?
Have you determined what you will need from the funding agency? Some funding agencies want to see a commitment by the applicant's institution in the form of cost-sharing. Some agencies want to support only part of a project which is also supported by other funding agencies.

From your institution

Is your institution willing to let you apply? (Will they support the project? Are they willing to cost-share?)
Do you have to file an "intent to apply"?
Is your institution willing to administer the grant?
Is your institution willing to put the necessary space and resources at your disposal?
Question of overhead.
Question of salary.
Question of patents and copyrights.
Question of equipment acquisition, use, and disposal.
Question of relative involvement of applicant and her/his institution in the project.
For government funds, is your institution willing to file assurance of compliance with civil rights act, affirmative action rulings, protection of human subjects, humane treatment of animals, and other relevant regulations?

From the prospective funding organization

Does the agency have printed materials to help acquaint you with its organization, programs, research priorities, and grant policies?

Does your interest match the purpose of the agency's program (mandate of the agency)?

Do you qualify? (eligibility, restrictions, and special stipulations). Some agencies have very specific eligibility requirements.

Is the agency really interested in your project?

> First find out as much as possible about the agency by sending for its annual report and/or other printed materials it may provide. Find out what projects the agency has funded in the recent past. (Ask the agency for a list, or look it up in one of the foundation directories or indexes.) Once you have some background information about the agency, it's a good idea to speak to a program officer (or other relevant administrator) at the agency in question *before* starting to write. Developing a good proposal is a lot of work. The best-thought-out and best-written proposal will not be funded by an agency that is not interested in the project. Some agencies have written documents describing their funding priorities for the next several (often 3 to 5) years. Determine whether your project is in keeping with the agency's mandate. Some agencies—especially certain private foundations—will help you develop your proposal, a service that is well-worth taking advantage of.

What aspects of your project will the agency support, and what aspects will it not support?

What parts of your project does the agency seem most enthused about?

Are there any obligations for the future? (payback clause)?

What amounts of money does the agency grant?

What are the total number of awards and amount of support provided by the agency? (What are your chances of getting support?)

Can the agency provide a list of past grantees and their projects?

What are the type, length, and amount of support per person? (Is it enough to complete your project?)

Are the funding level, indirect cost policy, and any restriction(s) acceptable to your institution?

Application information:

> —Is there a formal application kit?
> —Does the agency require a pre-application or a letter of inquiry?
> —When is the application due? Does the deadline refer to "date of postmark" or "date of arrival"?

Have there been recent changes in requirements or application procedure that differ from the information given in the agency's printed materials? (At NIH, check with the particular funding component (Institute or Center) from which you are requesting support about program changes and additional application instructions.)

Information about the review process:

> Who will review the application?
> Is a site visit required?
> What is the time lag between application and approval? Between approval and funding?

For information about the review process at private foundations, letters of inquiry, and preproposals, see Appendix IX.

RECAP FOR PART I: GETTING STARTED

Success in obtaining grant funding depends on:

- A good match between the proposed project and the mandate (mission) of the funding agency. Consult with the potential funding agency to be sure it is interested in your research idea.
- A good research idea
- A carefully thought-out approach to the project
- A well-written, focused proposal

Successful grant getters need:

- Research skills
- Salesmanship
- Communication skills
- Ingenuity and flexibility
- Administrative skills
- Good human relations
- Persistence, dedication, patience
- Political awareness and action
- Integrity

Successful grant getters should understand:

- The nature of the review process
- The concept of writing for the reader(s)
- How to respond to a set of instructions
- The basic elements of good expository writing

Beginning proposal writers should know about:

- Fellowships
- Grants
- Cooperative agreements
- Contracts
- Direct costs
- Indirect costs (overhead)
- Some NIH awards for beginning grant seekers
- Types of granting agencies
- Where to get information about available grants
- Information to gather before you decide to apply for a grant

~ PART II ~

UNDERSTANDING
THE REVIEW PROCESS

Introduction

Part II of this book deals predominantly with the review process at NIH. Information about proposal review at NSF is given in Appendices VII and VIII-A. Information about the review process at private foundations is given in Appendix IX and references therein.

The specifics of proposal review varies from agency to agency. It may be quite codified, formal, and stringent, as at NIH with its dual review system. Or it may be quite informal, as is the case at some private foundations. Nonetheless, some elements are common to many agencies because, like venture capital firms, banks, and other financial institutions, funding agencies want to be sure that their money is well invested and will get the highest possible return. Thus, virtually all funding agencies want to know about the innovative nature, feasibility, and likely outcome of the project; the reputation and quality ("track record") of the applicant, of her/his team, and of the institution with which s/he is affiliated; the resources available to the applicant/project; and other support available for the project.

A good grant proposal requires a good research idea—a unique, interesting, innovative, important, and well-defined problem for which you can suggest a sound and viable experimental approach that is likely to lead to a tangible solution, for example, an hypothesis that you can test and either prove or disprove.

The good idea must be

- Original/novel/innovative
- Feasible
  —Do-able by you and your staff
  —Do-able at your institution
  —Acceptable to your institution
  —Acceptable to the granting agency and relevant to the mission of the granting agency
  —In conformity with human and animal welfare policies and other funding agency requirements
- Conceptually significant: The successful resolution of the research idea (solution to the problem) should result in a substantive (nontrivial) finding that will benefit the profession or the public.

The best writing cannot turn a bad idea into a good grant proposal. However, bad writing can turn a good idea into a poor grant proposal. So planning, writing, and revising the proposal are important to the development of a successful application. These are the aspects of proposal preparation that this book is intended to teach.

Aside from the primary requirement—a good idea—several things will help you end up with a proposal that will "fly," that is, one that will receive a high-priority score and be funded. These are:

- Having a well-focused, well-written research proposal
- Having a long history ("track record") of concentration in a particular research field or problem or—if you are a new investigator—having good training and substantive preliminary results (pilot studies) in the area of the proposed research
- Being prepared to devote a substantial effort to the proposed work. (For new investigators, 75–100% is good, 50% is OK, and below 25% is "iffy" unless you have a very good reason! A smaller percent effort may be acceptable for very established investigators.)
- Maintaining a stable work group. (Funding agencies are not happy to have you spend their money for repeatedly interviewing and training new candidates.

ment in hiring and/or poor interpersonal skills and may be indicative of poor judgment in other areas.)

- Having an ample number of substantial publications (on which you are the first author[1]) in well-reviewed, competitive and (if you are in a nonclinical field) preferably basic science journals. A high ratio of abstracts to full-length papers is not a good sign. Papers in archive-type journals are less meaningful than those in prestigious peer-reviewed journals. Other publications, such as books, chapters in books, or review articles may, or may not, be considered indicative of your ability to do original work.

Understanding the review process will help you write a better grant application, just as understanding the job description helps you prepare for a job interview. Good expository writing requires that you write for the benefit of the readers. What do the readers, in this case the Reviewers, need or want to know? How can you help make the Reviewer's job easier? In addition, you should consider the wider audience—in this case the potential funding agency—which needs assurance that its money will be well spent. Thus, you must understand the review process, and the situation of the Reviewers and the potential funding agency within that process, to be able to write a good grant application.

THE NIH REVIEW SYSTEM

NIH has a dual peer review system.

The first level of review is by a **Scientific Review Group (SRG)**, constituted by scientific discipline or biomedical topic. The SRG is called an Initial Review Group (IRG) when pertaining to *grant* applications (as opposed to contracts). The IRGs are composed of sub-committees called Study Sections.

The Study Section

- Is constituted by scientific discipline or biomedical topic.
- Provides initial *scientific review* of grant applications.
- Assigns priority scores, based on scientific merit, to appropriate applications.
- Makes budget recommendations (but no funding decisions —funding decisions are the prerogative of each Institute or other NIH funding component, which has full discretionary powers).
- Does *not* set program priorities. (Program relevance is determined by the priorities of the potential funding Institute.)
- Has about 14–20 members, all scientists.
- Is headed administratively by a Scientific Review Administrator (SRA)[2] from the Division of Research Grants (DRG)—but discussions about the scientific merit of applications are led by a chairperson who is a *scientist* member of the Study Section. The SRA and the chairperson sit next to each other at Study Section meetings.
- Is only advisory.

The second level of review is by the **Advisory Council or Board** of the potential awarding component (Institute, Center, or other unit).

---

[1] Be aware of the distinction between being the first author and the senior author. The general understanding is that the first author actually did the major part of the work. In contrast, the senior author is often thought to be the director of the research group, who may or may not have done any work on the project, and whose name may have been added as the last author simply as a courtesy.

[2] Until fall 1991 the Scientific Review Administrator was called the Executive Secretary.

The council

- Evaluates applications against program priorities and relevance
- Concurs with or modifies Study Section action on grant applications—or defers the application for further review
- Makes recommendations—but no decisions—about funding to the Institute staff
- Advises on policy
- Has 12 or more members, both scientists and nonscientists
- Is only advisory

THE TRAVELS OF AN NIH GRANT APPLICATION

A grant proposal to NIH is

- Initiated by a principal investigator (PI)
- Submitted by her/his sponsoring institution to the NIH
- Received at NIH by the Referral Office of the Division of Research Grants

The Division of Research Grants (DRG)

When a grant proposal is sent to NIH, it first goes to the Referral Office of the *Division of Research Grants (DRG),* where it is assigned to a Study Section for initial review and to a funding Institute (or other funding component) on the basis of administrative guidelines. Here the grant is assigned a number, for example; 1 R01 EY 01234–01:

1	**R01**	**EY**	**01234**	**–01**
Status of grant proposal (1 = new, 2 = renewal, etc.)	Type of grant proposal (R = research, F = fellowship, etc.)	Funding Institute[3]	Identification number within the Institute	Year of project

(Sometimes there is a suffix following the "Year of project;" for example, A1 means amended or revised, S1 means supplement.)

The Division of Research Grants:

- Sets up Study Sections (both standing and, when necessary, ad hoc) to review applications for Research Grants (R01), Research Career Development Awards (RCDA, K04), FIRST Awards (R29), Academic Research Enhancement (AREA) Awards (R15), Small Business Innovative Research Grants (SBIR, R43, R44), and fellowships (NRSA, F32, F33).

  Many grant applications submitted to various agencies of the Public Health Service (PHS) must be submitted through the Referral Section of the NIH DRG. This includes applications intended not only for the NIH, but also for the Food and Drug Administration (FDA), Agency for Health Care Policy and Research (AHCPR), Health Resources and Services Administration (HRSA), and Centers for Disease Control and Prevention (CDC).

---

[3] See Appendix VI-A for a list of abbreviations of NIH funding components.

- Is not part of any Institute
- Is a separate body that answers to the Director of NIH
- Is advisory to the Institutes

Grant application assignment to a Study Section

At DRG the application is assigned for scientific review to one of approximately 100 Study Sections.[4]

- DRG has Referral Officers[5] who assign applications to specific Study Sections for review.
- Referral Officers rely heavily on the title, project description (abstract), and specific aims of an application to make Study Section assignments.
- The Referral Officers use specific guidelines to make assignments of grant applications to Study Sections and may discuss the appropriateness of a Study Section with the SRA of the relevant Study Section.[6]
- *You may suggest 3 Initial Review Groups that would be appropriate for your application.* Attach such correspondence to the application at the time of submission. Suggestions will be considered, but the final determination will be made by the DRG.
- If you think there has been a serious error in the Study Section assignment of your application, you may request corrective action by writing to the SRA of the Study Section.

Information about Study Section membership—and the advice of colleagues who are "savvy" about the grants process—can be of great help in directing a proposal to the most suitable Study Section. The book *NIH Advisory Committees: Authority, Structure, Function, Members* (last published in April, 1993), gives the mandate of each Study Section and lists its members. As of 1994, information about Study Section rosters is available only on-line.[7]

---

[4] The number of Study Sections changes periodically as new areas of investigation emerge or the application load in specific research areas increases. In spring 1993 there were 83 chartered Study Sections in DRG. Some of these were divided into subcommittees, making a total of 101 working DRG Study Sections. In addition, DRG had one Special Emphasis Panel (SEP) for Behavioral and Neurosciences. As this book went to press in mid-1994, DRG had been reorganized into 19 Initial Review Groups and 6 SEPs, one for each of the 6 DRG review sections. (For a listing of the review sections, see Appendix VI.) Each of the Initial Review Groups is divided into subcommittees called Study Sections—which, in June 1994 were approximately the same 100 operative Study Sections that existed prior to the reorganization (watch for possible changes!). The SEPs are permanently chartered Initial Review Groups (Study Sections) but do not have a standing membership; thus, every time the SEP meets, it has a different ad hoc group of Reviewers. Investigator-initiated research grant proposals such as the R01, R29 (FIRST Award), individual fellowship applications [F32 (postdoctoral fellowships), F33 (senior fellowships; often used for sabbaticals)], Research Career Development Awards (RCDA = K04), Academic Research Enhancement Awards (AREA = R15), Small Business Innovation Research Grants (SBIR = R43 & R44), and Shared Instrumentation grants (S10)— among other types of grant applications—are reviewed by Initial Review Groups within DRG.

In addition to the Initial Review Groups (IRGs) within DRG, there are (as of June 1993) some 69 Initial Review Groups in the Institutes (including the 3 Institutes that were transferred from the Alcohol, Drug Abuse, and Mental Health Administration (ADAMHA) in 1992). It is noteworthy that 45% of NIH peer review is done outside DRG, within review units of the individual Institutes. The Institute IRGs review Applications for Cooperative Agreements, Program Projects, Center Grants, Institutional Training Grants, Contracts, and responses to RFAs (Request for Applications). The Institutes also have SEPs and these special review groups may increase in number in the future. In this book I will discuss primarily the review process at DRG.

[5] The referral officers are generally scientists who have become Scientific Review Administrators and have had extensive experience running Study Sections.

[6] In the future, if electronic submission of grant proposals becomes the predominant mode of grant submission (see information about Project EGAD in Appendix I-A), Study Section assignment probably will be made predominantly by computer—using keywords assigned by the Principal Investigator.

[7] For information, call Dr. John C. James: 301-594-7270. Additional information from this book may be available on-line in the future.

Grant application assignment to an Institute or other funding component

At DRG your proposal is also assigned for management and possible funding to one, or in some cases two (dual assignment), of 21 funding components.[8] The Referral Officers use specific guidelines to make assignments of grant applications to Institutes (or other funding components).[9] The assignment is made according to the *overall mission* and *specific programmatic mandates* and interests of the Institute or other funding component.

You may suggest an NIH funding component that would be appropriate for your application.

- Attach such correspondence to the application at the time of submission.[10]
- Suggestions will be considered, but the final determination will be made by the DRG.

At the Institute the application is assigned to a member of the Institute program staff who

- Is your primary Institute contact for all matters dealing with your grant application before and after the review process
- Is responsible for administration of the grant if the application is funded
- Is expected to attend the Study Section meeting at which the application is reviewed—but only as an observer; i.e., s/he does *not* participate in the review and evaluation of the application
- Is prepared to defend and elucidate the recommendations of the Study Section to Council

The member of the Institute program staff assigned to your grant acts as an ombudsperson for the application with respect to procedures that affect the grant at NIH. It is the responsibility of that individual to respond to questions by the applicant. These questions may relate to priority scores, to items within the Summary Statement, or to rebuttals or may concern advice about the course of action to be taken when a proposal is not funded. In addition, s/he can be questioned about the relevance of potential research ideas—for future proposals—with respect to the research priorities of that Institute. The Institute program staff members are instructed to remain neutral in all grant dealings.

When assignment to a Study Section and a funding component is completed, a computer-generated snap-out mailer, indicating the assignments, is sent to the PI (see Appendix I-E, Fig. A1-1).

About the Study Section

Each Study Section is composed of about 14 to 20 scientists (including, when appropriate, research-oriented clinicians, community practitioners, ethicists, etc.) chosen by the SRA for

---

[8] The 21 funding components include the 17 NIH Institutes (counting the National Institute for Nursing Research, which was the National Center for Nursing Research (NINR) until June 10, 1993, and the 3 Institutes that were transferred from the former ADAMHA in 1992, the National Library of Medicine, the National Center for Human Genome Research, the National Center for Research Resources, and the John E. Fogarty International Center. There are also 3 non-funding components among the 24 NIH Institutes/Centers/Divisions: Division of Research Grants, Warren Grant Magnuson Clinical Center, and Division of Computer Research and Technology (see Appendix VI-A and Appendix I-F, Figure A1-6).

[9] If electronic submission of grant proposals becomes the normal mode of grant submission, assignment of potential funding component(s) will also be made by computer. Apparently, such assignment presents greater problems than Study Section assignment and will likely take longer to implement.

[10] Suggestions about funding component assignment should go into the same letter as suggestions about Study Section assignment.

their competence in particular scientific areas. One of these scientists is selected by the SRA to be the chairperson of the Study Section. The chairperson moderates the discussion of the scientific merit of the proposals during the Study Section meeting; the SRA attends to all administrative and policy aspects of the proceedings. Each Study Section meets 3 times a year, usually for 2 to 3 days at a time, and reviews 40 to 120 applications.

The Scientific Review Administrator (SRA):

- Is a Federal employee, usually a Ph.D. scientist, who is in charge of a Study Section.
- Nominates Study Section members (sometimes using recommendations of retiring members).
- Selects the chairperson for the Study Section.
- Performs administrative and technical review of applications.
- Selects primary and secondary Reviewers and Readers (Discussants) for each proposal.
- Manages the administrative aspects of the Study Section meeting.
- Prepares Summary Statements (often referred to as "Pink Sheets"[11]).
- Provides information about Study Section recommendations, when requested, to Institute staff, to Advisory Councils, and to PIs.

Criteria for selections of Study Section members

- Doctoral degree or equivalent.
- Demonstrated scientific expertise.
- Mature judgment.
- Balanced perspective and objectivity.
- Ability to work effectively in a group context.
- Interest in serving on a Study Section.

Other considerations for choice of Study Section members[12]

- Members must represent a wide range of expertise related to main subjects reviewed by that Study Section .[13]
- Members must represent different geographical areas (U.S. divided into 4 areas: Northeast, South, Midwest, West).
- There may be no more than one member from a given institution.
- Member may be on only 1 Study Section at a time.
- Member generally serves 4 years but may serve longer (a maximum of 2 *non*-consecutive terms (8 years) in a 12-year period).
- No more than 25% of members may be Federal employees. (In practice, the DRG aims to have no more than 1 Federal employee per Study Section.)
- The membership must have representation—insofar as possible—of both sexes and from diverse ethnic groups.
- NIH funding history of potential member.

---

[11] For reasons of ease of reproduction and recycling, the "Pink Sheets" are no longer printed on pink paper as of 1992.

[12] Be familiar with NIH procedures and requirements for consultants (Reviewers) about confidentiality and avoidance of conflict of interest (see *NIH Peer Review Notes*, February 1991, pp. 4).

[13] For example, selected areas of competence represented on the Surgery, Anesthesiology and Trauma Study Section include biochemistry, burn physiology and electrolyte metabolism, cardiovascular and pulmonary physiology, clinical anesthesiology, drug metabolism (anesthetics), general surgery, immunology and transplantation, nutrition, pharmacology, pulmonary embolism, shock and trauma, toxicology and anesthetic drugs, urology, and vascular surgery (taken from pp. 42 of *NIH Peer Review of Research Grant Applications*, February 1992).

The specific members, the chairperson, and the Scientific Review Administrator of every NIH Study Section are listed in an NIH publication entitled *NIH Advisory Committees: Authority, Structure, Functions, Members,* which is updated annually. It is wise to be familiar with the membership of the Study Section that will review your proposal.[14]

The Scientific Review Administrator of the Study Section assigns specific grants to particular Reviewers. Each grant application is assigned primary and secondary Reviewers who are responsible for its in-depth review. The Reviewers study the application carefully and sometimes do a great deal of homework and library work to determine the merits of the application.[15] In addition, the Scientific Review Administrator assigns two or more Readers (Discussants) to each application.[16] Readers, like primary Reviewers, must be very knowledgeable about the applications that they have been assigned and are expected to participate actively in the discussion. But, unlike the primary Reviewers, the Readers are not required to prepare a written report about the application—although some choose to do so.

The Scientific Review Administrators of Study Sections sometimes enlist ad hoc members for specific meetings when additional expertise in a particular field is necessary. These ad hoc members[17] may *not* vote on the disposition of the application or assign priority scores. The names of these ad hoc Reviewers are included in the roster of each meeting, which may be obtained from the Committee Management Office.[18] There is also an NIH Reviewers Reserve (NRR[19]), which is a pool of Reviewers who can be summoned to serve on a Study Section on an ad hoc basis. Reviewers from the NRR may vote like regular Reviewers. The Scientific Review Administrators of Study Sections also may request "outside" opinions about an application, by mail.

You will not be given, and should not ask for, the names of the primary and/or secondary Reviewers—or the Readers—of your application.

Each member of the Study Section is sent a copy of every application to be considered at the meeting except those in which they may have a conflict of interest. To enable them to participate in the discussion and rating of all applications, all Study Section members are expected to be familiar with all the applications. The primary and secondary Reviewers are responsible for thoroughly evaluating—in writing (according to a set of

[14] For up-to-date information about Study Section rosters, call the DRG Committee Management Office: 301-594-7265. NIH is also working to develop an on-line database system that will make such information accessible directly to the scientific community.

[15] As with any group of individuals, the Reviewers who make up a Study Section tend to represent the range of personality types. Some are conscientious and/or compulsive; others may be more casual. How much homework or library work a given Reviewer will do for a particular proposal will also depend, to some extent, on the pressures and time constraints of her/his own schedule (both work and home life) at the time of review. Because it is generally not possible for you to predict the situation of your Reviewer, it is critical that your application be clearly understandable on its own, that is, without an appendix—and without trips to the library, or the bother and expense of on-line literature searches by the Reviewer.

[16] According to the DRG *Handbook for Executive Secretaries, 1990,* page 82, each application must be assigned to at least two Readers. Dr. Donna Dean, Chief, Biological Review Section, assured me that this was still the official policy in 1993 (note that Executive Secretaries are now called Scientific Review Administrators); however, members of 2 different Study Sections, have told me that only one Reader is assigned to applications reviewed in their Study Sections. On the other hand, some SRAs apparently use 3 or more Readers.

[17] The ad hoc Reviewers are officially referred to as "Special Reviewers." They may *not* serve in consecutive rounds in the same *regular* Study Section.

[18] Committee Management Office: 301-594-7265.

[19] NRR members are nominated for a 4-year-term by SRAs, reviewed by the NRR Pool Coordinators, and approved by the Director of DRG. NRR members may serve on up to 2 NIH-chartered review committees during a grant cycle. The number of NRR members who participate in a particular review committee meeting is limited to no more than half the quorum, which is the majority of the chartered committee's authorized membership. However, the NRR members do *not* count toward the quorum. NRR members have the rights, privileges, and obligations of actual members and may accordingly make and vote on motions and assign priority ratings if they are present for the entire meeting.

guidelines provided by DRG)—the scientific merits of the applications assigned to them. (See pages 20–21). Reviewers must sign a Certification of No Conflict of Interest.[20]

The Primary Reviewers come to the Study Section meeting with a written report in which they have assessed, to the best of their ability, the

1. Scientific and technical significance of the proposed research
2. Originality/innovativeness of the proposed research
3. Adequacy of the outlined methodology
4. Qualifications and experience ("track record")—or potential, in the case of a new applicant—of the investigator(s) and of the staff
5. Suitability of the facilities (including availability of resources and scientific ambiance)
6. Appropriateness of the requested budget
7. Appropriateness of the requested time to carry out the project (usually 3 to 5 years)
8. Other factors: ethical matters, human subjects, animal welfare, biohazards, representation of both sexes and diverse ethnic groups in clinical studies, and conformity with other relevant regulations.

The instruction sheets that NIH Reviewers are asked to follow when they write their reports about each application for which they are a primary or secondary Reviewer are given in Appendix I-D-1 (*Guide for Assigned Reviewers' Preliminary Comments on Research Grant Applications (R01).*

Although the Readers are not required to bring a written report to the Study Section meeting, they are expected to provide substantial discussion about an application's major strengths and weaknesses. The Readers sometimes also help put an application into final perspective for the Study Section. Because funds are in such short supply, Study Section members want to be sure they support the best applications. The nonprimary Reviewers—who may have read a particular application only cursorily—especially value the additional opinions provided by the Readers about applications. Thus, Readers may have substantial influence on how nonprimary Reviewers vote, and, in some sense, may play a pivotal role in the review of an application. Because the Readers' input is often critical, the Scientific Review Administrator may—after review of an application—ask a Reader to provide one or more paragraphs of critique for inclusion into the Summary Statement. Some SRAs encourage Readers to arrive at the Study Section meeting with some written comments about the application.

As this book goes to press, a study (initiated in 4 Study Sections at the February 1994 review cycle), intended to streamline the review process, is underway at NIH.[21] The procedure under study, referred to as Triage, gives assigned Reviewers the option to designate as Noncompetitive (NC), those R01 and R29 applications which they think would score in the bottom 50% of priority scores for that review cycle. However, an objection from even a single member of the relevant Study Section brings the NC application back into full review. Thus, in a sense, an application can be designated NC only by unanimous decision

---

[20] Certification of No Conflict of Interest: "This will certify that in the review of applications and proposals by _____ on _____, I did not participate in the discussion of any application or proposal from an organization, institution, or university system where I am an employee, consultant, officer, director, or trustee, or have any financial interest. I was not involved in the review of any application or proposal in which there was a real or apparent conflict of interest."

[21] Triage was adopted for DRG-wide use in Sept. '94. See page xiv, footnote 27 on page 22, and *NIH Guide for Grants and Conracts*, Vol. 23 No. 34, Sept. 23, 1995, page 2.

of all members of the review group. Applications designated NC are not discussed at the Study Section meeting, thus saving time at the meeting or allowing more time for discussion of borderline applications. The study was continued in 12 Study Sections, at the June 1994 review cycle and at 52 Study Sections at the October review cycle and was adopted for all DRG review panels as of the February 1995 review cycle. A major concern about the new procedure is whether the Principal Investigators of NC applications are getting sufficient feedback from Reviewers in the modified Summary Statements associated with the new procedure. It should be noted that with the Triage procedure, use of the NRFC (Not Recommended for Further Consideration) voting category has been replaced by NC (see footnote 27, page 22). But NC is not considered a voting category. Watch the *NIH Guide for Grants and Contracts* and other science news publications for developments related to the Triage study.

At the Study Section meeting

Study Section meetings are open to the public—limited by space available—for approximately 45 minutes at the beginning of the first session of the first day of the meeting during the discussion of administrative details relating to Study Section business. Thereafter, the meetings are closed and confidential.

Any primary or secondary reviewer may designate up to 50% of R01 and R29 applications reviewed at a study section as "Noncompetitive" (NC) at current funding levels. If both reviewers concur, and if no other member of the Study Section objects, these applications are not discussed at the study section meeting and thus, do not receive a priority score. These applications are not routinely forwarded to the relevant Advisory Council (the second level of NIH peer review). This process is called Triage. Most of the triaging is expected to occur prior to the Study Section meeting but an application may also be designated NC during the meeting and any application so designated may be recalled to full review at any time before or during the meeting by any single member of the Study Section. Thus, an NC designation must be unanimous. For applications which have not been triaged, the primary and secondary Reviewers present[22] their reports aloud at the meeting, followed by comments by the assigned Reader(s). Then there is general discussion, by all the Study Section members, of the merits and pitfalls of the proposal, the qualifications of the principal investigator (PI), and the appropriateness of the proposed staff. All members are expected to be acquainted with the general substance of all of the grant applications to be reviewed and to participate in the discussion. Administrators from the relevant NIH Institute(s) are often present at the Study Section meetings. They may be asked to provide administrative information, for example, about the applicant's grant history, but they do not participate in the general discussion. Anytime during—or after—the discussion, which may take anywhere from 10 minutes to as long as an hour, a member of the Study Section may make a recommendation that the application be designated *Noncompetitive* (NC) or *Deferred for additional information.* If the recommendation is adopted, these applications are not further discussed by the Study Section, are not given priority scores, and are not considered by Council. If no "NC" designation or motion to "Defer" is proposed, or if the NC designation is not unanimous, or the motion to "Defer" is not carried, the application is assigned a numerical rating by each Study Section member (see below). These applications are informally referred to as the "Scored" applications.[23]

---

[22] At some Study Sections, Reviewers read their reports verbatim; in others, Reviewers only summarize their reports. The pattern is determined by the SRA and/or the chairperson.

[23] "Not Recommended for Further Consideration" (NRFC = "Nerfed") and "Deferred for additional information" are the 2 official voting categories at NIH Study Section meetings. "Scoring," that is, assigning a scientific merit

Possible actions taken on applications being reviewed:

1. Designated as Noncompetitive (NC)

- Reviewers are asked to use the "Noncompetitive" (NC) designation to mean that the application is in the bottom half of the applications assigned to that Study Section. (Note that the cut-off priority score—with respect to funding—is different in different review groups.)
- To be considered NC, an application must be so judged by at least two assigned reviewers/readers. If any member of the Study Section does not concur with the judgement, the application is returned to full review. Thus, the NC designation must be unanimous. An application can be called back into full review at any time before or during the Study Section meeting. Study Section members are advised to err—if they are in doubt—on the side of full review rather than NC.
- Note that NC is very different from the voting category "Not recommended for further consideration" (NRFC) which came into use in 1991 and was used for the last time in Autumn 1994 for R01 and R29 applications reviewed by DRG.[24] Whereas NRFC indicated that an application did not have substantial scientific merit,[25] *NC does not mean that an application lacks merit, but rather that it is not likely to be awarded in the current funding climate.* Thus, NC does not directly tell the PI anything about the quality of the application.
- Although NIH considers triage to be fully implemented as of the February 1995 review cycle, the agency says the process will undoubtedly continue to evolve, with modifications being made as issues become apparent and necessitate adjustments.

2. Deferred for additional information

The deferral mechanism is used when a basically good proposal is missing readily definable information that the Study Section members think they can obtain by mail or—in some cases—via a project site visit. For applications that are deferred, the Reviewers delineate for the SRA what additional information needs to be supplied by the PI to enable appropriate review by the Study Section. After the Study Section meeting, the SRA contacts the PI to convey this information. Deferred applications are generally re-reviewed at the next Study Section meeting if the PI has responded to the request for additional information.

3. Assigned a priority score

Priority score = 100 × average of individually assigned numerical ratings

For each application that is not designated "NC" or "deferred," each voting member of the Study Section individually records, by secret ballot, a numerical rating that reflects her/his personal evaluation of the scientific merit of the proposed research. The primary Reviewers may suggest an appropriate merit descriptor or priority score range for the ap-

---

rating, is the action taken by the reviewers on applications that are not relegated to 1 of the 2 voting categories, but "scoring" an application is not an official voting category. Use of the voting categories "Approval" and "Disapproval" was discontinued in fall 1991. Note, however, that a modification of peer review at NIH in 1994 render NRFC obsolete, as of the February 1995 review cycle.

[24] NIH is still using the NRFC (informally referred to as "Nerfed") voting category for fellowship and certain other types of applications and apparently may, in the future, re-introduce the NRFC designation (to co-exist with NC) for R01 and R29 applications. Keep your eye on the *NIH Guide for Grants and Contracts.*

[25] NRFC is used if an application (1) lacks new or original ideas, (2) has a diffuse, superficial or unfocused research plan, (3) shows inadequate knowledge of published relevant work, (4) lacks (a) clarity in the broad, long-term objectives, or (b) an acceptable scientific rationale, (5) shows (a) questionable reasoning in experimental approach, (b) lack of sufficient experimental detail, (c) lack of experience in the essential methodology, or (d) an uncritical approach, or (6) describes an unrealistically large amount of work for the requested time.

plication before individual numerical merit rating assignment. Reviewers by mail are asked to recommend a merit rating or a merit descriptor.

Numerical ratings are assigned according to a scale of 1.0 (best) to 5.0 (worst), in increments of 0.1.

The numerical ratings are later averaged and multiplied by 100 to generate priority scores.

Numerical Rating	Corresponding Merit Descriptor
1.0–1.5	Outstanding
1.5–2.0	Excellent
2.0–2.5	Very good
2.5–3.5	Good
3.5–5.0	Acceptable

The research proposed in scored applications is considered to be significant and substantial. The recommendation to assign a merit rating may be for the time and amount requested or for an adjusted time and amount. The budget is discussed *after* the individual confidential numerical rating assignment.

The NIH review procedures for Initial Review Group (Study Section) meetings are given in Appendix I-D.

A site visit to a principal investigator's laboratory

Occasionally, the Study Section may recommend a project site visit to the principal investigator's laboratory. Because site visits are costly, they are generally used for the more complex applications.

A site visit is:

- Recommended before a Study Section meeting if a primary Reviewer or the Scientific Review Administrator recognizes the need for additional information that cannot be obtained by mail or telephone. That is, when information needed to make a recommendation about an application can be obtained only at the proposed research or training site.
- Recommended at a Study Section or Council meeting in conjunction with a deferral action.
- Desirable when the application involves complex coordination of individuals or institutions, for example, Program Project Grants, and Training Grants.

The site visit is made by a special site visit committee. The Scientific Review Administrator selects the members of the project site visit team, accompanies them, and coordinates the proceedings. Typically, the site visit team (for an R01 application) is composed of 3 or more members of the Study Section and, when necessary, ad hoc consultants who are experts in critical aspects of the proposed work. Representatives from the potential awarding Institute also attend the site visit as observers. The site visit team reports its findings and recommendations back to the Study Section in time for its next meeting.

In the past, site visits, as their name implies, have been to the PI's laboratory. Because of increasing budgetary constraints, future site visits may be held in the Washington, DC, area.[26] In addition, NIH occasionally does Conference Call Reviews—a sort of site visit by phone.

---

[26] This situation is often referred to as a "reverse site visit" or "applicant interview."

After the Study Section meeting

At the end of each Study Section meeting, the Scientific Review Administrator prepares a Summary Statement for each grant application. Summary Statements have a specific format. All Summary Statements contain the primary and secondary Reviewers' reports, i.e., critiques of the project proposed in the grant application. (Reviewers are expected to modify their written critiques during the review of an application—for example, removing a criticism that was deemed to be invalid following group discussion.) Scored applications also have a "Description of Project" and a paragraph summarizing the study section discussion (including budget recommendations, if appropriate) about the proposal. NC applications do not contain these two paragraphs but have instead a standard explanation of the NC designation. Some Summary Statements contain notations about special points, such as a split vote,[28] a potentially hazardous experimental procedure, or concerns about proposed human studies or use of vertebrate animals.

In preparation for generating the Summary Statement:

- The numerical scores assigned by the individual Study Section members for each scored application are averaged[29] and multiplied by 100 to provide a three-digit rating—known as a *priority score*—for the proposal.
- Percentile ranks are then calculated for these averaged priority scores[30] The priority scores and percentile rankings are the primary, but not the only, determinants upon which funding decisions are based. Funding decisions are also influenced by Council and are also based on program considerations (program relevance and priorities) and availability of funds.
- Applications which are "Deferred for Additional Information" or designated "Noncompetitive" are not given priority scores or percentile ranks.

The priority score and percentile rank are sent to the PI, via a computer snap-out mailer (see Appendix I-E, Fig. A1-2), within 2 weeks after the Study Section meeting.

The Summary Statement is sent to the PI about 6 to 8 weeks after the Study Section meeting (sooner for NC applications). The Summary Statements for scored applications are generally also forwarded to the Council of the appropriate Institute (or other funding component) for further review and possible recommendation for funding. But applications which are "Deferred for additional information" or designated "Noncompetitive" are not sent to the Council/Board. In addition, some institutes do not routinely send all scored applications for Council review. However, Councils and Institutes have the flexibility to make special exceptions (based on program or policy considerations) and may request to see certain applications in the group (whether scored or not scored) that are not automatically sent to them.

---

[27] As part of the 1994 NIH Study of Peer Review, the nature of the Summary Statement has changed, e.g., See articles by Reif-Lehrer in *The Scientist;* 11/28/94 and *J. Nat'l Grantseekers Inst.,* Vol. 2, No. 1, 1995..

[28] A split vote refers to the situation at an NIH Study Section meeting when the members do not agree on a voting category for a particular grant application. If there are 2 or more dissenting members, they are required to write a Minority Report explaining their reasons for dissenting. If only 1 member of the Study Section gives a dissenting vote, a Minority Report is optional. In this case the SRA may designate whether such a report must be written. If the SRA does not request a Minority Report, the dissenting member has the option of writing one.

[29] In the process of averaging the numerical scores, the SRA has both responsibility and latitude to ignore unsubstantiated outlying scores. This avoids the problem of an occasional low score given for the wrong reasons. A very low score assigned to an application by a reviewer who thinks the other reviewers are missing a major fault in the application is not considered an outlying score. If a probable outlying score comes to light during the discussion at the Study Section meeting, other Reviewers may adjust their scores to compensate. If the SRA discovers an unanticipated outlying score after the Study Section meeting, s/he may discard the score after discussion with a supervisor or may decide on a re-review if the issues are serious.

[30] See *NIH Peer Review Notes,* October 1991, pages 2–3, part of which is reproduced in Appendix I-D-4.

Note, however, that all applications reviewed, whether given a priority rating, or designated "Noncompetitive," are included in the calculation of percentiles.[30]

The Council

Each Institute has a National Advisory Council composed of 12 to 16 individuals, approximately 25% of whom are lay people; the remainder are scientists. The Scientific Review Administrator of a Study Section attends the Council meeting when a grant application reviewed in her/his Study Section is discussed. The Council considers the Summary Statements from each Study Section and adds its own review based on judgments of both scientific merit and relevance to the program goals of the assigned Institute. In some cases the program relevance can alter the ranking position of the application for funding. The Council then makes recommendations on funding. Consideration by the Council constitutes the second half of the peer review.

Overall, and within the confines of availability of funds, the *awards are based on both scientific merit and program considerations.* Thus, it should not come as a shock if an application with a worse priority score (higher number) is funded in preference to an application with a better priority score (lower number). *It should be kept in mind that neither the Study Section nor the Council has the power to make funding decisions. Both of these groups are only advisory. Final decisions about funding are made by the Director of the relevant Institute or funding component.*

"For most applications the minimum time from receipt to award is approximately 10 months. The initial scientific merit review generally takes place within 4 months of receipt, after which the results for most applications recommended for further consideration are conveyed to Institute Advisory Councils. A copy of this Summary Statement is usually sent by the Institute to the investigator about 1 month before the Council meets. Council generally meets about 3 or 4 months after the initial review, and awards are made after[31] the Council review."[32]

SOME GRANTSMANSHIP ADVICE

Know your Study Section

Study Section members rotate on and off the Study Section every July in a staggered fashion that assures overlap. Check the membership in *NIH Advisory Committees: Authority, Structure, Functions, Members.*[33] Call the SRA of the Study Section for up-to-date information on the membership roster and the exact dates of the Study Section meeting. Alternatively, you can call the Committee Management Office at DRG (301-594-7265). This information is also available on-line (see Appendix XI).

If you submit an application and subsequently submit a revised application, the revision may or may not be reviewed by the same primary Reviewers and Readers.

Although the essence of the grant review process is reasonably consistent throughout all DRG Study Sections, the subtle factors that influence the scoring of proposals may differ from one Study Section to another and may change as the membership and workload changes. Each Study Section has a different "culture" (i.e., a set of unwritten but generally agreed upon policies) that is determined by the

---

[31] Awards can be made as early as within 1 month, or as late as 1 year, after Council review.

[32] This paragraph is copied verbatim from pp. 3 of the PHS-398 Instructions, 9/91 revision.

[33] *NIH Public Advisory Groups: Authority, Structure, Functions, Members* is reissued annually but is often 6 months behind schedule. My April 1993 issue arrived September 21, 1993. The most recent previous issue was dated October 1991. This unusually long delay between issues apparently resulted from the changeover from publication of 2 issues per year to 1 issue per year. The book is available electronically from NIH (see page 352). Printed issues will no longer be available. Now that this publication is on-line it may be kept more current.

Table 2–1 Increase in Number of Applications Reviewed (1975–1992)

Year	1975	1985	1990	1991	1992
	Total applications reviewed				
DRG/Total	15,228	23,881	24,314	23,283	24,708
DRG /R01s only	10,778	17,245	16,850	15,605	16,837
DRG/FIRST Awards*	0	1	1,653	1,745	1,743
All NIH (including all DRG)	17,045	28,608	29,529	30,642	31,145
All PHS (including all NIH)	22,176	32,177	36,714	38,028	37,826

*The FIRST Award, which replaced the R23 program, was initiated in 1985.

- Scientific Review Administrator
- Chairperson
- Membership (4–year staggered terms)
- Number of grants being reviewed
- Subject matter under review and the context

Think about the Reviewers' workload

As you can see in Table 2–1, the number of grant applications reviewed by DRG has increased by about 60% since 1975. The increase has been even greater at NIH than at PHS as a whole. This has created a tremendous increase in workload for Reviewers. Grant application writers should appreciate that although Reviewers receive an honorarium ($150 per day in 1993, plus expenses at the government rate for attendance at the Study Section meetings, usually 3 days per meeting; 3 meetings per year), they receive no financial compensation for the many hours of work they devote to reviewing proposals in preparation for the meeting.

To be a successful grant application writer, it is important to think about the Reviewers as real people who have many important obligations in addition to reviewing your proposal.

Make *your* Reviewers' jobs as easy as possible[34] *before*—and *during*—the Study Section meeting. Give the Reviewer good cause to become your advocate rather than your adversary:

- "You never get a second chance to make a first impression." The Reviewer is likely to form a first impression within seconds of pulling your application out of the box. Be certain that it's a *good* impression. Your application should look neat and should be responsive to *all* instructions in the instruction packet.
- Rarely will a Reviewer be able to read your application from start to finish in one sitting. Make it easy for Reviewers, who are likely to read your proposal in bits and pieces, to understand what you propose to do without having to do too much backtracking.
- Write accurately, clearly, and concisely, and follow the instructions meticulously.
- Never cause the Reviewer to have to guess what you plan to do or are trying to say.
  —Explain precisely and clearly what you plan to do.
  —Although some Reviewers may know more about a subject than the grantee, never take it for granted that the Reviewer will "know what you mean."

---

[34] The information below is just a brief summary. Much of the rest of this book is devoted to helping you make your Reviewer's job as easy as possible.

—Give all necessary information in the correct places, in logical order, according to the required format, and within the stipulated page limitations.

—Don't make the Reviewer have to search the library to find out how you plan to do your experiments.

Dr. Jane Koretz, who served as a member of the NIH Visual Science-A Study Section from 1989 to June 1993 and who was one of the readers for this book, commented here: "I strongly concur with what you are recommending to [grant application writers]. The heavy loads that Reviewers must cope with these days reduce Reviewers' patience with poor writing, implicit assumptions about the expertise of the Reviewers, and poor layout. A good guideline for applicants would be to assume that they are writing for a qualified scientist in a somewhat related field, rather than an expert directly in their area."

Keep up to date

Keep up to date with what is going on at NIH and at other funding agencies. With new directors at both NIH and NSF in 1993, things are likely to change rapidly at both agencies in the next few years. For example, in 1994 NIH adopted a "Triage" system in its DRG Study Section review of grant applications, changed the nature of the Summary Statement, began attempting to identify research that is high risk but is likely to have high impact on our knowledge base, and is considering a two-grant cap for researchers, considering fixed rate ("chunk") grants, and considering a "Just In Time" program whereby grant applicants would not have to provide certain administrative details (which have up to now been required in the application) until the application has been judged to be in the likely funding range.[35] Undoubtedly, many more changes are being considered. Watch for them.

- Get on the mailing list for the *NIH Guide for Grants and Contracts,* or access it weekly via computer (see Appendix XI, Resources).
- Maintain contact with—and establish a good relationship with—the administrators of your funding Institute.
- Understand current funding priorities for research relevance at your funding Institute—and at other organizations where you might seek financial support.
- Keep track of the funding situation—both nationally and within your NIH Institute.
- Visit the Office for Grants and Contracts (Sponsored Research) at your institution. Get to know the people and the resources. For example, do they publish a newsletter? Do they search the *Federal Register* for items of interest to members of their research community?
- Get on the mailing list or subscribe to other pertinent newsletters, e.g., those published by various professional organizations (see Appendix XI, Resources).
- Note the revision date on the grant application form you use, and be sure you use the latest version. (For example, the PHS-398, Rev. 9/91 was reprinted with corrections in 9/92.)
- Watch for changes in grant application instructions between revisions.

For information about the review process at private foundations, see Appendix IX and *Tips for Applying to Private Foundations For Grant Money*, by L. Reif-Lehrer, in *The Scientist*, listed in Appendix XI.

---

[35] See Liane Reif-Lehrer, "Science Community Gives Mixed Review To Triage." *The Scientist,* November 28, 1994, pages 1, 8–9 and article by Liane Reif-Lehrer in *Journal of the National Grantseekers Institute,* Vol. 2, No. 1, 1995.

RECAP FOR PART II: UNDERSTANDING THE REVIEW PROCESS

A fundable grant proposal requires that the PI have:

- A good research idea.
- A well-focused, well-written research proposal.
- A good "track record" and/or substantive preliminary results (pilot studies).
- A substantial percent effort.
- A stable work group.
- An ample number of substantial, preferably peer-reviewed, publications.

Understanding the review process will help you write a better grant application. NIH has a dual peer review system:

- Initial Review Group (Study Section).
- Advisory Council.

The travels of an R01 grant application to NIH:

- Initiated by PI.
- Submitted by her/his sponsoring institution.
- Received by Referral Office at DRG.
- Assigned a number, for example, 1 R01 EY 01234–01.
- Assigned to a Study Section; PI may suggest 3 suitable ones.
- Assigned to an Institute or funding component (possible dual assignment); PI may suggest an appropriate one.
- Assigned to a member of the Institute program staff (Institute contact for PI).
- Study section and funding component assignments sent to PI via snap-out mailer.

About the Study Section:

- Run by Scientific Review Administrator (attends to administrative and policy aspects of proceedings).
- 14 to 20 scientists (chosen by SRA according to selection criteria).
- One member is selected by SRA to be chairperson (moderates the discussion of the scientific merit of proposals).
- Study Section meets 3 times a year.
- SRA assigns specific grants to particular Reviewers (primary and secondary) and Readers (Discussants).

Primary Reviewers' reports assess:

- Scientific and technical significance of proposed research.
- Originality of research.
- Adequacy of methods.
- Qualifications/experience ("track record") — or potential (for new applicant) — of PI and staff (Pilot studies/preliminary data).
- Suitability of the facilities/resources/scientific ambiance.
- Appropriateness of the budget.
- Appropriateness of the requested time.
- Other factors/assurances and certifications.

Actions on R01 and R29 grant applications:

- Designated Noncompetitive (NC)
- Deferred for additional information and/or site visit

- Assigned a scientific merit rating via secret ballot on a scale of 1.0 (best) to 5.0 (worst). Priority score = 100 × average numerical (merit) rating.

Numerical Rating	Corresponding Merit Descriptor
1.0–1.5	Outstanding
1.5–2.0	Excellent
2.0–2.5	Very good
2.5–3.5	Good
3.5–5.0	Acceptable

Budget recommendations (made after individual merit rating assignment).
After the Study Section meeting:

- SRA prepares Summary Statements.
- Merit ratings are averaged and converted to priority scores.
- Percentile ranks are calculated.
- Priority score and percentile rank are sent to the PI (within 2 weeks).
- Summary Statement is sent to PI (within 6 to 8 weeks).
- Scored applications are sent to the Council for further review and possible recommendation for funding.

About the Council:

- Each Institute has a National Advisory Council.
- Each council has 12–16 members (scientists + 25% laypeople).
- The SRA of the Study Section attends the Council meeting during discussion of grant applications reviewed in her/his Study Section.
- The Council reviews the application's scientific merit and relevance to the program goals of the assigned Institute.
- The Council makes recommendations on funding.

Basis of awards:

- Scientific merit
- Program considerations
- Amount of funding available

Be aware:

- The Study Section and the Council are only advisory.
- Final funding decisions are made by program staff at Institutes/funding components.
- Program relevance can alter the ranking position of a proposal for funding.
- The time from application receipt to award is about 10 months.
- Keep up to date with funding/events/changes at NIH and other funding agencies. Get agency literature.
- Maintain contact with the potential funding agency.
- Get to know people/resources at your institutional office for sponsored research.
- Give the Reviewer good cause to become your advocate:
  —Think about Reviewers' workload.
  —Write accurately, clearly, and concisely.
  —Follow instructions and page limitations meticulously.
  —Put information in correct places, in logical order, and in the required format.
  —Write for the average Reviewer: a qualified scientist in a somewhat related field, not an expert in your field.

PART III

PARTS OF THE
GRANT APPLICATION

INTRODUCTION

The application form for an NIH investigator-initiated Research Grant (R01) is Public Health Service (PHS) Form 398. This form is revised approximately every 3 years, and the changes vary from minor to extensive, though the general overall format has not changed dramatically in the 30 years that I have been writing proposals—except for the introduction of page limits. The version used as an example in this book is dated 9/91, but NIH has already begun work on the 1994 revision, which is expected to be available in early 1995. Where I have referred to page numbers in the PHS-398, these refer to the 9/91 revision. Apparently the 9/94 revision has a somewhat different organization of sections—so the page numbers may no longer be useful when the new forms are published.

The PHS-398 packet contains application forms and instructions for Research Grants (R01) and other types of support such as FIRST Awards (R29), Research Career Development Awards (RCDA), and Training Grants [Institutional National Research Service Awards (NRSA[1])]. A different application packet, PHS 416-1, is used to apply for individual postdoctoral fellowships [Individual National Research Service Awards (NRSA)]. I will use as an example—and discuss in detail—in this book only the R01 application. However, many of the basic concepts presented can be adapted to other types of applications at NIH and also at other funding agencies. *If you know how to prepare a good NIH grant application and understand the principles of responding to a set of instructions, you should be able to prepare a good application to any other agency.*

It is important to become familiar with the different sections of the grant proposal and understand the purpose and importance of each.

Reproduced on the following pages are the parts of the R01 application from the PHS-398 (Rev. 9/91) and some suggestions for filling them out. The complete NIH instructions can be obtained from the NIH Grants Information Office and may be available in your institutional grants office. It is important that you read the latest version of the NIH instructions very carefully before writing your proposal.

ADMINISTRATIVE AND FINANCIAL INFORMATION

In the first part of the NIH grant application you are required to give various kinds of administrative and financial information, primarily on forms provided in the application kit. In addition, on page 2 of the form there is a space in which to write a description (abstract) of the Research Plan that you must present in Section C. The instructions in the kit are quite explicit about how to fill out the forms in the kit. Where I considered it important, I have reiterated some of the NIH instructions. In some cases, I have provided additional information that you may find helpful.

Copies of individually printed form pages from the PHS-398 packet are available from DRG and may also be available from the grants office at your institution.

Computer-generated facsimiles may be substituted for any of the forms in the PHS-398 packet, but they must have the exact wording and format of the original forms, including captions and spacing. One exception, with respect to spacing only, is Form page 7, "Other Support," where the spacing may be changed as described later. "Any deviations," aside from that mentioned for "Other Support," "may be grounds for the PHS to reject the entire application."[2]

---

[1] Institutional National Research Service Awards and Individual National Research Service Awards both have the same abbreviation: NRSA.

[2] See PHS-398 instructions (Rev. 9/91), page 9, right-hand column, paragraph 2, third sentence.

Face page (Form page 1, Fig. 3-1)

Title of application (Fig 3-1, item 1) maximum of 56 spaces

The title of an application is quite important. It is the first introduction of your project to the referral officers and to the Reviewers and Readers and thus helps formulate their first impression about your application. The title should be descriptive, specific, and appropriate, and should reflect the importance of your research project.

The title may also be used by the referral officers for routing the application to the appropriate Study Section and assigning the application to an appropriate funding component. For example, an application with a title about a particular study in animal cells might be assigned to the National Institute for General Medical Sciences for possible funding and would go to a Study Section that reviews a large number of applications with subject matter relevant to that Institute. In contrast, specifying that the study will be done in retinal cells is likely to route the proposal to a vision Study Section for review and to the National Eye Institute (NEI) for possible funding. The level of funding at these two institutes may be quite different!

Another reason to be thoughtful about the title is well-illustrated in a 1992 *Science* article[3] concerning "congressional flak" about some grants with trivial sounding titles that were funded by NSF and NIH. The article ends with a quote from Herb Simon, a Carnegie-Mellon economist and 1978 Nobel Laureate: "We ought to learn that when we write down a title of a project, it should reflect the importance of the research."

Dates of entire proposed project period (Fig. 3-1, item 6)

The review process at NIH generally takes about 9 months. NIH has accelerated review for certain types of proposals such as fellowships and applications about certain "hot" topics such as AIDS. Check with the office of sponsored research or office for grant administration at your institution or with the DRG Grants Information Office at NIH (301-594-7248).

Enter the correct starting date according to the table on page 8 of the PHS-398 instructions. Unless you have reason to do otherwise, indicate the earliest possible starting date for the submission deadline you plan to meet. For example, if you apply for the Feb. 1 deadline (new R01 or R29 application), the starting date would be Dec. 1.

Application Receipt Date[4]	Study Section Meets	Council Meets	Earliest Possible Start Date
Feb. 1/Mar. 1	June/July	Sept./Oct.	Dec.
June 1/July 1	Oct./Nov.	Jan./Feb.	April
Oct. 1/Nov. 1	Feb./Mar.	May/June	July

Direct costs (Fig. 3-1, items 7a and 8a) and total costs (Fig. 3-1, items 7b and 8b) for the first 12-month budget period and entire proposed project period.

You may be able to get help from the office of sponsored research or office for grant administration at your institution to develop your detailed budget.

---

3 Richard Stone, "Peer Review Catches Congressional Flak," *Science*, Vol. 256, May 15, 1992, page 959.

4 As of April 1, 1993, *all* individual NRSA (F-series fellowship applications) must be received at NIH on April 5, August 5, and December 5 and must be submitted on PHS 416-1 (rev. 10/91) forms to be eligible for review (see *NIH Guide for Grants and Contracts*, Vol. 22, No. 1, January 8, 1993, Part II of II, and Vol. 22, No. 7, February 19, 1993, pages 1-2).

AA

Form Approved Through 6/30/94
OMB No. 0925-0001

DEPARTMENT OF HEALTH AND HUMAN SERVICES
PUBLIC HEALTH SERVICE

GRANT APPLICATION
Follow instructions carefully. Type in the unshaded areas only.
Type density must be 10 c.p.i.

LEAVE BLANK FOR PHS USE ONLY.

Type	Activity	Number
Review Group		Formerly
Council/Board *(Month, Year)*		Date Received

1. TITLE OF PROJECT *(Do not exceed 56 typewriter spaces.)*

2a. RESPONSE TO SPECIFIC REQUEST FOR APPLICATIONS OR PROGRAM ANNOUNCEMENT ☐ NO ☐ YES *(If "YES," state number*
Number: Title: *and title)*

2b. TYPE OF GRANT PROGRAM

3. PRINCIPAL INVESTIGATOR/PROGRAM DIRECTOR

3a. NAME *(Last, first, middle)*   3b. DEGREE(S)   3c. SOCIAL SECURITY NO.

3d. POSITION TITLE   3e. MAILING ADDRESS *(Street, city, state, zip code)*

3f. DEPARTMENT, SERVICE, LABORATORY, OR EQUIVALENT

3g. MAJOR SUBDIVISION

3h. TELEPHONE AND FAX *(Area code, number and extension)*
TEL:
FAX: BITNET/INTERNET ADDRESS

4. HUMAN SUBJECTS   If "Yes," exemption no. **or**   IRB approval date   4b. Assurance of compliance no.
4a. NO ☐ YES

5. VERTEBRATE ANIMALS   If "Yes," IACUC approval date   5b. Animal welfare assurance no.
5a. NO ☐ YES

6. DATES OF ENTIRE PROPOSED PROJECT PERIOD
From (MMDDYY)   Through (MMDDYY)

7. COSTS REQUESTED FOR INITIAL BUDGET PERIOD
7a. Direct Costs ($)   7b. Total Costs ($)

8. COSTS REQUESTED FOR ENTIRE PROPOSED PROJECT PERIOD
8a. Direct Costs ($)   8b. Total Costs ($)

9. PERFORMANCE SITES *(Organizations and addresses)*

10. INVENTIONS AND PATENTS *(Competing continuation application only)*
☐ NO ☐ YES   If "YES," ☐ Previously reported ☐ Not previously reported

11. NAME OF APPLICANT ORGANIZATION

ADDRESS

12. TYPE OF ORGANIZATION
☐ Public: *Specify*   ☐ Federal   ☐ State   ☐ Local
☐ Private Nonprofit
☐ Forprofit *(General)*   ☐ Forprofit *(Small Business)*

13. ENTITY IDENTIFICATION NUMBER   Congressional District

14. BIOMEDICAL RESEARCH SUPPORT GRANT CREDIT
Code: Identification:

15. NAME OF ADMINISTRATIVE OFFICIAL TO BE NOTIFIED IF AWARD IS MADE
TELEPHONE
FAX
TITLE
ADDRESS

BITNET/INTERNET ADDRESS

16. NAME OF OFFICIAL SIGNING FOR APPLICANT ORGANIZATION
TELEPHONE
FAX
TITLE
ADDRESS

BITNET/INTERNET ADDRESS

17 PRINCIPAL INVESTIGATOR/PROGRAM DIRECTOR ASSURANCE: I agree to accept responsibility for the scientific conduct of the project and to provide the required progress reports if a grant is awarded as a result of this application. Willful provision of false information is a criminal offense (U.S. Code, Title 18, Section 1001). I am aware that any false, fictitious, or fraudulent statement may, in addition to other remedies available to the Government, subject me to civil penalties under the Program Fraud Civil Remedies Act of 1986 (45 CFR 79).

SIGNATURE OF PERSON NAMED IN 3a.
(In ink. "Per" signature not acceptable.)   DATE

18. CERTIFICATION AND ACCEPTANCE: I certify that the statements herein are true and complete to the best of my knowledge, and accept the obligation to comply with Public Health Service terms and conditions if a grant is awarded as the result of this application. A willfully false certification is a criminal offense (U.S. Code, Title 18, Section 1001). I am aware that any false, fictitious, or fraudulent statement may, in addition to other remedies available to the Government, subject me to civil penalties under the Program Fraud Civil Remedies Act of 1986 (45 CFR 79).

SIGNATURE OF PERSON NAMED IN 16.
(In ink. "Per" signature not acceptable.)   DATE

PHS 398 (Rev. 9/91)   Face Page   AA

Fig. 3-1 Face page from PHS-398 grant application packet

PI's signature (Fig. 3-1, item 17)

Be sure to sign *and date* the application.

Signature of official signing for applicant institution (Fig. 3-1, item 18)

Have the person sign early; if you wait until the last minute, s/he may be out of town!

A responsible institutional official will not sign an application that s/he considers incomplete. It is that person's responsibility to ensure that the entire content of the application (goals, budget, facilities available, regulated activities (assurances), etc.) is acceptable within the context of your institution's mission.

The person responsible for signing the application is often a knowledgeable grants officer at your institution and may be able to help you improve your application if given enough time. Bringing your application for signature at the last possible moment is unfair to yourself and to the official and undermines the official's ability to do her/his job properly.

Abstract page (Form page 2, Fig. 3-2)

Abstract of the Research Plan (Fig. 3-2, top)

The abstract serves several purposes:

- The abstract may be used in routing the application to the proper Study Section.
- The abstract is often the first thing read by the Reviewers. It helps to form their initial impression. It tells the Reviewer what the proposal is about.
- The NIH publication *Orientation Handbook for Members of Scientific Review Groups* (Interim revision: March 1992) suggests that Reviewers use the abstract on page 2 of the application to write the "Description" part of the Reviewer's Report. (See also the Guide for Assigned Reviewers' Preliminary Comments on Research Grant Applications" in Appendix I-D-1 of this book.) A well-written abstract helps the Reviewers do their homework more easily. All other things being equal, happy Reviewers tend to be more favorable Reviewers.
- The abstract is one of the major things read by members of the Study Section who are not primary Reviewers for that application. Although NIH Study Section Reviewers are rarely asked to be primary or secondary Reviewers on more than 10 to 20 applications, they may be involved in the review process for as many as 100 or more grant applications. Because Reviewers also have full-time jobs, it may not be possible for them to read so many grant applications completely and thoroughly in the allotted time (usually about 6 weeks). Conscientious Reviewers read very carefully the applications for which they are specifically responsible and sometimes do many hours of homework before they write the reviews. For the remaining numerous applications, Reviewers have to pick, choose, and scan so that they can be sufficiently knowledgeable about the proposal to participate in the discussion during the Study Section meeting. The abstract (Form page 2 of the application) and the Specific Aims (Section C, item 1 of the application) are essential for this process. It is on the basis of these two sections that the Reviewers usually decide what other parts of a grant proposal to read more carefully.
- The abstract helps the Reviewer to remember what your grant is about at the time of the Study Section meeting. Often days, or even weeks, have passed between the time the Reviewer reads a grant proposal and when the Study Section meets. By the time of the meeting, the Reviewer has read a large number of applications. Exceptionally good and extremely bad applications tend to be better retained in the Reviewer's memory. For the remaining applications the Reviewer may rely on the abstract to help her/him recall the contents of the proposal. Underlining key

BB Principal Investigator/Program Director *(Last, first, middle):* _____

DESCRIPTION: State the application's broad, long-term objectives and specific aims, making reference to the health relatedness of the project. Describe concisely the research design and methods for achieving these goals. Avoid summaries of past accomplishments and the use of the first person. This abstract is meant to serve as a succinct and accurate description of the proposed work when separated from the application. **DO NOT EXCEED THE SPACE PROVIDED.**

PERSONNEL ENGAGED ON PROJECT, INCLUDING CONSULTANTS/COLLABORATORS. *Use continuation pages as needed* to provide the required information in the format shown below on **all** individuals participating in the project.

Name _____ Degree(s) _____ Social Security No. _____
Position Title _____ Date of Birth (MM/DD/YY) _____ Role on Project _____
Organization _____ Department _____

Name _____ Degree(s) _____ Social Security No. _____
Position Title _____ Date of Birth (MM/DD/YY) _____ Role on Project _____
Organization _____ Department _____

Name _____ Degree(s) _____ Social Security No. _____
Position Title _____ Date of Birth (MM/DD/YY) _____ Role on Project _____
Organization _____ Department _____

Name _____ Degree(s) _____ Social Security No. _____
Position Title _____ Date of Birth (MM/DD/YY) _____ Role on Project _____
Organization _____ Department _____

Name _____ Degree(s) _____ Social Security No. _____
Position Title _____ Date of Birth (MM/DD/YY) _____ Role on Project _____
Organization _____ Department _____

Name _____ Degree(s) _____ Social Security No. _____
Position Title _____ Date of Birth (MM/DD/YY) _____ Role on Project _____
Organization _____ Department _____

Name _____ Degree(s) _____ Social Security No. _____
Position Title _____ Date of Birth (MM/DD/YY) _____ Role on Project _____
Organization _____ Department _____

Fig. 3-2 Abstract page (Form page 2 from PHS-398 grant application packet)

words may also help the Reviewer remember the most important parts of your proposal. The abstract should be well thought out, clear, and concise, and should realistically represent the contents of the total grant application.

- The abstracts of all funded research grant applications are sent to the National Technical Information Service (NTIS), U.S. Department of Commerce (see Appendix I-C). NTIS uses the information for:
  —Dissemination of scientific information
  —Scientific classification
  —Program analysis
  —Public access to information about funded proposals

Note that the small print instructions above the box for the abstract specify that you:

1. State the *broad, long-term objectives* of the proposal.
2. State the *Specific Aims.*
3. Make reference to the *health-relatedness* of the project.
4. Describe the Research Design and Methods concisely.
5. Avoid summaries of past accomplishments.
6. Do *not* use the first person. Not using first person applies only to the abstract. It is acceptable to use first person in the Research Plan.
7. *Do not exceed the space provided.*
8. The abstract "should serve as a succinct and accurate description of the proposed work [even] when [the abstract is] separated from the application."

It is easiest to satisfy the instructions and save your own time by writing the abstract as follows:

"The *broad, long-term objectives* of this proposal are ... . The *Specific Aims* are 1.) ... 2.) ... 3.) ... . The *health-relatedness* of the project is ... . The *research design* is ... . The *methods* to be used are ...."

In keeping with points 5 and 6 of the instructions, do not begin the abstract with a sentence such as "For the past 5 years I have been studying ... ."

In keeping with point 7, do not try to fit more words into the box by changing to smaller print.[5] Use 10- or 12-point letters (see page 10, left column, paragraph 2 in the NIH instructions), and keep the text within the outline of the "box." Use the strategies in Appendix X to help you shorten your abstract. *It is not necessary to fill the box! When you have nothing more to say, stop writing!*

Write the abstract of the Research Plan last—after you have finished writing the final draft of the rest of the grant proposal. This will ensure that the abstract is both an accurate summary of—and an appropriate introduction to—the *final draft* of the proposal.

Key personnel (Form page 2, Fig. 3-2, bottom)

Use an additional page in the same format if more space is needed. Key personnel will be more clearly defined in the new PHS-398 Forms that are scheduled to be released in early 1995. Watch for changes about this part of the application.

"List all individuals, at the applicant institution or elsewhere, including the principal investigator, collaborating investigators, individuals in training, and support staff who will participate in the scientific execution of the project whether or not salaries are requested."

---

[5]NIH now returns applications with type sizes that are not in keeping with NIH instructions.

For each individual, list

- Name
- All degrees
- Social Security number (optional)
- Position title (within her/his own organization; e.g., assistant professor, staff researcher, predoctoral student, postdoctoral researcher)
- Date of birth (month, date, year)
- Role on project (e.g., principal investigator (PI), consultant, graduate research assistant)

Table of Contents (Form page 3, Fig. 3-3)

Fill in the page numbers on this form in the *last* draft of the proposal. If there is an appendix, list the appendix items in the space provided.

A separate table of contents for the Research Plan, listing all subheadings, helps the Reviewer find topics quickly in an application that is long and/or complex. The stringent page limitations of the NIH application form will, in most cases, preclude the use of such an additional table of contents for the Research Plan of NIH applications. However, an extra table of contents for the Research Plan may be useful for other types of grant proposals.

Subheadings in a table of contents should be informative:

Not: Experiment 1   *But:* Testing the effects of substance X on cell viability.

Detailed budget for initial budget period (usually the first 12 months) (Form page 4, Fig. 3-4)

Read carefully the NIH (or other agency) instructions for this section.

The budget should be reasonable, believable, well-researched, and superbly justified. Develop the budget *after* you have planned the project and can calculate what you will need to carry out the work.

Be sure the budget accurately reflects the proposed research. Don't "underbudget." (Don't try to give NIH a bargain; Reviewers will think you're naive.)

Don't "overbudget." (Don't be an opportunist or a "thief." Reviewers spot "padded" budgets.)

Discuss with the appropriate personnel at your institution which items are considered direct as opposed to indirect costs.

Be aware of budgetary guidelines[6] and restrictions imposed by your institution and by

---

[6] As of FY 1993, NIH funding components use the following guidelines to make funding decisions:
- Budgets of noncompeting grants must, on average, amount to not more than 4% more than the prior budget period, not counting nonrecurring costs such as equipment.
- The average total cost of all competing grants in FY 1994 will be no more than 4.19 percent (i.e., the Biomedical Research and Development Price Index) over the average total cost of all competing grants from FY 1993. Some funding components may provide smaller increases.
- Funding decisions will be based on the total costs (direct plus indirect).
- PIs of awards that are reduced 25% or more below Study Section recommendations may have to submit a revised statement of Specific Aims and a revised budget, countersigned by the official who signed the initial application at the PI's institution.
- On average, research grants will be funded for no more than 4 years.

See *NIH Guide for Grants and Contracts,* Vol. 21, No. 43, November 27, 1992, page 2 and Vol. 23, No. 6, February 11, 1994, page 2. Moreover, if you request more than $500,000 in direct costs in any one year, you must contact the appropriate Institute or the Referral Office (301-594-7250) early in your planning. See *NIH Guide for Grants and Contracts,* Vol. 22, No. 45, December 17, 1993, page 2.

Type the name of the principal investigator/program director at the top of each printed page and each continuation page. (For type specifications, see **Specific Instructions** on page 10.)

RESEARCH GRANT
TABLE OF CONTENTS

PAGE NUMBERS

Research Plan

*Type density and size must conform to limits provided in Specific Instructions on page 10.

Appendix *(Five collated sets. No page numbering necessary for Appendix)*
    Number of publications and manuscripts accepted or submitted for publication *(Not to exceed 10)* _____
    Other items (list):

☐ Check If Appendix
is Included

Fig. 3-3 Table of contents (Form page 3 from PHS-398 grant application packet)

DD   Principal Investigator/Program Director *(Last, first, middle):* Scientist, Jane X.

DETAILED BUDGET FOR INITIAL BUDGET PERIOD
DIRECT COSTS ONLY

FROM	THROUGH
12/01/93	11/30/94

PERSONNEL *(Applicant organization only)* (1) NAME	ROLE ON PROJECT	TYPE APPT. *(months)*	% EFFORT ON PROJ.	INST. BASE SALARY	DOLLAR AMOUNT REQUESTED *(omit cents)* SALARY REQUESTED	FRINGE BENEFITS	TOTALS
Jane X. Scientist (a)	Principal Investigator						
"	"	9	25	$40,837	$0	$0	$0
John Y. Tech (b)	Senior Lab Technician	3	100	$13,612	$13,612	$3,811	$17,423
Tom Z. Grad (c)	Graduate Lab Ass't	12	100	$18,727	$18,727	$5,712	$24,439
Ann W. Help (d)	Undergrad Lab Ass't	12	100	$14,009	$14,009	$4,378	$18,387
		12	100	$ 6,650	$ 6,650	$0	$ 6,650
SUBTOTALS ⟶					$52,998	$13,901	$66,899

CONSULTANT COSTS

EQUIPMENT *(Itemize)* (2)   Inverted microscope with DIC, epifluorescence, & photo capabilities ($32,140) (a); Leitz micromanipulator ($8,540) (b); New Brunswick G76 water bath($3,425) (c); JAIO rotor (1/2 share = $2,330) (d)

$46,435

SUPPLIES *(Itemize by category)* (3)

Photo supplies (a)	$2,465	Enzymes (b)	$3,150
Radioisotopes (c)	$2,280	Chem reagents (d)	$2,880
Media (e)	$1,990	Disposable supplies (f)	$4,270
Miscellaneous (g)	$3,500		

$20,535

TRAVEL (4)   2 National research conferences; PI will present research results.   ABC Mtg., Washington, DC. TDY Conf., San Francisco, CA $ 2,225

PATIENT CARE COSTS	INPATIENT
	OUTPATIENT

ALTERATIONS AND RENOVATIONS *(Itemize by category)*

OTHER EXPENSES *(Itemize by category)* (5)   Publication costs, $500 (a); photocopying and laser printing, $500 (b); Computer connection/services, $1,000 (c) $ 2,000

SUBTOTAL DIRECT COSTS FOR INITIAL BUDGET PERIOD $138,094

CONSORTIUM/CONTRACTUAL COSTS
  DIRECT COSTS $ _____
  INDIRECT COSTS $ _____   TOTAL ⟶

TOTAL DIRECT COSTS FOR INITIAL BUDGET PERIOD *(Item 7a, Face Page)* ⟶ $ 138,094

Fig. 3-4   Detailed budget for initial budget period (Form page 4 from PHS-398 grant application packet)

the funding agency. For example, NIH imposes a cap on the amount of salary that can be charged to a grant application or contract proposal for a given individual.[7]

Footnote budget items on the budget page, and refer to these numbers for the relevant explanations in the Budget Justification section (see the example on the sample budget page, Fig. 3-4).

Personnel

List the names and types of appointment of all applicant organization employees to be involved in the project during the 12-month budget period.[8]

List the principal investigator first.

List all collaborating investigators, then individuals in training, and finally support staff.

List personnel even if no salary is requested.

Note: Although the terms "co-principal investigator" and "co-investigator," are commonly used by grant application-writers, NIH does not officially recognize these titles. It is preferable to refer to individuals in such positions as "Investigators" or "Collaborating Investigators."

Role on project

List each individual's role: e.g., principal investigator, consultant, graduate research assistant.

Type of appointment (months)

List the number of months per year for which the individual has a contractual appointment at the applicant organization—or, if there is no contractual appointment, the number of months for which salary is being requested.

NIH assumes that the appointments are full-time for that period. If this is not the case, type an asterisk (*) after the number of months, and explain the extent of the appointment (e.g., ½ time or ¾ time) in the Budget Justification section.

If the 12-month year is divided into academic and summer periods, identify and enter *on separate lines* the type of appointment for each period.

Percent effort on the project

For each individual, specify the percentage of the appointment at the applicant institution to be devoted to this project. If an investigator has other institutional responsibilities, such as teaching, the *total percent* devoted to *all* research activities must be *less than* 100%.

Institutional base salary

For each individual, list the annual compensation from the applicant organization regardless of the individual's activity, but excluding income that the individual is permitted to earn outside of duties to the applicant organization.

You may leave this column blank in the application, but NIH may request this information before making an award.

Salary requested

Multiply the base salary by the percent effort on the project. If a lesser amount is requested for any position, explain in the Budget Justification.

Congress has imposed and may continue to impose salary caps (upper limits); check with your grants office, the *NIH Guide for Grants and Contracts,* and the NIH/DRG

---

[7] See information about NIH salary caps in Appendix I-D-5.

[8] For salary limitations on grants and contracts see page 17, bottom of left-hand column of instructions in PHS-398, (Rev 9/91) and Appendix I-D-5.

Grants Information Office for the latest advisory.[8] For noncontractual appointments, see NIH instructions.

If you want to omit specific salary amounts, see NIH instructions.

Fringe benefits

Fringe benefits must be in accordance with the existing rate agreement for each position and must be treated consistently with respect to all sponsors.

Consultant costs

Provide names and affiliations of consultants[9] even if no costs are involved. Exclude consultants involved in consortium/contractual arrangements. Include physicians who consult on patient care and people who serve on external monitoring boards or advisory committees to the project.

Describe briefly in the Budget Justification:

- Services to be performed
- Number of days of consultation anticipated
- Rate of compensation
- Other related costs: e.g., travel and per diem.

Provide biographical sketches for each consultant on the project. Place the biosketches with those of other participants on the project.

Provide letters from consultants attesting to their willingness to work on the project. These letters should contain sufficient detail to convince the reviewers that (1) the consultant understands your project and (2) s/he understands and agrees to her/his specific role in the project. Place these letters in Section 7 of the Research Plan.

Equipment

- Be aware of the "Buy American" provision which states that equipment purchased with grant money should be American-made whenever possible. (See *NIH Guide for Grants and Contracts*, Vol. 23, No. 7, February 18, 1994, page 2.)
- List separately each item requested that has a unit acquisition price of $500 or more.
- Include the shipping costs with the price of the item, and specify this in the Budget Justification. Shipping costs may be substantial for large pieces of equipment.
- Justify in the Budget Justification.
  If you need an expensive piece of equipment:
  —Get a written cost estimate to include in Budget Justification.
  —Try to split the cost with another funding agency, a colleague, another department, or some other source, or consider applying for a Shared Instrumentation Grant. If you must ask for the full cost of the equipment, write a very cogent and well-thought-out justification.
- List (under "Other Expenses") the cost of any necessary service agreements/contracts.
- Check that requested items are not contradictory to items listed under "Facilities" and "Major Equipment" on the Resources and Environment Form page 8 (see example under "Budget Justification" below).

---

[9] Except under very particular circumstances, staff members and employees of the applicant's institution may not act—or be listed—as paid consultants on the applicant's grant application.

Supplies

- Itemize supplies in separate categories such as glassware, chemicals, radioisotopes, etc., *if* the category total exceeds $1000.
- Categories in amounts less than $1000 should be combined as "Miscellaneous Supplies."
- For animals, give
  —Species
  —Number to be used
  —Unit purchase cost
  —Unit care cost
  —Number of care days
- Purchase, housing, and disposal costs for animals are usually also listed under "Supplies." However, depending on the grantee institution's accounting practices, these charges may be listed under "Other Expenses."

Travel

- On the budget page, specify number of trips, number of persons who will travel, and total costs.
- For each trip, specify in the Budget Justification:
  —Person(s) who will travel
  —Purpose of travel (e.g., will you present a paper/poster about your research?)
  —Destination (Professional organizations generally know where their annual meetings will be for the next 3 to 5 years.)
  —Estimated cost (Travel agents can provide approximate costs to these destinations.)

Reviewers are less likely to recommend budget cuts if it seems obvious that the PI has carefully researched the travel plans rather than just filled in some "guestimate" figure ending in 3 zeros.

Patient care costs
See NIH instructions.

Alterations and renovations
See NIH instructions.

Other expenses
Itemize by category and unit cost:

- Publication costs
  —Drafting
  —Photographs
  —Page charges
  —Reprints
- Books and professional journals
- Computer charges
- Rentals and leases
- Equipment maintenance
  —Service contracts
  —Repairs

- Fees for services
- Office supplies
- Postage
- Reimbursement for tuition remission that is given in lieu of all or part of salary for students who work on the project (detail in the Budget Justification).
- Reimbursement for expenses incurred by human subjects who participate in the project (detail in the Budget Justification). Note that this is different from *patient care costs* listed above.

Consortium/contractual costs
See NIH instructions, and consult your grants office.

Budget for total project period (Form page 5, Fig. 3-5, top)

Account for (i.e., include and justify) annual raises for personnel (cost-of-living, merit, promotion) and predictable changes in fringe benefit rate. Check guidelines at your institution's office for sponsored research and/or NIH to determine appropriate percentages to use to calculate these increases.

Think about new expenses that may arise in later years of the project—e.g., repairs, replacements, beginning new experiments that require new supplies, additional personnel.

On Form page 5, identify with an asterisk (*) any significant increase or decrease in any category, including personnel effort, over the initial budget period. Explain such changes in the Budget Justification.

Budget Justification (Form page 5, Fig. 3-5, bottom)

Justify *everything* in the budget that is not obvious, keeping in mind that what is obvious to you may not be obvious to the Reviewers. The Reviewers will be in a better mood if they do not have to puzzle over things such as unexplained changes in budget for subsequent years. Any changes should be specifically pointed out; it is to your *disadvantage* if the Reviewers think that you are trying to "pull a fast one" by slipping extra items into future year budgets.

Dr. Jane Koretz, who served as a member of the NIH Visual Science-A Study Section from 1989 to June 1993 and who was one of the readers for this book, commented here: "In these cost-conscious times, the budget justification is *crucial*.[10] It is essential that each expense be well justified, even if the need for something or someone appears to have already been implicitly justified in the Research Design and Methods section. Items will be cut by the Study Section or Council in the absence of appropriate justification."

A PI should also consider that the care illustrated in the writing of the Budget Justification tells the Reviewers a great deal about the care and conscientiousness with which the PI approaches her/his work and also is indicative of the PI's awareness of—and sensitivity about—good resource management.

There are *no* page limits for the Budget Justification in an NIH application.[11] If this section is written *concisely*, in clear outline form, underlining to make key words stand out and using appropriate formatting, such as indentation, to delineate secondary information (for example, details about how you arrived at the final figures), then each Reviewer can choose what to read and what to ignore. The budget discussion at the Study Section meeting occurs after the members have *privately* assigned priority scores on their individual scoring sheets. During the budget discussion, Reviewers, for the most part, should

---

[10] The italics are Dr. Koretz's.
[11] At NSF the Budget Justification has been limited to 3 pages, as of 1992.

EE   Principal Investigator/Program Director *(Last, first, middle):* _____

BUDGET FOR ENTIRE PROPOSED PROJECT PERIOD
DIRECT COSTS ONLY

BUDGET CATEGORY TOTALS		INITIAL BUDGET PERIOD *(from page 4)*	ADDITIONAL YEARS OF SUPPORT REQUESTED			
			2nd	3rd	4th	5th
PERSONNEL: *Salary and fringe benefits* *Applicant organization only*						
CONSULTANT COSTS						
EQUIPMENT						
SUPPLIES						
TRAVEL						
PATIENT CARE COSTS	INPATIENT					
	OUTPATIENT						
ALTERATIONS AND RENOVATIONS						
OTHER EXPENSES						
SUBTOTAL DIRECT COSTS						
CONSORTIUM/ CONTRACTUAL COSTS						
TOTAL DIRECT COSTS						

TOTAL DIRECT COSTS FOR ENTIRE PROPOSED PROJECT PERIOD *(Item 8a)* ⟶ $.

JUSTIFICATION (Use continuation pages if necessary):

From Budget for Initial Period: Describe the specific functions of the personnel, collaborators, and consultants and identify individuals with appointments that are less than full time for a specific period of the year, including VA appointments.

For All Years: Explain and justify purchase of major equipment, unusual supplies requests, patient care costs, alterations and renovations, tuition remission, and donor/volunteer costs.

From Budget for Entire Period: Identify with an asterisk (*) on this page and justify any significant increase or decrease in any category over the initial budget period. Describe any change in effort of personnel.

For Competing Continuation Applications: Justify any significant increases or decreases in any category over the current level of support.

Fig. 3-5 Budget for total project period (Form page 5 from PHS-398 grant application packet)

not have to refer to sections of the proposal other than the budget and Budget Justification; nor should they have to waste time doing arithmetic—do it for them. Show your work, not just the answer, and be sure it is correct (but exclude absurd levels of detail). There may be one Reviewer in the crowd who pulls out a pocket calculator and checks the math; incorrect calculations detract from your credibility!

It may be easier to type: "Please see continuation pages" on the bottom of Form page 5 and begin the Budget Justification on a new page. Use continuation sheets provided in the PHS-398 kit. (Type your name—*last name goes first*—and Social Security number (optional) onto the sample continuation page provided in the application packet *before* you photocopy the page! Or simulate the continuation sheet form on your computer.)

An indented format makes it easy for Reviewers to find increasing levels of detail in the Budget Justification.

— — — — — — — — — — — — — —
— — — — — — — — —
— — — — —

For example:

(4) **Supplies:** $10,856

   (a) Animals $7,950

      z Rats .... $ xxx
        x/wk for y weeks for the __ experiments

      x Rabbits .... $ yyy
        y/wk for x weeks for the __ experiments

   (b) Chemicals $1,006

      ___, 3 gm per month for x months at $x/gm .... $ xyz

      ___, 7 gm per month for x months at $x/gm .... $ zzz

   (c) Glassware $1,900

Justify everything

Footnote budget items on the Form Budget pages 4 and 5, and use corresponding numbers for explanations in the Budget Justification section (see Fig. 3-4).

Justify all personnel.

- The personnel category is likely to be the largest item in your budget. Justify it accordingly!
- Specify what *unique* role each person will play in the execution of the research. Describe each person's specific functions in the project. Show how the person's qualifications match her/his role in the project. Give the Reviewers good reasons to invest funds in this individual.
- Try to avoid using "To be named;" if you must use it, explain what sort of individual will be recruited (i.e., qualifications: field, specialty within the field, years past B.A. or Ph.D., etc.).

Explain and justify annual increases in budget items/categories.

If you request a piece of equipment in the Budget, explain why this equipment is necessary for this project. For example, why is it critical for the experiments? Do not just say that it will let you do an experiment better or faster.

If a piece of equipment is to be shared—or made available to other investigators for their work—it is sometimes helpful to mention this. However, you should give good reasons why *you* are requesting the total cost (rather than sharing it).

Check Equipment requests against the Resources and Environment page to be sure they are not contradictory. Justify *particularly well* equipment also listed under "Major Equipment" on the Resources and Environment page; for example, if you say that your institution has five balances (because you want to convince the Reviewer what a good facility it is), you must present a very strong argument for purchasing a sixth one with the requested grant funds.

Justify and explain new equipment requests in later budget years.

- If you are requesting a Model XYZ Microscope in the third-year budget and on the Resources and Environment page you write that you have a Model XYZ microscope, explain that the microscope that you now use belongs to Dr. X. She will be moving to another university in the third year of your project period and will be taking the microscope with her. Therefore, you will need a microscope at that time.
- If you ask for a piece of equipment in the third year and justify the request by saying that piece of equipment isn't available at your institution, then you should explain why you're not asking for it in the first year. For example, the project for which you need the piece of equipment is not scheduled to begin until the third year.

Without a very good explanation, Study Section members are unlikely to recommend purchasing an expensive piece of equipment in the last year of a project period. Although you may plan to continue your research for many years, your future applications may not get funded. A granting agency is unlikely to invest a large sum of money for just one year of research!

For expensive equipment, it's a good idea to provide a written quote from the company. NIH has apparently increasingly been requesting such formal quotes. Save them the effort and the wait for the information; provide it at the start. Be sure to include the shipping cost; this is especially important if the item is large and/or heavy.

If not included in the quote, add an inflation factor and estimate what the price might be at the time the item is to be purchased. Remember, about a year is likely to elapse between the time you obtain the quote and the time the grant is funded!

For supplies that cannot be obtained via readily available catalogs, if there has been a drastic price increase or if you are requesting money for a large quantity of a particular item, it may help to include receipts of previous purchases or other proof of price and/or actual usage. Reviewers sometimes forget about inflation. It pays to face them with proof of the facts. A little telephone and library research toward creating a realistic budget is time well spent.

Justify all travel.

- Specify who will travel and whether or not that person will present a paper.
- Estimate expenses based on actual meeting places. Find out where meetings will be held and how much it costs to get there.
- Specify that costs are based on shared room, tourist class fare, etc.

In these times of tight funding, travel sometimes is not considered a very high-priority item. Many Reviewers consider one meeting per year per senior investigator reasonable. If you are requesting money for more than one meeting per senior person, it is imperative to justify why it is important for that individual to go to two meetings and how you think she/he will benefit from attendance.

Justify *all* other expenditures.

Justify consortium and contractual (subcontract) costs thoroughly both here and in Section 8 of the Research Plan.

Justify the budget for the total project period

- Justify any significant increases in any category over the first 12–month budget period. *Identify such significant increases* with *asterisks* against the appropriate amounts.
- Specify: " 'Other Expenses' is increased by an *extra* $1000 (above the annual 4% increase) in year 03 to pay for sharpening our diamond knife (purchased in 19xx)."
- Or state, for example, "No additional equipment is requested in subsequent years."
- Don't give the Reviewers the opportunity to think you are trying to "put one over" on them.

Sample budget justifications are given in Appendix IV.

Biographical sketches (biosketches) (Form page 6, Fig. 3-6)

Maximum of 2 pages per person.

Photocopy the biosketch form *before* filling it out (except for your name and Social Security number (optional) at top right corner of the page).

Provide a biosketch for the principal investigator and all other key professional personnel listed on page 2—and be sure that all the biosketches provided are in the *same format*, including the publications. Note that postdoctoral training should be listed under "Education," not under "Research and Professional Experience."

Research and professional experience includes:

- Previous employment— in chronological order *(present position LAST)*
- Experience
- Honors
- Present membership in any federal government Public Advisory Committee
- Give complete references (including titles) to *all* publications *of the past 3 years* and *representative* earlier publications *pertinent* to this application. Because there is a two-page limit for each complete biosketch, choose publications wisely. *List them in chronological order.*

Note: Your own publications may appear in 3 places: Biosketch, Progress Report (Section C, item 3), and Literature Cited (Section C, item 9). In an elegant, carefully prepared proposal, references in all 3 bibliographies are presented in identical format. Avoid the temptation to simply collect biosketches from collaborating investigators and insert them in your proposal without reworking them into the same format—and/or without changing the name of the principal investigator in the upper right corner of the page.

Other support (Form page 7, Fig. 3-7)

Read carefully the *definition* of "Other Support" provided in the instructions and on the Other Support Form in the PHS-398 application kit (Rev. 9/91). Read carefully the *instructions* given on the Other Support Form provided in the application kit. Provide information about *all* active or pending sources of project-specific support to the principal investigator or any other key personnel on the project, *whether related to this application or not.*

FF   Principal Investigator/Program Director *(Last, first, middle):* _____

BIOGRAPHICAL SKETCH

Give the following information for the key personnel and consultants and collaborators. Begin with the principal investigator/program director. Photocopy this page for each person.

NAME	POSITION TITLE

EDUCATION *(Begin with baccalaureate or other initial professional education, such as nursing, and include postdoctoral training.)*

INSTITUTION AND LOCATION	DEGREE	YEAR CONFERRED	FIELD OF STUDY

RESEARCH AND PROFESSIONAL EXPERIENCE: Concluding with present position, list, in chronological order, previous employment, experience, and honors. Key personnel include the principal investigator and any other individuals who participate in the scientific development or execution of the project. Key personnel typically will include all individuals with doctoral or other professional degrees, but in some projects will include individuals at the masters or baccalaureate level provided they contribute in a substantive way to the scientific development or execution of the project. Include present membership on any Federal Government public advisory committee. List, in chronological order, the titles, all authors, and complete references to all publications during the past three years and to representative earlier publications pertinent to this application. DO NOT EXCEED TWO PAGES.

Fig. 3-6 Biographical sketches (Form page 6 from PHS-398 grant application packet)

GG _____   Principal Investigator/Program Director *(Last, first, middle):* _____

OTHER SUPPORT
(Use continuation pages if necessary)

FOLLOW INSTRUCTIONS CAREFULLY. Incomplete, inaccurate, or ambiguous information about OTHER SUPPORT could lead to significant delays in the review and/or possible funding of the application. If there are changes in the information after submission, notify the scientific review administrator of the initial review group before the review; if changes occur after the review, notify the appropriate Institute.

Other support is defined as all funds or resources, whether Federal, non-Federal, or institutional, available to the principal investigator/program director (and other key personnel named in the application) in direct support of their research endeavors through research or training grants, cooperative agreements, contracts, fellowships, gifts, prizes, and other means. Key personnel are defined as all individuals who participate in the scientific development or execution of the project. Key personnel typically will include all individuals with doctoral or other professional degrees, but in some projects will include individuals at the masters or baccalaureate level provided they contribute in a substantive way to the scientific development or execution of the project.

Reporting requirements are: for each of the key personnel, describe (1) all currently *active* support and (2) all applications and proposals *pending* review or award, whether related to this application or not. If the support is part of a larger project, identify the principal investigator/program director and provide the data for the relevant subproject(s). If an individual has no active or pending support, check "None." Use continuation pages as needed to provide the required information in the *format* as shown below.

Name _____   Active _____   Pending _____   None _____

a. Source and identifying no. _____   P.I. _____

Title _____   _____

b. Your role on project _____   % Effort _____

c. Dates and costs of entire project _____

d. Dates and costs of current year _____

e. Specific aims of project _____

_____

_____

_____

_____

f. Describe scientific and budgetary overlap _____

_____

_____

_____

g. Describe adjustments you will make if the present application is funded (budget, % effort, aims, etc.)

_____

_____

_____

Fig. 3-7 Other support (Form page 7 from PHS-398 grant application packet)

Inaccurate reporting of "Other Support" is a major problem at NIH! Despite specific requests for information in the PHS-398 instructions, many applicants still fail to provide information about *all* active and *pending* applications.

Incomplete, inaccurate, or ambiguous information "could lead to delays in the review and/or possible funding of the application."

It is important to be totally candid when completing this section of the application. With current tight funding, Reviewers look very closely at the "Other Support" section. PI's should be careful not to indicate that there is no overlap between the project under review and other grants the applicant holds when it would be more accurate to explain that there are certain similarities (e.g., in the system or the methods) but there is no overlap in the Specific Aims. In this era of computerized databases it is easy for funding agencies to track grant support for an applicant. Discrepancies between the information that you provide and that which surfaces from such databases almost always have a very negative impact on your reputation and credibility. Moreover, dishonesty on the part of, for example, one scientist, often affects the reputation of the entire scientific community!

If there are changes in support after you submit the application but before review by the Study Section, notify the Scientific Review Administrator (SRA) of the Study Section. If there are changes in support after the Study Section meeting, notify the Institute personnel.

Provide information for all key personnel named on page 2 of the application form.

Use continuation pages if necessary. Do *not* use a separate page for each item of "Other Support." Simulate the "Other Support" Form (excluding the instructions) on the computer, and place, consecutively, as many items per page as good formatting and the page margins permit. *But information must be provided in the format given on Form page 7.*

List separately

1. Current active support
2. Applications pending review or funding
3. Applications planned or in preparation

Include[12]

- Federal, nonfederal, institutional support
- All types of
    —Grants (research, training, etc.)
    —Cooperative agreements
    —Contracts
    —Fellowships
    —Gifts
    —Prizes }—only those that support the specific project
    —Other means of support
- Support administered through another institution

If your support is part of a larger project, give the principal investigator/program director and other data for the relevant subprojects.

For each item, give:

- Name of relevant key personnel
- Source of support
- ID number

---

[12]The information to be included under "Other Support" may be slightly different in the 9/94 PHS-398. Read the instructions carefully when the new forms are issued. Also, NIH is apparently considering requesting certain administrative information later in the review process rather than with the application. Watch for possible changes in the *NIH Guide for Grants and Contracts.* (See Liane Reif-Lehrer, *J. National Grantseekers Inst.,* Vol. 2, No. 1, 1995.)

- Name of principal investigator (PI)
- Title
- Role on project of relevant key personnel
- Percent effort on project for relevant key personnel
- Dates and costs of entire project period
- Dates and costs of current year
- Specific Aims of the project
- Description of any scientific and/or budgetary overlap with the present application
- Description of adjustments you will make if the present application is funded (budget, percent effort, aims, etc.)

If you have no other support, check "None."

Resources and environment (Form page 8, Fig. 3-8)

Read carefully the instructions given on the "Resources and Environment" Form (Form page 8) provided in the application kit. Use continuation pages if necessary.

Facilities
- Check in the appropriate boxes on the Form, the facilities available at the applicant organization.
- Check "Other" to describe facilities available at other performance sites listed in item 9 on the Face Page.
- Indicate the capacity of the facilities (for laboratory, office, and other spaces, give total number of square feet available to the project).
  —Explain pertinent capabilities of the facilities.
  —Describe relative proximity of the facilities.
  —Detail the extent of availability to the project.
  —Include an explanation of any consortium/contractual arrangements with other organizations.

Major equipment
List major equipment items in the space provided (compare to budget requests!).

- Note location and pertinent capabilities of each item.
- Specify extent of availability for this project.

Additional information
Provide additional relevant information in the space at the bottom of the page.
Describe the work environment.

- Colleagues
- Occasional collaborators not listed under key personnel
- Potential for interaction with other scientists
- Library facilities
- Seminars and journal clubs
- Outside speakers

Identify support services, and specify the availability of each for this project.

- Consultants
- Secretaries
- Analytical laboratory

HH   Principal Investigator/Program Director *(Last, first, middle):* _____

RESOURCES AND ENVIRONMENT

FACILITIES: Mark the facilities to be used at each performance site listed in Item 9, Face Page, and briefly indicate their capacities, pertinent capabilities, relative proximity, and extent of availability to the project. Use "Other" to describe the facilities at any other performance sites listed in Item 9 on the Face Page and at sites for field studies. Use continuation pages if necessary. Include an explanation of any consortium/contractual arrangements with other organizations.

☐ Laboratory:

☐ Clinical:

☐ Animal:

☐ Computer:

☐ Office:

☐ Other (_____):

MAJOR EQUIPMENT: List the most important equipment items already available for this project, noting the location and pertinent capabilities of each.

ADDITIONAL INFORMATION: Provide any other information describing the environment for the project. Identify support services such as consultant, secretarial, machine shop, and electronics shop, and the extent to which they will be available to the project.

PHS 398 (Rev. 9/91)   (Form Page 8) Page _____   HH

Fig. 3-8 Resources and environment (Form page 8 from PHS-398 grant application packet)

- Electron microscopy laboratory
- Electronics shop
- Histology laboratory
- Machine shop
- Photographic services
- Other general service facilities

THE RESEARCH PLAN

Introduction

The Research Plan is the main (science) part of the grant application and the most important for the review process.

Writing the Research Plan (Section C in an NIH application) requires much planning and care. It pays to allow yourself plenty of time. It is also wise—especially if you are a first-time applicant—to contact Institute program personnel before you begin to write, and discuss with them:

- The application process
- The relevance of your project in relation to the mandates and program priorities of that Institute
- What help the Institute personnel might be able to provide in the application process

The NIH instructions state: "Reviewers often consider brevity and clarity in the presentation to be indicative of a focused approach to a research objective and the ability to achieve the Specific Aims of the project."

You are expected to include sufficient information in the Research Plan to permit an effective review without reference to any previous application. However, you should be aware that, in the case of renewal applications—and certainly revised applications—the Reviewers are almost certain to have the Summary Statement for the previous application and may occasionally also get—or can request—a copy of that application.

New proposers/new proposals

Reviewers tend to make allowances for first-time applicants. They understand that novices do not have track records or long lists of publications. However, in these times of tight funding, some substantive pilot experiments and preliminary data, to convince the Study Section members that you really can do the project, are essential. Likewise, one or more good papers on which you are the sole—or at least first—author are a big plus.

If you are a seasoned investigator, applying for a *new* grant, Reviewers will want to know why you are expanding into new areas or changing direction. Include a few sentences of rationale in the "Background and Significance" section and have ample and substantive preliminary data for the new project. If the new project is in addition to an ongoing one (for which you are funded), make it clear in the Budget Justification that you have the time and personnel to do justice to both projects.

Renewals

Although Study Section review criteria remain the same, there may be subtle differences in the expectations of the Study Section members for first renewals (the second application to the same agency) compared to second renewals (the third application to the same agency). A first renewal that shows somewhat expanded horizons and new Specific Aims related to those of the initial proposal may be acceptable if the principal investigator has made sufficient progress in the form of substantive original research publications. By the time of the second renewal, Reviewers may look for somewhat more than just "linear" progress. The principal investigator would do well, at this stage, to demonstrate some maturity of outlook: a realistic assessment of whether the project is worthy of a long-term study or is perhaps in need of a more effective new direction, awareness of and incorporation of appropriate new technology—perhaps from other fields of science, new approaches to the problem, a broader conceptual base, or a more encompassing hypothesis.

Collaborators

In these times of tight funding, NIH, NSF, and many other agencies generally are not anxious to spend their limited resources for training investigators in new fields after the investigators have finished their postdoctoral training. Dr. Jane Koretz, who served as a member of the NIH Visual Science-A Study Section from 1989 to June 1993 and who was one of the readers for this book, commented here: "The current expertise of the PI is a crucial factor. The time of 'trust me' proposals is long gone, and no one will believe that the PI will be able to pick up and successfully use a new technique in her/his spare time." Thus, for example, if you are a biochemist and your project requires some electron microscopy, consider getting a collaborator. As described earlier in this book, be sure to provide a letter confirming the collaborator's willingness to work on the project, as well as a biographical sketch for the collaborator.

General Instructions for the Research Plan

Type (print) the Research Plan on the continuation pages provided in the application packet.

- Type your name and Social Security number (optional) onto the sample continuation page provided in the application packet *before* you photocopy the page! Or simulate an identical form using your computer. *Note that as of the 9/91 revision of the PHS 398, NIH specifies that the format for the principal investigator's name be "Last name," first, then "First name," then "Middle name or initial."*
- If you photocopy, make as many of these continuation pages as you think you will need for your application. Save the original in case you need extra copies.
- Stay within the margins indicated on the sample page. Your application is photocopied at NIH in a somewhat smaller format!
- Be sure to use an easy-to-read type style and a permissible type size (see the NIH Instructions (page 10, left column, paragraph 2 in the 9/91 revision of the PHS-398; note that the instructions specify the allowable characters per horizontal inch and the number of lines per vertical inch).

Page limits

There is a *25-page limit* for items 1 through 4 of the Research Plan.

Applicants should resist the temptation to use the Appendix to supply information that they could not accommodate within the page limits. The Appendix should be limited to material that is supportive of the application, not integral to it and the application—exclusive of the Appendix—should be able to stand on its own. Making the application complete and clear within the imposed page limits is one of the obligations of—and challenges to—the writer of the grant application.

The 25 pages must include all tables and charts as well as reduced versions of any materials (other than reprints/publications) provided in the Appendix, such as electron micrographs, photographs of gels, etc.

Your application may be returned if you exceed the page limitations.

DRG may electronically scan your proposal and return it without review if you have not adhered to the type size or page limit restrictions! Proposals have been returned for being as little as a half page over the allowed limit.

You may use any page distribution within the 25-page overall limit; but NIH recommends:

1. Specific Aims: 1 page
2. Background and Significance: 2–3 pages
3. Progress Report/Preliminary Studies: 6–8 pages for narrative portion
   - Progress Report: for *renewal* applications. *Required*
   - Preliminary Studies: for *new* applications. "Useful but *optional,*" according to NIH instructions[13]

   Submit a *maximum* of 10 manuscripts (5 copies of each) in the Appendix.
4. Research Design and Methods, 25 minus the number of pages used for items 1–3 (i.e., 13-16 pages)

Parts of the Research Plan

Optional additional table of contents for the Research Plan

In addition to the Table of Contents in the PHS-398 packet (Form page 3) it is sometimes desirable to provide an additional Table of Contents specifically for the Research Plan, including all subheadings. The Reviewers can use this detailed Table of Contents to locate specific items quickly when they are reviewing your grant application and during the discussion at the Study Section meeting.

The *extra* Table of Contents is not useful for proposals with severe page limitations (if you are short of space).

If included with an NIH proposal, put the Table of Contents *before* the Research Plan and mark it "For convenience of Reviewers." (Be careful about page limitations.)

Subheadings in a Table of Contents should be informative:

Not: Experiment 1   *But:* Testing the effects of substance X on cell viability.

The words "Experiment 1" may mean a lot to you, but they convey nothing to the Reviewer, except perhaps that it was the first experiment that you did.

Summary of the general information required in parts 1–4 of the Research Plan for an NIH application

The type of information shown below is generally required—in some form—in many types of grant applications.

Introduction:	At NIH, required only for revised and supplemental applications (see below)
Specific Aims:	What you intend to do
Background and Significance:	What has already been done in the field Why is the work important
Preliminary Studies or Progress Report:	What *you* have done already on this project
Research Design and Methods:	How you will fulfill the aims How you will do the work

---

[13] On seeing this statement, a member of a Study Section remarked, "Preliminary data in a new grant application are about as optional as breathing."

INTRODUCTION

In an NIH application, include only for:

- Revised application *(Do not exceed 3 pages)*
  - —Delineate all significant changes made.
  - —Respond to *all* criticism in the Summary Statement for the previous application. Be polite and direct. Do not use an adversarial tone. Whether your proposal is returned to the same Reviewers or different Reviewers, a "sour grapes" or "cry baby" response to the critique in the Summary Statement will probably elicit a negative response from Reviewers and may hinder your chance to improve your priority score.
  - —Highlight changes made in the text of the revised Research Plan by use of
    - Brackets
    - Indents
    - Different typography. (Do *not* use shading or underlining.)
      Failure to highlight changes creates an unnecessary burden on Reviewers and may irritate them!
  - —Incorporate into the Progress Report/Preliminary Studies any work done since the prior version was submitted.
    "*A revised application will be returned if it does not address criticisms in the previous Summary Statement and/or an Introduction is not included and/or substantial revisions are not clearly apparent.*"
- Supplemental application *(Do not exceed 1 page)*
  - —Explain the significance with respect to the original proposal.
  - —See page 20, left column, of the NIH instructions.

1. SPECIFIC AIMS (recommended maximum: 1 page)

All other things being equal, a proposal that is hypothesis-driven is likely to be more favorably received than one that is not. "Fishing expeditions" are unlikely to be funded. Proposals referred to by the Study Section members as being primarily "descriptive" are also not likely to get good scores.

1. State the *broad, long-term objectives of the proposal.*
2. Describe concisely and realistically:
   a.) What the specific research described in the application is intended to accomplish;
   b.) Any hypotheses[14] to be tested, or clear, specific questions to be addressed.
      Avoid grandiose designs.
      If appropriate, state hypotheses—or questions to be addressed—in the form of short bulleted statements rather than narrative paragraphs.
      "To study the effect of substance X on system Y" is *not* a good specific aim! The statement is too vague.
      Understand the difference between
      - *Broad, long-term objectives,* for example, "Eradicate diabetes" (hard to quantify progress) and
      - *Specific Aims,* for example, "Develop a method to continuously measure blood sugar levels" (something that could be crossed off a list of *n* items needed to further the broad, long-term objectives).

---

[14] A hypothesis is defined as "a proposition tentatively assumed in order to draw out its logical or empirical consequences and so test its accord with facts that are known or may be determined" (*Webster's Third New International Dictionary*). Simply placing the phrase "The hypothesis is…" before a string of words does not make the statement a hypothesis. A hypothesis generally states a problem in a form that can be tested and also generally predicts a possible outcome. For a more extensive discussion of the nature of a hypothesis, see Locke et al. cited in Appendix XI.

Be careful not to include methods as aims unless the major goal of the proposal is to develop a new method. However, a proposal whose primary aim is to develop a new method will probably not be funded unless subsequent aims within the proposal involve using the method once it is developed. Such a proposal would also need to be backed up with alternative methods to fulfill the subsequent aims. In general, it should be kept in mind that a Specific Aim that, if not successfully accomplished, prevents successful completion of the rest of the project is a dangerous Specific Aim!

2. BACKGROUND AND SIGNIFICANCE (recommended maximum: 2–3 pages)

1. *Briefly* sketch the *Background* for the proposal.
2. Critically *evaluate* the existing knowledge in the field.
3. Specifically identify the *gaps* the project is intended to fill.
4. State *concisely* the importance of the research by *relating* the Specific Aims to the broad, long-term objectives.
5. Reference this section (especially the Background).
   The references go into "Literature Cited," item 9 of the Research Plan (which has a limit of 6 pages; this limit is subject to change. Read the instructions carefully, and follow the *NIH Guide for Grants and Contracts*).

Use this section of the grant application to demonstrate your understanding of the subject and justify the need for the proposed research. Do not simply delineate the Background (any clever high school student can probably do that!), but evaluate the existing knowledge (a clever high school student probably cannot do that!). State clearly why the information to be obtained is useful, that is, what you can do with the information after you get it. If appropriate, explain the clinical relevance of your proposed research. In the Background section, make it clear which previous work was done by others and which by you, the PI.

Background discussions should avoid fanning the flames of scientific controversies. Someone on the Study Section may have a strong bias in the debate that may not coincide with yours. Discuss all sides and aspects of the issue, remain strictly scientific and unbiased, and let the data speak for you. If you think you are correct, do *not* compromise your position, but state it politely and with respect for the opinions and publications of others. They may be your Reviewers!

References that are cited by author and year in the text and listed in alphabetical order (and numbered) in the bibliography are more meaningful to the Reviewer than references cited by number. References cited only by number cause the Reviewer to have to flip back to the bibliography pages frequently to determine what the reference is. However, the author/year method of citation takes up valuable space in the context of the current page limitations. In addition, the author/year method of citation can interrupt the flow of text for the reader, especially when there are multiple citations at a given place. You will have to make a judicious decision about the best way to cite references in your application, considering the positive and negative aspects of each method.

If you refer to a long article (for example, a review article), put a note in the text to the effect that "discussion pertinent to the subject may be found on pp. 15–18, 29–32, and 56 in Gooding and Slade, 1959 (reference 43)." The Reviewer may want to check a statement without wading through a 63-page article to find it. If the article is not readily attainable, ask the SRA for permission to provide photocopies of the pertinent pages for the Reviewers[15] (see the section on bibliography below).

---

[15] If permission is granted, ask the SRA how many copies you should send and where in the application they should be placed.

3. PRELIMINARY STUDIES (recommended maximum: 6–8 pages)[16]

New applicants may use this section to provide information that will help to establish their experience and competence to pursue the proposed project.

Although the NIH instructions state that this section is *optional* for *new* applications, it is imperative that you provide preliminary data that show that your project is feasible—and do-able by you. The chances of a new grant application without any preliminary data getting funded are pretty remote. (See footnote 13 earlier in this part).

1. Discuss preliminary studies *by the principal investigator (PI),* that are pertinent to the application.
2. Provide any other information that will help to establish the experience and competence of the principal investigator to pursue the proposed project.
3. Give titles and complete references to appropriate publications and manuscripts *submitted or accepted* for publication.
   Submit 5 copies each of *no more than 10* such items as an appendix. (Submit them as collated sets.)

Give any relevant preliminary data you have available. They do not have to be in final format, but they must have a clear connection to the proposed work and should be clear and neat. Any evidence that the project is realistic and/or that you can handle it is valuable. Data that indicate that your basic premises—your hypotheses—are correct are especially helpful for bridging the credibility gap for new applicants. A photocopy of a curve from even a single experiment that you have done is better than no preliminary data, but make it understandable to the Reviewers. Explain what is in the figure, and label the coordinates properly. A curve derived from an in-house experiment, labeled with lab jargon with which you are familiar, may not be comprehensible to someone else. Be careful about inclusion of preliminary data in this section that preempt experiments that you have proposed, in the application, to carry out in the forthcoming project! Inclusion of preliminary data that have no relevance to the project described in the application is likely to count against you.

In renewal applications, the "Preliminary Studies" section is replaced by the Progress Report.

3. PROGRESS REPORT (recommended maximum: 6–8 pages)[17]

A progress report is required for competitive renewal and supplemental applications (in place of Preliminary Studies).

The Progress Report is a very important part of the proposal because it lends credibility to what you proposed in the previous application and helps the Reviewers decide whether you did a good job.

1. Give beginning and ending dates of period covered since the last competitive review (i.e., the date your funding began, to the date of submission of the proposal for which you are writing this Progress Report).
   (Note that this does not coincide with project period dates. Remember that you are reapplying about a year before the present project period is up. Also, the beginning date for the Progress Report will be the day after the ending date for the previous Progress Report.)
2. List all personnel who have worked on the project in this period.
   • Name

---

[16] For the narrative portion. Does not include list of publications.
[17] For the narrative portion. Does not include list of professional personnel or list of publications.

- Title
- Birth date
- Social Security number (optional)
- Dates of service
- Percentage of appointment devoted to this project

3. Summarize Specific Aims of preceding application, and provide a succinct account of progress (published and unpublished) toward their achievement.

> Summary of Specific Aim (1) of the previous proposal:
>
> "SA (1) has been accomplished in that . . . and a publication describing the results appeared in . . ." (give reference).
>
> Summary of Specific Aim (2) of the previous proposal:
>
> "SA (2) was not pursued after some initial experiments because we ran into an unexpected, serious experimental difficulty that did not show up in our preliminary experiments." (State briefly what the difficulty was.)
>
> Summary of Specific Aim (3) of the previous proposal:
>
> "SA (3) was started in the last year of the project period. One publication has resulted (give reference), but the project has evolved into a more extensive one than originally anticipated; new methodology, described in the current proposal, will have to be employed to further evaluate . . ." (Then, in the "Specific Aims" section of the renewal application, one specific aim would be related to the continuation of this work.)
>
> Summary of Specific Aim (4) of the previous proposal:
>
> "Work relating to SA (4) has just begun. The figure below shows the results of the first 3 experiments and indicates . . . . We expect this aspect of the project to be complete by the end of the current project period."

- Number items in the Progress Report to correspond to numbers of Specific Aims of the *preceding* proposal so that the Reviewer can easily follow along in the preceding application.
- Although the instructions specify that you "include sufficient information in Section C to facilitate an effective review *without* reference to any previous application," Reviewers are generally provided with the Summary Statement for your previous proposal and may also occasionally be sent the previous proposal. Reviewers may also specifically request to see the previous proposal.

4. Summarize the importance of the findings. (Don't just list the findings!)
5. Discuss any changes in original Specific Aims. Clearly note which of the original aims of the previous proposals have been accomplished, which have not, and why (as illustrated above). *Account for every Specific Aim listed in the original application!* A budget cut is a common reason why a Specific Aim was not accomplished. If that is the case, be sure to explain this.
6. List titles and complete references to all publications, manuscripts *submitted or accepted* for publication, patents, invention reports, and other printed materials that have resulted since the last competitive review. Clearly distinguish between

peer-reviewed original papers (research reports), reviews, books, and abstracts: Group them using subheadings. In addition, in listing your publications in the Progress Report, you may want (within the category of peer-reviewed original papers) to list first the papers on which you are the sole author.

Submit 5 copies each of *no more than 10* such items as an Appendix. (Submit them as collated sets.)

If you are the sole author or first author on only a few papers—or have only few publications—and if you have a valid reason, explain why. An enforced move to another laboratory, a long illness, or an equipment supplier who went out of business before delivering your order, may be acceptable. Problems with techniques or staff turnover are likely to make the Reviewers wonder about your ineptitude or lack of good public relations and are thus better left unsaid.

Study Section members do not like PIs who suffer from "apublishanemia" or have a high A:P ratio[18] (where "A" stands for "abstracts," and "P" stands for "peer-reviewed publications"). Obviously, you must think about your publication record long before it is time to write the renewal application. The official instructions (9/91 revision) state that only submitted or accepted published papers should be listed. However, if you have only a small number of publications, but have a paper that is in preparation but is essentially complete, call your SRA and ask for permission to submit copies. For each such paper listed, submit preprints in the Appendix, and indicate in the list of publications that the preprint is provided in the Appendix.

4. RESEARCH DESIGN AND METHODS (limit of 25 pages minus the number of pages used for items 1–3 – 13–16 pages)

The Research Design and Methods section is an important part of the Research Plan. You have said in the "Specific Aims" section what you propose to do; now you are telling the Reviewers how you propose to do it. Explain why the particular approach that you describe was chosen to address the problem that you plan to research. Convince the Reviewers that you can do what you propose and that the necessary facilities and equipment are available to you.

It is especially important to be very focused—and very clear—in this section of the proposal. Many grant application writers, totally absorbed in their own project and thus forgetting the needs of the Reviewers and the funding agency, begin this section of the Research Plan with a "shopping list" of methodologies they plan to use—without providing a context within which these methods will be used. This is a major problem for Reviewers and is well illustrated by the *New Yorker* cartoon reproduced on page 60. The 1986 change in the title of this section from "Methods" to "Experimental Design and Methods" and the further change in the 1991 revision of the PHS-398 Form to Research Design and Methods should send a message to grant application writers that NIH has not been getting adequate descriptions of research design in proposals.

You should restate—or at least summarize—the relevant Specific Aim at the beginning of each subsection of the Research Design and Methods section. In addition, providing a one- or two-sentence rationale for each aim (without including extensive Background or progress report material) is also a big help for Reviewers. A brief introductory or closing paragraph, indicating the relationship of the Specific Aims to each other as well as to the overall objective of the proposed work also helps to focus the point of the work for the reader.

- Outline the research design and methods to be used to accomplish the Specific Aims of the project.

---

[18] Thanks to Dr. Robert Silber, formerly of New York University Medical School, for the comment about the A:P ratio.

Misunderstood directions.
Drawing by Stevenson; © 1976, *The New Yorker Magazine*, Inc.

- Number the research designs and the methods in this section to *correspond* to the numbers of the Specific Aims in *this* proposal.
- Use subnumbering within this section when describing several methods applicable to the same Specific Aim. But don't overuse subnumbering, and be sure that the numbering system is very clear and does not confuse Reviewers by overlapping with numbers used in a different section of the proposal.
- *Distinguish between the overall research design and the specific methods:*

> Research design for SA (1): To label Q-protein with fluorescent probes at specific amino acid sites and use the probes as indicators of changing inter-molecular interactions associated with the functions of Q-protein in the presence of X-protein.

> Methods for SA (1):
> A. Techniques for labeling proteins with probe reagents
>   1. Covalent labeling (Reference and/or describe the method briefly.)
>   2. Noncovalent labeling (Reference and/or describe the method briefly.)
> B. Determination of specificity of labeling
>   1. Separation and identification of fluorescent peptides by HPLC and gel electrophoresis after enzymatic digestion of protein
>   2. Analysis of labeled peptides on amino acid analyzer/sequencer

- *Do not repeat* identical procedures that apply to more than one Specific Aim. Describe them once, and then refer the Reader back to that section—or group such procedures in a section of "General Procedures" and refer to them as appropriate.
- Describe and/or reference protocols.

—Reference, but do not describe, well-known procedures.

"Cookbook" repetitions of techniques copied from published papers do not convince Reviewers of your expertise. If you find it necessary to detail such a technique, describe it in the context of your specific research problem and experiments.

—Describe and reference procedures that are new or unlikely to be known to Reviewers. If in doubt, give a reference to the methodology, and ask the Scientific Review Administrator for permission to provide 3 copies of the actual reference (a reprint or a photocopy of the article) in the Appendix for use by the primary Reviewers/Readers. Providing reprints for Reviewers is especially important if the source is not readily available.

- For new methods, explain *why* they are *better* than existing methods.
- Discuss all applicable *control experiments.*
- Explain how the data are to be *collected, analyzed,* and *interpreted.*
- Discuss potential *difficulties* and *limitations* of the proposed procedures and *alternative approaches* to achieve the aims.
- Point out procedures, situations, or materials that may be *hazardous* to personnel and describe *precautions* to be exercised.
- Provide a tentative *sequence* or *timetable* for the project. (Be realistic, not exact.)

    In many cases, this timetable deserves no more than ⅓ to ½ page. Reviewers do not want a blow-by-blow account of what you will do when. They simply want (1) assurance that you have really thought through the project and (2) some indication of approximately when various aspects of the project will be started and finished. Some applicants use diagrammatic or tabular formats for presenting the necessary information.

- Document proposed collaborative arrangements with a letter from the individual with whom you propose to work. The letter should demonstrate that the collaborator understands your project and should define what role that individual will play in the project. Biographical sketches must also be obtained from collaborators. The letters of collaboration should be placed in Section 7 of the Research Plan. The biographical sketches should be placed with the biosketches of the principal investigator and other key personnel.

An explanation of how the data are to be *interpreted* is especially important and is, in my experience, often omitted from proposals.[19] Describe *briefly* what might be expected in a given set of experiments. For example: "If the data come out thus and so, then it means . . . and we will do . . .; on the other hand, if the data turn out to be . . ., it might mean . . . and we will proceed as follows . . . ." Don't speculate on experimental outcomes for which you can propose no further experimental progress.

A discussion of *alternative approaches* can sometimes save your proposal if a Reviewer is not convinced that your primary approach will yield the desired results. Grant application writers should also be aware that Reviewers, who are generally chosen because they are eminent—or at least established investigators—in their field of research, may have access to very up-to-date, as yet unpublished and even unreported information about developments in your field. Thus, they may know about data that may put your approach into question. Discussion of alternative approaches to your project may rescue your proposal under these circumstances.

---

[19] Dr. Donna Dean, Chief of the Biological and Physiological Sciences Review Section in the Division of Research Grants at NIH, who was one of the readers for this book, commented here: "[The next several paragraphs] are the most important in the entire book and probably contain the most significant advice in grant proposal writing."

A discussion of the *difficulties* and *limitations* of the procedures you have proposed is also very important—as can be discerned from the excerpts from 3 Summary Statements (SS) (reproduced in Appendix V) shown below.

SS1: A major potential problem in this research, the contamination of material from . . ., is serious. The principal investigator is fully aware of such criticism and has diligently attempted to deal with it. This is a major strength in the proposal. Nonetheless, questions remain. In particular, the separation . . . may require further analysis. The principal investigator might be encouraged, insofar as possible, to carry out . . . analysis on the material obtained by the . . . procedure of . . . . The alternative mode of preparation of . . . is an important complementary method. This should ensure more complete . . . .

SS2: A problem of the previous application was that there was concern about several limitations of the proposed methodology. However, the investigators have added a substantial amount of text indicating that they are well aware of these limitations and do, in fact, have a great deal of insight into the ways of solving any potential problems that arise. It is now clear that the research will provide a substantial amount of new and important data.

SS3: In any investigation which requires the use of . . . , the question of . . . introduced by . . . always arises. Dr. . . . is keenly aware of potential pitfalls, and is prepared to deal with them.

Note that the PI's ability to point out possible problems to be encountered in the project is an asset rather than a liability. If you don't call attention to the problems and state how you will deal with them, the Reviewers will find them!

Some years ago, I asked a Program Officer at one of the NIH Institutes what he would say to proposal writers about preparing a good "Methods" section. He said: "Try to convince the Reviewer that you have not merely gone to the library but that you really understand and know how to carry out the research and are familiar with the techniques and their shortcomings."

5. HUMAN SUBJECTS (no page limit; be brief)

Research involving human subjects, as defined in Department of Health and Human Services (DHHS) regulations (45CFR46), is research that involves direct interaction or intervention with *living* persons, including acquisition or recording of private information, except as waived or exempted by the DHHS regulations. Human studies research requires *prior* assurance to the NIH Office for Protection from Research Risks (OPRR) of compliance with DHHS regulations and certification of Institutional Review Board (IRB) review and approval.

The DHHS regulations for protection of human subjects extend to the use of human organs, tissues (e.g., biopsy specimens, tissues that have been surgically removed for medical reasons), and body fluids, as well as graphic, written, or recorded information (e.g., data collected from patient chart records), *if* any of the aforementioned are derived from individually identifiable human subjects. Certain studies involving human subjects (e.g., surveys in which the investigator does not record any identifiers or sensitive information) are exempt from the DHHS regulations. A list of exemptions and more detail about the DHHS regulations are given in the PHS-398 instructions.

The use of autopsy material is governed by state and local law and is not directly regulated by DHHS regulations (45CFR46) for the protection of human subjects. Approval from an appropriate IRB is required to *receive* an NIH award, but not to *apply* for an award. The Division of Human Subject Protections (DHSP) of the NIH OPRR administers the DHHS regulations (45CFR46) for protection of human subjects.

Additional Information about Studies Involving Human Subjects

- Need approval from IRB
  Approval from an appropriate IRB is required to *receive* an NIH award, but not to *apply* for an award. Certification of IRB review and approval is required at the time of—or within 60 days of—application by those institutions that *do not have* an OPRR-approved assurance that applies to the research in question (e.g., a Multiple Project Assurance). Check with the appropriate office at your institution to find out the procedures and amount of time required to get approval to conduct human studies.
- See the regulations about use of Human Subjects in NIH Instructions (pages 11–13, 22–23, and 25–26). See also *NIH Guide for Grants and Contracts*, Vol. 22, No. 12, March 26, 1993, pages 2–3 (2 articles).
- A copy of the Federal Policy for the Protection of Human Subjects is in the *Federal Register* (Vol. 56, No. 117, Tuesday June 18, 1991, pages 28001–32). The Federal policy uniformly applies to 16 Federal agencies and departments, including DHHS. DHHS regulations additionally provide for vulnerable subject populations such as pregnant women, fetuses, children, and prisoners.
- Free copies of the items listed below are available from the Education Program Director of DHSP (while supplies last), call 301-496-8101.
  — 45 CFR 46 (DHHS regulations that state minimum standards for protection of human subjects)
  — The Belmont Report (a review of basic bioethical principles that apply to the conduct of human studies research)
  — A VHS videotape that covers historical information on events leading to current protections of human subjects
- IRB Guidebook
  Topics include:
  — Introduction for new IRB members and investigators
  — The Belmont Report
  — Institutional administration
  — Regulations and policies
  — Basic IRB review
  — Consideration of research design
  — Overview of biomedical and behavioral research
  — Special categories of subjects
  — Glossary of terms
  — Answers to some frequently asked questions about DHHS regulations and policies

  The IRB Guidebook is available for $31 from:
  Superintendents of Documents
  P.O. Box 371954
  Pittsburgh, PA 15250-7954
  or from
  202-783-3328 (in Washington, DC)

If you need additional information about studies involving human subjects, contact your institutional IRB or the NIH DRG Grants Information Office at 301-594-7248.

If your studies involve human subjects:

- Check Item 4a on the Face page.

- State whether any of the research involving human subjects will be carried out at collaborating site(s) or other performance site(s).
- Assure the Reviewers that your experiments using human subjects are necessary, well thought-out, and scientifically sound. Either in this section [under (1) below] or in the Research Plan, indicate how many patients per year will be available for your studies and demonstrate that this number is sufficient to provide a statistically significant answer to your questions.
- In this section, address the 6 points specified on pages 22–23 of the NIH Instructions and outlined below:
  (1) Detailed description of the proposed involvement of human subjects as previously outlined in the Research Design and Methods section.
    - Characteristics of subject population
      —Anticipated number of subjects
      —Ages (age ranges)
      —Health status
      —Sex
      —Gender and racial/ethnic composition of the subject population
    - Criteria for inclusion or exclusion of any sub-population
        Provide a clear rationale for exclusion of one gender and/or minorities. NIH is now paying particular attention to inclusion of diverse groups in clinical studies and asks Reviewers to address this issue directly during the review process. It is essential that applications include plans for recruitment of appropriate groups or provide a reasonable rationale for exclusion of a particular group. For example, women would not expect to be included in a study about prostate cancer, but men should perhaps be included in a study on breast cancer. Reviewers are now required to "code" applications with respect to the PI's consideration of this issue (see the coding table at the end of Appendix I-D-3).
    - Give a rationale for the involvement of
      —Fetuses
      —Pregnant women
      —Children
      —Human *in vitro* fertilization
      —Prisoners or other institutionalized or "vulnerable" individuals
  (2) Identify sources of research material obtained from individually identifiable *living* human subjects:[20]
    - Specimens
    - Records
    - Data
    (Specify whether you will use existing material or gather material especially for this research.)
  (3) Describe plans for recruitment and for consent procedures:
    - How subjects will be recruited
    - Circumstances under which consent will be sought and obtained
    - Who will seek consent

---

[20] If your research deals with, for example, human fetuses but also involves information (which includes individual identifiers) from records about the still-living parents of the fetuses, you may need to get Human Subjects approval. In general, if after reading the PHS-398 instructions carefully, you are still in doubt as to whether or not you need Human Subjects approval, ask your IRB. If the IRB can't help, call the NIH/DRG Grants Information Office (301-594-7248) for advice. If they cannot answer your question, they will put you in touch with an appropriate person at the Office for Protection from Research Risks (OPRR).

- Nature of information to be provided to prospective subjects
- Method of documenting consent
- State whether the IRB has authorized a modification or waiver of the elements of consent or the requirement for documentation of consent.

(4) Describe potential risks:
- Physical
- Psychological
- Social
- Legal
- Other

Assess likelihood and seriousness of each risk. Where appropriate, describe alternative treatments and procedures that might be advantageous to the subjects.

(5) Describe procedures to protect against or minimize potential risks, include risks to confidentiality, and assess their likely effectiveness:
- Provisions for ensuring necessary medical/professional intervention in case of adverse effects to subjects
- Provisions for monitoring the data collected to ensure safety of subjects

(6) Discuss *risk/benefit ratio:*
- Anticipated benefits to subjects
- Importance of knowledge that may be expected to result (benefit to society)

If an investigational drug, device, or biologic is involved:

- Name the test item(s) involved, and state whether
  —30-day interval between submission of applicant certification to the Food and Drug Administration (FDA) and its response has elapsed or been waived
  —Use of test item has been withheld or restricted by FDA
- If you have designated exemptions from the Human Subjects regulations on the Face Page, provide information to show propriety of exemption.

6. VERTEBRATE ANIMALS (no page limit; be brief)

The Division of Animal Welfare (DAW) of the NIH Office for Protection from Research Risks (OPRR) administers the PHS Policy on Humane Care and Use of Laboratory Animals via a multifaceted approach that includes (1) review and approval of (a) assurances, and (b) reports from institutions certifying that required internal semiannual inspections of animal facilities and evaluation of programs have been conducted, (2) review of research protocols by Institutional Animal Care and Use Committees (IACUCs), (3) requirements for prompt reporting of serious noncompliance, (4) evaluations of allegations of noncompliance, (5) conduct of special reviews or site visits at selected institutions, and (6) a nationwide education program about appropriate treatment of laboratory animals.

Use of vertebrate animals requires approval from an IACUC. Processing of your application by NIH cannot be completed without certification of IACUC approval. Check with the appropriate office at your institution to find out the procedures and amount of time required to get approval to conduct vertebrate animal studies.

See regulations for use and care of vertebrate animals in NIH Instructions (pages 13, 23, 26–27). If you need additional information, contact your institutional IACUC or the NIH DRG Grants Information Office at 301-594-7248.

For information about public opinions and/or reservations about animal use, call the NIH Office of Laboratory Animal Research (OLAR), 301-402-1058.

If your studies involve vertebrate animals:

- Check Item 5a on the Face page.
- State whether any of the research involving vertebrate animals will be carried out at collaborating site(s) or other performance site(s).
- Assure the Reviewers that your animal experiments are necessary, well-thought-out, and scientifically sound.
- Address, in this section, the 5 points specified on page 23 of the NIH Instructions and outlined below:

    (1) Describe in detail the proposed use of animals. Identify:
        - Species
        - Strains
        - Ages
        - Sex
        - Number of animals to be used
    (2) Justify:
        - Use of animals
        - Choice of species
        - Number to be used (give additional rationale if animals are scarce, costly, or to be used in large numbers).
    (3) Describe veterinary care of animals.
    (4) Describe procedures to minimize the animals' discomfort, distress, pain, and injury. Discuss the use of:
        - Analgesics
        - Anesthetics
        - Tranquilizers
        - Comfortable restraining devices
    (5) Describe euthanasia methods.
        - Give reasons for selection.
        - State whether methods to be used are consistent with recommendations of the Panel on Euthanasia of the American Veterinary Medical Association. If not, justify.

7. CONSULTANTS/COLLABORATORS

- List all consultants and collaborators, whether or not salaries are requested.
- Provide, in this section, a letter from each such person, confirming her/his role in the project. (Do not put the letters in the Appendix.)
- Provide a biosketch for each such person. Place the biosketches with those of other participants in the project.

8. CONSORTIUM/CONTRACTUAL ARRANGEMENTS

- Justify consortium and contractual (subcontract) costs thoroughly both here and in the Budget Justification.
- Provide a detailed explanation of the arrangements between the applicant and collaborating organization:
    — Programmatic
    — Fiscal
    — Administrative
- Provide a statement that the applicant and collaborating organization have estab-

lished or are prepared to establish written interorganizational agreements that will ensure compliance with all pertinent Federal regulations and policies.

- Provide copies of written agreements or letters (signed by the applicant PI and an authorized official of the collaborating organization) confirming inter-organizational agreements.
- If the majority of the work is not being done at the applicant organization, explain why that organization should be the grantee. Assure the Reviewers that the applicant organization intends to have a substantive role in the project.

9. LITERATURE CITED (BIBLIOGRAPHY) (maximum: 6 pages)

- Acknowledge the work of others, including your competitors. Do not let the Reviewers think that you are biased or arrogant.
- Be thorough, relevant, and current.
- Reviewers are interested in how up to date you are.

    A grant application submitted in November 1995 in which the latest reference cited is from March 1994 does not sit well with the Study Section unless you specifically point out that no publications in the field have appeared in the interim.
- Article *titles must be included* in the bibliography. Also include: names of *all* authors (do not use "et al."), title of book or journal, volume number, page numbers (beginning and ending), and year of publication.
- Use a consistent format throughout Section 9. If possible, the format should also be the same as that used in the list of publications in the Biographical Sketches and in the Progress Report.
- Be sure every citation in the text is listed in the bibliography.
- Be sure every citation in the bibliography is referred to in the text.
- Do not scatter citations throughout the text. List them in this section of the Research Plan.
- This section may include, *but not replace*, the list of publications in the Progress Report.

Choose wisely what you will include within the 6-page limit. Your choice of citations will tell the Reviewer about your quality as a scientist—your ability to evaluate the work of others and to distinguish the important from the mundane.

The use of the author/year citation system in the text is much more meaningful to Reviewers than number citations; the author/year citation system saves Reviewers the time to flip back to the bibliography whenever they come to a numbered citation. If you use the author/year citation system, you should present the references in alphabetical order (by first author) in the bibliography. In addition, number the articles in the bibliography. The numbers make it easier for Reviewers to refer to them during the discussion (e.g., "Doesn't Homenflof have more recent references on . . . than those cited at numbers 37 to 41 on p. 80?"). The disadvantages of the author/year system are (1) it takes up more space and (2) multiple citations cause a long break in the text that can break one's train of thought and can thus be annoying or confusing to the reader.

If the bibliography contains obscure or foreign journal references that you went to a lot of trouble to obtain and that are likely not to be readily available to the Reviewer— and if the reference is important in the context of the proposal—you may wish to get permission from the Scientific Review Administrator of the Study Section to provide 3 or more copies of the article—or at least, the (English) summary of the article—for the primary Reviewers/Readers.

APPENDIX

The Appendix is Section D in an NIH application.

Submit 5 collated sets. (*Note:* This is in contrast to the body of proposal, for which you must submit 6 sets.)

The Appendix is *not* to be used to circumvent the page limitations in the Research Plan and the proposal must be understandable without reference to the Appendix.

What to put into the Appendix

1. Questionnaires
2. Graphs, diagrams, tables, charts, oversized documents, photographs, and other materials that do not reproduce well. *Reduced copies of such items must also be incorporated in the relevant section in the Research Plan and are counted toward the 25-page limitation for Sections 1–4 of the Research Plan.*
3. *Maximum of 10 documents* that have resulted from the project since the last competitive review such as:
   * Publications or manuscripts *submitted or accepted* for publication
   * Patents
   * Invention reports
   * Other printed materials
     New applicants may provide similar Background materials to document preliminary studies.
4. Materials intended to help the primary Reviewers by saving them a trip to the library. Submit such materials only after getting permission from the Scientific Review Administrator. These reprints or abstracts need only be submitted in triplicate—unless the SRA requests otherwise.

How to prepare the Appendix for the final draft

* Be sure each Appendix item is referred to in the text of the application.
* Be sure each Appendix item referred to in the text of the application is provided in the appendix and entered in the list of Appendix items.
* Identify each Appendix set and each item within each set—with the name of the principal investigator/program director, Social Security number (optional), project title, and title of item.
    Individual manuscripts within the Appendix should be stapled; the rest of the application should *not* contain staples.
* Provide a list of Appendix items in 2 places:
    — At the bottom of Form page 3 (Table of Contents)
    — On a separate sheet at the front of each collated Appendix set
* Do not number Appendix pages.
* Do not mail the Appendix separately.

Note: Unlike the rest of the proposal, the Appendix is not duplicated by NIH. The Appendix is given, in original form, to selected members of the Study Section, usually only the primary Reviewers/Readers. The remaining copies are available at (or before) the Study Section meeting for other members who request to see the Appendix.

Note: "An application may be returned if the Appendix fails to observe the limitations on content."

CHECKLIST (FORM PAGES II AND JJ, FIG. 3-9A, AND 3-9B)

- The Checklist is part of Section E in an NIH application (2 Form pages in the application kit).
- The Checklist is required as the *last 2 pages* of the signed original of the application.
- Number the Checklist pages appropriately.
- Fill out the Checklist according to the detailed instructions given in the PHS-398 packet.
- Duplicate the Checklist pages for the other 5 copies of the application.
- The Checklist is an integral part of your application and thus, part of the review process.

Parts of the Checklist

1. ASSURANCES AND CERTIFICATIONS

See 9/91 NIH Instructions, pages 24–32[21]

Each application to NIH requires that the assurances and certifications listed below be provided as appropriate. After the assurances and certifications are made by your institution, they are attested to by checking the appropriate boxes on the Face page and on the first page of the Checklist and are verified by the signature of the official signing for the applicant organization on the Face page of the application. In addition, specific information related to human subjects, inclusion of minorities and both genders in study populations, and use of vertebrate animals must be provided within the Research Plan of the application.

Note that items a–d below are project- and application-specific; in contrast, item e–l are institution-level clearances. Investigators are expected to be aware of the legal requirements for all items in both categories.

All required Assurance of Compliance forms are available from the Grants Information Office, Division of Research Grants, NIH, 301-594-7248.

a. *Human subjects*
Enter the appropriate information in item 4 on the Face page.

b. *Vertebrate animals*
Enter the appropriate information in item 5 on the Face page.

c. *Inventions and patents*
Include in competing continuations *only;* enter the appropriate information in item 10 on the Face page.

d. *Debarment and suspension*
See NIH Instructions.

e. *Drug-free workplace*
See NIH Instructions.

---

[21] See also:
- Assurances and information about misconduct in science: *NIH Guide for Grants and Contracts*, Vol. 18, No. 41, Nov. 17, 1989, page 1, *NIH Guide for Grants and Contracts*, Vol. 20, No. 9, Mar. 1, 1991, page 3, *FASEB Newsletter*, Vol. 25, No. 7, Oct./Nov. 1992.
- NIH "Final Rules" about grantee requirements for drug-free workplace (See *NIH Guide for Grants and Contracts*, Vol. 19, No. 32, Sept. 7, 1990, page 1.)

II   Principal Investigator/Program Director *(Last, first, middle):* _____

CHECKLIST

TYPE OF APPLICATION

☐ NEW application. *(This application is being submitted to the PHS for the first time.)*

☐ REVISION of application number: _____
   (This application replaces a prior unfunded version of a new, competing continuation, or supplemental application.)

☐ COMPETING CONTINUATION of grant number: _____
   (This application is to extend a funded grant beyond its current project period.)

☐ SUPPLEMENT to grant number: _____
   (This application is for additional funds to supplement a currently funded grant.)

☐ CHANGE of principal investigator/program director.
   Name of former principal investigator/program director: _____

☐ FOREIGN application, city and country of birth and present citizenship of principal investigator/program director. *(This information is required by the U.S. Department of State.)* _____ .

1. ASSURANCES/CERTIFICATIONS

The following assurances/certifications are made by checking the appropriate boxes and are verified by the signature of the OFFICIAL SIGNING FOR APPLICANT ORGANIZATION on the FACE PAGE of the application. Descriptions of individual assurances/certifications begin on page 24 of Specific Instructions.

a. Human Subjects *(Complete Item 4 on the Face Page)*
   ☐ Full IRB Review   ☐ Expedited Review

b. Vertebrate Animals *(Complete Item 5 on the Face Page)*

c. Inventions and Patents *(Competing Continuation Application Only—Complete Item 10 on the Face Page)*

d. Debarment and Suspension   ☐ No   ☐ Yes *(Attach explanation)*

e. Drug-Free Workplace *(Applicable only to new or revised applications being submitted to the PHS for the first proposed project period, Type 1)*
   ☐ Yes   ☐ No *(Attach explanation)*

f. Lobbying

   With Federal appropriated funds   ☐ No

   With other than Federal appropriated funds   ☐ No   ☐ Yes
      (If "Yes," see page 29 and attach Standard Form LLL, "Disclosure of Lobbying Activities," to the application behind the second page of the Checklist.)

g. Delinquent Federal Debt   ☐ No   ☐ Yes *(Attach explanation)*

h. Misconduct in Science (Form PHS 6315)   ☐ Filed   ☐ Not Filed
   If filed, date of Initial Assurance or latest Annual Report _____

i. Civil Rights Form HHS 441	j. Handicapped Individuals Form HHS 641	k. Sex Discrimination Form HHS 639-A	l. Age Discrimination Form HHS 680
☐ Filed	☐ Filed	☐ Filed	☐ Filed
☐ Not Filed	☐ Not Filed	☐ Not Filed	☐ Not Filed

Fig. 3-9A   Checklist, first page (Form page II from PHS-398 grant application packet)

JJ   Principal Investigator/Program Director *(Last, first, middle):* _____

CHECKLIST *(Continued)*

2. PROGRAM INCOME *(See instructions, page 32.)*

All applications must indicate (Yes or No) whether program income is anticipated during the period(s) for which grant support is requested.

[ ] No   [ ] Yes   If "Yes," use the format below to reflect the amount and source(s) of anticipated program income.

Budget Period	Anticipated Amount	Source(s)

3. INDIRECT COSTS

Indicate the applicant organization's most recent indirect cost rate established with the appropriate DHHS Regional Office, or, in the case of forprofit organizations, the rate established with the appropriate PHS Agency Cost Advisory Office. If the applicant organization is in the process of initially developing or renegotiating a rate, or has established a rate with another Federal agency, it should, immediately upon notification that an award will be made, develop a tentative indirect cost rate proposal. This is to be based on its most recently completed fiscal year in accordance with the principles set forth in the pertinent *DHHS Guide for Establishing Indirect Cost Rates*, and submitted to the appropriate DHHS Regional Office or PHS Agency Cost Advisory Office. Indirect costs will **not** be paid on foreign grants, construction grants, grants to Federal organizations, and grants to individuals, and usually not on conference grants. Follow any additional instructions provided for Research Career Development Awards, Institutional National Research Service Awards, and the specialized grant applications listed on page 6.

[ ] DHHS Agreement dated: _____   [ ] No Indirect Costs Requested.

[ ] DHHS Agreement being negotiated with _____ Regional Office.

[ ] No DHHS Agreement, but rate established with _____   Date _____

CALCULATION*

(The entire grant application, including the Checklist, will be reproduced and provided to peer reviewers as CONFIDENTIAL information. Supplying the following information on indirect costs is OPTIONAL for forprofit organizations.)

a. Initial budget period:

    Amount of base $ _____ x Rate applied _____ % = Indirect costs (1) $ _____

b. Entire proposed project period:

    Amount of base $ _____ x Rate applied _____ % = Indirect costs (2) $ _____

        (1) Add to total direct costs from form page 4 and enter new total on FACE PAGE, Item 7b.

        (2) Add to total direct costs from form page 5 and enter new total on FACE PAGE, Item 8b.

*Check appropriate box(es):

[ ] Salary and wages base   [ ] Modified total direct costs base   [ ] Other base (Explain below)

[ ] Off-site, other special rate, or more than one rate involved (Explain below)

Explanation *(Attach separate sheet, if necessary.)*:

Fig. 3-9B Checklist, second page (Form page JJ from PHS-398 grant application packet)

f. Lobbying

The applicant organization must make a certification (See NIH Instructions, pages 29–30). If required, obtain Standard Form-LLL from the DRG Grants Information Office, complete it, and attach it to the application behind the second page of the Checklist.

g. Misconduct in science

The applicant organization must submit an annual assurance (see NIH Instructions, pages 30–31). The date of the Initial Assurance or latest Annual Report submission to the Office of Scientific Integrity should be indicated in Item h on the first page of the Checklist.

h. Civil rights

Certify that the applicant organization has filed an Assurance of Compliance (Form HHS 441) with Title VI of the Civil Rights Act of 1964. *(Does not apply to foreign applicant organizations.)*

i. Handicapped individuals

Certify that the applicant organization has filed an Assurance of Compliance (Form HHS 641) with section 504 of the Rehabilitation Act of 1973 (amended). *(Does not apply to foreign applicant organizations.)*

j. Sex discrimination

Certify that the applicant organization has filed an Assurance of Compliance (Form HHS 639–A) with section 901 of Title IX of the Education Amendments of 1972 (amended). *(Does not apply to foreign applicant organizations.)*

k. Age discrimination

Certify that the applicant organization has filed an Assurance of Compliance (Form HHS 680) with the Age Discrimination Act of 1975. *(Does not apply to foreign applicant organizations.)*

Recombinant DNA

Although recombinant DNA is no longer listed with other assurances, NIH continues to have—and to update—guidelines for research involving recombinant DNA. *All research involving recombinant DNA techniques that is supported by the DHHS must meet the requirements of these guidelines.* This issue is discussed on page 35 in the 9/91 revision of the NIH Instructions.

Recombinant DNA molecules are defined as

"1. Molecules which are constructed outside living cells by joining natural or synthetic DNA segments to DNA molecules that can replicate in a living cell; or
2. DNA molecules that result from the replication of the DNA molecules described in (1) above."

Guidelines concerning recombinant DNA research are available from the Office of Recombinant DNA Activities, NIH, Bethesda, MD 20892.

2. PROGRAM INCOME

See page 32 of the 9/91 revision of the NIH instructions. Fill out the top of the second page of the Checklist.

3. INDIRECT COSTS

Consult your Office of Sponsored Research to get the information needed to fill out this section.

Fill in the indirect costs in item 3 on the second page of the Checklist.

PERSONAL DATA ON PRINCIPAL INVESTIGATOR (FORM PAGE KK, FIG. 3-10)

Section F in an NIH application

- Data provided by you are confidential.
- Providing personal data is optional. If you do not wish to provide the requested information, fill in your name at the top, check the last box on the page, and attach the form without filling out the information.
- *Do not duplicate this form.* Provide only one copy.
- Do *not* give this form a page number.
- Attach this form to the signed *original* of the application, following the *Checklist.*
- This form gets separated from the rest of the application before duplication.
- This form is *not* part of the review process.

SOME IMPORTANT CONSIDERATIONS

Incomplete applications

An application will be considered incomplete and *returned to the principal investigator if:*

- It is illegible.
- It does not conform to the instructions.
- The material presented is insufficient to permit adequate review.

Simultaneous submission of applications

You may not simultaneously submit identical applications to different agencies within the PHS or to different Institutes within an agency.

Exceptions:

- Research Career Development Award applications may propose work identical to that proposed in an individual research grant application.
- An individual research grant application may propose work identical to a subproject that is part of a Program Project or Center Grant application.

The PI must fully disclose simultaneous submissions under "Other Support," *in both applications.*

Sending additional information after submission of the proposal[22]

You may send additional or corrective material pertinent to an application after the submission deadline (required application receipt date)—as late as 4 weeks *before* the Study Section meeting, *only* if it is specifically solicited—or agreed to—by prior discussion with an appropriate Public Health Service staff member, usually the Scientific Review Administrator of the Study Section. Be sure that the SRA concurs that the material you plan to

---

[22] See also the section of this book called "Tracking the Application" and the PHS-398 Instructions, page 7, right-hand column, next-to-last paragraph, last sentence.

Attach this form to the signed original of the
application after the CHECKLIST. Do not duplicate.

PERSONAL DATA ON
PRINCIPAL INVESTIGATOR/PROGRAM DIRECTOR

The Public Health Service has a continuing commitment to monitoring the operation of its review and award processes to detect—and deal appropriately with—any instances of real or apparent inequities with respect to age, sex, race, or ethnicity of the proposed principal investigator/program director.

To provide the PHS with the information it needs for this important task, complete the form below and attach it to the signed original of the application after the Checklist. *Do not attach copies of this form to the duplicated copies of the application.*

Upon receipt and assignment of the application by the PHS, this form will be separated from the application. This form will *not* be duplicated, and it will *not* be a part of the review process. Data will be confidential, and will be maintained in Privacy Act record system 09-25-0036, "Grants: IMPAC (Grant/Contract Information)." All analyses conducted on the data will report aggregate statistical findings only and will not identify individuals.

If you decline to provide this information, it will in no way affect consideration of your application.

Your cooperation will be appreciated.

DATE OF BIRTH *(month/day/year)*   SEX

☐ Female   ☐ Male

RACE AND/OR ETHNIC ORIGIN *(check one)*

Note: The category that most closely reflects the individual's recognition in the community should be used for purposes of reporting mixed racial and/or ethnic origins.

☐ *American Indian or Alaskan Native.* A person having origins in any of the original peoples of North America, and who maintains a cultural identification through tribal affiliation or community recognition.

☐ *Asian or Pacific Islander.* A person having origins in any of the original peoples of the Far East, Southeast Asia, the Indian subcontinent, or the Pacific Islands. This area includes, for example, China, India, Japan, Korea, the Philippine Islands, and Samoa.

☐ *Black, not of Hispanic origin.* A person having origins in any of the black racial groups of Africa.

☐ *Hispanic.* A person of Mexican, Puerto Rican, Cuban, Central or South American, or other Spanish culture or origin, regardless of race.

☐ *White, not of Hispanic origin.* A person having origins in any of the original peoples of Europe, North Africa, or the Middle East.

☐ Check here if you do not wish to provide some or all of the above information.

Fig. 3-10 Personal data on principal investigator (Form page KK from PHS-398 grant application packet)

send is acceptable and that the time of submission is acceptable. Some SRA's have cutoff dates for acceptance of additional materials.

If permission is granted, send 6 copies (if it is months before the Study Section meeting) to 25 copies (if it is only a few weeks before the Study Section meeting) of the item, along with a cover letter to the Scientific Review Administrator of the assigned Study Section.

Address the materials to the Scientific Review Administrator of the Study Section to which your application has been assigned. Your materials are likely to get lost if you address them simply to "Division of Research Grants."

Enclose a self-addressed, stamped postcard to receive acknowledgment that the materials you sent were received by the Scientific Review Administrator. Call the SRA if your postcard is not returned within 2 weeks.

At the same time, send a copy of the letter and the item(s) to the Institute program staff ombudsperson for your application. Indicate that the materials are "For your information."

Use/and availability of information contained in grant applications

- NIH may use the information contained in proposals for
  — Reviewing applications
  — Monitoring grantee performance
  — Identifying candidates to serve as regular or ad hoc Reviewers for Study Sections, Councils, etc.
  — Analyzing costs of proposed grants
- The Privacy Act of 1974 allows certain disclosures discussed on pages 33–35 of the NIH Instructions and permits principal investigators and program directors to request copies of records pertaining to their grant applications from the NIH component responsible for funding decisions. Established procedures permit principal investigators and program directors to request correction of inaccurate records. NIH will amend such records if it concurs that the records are incorrect.
- NIH makes information about *awarded* grants available to the public, including the title of the project, the grantee institution, the principal investigator or program director, and the amount of the award. *The abstracts of all funded research grant applications* are sent to the National Technical Information Service (NTIS), U.S. Department of Commerce, and *are available to the public from NTIS.*
- The Freedom of Information Act and implementing DHHS regulations require the release, upon request, of certain information about grants that have been awarded, irrespective of the intended use of the information. For information about the types of information that are generally available and *not* available for release, see page 35 of the 9/91 NIH Instructions. *Final determination about information release is made by NIH.* The principal investigator or program director of the grant in question is consulted and/or informed about any such release of information.

From the above regulations it becomes obvious that if you are unable to obtain a good example of a successful grant proposal (to use as a learning model) from colleagues, you can search NTIS files for an abstract of a proposal in a field close to yours and then request to see the corresponding proposal. Although this is a way to get a successful proposal to read, reading another scientist's current proposal is fraught with ethical dilemmas, because once you read someone else's good idea(s), it is not possible to completely delete the information from your brain. Thus, if you use this mechanism to obtain a proposal, you must be very careful not to inadvertently "borrow" ideas from the proposal. Moreover, the principal investigator of the proposal will be informed that you requested her/his application, and s/he may have negative feelings about your request. If you decide to obtain a proposal in this manner, it is probably wiser to get an older, rather than a current, proposal.

NONCOMPETING CONTINUATION APPLICATIONS [22]

Noncompeting continuation applications must be submitted annually (throughout a funded project period) 2 months before the beginning date of the next budget period. Applications for continuing support must be submitted on the forms provided in the PHS-2590 packet, which was last revised on 9/91 and is approved through 6/30/94. DRG generally mails a computer-generated Face page completed through item 6, and a mailing label to the applicant organization about 4 months before the end of the current budget period. If you do not receive these materials at the appropriate time, call 301-594-7180.

Read and follow the PHS-2590 instructions carefully, and prepare the application accordingly, following the outline and numbering system prescribed in the PHS-2590. This packet contains many of the same parts as the PHS-398. Therefore, I have highlighted only a few items below. Submit the completed original application and 2 copies—signed by both the PI and the official signing for the institution—directly to the awarding component that is funding the grant. Use the mailing label supplied.

In developing the budget for the next budget period, you should, in general, not exceed the amount shown for that year on the latest "Notice of Grant Award." If funding requirements have changed since the award notice, you should discuss such changes with your Program Officer at the awarding Institute. If the Program Officer concurs that the changes are necessary, you may exceed the original projected budget, but be sure to fully explain and justify any significant changes.

Provide biographical sketches for all new key personnel and consultants/collaborators.

Use Form page 6 and continuation pages to write the Progress Report Summary.

The Progress Report Summary is the record of your accomplishments in the preceding year and serves as the basis for continuing support for the project. Contrary to commonly held beliefs, the noncompeting applications are read by the staff at the awarding agency and should be prepared carefully and with attention to the needs of the readers at the awarding agency.

The Progress Report Summary is also used by the awarding component staff to:

- Prepare annual reports
- Plan programs
- Communicate scientific accomplishments supported by the agency

Therefore, the language used in the Progress Report Summary should be readily understandable to a biomedical scientist who may *not* be a specialist in the project's research field. Aim for the style used in articles in *Scientific American*.

Parts of the Progress Report Summary

1. Specific Aims (maximum of 250 words)
   - Summarize the Specific Aims of the project *as funded.*

---

[22] NIH implemented some changes in the noncompeting award process in October 1994. The changes affect primarily the financial and administrative aspects of the applications. (See article by Liane Reif-Lehrer in *Journal of the National Grantseekers Institute*, Vol. 2, No. 1, 1995). Further streamlining is under consideration by the agency. Keep up to date with additional changes that are likely to occur.

- Unless otherwise specified, the budget awarded is based on the assumption by the awarding agency that the funds provided are adequate to accomplish the Specific Aims of the original proposal. In some cases, however, Study Section or Council recommendations or budget modifications (usually reductions) made by the awarding component may require a change in the scope of the aims compared to those in the original competing application.

2. Studies and results (maximum of 750 words)
   - Describe results obtained in the past year with respect to the Specific Aims.
   - Discuss significant negative results and technical problems.

3. Significance (no page limit specified; probably deserves ½ page)
   - Use lay language.
   - Discuss the potential impact of your findings on health.

4. Plans (no page limit specified; probably deserves 1–2 pages)
   - Summarize plans for the next budget year to address the aims listed in Specific Aims.
   - Discuss any modifications to your original plans.
     Also fill out the table on Form page 7 about personnel and study subjects.

5. Human subjects
6. Vertebrate animals
7. Publications
   - Report only publications (submitted, accepted for publication, or published) resulting directly from this grant and not reported previously.
   - Provide 1 copy of each such manuscript or publication.
8. Inventions and patents

There is also a 1-page (Form page 8) Checklist (dealing with assurances and certifications, program income, and indirect costs) that must be filled out and included as the *last* page of the application.

The PHS-2590 Instructions state: "PHS estimates that it will take approximately 20 hours to complete this application for a regular research project grant. Items such as human subjects are cleared and accounted for separately, and are therefore also not part of the time estimate for completing this form." This is, in my experience, a reasonable estimate of the time it takes to complete this form. Parts 1 through 4 of the Progress Report Summary should be no longer than about 5 single-spaced pages. If you wish to submit any sizable inclusions (such as large data sets, figures, tables) pertinent to your progress, consult the Institute program staff person responsible for your application, and discuss the appropriateness of the intended submission.

Recap for Part III: Parts of the Grant Application

Application form for NIH grants: PHS-398

- For Research Grants (R01), FIRST Awards (R29), Research Career Development Awards (RCDA), Training Grants [Institutional National Research Service Awards (NRSA)]
- Revised approximately every 3 years
- 1994 revision expected to be available in early 1995

Other funding agencies have different applications and instructions. If you know how to prepare a good NIH grant application and understand the principles of responding to a set of instructions, you should be able to prepare a good application to any other agency.

Parts of the grant application

Administrative and financial information:
Face page

- Title of application: 56 spaces, descriptive, specific, and appropriate
- Dates of entire proposed project period
- Direct costs and total costs
- PI's signature
- Signature of official signing for applicant institution

Abstract of Research Plan

- Broad, long-term objectives
- Specific Aims
- Health-relatedness
- Research design and methods
Write the abstract last.

Key personnel

List specified information.

Table of Contents

- Fill in page numbers in final draft.
- List appendix items.
Consider a separate Table of Contents for the Research Plan.

Detailed budget for first 12 months

- Reasonable
- Believable
- Well-researched
- Superbly justified
Develop the budget after you plan the project.

Budget for total project period

- Research budget carefully.
- Provide quotes for large equipment.
- Include costs of service contracts and shipping.

Budget Justification

- Justify everything that is not obvious.
- Justify significant increases in future years.
- Care demonstrated in writing the Budget Justification tells reviewers about the care and conscientiousness of the PI's research and resource management.
- Use an outline form.
- There are *no* page limits—but be brief.

Biographical sketches

- Photocopy a form for each key professional person.
- Put postdoctoral training under "Education."
- Give complete references (including titles) to *all* publications of the past 3 years and representative earlier publications pertinent to the application.
- 2-page limit per person.

Other support

- Provide information about *all* active or pending support to the PI or other key personnel, whether related to this application or not.
- Incomplete/inaccurate/ambiguous reporting may delay review and/or funding.
- Report any changes in support that occur after proposal submission.

Resources and environment

- Facilities
- Major equipment
- Work environment
- Support services

Research Plan

Main (science) part of application

Introduction:	At NIH, required only for revised and supplemental applications (see below).
1. Specific Aims:	What you intend to do.
2. Background and Significance:	What has already been done in the field. Why the work is important .
3. Preliminary Studies or Progress Report:	What *you* have done already on this project.
4. Research Design and Methods:	How you will fulfill the aims. How you will do the work.

There is a 25-page limit for parts 1–4 of the Research Plan (must include tables/charts and reduced versions of appendix materials other than reprints/publications).

Include sufficient information for effective review without reference to previous application.

Use collaborators for aspects of the project that are outside your field.

1. Specific Aims (1 page)

- State broad long-term objectives.
- Describe what research is intended to accomplish.

2. Background and significance (2–3 pages)

   • Sketch Background.
   • Evaluate existing knowledge.
   • Identify gaps project is intended to fill.
   • State importance of research.
   • Include citations (list references in Research Plan/Item 9, "Literature Cited," 6-page limit).

3. Preliminary Studies/Progress Report (6–8 pages)
   New applicants: Discuss preliminary studies and other information that will help establish experience and competence of PI. List publications and manuscripts submitted or accepted for publication.
   Renewals: Require a Progress Report

   • Provide an account of progress for Specific Aims of the preceding application.
   • Summarize importance of the findings.
   • List publications and manuscripts submitted or accepted for publication.

4. Research design and methods (13–16 pages)

   • Summarize Specific Aims.
   • Give a one- or two-sentence rationale for each aim.
   • Describe research design for each aim.
   • Describe and/or reference methods.
   • Explain why proposed approach was chosen.
   • Convince Reviewers that you can do what you propose.
   • Indicate relationship of Specific Aims to each other and to overall objective.
   • Discuss
     —Control experiments
     —How data will be collected, analyzed, and *interpreted*
     —Potential difficulties and limitations of proposed procedures
     —Alternative approaches to achieve aims
     —Hazardous procedures/situations/materials and precautions to be exercised
     —Tentative sequence/timetable for project.

5. Human subjects:

   • Requires IRB approval
   • Address 6 points specified on pages 22–23 of the NIH Instructions.
   • Assure Reviewers that human subjects experiments are necessary, well-thought-out, and scientifically sound.
   • Indicate how many patients per year will be available for studies, and demonstrate that this number is sufficient to provide a statistically significant answer to your questions.

6. Vertebrate animals:

   • Requires IACUC approval
   • Address 5 points specified on page 23 of NIH Instructions.
   • Assure Reviewers that animal experiments are necessary, well-thought-out, and scientifically sound.

7. Consultants/collaborators:

   • List whether or not salaries are requested.

- Provide a letter from each, confirming her/his role in the project.
- Provide a biosketch for each.

8. Consortium/contractual arrangements:

- Justify and explain arrangements (programmatic, fiscal, administrative).
- Provide copies of written agreements.

9. Literature cited (Bibliography, 6 pages)

- Be thorough, relevant, and current.
- Choose wisely.
- Include titles.
- Use a consistent format.

Appendix:

- Questionnaires
- Graphs, diagrams, tables, charts, oversized documents, photographs and/or other materials that do not reproduce well. (Reduced copies must appear within the Research Plan.)
- Maximum of 10 publications/manuscripts or other documents resulting from the project.
- Materials that save primary Reviewers time (only with permission from SRA).
- Do not use Appendix to circumvent page limits for Research Plan.
- Proposal must be understandable without reference to Appendix.

Checklist

- 2 Form pages
- Assurances and certifications, made by PI's institution, are attested to by checking appropriate boxes on Face page of application and first page of Checklist (verified by signature of official signing for applicant organization on Face page). Specific information related to human subjects, inclusion of minorities and both genders in study populations, and vertebrate animals must also be provided within Research Plan.
- Required as last 2 pages of application.
- Assurance of compliance forms (available from DRG Grants Information Office: 301-594-7248)
    —Human subjects
    —Vertebrate animals
    —Inventions and patents
    —Debarment and suspension
    —Drug-free workplace
    —Lobbying
    —Misconduct in science
    —Civil rights
    —Sex discrimination
    —Age discrimination
    —Recombinant DNA (not listed with other assurances; see NIH instructions, page 35)
- Program income
    —Page 2 of Checklist
    —See page 32 of NIH Instructions.
- Indirect costs

—Page 2 of Checklist

—Consult your institution's Office of Sponsored Research.

Personal data on principal investigator:

- Form page: optional/confidential.
- Not part of the review process.
- Provide only one copy (no page number).

SOME IMPORTANT CONSIDERATIONS

- Incomplete applications may be returned without review.
- Simultaneous submission of applications is not permitted (except R01 & RCDA and R01 & a subproject of a Program Project or Center Grant application; these require full disclosure of simultaneous submission under "Other Support," in *both* applications).
- Sending additional information after proposal has been submitted is permitted *only* if solicited—or agreed to—by SRA.
- Use/availability of information contained in grant applications is explained in the NIH Instructions, pages 33–35.
  —Privacy Act of 1974
  —Information about awarded grants is available to the public from NTIS.

NONCOMPETING CONTINUATION APPLICATIONS

- Submitted annually (throughout a funded project period) on PHS-2590 form
- DRG sends PI a computer-generated Face page, completed through item 6, and a mailing label 4 months before due date.
- Do not exceed the budget amount shown for that year on the latest "Notice of Grant Award" unless agreed to by Program Officer at awarding Institute.
- Provide biographical sketches for new key personnel and consultants.
- Submit a Progress Report Summary (5 single-spaced pages for Parts 1–4). Include publications not previously reported, and provide 1 copy of each such manuscript or publication.
- List inventions and patents.
- Complete Checklist, and include it as the *last* page of the application.
- Submit original and 2 copies of application.

PART IV

Planning the Research Plan

INTRODUCTION

The most important part of a grant application is the proposal idea: the major subject and content of the proposed research (the Research Plan, Section C of the NIH grant application). The Research Plan should be innovative, have a clear rationale, and have obvious significance; it should be focused, well thought out, and timely. It should address a specific problem or set of related problems that can be solved by a logical sequence of experiments. Don't try to incorporate every idea you have about all interesting topics into one grant proposal.

For applications to NIH and other organizations that are primarily committed to solving problems related to health, clinical relevance is also helpful. But an artificial or overly tenuous, circuitous health-relatedness should not be invented for the proposal. Consult the funding agency to determine whether your ideas are considered to have a high priority in the view of that agency. Some NIH Institutes publish documents that indicate their research priorities. For example, the National Eye Institute has periodically published a 5-year plan of its program priorities.[1] A variety of NIH publications, many of them free of charge, including the *NIH Guide for Grants and Contracts*, are also good places to get ideas of current interests at NIH. (There is no charge for being on the mailing list for the *NIH Guide* and it is also available via electronic medium. See Appendix XI, "Resources.")

Although it is important that you have expertise (a "track record") in the proposed field of research, do not be discouraged if you are a new entrant into the field. If your training was good and your proposal idea is good, well thought out, and well presented (well written), you stand a good chance of getting funded. However, pilot experiments and presentation of preliminary experimental results are imperative.[2] Although the success rate[3] for R01 competing continuations tends to be about twice that for new R01 applications,[4] the numbers of proposals funded and the total dollar amount spent by NIH is about the same for new and competing continuation R01s (Table 4-1).

Be aware also that success rates vary from one granting agency to another and from one NIH funding component to another (Table 4-2). At NIH the variability depends not only on the difference in appropriations for the various funding components but also on how much of the funding is obligated for non-competing renewals committed to in prior years and on how each funding component chooses to use its funds. For example, funding components that fund many large programs such as PPGs fund fewer R01s, R29s, etc. and vice versa.

A clear, concise, but adequately detailed description of the research design and methods to be used to achieve the proposed research goals is essential in Section C, item 4 of the application. Do not plunge the Reviewer into a long "shopping list" of methods that you plan to use without providing a context (research design) within which you will use these methods. Don't present a global set of experiments. Experiments should be feasible

---

[1] Their previous such report was dated 1983–1987. The National Eye Institute has recently issued a new 5-year plan for 1994–1998.

[2] Some agencies provide small grants that support pilot projects. For example, NIH has a Small Grants Program, and NSF has a Small Grants for Exploratory Research (SGER) Program. For small businesses, various government agencies have a Small Business Innovation Research Grant Program that provides Phase I funding for pilot projects.

[3] The success rate is the number of competing project grants awarded as a percentage of the sum of the number of applications reviewed and the number of funded carryovers. For practical purposes, this is approximately equal to 100 times the number of grants awarded divided by the number of grant proposals reviewed.

[4] For fiscal year 1992 the success rate (including carryovers) was 20.7 for new R01s and 41.8 for R01 competing continuations.

Table 4-1 R01 and R29 Applications and Awards for 1990 –1992*

Year	1990	1991	1992
Total R01 applications submitted (including Competing Continuations)	17,117	16,773	17,944
Total R01 grants awarded (including Competing Continuations)	3,448 (20.1)	4,168 (24.8)	4,765 (26.6)
Total new R01 applications submitted	11,900	11,476	12,352
Total new R01 grants awarded	1,830 (15.4)	2,238 (19.5)	2,590 (21.0)
Total R01 Competing Continuation applications submitted	5,217	5,297	5,592
Total R01 Competing Continuation grants awarded	1,618 (31.0)	1,930 (36.4)	2,175 (38.9)
Total FIRST Award (R29) applications submitted	1,712	1,615	1,818
Total FIRST Award (R29) grants awarded	425 (24.8)	452 (28.0)	579 (31.8)
Ratio of new R01 applications to R01 Competing Continuations submitted	2.28	2.17	2.21
Ratio of new R01 grants awarded to R01 Competing Continuations awarded	1.13	1.16	1.19

* The figures in the table are numbers of proposals, except where otherwise indicated. The success rates (not including carryovers) are given in parentheses. (The success rate is the number of competing project grants awarded as a percentage of the sum of the number of applications reviewed and the number of funded carryovers. For practical purposes, this is approximately equal to 100 times the number of grants awarded divided by the number of grant applications reviewed.) Note that because NIH statistics are gathered by fiscal year and because the review process takes about 9 months, the number of grants awarded is generally those submitted in the year preceding the award year. As this book goes to press, NIH is trying to get data on the difference in success rates between *new (first-time)* PIs and *veteran* PIs (a veteran PI being defined as a PI who has submitted at least one NIH grant application, whether or not that application was funded). Because of the uncertainty of identifying new versus veteran PIs, these data are difficult to obtain and were not yet available.

and designed in such a way that they answer specific questions and that one experiment leads logically to the next. It is extremely important to provide the Reviewers with alternative procedures to be used to achieve the specific aims, should one approach turn out to be unfruitful. If the experiments proposed are sequentially dependent on each other, defining alternative approaches becomes even more important. If a project hinges, for example, on one early experiment, and no alternative approaches are given, the project is unlikely to be funded.

A realistic grasp of what personnel, equipment, supplies, and so forth will be required to do the project and how much can be accomplished in the requested time is absolutely necessary. A reasonable budget reflects your thoughtfulness and knowledge about the costs associated with your research. Reviewers may consider you naive if you underbudget—or greedy if you overbudget. Likewise, Reviewers become wary if you propose 10 years of work in a 3-year grant request or attempt to draw a 1-year project out to 3 years. A concise schedule indicating the aspects of the project planned for each of the proposed years (at the end of Research Design and Methods section) is a help to the Reviewer, but a detailed analysis of what you will do week by week or month by month is unnecessary. Exaggerated detail

Table 4-2   R01 and R29 Grants Awarded (FY 1992) by NIH Funding Component*

Institute/ Center	Traditional Research Project Applications (R01)				First Applications (R29)			
	Total	Revised	Base**	Success Rate**	Total	Revised	Base**	Success Rate**
NCI	682	254	2,495	27.3	59	24	187	31.6
NEI	203	72	645	31.5	9	3	31	29.0
NHLBI	487	202	1,907	25.5	71	30	240	29.6
NIA	202	61	770	26.2	23	8	59	39.0
NIAAA	124	52	394	31.5	9	1	20	45.0
NIAID	364	158	1,523	23.9	63	22	179	35.2
NIAMS	108	44	651	16.6	19	8	80	23.8
NICHD	300	123	1,184	25.3	28	8	98	28.6
NIDR	67	37	266	25.2	20	10	36	55.6
NIDDK	460	204	1,491	30.9	51	24	155	32.9
NIDA	167	64	551	30.3	19	7	34	55.9
NIEHS	103	40	373	27.6	10	2	25	40.0
NIGMS	727	227	2,109	34.5	79	26	230	34.3
NIMH	258	118	1,089	23.7	52	28	152	34.2
NINDS	352	143	1,382	25.5	39	16	151	25.8
NINR	30	14	220	13.6	8	5	26	30.8
NIDCD	94	27	318	29.6	13	6	31	41.9
NCHGR	29	4	153	19.0	1	—	3	33.3
NCRR	12	3	58	20.7	1	—	2	50.0
All I/Cs	4,769	1,847	17,579	27.1	574	228	1,739	33.0

* The numbers in the table are numbers of applications, except for success rates, which are given as a percent.

** The success rate is the number of grants awarded divided by (total number of applications reviewed + funded carryovers + applications returned as a result of triage review[5]). The denominator is referred to as the "Base."

often provides—to your disadvantage—comic relief for the Reviewers and detracts from your credibility as an experienced, professional scientist.

THINGS TO THINK ABOUT BEFORE YOU WRITE THE RESEARCH PLAN

Writing a good grant application is a long and painstaking process. Before you devote any effort to that task, be sure that your idea is a good one and is of interest to the funding agency to which you plan to apply for support. Although bad writing can sometimes undermine a good idea, the best writing will not turn a poor idea into a funded proposal. Likewise, a well-written proposal about a superb idea will probably not be funded by an

---

[5] Triage review refers to applications submitted in response to RFAs but deemed *not* to be responsive to the RFA during the referral process (prior to review). There are apparently fewer than 100 such applications per year; thus, the contribution of such proposals to the calculation of the success rates is small.

agency that is not interested in the project. Thus, discussion of your ideas with more established and experienced colleagues and with administrators from the potential funding agency—before you write the proposal—can save you hours of valuable time.

NIH states in its application kit: "Applicants should be aware of the availability of pre-submission advice from staff of the Institute to which an application may be assigned. Because Institute staff can provide helpful comments and advice regarding the general approach taken in preparing an application, applicants are *encouraged*[6] to contact staff of the relevant Institute. Initial contact points for staff of the various agencies or Institutes within the NIH are listed [on pages 4–5 of the 9/91 PHS-398 Instruction booklet]."

Some private foundations will actually work with you to develop your proposal if they determine that your idea is appropriate to their mandate.

Having colleagues critique your application—after you have written a fairly good complete draft—is also important and can help you avoid pitfalls in your logic or science and can also help you test for clarity in your presentation: You understand your subject well and know what you want to say; do others perceive what you intend them to? It's important to remember that there is no communication when there is a gap between the intention of the writer (speaker) and the perception of the reader (listener).

Plan to have at least 3 people review your grant before you write your final draft:

1. Someone who understands your specific research—to check for accuracy.
2. Someone who understands science and research but does *not* know about your specific research—to check for clarity.
3. Someone who is a good editor.

Make an appointment with appropriate readers early in the process. This gives the readers a chance to block out a time to devote to reading your proposal and creates for you a convenient pre-deadline target date by which to finish a good second draft of your proposal. Plan to give the readers at least 2 to 4 weeks to read your proposal, and allow at least 4 weeks after that to implement their suggestions.

Before you plan your project—and again before you begin to write your grant proposal—carefully read the instructions for completing the application, in the case of NIH the PHS-398 packet. Some aspects of the instructions are changed occasionally by NIH *without printing new editions of the instruction booklet.* These changes are sometimes delineated on loose sheets added into the application kits and are also announced in the *NIH Guide for Grants and Contracts.* The changes may be important. So always read the additional instruction sheets that you may find in the grant application kit and keep up to date with the *NIH Guide.* Do not assume that you know the instructions by remembering them from the last time you submitted an application. Whatever instructions you are following, be they from NIH or another agency, it is wise to make a detailed outline of the information to be provided and the order in which the agency wants you to provide it.

After you have read the instruction booklet but before you begin writing your own proposal, read one or more well-written, successful applications that have received good (i.e., low) priority scores and have been funded for 3 or more years. You will be able to find such proposals at many research institutions. Perhaps the PIs will allow you to read not only the proposals, but also the corresponding Summary Statements. Reading these documents will give you a better idea of what the instructions mean and what Study Sections do and don't like. Careful reading of the depersonalized Summary Statements in Appendix V of this book

---

[6] This paragraph is copied verbatim from page 3 of the PHS-398 Instructions, 9/91 revision. The word "encouraged" is in boldface type in the original.

will also give you a sense of what Reviewers look for when they review grant applications. If you cannot find a good model proposal to read at your institution, reread the section in Part III of this book entitled, "Use/Availability of Information Contained in Grant Applications."

OTHER PRELIMINARY CONSIDERATIONS

Think about the various aspects of proposal preparation:

- Deciding what you are going to do (propose)
- Doing a feasibility analysis (facilities, resources, institutional support for the project, etc.)
- Deciding where to apply for funding
- Making contact with the funding agency. Finding out whether the agency is interested in—and has funds available for—your project
- Planning the project
- Arranging for appropriate collaborators and/or consultants, if necessary
- Doing preliminary (pilot) studies
- Describing what you are going to do (writing the proposal)
- Developing a realistic budget
- Arranging for colleagues who will read your proposal

Write down the answers to the following questions:

- What is to be done? What is the hypothesis to be tested or question(s) to be answered?
- Is the work original? (Have you done a thorough library or computer search?)
- Are you and your team aware of what has been done in this and related fields? (Background)
- Why is the work worth doing? (Significance)
- What is the long-range goal?
- What are the specific aims/objectives?
- Do the specific aims/objectives lead toward accomplishment of the long-range goal?
- Is the methodology innovative or at least "state-of-the-art?"
- Who will do the work? (The reputation of the PI and her/his team)
- Why should the granting agency let *you* do the project? (What are your unique qualifications?)
- How long will the work take?
- How much will the project cost (budget) and why (budget justification)?
- Where will the work be carried out (project site)?
- What facilities will the work require? Do you have access to such facilities?
- Is the environment conducive to carrying out your project expediently?
- What are the expected results?
- What are your contingency plans (alternative methods) in case you hit a snag?
- What is the cost/benefit ratio for the project?
  —How will the project benefit your institution?
  —How will the project benefit the granting institution?
  —How will the project benefit society? (e.g., health relatedness)
  —For corporation grants: How will the project make money for, or add to the stature of, the corporation?
- What other funds are available to support your project? (Cost-sharing? Other funding agencies?)
- If applying to an agency other than NIH, does the agency require a pre-application?

RECAP FOR PART IV: PLANNING THE RESEARCH PLAN

Before you write the Research Plan:

- Be sure your idea is good. Discuss your project with established, experienced colleagues.
- Consult the funding agency to determine whether your project has high relevance priority.
- Outline your project.
- Analyze your "track record" and plan and organize pilot experiments and preliminary experimental results accordingly.
- Research how much time and what personnel, equipment, supplies, etc. will be required to do the project (reasonable budget and schedule).
- Get pre-submission advice from staff of the potential funding agency. Some agencies will help you develop your proposal.
- Plan to have colleagues critique your application. (Make appointments with at least 2 or 3 people well in advance, and commit to getting a good draft to them by a specific date.)
- Read and outline agency instructions for completing the application.
- Read one or more applications that have been funded by the potential funding agency.
- If available, read Summary Statements or Reviewers' reports from the potential funding agency.
- Gather all the information you will need.
- Plan the Research Plan.
  - —Be sure your project idea is innovative.
  - —Have a clear rationale and obvious significance.
  - —Be sure the proposal is focused, well thought out, and timely.
  - —Address a specific problem or set of related problems that can be solved by a logical sequence of experiments.
  - —If appropriate for your project, demonstrate clinical relevance if the potential funding agency is committed to solving problems related to health.
  - —Provide a context (research design) within which you present the methods to be used.
  - —Include description of experiments that are feasible and designed to answer specific questions.
  - —Explain alternative approaches.

PART V

Writing the Research Plan

INTRODUCTION

In the current climate of tight funding it is imperative to write a superior (competitive) grant application. "A superior application will state a project purpose clearly, document its need compellingly, describe its uniqueness or appropriateness convincingly, set forth its methods competently and discuss anticipated outcomes conservatively but confidently. The best applications will capture the imagination."[1]

The way you write your grant application tells the reviewer a lot about you—as a scientist and as a person.

- Do you show originality of thought?
- Do you plan ahead—and do so with ingenuity?
- Do you think logically and clearly?
- Are you up to date in all matters relevant to your project?
- Do you have good analytical skills?
- Do you recognize limitations and potential pitfalls?
- Do you think about alternative procedures in case your proposed project does not go according to expectation?
- Do you have good managerial skills? How do you handle a budget?
- Are your interpersonal skills good enough to allow you to maintain a stable work group and to get help from colleagues and other department personnel?
- How meticulous are you? How much care do you give to detail?

Begin to write your grant proposal EARLY.

The 10/88 revision of the PHS-398 Instructions states, "PHS estimates that it will take from 10 to 15 hours to complete this application. This includes time for reviewing the instructions, gathering needed information, and completing and reviewing the form." The 9/91 revision states, "The PHS estimates that it will take approximately 50 hours to complete this application for a regular research project grant. This estimate does not include time for development of the scientific plan. Items such as human subjects are cleared and accounted for separately, and are therefore also not part of the time estimate for completing this form." I have heard occasional stories of proposals that were written a week before the deadline and were funded. However, in my experience and that of many of my colleagues it usually takes an appreciably longer time—several weeks to several months—to prepare a good grant application. And this is not counting the many months that may be required to accumulate the preliminary data on which the proposal is based! Moreover, it is important also to set aside time to have others read the proposal (about 1 month), for you to consider—and act on—their relevant suggestions (about 1 month), and for the grants office at your institution to check over the administrative aspects of the proposal (generally between 5 days and 2 weeks). A hastily prepared application is often a poorly prepared application.

Think about the time required to do each of the following:

- Compile the relevant data.
- Prepare tables, figures, and/or photographs.
- Finish the various stages of the project: outline, first draft, second draft, etc. Set deadlines for yourself for finishing each stage.
- Have others read your proposal. Have a good second draft of the proposal ready to send to colleagues for appraisal at least 9–10 weeks before the grant application

---

[1] Excerpted from a Capitol Publications brochure. Reprinted with permission of Capitol Publications, Inc., 1101 King Street, Suite 444, Alexandria, VA 22314 (800 221-0425).

is due at your institution's grants administration office (often 1–2 weeks before the grant proposal is due at NIH).

    —*NEW* R01 and R29 grant applications are due Feb. 1, June 1, Oct. 1.

    —*RENEWAL* R01 and R29 applications are due Mar. 1, July 1, Nov. 1.

    —*REVISED* R01 and R29 applications are due Mar. 1, July 1, Nov. 1.

    A missed deadline[2] may cost you 4 months of time!

After you have finished your pilot experiments, leave yourself ample time to:

- Think
- Plan
- Prepare
- Outline
- Make tables and figures (diagrams, photographs, etc.)
- Write the first draft
- Revise the first draft to generate a good second draft
- Get help: Have pre-reviewers (colleagues/consultants) read the second draft
- Revise the second draft using the relevant pre-reviewers' comments
- Polish the final draft
- Get administrative approval
- Photocopy, assemble, etc.
- Mail (in time to be *received* by the deadline)

Read and follow instructions meticulously.

- Keep to the *page limits.*
- Stay within the recommended margins (at NIH, applications get copied and somewhat reduced).
- *Put information only where it belongs.* (Don't put Background information into Specific Aims or Specific Aims into Research Design and Methods, etc.)

Use a checklist.

Use the printed administrative checklist that NIH requires as the last page of the application to see that you have attended to all administrative matters. Use the general checklist provided in Appendix III of this book:

- When you plan the proposal (before you begin writing)
- Before you finish the second draft
- Before you finish the final draft

OUTLINING THE RESEARCH PLAN

Make an outline for each section of the proposal. The time you spend making an outline will probably be regained many times over in the time you save at the writing and editing stages. Many good writers spend 60% of their time making an outline, 10% writing, and 30% revising.

---

[2] For grant applications processed through the NIH, Division of Research Grants (DRG), applications must be *received* by the published application receipt dates. However, an application received after the deadline may be acceptable if it carries a legible proof-of-mailing date assigned by the carrier and the proof-of-mailing date is not later than one week prior to the deadline date. The instructions on page 8 of the 9/91 PHS-398 packet ("Applications must be **postmarked no later than the due date** and must be received at NIH in time for orderly processing. ... If the due date falls on a weekend or holiday, the due date will be extended to the next workday") pertain only to PHS agencies and programs that do not utilize the NIH Division of Research Grants (DRG) for review. This confusion is clarified in the *NIH Guide for Grants and Contracts*, vol. 21, No. 38, Part I of II, October 23, 1992, and in the second printing (9/92) of the 9/91 PHS-398.

- Use index cards, 3M Post-it notes, or an outline processor.[3] (Word processors are very useful *but are not a substitute for making an outline.* Make an outline on your word processor, and then write from the outline.)
- Your outline should fit *logically* into the obligatory outline given in the NIH (or other agency) instructions.
- *Outlines are much easier to revise than text.*
- Check the outline for logical progression of ideas, parallel construction, and adequacy of detail.
- *Don't begin to write until you are 99.99% happy with your outline.*

GETTING READY TO WRITE

- Plan to include well-designed and carefully labeled tables and figures. Prepare *figures, tables,* and *photographs* (plates) *before* you write the proposal.
  - —Use them as a guide to organize your material (sequence).
  - —Be sure they are referred to in the text.
  - —Be sure they are labeled with an informative title and have a clear legend in a type size that conforms to NIH (or other agency) specifications. The reader should be able to understand the essence of a table or figure without referring to the text. For graphs, coordinates should be clearly labeled.
  - —Be sure they are interpreted in the text.
  - —Be sure the units, abbreviations, and other terminology, as well as the findings depicted in the legends to figures and tables, agree with the corresponding discussion in the text.
  - —Be sure that all figure legends, coordinate labels, and other text on figures and photos that have been reduced on a computer or photocopy machine remain legible, that is, have not become too small to read easily.
- Plan to *refer to the literature* thoughtfully, thoroughly, and selectively.

WRITING THE FIRST DRAFT

Refer to the advice given below and in Appendix X before writing and revising the first draft of your proposal.

- *Follow the outline.*
- Try to write each section at one sitting; if the section is long, try to write each subsection at one sitting. If you must take a break, reread what you wrote so that you do not introduce changes in tense or style into the text.
- Unless otherwise noted in the instructions of the agency to which you are applying, it is acceptable to use the first person when writing the research plan. Note, however, that for an NIH application the first person is *not* to be used in the *Description (Abstract)* of the proposal.
- Don't worry about niceties in the first draft; just let the sentences flow. During this process, do not allow yourself to be interrupted to look up details. Keep a pad at your side, and jot down things that you need to check or find later.
- Wr*ite to express, not to impress!*
- Never assume that the Reviewers will know what you mean.
- Don't be afraid to repeat words. In expository writing, it is important to "call a

---

[3] A type of software program that facilitates creation of an outline.

spade a spade" every time you refer to it—rather than taking the risk of confusing the Reader or Reviewer by varying what you call something.

- Convince your Reviewers that your project has a high likelihood of succeeding by providing good pilot data and sound plans for evaluating your progress, not by lauding yourself.

REVISING (SELF-EDITING) THE FIRST DRAFT

When you revise the first draft, think about:

- Accuracy
- Clarity
- Consistency
- Brevity
- Emphasis/impact
- Style
- Tone
- Presentation

Each of these subjects is discussed briefly below and also in Appendix X.

Be accurate

- Provide correct information to maintain your credibility.
- Convey correctly the information you provide.
  —Use words correctly.
  —Don't call something a fact unless it *is* a fact.
  —Don't use superlatives unless you are certain that they apply.

Be clear

The Reviewer should be able to

- Understand easily what you wrote
- Perceive easily how you got from point A to point B

Keep in mind that the Reviewer is likely to be less familiar with your project than you are. What seems perfectly clear to you may be confusing to a Reader who is not as involved with the project as you are. This is well illustrated in the *New Yorker* cartoon on page 60.

Having colleagues read and critique your application can be very useful for catching unwarranted assumptions and other unclear exposition in your proposal.

To achieve clarity:

- Use a logical sequence of presentation.
- If you discuss 3 topics, give similar information—in the same sequence—about each topic e.g., Method 1 should go with Specific Aim 1).
- Don't use "big" words (never send your reader to the dictionary).
  —Just because someone knows a lot about science does not mean that s/he has a large vocabulary.
  —Many scientists now come from abroad and are not native English speakers.
- Don't use jargon! Terminology limited to a given field may be unfamiliar—and irritating—to a Reviewer who is not in that field.
- Don't use the words "former" and "latter"—it slows the reader down.

- Use acronyms and abbreviations sparingly and only if they are in fairly common usage. Acronyms and abbreviations defined many—or even just several—pages earlier or use of multiple unfamiliar acronyms and abbreviations makes for slow reading and can be annoying to Reviewers.
- Be sure sentences and paragraphs are not too long. Sentences of 17 to 23 words tend to make for easy reading. Paragraphing should be done around topics; however, paragraphs may have to be split to avoid overwhelming the Reader with a large solid block of text that provides no relief (in the form of white space) for the reader.
- Start paragraphs with clear, informative *topic sentences.*[4] What are you going to tell the reader in that paragraph?
- Don't disappoint the reader. Be aware that a topic sentence, a subheading, or a heading is essentially a promise to the reader about what s/he will find in the text that follows. Thus, in the paragraph below, taken from an actual grant proposal, the writer has broken his promise to the reader. The subheading promises a discussion of alternative approaches, but none is forthcoming in the paragraph!

  > "*Alternative Approaches:* All the approaches planned for years 1–5 of the proposed project are very low-cost strategies. Each will be carefully evaluated to gauge its effectiveness and those which prove most successful will be repeated, and where possible expanded."

- *Avoid ambiguity.* Think about possible gaps between what you *intend* to convey and what the reader may *perceive.*
  —Misplaced modifiers
  —Uncommitted pronouns
  —Words or phrases that can be interpreted in more than one way
  —Complex sentences

  See Appendix X.

- *Avoid irrelevant information,* that is, information that is irrelevant in a given context.
  —Irrelevant information may confuse the reader.
  —Irrelevant information may annoy the reader.
  —Don't "pour out" all you know just to impress the reader.
  —Think about what the reader needs (wants) to know in relation to *this* section of *this* proposal about *this* subject (project).

  > Some rules of thumb that may help you avoid putting information in the wrong section of a proposal:
  >
  > If it's future tense, it probably doesn't belong in the Background Section or Progress Report.
  > If it's past tense, it probably doesn't belong in the Methods Section.

Irrelevant information is a weak point in proposals. Novice grant application writers are particularly prone to buttress their proposals with additional information for fear that they are not saying or doing enough. But irrelevant information tends to depress rather than impress Reviewers. Limit yourself to the relevant, strong points about your project. If your application is complete and you have responded to everything in the instructions, Reviewers will be thankful for having to read less rather than more!

---

[4] When long paragraphs are broken into two or more paragraphs to avoid presenting the Reader with a large block of uninterrupted print, the continuation paragraphs may not need topic sentences.

Be consistent

Consistency helps the reader understand the proposal; it is important in all aspects of the proposal.

- In the outline form, are your headings I, II, III; A, B, C; and 1, 2, 3 at the same levels of importance?
- Although it is difficult, you should maintain a good outline within the confines of the one imposed by the NIH (or other agency) instructions.

> *An outline processor can help immensely.* Some word-processing programs have built-in outline processors.

- Text should agree with the information in figures and figure legends (including the units you use).
- Terminology and abbreviations should be the same throughout.

> Do not use different words for the same thing just for literary reasons. Use of different terms for the same thing may create ambiguities—which can slow the reader down.

- Tenses should be uniform throughout the document or at least throughout a section of the document.
- Subjects and verbs should agree (singular or plural):

> The *group* of scholars *is* getting an award.
> The *scholars are* getting an award.
> Be aware that the word "data" is plural; the data are ...

Software programs generically called grammar checkers may help detect some grammatical errors.

- Appropriate sections of the proposal should agree with each other:
  —Body of proposal with Description (Abstract)
  —Specific Aims with Methods
  —Methods with Budget
  —Budget requests with Facilities Available

> If you ask for a microscope in the Budget and then say in the "Resources and Environment" section that your department has 3 microscopes, you had better have a very good justification for why you need another microscope.

- Separate clearly what you say you
  —Have done (Progress Report)
  —Are doing now (time between writing proposal and, you hope, funding)
  —Propose to do in next project period
  —Want to do (or should do) in the future but are *not* planning to do in the next project period. That is, if you want to discuss future projects (e.g., to discuss long-range goals or establish significance), be very explicit about designating what might be a direction for a subsequent renewal project period but is not a current aim.

Be brief (concise but complete)

In the case of a competitive renewal application, the Reviewers may be provided with a copy of your previous research proposal. Nevertheless, the instructions specify that the present application must be complete by itself.

In expository writing, the Reader wants the *maximum* information in the *minimum* number of words.

Avoid information that is irrelevant in the context of the proposal.

- Don't discuss things just to show how much you know. Limit yourself to information that relates to your project.
- Don't overwhelm the Reviewer with a "shopping list" of facts or findings devoid of any effort on your part to summarize, compare, contrast, or evaluate. Beware of this tendency especially, for example, in the "Background and Significance" section.
- Don't put information in an inappropriate part of the proposal. For example, the 2 excerpts below were found in the Progress Report of a proposal. The first excerpt would be more appropriately placed in the Background section; the second is likely to fit better into the Methods section.

> *Excerpt 1:* "X-cell cultures, on the other hand, are characterized by _____. These cells are presumed to derive from _____, based on a number of criteria such as _____. Substance Y, however, is not a useful marker in _____ cultures because _____."

> *Excerpt 2:* "The _____ was next used to determine if _____. We purified the _____ by separating _____ on an SDS gel and transferring these to _____ The _____ was then stained with _____, and the band of _____ was cut out. This strip was then de-stained and reacted with _____ Following an x-hour incubation, the _____ was eluted from the strip using a _____ buffer. This _____ was then used on _____"

- Don't provide information that is not useful to the Reviewer or that detracts from your image. Some foundation applications require a free-form biographical sketch. Think about what the agency would want to know about you in the context of the proposal. Steer clear of personal details, especially those that do not show you in the best light. For example, the statement "I was an awkward child" may well suggest to the Reviewer that the writer grew into an awkward adult. Awkward adults do not tend to do well in a laboratory situation.

Avoid redundancy and unnecessary words.

- They waste your space (page limitations).
- They waste the Reviewer's precious time.
- They may irritate the Reviewer.
- They may confuse the Reviewer. (Why is the writer telling me this again?)

Sentence redundancy may give the Reviewer the idea that you are an insecure person. Say it once and say it right. One exception to this suggestion is redundancy for purpose of emphasis. For example, when there are *no* page limits, it is often useful to formulate expository reports (including oral presentations) so that you:

1. Tell the Readers (listeners)—in outline form—what you are going to tell them.
2. Tell them—in appropriate detail—what you want to tell them.
3. Tell them briefly (summarize) what you told them.

See Appendix X.

Think about emphasis and impact

Don't begin a paragraph with unimportant words. In a compound sentence, put the important phrase first.

If you want to stress that the work was done *in the previous project period,* write:

> *In the previous project period,* three approaches were developed to solve ...

If you want to stress that *three approaches were developed,* write:

> *Three approaches were developed* in the previous project period to solve ...

Think about style

- Use simple (but not simple-minded/simplistic) words.
- Use short, direct sentences (about 17 to 23 words is a reasonable length), but avoid a choppy first-grader sound by judicious use of transition words (Although, However, Nevertheless, etc.).
- Use short paragraphs that begin with *informative topic sentences.*
- Avoid modifiers that do not add to the critical essence of what you want to say:

  > This *cleverly conceived* experiment ...

- Avoid an undue amount of self-praise. Let your data speak for you.

  > Our *tremendously unique* method for ...
  > Our laboratory is the *best known in the world* for ...
  > We have *by far the largest* collection of ... in the country.

- Replace "opinion" modifiers with quantitative modifiers.

  > Not: *most* or *many.* But: 68–70%

- Don't overstate your case. Avoid superlatives unless you are very sure "it" really is *best, most,* etc.
- Try not to split infinitives, unless splitting the infinitive avoids ambiguity or improves the flow of the sentence.

  > Consider the difference in meaning in the sentences below:
  > She will try *to* **more than** *justify* the cost of the computer.
  > She will try *to justify* **more than** the cost of the computer.
  > She will try **more than** *to justify* the cost of the computer.
  > These sentences do not have identical meanings. To achieve clarity (get the correct meaning), the modifier words "more than" must be located close to the word they are intended to modify, in this case, "justify."

  See Appendix X.

- *Avoid pompous language*
  —Don't write: "Nosocomial infection." Write "Hospital-acquired infection."
  —Don't write "Iatrogenic condition." Write "Physician-induced condition."
  (Your Reviewer may not be an M.D.)

  > Avoidance of unnecessary, "heavy" medical jargon is especially important if you are a physician-researcher proposing a project that involves a lot of basic science. Such a proposal is likely to have at least one Ph.D. Reviewer. Sending this Reviewer on frequent trips to a medical dictionary wastes her/his time!

On the other hand, failure to use the proper terminology in a given field may be perceived by some reviewers as a lack of familiarity with the subject. There is a fine line here, and a PI must make an educated judgment about such issues. Assessments of likely Study Section assignments and familiarity with the work of the members of those review groups can sometimes help you to decide how much or how little jargon to use.

Think about tone

Attitude, mood, and tone can be "contagious."

Avoid words that have a negative tone, such as "unfortunately."
Be positive.

Not: I won't be able to finish this project by the end of the first year.

But: I will be able to finish this project by March of the second year.
or
I expect to finish this project by March of the second year.
or
I plan to finish this project by March of the second year.

Think about presentation

Some scientists think that if they have a superb project idea, they do not have to worry about the presentation. This shows a naive view of human psychology. Although an attractive presentation will not fool any Reviewer into mistaking a poor proposal for a good proposal, a well-formatted, easy-to-read proposal can certainly affect the attitude of the Reviewer as s/he reads your proposal, all the more so because s/he may already have read numerous other proposals—or there may be 100 more applications waiting to be reviewed/read after yours.

Strictly adhere to the page limitations. If you are strapped for space, consider that 12 letters per horizontal inch type allows more text on a page than 10 letters per inch, but don't antagonize your Reviewer by using smaller than 10 or 12 point type (to circumvent the page limitations!) or fancy fonts that are hard to read. Choose a type style and size that result in a neat and legible document. Good "letter-quality" print (black ink, white paper) should be used in all drafts that will be read by others; do not use dot-matrix print.

NIH specifies, on page 10 of the PHS-398 instructions (rev. 9/91), the type style and size limitations for proposal preparation: *"applications not meeting the dictated size requirements may be returned without review."*

- Face page: Type density must be 10 characters per inch (cpi).
- Rest of application:
  —Type must be clear and readily legible.
  —Type must be standard size. That is, 10 to 12 point (about ⅛ inch in height for uppercase letters).
  —For constant-spacing type, do not exceed 15 cpi.
  —For proportional-spacing type, do not exceed an average of 15 cpi.
  —Do not have more than 6 lines of type per vertical inch.
  —Figures, charts, tables, figure legends, and footnotes may be in smaller type but must be clear and readily legible. In making this judgment, take into account that the copies of your proposal that are sent to the Reviewers have been repro duced by NIH in a format that is about a half inch less in each dimension than the one you submit.

Note the readability of the type and size of the font you choose:

- This is New York 12 point. It is a serifed font and is easy to read, but it is fairly spread out and takes up a lot of space. Apparently, many people find it easier to read a serifed font.
- This is New York 10.
- This is New York 9. This is too small.
- *This is Zapf Chancery 12.* This is too ornate for use in a grant application.
- This is Helvetica 10. This is too small.
- This is Helvetica 12. This is a condensed, nonserifed font. It takes up a lot less space than New York 12 point.

It is very difficult to read a page of small text that has no visual relief in the form of some white space. For dense text it is helpful to skip a line between paragraphs. If you do this, do not indent the beginnings of paragraphs.

Consider placing tables and figures to relieve the look of densely packed text and let text flow around the tables and figures. But be sure the tables and figures are as close as possible to the text that refers to them.

If it seems appropriate, consider presenting your proposal in a two-column-per-page format and reducing tables and figures to fit into one column width. A few Reviewers have told me that they find this format easier to read and digest. But this is a matter of taste. Check with your SRA.

Although many people prefer the neat look of text justified at both margins, I have heard from several Reviewers that they find text with a ragged right margin easier to read—especially if one is frequently interrupted. Apparently, the pattern recognition of the irregular margin helps some readers—especially people who are very fast readers—to keep their place.

Further suggestions for editing your first draft

Use computer aids to help you improve the first draft.

- Outline processors
- "Search mode" in word processors to find overused words
- Spell checkers (These are now integrated into many word-processing programs.)

    Be aware that spell checkers do not catch words that are correctly spelled but incorrectly used, such as "there" instead of "their" (or vice versa) or "Principle Investigator" instead of "Principal Investigator." Thus, even after you spell-check your proposal, you must proofread it to be sure that all word usage is correct.

- Stylistics and grammar checkers (Some computer programs can check for passive versus active verb constructions, sentences and paragraphs that are too long, vague phrases, incorrect punctuation, missing spaces, overused words, etc.)

Be sure the grant proposal is short but thorough; do not repeat, but rather refer to, material in other sections. For example, say "See section Y, page X."

Print out a clean copy of the first draft and check again for:

- Lack of logical flow
- Bad grammar (especially the kind that causes ambiguity. A grammar checker software program may help.)
- Jargon
- Insufficient references

- Circular sentences

  "The important conclusion from these findings is . . ." But instead of giving a conclusion, you repeat the findings!

- Sentences and paragraphs that are too long (A grammar checker software program may be of help.)
- A messy presentation (e.g., too many typos or spelling errors)

  The Reviewer may extrapolate: Carelessness in writing indicates carelessness in experimentation!

Then read the proposal again[5] and ask yourself:

- Is my organization good? (It should be if you made a good outline at the start.)
- Is my proposal convincing? (Is it authoritative and persuasive without being arrogant?)
- Did I adequately examine, analyze, and interpret the information presented, rather than just list it?
- Did I add my own thoughts and insights about information obtained from the published literature?
- Did I give sufficient credit to the work of others?
- Is the proposal easy to read?
- Did I miss any ambiguities (things that are obvious to you but may not be to the Reviewer[6])?
- Is the proposal up to date? (Have you rechecked for new developments in your field that may have occurred since you began work on the proposal—perhaps several months ago?)
- Is the bibliography up to date?

GETTING HELP AFTER YOU HAVE A GOOD SECOND DRAFT

Preparing a draft for the pre-reviewers

When you have edited your first draft in accordance with each of the above criteria; check a single-spaced version with margins designated by NIH (or other funding agency) to be sure that you are within the designated page limits. Then print out a second draft for the readers. It should be double-spaced and have wide margins to make it easy for the readers to insert suggested changes. (Alternatively, you may prefer to suggest to the readers that they insert circled numbers within the manuscript and use these numbers to make relevant comments or changes on separate sheets of paper.)

Getting help from others when you have a good second draft

The best stage at which to get help with your application is when you have a clean, comprehensible draft but one that is not yet at the point at which you will feel resentful about making suggested changes.

---

[5] If you can afford the time, it is good to put the proposal away for a few days before this rereading. The effort is likely to be more fruitful if you have taken a break from working on the document.

[6] A senior professor who attended one of my workshops remarked to me, "I never notice my ambiguous statements because every time I read my own proposal, I know exactly what I mean."

Have at least 3 people review your grant before you write your final draft:

1. Someone who understands your specific research—to check for accuracy.
2. Someone who understands science and research but does **not** know about your specific research—to check for clarity.

> If your institution has an in-house "Study Section," take advantage of this generous service.

3. Someone who is a good editor—to help you polish the proposal.

> If your institution has an in-house editorial service, take advantage of this service.

In addition you may be able to get help from your potential funding agency and from your institutional Grants Office (Office for Sponsored Research).

When you send your proposal to others for critique, send only those parts that are appropriate for the particular reader(s). For example, if your reader is an eminent scientist in your field with whom you have had only professional contact, send only the Research Plan. If your reader is a kindly mentor whom you have known for some time, you might consider also sending the budget and budget justification—or even the whole application. If you are submitting the application to your institutional grants office, you may want to send everything *except* the Research Plan—unless the staff requires the whole application.

Colleagues

Try to make an "I'll read your grant, if you read mine" agreement with a responsible, conscientious colleague who is intimately familiar with your field of research and who is a successful grant getter.

- Ask ahead of time.
- Give your colleague(s) *at least* 2 to 4 weeks to read your proposal.

People who know your field can make valuable scientific suggestions, but someone who is not totally familiar with your specific area of research may be a better judge of clarity (and may, in some cases, better simulate the secondary Reviewer). Likewise, someone who is a successful proposal writer (preferably with multiple successes) and has had experience as a Reviewer can have valuable comments even if he/she knows little about your field. Lastly, someone with good editorial skills can help with the final polishing of the proposal. It is optimal for the success of your grant proposal to have it read by each of these types of critics.

Your choice of readers is extremely important. To make the pre-review process a worthwhile endeavor, you must choose readers who are knowledgeable and savvy, conscientious, and candid. In addition, they should have an eye for detail. A colleague who reads your proposal in an hour and tells you "it's fine" has probably not helped you very much. As a consultant, I spend at least 30 hours to critique an R01 proposal! *Assure your readers that you invite harsh criticism and are not afraid of a lot of red ink.*

The value of having your proposal read by several readers is well illustrated by my experience with the manuscript for this book. I sent the main part of the book to the five readers named in the acknowledgments section. Each of them made extremely valuable and cogent suggestions for improving the text. But, interestingly, there were very few suggestions or corrections that overlapped, that is, were made by more than one reader. This illustrates that people bring very different expertise, criteria, and perspectives to what they read. Thus, it will generally benefit your proposal to have more, rather than fewer, readers.

If you are mailing your manuscript to the readers, always enclose for each reader:

- A cover letter or note
  —Thank the person in advance for taking her/his precious time to read your proposal.
  —Suggest an appropriately far off date for the return of your proposal.
  —Specify when the person can best reach you in case of questions (provide phone and fax numbers).
- A self-addressed return envelope (large enough—with the correct amount of postage—to accommodate the original proposal and the extra sheets the reader may wish to enclose). The U.S. Postal Service 2-day priority mailers are often a convenient way to send manuscripts, if the pre-reviewer retains a photocopy of her/his comments. Otherwise, express mail or registered mail should be used so the package can be traced if lost.

Funding agency staff members

Applicants can get various degrees of pre-submission advice from their potential funding agency. Some foundations will actually work with you to prepare your proposal.

At NIH, applicants can get pre-submission advice regarding the general approach taken in preparing an application (see pages 3–5 of the PHS-398 Instruction booklet, 9/91 revision), and a staff member may discuss with you the appropriateness of various components of your application. But for the most part, agency pre-review will be only with respect to form and adequacy of the presentation (i.e., for grantsmanship, not for scientific merit). If you wish to use this service, the grant application must be sent to the agency several months before the required submission date! (Call to ask when to send the proposal.) *Do not count on agency personnel to make suggestions about material (scientific) content, give "estimates" on fundability, or do editing.*

Office for sponsored research at your institution

At many institutions, personnel in the office for sponsored research will check the administrative parts of your application. This is a valuable service. *Give them ample time to do the best possible job for you.* Some institutions have people in this office who can help with more than the administrative details. If such help is available, take advantage of it.

Consultants

Consultants can help you organize your ideas, write, rewrite, critique, and/or generally improve the presentation of your idea in your application. Consultants are unlikely to help you with your research idea. Therefore, before you spend money on a consultant, be sure that your idea is good and feasible (check with knowledgeable colleagues), the science is sound, and the intended granting agency is interested in—and enthusiastic about—the idea.

It's a good idea not to change the draft you gave to the readers while the readers have that draft. It will be harder to locate changes suggested by the readers if you have generated a new draft! Furthermore, this is a good time for you to get some distance from the proposal.

REVISING THE SECOND DRAFT AFTER IT COMES BACK FROM THE READERS/PRE-REVIEWERS

Revise the second draft after you get all the copies back from the readers/pre-reviewers.

A conscientious reading of a grant proposal is a lot of work. You owe your readers the courtesy of *seriously considering* their suggestions. However, you need *not* feel obliged to *use* all their suggestions! You are responsible for the proposal. You should feel comfortable with the proposal that you submit. You must decide which of the readers' suggestions are useful and appropriate.

Incorporate only those of the readers' suggestions that you consider pertinent. But be open-minded in your assessments. Sometimes another person's comment wounds your ego. Reread that comment a day later; you may find that the reader made a good point. Remember that the objective is to get funded.

While reading the pre-reviewers' edits, you may find that the comments suggest other changes to you that you had not thought of before. This technique tends to work better if you have put the proposal aside for a while. Leave your mind open for this process.

When you have finished this revision process, you should have a pre-final draft of your proposal.

This is your last opportunity to make changes. Be sure you are satisfied overall with your proposal before you do the final polishing and checking.

See Appendices I-D, II, III, and X.

The final copy of the proposal should look neat. Spelling and grammar should be correct. Poor grammar makes extra work for the Reviewers and, if they are of the "old school," may sour them about the applicant. Above all, some grammatical errors can lead to misunderstandings about your science!

Certain spelling and grammatical errors or a large number of such mistakes may provide comic relief during the long and tedious Study Section meetings. Be sure your proposal is not used for this purpose. An occasional minor error is no calamity, and a neatly "whited-out" correction is perfectly acceptable. But a sloppy-looking—or carelessly written—grant application may give the Reviewers the idea that this is a reflection of how you do your science. If a Reviewer feels that an applicant could not be bothered putting out a decent final product, the Reviewer is likely to start her/his review of your grant proposal with a negative attitude.

If all of the above are in order, it is time to prepare your application for submission.

Recap for Part V: Writing the Research Plan

The way you write your grant application tells the reviewer a lot about you.

To be competitive, write a superb grant application.

Begin to write your grant proposal early. It may take several weeks to several months to prepare a good application—not counting time to accumulate preliminary data or time to have others read the proposal.

Prepare before you write:

- Read and follow instructions meticulously.
- Set deadlines for yourself for finishing the various stages of the project.
- Use a good checklist when you plan the proposal.

Writing the Research Plan:

- Make an outline.
- Compile and analyze relevant data.
- Prepare tables, figures, and photographs.
- Write the first draft.
  - —Write to express, not to impress.
  - —Provide alternative approaches for the project.
  - —Don't put information in an inappropriate part of the proposal.
  - —Avoid ambiguity and irrelevant information.
  - —Be quantitative and specific.
  - —Be consistent (tenses, nomenclature—including abbreviations).
  - —Be concise but complete (avoid redundancy and unnecessary words).
  - —Use simple (but not simple-minded or simplistic) words.
  - —Use short, direct sentences.
  - —Use short paragraphs that begin with informative topic sentences.
  - —Avoid pompous language and self-praise (let your data speak for you).
  - —Be positive.
  - —Stay within the recommended margins.
  - —Strictly adhere to the page limitations and instructions about type size.
- Revise the first draft to generate a good second draft.
  - —Consider accuracy, clarity, consistency, brevity, emphasis and impact, style, tone, and presentation.
  - —Use computer aids to help you improve the first draft.
  - —Use a good checklist to see that everything is perfect.
- Print out a good second draft.
- Have colleagues and/or consultants critique the second draft.
- Revise the second draft using the relevant comments of pre-reviewers.
- Generate a pre-final draft.

PART VI

SUBMITTING AND TRACKING THE GRANT APPLICATION

Now that you have finished filling out most of the administrative forms of the application and have finished writing the Research Plan, you are ready to finalize the application.

POLISHING AND CHECKING THE PRE-FINAL DRAFT OF THE GRANT APPLICATION

- Have you rechecked the budget calculations?
- Have you checked that budget totals are entered in items 7 and 8 of the Face page?
- Is the budget adequately justified?
- Have you signed the application (*before* photocopying)?
- Has the responsible institutional official signed the application (*before* photocopying)?
- Are your name (last name first!) and Social Security number (optional) filled in on the top right corner of each page?
- Are the pages all numbered consecutively and correctly?

> (NIH does not permit page numbers with suffixes (e.g., pages 5A, 5B, 6a, etc.); Some other agencies permit and even request such numbering. Check the instructions.

- Do you have a table of contents? Are the page numbers entered *in accordance with the page numbers of the final draft* on the text pages? In the table of contents? Have you remembered to list the appendix items?
- Have you compared the project description (Abstract; Form page 2 in an NIH application) with the final version of the application to be sure it is appropriate and parallel in content?
- Do you have a tentative timetable for your project (at the end of the Research Design and Methods section?)
- Do you have a Biographical Sketch (maximum of 2 pages per person) for each professional person listed under "personnel" and under "Consultants/Collaborators"?
- Do you have a letter of collaboration for each "consultant" and "outside collaborator"? Have you placed the letters in Section 7 of the Research Plan?
- Do you have the necessary documentation for Consortium or Contractual Arrangements?
- Have you completed the necessary forms concerning
  —Other Support
  —Resources and Environment

  > Be sure "Facilities" and "Equipment" are not at odds with equipment asked for in the budget.

  —Personal Data on the Principal Investigator
  —Are the 2 NIH Checklist pages filled in and included? Have you numbered them as the last 2 pages of the application?
  Are the forms in the correct places in the application?
- Have the dates of the various institutional agreements and assurances been filled in on the Face page and Checklist pages?
- Have the indirect costs been calculated on the Checklist pages and filled in on the Face page?
- Is the Appendix complete and in (collated) order? Is each Appendix item labeled correctly? Have you included a list of Appendix items on Form page 3 (Table of Contents)?

Have you included a list of Appendix items as a cover sheet for each copy of the Appendix?

- Have you made a final check of all items against the NIH checklist?
- Have you checked the formatting of each page (including margins)?
- Have you checked that no page limits have been exceeded in the final formatted draft?

PREPARING THE APPLICATION FOR SUBMISSION

- Print out a final draft.
- Make the appropriate number of photocopies of the application and the Appendix.

  Aside from the 5 photocopies of the application and 4 photocopies of the Appendix required by NIH, you will need extra copies of the application for yourself and for the grants office, and perhaps other administrative offices at your own institution.

  —Use paper clips or rubber bands to fasten pages together. (Do not staple or bind!)
  —Use folders or lower halves of manila envelopes to keep copies neat.
  —Label items: "Original Application," "Original Appendix," etc.
- If you wish, you may provide a cover letter requesting (suggesting) up to 3 specific Study Sections that could review your application—and the reason you are making the request—and attach it (with a paper clip) to the front of the original copy of the application. You may also suggest a potential funding component in this letter.
- If the application is in response to an RFA (Request for Application), read carefully and follow the instructions below the mailing label (in the middle of the application kit just after the personal data form).
- Include a self-addressed and *stamped* postcard that someone at NIH can drop in the mail to confirm receipt of application. Attach the postcard to the original copy of your proposal. The postcard can read simply:

  "Grant Application: (Fill in your grant proposal title) by (Fill in your name) was received at DRG

  "by _____

  "on (date) _____

  "Thank you."

MAILING THE APPLICATION

Mail the *original* + 5 copies of the application = 6 complete sets.[1]
    Mail 5 complete sets of the Appendix.

---

[1] Some NIH proposals with expedited review processes may require submission of a greater number of copies of the proposal. If in doubt, call the Program Officer at the relevant Institute.

- Use a box from bond paper or something similar to pack the application so that it arrives at NIH in good condition.
- Use the mailing label provided in the middle of the application kit (just after the personal data form and before the first page with the vertical crimson stripe).

  Note: If you use Express Mail or courier service, change the zip code on the NIH mailing label to 20816.

- Use the proper amount of postage. (Weigh it; don't guess.)
- Mail the application in ample time.

  For grant applications processed through the NIH, Division of Research Grants, applications must be *received* by the published application receipt dates. However, an application received after the deadline may be acceptable if it carries a legible proof-of-mailing date assigned by the carrier and the proof-of-mailing date is not later than one week prior to the deadline date.[2]

- Get a legible proof-of-mailing receipt from the Post Office or commercial mail carrier.

On arrival at NIH, each application is stamped with the arrival date in large letters. It is important that your application arrive on time. If you cannot mail the application early enough to use regular mail, use U.S. Postal Service Express Mail or a private express delivery service such as Federal Express.

TRACKING THE APPLICATION

Follow the travels of your application after it is sent to the granting agency—in this case, NIH:

- Did you get the self-addressed postcard back after about 2 weeks?
- Did you receive the snap-out mailer with your proposal ID number and Study Section assignment from NIH after about 6 weeks (see Appendix I-E, Fig. A1-1)?
- What are your Study Section and Institute assignments?
  If an application is assigned to a Study Section or funding component that you consider inappropriate, you should immediately contact the Referral Office (301-594-7250) to discuss the possibility of reassignment and follow up with a written request to the Referral Office. As with suggestions for Study Section assignments submitted with the original proposal, requests for reassignment will be considered carefully, but the final decision rests with NIH.
- When does your Study Section meet?

---

[2] Page 8 of the 9/91 PHS-398 packet reads, "Applications must be **postmarked no later than the due date** and must be received at NIH in time for orderly processing. . . . If the due date falls on a weekend or holiday, the due date will be extended to the next workday." However, the *NIH Guide for Grants and Contracts*, Vol. 21, No. 38, Part I of II, October 23, 1992, contains the following "Reminder": "[NIH] guidelines governing receipt dates for applications have not changed and may be found on page 4-14 of the PHS Grants Policy Statement (rev. 9/91). Item 2 in the first full paragraph in the instructions on page 8 of the revised PHS application (rev. 9/91) is applicable to PHS agencies and programs that do not utilize the NIH Division of Research Grants (DRG). For grant applications processed through NIH, DRG, the Division of Research Grants system requires that applications must be **received** by the published application receipt dates. However, an application received after the deadline may be acceptable if it carries a legible proof-of-mailing date assigned by the carrier and the proof-of-mailing date is not later than one week prior to the deadline date." This clarification notice is an example of the importance of reading the *NIH Guide for Grants and Contracts* on a regular basis! This matter was later clarified in the second printing (9/92) of the PHS-398 (Rev. 9/91).

- Who are the members of the Study Section?

> As soon as you get your assignment, you may want to call your Scientific Review Administrator to find out whether there is anyone on the Study Section who is not listed in the NIH list of Study Section members. Then, if there is someone on the Study Section you consider to have a conflict of interest with respect to your project, you can alert the SRA not to send your proposal to that individual for review.

It is *your responsibility* to contact the Division of Research Grants (DRG) Referral Office if you do not get, within 6 weeks of submitting the application, the Study Section assignment (including the name, address, and phone number of the Scientific Review Administrator and the number assigned to your application).

In the months between submission of your application and the Study Section meeting, things may happen that might help your proposal get a better review. You may get some new exciting data, an additional paper may be accepted for publication, you may get a promotion, or something else may occur that would strengthen your application. It is to your advantage to inform the Study Section about such matters.

If you have something to send, contact the Scientific Review Administrator of your assigned Study Section and ask for permission to send supplementary materials. If permission is granted, write a letter (enclose new data, reprints, preprints, etc., at least in triplicate) to the Scientific Review Administrator of the Study Section asking him/her to release this additional information to the Reviewers. However, do not send data just to impress the Reviewers that you are working hard. Use good judgment about what is important for the review process. Do not send data that you would not have put into the original grant application. Do not abuse the option to send additional data, and do not send too much material; try to keep it to 1 to 2 pages. You should be aware that even if you do get permission to send additional material, the Reviewers have the option not to consider it![3]

In fairness to the Scientific Review Administrator, staff, and the Study Section, the optimal time to send such additional data is more than 6 weeks before the Study Section meeting. However, if an experiment that will help the status of your grant proposal comes out a week before the meeting, call the SRA. *If you get permission,* send the materials by Express Mail; there is no harm in trying.

If you do send material close to the time of the Study Section meeting, ask the SRA how many copies s/he would like to have to save NIH the task of making photocopies. Some SRAs send additional materials only to the primary Reviewers/Readers. Some may send them to all Study Section members.

Enclose a self-addressed, *stamped* postcard with the materials you send so that you can get acknowledgment of receipt of the materials.

If you get permission and send additional materials to the Scientific Review Administrator, also send a copy of the materials and the cover letter to the Institute program staff person who is responsible for your application.

Applicants are automatically notified of the status of their application, including their priority score and percentile ranking (if the application was scored), by means of a computer-generated snap-out mailer (Appendix I-E, Fig. A1-2). You should receive this mailer within 2 weeks of the end of the Study Section meeting.

Prompt access to your priority score and percentile ranking can give you an appreciable head start on revising an application that is not likely to be funded. The snap-out

---

[3] See PHS-398 Instructions, page 7, right-hand column, next-to-last paragraph, last sentence.

mailer also provides the name of the Program Official from the potential funding component who is responsible for your application.

Do not call the Scientific Review Administrator for information about priority scores. The SRA needs time to recover from the Study Section meeting, average scores, calculate percentiles, and prepare the Summary Statements. The SRA has to prepare some 60 to 100 or more of these reports within the month after the meeting. In the past, the SRA had to synthesize these Summary Statements from 2 or 3 written reports of the primary Reviewers, notations of the Readers (Discussants), and what she/he remembers of (or took notes about) the discussion during the meeting that follows the oral reading of the Reviewers' reports. It was no easy task![4] This burden has perceptibly decreased by the adoption of triage[4]—and associated modifications in the form of the summary statements[5]—for DRG-wide use for all Investigator-initiated research grant (R01) and "FIRST Award" (R29) applications reviewed by DRG as of February 1995 Study Section meetings. The modified Summary Statements consist primarily of the individual reviewer's reports (critiques). Reviewers are expected to modify their written critiques during the review of an application—for example, removing a criticism that was deemed to be invalid following group discussion. Under the new system, SRAs edit Summary Statements "lightly"—only to eliminate bad grammar and unnecessarily hurtful comments—but are no longer required to integrate the reviewers' reports into a cohesive Summary Statement. Summaries of the Study Section discussion (including budget recommendations, if appropriate) are included only for applications that underwent full review by the study section. (Because NC applications are not discussed at the Study Section meetings, their summary statements do not contain a paragraph summarizing the discussion by the study section members about the application. Instead, they contain a standard explanation of the NC designation.) Summary Statements for scored applications continue to have a "Description of Project," but NC applications no longer contain this paragraph. The separate paragraph about investigators has been eliminated from all Summary Statements.

Do not call the assigned Program Official on the day after the Study Section meeting! Wait at least until after you receive the snap-out mailer containing your priority score.

After you receive the snap-out mailer, you may contact the assigned Program Official if you need more details about the review and for information about the likelihood of funding. This information can be useful for planning ahead, for example, starting to revise the proposal, planning a totally new project—or perhaps even contemplating career moves if the grant is not likely to be funded!

You should receive your Summary Statement 4 to 6 weeks after the Study Section meeting (or sooner, if your proposal was designated NC). Mark your calendar, and call the SRA if you have not received it on time.

---

[4] See September 23, 1994 *NIH Guide for Grants and Contracts.* Be aware that although NIH considers triage to now be fully implemented, the agency says the process will undoubtedly continue to evolve, with modifications being made as issues become apparent and necessitate adjustments.

[5] See Reif-Lehrer, L., article about changes at NIH *Journal of the National Grantseekers Institute,* Vol. 2, No. 1, 1995 and Reif-Lehrer, L., "Science Community Gives Mixed, Review To 'Triage,'" *The Scientist,* Vol. 8, No. 23, November 28, 1994, pages 1, 8–9

RECAP FOR PART VI: SUBMITTING AND TRACKING THE GRANT APPLICATION

Prepare the application for submission:

- Polish the pre-final draft. (Use a good checklist.)
- Generate a final draft.
- Incorporate final draft of Research Plan into whole application.
- Assemble rest of application packet.
- If application is in response to an RFA (Request for Application), follow instructions below mailing label in application kit.
- Sign and date application.
- Get administrative approval for application from your institution's grants office.
- Photocopy the application (correct number of copies for the funding agency plus extra copies for yourself, the grants office, and other administrative offices at your own institution).
- Organize pages, fasten them together (do not staple or bind!), label items ("Original Application," "Original Appendix," etc.).
- Provide a cover letter (optional).
  —Suggest up to 3 Study Sections for application review.
  —Suggest appropriate funding component.
  —Give reasons for requests.
  —Paper-clip cover letter to front of original copy of application.
- Include self-addressed and stamped postcard for acknowledgment of receipt of application by funding agency.

Mail the application:

- Pack application well.
- Use mailing label provided in application kit.
- If using Express Mail or courier service to NIH, change zip code on mailing label to 20816.
- Mail in time to be received by the deadline.
- If using U.S. Post Office or commercial delivery service, get a legible proof-of-mailing receipt.

Follow ("Track") the travels of your application—in this case at NIH:

- Did you get acknowledgment-of-receipt postcard within 2 weeks after mailing application?
- Did you get snap-out mailer with application ID number and Study Section assignment? (Contact DRG if not received within 6 weeks after submitting application.)
- When does your Study Section meet?
- Who are the members of the Study Section?
- If you get new pertinent results, consider sending additional information. (Get permission from SRA.)
- Did you get snap-out mailer with priority score and percentile ranking (if the application was scored) within 2 weeks after end of Study Section meeting?
- Did you receive Summary Statement 4 to 6 weeks after Study Section meeting? If not, call SRA.

PART VII

SUMMARY STATEMENTS, REBUTTALS, AND REVISIONS

SOME HINTS ABOUT THE SUMMARY STATEMENT/"PINK SHEETS"

In the past, the Summary Statement (also known as the "Pink Sheets") was an integration of the reports of the primary Reviewers and comments of the Readers/Discussants.[1] Sometimes one could detect the "cut-and-paste" nature of the "Pink Sheets" and even distinguish between the comments of different Reviewers. Did they agree or disagree? What were their individual "gripes" with your proposal? Things have changed (see page 112).

Most Summary Statements have some good things to say about the proposal under review and also some negative things. It is a common and human response for PIs who find criticism of their proposal in the Summary Statement to respond with negative feelings or comments about the Reviewers. These comments may range from an exasperated "The Reviewers did not understand this at all" to some exclamation implying that the Reviewers are just short of retarded. It is wise to keep such thoughts to oneself for a day or two and then try to re-read the Summary Statement in a more dispassionate frame of mind. Although occasional mishaps do occur, Reviewers are chosen carefully, are—on the whole—fairly bright people, and—unless they are new Study Section members—have read many proposals. It is important not to let your wounded ego get in the way of carefully considering the Reviewers' comments. The following story, which was told by a physician-writer who spoke at a writing workshop I attended, may help to make the point:

> The writer gave his editor a book manuscript. The editor gave it back saying it needed more work. This happened multiple times. Finally, the writer got annoyed and said to the editor, "If you're so smart, why don't *you* rewrite the book." The editor responded, "I'm not a writer and I can't write, but I read a lot of manuscripts and this one stinks." The writer rewrote the manuscript several more times. When it was finally published, it became a best seller!

There is an art to reading between the lines of the Summary Statement. Learn to interpret the "Pink Sheets" and to use them to write a better revision. If you are a novice grant application writer, it may be useful to have an experienced and successful PI read your Summary Statement. In any event, as you read your Summary Statement, you should consider the following possibilities before deciding what action to take in response to the critique:

- Comments that represent the proposal inaccurately often result from unclear writing by the principal investigator.
- Criticisms about protocols, techniques, or data analysis often indicate that the principal investigator didn't do enough homework.
- If the critique questions the ability of the principal investigator to carry out the proposed work, an appropriate collaborator may be in order.
- If the critique questions the choice of problem, it may mean that the significance was poorly explained (rewrite) *or* that the problem per se lacks merit (pick a new problem).
- If the *Summary Statement ("Pink Sheet")* is not sufficiently explicit about what the Study Section did and did not like about your proposal, you can sometimes get additional information by contacting the Scientific Review Administrator of your Study Section and/or the Institute program staff.

If your priority score was just beyond the payline,[2] your Summary Statement may be quite positive and may provide relatively little information for you to use in writing a re-

---

[1] The triage procedure under study at NIH in 1994 was adopted, and Summary Statements changed.
[2] The highest (worst) priority score for a funded proposal for that review cycle, keeping in mind that 500 is the worst score; 100, the best score.

vised application. The Institute program staff member responsible for your application is likely to have been present during the Study Section review of your application and may be able to provide some insight into what the Reviewers did and did not like about your project and may be able to make suggestions about rewriting your proposal if you plan to submit a revised application.

It is important to understand, however, that a major reason why some grants do not get funded is that the ideas, although perhaps good, are not quite good enough to compete in the present funding climate. Applicants themselves often find it difficult to comprehend that a second or third revision for which the priority score has not markedly improved may be based on a less-than-great idea. On the other hand, if, after checking with knowledgeable colleagues, you are convinced that your project idea is superb, you should be tenacious about reapplying. Among applications reviewed by DRG in 1992, there were four A6 applications (6th revision = 7th application submitted), 2 of which were funded, and one A7 application (7th revision = 8th application submitted), which *was* funded! But watch out for possible future caps on the number of permissible revisions.

REBUTTALS

When you receive your Summary Statement, you may not agree with what the SRA and Reviewers have written. "They totally misunderstood _____ ," is a common response from unsuccessful proposal writers! It is important to consider that the fault may lie with your writing. If "they" misunderstood, perhaps you did not explain the project clearly enough! However, if after recovering from the initial pain, you still think that the review was flawed, you may wish to write a rebuttal. But consider that unless your priority score was close to the funding level, or your proposal was really grievously misjudged—the rebuttal process may just cost you time that you could spend more fruitfully by revising your application.

If you want to write a rebuttal, contact an appropriate staff member at the assigned Institute or other funding component for information about procedures to seek redress of your concerns. Detailed information about communicating concerns about the review of an application is available from the Grants Information Office, Division of Research Grants, NIH, Bethesda, MD 20892, (301-594-7248).

If you decide to write a letter of rebuttal, be sure that it is constructive and written in a positive tone.

Do not *complain* to the granting agency. Do not berate the Institute staff about what is in the "Pink Sheets," no matter how "right" you are.

- The Institute staff does not initiate the critique.
- The Institute staff is only the intermediary between the Study Section and the principal investigator.
- The Institute staff generally does not communicate with the Study Section about an application once the Study Section meeting is over.
- The Institute staff consists of professionals. They are also human beings; it is important to treat them with courtesy and respect.

Intrusion of sarcasm, righteous indignation, and/or "sour grapes" statements in a letter of rebuttal helps no one, least of all you!

Under no circumstances should you attempt to contact individual Study Section members. Never put a Study Section member in a compromising position either by trying to influence him/her personally before the Study Section meeting or by asking for the results of the deliberations of the Study Section after the meeting.

WHAT TO DO IF YOUR APPLICATION IS NOT FUNDED

It is painful to deal with rejection. It is common for grant application writers to respond with some negative reaction to Summary Statements bearing bad news about the outcome of their efforts. Many people find—after their disappointment subsides and they reread the Summary Statement—that the Reviewers were not as far off the mark as had initially appeared. However, a major reason for not getting funded may simply be that there was not enough money to fund all the good applications. Although this knowledge does not help your particular situation and may do little to salve your wounded ego, it should help you to understand that the best next step is to give yourself a few days to recover from the disappointment and then begin to plan realistically what needs to be done. For many grant seekers, this next step is to prepare to write a revised and improved proposal that is responsive to the Reviewers' comments or to plan a new proposal, perhaps to a different funding agency.

SUBMITTING A REVISED APPLICATION

If you have funds to tide you over for another grant cycle, revise the proposal and try again. As funding decreases, it is becoming more the rule than the exception to have to revise at least once (see Table 7-1)—and even twice.

Some scientists have been funded on the eighth try, that is, the original proposal and 7 revisions (See Table 8-1)! So persistence is extremely important. However, as a rule of thumb, priority scores for revised applications rarely improve by more than 50 points. So if your priority score is more than 50 points away from the payline, you will need to seriously consider making major changes in the proposal, preparing a totally new proposal about some other project, or reworking the old proposal for another funding agency.

A revised application requires an Introduction (see below) and must be responsive to the critique in the Summary Statement. In writing the 3-page Introduction section, please consider the advice given earlier for writing rebuttals. The way you respond to constructive criticism, the manner in which you deal with criticism that you consider invalid, and the general tone of your response are all important factors in the way Reviewers will view your revised proposal. It is a courtesy to overworked Reviewers to thank them for praise they bestow on your proposal and to be open-minded about criticism. If you disagree with comments in the Summary Statement, it is a good idea to leave such comments for last and then state your counter-opinion firmly but politely and, whenever appropriate, back up your arguments with sound data and references to published work. Insults or other negative comments to or about the Reviewers rarely, if ever, produce a positive effect and serve only to sour the Reviewers and other Study Section members about you

Table 7-1   R01 Applications Reviewed by DRG Study Sections: FY1985 Compared to FY1993*

Type of Application	FY1985	FY1993	Number increase	Percent increase
Total R01s	14,258	15,435	1,177	8.3
Amended R01s	3,646	5,713	2,067	56.7
Total R01s minus amended R01s	10,612	9,722	−890	−8.4

*The data in the table are taken from *NIH Peer Review Notes,* October 1993. Note that the increase in workload is more than accounted for by amended proposals.

and your proposal. Likewise, flattery, in the form of excessive compliments to the Reviewers, is more likely to turn the Reviewers off than on. Be neutral and make it clear that you have carefully considered the comments in the Summary Statement.

To make the Reviewers' job as easy as possible, summarize in the Introduction, the changes that you have made in the proposal—do not repeat them. If your revisions are so extensive that you cannot mark them in the manner requested in the PHS-398 Instructions, clearly indicate this in the Introduction.

If you prepare a *revised application*, get help from the Institute program staff member responsible for your application.

- Be sure the revised application has substantive improvements.

  "A revised application will be returned if substantial revisions are not clearly apparent."

- Be sure the revised application is responsive to all questions and criticisms raised in the Summary Statement. Being responsive means acknowledging and responding to—not necessarily agreeing with—all the comments.
- Indicate all substantive changes you have made in the revised application.
  —"Highlight these changes within the text of the Research Plan by appropriate bracketing, indenting, or changing of typography." *Do not underline or use shading!*
  —Discuss these changes in Section C: Research Plan, Introduction (3-page maximum).
- "Incorporate into the Progress Report/Preliminary Studies of the revised application any [pertinent] work done since the prior version was submitted."
- Note that the deadline for submission of revised applications is the same as for competitive renewals: March 1, July 1, November 1.

If you submit a revised application, remember that the composition of the Study Section changes with time. Although a resubmitted grant application is frequently returned to the same Reviewers, this is not always the case.

RECAP FOR PART VII: SUMMARY STATEMENTS, REBUTTALS, AND REVISIONS

Some hints about the Summary Statement ("Pink Sheets"):

- Summary Statements combine primary Reviewers' reports, Readers' comments, and sometimes a summary of the Study Section discussion.
- Ask an experienced, successful grantee to read your Summary Statement.
- Before blaming the Reviewers for negative comments about your proposal, ask yourself:
  —Was my writing unclear?
  —Did I do enough homework?
  —Should I have enlisted the help of a collaborator?
  —Was the significance poorly explained?
  —Did project fit mandate of the funding agency?
  —Does problem per se lack merit?
- If the Summary Statement is not sufficiently explicit, contact the SRA or Institute program staff. Never try to contact individual Study Section members!

If you think your application was grievously misjudged, write a rebuttal:

- Contact a staff member at the assigned Institute or grants information office about procedures.
- Do not complain or berate the granting agency.
- Do not be sarcastic.

What to do if your application is not funded:

- If your priority score is more than 50 points away from the payline, seriously consider:
  —Preparing a new proposal.
  —Reworking the old proposal for another funding agency.
- If your priority score is less than 50 points away from the payline, submit a revised application at least once—and even twice (if you have funds to tide you over for another grant cycle or two).

If you prepare a *revised application:*
- Get help from the Institute program staff.
- Write an Introduction (3-page maximum):
  —Summarize changes made in proposal.
  —Be responsive to critique in Summary Statement.
  —Back up your arguments with sound data and references to published work.
  —Do not indulge in "sour grapes."
  —Do not flatter or excessively compliment Reviewers.
- Indicate changes in body of proposal by bracketing, indenting, or changing typography." *Do not use underlining or shading.*
- Incorporate into progress report/preliminary studies, pertinent work done since prior version of application was submitted.
- Do not submit a revised application unless you have made *substantive* changes.
- Deadline for submission of revised applications is the same as for competitive renewals.

PART VIII

SOME FINAL WORDS

Don't Get Discouraged

Writing a good grant proposal is a readily learnable skill.

Writing a grant proposal, like many other things in life, is not as daunting as it first appears. If you have a good idea, start early, and simply "put one foot in front of the other"—and follow the instructions—you will get the job done little by little. If you do your homework thoroughly, follow the advice given in this book about the writing, and get help and advice from wisely chosen colleagues, you are likely to put together a good proposal that stands a good chance of being funded.

If you can't seem to get funded by NIH or some other government agency, try private foundations and/or business and industry.

Be Persistent

REVISE, revise, revise! If you want to get granted, you must be persistent.

In the last 3 years, 25% or more of the Study Section workload consisted of reviewing revised proposals! Some people revise more than once before being funded. See Table 8-1 and the excerpts from the minutes of the November 1992 DRG Advisory Committee Meeting (Appendix I-D-6) for some statistics on revised proposals (amended applications). Check the current statistics at NIH (Tel: 301-594-7185 or 301-594-7328; Fax: 301-594-7394).

In the past decade, new Research Project Grants (RPGs) have accounted for about the same percentage of the research project dollars as competing continuations (renewals). As in the previous 10 years, 1990 success rates for renewals were about twice as high as for new RPGs (37.2% compared to 18.9%). Success rates for fiscal 1992 were 20.7% for new R01s and 41.8% for R01 renewals.

Table 8-1   Initial and Revised R01 Applications Reviewed by DRG in 1992

Submission category*	Number Reviewed**	Number Awarded**
Original (non-revised) applications	11,551	2,575
1st Revisions (A1)	3,737	1,093
2d Revisions (A2)	1,211	388
3d Revisions (A3)	308	101
4th Revisions (A4)	78	22
5th Revisions (A5)	18	6
6th Revisions (A6)	4	2
7th Revisions (A7)***	1	1

* The funding component with the lowest revision *rate* was the National Center for Human Genome Research: 106 applications were reviewed in 1992, 24 of these (22.6%) were revisions. The funding component with the highest revision *rate* was the National Institute for Nursing: 134 applications were reviewed in 1992, 52 of these (38.8%) were revisions. The National Cancer Institute had the greatest *number* of revised proposals: Of 2,508 applications reviewed, 756 (30.1%) were revisions.

** It should be noted that NIH summarizes applications by fiscal year of review, while awards are summarized by fiscal year of requested start date.

*** Note that for every revised application there was an original application; thus, for an A7 application the PI has submitted 8 applications!

It should also be noted that NIH may in the future limit the number of revisions permitted. Keep aware of this and other impending changes in peer review.

For additional information about the statistics given in this table, contact Dr. William McGarvey, 301-594-7328 or Mr. Robert Moore, 301-594-7185.

The Robert Wood Johnson Foundation states in its guidelines for grant applicants: "Unsuccessful applicants should approach the foundation again, and, if necessary, again. *Most grantmakers regard tenacity as a virtue, and we are certainly among them.*"

Think of tenacity as a prerequisite for doing research. If you really want to do what you want to do, you must keep trying until you succeed in getting funding.

"The One Truth: If you don't submit a grant [proposal], you won't get a grant." [1]

THE GRASS IS ALWAYS GREENER . . .

If you think life is tough in the sciences, talk to people in other fields, especially in the arts and humanities. Scientists have the advantage of getting referees' comments, Reviewers' reports, and Summary Statements to help them improve their papers and grant proposals. Literary writers often get rejection slips *without* any feedback! A professor of creative writing at one of the large universities in Boston submitted a book to over 100 publishers before it was finally published by a fairly prestigious university press.

AD HOC REVIEWING: A CHANCE TO SEE PEER REVIEW FROM THE INSIDE

If you get a chance to be an ad hoc reviewer on a Study Section (i.e., on a one-time basis), do it! Watching the peer review system work, from the inside—and observing and experiencing the enormous task of the Reviewers—will not only be enlightening but is almost guaranteed to improve your writing of your own grant applications. When you get to the appropriate stage of your career, you should consider it an obligation to serve on a Study Section. Others have reviewed your proposals. You should repay the favor by reviewing the proposals of younger scientists.

GOOD LUCK!

---

[1] I found this good advice on the last page in a set of materials entitled *Research Manual: A Guide to the Grants Process at Purdue University,* "for use at the Fall research Orientation, hosted by the Division of Sponsored Programs" in September 1991. The book was put together by Gary Isom, Director of the Purdue University Division of Sponsored Programs and was provided to me by Dr. Willis Tacker, Professor of BioEngineering and Associate Director of the Division of Sponsored Programs at Purdue. The quote is from "Tips on Successful Grant Writing" by Connie Weaver, Department of Foods and Nutrition, Purdue University.

RECAP FOR PART VIII: SOME FINAL WORDS

- Don't get discouraged.
    - Be persistent.

        —Writing a good grant proposal is a readily learnable skill.
        —If you don't get funded by NIH or some other government agency, try private foundations, business, and industry.
        —REVISE, revise, revise!

    - "If you don't submit a grant [application], you won't get a grant."
    - Try to be an ad hoc reviewer on a Study Section.

Useful Information

A. Impending Changes in Procedure for Submission and Processing of Grant Applications at NIH and NSF

NIH Electronic Grant Application Development (EGAD) Project

The National Institutes of Health, Division of Computer Research and Technology, in conjunction with the Division of Research Grants, began some years ago to develop a computer software program to facilitate the processing of R01 grant applications to the National Institutes of Health (see Liane Reif-Lehrer, "NIH Sees Computerization as Remedy for Paper Flood," *The Scientist*, May 30, 1988, page 21). The program was subsequently enlarged and formalized into the EGAD (Electronic Grant Application Development) Project under the leadership of Dr. John Mathis, who was formerly a DRG Executive Secretary (referred to, as of 1991, as a Scientific Review Administrator). The EGAD Project is intended to enhance the effectiveness of the extramural program activities of the PHS at both the applicant and federal levels. The specific aims of the EGAD Project are to (1) simplify application preparation, submission, and peer review, administration of awarded grants, and overall information management by reducing paper-dependent tasks; (2) reduce errors and costs by use of automated data capture; and (3) increase efficiency and productivity by eliminating tasks such as photocopying and facilitating data storage and retrieval.

The first step of the EGAD Project has been to develop software called the Automated Grant Application System (AGAS) that enables preparation of grant applications in an electronic medium. AGAS is a free-standing personal computer-based program (DOS and Macintosh versions) that guides the user through the entry of all the required application data and then formats the data for transmission to NIH. It is a form-independent system that treats the application as a set of data, not a set of form pages. The program contains context-sensitive help, extensive error-trapping procedures that prevent submission of incomplete applications, and electronic sign-off via a confidential code. The transmission of applications will be possible (i.e., authorized) only via the grants office (or other relevant office) at the applicant organization. Eventually, applications will be moved from one computer to another without intermediate transfer to paper. Ultimately, Reviewers' reports, Summary Statements, award notices, etc. will also be created and sent via electronic medium.

The AGAS program was tested at 4 sites in 1993. But in early 1994, NIH decided to put the AGAS project out for commercial development. See NIH Guide for Grants and Contracts, Vol. 23, No. 11, March 19, 1994, page 11. Watch for developments of commercially available programs in the future.

For further information about AGAS or the EGAD Project, contact Dr. John Mathis, 301-594-7038; Fax: 301-594-7068, Mr. Robert Reifsnider, 301-594-7038, or Mr. James T. Lowrie, 301-594-7090 or 301-594-7063.

THE NSF ELECTRONIC PROPOSAL SUBMISSION (EPS) PROJECT

This project is the initial phase of NSF's transition from paper-based to electronic processing of proposals. The ultimate goal is to use electronic communications technology for the relevant aspects of the proposal submission, review, and award processes.

NSF has worked with the NIH to coordinate the EPS Project with the EGAD Project so that electronic submission will be similar for both agencies. Moreover, NSF has designed its software so that it will be able to be used in the preparation of a proposal to any agency.

For information about participation in the EPS Project, required capabilities and restrictions, establishment of an account, or preparation and submission of a proposal by electronic means, see Appendix VIII-D or contact Mr. Jerald Stuck, 703-306-1144.

B. Other Impending or Recent[1] Changes at NIH and NSF

NIH

Watch for developments in the items listed below in the *NIH Guide for Grants and Contracts* and other NIH publications and professional organization newsletters.

High-risk/innovative research identification

As of the fall 1993, DRG Study Sections have attempted to identify high-risk/innovative research proposals.[2] Such proposals are considered for funding even though they may be somewhat beyond the normal funding payline. A tracking system to monitor and assess the results of this new procedure will also be developed. (See details in Section D-9 of this appendix.)

Investigator-initiated Interactive Research Project Grants (IRPGs)

IRPGs are intended to promote a new kind of formal interaction, based on the initiative of applicants, to enhance existing interactions with colleagues or to develop new collaborative relationships. The IRPG program encourages the coordinated submission[3] of related research project grant applications (R01s) and, to a limited extent, FIRST award (R29) applications from two or more investigators who wish to collaborate on research but do not require extensive shared physical resources. In contrast to program projects, in which some researchers fear a loss of autonomy, IRPG PIs retain control of their own projects.

IRPG applications must share a common theme and describe the objectives and scientific importance of the interchange of, for example, ideas, data, and materials among the collaborating investigators. Applicants may be from one or several institutions. Appli-

---

[1] Please be aware that the words "impending" and "recent" used here refer to Summer 1993, when this Appendix material was collected.
[2] See *NIH Peer Review Notes*, June 1993, pages 9–10.
[3] Submission of IRPGs must be concurrent and cross-referenced.

cations are reviewed independently for scientific merit. Applications that are judged to have significant and substantial merit are considered for funding both as independent awards and in the context of the proposed IRPG collaboration. An IRPG package may consist of a combination of R01s and R29s, or R01s only, but may not consist solely of R29 applications. Applications for both new (Type 1) and competing renewal (Type 2) awards may be submitted as IRPGs.

Applications must be tightly focused, and the interactions and benefits of the proposed linkages must be made explicit. The IRPG mechanism can be used constructively to support collaborative efforts designed to accelerate the development of fundamental knowledge and/or enhance the clinical application of that knowledge. The IRPG also may fit well with clinical applications that propose limited, testable research questions or focused therapeutic and related correlative laboratory studies. However, the IRPG mechanism is not appropriate for large epidemiologic studies or for multi-institutional clinical trials using common protocols.

IRPG applications must be identified by checking "yes" on line 2a of the PHS-398 Face page, citing announcement PA-93-078, and including the phrase "investigator-initiated IRPG." Receipt dates for IRPG applications, whether new (Type 1), competing renewal (Type 2), or revised applications, are February 15, June 15, and October 15 of each year. Each application must be complete. All R01 or R29 applications constituting the proposed IRPG cohort must be submitted *in a single package*, whether or not the applications arise from the same institution—but should not be collated into a single IRPG "package." A *cover letter* must list the total number of applications submitted for the IRPG cohort, indicating the principal investigator of each. *Failure to follow the instructions regarding submission date and packaging may lead to a delay in review.*

Particular attention must be paid to completion of Section 7 of the Research Plan, "Consultants and Collaborators," for each IRPG application. In addition to those collaborations that would be necessary to carry out the proposed research, whether or not the IRPG mechanism is involved, within Section 7, each application that is a component IRPG must provide an identical statement (titled "IRPG Interactions") regarding the IRPG collaboration. This section should list each application that is part of the IRPG, including title, principal investigator, and other participating scientists. The single *program coordinator* who is responsible for coordinating the collaborative efforts among the research projects and for promoting interaction and communication among the principal investigators should be identified here. This section should further discuss the intended interactions among the components of the IRPG and the perceived benefits of supporting all of the components of the IRPG as a combined effort.

Requests for limited shared resources, if any, should be included in this part of Section 7. This should *include costs and full budget justification*. Two tables should also be included:

Table I: Should be identical in all applications of the IRPG cohort and should specify the percent utilization and dollar amount requested of each interactive resource by each IRPG in the proposed cohort.

Table II: Should detail the distribution of effort for all of that application's personnel on all shared activities and/or resources.

Sample formats for these tables may be obtained from the funding component contacts listed below.

Applications will be reviewed independently for scientific and technical merit by—for the most part—DRG Study Sections. Component applications may be assigned to different Study Sections for initial review and to different Institutes/Centers for funding consideration. Reviewers will read Section 7 and will assess the intended collaborations just as they do the proposed collaborative arrangements in any other application. As appropriate, the effectiveness and merit of the collaborations may contribute to the overall assessment of each application. In addition, budget recommendations related to the appropriateness of collaborative arrangements and core utilization will be assessed for each application.

Applications will compete for available funds with all other applications found to have significant and substantial merit. The following will be considered in making funding decisions:

- Quality of the proposed project as determined by peer review
- The interactive nature of the program and of the component IRPGs
- Availability of funds
- Program balance among research areas

The IRPG package should be sent to:

Division of Research Grants
National Institutes of Health
Westwood Building, Room 240
Bethesda, MD 20892

For Express Mail or courier delivery, add "5333 Westbard Ave." and use zip code **20816** instead of 20892.

For further information regarding the format for submission of an IRPG package, contact the NIH DRG Referral Office (301-594-7250).

For other information, contact:

Name	Funding Component	Telephone Number (Area Code 301, except as noted)
Dr. Kenneth Warren	NIAAA	443-4375
Dr. Miriam Kelty	NIA	496-9322
Mr. Allan Czarra	NIAID	402-0160
Dr. Michael Lockshin	NIAMD	496-0802
Dr. Marvin Kalt	NCI	496-4218
Ms. Hildegard Topper	NICHD	496-0104
Dr. Norman Braveman	NIDR	594-7648
Dr. Walter Stolz	NIDDK	594-7277
Ms. Eleanor Friedenberg	NIDA	443-2755
Dr. Thor Fjellstedt	NIEHS	919-541-0131
Dr. Milton Corn	NLM	496-4621
Dr. Anthony Pollitt	NIMH	443-4673
Dr. Mary Lucas	NINR	594-3290
Dr. Louise Ramm	NCRR	594-0630

See also *NIH Guide for Grants and Contracts*, Vol. 22, No. 16, April 23, 1993, pages 7–11.

Electronic access to NIH/DRG Study Section rosters

DRG has developed a system that permits electronic access to DRG Study Section rosters by the extramural research community and other interested parties.[4] Initially, rosters are available only for chartered review committees, not for special Study Sections, Special

---

[4] See *NIH Peer Review Notes*, June 1993, pages 10–11.

Emphasis Panels (SEPs), or ad hoc review groups, nor for Institute Study Sections;. Rosters lists only regular members of Study Sections. Special Reviewers for specific Study Section meetings or members who were absent at a particular meeting will not be indicated. The system is on-line and accessible to PIs by the time this book comes out. For information about the initial stages of this project, call Dr. John C. James (301-594-7270). This electronic roster project has replaced the annual book *NIH Advisory Committees: Authority, Structure, Function, Members*. For information about the overall project, call Ms. Susan Feldman (301-496-2123).

Electronic availability of NIH New Grants and Awards

NIH New Grants and Awards Available Electronically (from *NIH Peer Review Notes*, June, 1993, page 11).

The publication, *NIH New Grants and Awards,* is now available through a computer program. This electronic access was developed to be more responsive to the data information needs of the biomedical and behavioral sciences community.

On April 1, 1993, the listing of the January and February 1993 NIH awards was made available on the electronic NIH Grant Line; the March 1993 awards were added on April 15. Monthly listings, thereafter, will be available on the 15th of each succeeding month.

The preceding month's listing will be interpolated into another file, and eventually a cumulative file will list the awards made for a fiscal year. The on-line information will be in a report format that lends itself easily to paper copies and data can be manipulated to satisfy specific requirements.

The automated system also contains other information that may be of interest. Detailed instructions for accessing all files on the electronic NIH Grant Line are as follows.

NIH Grant Line Access

Configure terminal emulator as: 1200 or 2400 baud, even parity, 7 data bits, 1 stop bit, Half Duplex.

Using the procedure for your communication software, dial 1-301-402-2221. When a response is received indicating connection, type **,GEN1** (the comma is mandatory) and press **<ENTER>**. The NIH system will prompt for "INITIALS?", type **BB5** and press **<ENTER>**. A prompt for "ACCOUNT?" will be received, type **CCS2** and press **<ENTER>**.

Messages and a menu are displayed to read bulletins and download files.

The system is menu-driven with easily understood commands. To execute a command, type only its first letter. Most current and historical files are located in the section called FILES; type **F** to access any of the files arranged into directories. For an overview of the information available, type **D** for **Directory**. *NIH New Grants and Awards* are in the directory **NIHINFO**. *Note:* One of the "download" options is to mail files to your Internet address.

NIH Grant Line Via Internet Access

To access the Grant Line in an interactive Internet session, use Telnet to **WYLBUR.CU.NIH.GOV**. When a message is received that the connection is open, type, **GEN1** (the comma is mandatory). At the "INITIALS?" prompt, type **BB5**; at "ACCOUNT?" prompt, type **CCS2**. This accesses the DRGLINE Bulletin Board (also known as the NIH Grant Line).

If you have any questions or comments about *NIH New Grants and Awards*, call or write to:

Ms. Carolyn R. Stelle
Information Systems Branch
DRG/ NIH
WW Bldg., Room 125
Bethesda, MD 20892
301-594-7015

For general information about the NIH Grant Line, call Dr. John C. James, 301-594-7270.

New guidelines about the support and conduct of therapeutic human fetal tissue transplantation research

The 5-year moratorium on Federal funding for therapeutic transplantation research that uses human fetal tissue derived from induced abortions was formally revoked on February 1, 1993. New guidelines about support and conduct of therapeutic human fetal tissue transplantation research were enacted on June 10, 1993 (Public Law 103-43). For further information, see *NIH Guide to Grants and Contracts*, Vol. 22, No. 32, September 3, 1993, pages 3–4, or contact F. Wm. Dommel, Jr., JD, Senior Policy Advisor, Office for Protection from Research Risks, Bldg. 31, Room 5B63, Bethesda, MD 20892, 301-496-7005.

NSF

Relocation of NSF from Washington, DC to Arlington, VA

In 1993, NSF headquarters moved to Arlington, Virginia. NSF area code 202 phone numbers are incorrect. All new NSF phone numbers have a 703 area code.
    The new address and main information number for NSF are:

National Science Foundation
4201 Wilson Blvd.
Arlington, VA 22230
703-306-1144

Reorganization of the NSF Division of Research Grants

Two new NSF Divisions; were established on May 2, 1993, to replace the former Division of Grants and Contracts (DGC) in the NSF Office of Budget, Finance and Award Management.

Division of Grants and Agreements (DGA)

- Responsible for business, policy, and financial review, issuance, and administration of all NSF grants and cooperative agreements and all other transactions involving awards of NSF funds.
- Provides advice and guidance to the performer research community on the business and administrative aspects of NSF proposal generation and award systems.

Division Director: Mr. Wm. B. Cole, Jr.

Division of Contracts, Policy and Oversight (CPO)

- Responsible for performing previous DGC contract management functions, developing proposal and award policy, performing cost analysis and establishing

NSF indirect cost rates for NSF awards, and resolving audit findings arising under or in the oversight of NSF awards.

Division Director: Mr. Robert B. Hardy

C. Miscellaneous

AVAILABILITY OF NIH GRANT APPLICATION FORM TEMPLATES ON COMPUTER DISKS

NIH DRG Grants Information Office (301-594-7248) keeps a list of individuals who have developed and are willing to share NIH forms on software. If you contact these individuals, please send a blank formatted disk and a padded, self-addressed envelope (or disk mailer) with sufficient postage ($0.75 in 1993) to return the disk to you without expense to them!

Dr. John Livesey, University of Washington, Seattle

PHS-398 templates have been created by Dr. John Livesey and colleagues at the University of Washington, Seattle. *The data must be entered in Microsoft Excel,* and then the Excel table must be copied as a "photograph" and pasted into Microsoft Word, where it can be further edited *only to a very limited extent.*

The templates are available at no cost. These templates are provided without warranty or support of any kind. NIH has not sanctioned their use, but Dr. Livesey's research group has used previous versions of these templates for years with success. Send a single formatted 3.5-inch disk (marked either DOS or MAC) or a 5.25-inch DOS disk and a self-addressed disk mailer with adequate return postage to:

John C. Livesey, Ph.D.
Assistant Professor
Grant Application Templates
Radiation Biology, RC-09
1959 N.E. Pacific Street
University of Washington
Seattle, WA 98195
206-548-4090
Fax: 206-548-6218
E-mail: Livesey@u.washington.edu (Internet) or Livesey@MAX (BITNET)

Send an e-mail message to Dr. Livesey if you wish to be added to his electronic mailing list; notices of updates, etc. will be distributed only in this manner.

GrantFormPak S398

Forms are available for WordPerfect for DOS and Windows from

Envisage, Inc.
5111-6 Baymeadows, Suite 315
Jacksonville, FL 32217-4860
904-739-0060
Fax: 904-731-1993

Cost: $189.95 for nonspreadsheet version; $249.95 for spreadsheet version.

AVAILABILITY OF ABSTRACTS OF FUNDED NIH RESEARCH GRANT APPLICATIONS

The abstracts of all funded NIH research grant applications (including SBIR, etc.) are sent to the National Technical Information Service (NTIS), U.S. Department of Commerce on magnetic tape via a subfile called CRISP.[5] NTIS collects but does *not* disseminate information about PHS abstracts.

The primary mission of NTIS is to collect and disseminate to the public the broad scientific, technical, engineering, and business information that is produced with Federal support but is not peer-reviewed or published in journals (the so-called "grey literature"). NTIS stores the information on the Federal Research In Progress (FEDRIP) Database, which NTIS manages. The PHS CRISP subfile is added to the FEDRIP Database, where it is merged with data from 11 government sources. NTIS issues a monthly update tape to various commercial and university sources. NTIS is self-supporting and *charges for its services.* Information collected by NTIS is available to the public from the sources listed below:

Electronic access:

DIALOG (Fee for service)
3460 Hillview Ave.
Palo Alto, CA 94303
1-800-334-2564 (1-800-3-DIALOG)
415-858-3792

Access to DIALOG is available via many local public libraries, but users must pay for the service. Almost all academic libraries subscribe to DIALOG and may or may not charge users for the service.

Knowledge Express (fee for service)
900 West Valley Rd., Suite 401
Wayne, PA 19087
1-800-248-2469
215-293-9712

NERAC, Inc. (fee for service)
1 Technology Drive
Tolland, CT 06084
203-872-7000

Batch Searching and Selected Dissemination of Information (SDI) services.

Federal Depository Libraries:

There are some 1400 such libraries across the United States. Many of them are housed in existing state or law libraries. The latter must provide *free* public access to the Federal Depository Library materials even if the library which houses the Federal Depository collection is a nonpublic library.

Although much of the information collected by NTIS is available in Federal Depository Libraries, many of the collections tend to be incomplete in comparison to the information available on the NTIS FEDRIP Database

For more information about NTIS, a free copy of the catalog of services, or a free copy of the FEDRIP Search Guide (PR847), contact:

[5] CRISP stands for Computer Retrieval of Information on Scientific Projects, a database of information about all NIH-funded grants. For information about CRISP, call Ms. Seu Lain Chen at NIH (301-594-7267).

National Technical Information Service
US Department of Commerce
Springfield, VA 22161
1-800-553-6847
703-487-4600
Fax (Research Service): 703-321-8547

CONGRESSIONAL FELLOWS PROGRAM

A program whereby scientists spend 1 year on Capitol Hill, working with members of Congress or Congressional Committees as legislative assistants.

Administration: American Association for the Advancement of Science (AAAS) is the umbrella organization; 20 societies belong and select fellows and pay for their stipends. Stipends, application procedures, timetables, and deadlines vary according to the sponsoring society. In 1992–93 the AAAS sponsored 2 fellows. The stipend was $38,000 plus a relocation and travel expense allowance.

Eligibility: Targeted to postdoctoral fellows but also accepts older candidates (up to mid-career senior scientists). Fellows must have exceptional competence in science/engineering, know about nonscience areas, and have a sensitivity to political and social issues.

For information, contact:

Ms. Claudia J. Sturges
Senior Program Associate
Directorate for Science and Policy Programs
AAAS
1333 H St. NW
Washington, DC 20005
202-326-6600
Fax: 202-289-4950

NATIONAL TECHNICAL TRANSFER CENTER

A congressionally funded information center with the mission to put people in contact with researchers in a federal laboratory or facility. The services are free. In 1993, NTTC had over 700 laboratories/facilities in their database. There are also 6 regional Technical Transfer Centers in the United States. The regional centers deal with research in the private sector as well as with government laboratories and facilities.

For further information, contact:

National Technical Transfer Center (NTTC)
Wheeling Jesuit College
Wheeling, WV 26003
1-800-678-6882
Fax: 304-243-2539
See also Appendix XI.

"RAPID" (RAPID ASSESSMENT POST-IMPACT OF DISASTER) PROGRAM—NIMH

A National Institute of Mental Health program. Grants are 1-year, nonrenewable and provide a maximum of $50,000 for study of the effects of catastrophic events on mental

health. Accelerated review time for proposals is 5 to 6 weeks.
For information, call Susan D. Soloman, 301-443-3728.

UNITED STATES ARMY RESEARCH OFFICE BIOSCIENCES RESEARCH PROGRAM

Supports basic research in the biological sciences, exclusive of medical, behavioral, and social science research. Average grant size is $60,000/year for 3 years. Funds about 12 new grants per year, with continuing support for about 24 more.

For information, contact:

Shirley R. Tove, Head
Biology Branch
Chemistry and Biological Sciences Division
Army Research Office
P.O. Box 12211
Research Triangle Park, NC 27709-2211

STRATEGIC ENVIRONMENTAL RESEARCH DEFENSE PROGRAM (SERDP)

A Federal program set up in 1990 to help solve the defense-related environmental problems of the nation by funding environmental research. A goal of the SERDP is to transfer technology—in both directions—between government agencies and the commercial and private sector (including universities). The program is a joint effort of the Department of Defense, the Department of Energy, and the Environmental Protection Agency.

To be eligible, projects must be of interest to one of these 3 agencies and must be related to defense needs. The National Oceanic and Atmospheric Administration (NOAA) helps to oversee the program.

An information packet is available from:

Dr. Robert Oswald, Ph.D.
Director of Research and Development,
U.S. Army Corps of Engineers and Executive Director of SERDP
202-272-0254

D. NIH Documents/Excerpts of NIH Documents

In the documents in this section the underlines are from the original document. I have put some of the text into italic type to call attention to important points.

1. GUIDE FOR ASSIGNED REVIEWERS' PRELIMINARY COMMENTS ON RESEARCH GRANT APPLICATIONS (R01) (NIH DOCUMENT, MARCH 1992)[6]

Please use the following guidelines when preparing written comments on research grant applications assigned to you for review.

<u>DESCRIPTION</u>: Use the assigned abstract on page 2 of this application unless inappropriate. *Do not make evaluative statements in this section.*

<u>CRITIQUE</u>: <u>Do not include descriptive information in this section</u>. Provide *analysis of the strengths and weaknesses of the research plan*, which consists of Specific Aims, Background

---

[6] These instructions may change in 1994–95 if changes in peer review under study in 1994 are adopted.

and Significance, Progress Report/Preliminary Studies, and Experimental Design and Methods. *For deferred and/or amended applications, evaluate progress, changes, and responses to the critique* in the Summary Statement from the previous review. Indicate whether the application is improved, the same or worse than the previous submission.

GENDER AND MINORITIES: For all research involving human subjects and human tissues, *including autopsy material, evaluate the proposed gender and minority composition* of the study population and its appropriateness to the scientific objectives of the study. If the *representation* of gender or minorities in a study design is inadequate to answer the scientific question(s) addressed AND the *justification* for the selected study population is inadequate, the reviewer should consider it a *scientific weakness or deficiency* in the study design. Recommendations on this policy will be made in a section at the end of the Critique sub-headed: "Gender and Minority Subjects."

INVESTIGATORS: Assess the *competence of the principal investigator and key personnel* to conduct the proposed research.

RESOURCES AND ENVIRONMENT: Evaluate any *special attributes or deficiencies* relevant to the conduct of the proposed studies.

BUDGET: *Evaluate the direct costs only.* For all years, determine whether all items of the budget are *appropriate and justified.* Provide a *rationale* for each suggested modification in amount or duration of support. For supplemental applications, comment on the requested budget in relation to the parent grant.

OTHER CONSIDERATIONS:
Overlap: Identify any apparent *scientific or budgetary overlap* with active or pending support.

Foreign: If the applicant organization is foreign, comment on any *special talents, resources, populations, or environmental conditions that are not readily available in the United States* or that provide augmentation of existing United States resources. In addition, indicate whether similar research is being performed in the United States and whether there is a need for such additional research. These criteria do not apply to applications from U.S. organizations for projects containing a significant foreign component.

Human Subjects
    Exemptions Claimed: Express any comments or concerns about the appropriateness of the exemption(s) claimed.

    No Exemption Claimed: Express any comments or concerns about the *appropriateness of the responses to the six required points,* especially whether the risks to subjects are reasonable in relation to the *anticipated benefits to the subjects* and in relation to the importance of the knowledge that may reasonably be expected to result from the research.

    Animal Welfare: Express any comments or concerns about the *appropriateness of the responses to the five required points,* especially whether the procedures will be limited to those that are unavoidable in the conduct of scientifically sound research.

    Biohazards: Note any materials or procedures that are *potentially hazardous* to research personnel and indicate whether the *protection proposed* will be adequate.

<u>SUMMARY AND RECOMMENDATION:</u>

Briefly *summarize the strengths and weaknesses* of the application and *provide a recommendation* of a level of merit (or numerical rating) or deferral, or not recommended for further consideration.

Note: Your *written comments* will be destroyed after being incorporated into the Summary Statement. However, they *should not bear personal identifiers* because, under the *Privacy Act* of 1974, principal investigators may, upon request, gain access to documents relating to the review of their grant applications. In the rare event that your comments must be made available to a principal investigator, *you will be notified promptly* by NIH staff.

2. REVIEW PROCEDURES FOR INITIAL REVIEW GROUP MEETINGS (NIH DOCUMENT, MARCH 1992)

The underlines are from the original document. I have put some of the text into italic type to call attention to important points.

Review procedures

The Initial Review Group (IRG) evaluates the scientific merit of each grant application *according to specific criteria.* The principal criteria for the initial review of research project grant applications based on the Public Health Service (PHS) Scientific Peer Review Regulations, include:

- scientific and technical, or medical *significance and originality* of the goals of the proposed research;
- *appropriateness and adequacy* of the *experimental approach and methodology* proposed to carry out the research;
- *qualifications and research experience* of the principal investigator and staff, particularly but not exclusively in the area of the proposed research;
- availability of *resources* necessary to conduct the research;
- the proposed *budget and duration* in relation to the proposed research; and
- where an application involves activities that could have an adverse effect on *humans, animals, or the environment,* the adequacy of the proposed means for *protecting* against or minimizing such effects.

The specific *criteria* will *vary* with types of applications reviewed, such as the National Research Service Awards (fellowships), Research Career Development Awards, or Small Business Innovation Research grants.

In addition, *for renewal and supplemental* applications, *preliminary data* and/or *progress* to date must be evaluated. For amended applications, response to the previous review must be evaluated. The reviewers should indicate *whether the application is improved,* the same or worse than the previous submission.

During the meeting, the Chairperson of the IRG, following an agenda prepared by the Scientific Review Administrator (SRA), introduces each application, calls upon the individuals assigned by the SRA to *present their written comments,* and invites discussion. The assigned discussants are then called upon for their comments and group discussion follows.

After sufficient discussion has ensued, the Chairperson calls for a *priority rating* to be *assigned* to the application if it appears from discussions that the application has significant and substantial scientific and technical merit. No vote for approval is taken by the initial review group. Ratings will be assigned only by regularly appointed members of the IRG and members of the Reviewers Reserve.

If it appears that the application does not have significant and substantial scientific merit, a motion may be made by the review group that the application <u>not be recommended for further consideration.</u> This action is made by *majority vote* of the review committee. In addition, if there are *serious concerns regarding the use of human subjects or animal welfare or biohazards,* a motion may be initiated that the application <u>not be recommended for further consideration.</u>[7]

If additional information is needed before a review group can make a recommendation, a motion for <u>deferral</u> may be entertained. The review group, by majority vote, may defer an application for additional information or a project site visit. The vote for deferral or that no further consideration be given to an application will be made by regularly appointed members of the IRG and members of the Reviewers Reserve.

Minority opinion

If a reviewer initiates a motion that the application be "not recommended for further consideration" and the motion is seconded, the Chair will ask for additional discussion before calling for a vote on the motion. If the motion <u>passes</u>, the application is not scored; if the motion <u>fails</u>, the Chair instructs the reviewers to score the application. If the vote is not unanimous, two or more dissenting members <u>must</u> provide a *minority report;* one dissenting member <u>may</u> provide a minority report. Regardless, all reviewers should assign a score to reflect their individual opinion of the scientific merit of the application.

For any motion that an application be "not recommended for further consideration" and that does not pass unanimously, the full action of the committee must be recorded: number of votes for the motion, number of votes against the motion, and number of abstentions and number assigning a score. *Reviewers are encouraged not to abstain.* However, if a reviewer is unable to assess the merit of an application without additional information, as evidenced by his/her prior discussion or recommendation for deferral, that reviewer should abstain from voting on the motion. No minority report is needed when a motion for <u>deferral</u> is voted against by two or more reviewers.

Numerical rating

For each application which the majority of members believes has *significant and substantial scientific merit,* each member (including dissenting members) records a numerical rating that reflects the member's opinion of the merit of the application. Numerical ratings range with increments of 0.1 as follows:

1.0–1.5	Outstanding
1.5–2.0	Excellent
2.0–2.5	Very good
2.5–3.5	Good
3.5–5.0	Acceptable (has significant and substantial scientific merit and is worthy of further consideration)

Abstaining members do not assign a numerical rating and are not counted in calculating the average of the individual ratings.

---

[7] These instructions may change in 1994–95 if changes in peer review under study in 1994 are adopted.

The budget recommendation should be based upon careful scrutiny of direct costs of the proposed research for each year of support requested. In accordance with policy articulated in the *NIH Financial Management Plan* which was submitted to Congress in June 1991, reviewers are urged to closely examine the proposed cost elements for the current year and all future years to ensure that each cost item is reasonable, necessary, and consistent with the research activities to be conducted. *Particular attention should be given to the need for all personnel listed in the application and their percent effort in relation to the workscope, the justification for requests in all budget categories, and addition of personnel, equipment, etc., in future years. The IRG must recommend the duration and amount of support that is scientifically justified.*

Overlap

Reviewers will identify any apparent scientific or budgetary overlap with active or pending support. However, *potential overlap must not be reason for altering the budget nor may it affect the priority score.* Information regarding potential overlap is included in an Administrative Note in the summary statement.

Foreign organizations

In addition to the regular review criteria, *foreign applications are evaluated in terms of special opportunities for furthering research programs* through the use of special talents, resources (human subjects, animals, diseases, equipment or technologies), populations or environmental conditions in the applicant country which are not readily available in the United States or which provide augmentation of existing United States resources. In addition, notice is taken whether similar research is being done in the United States and whether there is a need for additional research in the area of the proposal. *These special review criteria are not applied to applications from domestic institutions which include a significant foreign component.*

Research involving human subjects

Applicant organizations have the primary responsibility for safeguarding the rights and welfare of individuals who participate as subjects in research activities supported by the NIH. However, the NIH also relies on its IRGs and National Advisory Councils or Boards to evaluate all applications and proposals involving human subjects for compliance with the Department of Health and Human Services human subject regulations.

The regulations *define "human subject"* as a "living individual about whom an investigator obtains (1) data through intervention or interaction with the individual, or (2) identifiable private information." The regulations extend to the use of human organs, tissue and body fluids from individually identifiable human subjects as well as to graphic, written, or recorded information derived from individually identifiable human subjects. The use of autopsy materials is governed by applicable state and local law and is not directly regulated by the Federal human subject regulations.

The Department will *fund research covered by these regulations only if the institution has filed an assurance* with the NIH Office for Protection from Research Risks and has certified that the research has been approved by an Institutional Review Board (IRB) and is subject to continuing review by the IRB. When research involves only minimal risk and meets certain other conditions, the IRB may waive the requirement for obtaining informed consent. In addition, certain research that poses little or no risk to human subjects is exempt from IRB review and approval. In such cases, however, *adherence to ethical standards and pertinent laws is still required.*

The review by the IRG is expected to reflect existing codes adopted by <u>disciplines</u> relevant to the research or the collective standards of the professions represented by the membership. *The evaluation by IRG members is to take into consideration the investigator's response to the following six points:*

1. Provide a detailed description of the proposed involvement of human subjects in the work previously outlined in the experimental design and methods section. Describe the characteristics of the subject population, including their anticipated number, age range and summarize the gender and racial/ethnic composition of the population and health status. Identify the criteria for inclusion or exclusion of any subpopulation. If women and/or minority groups are not fully represented in the study population, provide a rationale for their under-representation. If gender representation and/or inclusion of minorities is not addressed, provide a clear rationale for their exclusion. Explain the rationale for the involvement of special classes of subjects, if any, such as fetuses, pregnant women, children, prisoners or other institutionalized individuals, or others who are likely to be vulnerable, as well as human <u>in vitro</u> fertilization.

2. Identify the sources of research material obtained from individually identifiable living human subjects in the form of specimens, records, or data. Indicate whether the material or data will be obtained specifically for research purposes or whether use will be made of existing specimens, records, or data.

3. Describe plans for the recruitment of subjects and the consent procedures to be followed, including the circumstances under which consent will be sought and obtained, who will seek it, the nature of the information to be provided to prospective subjects, and the method of documenting consent. State if the IRB has authorized a modification or waiver of the elements of consent or the requirement for documentation of consent. The consent form, which must have IRB approval, should be submitted to the PHS only on request.

4. Describe any potential risks—physical, psychological, social, legal, or other, and assess their likelihood and seriousness. Where appropriate, describe alternative treatments and procedures that might be advantageous to the subjects.

5. Describe the procedures for protecting against or minimizing any potential risks, including risks to confidentiality, and assess their likely effectiveness. Where appropriate, discuss provisions for ensuring necessary medical or professional intervention in the event of adverse effects to the subjects. Also, where appropriate, describe the provisions for monitoring the data collected to ensure the safety of subjects.

6. Discuss why the risks to subjects are reasonable in relation to the anticipated benefits to subjects and in relation to the importance of the knowledge that may reasonably be expected to result.

If the application designates exemptions from the human subjects regulations, sufficient information must be provided to allow a determination that the designated exemptions are appropriate. If a test article (Investigational New Drug, device, or biologic) is involved, the test article must be named and it must be stated whether the 30-day interval has elapsed or has been waived and/or whether use of the test article has been withheld or restricted by the Food and Drug Administration.

Based on this evaluation, the IRG may:

- score an application without restrictions;
- score an application, but record comments or expressions of concern to be communicated to the institution and principal investigator;

- score an application, but limit the scope of the work proposed, impose restrictions, or eliminate objectionable procedures involving human subjects;
- defer for clarification; or
- recommend no further consideration be given to the application[8] if the research risks are sufficiently serious and protection against the risks so inadequate as to consider the proposed research unacceptable.

Any comments or concerns that IRG members may wish to express regarding the adequacy of protections afforded human subjects will be presented as a special note (HUMAN SUBJECTS) in the summary statement. A *"concern"* is an IRG finding regarding human subjects that requires resolution by program staff prior to award; a *"comment"* is an IRG observation that will be communicated in the summary statement as a suggestion to the principal investigator. *No awards will be made until all expressed concerns about human subjects have been resolved to the satisfaction of the NIH.* Specific concerns and policy interpretation requests may be addressed to the Office for Protection from Research Risks, which is responsible for the administration and interpretation of DHHS policy and regulations for the protection of human subjects of research.

Gender and minorities inclusion in clinical research

NIH and ADAMHA[9] policy requires that, for all research involving human subjects and human tissues, including autopsy materials, applicants *must include in study populations appropriate representation of gender and minorities* in all research involving human subjects and human tissues so that research findings can be of benefit to all at risk of the disease, disorder or condition under study. This policy is intended to apply to males and females of all ages. If gender or minority representation is not included or inadequately represented in the research plan, a clear and compelling rationale must be provided in the application.

The assessment of scientific and technical merit of applications must include an evaluation of the proposed gender and minority composition of the study population and its appropriateness to the scientific objective. *If the representation of gender or minorities in a study design is inadequate to answer the scientific question(s) addressed AND the justification for the selected study population is inadequate, the reviewer should consider it a scientific weakness or deficiency in the study design and it must be considered in assigning a numerical rating.* For all studies on human subjects, recommendations on compliance with policy will be made in a section at the end of the Critique sub-headed: "Gender and Minority Subjects."

Research involving vertebrate animals

Although the recipient institution and investigator bear the major responsibility for the proper care and use of animals, NIH staff, IRGs, and Councils and Boards share this responsibility. Care and use of vertebrate animals in research must conform to applicable law and Public Health Service policy, especially the *Principles for Use of Animals*. These principles can be summarized as two broad rules:

---

[8] These instructions may change in 1994–95 if changes in peer review under study in 1994 are adopted.

[9] ADAMHA as such ceased to exist in 1992 when its 3 research Institutes were transferred to NIH. The rest of the components of ADAMHA became SAMHSA.

- The project should be *worthwhile and justified* on the basis of anticipated results for the good of society and the contribution to knowledge, and the work should be planned and performed by *qualified* scientists;
- Animals should be confined, restrained, transported, cared for, and used in experimental procedures in a manner to *avoid any unnecessary discomfort, pain, or injury.* Special attention must be provided when the proposed research involves dogs, cats, nonhuman primates, large numbers of animals, or animals that are in short supply or are costly.

The evaluation by IRG members is to take into consideration the investigator's response to the following five points:

1. Provide a detailed description of the proposed use of the animals in the work previously outlined in the experimental design and methods section. Identify the species, strains, ages, sex and *numbers* of animals to be used in the proposed work.
2. *Justify* the use of animals, the choice of species, and the numbers used. If animals are in short supply, costly, or to be used in large numbers, provide an additional rationale for their selection and their numbers.
3. Provide information on the veterinary care of the animals involved.
4. Describe the Procedures for *ensuring* that discomfort, distress, pain, and injury will be limited to that which is unavoidable in the conduct of scientifically sound research. Describe the use of analgesic, anesthetic, and tranquilizing drugs and/or comfortable restraining devices where appropriate to minimize discomfort, distress, pain, and injury.
5. Describe any euthanasia method to be used and the reasons for its selection. State whether this method is consistent with the recommendations of the Panel on Euthanasia of the American Veterinary Medical Association. If not, present a justification for not following the recommendations.

Any comments or concerns that IRG members may wish to express regarding the appropriateness of the choice of species and numbers involved, the justification for their use, and the care and maintenance of vertebrate animals used in the project will be discussed in a special note (<u>ANIMAL WELFARE</u>) in the summary statement. A *"concern"* is an IRG finding regarding animal care or use that requires resolution by program staff prior to award; a *"comment"* is an IRG observation that will be communicated in the summary statement as a suggestion to the principal investigator. Questions may be directed to the Office for Protection from Research Risks. *No award will be made unless the applicant institution has given the NIH Office for Protection from Research Risks an acceptable assurance of compliance with the PHS policy and all concerns or questions raised by the IRG have been resolved to the satisfaction of the NIH.* If concerns are expressed regarding the proper use and care of animals a recommendation may be made that no further consideration be given to the application.

Biohazards

The investigator and the sponsoring institution are responsible for protecting the environment and research personnel from hazardous conditions. As with research involving human subjects, reviewers are expected to apply the collective standards of the professions represented within the IRG in identifying potential hazards, such as inappropriate handling of oncogenic viruses, chemical carcinogens, infectious agents, radioactive or explosive materials, or recombinant DNA.

If applications pose special hazards, these hazards will be identified and any concerns about the adequacy of safety procedures highlighted as a special note (BIOHAZARD) on the summary statement. *No awards will be made until all concerns about hazardous procedures or conditions have been resolved to the satisfaction of the NIH.*

Avoiding conflicts of interest during IRG meetings

At the beginning of each meeting, the Scientific Review Administrator orients the members by explaining the *NIH conflict of interest policy.* A member must leave the room when an application submitted by his/her own organization is being discussed or when the member, his/her immediate family, or close professional associate(s) has a financial or vested interest even if no significant involvement is apparent in the proposal being considered. If the member is available at the principal investigator's institution for discussions is a provider of services, cell lines, reagents, or other materials, or writer of a letter of reference, the member must be absent from the room during the review. Members are also urged to avoid any actions that might give the <u>appearance </u>that a conflict of interest exists, even though he or she believes there may not be an <u>actual </u>conflict of interest. Thus, for example, a member should not participate in the deliberations and actions on any application from a recent student, a recent teacher, or a close personal friend. *Judgment must be applied* on the basis of recency, frequency and strength of the working relationship between the member and the principal investigator as reflected, for example, in publications. Another example might be an application from a scientist with whom the member has had long-standing differences which could reasonably be viewed as affecting the member's objectivity. Another example which might be considered is the review of a project which closely duplicates work ongoing in the member's laboratory.

The term *"own organization"* includes the entire system in which the member is an employee, consultant, officer, director, or trustee or has a financial interest; or with which the member is negotiating or has any arrangement concerning prospective employment. However, it has been determined that the interest involved is too remote or too inconsequential to affect the integrity of a review of an application from one of the following list of multi-campus state institutions, where the interest consists solely of employment as a faculty member at a separate campus of the same multi-campus institution. These multi-campus institutions are:

ALABAMA
The University of Alabama system and other Alabama State owned institutions of higher education.
Multi-campus Institutions: The University of Alabama system consisting of the University of Alabama, The University of Alabama at Birmingham, and The University of Alabama at Huntsville.

CALIFORNIA
The California Community Colleges, the California State Universities and Colleges, and the University of California.
Multi-campus Institutions: The campuses of the University of California.

COLORADO
The Colorado State University, University of Colorado, and other Colorado State owned institutions of higher education.
Multi-campus Institutions: The system consisting of Colorado State University, the University of Southern Colorado, and Fort Lewis College.

CONNECTICUT

The Connecticut Community Colleges, Connecticut State University, the Connecticut Technical Colleges, and the University of Connecticut.

ILLINOIS

The Illinois Community Colleges, Illinois State University, Southern Illinois University, the University of Illinois, and Western Illinois University.

INDIANA

The Indiana University and the other Indiana State owned institutions of higher education.

Multi-campus Institutions: The Indiana University system consisting of eight universities on nine campuses, with the exception of the system-wide schools: the School of Business; the School of Dentistry; the School of Medicine; the School of Nursing; and the School of Public and Environmental Affairs.

IOWA

The Iowa State University, and the University of Iowa.

KANSAS

Fort Hays State University, Kansas State University, the Kansas Technological Institute, Pittsburgh State University, the University of Kansas, and Wichita State University.

LOUISIANA

Louisiana State University, and other Louisiana State owned institutions of higher education.

MASSACHUSETTS

The University of Massachusetts, and other Massachusetts State owned institutions of higher education.

MICHIGAN

Michigan State University, the University of Michigan, and Wayne State University.

MINNESOTA

The Minnesota Community College system, the Minnesota State University system, and the University of Minnesota.

MISSOURI

The University of Missouri, and other Missouri State owned institutions of higher education.

NEBRASKA

The University of Nebraska, and other Nebraska State owned institutions of higher education.

Multi-campus Institutions: The University of Nebraska system consisting of the University of Nebraska–Lincoln, the University of Nebraska at Omaha, and the University of Nebraska Medical Center.

NEW YORK

The City University of New York system, and the State University of New York system.

Multi-campus Institutions: The campuses of the State University of New York.

NORTH CAROLINA

North Carolina State, the University of North Carolina, and other North Carolina State owned institutions of higher education.

OREGON

Multi-campus Institutions: The Oregon system of higher education consisting of the University of Oregon, Oregon State University, Oregon Health Sciences University, Portland State University, Western Oregon State College, Southern Oregon State College, Eastern Oregon State College, and the Oregon Institute of Technology.

PENNSYLVANIA

Lincoln University, Pennsylvania State University, Temple University, the University of Pittsburgh, and the other State owned colleges and universities in Pennsylvania.

TENNESSEE

Multi-campus Institutions: The campuses of the University of Tennessee.

TEXAS

East Texas State University
Lamar University System
Midwestern University
North Texas State University
Pan American University
Stephen F. Austin State University
Texas A & M System
Texas Southern University
Texas State University System
Texas Tech University
Texas Woman's University
University of Houston System
University of Texas System
University System of South Texas
West Texas State University
Multi-campus Institutions: The separate universities comprising the University of Texas System

UTAH

Utah State University and the University of Utah.

WISCONSIN

Multi-campus Institutions: The separate universities comprising the University of Wisconsin system.

In all other cases, a reviewer from any State owned institution must leave the room during the review of an application from any other campus of that institution or any other State-owned institution. Thus, the College Park and Baltimore campuses of the University of Maryland constitute a conflict, as do the University of Florida, Florida State University, and the University of South Florida.

Each of the Harvard-affiliated organizations is considered a distinct and separate entity, so that persons from one are not in conflict if reviewing applications from another, provided they have no professional or personal relationships with the other institution. Thus, a member from Massachusetts General Hospital can review an application submitted from Beth Israel Hospital.

Harvard-affiliated institutions include:
Beth Israel Hospital
Brigham and Women's Hospital

Cambridge Hospital
Center for Blood Research
Children's Hospital
Dana Farber Cancer Institute
Forsyth Dental Center
Harvard Community Health Plan
Massachusetts Eye and Ear Infirmary
Massachusetts General Hospital
Massachusetts Mental Health Center
McLean Hospital
Mount Auburn Hospital
New England Deaconess Hospital
New England Regional Primate Research Center
West Roxbury/Brockton Veterans Administration Center

Reviewers who are supported as investigators of the Howard Hughes Medical Institute may not review applications submitted by other investigators who receive support from this institute.

A reviewer must leave the room during discussion of an application if he/she is a member of, or has a financial interest in a for-profit organization submitting the application. This includes ownership of stock in, or being a consultant for a for-profit organization. A reviewer should also leave the room during discussion of an application if being present would give the appearance of a conflict of interest. Examples would be an application from a for-profit organization that provides substantial financial funding to the reviewer's organization or laboratory.

Prior to the IRG meeting, each reviewer will receive a certificate of Conflict of Interest and confidentiality and a list of applications which will be reviewed. Reviewers must notify the Scientific Review Administrator of any conflict of interest prior to the meeting and certify that the confidentiality of the review procedures will be maintained.

At the end of the IRB meeting, the SRA will obtain written certification from all members that they have not participated in any reviews of applications when their presence would have constituted a real or apparent conflict of interest and that the confidentiality of actions will be maintained. In addition, *each study section keeps a log, prepared by the Grants Assistant and maintained in the study section office, of which members left the room because of potential conflict of interest and for which applications.*

Confidentiality and communications with investigators

All materials pertinent to the *applications being reviewed are privileged communications* prepared for use only by consultants and NIH staff, and should not be shown to or discussed with other individuals. Review group members must not independently solicit opinions or reviews on particular applications or parts thereof from experts outside the pertinent initial review group. Members may, however, suggest scientists from whom the SRA may subsequently obtain advice. Consultants are required to leave all review materials with the SRA at the conclusion of the review meeting. Privileged information in grant applications shall not be used to the benefit of the reviewer or shared with anyone.

Under no circumstances shall consultants advise investigators, their organizations, or anyone else of recommendations or *discuss the review proceedings.* The investigator may be led into unwise actions on the basis of premature or erroneous information. Such advice also represents an unfair intrusion into the privileged nature of the proceedings and invades the privacy of fellow consultants serving on review committees and site visit teams. A breach of confidentiality could deter qualified consultants from serving on review committees and inhibit those who do serve from engaging in free and full discussion of recommendations.

Except during site visits, there must be no direct communications between consultants and investigators. Consultants' requests for additional information and telephone inquiries or correspondence from investigators must be directed to the SRA, who will handle all such communications.

Misconduct

"Misconduct" or *"misconduct in science"* is defined at 42 CFR 50.102 as fabrication, falsification, plagiarism, or other practices that seriously deviate from those that are commonly accepted within the scientific community for proposing, conducting or reporting research. It does not include honest error or honest differences in interpretation or judgments of data.

Review of grant/cooperative agreement applications and contract proposals for scientific merit will ordinarily not be delayed by concerns about possible misconduct or by a pending or ongoing inquiry or investigation. To avoid influencing the review process, PHS awarding units generally will not inform members of scientific or objective review groups about instances of possible misconduct or the status of ongoing investigations. However, if certain instances have received such extensive publicity that the review may be compromised, the agency-level Misconduct Policy Officer (MPO) should consult with the Office of Scientific Integrity (OSI) as to whether the review should be deferred or the reviewers be informed about the status of activities with regard to the possible misconduct. Findings from completed investigations should be shared with scientific review groups whenever an accurate disclosure of the facts in the case is necessary to the objectivity and thoroughness of the review process.

During the conduct of the initial review of applications, the Initial Review Group (IRG) may identify instances of suspected or possible misconduct; e.g., suspicions regarding possible plagiarism or questionable data in support of the proposed research. The SRA of the IRG, in consultation with the IRG chairperson and Section Chief, must first determine, from the discussions of the IRG, if the review may proceed. Generally, what appears to be a relatively "minor" impropriety such as the unattributed use of small amounts of textbook material in the Background section of the application would not prevent the IRG from providing a fair review. The general principle is that if the IRG is able to provide an unbiased technical/scientific merit review, unaffected by the suspicions of misconduct, it should do so. Subsequently, the concerns of the IRG will be forwarded by the SRA through the Section Chief and cognizant MPO to the OSI for resolution.

In all such cases of suspected misconduct, it is essential that the SRA stress to the reviewers the seriousness of such allegations and the potential harm that may result if confidentiality is not strictly maintained. In addition, it is important for the SRA to assure the consultants that the *suspicion of misconduct in sciences identified will be taken seriously and pursued by the PHS.* If it is determined that a fair review of an application cannot be carried out by any appropriate initial review group because of the existence of reviewers' concerns about possible misconduct, immediate deferral of the application is the correct course of action.

In no instance shall the SRA or an IRG member communicate the IRG's concerns to the principal investigator or applicant institution. Instead immediately following the IRG meeting, it is the responsibility of the SRA to communicate these concerns to the Section Chief and the cognizant MPO. As soon as possible thereafter, formal written communication of the concerns and the precise details of the IRG discussion will be forwarded to the OSI by the SRA through the Section Chief and the cognizant MPO. Any subsequent communications with the principal investigator and/or applicant institution will be done only through the OSI for resolution.

The OSI will attempt to resolve the concerns so that the review may be completed during the next review cycle. If the IRG's concerns are subsequently allayed, review of the application should proceed to conclusion at the subsequent meeting. However, if the concerns remain, and if it is not appropriate or possible for the review to proceed, the application should be deferred while the OSI proceeds with the necessary steps to examine the identified issues.

It is important that the preparation of the summary statement be carefully monitored by the Section Chief in consultation with the MPO and OSI to ensure that only appropriate details of the IRG's concerns are expressed in that document. In addition, the SRA should carefully monitor the priority scoring of the reviewers for that application. If it appears that the scoring has been influenced by concerns of possible misconduct, the SRA, in consultation with the Section Chief, MPO and the OSI, should administratively defer the application for resolution of the identified issues.

3. NIH GUIDANCE ON THE INCLUSION OF MINORITIES AND WOMEN IN CLINICAL RESEARCH STUDY POPULATIONS

(Instruction and Information Memorandum OER 90-5; Attachment 5)

Office of Extramural Research
National Institutes of Health
December 1990

The National Institutes of Health (NIH) has a strong commitment to research on health problems related to minorities and women. Since 1986, published NIH policies have been in place to include minorities and women in study populations whenever possible. These policies have been recently updated, republished in collaboration with the Alcohol, Drug Abuse, and Mental Health Administration (ADAMHA) in the *NIH Guide for Grants and Contracts* (August 24 and September 28, 1990), and widely distributed to the extramural research community under the title "Inclusion of Minorities and Women in Study Populations."

Therefore, all applicants who submit applications for research grants and cooperative agreements and proposals for contracts relevant to the NIH mission and the mandates of its individual Institutes and Centers (ICDs) must adequately follow the NIH Policy by including minorities and women in study populations so that research findings can be of benefit to all persons at risk of the disease, disorder or condition under study.

The NIH guidance about inclusion of minorities and women in study populations has been developed in the form of Questions and Answers as a means of implementing the NIH policy and to assist you in the preparation of grant applications and contract proposals. The word "application" in this document refers to grant and cooperative agreement applications and contract proposals. If you have any questions about this policy, please contact the appropriate NIH Representative from any specific Institute, Center, or Division's research program.

1. What is the policy on inclusion?

NIH and ADAMHA policy is that applicants for NIH/ADAMHA clinical research grants, cooperative agreements and contracts will be required to include minorities and women in study populations so that research findings can be of benefit to all persons at risk of the disease, disorder or condition under study; special emphasis should be placed on the need for inclusion of minorities and women in studies of diseases, disorders and conditions which disproportionately affect them. This policy is intended to apply to males and females of all ages. *If women or minorities are not included or are inadequately represented in clinical research, particularly in proposed population-based studies, a clear compelling rationale should be provided.*

2. What is included in clinical research under this policy?

For the purpose of this policy, clinical research includes human biomedical and behavioral studies of etiology, epidemiology, prevention (and preventive strategies), diagnosis, or treatment of diseases, disorders or conditions, including but not limited to clinical trials.

The usual NIH policies concerning research on human subjects also apply. Basic research or clinical studies in which human tissues cannot be identified or linked to individuals are excluded. However, every effort should be made to include human tissues from women and racial/ethnic minorities when it is important to apply the results of the study broadly, and this should be addressed by applicants.

3. What are the main reasons for emphasizing the inclusion of minorities and women in study populations?

a. The disease under study is either unique to or disproportionately affects minorities or women, or
b. A gap in knowledge exists regarding the magnitude of the impact of the disease under study on minorities and women, though it is known to be significant, or
c. There is no evidence or scientific reason to exclude them from the study, based on expected outcome measures, or
d. The population to which the study results will be applied or extrapolated includes various subpopulations and both genders.

Thus, minorities and women should be included in such study populations unless strong scientific or practical reasons are provided for excluding them.

4. What level of inclusion is necessary in a specific study?

Scientific, ethical, logistical, cost, and possible other factors may result in one of several eligibility and recruitment plans with respect to inclusion of minorities and women, for example:

a. inclusion, with a specific major goal to test for a difference between groups;
b. inclusion, with the goal to be representative of the community or some other demographic group;
c. inclusion, with the goal of over-representation (or under-representation) compared to the community or some other demographic base;
d. inclusion, but without special goals; and
e. exclusion.

Investigators are expected to indicate their plans and the scientific, ethical, logistical, cost, and possible other factors that resulted in these plans.

5. What kinds of justification are acceptable for not including adequate representation of women?

Depending on the specific research questions, design, and resources available, some examples of possible justifications could be:

    a. The only population available with the needed clinical characteristics is all or predominantly male, or the clinical condition of interest is predominantly or exclusively a male condition.

    b. Experimental procedures/treatments present unacceptable risk for women of child-bearing age.

    c. Gender differences may not be germane for pilot or feasibility studies which will evaluate instrumentation, possible approaches or techniques, etc.

    d. The condition under study is of such low prevalence/incidence in women that the probability of obtaining enough cases for study is too low to justify the effort.

    e. Research is proposed with a pre-defined unique but unrepresentative population (e.g., an extensive registry of patients with a condition of interest) and would not be feasible or would be prohibitively expensive if a different sample was used.

    f. The scientific condition under study has already been extensively studied in women and additional study in men is required.

Each of these justifications would be evaluated in Initial Review Groups in the context of the specific scientific goals and issues being addressed. Depending on the details, these justifications may or may not be considered adequate and compelling.

6. What minorities are to be included?

Applicants/offerors are urged to assess carefully the feasibility of including the broadest possible representation of minority groups. However, NIH recognizes that it may not be feasible or appropriate in all research projects to include representation of the full array of United States racial/ethnic minority populations (i.e., Native Americans [including American Indians or Alaskan Natives], Asian/Pacific Islanders, Blacks, Hispanics). The rationale for studies on single minority population groups should be provided.

7. What kinds of justification are acceptable for not including adequate representation of racial/ethnic minorities?

Depending on the specific research questions, design, and resources available, some examples of possible justifications could be:

    a. There is only one minority group living in the area in sufficient numbers to participate.

    b. The condition/disease/disorder is characteristic of only one minority group.

    c. Racial/ethnic differences may not be germane for pilot or feasibility studies which will evaluate instrumentation, possible approaches or techniques, etc.

    d. The scientific condition under study has already been extensively studied in some minority groups and additional study in other groups is required.

    e. The scientific question requires the use of the same or a comparable study population as that used in an earlier study.

As in the previous answer, each of these justifications would be evaluated by IRGs in the context of the specific goals and issues being addressed. Depending on the details, these justifications may or may not be considered adequate and compelling.

8. How do I describe my study population, and where does this information go in the application?

Applications must include a description of the composition of the proposed study population in terms of the gender and racial/ethnic group, together with a rationale for its choice. In addition, gender and racial/ethnic issues should be addressed in developing a research design and sample size appropriate for the scientific objective of the study. *This information should be included in the form PHS-398 in Section 2, A-D [as of 9/91: Section C, 1-4] of the Research Plan AND summarized in Section 2, E [as of 9/91: Section C, 5], Human Subjects.*

RFPs for contracts will provide instructions concerning inclusion of minorities and women in study populations.

9. Do these policies require that sample sizes be sufficiently large to provide statistical power to assess gender and racial/ethnic effects?

The research goals and scientific hypotheses (as well as ethical, feasibility, and other factors) must dictate the sample sizes. Applications must employ a study design with gender and/or minority representation (by age distribution, risk factors, incidence/prevalence, etc.) appropriate to the scientific objectives of the disease, disorder or condition being studied.

It is not an automatic requirement for the study design to provide statistical power to answer the questions posed for men and women and racial/ethical groups separately; however, whenever there are scientific reasons to anticipate differences between men and women or minorities with regard to the hypothesis under investigation, applications should include an evaluation of gender and minority group differences in the proposed study.

10. What types of differences in gender or minority composition might influence study outcomes?

There may be biological, behavioral, socioeconomic or cultural differences due to gender or minority status which might be hypothesized to impact on study outcome variables. If any differences are known to exist, they should be considered in determining appropriate sample sizes and statistical power for the study.

Pilot studies might be appropriate to begin looking for potential differences, especially if no prior work has been done. If no differences are known or anticipated, it should be feasible to include minorities and both genders in representative numbers in the study.

11. Is the establishment of outreach programs to assist with the recruitment of minorities and women into study populations an acceptable expense?

The establishment of outreach programs to assist with the recruitment of minorities and women can be considered an acceptable expense for clinical trials, demonstration and education research, and epidemiologic and other community-based studies provided that the costs are not excessive and are adequately justified.

12. Is increased study cost an acceptable rationale for not including minorities and women?

Initial peer review focuses on the scientific merit of the application. Costs are reviewed according to NIH peer review procedures. Depending upon the relevance of minorities and women to the research question(s) being asked, the increase in study cost may be appropriate and acceptable. Therefore, *increased study cost may be unacceptable as the sole rationale for excluding minorities and women in study populations.*

13. In multi-center clinical studies, must each study site meet the inclusion requirement independently?

The answer will depend on the study goals and hypotheses and the locations of the study sites. Recruitment of women or minority groups may be uneven at different sites, but, when combined, meet the study goals. This could be acceptable if the minority and women populations from the contributing centers do not have some relevant unique characteristics, other than being from those centers, that could limit the value of the study results.

14. What is the role of minority institutions in clinical trials, demonstration and education research, and epidemiologic and other community-based studies?

The focus of the NIH policy is on the participation of minorities and not minority institutions. However, minority institutions should be encouraged to participate in all Institute-supported research, including clinical trials, demonstration and education research, and epidemiologic and other community-based studies. In addition, *non-minority institutions should be encouraged to consider collaborating with minority institutions,* since it is likely that the involvement of minority institutions will enhance the recruitment of minority subjects and add cultural sensitivity to the development, recruitment, and management aspects of interventions involving minority populations.

15. Will Peer Reviewers evaluate applications for conformance to this policy?

Yes. *Peer Reviewers will address specifically whether the research plan in the application conforms to these policies,* using questions such as these. Is clinical research involved? Is there sufficient information on gender and minorities? Is gender and minority composition germane to the research goals? Is there adequate representation of women and minorities, and if not, is there adequate justification for the selected study population?

If the representation of women or minorities in a study design is inadequate to answer the scientific question(s) addressed AND the justification for the selected study population is inadequate, it will be considered a scientific weakness or deficiency in the study design and will be reflected in assigning the priority score to the application.

Executive Secretaries of the Initial Review Groups (IRG) will request written clarification from the applicant when the application does not describe and justify the gender or minority composition of the study population. *If such information is not contained within the application, and is not provided upon request, the application will be deferred without IRG review* until it is complete, or be returned to the applicant. In the case of responses to *RFAs with single receipt dates,* applications *which are not brought into compliance will be returned without review, rather than deferred.*

16. Does the policy apply to foreign projects funded by NIH?

For foreign awards, the policy on inclusion of women applies fully; since the definition of minority differs in other countries, the applicant must discuss the relevance of research involving foreign population groups to United States' populations, including minorities.

17. How will conformance to this policy affect funding of projects?

Regardless of the priority score, percentile ranking or program relevance of the proposed research, the NIH and ADAMHA *funding components will not fund/award grants that do not comply with this policy.*

18. Where can I get additional information about this policy?

Applicants should contact NIH program staff for additional guidance in interpreting this policy in the context of any specific NIH Institute, Center or Division's research program.

Coding table for reviewers concerning inclusion of diverse groups in clinical studies

Inclusion of Women and Minorities in Study Populations

Recommend the appropriate code:

Research	Code	
	Women	Minorities
Not clinical*	60	70
Not germane	61	71
Included & adequate	62	72
Not included but justified	63	73
Not included and not justified	64**	74**

*Human biomedical and behavioral studies of the etiology, epidemiology, prevention (and preventive strategies), diagnosis, or treatment of diseases, disorders, or conditions. Includes but is not limited to clinical trials.
**Codes barring an award.

4. CALCULATION OF PERCENTILES

(This section is taken from *NIH Peer Review Notes*, October, 1991, pages 2–3.)
The percentile value represents the relative rank for each priority score on a scale from 1.0 to 100.0. Following the NIH convention of assigning the order of priority scores for scientific merit inversely to the numerical scale, the lowest percentile value represents the judgment of highest scientific merit.

The calculated percentile value for a given application specifies the percent of applications with score equal to or better (lower number) than that application, i.e., a cumulative percent distribution.

The formula for calculating the percentile is the following:

$$p = 100\,(\,k - \tfrac{1}{2}\,)/N$$

where p = percentile value.
100 = the percentile scale (a constant).
k = numerical rank of priority score.
N = number of applications in base.

Consider the following set of scores as an example from a pool of 80 applications, 14 of which were not recommended for further consideration.

Rank	Priority Score	Percentile
1	108	0.6
2	115	1.9
3	118	3.1
4	120	4.4
//	//	//
66	478	81.9

The percentile for priority score 118 above is calculated as follows:

$$p = 100(3 - \tfrac{1}{2})/80$$
$$= 100(2.5)/80$$
$$= 250/80$$
$$= 3.125$$
$$p = 3.1$$

As may be seen, for a given N, the percentile intervals are approximately equal, considering rounding to the nearest 0.1, and the interval (in this example, 1.25) × the number of applications (80) = 100. This relationship holds without regard to the distribution of priority scores and without regard to the number of applications "not recommended for further consideration," since these are included in the percentile base.

Notes added by LRL:

All applications reviewed, whether given a priority rating or designated "Noncompetitive" (NC), are included in the calculation of percentiles. Thus, in the equation shown above, N includes all applications reviewed in the 3 last meetings of *that* Study Section, including those that are "NC." Because the "NC" applications are not scored and not given a percentile rank and are simply aligned below all scored applications, it does not matter that they do not have a numerical score.[10]

Most applications reviewed by ad hoc Study Sections, special committees, or NIH Institute/Center review groups are also assigned percentiles. However, applications for set-aside funds such as RFAs, SBIR grants, or AREA grants are not assigned percentiles. In the 1990s, about 5–7 % of research project grants were paid out of percentile order for reasons of program priorities. Note that applications with *similar* percentiles, but assigned to different funding components, may have *different* funding outcomes because the different funding components may have different amounts of money for funding competing awards. (See "NIH Scientific Merit Review: Terminology and Practices," *NIH Peer Review Notes*, October 1993, pages 11–13.)

---

5. SALARY LIMITATION ON GRANTS AND CONTRACTS

(This information is taken from *NIH Guide for Grants and Contracts*, Vol. 23, No. 7, February 18, 1994, pages 3–4.) For questions, call the Grants Management Office of the NIH Awarding Component.

This notice provides updated information regarding the salary limitation as it relates to NIH grant and cooperative agreement awards (hereafter called 'grant'). This information also applies to extramural research and development contract awards. In addition, this notice describes a change in the way that NIH Institutes and Centers (I/Cs) are treat-

---

[10] These instructions may change in 1994–95 if changes in peer review under study in 1994 are adopted.

ing salaries in excess of the limit for any future years in competing grant awards. The last notice in the NIH Guide for Grants and Contracts regarding the salary limitation was in Vol. 20, No. 47, December 20, 1991, pages 2–3.

Fiscal Year (FY) 94 is the fifth consecutive year for which there is a legislatively mandated provision for the limitation of salary. Specifically, the Department of Health and Human Services (HHS) Appropriations Act for FY 94, Public Law 103-112, restricts the amount of direct salary an individual under a grant or applicable contract issued by the NIH to a RATE of $125,000 per year. Direct salary is exclusive of fringe benefits and indirect costs/general and administrative expenses. The salary limit of $125,000 has not increased from the FY 93 level.

The NIH will continue to apply the limits to all grant and applicable contract awards and all funding amendments to existing awards made with FY 94 funds. Therefore, NIH grant and applicable contract awards for applications/proposals that request direct salaries of individuals in excess of a RATE of $125,000 per year will be adjusted in accordance with the legislative salary limitation, and will include a notification such as:

According to the HHS Appropriations Act, "None of the funds appropriated in this title for the National Institutes of Health . . . shall be used to pay the salary of an individual, through a grant or other extramural mechanism, at a rate in excess of $125,000 per year."

The following are examples of the adjustments that NIH will make when salaries exceed the limit:

EXAMPLE 1. INDIVIDUAL WITH FULL-TIME APPOINTMENT

Individual's institutional base* salary for a FULL-TIME (twelve month) appointment	$150,000
Research effort requested in application/proposal	50%
Direct Salary requested	$75,000
Fringe benefits requested (25% of salary)	$18,750
Subtotal	$93,750
Applicant organization's indirect costs at a rate of 45% of subtotal	$42,188
Amount requested - salary plus fringe benefits plus associated indirect costs	$135,938

If a grant/contract is to be funded, the amount included in the award for the above individual will be calculated as follows:

Direct salary—restricted to a RATE of $125,000 multiplied by effort (50%) to be devoted to project	$62,500
Fringe benefits (25% of allowable salary)	$15,625
Subtotal	$78,125
Associated indirect costs at 45% of subtotal	$35,156
Total amount to be awarded due to salary limitation	$113,281
Amount of reduction due to salary limitation ($135,938 requested minus $113,281 awarded)	$22,657

*   An individual's institutional base salary is the annual compensation that the applicant organization pays for an individual's appointment, whether that individual's time is spent on research, teaching, patient care, or other activities. Base salary excludes any income that an individual may be permitted to earn outside of duties to the applicant organization.

EXAMPLE 2. INDIVIDUAL WITH HALF-TIME APPOINTMENT

Individual's institutional base salary for a HALF-TIME appointment (50% of a full-time twelve month appointment)	$65,000
Research effort requested in application/proposal	30%
Direct Salary requested	$19,500
Fringe benefits requested (25% of salary)	$4,875
Subtotal	$24,375
Applicant organization's indirect costs at a rate of 45% of subtotal	$10,969
Amount requested—salary plus fringe benefits plus associated indirect costs	$35,344

If a grant/contract is to be funded, the amount included in the award for the above individual will be calculated as follows:

Direct salary—restricted to a RATE of $125,000 multiplied by 50% appointment by 30% effort to be devoted to project	$18,750
Fringe benefits (25% of allowable salary)	$4,688
Subtotal	$23,438
Associated indirect costs at 45% of subtotal	$10,547
Total amount to be awarded due to salary limitation	$33,985
Amount of reduction due to salary limitation ($35,344 requested minus $33,985 awarded)	$1,359

Other important points relating to both NIH grants and contracts are:

- An individual's base salary, per se, is NOT constrained by the legislative provision for the limitation of salary. The rate limitation simply limits the amount that may be awarded and charged to NIH grant and applicable contract awards. An institution may supplement an individual's salary with non-federal, funds.
- The salary limitation does NOT apply to payments made to consultants under an NIH grant or contract although, as with all costs, such payments must meet the test of reasonableness.
- The salary limitation provision DOES apply to those subawards/subcontracts for substantive work under an NIH grant or contract.

The following three paragraphs apply to GRANT applications/awards only:

- COMPETING grant applications submitted to the NIH may continue to request funding at the regular/actual rates of pay of all individuals for whom reimbursement is requested, even when these rates exceed the salary limitation. NIH staff will make necessary adjustments to requested salaries prior to award.
- There is a change in the way that NIH I/Cs are treating salaries in excess of the limit for any FUTURE years beginning with COMPETING grant awards funded with FY 94 funds. Based upon experience and the expectation that the salary restriction will continue in future appropriations (although the amount of the limitation may change with future appropriations), NIH awards for COMPETING applications will reflect adjustments to all years of a project, including future years, so that no funds are awarded or committed for salaries over the limitation.
- With regard to NON-COMPETING continuation grant applications submitted to NIH, these applications should request funds for salaries at rates of pay that

DO NOT exceed the salary limitation. If the current committed level includes funds for salaries at a rate that exceeds the salary limitation, the excess may not be rebudgeted for any other purpose, and NIH staff will delete it from the award.

---

6. AMENDED APPLICATIONS

(This section is excerpted from NIH DRG Scientific Review & Information Systems, Advisory Committee Minutes, November 16 & 17, 1992, Item X, pages 16 and 20.)

Ms. Lucille Nierzwicki, Chief, Statistics, Analysis, and Evaluation Section, DRG Information Systems Branch, noted the great increase in the number and percent of amended applications in recent years. From FY 1981 through FY 1991, the percent of reviewed research project applications that were amendments doubled from 15 percent to 30 percent, and the percent of awards that were amendments almost tripled, from 13 percent to 36 percent. During this period, the number of amended applications increased from approximately 2,500 in FY 1981 to 6,400 in FY 1991. The number of awards based upon amended applications followed a similar trend, increasing from 700 to 2,000. Of the 2,000 awards, 1,400 were first-time amendments.

The number of original competing research project grant applications reviewed has declined from a high point of 15,700 in FY 1988 to 14,600 in FY 1991, while the number of amended applications has increased from 4,600 to 6,400 during this same period. Thus most of the growth in research project applications has been the result of the submission of amendments to previously submitted applications. In the various grant mechanisms, the largest fraction of amendments as a percentage of competing applications is the research project grant (R01, 33 percent in FY 1991). This is followed by the FIRST award; (R29, 29 percent), program projects (P01, 28 percent), training grants, (T32, 25 percent), Small Business Initiatives (R43, 20 percent), fellowships (F32, 9 percent) and Small Grants (R03, 6 percent).

How long before an applicant submits an amendment? In FY 1982, 51 percent of the amended applications came in within two rounds. By FY 1992, over 68 percent were able to submit amendments and have them reviewed within two rounds.

Amendments have quite a high success rate as compared with original applications. In FY 1991, first amendments had a success rate of 29 percent, second amendments a success rate of 36.8 percent, and original applications a success rate of 19 percent.

In the data on the success of the first amendments based on their original priority score, applications with priority scores from 113-200 had a very good chance (53 percent) of being funded when amended. Surprisingly, even those applicants with the poorest scores or even disapprovals, 8 to 10 percent in FY 1991 were funded after their first amendment. From DRG's perspective, workload has increased dramatically in the past few years. From the point of view of the applicant, they have been able to increase their success rate by submitting amendments.

Assigned discussants

Dr. Osborn noted that one reason for the high success rate of first amendments is the number that, in the initial review, had excellent scores. She was particularly appalled to learn that an application with a 113 priority score did not get funded the first time around because of the severe constriction in funding.

Dr. Braciale, the second discussant, speculated that morale among Study Section members has probably deteriorated because they see excellent applications coming back. There was general agreement with this view.

Dr. Ruh, the third discussant, wondered if there was any way to measure disruption of science in an individual's laboratory, this is of major concern to many scientists. In addition, Dr. Ruh wondered how many amended applications that are eventually successful have had a reduction in years as a result of the Study Section deliberation.

Ms. Nierzwicki felt that on the average applications had not been reduced in time, but this topic needs additional study.

Discussion

Lack of continuity is another problem amended applications create for the SRA's. Some Study Section members who previously reviewed the application have left the Study Section. Also, there is the question whether it is reviewed by the same or a different Study Section.

7. EXPERIENCES IN RECRUITING MINORITIES FOR STUDY SECTIONS AND NIH MINORITY PROGRAMS: THE PIPELINE FOR MINORITIES

(This section is excerpted from NIH DRG Scientific Review & Information Systems, Advisory Committee Minutes, April 12 and 13, 1993, Item VII and VIII, pages 12 and 13.)

From experiences in recruiting minorities for Study Sections:

Dr. Dean briefly summarized the restrictions on membership to a Study Section, including: (1) at least 1 year's lapse of service between appointments; (2) with the exception of chairpersons, no unbroken service greater than four years; (3) no excessive service on Departmental committees, i.e., serving more than 8 years out of 12 in the same time period; (4) not more than 1 member from the same institution; (5) no service on two committees concurrently; (6) no more than 15 percent membership from New York, Massachusetts, California, or Texas; (7) adequate representation of women and minorities on the nomination slate for NIH clearance; (8) at least 1 year's lapse between people from the same institution; (9) only rare and special nominees at the assistant professor level or lower; and (10) not more than 25 percent Federal employees. (With DRG, not more than one member of the study section may be a Federal employee.) Items 1–5 are from the Department of Health and Human Services, 6–7 from the NIH, and 8–10 from DRG. Exceptions must be justified by a waiver, which must be approved at the level of the sources of the policy.

From NIH minority programs: the pipeline for minorities:

The statistics regarding minority science faculty are also disturbing. Dr. Walter Massey, at the National Science Foundation (NSF), indicated in the *Science* issue on Minorities that when he started at Brown University in 1970, there were 15 African-American faculty members. In 1993 that number was only 17. At the University of Chicago in 1973 there were 17 tenured or tenure track African-American faculty members; some 20 years later, only 21 out of 1,266 faculty members were African-American. African-Americans comprise just slightly over 5 percent and Hispanics only about 2.5 percent of medical school faculty in the United States. In 1987, only 1 percent of full-time faculty in the natural sciences in the United States were African-Americans, and the statistics have not improved. From these statistics, one can see that there is clearly a pipeline problem that needs fixing.

NIH has been criticized for not awarding enough grants to minority investigators. But NIH does not receive many applications from minority researchers. The low number of applications and awards to minorities is a reflection of the output of the pipeline. In 1991, based on those who reported their race, 2.9 percent of the research project grants went to under-represented minorities. Their success rate did not differ significantly from that of the general pool of applicants, but the application rate is dismal.

8. NIH FIRST AWARD (R29) GUIDELINES

FIRST AWARD

FIRST INDEPENDENT RESEARCH
SUPPORT AND TRANSITION (FIRST)
AWARD
GUIDELINES

JUNE 1992

National Institutes of Health
Public Health Service
Department of Health and Human Services

THE FIRST INDEPENDENT
RESEARCH SUPPORT AND TRANSITION (FIRST) AWARD (R29)
(This document replaces the previous September 23, 1991 announcement)

The National Institutes of Health (NIH) announces the continuing availability of the FIRST Award (R29). Based on earlier review experiences the objectives and features of the R29 mechanism are further defined and clarified.

I. Objective

The objective of the FIRST Award is to provide a sufficient period of research support for newly independent biomedical investigators to initiate their own research and demonstrate the merit of their own research ideas. These grants are intended to underwrite the first independent investigative efforts of an individual; to provide a reasonable opportunity to demonstrate creativity, productivity, and further promise; and to help in the transition to traditional types of NIH research project grants. The award is not intended for persons in mid-career who may be in transition to another endeavor. FIRST Awards generally will provide funds for 5 years during which time the newly independent investigator can establish his or her own research program and make significant and innovative contributions to laboratory or clinical science disciplines in biomedical research.

II. Eligibility

To be eligible for a FIRST Award, the proposed principal investigator (PI) must be genuinely independent of a mentor yet at the same time must be at the beginning stages of his or her research career with, for example, no more than five years research experience since completing postdoctoral research training or its equivalent. If the applicant is in the final stages of training, it is permissible to apply, but no FIRST Award will be made to persons in training status. In addition, the proposed PI must otherwise be eligible to serve in the same capacity on a traditional research project grant (R01) awarded to the applicant institution. The applicant investigator must never have been designated previously as PI on any PHS-supported research project OTHER THAN a PHS small grant (R03), an Academic Research Enhancement Award (R15) or certain research career awards (K series) directed principally to physicians, dentists or veterinarians with little research experience. (Current or past Research Career Development Awardees are not eligible.) Sub-project leaders on multicomponent awards such as Program Project grants (P01), Center grants (P50) or Minority Biomedical Research Support grants (S06) may also be eligible; however potential applicants in these categories are urged to contact the appropriate person from the awarding unit listed in VIII below. An important principle to remember with regard to eligibility is that the more extensive the prior independent research experiences, regardless of funding sources, the greater likelihood there will be diminished enthusiasm among reviewers for the FIRST Award application.

III. General features

A. Pre-Award

1. Only domestic organizations and institutions are eligible to receive FIRST Awards.
2. A FIRST Award is for a distinct research endeavor and may not be used merely to supplement or broaden an ongoing project at the applicant institution.
3. An individual may submit only one FIRST Award application to the Public Health Service (PHS) for any particular receipt date and may not submit any other type of research grant application (including research career applications) to the PHS during that particular review cycle. However, applications for an R03 and an R15 may be submitted simultaneously with a FIRST application provided they are on separate topics. Applications for other projects may be submitted while the FIRST Award is in force provided that the time and effort is less than 100% on the FIRST Award.
4. FIRST Award applications must request 5 years of research support. Applications submitted to the NIH in which the request is for less than 5 years of support will be designated as R01s and so reviewed unless the applicant withdraws the application.
5. The principal investigator must make a commitment of no less than 50% effort to the proposed project.

    Up to 100% effort may be requested if a greater commitment of the principal investigator is required to do the research. The request for effort of the applicant investigator will be reviewed and reductions may be recommended.
6. Application page limitations apply to the Research Plan (Section C) of the PHS-398 application form. Sections 1–4 of the Research Plan, as described on page 20 of the instructions for the PHS-398 (Rev. 9/91), are limited to a total of 25 pages including tables, figures and chemical structures. Applications exceeding the 25-page limitation will be returned.

    If appendix material is submitted, five collated sets must be included with the application package. Identify each of the five sets with the name of the principal investigator and the project title. This material will not be routinely duplicated and will be used in a limited way by members of the initial review group.

7. In very unusual circumstances, FIRST Awards may be recommended by the initial review group or the awarding Institute for periods of less than five years.

B. Post-Award

1. The total direct cost award for the 5-year period may not exceed $350,000. The direct cost award in any budget period should not exceed $100,000. Indirect costs will be paid to the grantee institution in accord with applicable policy of the Department of Health and Human Services (DHHS).

   The authority to carry over unobligated direct cost funds from one budget period to the subsequent one under certain conditions will be a feature of this award and may be accomplished at the discretion of the principal investigator and the grantee institution. If funds have been restricted by a specific term or condition on the Notice of Grant Award, they may not be automatically carried over without the prior approval of the awarding unit.

   Carryover is effected by notification on the financial status report, which the grantee submits within 90 days of the termination of each budget period. A revised Notice of Grant Award will not be issued to reflect the carryover. Indirect costs will be paid to the awardee institution in accord with applicable DHHS policy.

2. FIRST Awards are not renewable; however, a PI may submit a traditional research project grant (R01) application to continue and extend the research supported by a FIRST Award. In this case, the application will be considered a competing continuation (renewal) application.

3. Grantee Institutions may extend the final budget period of the project one time for a period up to one year beyond the original termination date shown on the Notice of Grant Award. Such an extension may be made only when any one of the following applies:

   a. additional time beyond the established expiration date is required to assure adequate completion of the originally approved project scope or objectives;

   b. continuity of Public Health Service (PHS) grant support is required while a competing application is under review; or

   c. the extension is necessary to permit an orderly phase-out of a project that will not receive continued support.

   The fact that funds remain at the expiration of the grant is not in itself sufficient justification for an extension without additional funds.

   The grantee institution must notify the awarding unit of the extension prior to the expiration date of the project period. Upon notification, the awarding unit will issue a revised Notice of Grant Award to change the termination date.

   Grantees may not extend project periods previously extended by the awarding unit.

4. Replacement of the PI on a FIRST Award will not be approved. Transfer of the FIRST Award with the principal investigator to another institution for the remaining performance period may be requested.

5. Except as indicated above, all relevant portions of the PHS Grant Policy Statement are applicable to these awards.

IV. Additional documentation

A. The following are to be addressed in a *letter* or memorandum from a suitable department head or dean and *should be included with the application:*

Eligibility of proposed principal investigator independently to lead a research project at the applicant institution. Is this person otherwise qualified to be the PI on a traditional research project grant (R01)?

Details of intended commitment of the institution to the project for the five-year period.

B. In addition, *three letters of reference* are needed. An applicant submitting a REVISED APPLICATION MUST AGAIN SUBMIT REFERENCE LETTERS. Reference letters must be submitted with the application. Such letters are critically important and should reflect the investigator's research originality and potential for independent investigation. When the application is from the institution where the proposed PI received postdoctoral research training, it must be made absolutely clear that the FIRST Award would be to support a research endeavor independent of that conducted in the former training environment.

FIRST applicants are to request the letters of reference well in advance of the application submission, advising the referees to return the *reference letters* to the applicant in *sealed envelopes* as soon as possible. To protect the utility and confidentiality of reference letters, *applicants are asked not to open envelopes. The sealed envelopes must be attached to the front of the original applications.* Applications received without the three reference letters will be returned to the applicant.

C. *A list of individuals providing letters of reference must be included as Section 10 of the Research Plan.* Provide the names, title, and institutional affiliation for each individual.

V. Review criteria

Review criteria and procedures are those of the regular NIH system of dual peer review: evaluation for scientific and technical merit by an initial review group (Study Section) taking into consideration the investigator's stage of development and merit of the proposed research, followed by recommendation of the cognizant national advisory council or board. In addition, the PI must demonstrate the potential to carry out independent research and clear evidence of ability to develop a sound research plan. The quality of education, scientific training, research experience, commitment to a research career, as well as the institutional commitment, will also be important in the review process.

VI. Implementation

All awarding units of the NIH are authorized to use this mechanism. It should be noted that these applications compete for funding with traditional types of NIH research project grants and that the NIH has no special set-aside funds for FIRST Awards.

VII. How to apply

A. Applicants must use the PHS-398 (Rev. 9/91) application form and must provide relevant information on eligibility. (See Section II.) The acronym "FIRST" should be typed on line 2a. and "R29" on line 2b. of the application Face page.

B. Applications must be submitted to the Division of Research Grants (DRG) in accordance with regular receipt dates. (See below.) Assignment to the most appropriate Institute and Initial Review Group will be carried out by the DRG according to established guidelines.

The following table indicates the review and award cycle dates:

Application Receipt Dates	Initial Review Dates	Council Review Dates	Earliest Start Date
February 1	June	Oct/Nov	December 1
June 1	Oct/Nov	Jan/Feb	April 1
October 1	Jan/Feb	June	July 1

VIII. Participating Institutes

Additional information may be obtained by contacting:

National Institute on Aging (NIA)
Associate Director
Office of Extramural Affairs, NIA
NIH, Gateway Bldg., Room 2C218
Bethesda, MD 20892
301-496-9322

National Institute of Allergy & Infectious Diseases (NIAID)
Deputy Director
Extramural Activities Program, NIAID
NIH, Solar Bldg., Room 4C07
Bethesda, MD 20892
301-496-7291

National Institute of Arthritis & Musculoskeletal & Skin Diseases (NIAMS)
Deputy Director
Extramural Activities Program, NIAMS
NIH, Bldg. 31, Room 4C32
Bethesda, MD 20892
301-496-0842

National Cancer Institute (NCI)
Referral Officer, NCI
EPN Rm. 636
Bethesda, MD 20892
301-496-3428

National Institute of Child Health & Human Development (NICHD)
Special Assistant to the Director, NICHD
Bldg. 31, Room 2A03, NIH
Bethesda, MD 20892
301-496-0104

National Institute of Deafness & Communication Disorders
Associate Director for Extramural Activities, NIDCD
NIH, EPS Bldg., Room 400
Bethesda, MD 20892
301-496-8693

National Institute of Dental Research (NIDR)
Director, Extramural Programs, NIDR
NIH, Westwood Bldg., Room 503
Bethesda, MD 20892
301-594-7638

National Institute of Diabetes, & Digestive & Kidney Diseases (NIDDK)
Director
Division of Extramural Activities, NIDDK
NIH, Westwood Bldg., Room 657
Bethesda, MD 20892
301-594-7527

National Institute of Environmental Health Sciences (NIEHS)
Science Administrator
Division of Extramural Research and Training, NIEHS
P.O. Box 12233
Research Triangle Park, NC 27709
919-541-7723

National Eye Institute (NEI)
Extramural and Collaborative Program, NEI
Bldg. 31, Room 6A04, NIH
Bethesda, MD 20892
301-496-9110

National Institute of General Medical Sciences (NIGMS)
Deputy Associate Director
Office of Program Activities, NIGMS
NIH, Westwood Bldg., Room 938
Bethesda, MD 20892
301-594-7751

National Heart, Lung, and Blood Institute (NHLBI)
Deputy Director
Division of Extramural Affairs, NHLBI
NIH, Westwood Bldg., Room 7A17
Bethesda, MD 20892
301-594-7454

National Library of Medicine (NLM)
Extramural Programs, NLM
Bldg. 38A, Room 5N505
Bethesda, MD 20892
301-496-4621

National Institute of Neurological Disorders and Stroke (NINDS)
Deputy Director
Extramural Activities Program, NINDS
NIH, Federal Bldg., Room 1016A
Bethesda, MD 20892
301-496-9248

National Center for Human Genome Research (NCHGR)
Chief
Research Grants Branch, NCHGR
NIH, Bldg. 38A, Room 605
Bethesda, MD 20894
301-496-0844

National Institute for Nursing Research (NINR)
Director
Division of Extramural Programs, NINR
NIH, Bldg. 31, Room 5B03
Bethesda, MD 20892
301-496-0523

National Center for Research Resources (NCRR)
Deputy Director for Extramural Resources, DRR
Bldg. 12A, Room 4007
Bethesda, MD 20892
301-496-6023

Prepared by
GRANTS INQUIRIES OFFICE
DIVISION OF RESEARCH GRANTS
NATIONAL INSTITUTES OF HEALTH

9. REVIEWER GUIDANCE FOR TRIAL TO IDENTIFY HIGH RISK/HIGH IMPACT RESEARCH APPLICATIONS (HR/HI)

This document was issued by NIH DRG on June 7, 1994.

Background

The NIH system for identifying the most meritorious and scientifically sound research applications and selecting from them those which are offered support, has been criticized as too conservative and ignoring new and exciting research ideas. The contrary view, one held by many study section, review committee, and Council/Board members, is that these risky but potentially exciting research projects are routinely identified in the standard review process, and their special characteristics are routinely considered when scientific and technical merit is assessed by Initial Review Groups (IRGs). Unfortunately, there are very few data to support either position.

In a trial beginning with study section meetings in June/July 1994, those applications which involve high risk research with the potential for high scientific impact, i.e., High Risk/High Impact (HR/HI) research applications will be identified. Scientific Review Administrators (SRAs) will document such a finding in a special section of the summary statement for the attention of councils and program staff.

HR/HI identification may also be made by program staff and Council/Boards subsequent to the initial review process. Thus, by attending IRG meetings, program staff will have an opportunity to hear relevant discussions and provide information at later stages of review within the Institute or Center (IC) and by the Council/Board. Program staff should be able to discuss, for example, why the IRG might not have made the HR/HI designation initially. For all levels of HR/HI designation, the program staff will be the contact point in follow-up with the applicant.

Clearly, identifying a project as HR/HI is no guarantee that it will have a greater chance to be funded. However, it may provide the NIH a better sense of the risks and promises of projects when funding decisions are made.

The first set of applications from the trial procedure will be presented to councils in September/October of 1994. After three review rounds, a determination will be made as to whether changes in process are needed and whether, or to what extent, this procedure should be implemented NIH-wide.

Objectives of the trial

The goal of this trial is to determine on a limited basis, whether:

1. IRGs can identify HR/HI applications;
2. Councils can provide oversight by evaluating IRG findings or independently identify additional applications; and
3. Program staff will find such information useful.

Summary of HR/HI procedures

HR/HI research projects are not expected to be identified at a high frequency, nor are investigators likely to self-identify their projects as high risk.

1. In preparing reviewer comments prior to the meeting please determine if the research plan meets the criteria for designation as HR/HI.
2. At the meeting, the recommendation for this designation must not be introduced into the discussion of the scientific merit of the research plan. Thus, the assigned reviewers and readers will present their critiques, followed by a discussion of the scientific merit, assignment of the priority score and determination of the appropriateness of the budget. The discussion to recommend identification as HR/HI will come <u>after</u> the merit review and assignment of priority scores.
3. For an HR/HI designation the agreement of at least two members of the IRG is required.

Criteria for HR/HI designation

A given project could have either high risk, high impact, or both, but it is the combination that is critical for this trial. It is obvious that the application identified as high risk without a potential for high scientific impact is a poor candidate for support, and the application without high risk but with a potential for high impact is an excellent candidate. What is of interest here are research grant applications with both characteristics, some of which could be lost to conservatism and might deserve special consideration for funding.

Examples of HR/HI research:

- If the investigator is correct, the hypothesis would cause a "paradigm shift" for this area of science.
- Results of these studies might well revolutionize current concepts.
- This new approach, though risky and speculative, would be a major contribution if it were feasible.
- This new and/or unusual approach is fraught with uncertainty; however, if successful it would remove a significant obstacle to progress.

Examples of research which should NOT be designated as HR/HI:

- Proposed studies are novel.
- Proposed approach is promising and well-considered.
- Ideas presented are exciting, there is confidence that the studies will result in meaningful data.
- Good data and excellent progress give increasing evidence that this new concept is valid.
- This unusual research investigation is not well planned or justified and, even if successful, will not have much significance.

---

10. EXAMPLE OF AN NIH STUDY SECTION AGENDA

XYZ STUDY SECTION MEETING

ABC INN
ROCKVILLE, MARYLAND
JUNE X–Y, 199X

AGENDA

June X	8:00 A.M.	Open Meeting
		Introduction of new members
		Administrative Report
		Minutes of the previous meeting
		Confirmation of dates of future meetings
		Other business
	8:45 A.M.	Meeting Closed to Public*
		Review of Applications

Schedule for each day, times approximate:

8:00 A.M.	Review of applications: approximately in alphabetical order
10:30	Coffee break
10:50	Continue reviews
12:30 P.M.	Lunch
1:30	Continue reviews
4:00	Break
4:20	Continue reviews
6:00 P.M.	Adjourn

NEXT MEETINGS: October X–Y, 199X, February X–Y and June X–Y, 199Y.

---

* Closed to the public, in accordance with the provisions set forth in sections 552b(c)(4) and 552(c)(6), Title 5, U.S.C. and Section 10(d) of Public Law 92-463.

E. ILLUSTRATIONS

| FROM | IRG: (VR)
Virology Study Section
Dr. Stephanie Administrator, SRA
DRG/National Institutes of Health
RM A24, 5333 Westbard Avenue
Bethesda, MD 20892 (301)594-0012 | U.S. Mail
Postage & Fees Paid
U.S. Dept. of H.H.S.
HHS 396 |

1/22/94

A grant application has been received by NIH and assigned to an Initial Review Group (IRG) for scientific merit evaluation and to an Institute for funding consideration. The initial peer review should be completed by 03/94 and a funding decision should be made shortly after a the appropriate national advisory group meets in 05/94. For questions about the assignment, contact the referral office (301) 594-1234. For questions prior to the review, contact the IRG Scientific Review Administrator (SRA) or the individual listed above. For questions after the review, contact the institute listed below.

PRINCIPAL INVESTIGATOR: Alicia X. Scientist, PhD   COUNCIL: 05/94
TITLE: Targeted Eradication of XYZ-Infected Cells
ASSIGNMENT NUMBER: 2R01_____-04A2 IRG: Virology

| Nat'l Inst Allergy/Infectious Dis
Extramural Activities WW703
National Institutes of Health
Bethesda, MD 20892 (301) 496-7291 | TO | Alicia X. Scientist, PhD
Department of Cell Biology
University of America
Anytown, CA 94220 |

Fig. A1-1. NIH first snap-out mailer (Study Section Assignment). You should receive this mailer within 6 weeks of submitting the application.

| FROM | Ashley Administrator, PhD
Bacterial Pathogenesis
Bacteriology and Mycology Branch
DMID-NIAID
NIH Bethesda, MD 20892
(301) 594-7728 |

03/09/94

The first phase of the peer review of your application (2R01_____-04A2) is complete. The Initial Review Group (IRG) accorded your application a PRIORITY SCORE of 363. The PERCENTILE SCORE is 73.8. This initial information will be followed in about 6-8 weeks by the IRG Summary Statement, which will contain specific evaluative comments and budget recommendations. Until then, no additional information will be available. After you receive your Summary Statement you may contact me to discuss the possibility of funding, or for advice on revising/resubmitting your application. Should a revised application be indicated, it must respond specifically to the critical comments in the Summary Statement, as detailed in the instructions for form PHS 398, or it will be returned without review.

| TO | Alicia X. Scientist, PhD
Department of Cell Biology
University of America
Anytown, CA 94220 |

Fig. A1-2. NIH second snap-out mailer (priority score/percentile). You should receive this mailer about 2 weeks after the Study Section meeting.

1. DATE ISSUED *(Mo./Day/Yr.)* 01/30/93	2. CFDA NO. 93 361		DEPARTMENT OF HEALTH AND HUMAN SERVICES

3. SUPERSEDES AWARD NOTICE dated ___ except that any additions or restrictions previously imposed remain in effect unless specifically rescinded.

PUBLIC HEALTH SERVICE

NATIONAL INSTITUTES OF HEALTH
NATIONAL CENTER FOR NURSING RESEARCH
NOTICE OF GRANT AWARD
AUTHORIZATION *(Legislation/Regulation)*

4. GRANT NO. 1 R01 NR03047-01A1 Formerly:	5. ADMINISTRATIVE CODES AC3

42 USC 241   42 CFR 52

6. PROJECT PERIOD *Mo./Day/Yr.* From 02/01/93	Through 01/31/96

RESEARCH

7. BUDGET PERIOD *Mo./Day/Yr.* From 02/01/93	Through 01/31/94

8. TITLE OF PROJECT (OR PROGRAM) *(Limit to 56 spaces)*
ADAPTATION TO THE INTERNAL CARDIOVERTER DEFIBRILLATOR   NURS

9. GRANTEE NAME AND ADDRESS

a. PINE VALLEY UNIVERSITY
1207 RIVER ROAD
b. PINE VALLEY, PA 12345

10. DIRECTOR OF PROJECT *(PROGRAM DIRECTOR / PRINCIPAL INVESTIGATOR) (LAST NAME FIRST AND ADDRESS)*

MARTIN, RUTH B.   DSN
PINE VALLEY UNIVERSITY
CHARLES TYLER SCH OF NURSING
1207 RIVER ROAD
PINE VALLEY, PA 12345

JAN 27 1993

11. APPROVED BUDGET *(Excludes PHS Direct Assistance)*

I   PHS Grant Funds Only

II Total project costs including grant funds and all other financial participation   [I]

(Select one and place NUMERAL in box.)

a. Salaries and Wages ...... $ 77.538	
b. Fringe Benefits .... $ 17.997	
c. Total Personnel Costs .... $	95.535
d. Consultant Costs	3.980
e. Equipment	6.300
f. Supplies	9.570
g. Travel	1.560
h. Patient Care—Inpatient	0
i. —Outpatient	0
j. Alterations and Renovations	0
k. Other	6.602
l. Consortium/Contractual Costs	147.490
m. Trainee Related Expenses	
n. Trainee Stipends	0
o. Trainee Tuition and Fees	0
p. Trainee Travel	0
q. TOTAL DIRECT COSTS ➡	$ 271.037
r. INDIRECT COSTS (Rate ___ % of S&W/TADC)	$ 95.331
s. TOTAL APPROVED BUDGET	$ 366.368
t. SBIR Fee	$ 0
u. Federal Share	$ 366.368
v. Non-Federal Share	$

12. AWARD COMPUTATION FOR FINANCIAL ASSISTANCE

a. Amount of PHS Financial Assistance *(from Item 11.u.)* .... $	366.368
b. Less Unobligated Balance From Prior Budget Periods .... $	0
c. Less Cumulative Prior Award(s) This Budget Period .... $	0
d. AMOUNT OF FINANCIAL ASSISTANCE THIS ACTION .... $	366.368

13. RECOMMENDED FUTURE SUPPORT *(SUBJECT TO THE AVAILABILITY OF FUNDS AND SATISFACTORY PROGRESS OF THE PROJECT):*

YEAR	TOTAL DIRECT COSTS / STIPENDS	YEAR	TOTAL DIRECT COSTS / STIPENDS
a. 02	305.539	d.	0
b. 03	286.586	e.	0
c.	0	f.	0

14. APPROVED DIRECT ASSISTANCE BUDGET *(IN LIEU OF CASH):*

a. Amount of PHS Direct Assistance .... $	
b. Less Unobligated Balance From Prior Budget Periods ... $	
c. Less Cumulative Prior Award(s) This Budget Period ... $	
d. AMOUNT OF DIRECT ASSISTANCE THIS ACTION ...... $	

15. PROGRAM INCOME SUBJECT TO 45 CFR PART 74, SUBPART F, OR 45 CFR 92.25, SHALL BE USED IN ACCORD WITH ONE OF THE FOLLOWING ALTERNATIVES: (Select One and Place LETTER in box.)

a. DEDUCTION
b. ADDITIONAL COSTS
c. MATCHING   [B]
d. OTHER RESEARCH *(Add / Deduct Option)*
e. OTHER *(See REMARKS)*

16. THIS AWARD IS BASED ON AN APPLICATION SUBMITTED TO, AND AS APPROVED BY, THE PHS ON THE ABOVE TITLED PROJECT AND IS SUBJECT TO THE TERMS AND CONDITIONS INCORPORATED EITHER DIRECTLY OR BY REFERENCE IN THE FOLLOWING:
a. The grant program legislation cited above.   b. The grant program regulation cited above.
c. This award notice including terms and conditions, if any, noted below under REMARKS.
d. PHS Grants Policy Statement including addenda in effect as of the beginning date of the budget period.
e. 45 CFR Part 74 or 45 CFR Part 92 as applicable.
In the event there are conflicting or otherwise inconsistent policies applicable to the grant, the above order of precedence shall prevail. Acceptance of the grant terms and conditions is acknowledged by the grantee when funds are drawn or otherwise obtained from the grant payment system.

REMARKS: *(Other Terms and Conditions Attached –* [X] Yes [ ] No *)*

GRANT SPECIALIST: NANCY D. CURLING, (301) 496-0237
PROGRAM OFFICIAL: DR. MARY D. LUCAS (301) 402-3290

BASE X RATE ($ 167.247 x 57.00)

THIS GRANT IS AWARDED UNDER TERMS AND CONDITIONS OF THE FED. DEMO. PROJECT.

PHS GRANTS MANAGEMENT OFFICER: *(Signature)* *Sally A. Nichols*	*(Name-Typed/Print)* SALLY A. NICHOLS	*(Title)* GRANTS MANAGEMENT OFFICER

17. OBJ. CLASS. 41.4A	18. CRS - EIN 1580566256A1	19. LIST NO.:

	FY-CAN	DOCUMENT NO.	ADMINISTRATIVE CODE	AMT. ACTION FIN. ASST.	AMT. ACTION DIR. ASST.
20. a. 93 8426901	b. R1NR03047A	c.	d.	e.
21. a.	b.	c.	d.	e.
22. a.	b.	c.	d.	e.

PHS-5152-1 (Rev. 7/92)   *(Note: See reverse for payment information.)*   135

Fig. A1-3A. NIH Notice of Grant Award, page 1. The grant award notice may have more than 2 pages, for example, if there are budgets for subcontracts.

```
                    PAGE TWO

                    TERMS OF AWARD


        GRANT NUMBER   1 R01 NR87654-01A1
GRANTEE INSTITUTION    PINE VALLEY UNIVERSITY
               P.I.    RUTH B. MARTIN
                       YEAR 1      YEAR 2      YEAR 3
=====================================================
Salaries               77,538      99,509     101,144
Fringe Benefits        17,997      23,342      23,725
PERSONNEL              95,535     122,851     124,869
CONSULTANTS             3,980       4,053       3,248
EQUIPMENT               6,300           0           0
SUPPLIES                9,570       5,790       3,290
TRAVEL, D.              1,560       3,200       1,700
TRAVEL, F.                  0           0           0
INPATIENT                   0           0           0
OUTPATIENT                  0           0           0
ALTERATIONS                 0           0           0
THIRD PARTY-DC        100,957     111,817     102,056
THIRD PARTY-IC         46,533      51,859      47,486
OTHER                   6,602       5,969       3,937
-----------------------------------------------------
TOTAL DIRECT COSTS    271,037     305,539     286,586
```

THIS AWARD REFLECTS THE BUDGET AND THE BUDGET PERIOD NEGOTIATED
BETWEEN NANCY CURLING OF THE NATIONAL CENTER FOR NURSING RESERCH
AND RUTH B. MARTIN ON JANUARY 7, 1993.

THREE COPIES OF ANY REPRINTS OF PUBLICATIONS NOT PREVIOUSLY SUBMITTED
SHOULD ACCOMPANY THE ANNUAL PROGRESS REPORT.

INDIRECT COSTS FOR _____ UNIVERSITY AND THE UNIVERSITY OF _____ ARE
AWARDED AS DIRECT COSTS AND ARE BASED ON THE APPROVED BUDGET USING THE
THIRD PARTY'S NEGOTIATED INDIRECT COST RATES AVAILABLE AT THE TIME OF
AWARD. THE AMOUNT OF INDIRECT COSTS CHARGED MUST BE BASED UPON ACTUAL
DIRECT COST EXPENDITURES, BUT IS LIMITED TO THE AMOUNT AWARDED. NO
ADDITIONAL FUNDS WILL BE AWARDED FOR INDIRECT COSTS TO _____ UNIVERSITY
AND THE UNIVERSITY OF _____ .

Fig. A1-3B. NIH Notice of Grant Award, page 2.

F. ORGANIZATIONAL STRUCTURE DIAGRAMS

Department of Health and Human Services:
A Department of the Executive Branch of the U.S. Government.

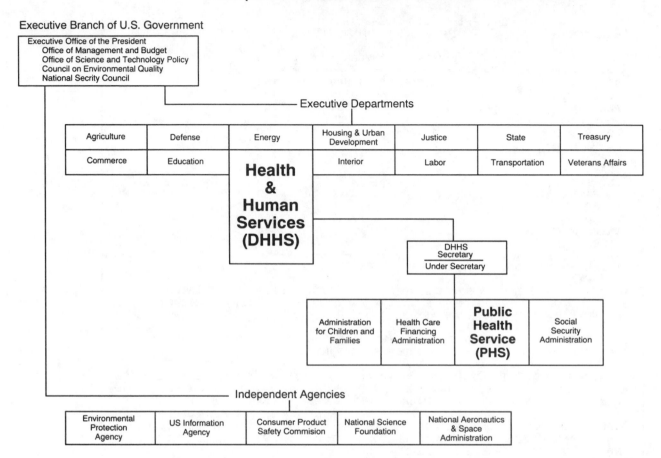

Fig. A1-4. Department of Health and Human Services (DHHS) showing the agencies that make up the DHHS and where the DHHS fits into the structure of the U.S. government.

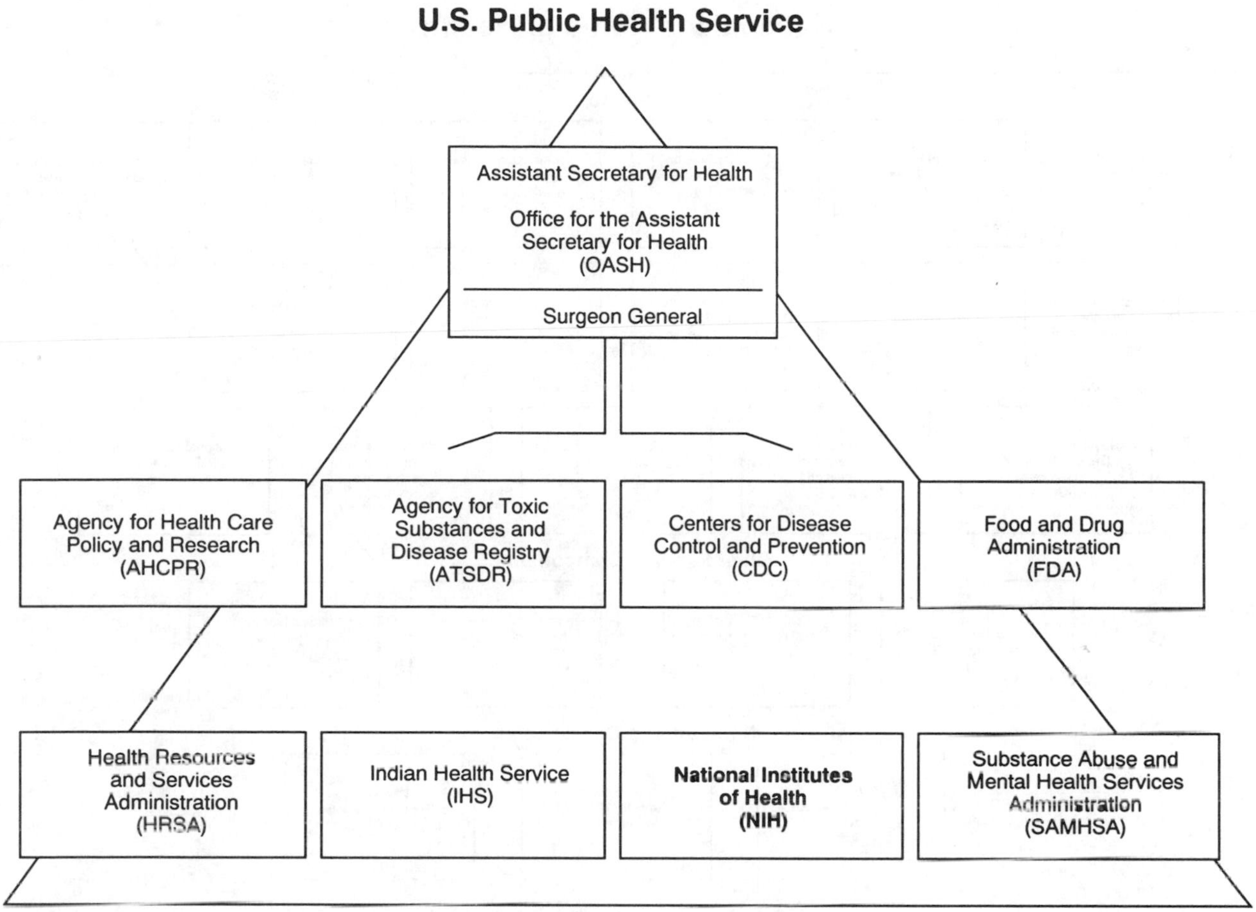

U.S. Public Health Service

Fig. A1-5. Public Health Service (PHS) showing the agencies that make up the PHS and where NIH fits into the PHS.

National Institutes of Health

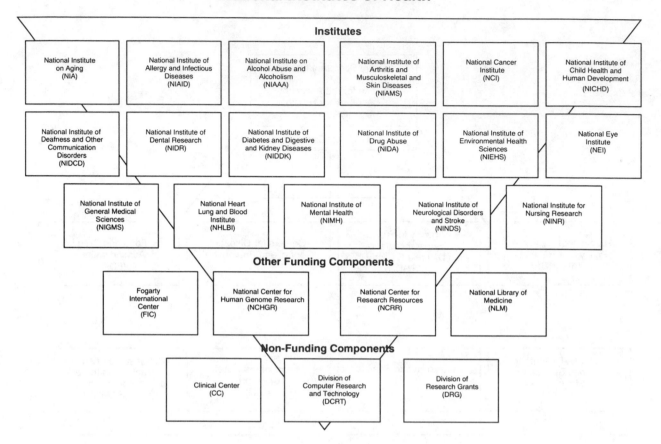

Fig. A1-6. National Institutes of Health (NIH) showing the Institutes and other components. Note that the 3 Institutes (NIAAA, NIDA, and NIMH) that moved from ADAMHA to NIH in 1992, are included.

NIH Division of Research Grants (DRG)

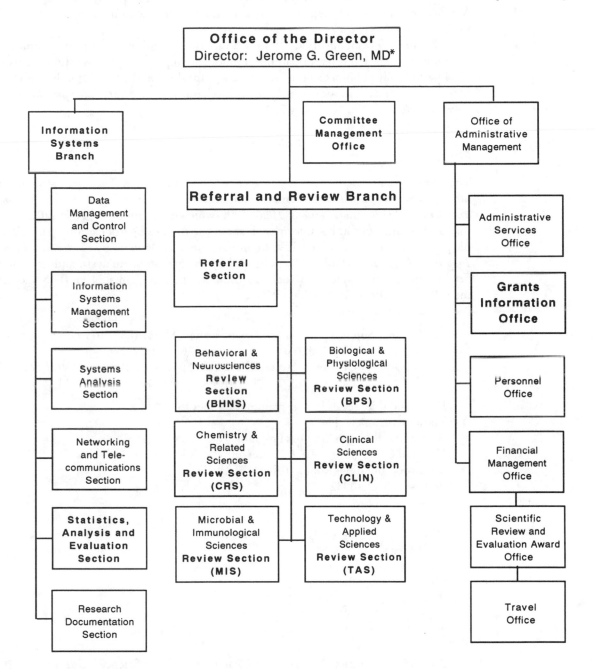

Fig. A1-7. National Institutes of Health, Division of Research Grants (NIH/DRG), showing the Referral and Review Sections. This organizational diagram is adapted from the diagram of DRG in the brochure entitled *DRG Organization & Functions,* published by NIH/DRG, July 1993. The 6 Review Sections shown in the center of the diagram are those that resulted from the early 1994 reorganization of DRG. * Dr. Green retired in March 1995.

G. Some NIH Awards

A variety of awards and their deadline receipt dates are listed on pages 6 and 7 of the PHS-398 (rev. 9/91) packet.

The funding components at NIH use a variety of award mechanisms to support extramural research. However, not all the components support all the award mechanisms. NIH periodically publishes a list of activity codes for the awards. This list indicates which funding components support which award mechanisms. See *NIH Guide for Grants and Contracts*, Vol. 23, No. 1, January 7, 1994.

For minorities

There are also a number of minority-targeted grant opportunities. These are listed, among other places, on pp. 110–111 of an NIH publication, *DRG Peer Review Trends: Workload and Actions of DRG Study Sections, 1980–1990,* which is put out by the NIH DRG Information Systems Branch. For information about the trends of participation by racial/ethnic groups in competition for NIH extramural grants see *Minorities in Extramural Grant Programs: Fiscal Year 1982–1991*, published by the Statistics, Analysis, and Evaluation Section, Information Systems Branch, Division of Research Grants, NIH. (U.S. Government Printing Office: 1993—351-597).

See also announcements about:

1. Research Supplements for Underrepresented Minorities, *NIH Guide for Grants and Contracts*, Vol. 22, No. 43, November 26, 1993, pages 2–11.
2. Minority High School Student Research Apprentice Program, *NIH Guide for Grants and Contracts*, Vol. 22, No. 35, October 1, 1993, pages 9–11, or call:

Direct inquiries regarding programmatic issues to:
Marjorie A. Tingle, Ph.D.
Biomedical Research Support Program
National Center for Research Resources
Westwood Building, Room 10A–11
Bethesda, MD 20982
301-594-7947

Direct inquiries regarding fiscal matters to:
Ms. Mary V. Niemiec
Office of Grants and Contracts Management
National Center for Research Resources
Westwood Building, Room 849
Bethesda, MD 20982
301-594-7955

See also: "Minorities '93: Trying to Change the Face of Science," *Science*, Vol. 262, No. 5136, November 12, 1993.

Also note the availability of *Minority On-Line Information System (MOLIS)*, an on-line database retrieval system for information about 104 historically Black colleges and universities and 32 Hispanic-serving institutions. The information provided is in the following categories: research centers and equipment, pre-college programs, education programs, scholarships and fellowships, faculty profiles, etc. The service is operated by a private company, Federal Information Exchange, Inc., but is financially supported by a coalition of Federal agencies. The service is free and can be accessed directly via modem (1-800-783-3349, 1-800-232-4879; within Maryland, call: 301-258-0953) or via the Internet. For information and a free User Guide, call 301-975-0103, fax to 301-975-0109, or write to Federal Information Exchange, 555 Quince Orchard Rd., Suite 200, Gaithersburg, MD 20878.

For women

For information about the trends of participation by women in competition for NIH extramural grants see *Women in Extramural Grant Programs: Fiscal Year 1982–1991*, published by the Statistics, Analysis, and Evaluation Section, Information Systems Branch, Division of Research Grants, NIH.

For novice PIs and/or new projects

For additional information about any of the NIH Grant Programs listed below, or about other NIH grant programs, contact the Grants Information Office, Division of Research Grants (DRG), NIH, 5333 Westbard Ave., Bethesda, MD 20892, 301-594-7248; Fax: 301-594-7384.

NIH publishes a booklet, *Activity Codes, Organization Codes, and Definitions Used in Extramural Programs* (latest edition: September, 1992 was edited by E. Farley, 1-301-594-7296; editor for next edition: Felicia Shingler, 1-301-594-7255). The booklet may be obtained by calling 301-402-0168.

NIH also publishes brochures about specific programs. For example, the Grants Information Office publishes a 158-page booklet about the K Awards.

Another useful resource is Samuel M. Schwartz and Mischa E. Friedman, *A Guide to NIH Grant Programs,* Oxford University Press, New York, 1992, Appendix 2 and 3.

NIH FIRST Award (R29)

(see also Appendix I-D-8)

- NIH established the FIRST Award to provide newly independent investigators with research support that will permit them to initiate their own research programs and demonstrate the merit of their own research projects. The award is intended as a transition to more traditional forms of support such as by R01 grants.
- The FIRST Award is *not* intended for mid-career scientists who want to change field, is available only to domestic organizations, and may *not* be used to supplement funds for projects already supported by other funds.
- Principal Investigators must generally be less than 5 years past post-doctoral training and must never have been a Principal Investigator (PI) on a regular NIH research grant.
- Applicants may apply during the final stages of training but may not receive awards while still in training status.
- *No* sponsor is required, but the applicant must provide 3 letters of reference and 1 letter or memo from the department head or dean at the sponsoring institution.
  — Letters of reference
    • Get letters from relatively senior people if possible.
    • It's good to get a letter from the person with whom you trained most recently.

If you are applying from the same institution where you have just finished training, your ex-mentor must assure that you will now be independent of her/him and must spell out who will do what if you will continue to work on the same project.

- Submit the letters with your application (after Section 9 of the research plan).

—Letter or memo from department head or dean at the sponsoring institution that attests that:

- You are now an independent researcher, eligible to conduct—and capable of conducting—independent research.
- The institution is committed to supporting your research efforts if you receive funding.

- Provides funds, not to exceed $350,000 (in direct costs) for 5 years; direct costs may not exceed $100,000 in any budget year.
- The PI must commit at least 50% time and effort to the project funded by the FIRST Award.
- The FIRST Award is *not* renewable.
- Potential applicants should call the relevant contact person listed at the end of the R29 Guidelines, available from the Office of Grants Inquiries (301-594-7248), and reproduced in Appendix I-D-8.

NIH pilot projects or feasibility studies (R21)

- Usually solicited by program announcement in the *NIH Guide to Grants and Contracts.*
- To support conceptually creative, novel, high-risk/high-payoff, scientifically sound research that may produce innovative advances in science or improve human health but may not be developed sufficiently to compete as a standard R01 application.
- Awards generally limited to $50,000 per year for a maximum of 2 years.

NIH small grants programs (R03)

- Available only through those Institutes/funding components that have announced sponsorship of this program
- Funds are for pilot studies, tentative ideas, high-risk projects not yet ready for the R01 mechanism of funding.
- Funding is for 1 to 2 years and is nonrenewable.
- Maximum award is $50,000 in direct costs.
- Number of copies of the application to be submitted and application due dates vary with the sponsoring Institutes/funding components.
- Some Institutes/funding components have different page limits for the Small Grants Program—even though the PHS-398 is used for the application.
- Some Institutes/funding components have an expedited review procedure for the Small Grants Program.
- R03 applications may or may not be reviewed by Division of Research Grants Study Sections and may or may not go to Council for the second level of review. For example, at the National Heart, Lung, and Blood Institute (NHLBI), small grant applications are reviewed for scientific merit by a committee convened by the Division of Extramural Affairs within NHLBI, and the second level of review is conducted by NHLBI senior program staff.

NIH Academic Research Enhancement (AREA) Award (R15)

- To stimulate research in educational institutions that award degrees to a significant number of potential research scientists but that have in the past not been major recipients of NIH awards.
- To support new or expanded health-related research projects by faculty in such institutions
- Eligible institutions: Accredited domestic health professional schools and other academic institutions offering baccalaureate or advanced degrees in the sciences related to health
- Preference is given to applications submitted by institutions that have granted baccalaureate degrees to 25 or more students who have gone on to obtain academic or professional doctoral degrees in the health-related sciences in the period 1983–1992.
- Eligible minority and women's educational institutions are encouraged to participate in the program.
- Eligible institutions must have received less than $2 million in research grants and/or cooperative agreements (direct and indirect costs) in 4 or more years between FY 1986 and FY 1992.
- Area grants may be used for:
    - —Pilot research projects and feasibility studies
    - —Development, testing, and refinement of research techniques
    - —Secondary analysis of available data sets
    - —Other similar discrete research projects that demonstrate research capability
- PI may not have any other NIH support at the time of award of the AREA grant.
- AREA grants are not renewable for the same project.
- About 130 AREA grants totaling $13 million were awarded in 1993.
- There is one receipt date for submission of AREA grant applications, usually in June.

Contact the Grants Information Office (301-594-7248) for AREA Program Guidelines. For additional information, contact Research Training and Special Programs Office, NIH, Bldg. 31, Room 5B44, Bethesda, MD 20892, 301-496-1968; Fax: 301-496-0166.

Small Business Innovation Research (SBIR) Grant (At NIH: R43, R44)

SBIR grants are available to small businesses that can meet federal research and development needs. To be eligible, (1) a small business concern must have 500 or fewer employees, (2) the business must be at least 51% owned by U.S. citizens or lawfully admitted resident aliens, and (3) a specified fraction of the grant project must be carried out at the small company (approximately two-thirds in Phase I; one-half in Phase II).

The grants are administered under the overall policy guidance of the Small Business Administration (SBA) and are intended to (1) stimulate technological innovation, (2) increase private sector commercialization of innovations derived from federal research and development, and (3) foster and encourage participation in technological innovation by small business concerns owned by women and socially and economically disadvantaged persons.

Federal government agencies with research—or Research and Development (R&D)—budgets in excess of $100 million are required, under the Small Business Research and Development Enhancement Act of 1992,[11] to establish SBIR Programs to sup-

---

[11] PL 102-564 (10/28/92). The program began with the Small Business Innovation Research Development Act of 1982.

port cutting-edge research and development on the nation's most pressing scientific and engineering problems.

Awards are made in fields spanning the entire spectrum of federal research and development, for example, advanced composite materials, agriculture, aquaculture, avionics, bioremediation, education, energy, environmental monitoring, manufacturing process control, medical devices, navigation, optical computing, parallel processing software, space propulsion systems, and transportation.

Funding is derived from a fixed percentage of each participating agency's R&D budget. In 1993, 11 agencies participated: the departments of Agriculture, Commerce, Defense, Education, Energy, Health and Human Services, and Transportation, the Environmental Protection Agency (EPA); the National Aeronautics and Space Administration (NASA); the National Science Foundation (NSF); and the Nuclear Regulatory Commission (NRC). The agencies involved in the SBIR Program have discretion in the administration and funding levels of awards.

The SBIR Program consists of 3 phases. Awards are announced annually and vary with the funding agency. The *award amounts indicated below are for DHHS (NIH)* for the 1993 calendar year *receipt* dates of April 15, August 15, and December 15.

- Phase I (R43):
    —To evaluate/establish the technical merit and feasibility of research and development ideas that may ultimately lead to a commercial product or service
    —Federally funded
    —Awards: up to $75,000[12] (for direct plus indirect costs) plus a fixed fee for a 6-month period
- Phase II (R44):
    —Only applicants who have received Phase I support may apply for a Phase II grant.
    —To support in-depth development of research and development ideas whose feasibility has been established in Phase I and that are likely to result in commercial products or services
    —Federally funded
    —Awards normally provide up to $500,000[13] (for direct plus indirect costs) plus a fixed fee for a performance period generally not to exceed 2 years. [For some fully justified awards for projects involving clinical trials, clinical evaluations, requirements imposed by the FDA, or special equipment, the NIH Phase II award may be as high as $600,000 (for direct plus indirect costs) plus a fixed fee.]
- Phase III:
    —To pursue the commercial application of the research and development supported by Federal funds in Phase I and II
    —Funded by nonfederal sources.
    —In some federal agencies, Phase III may involve follow-on non-SBIR-funded R&D or production contracts for products or processes intended for use by the U.S. government.

The NIH SBIR grant application forms are PHS-6246-1 for Phase I and 6246-2 for Phase II. The application forms are included in the PHS solicitation documents.

---

[12] Note that the figures given here are for NIH SBIR. The amounts of the awards vary from agency to agency but may not exceed $100,000 for Phase I.

[13] Note that the figures given here are for NIH SBIR. The amounts of the awards vary from agency to agency but may not exceed $750,000 for Phase II.

Note that NIH SBIR Contracts are also available (Phase I: N43; Phase II: N44), as are NIH SBIR Cooperative Agreements (Phase I: U43; Phase II: U44)

To keep informed about the details of upcoming SBIR program solicitations, get on the mailing list for the quarterly SBA pre-solicitation announcement:

Office of Innovation, Research and Technology
U.S. Small Business Administration
409 3rd Street, SW (6th Floor)
Washington, DC 20416
202-205-7777

Technical abstracts of SBIR awards are cataloged in the Federal Research in Progress (FEDRIP) database, which is available on-line through the U.S. Department of Commerce, National Technical Information Service (NTIS) via DIALOG, a private information service. About 10,000 projects are in the database. This includes all SBIR awards since the beginning of the SBIR Program in 1983, except Phase I awardees that do not go on to Phase II within 3 years, which are deleted from the system.

For information about NTIS, contact National Technical Information Service, U.S. Department of Commerce, Springfield, VA 22161, 1-800-553-6847; 703-487-4600.

For information about DIALOG, call 1-800-334-2564.

To receive a free copy of the FEDRIP Search Guide, call 703-487-4650; ask for PR 847.

Periodic conferences to help familiarize potential applicants with the SBIR Program are held in major cities. These conferences also present an opportunity for small business personnel to meet representatives of large corporations who attend the meetings. Topics include, for example:[14]

- Starting and financing the small high-tech firm
- Understanding government accounting requirements
- Creating and managing a joint venture
- Negotiating an SBIR contract
- Marketing techniques for small high-tech firms
- Planning for government audits
- Developing effective high-tech business plans
- Understanding federal procurement regulations
- Patents and nondisclosure agreements
- Financing via SBIR Phase III commitments
- International market opportunities
- SBIR proposal preparation
- U.S. and foreign licensing
- Seeking venture capital
- Finding corporate partners and closing the deal

For information about the conferences, contact Department of Defense/National Science Foundation, National SBIR Conferences (NSBIR), 1201 East Abington Drive, Suite 400, Alexandria, VA 22314. Conferences are run by Foresight Science and Technology, Inc., 6064 Okeechobee Blvd., P.O. Box 170569, West Palm Beach, FL 33417. There is a hotline to call for further information, 407-791-0720; Fax: 407-791-0098.

---

[14] These topics are from the 1993–1994 SBIR Conference announcement.

Small Business Technology Transfer Program (STTR)

STTR grants are designed to support small business concerns doing cutting-edge research and development on the nation's most pressing scientific and engineering problems who wish to enter into partnerships with research centers at universities and private research institutions. Eligibility for the small business concern is as described above for the SBIR program except that at least 40% of the project must be performed by the small business and at least 30% of the project must be performed by the research institution.

The grants are administered under the overall policy guidance of the SBA.

Federal government agencies with research or Research and Development (R&D) budgets in excess of $1 billion are required to establish STTR Programs. The SBA's STTR Program Policy Directive was published in the Federal Register on Tuesday, August 10, 1993, Vol. 58, No. 152, beginning at page 42607.

Awards are made in fields spanning the entire spectrum of federal research and development, as described above for the SBIR Program.

Funding is derived from a fixed percentage of each participating agency's R&D budget. For Fiscal Year 1994, 5 agencies will be participating: the departments of Defense, Energy, and Health and Human Services, the National Aeronautics and Space Administration (NASA), and the National Science Foundation (NSF). The agencies involved in the STTR Program have discretion in the administration and funding levels of awards.

The STTR Program, which consists of 3 phases, is a pilot program scheduled to begin in fiscal year 1994. NIH will award only Phase I awards (about 40) in fiscal year 1994. Future awards will be announced.

- Phase I (R41):
  —To establish the technical merit and feasibility of ideas that have potential for commercialization
  —Federally funded
  —Award level and time: up to $100,000 (direct costs plus indirect costs plus a negotiated fixed fee) for a period normally not to exceed 1 year
- Phase II (R42):
  —Only applicants who have received Phase I support may apply for a Phase II grant.
  —To support in-depth development of cooperative research and development projects between small business concerns and research institutions, the feasibility of which have been established in Phase I and that have potential for commercialization
  —Federally funded
  —Award level and time: up to $500,000 (direct costs plus indirect costs plus a negotiated fixed fee) for a period normally not to exceed 2 years
- Phase III:
  —To pursue (generally with the use of nonfederal funds) the commercialization of the results of the research or R&D funded in Phases I and II
  —In some federal agencies, Phase III may involve follow-on non-STTR-funded R&D or production contracts for products or processes intended for use by the U.S. government.

The NIH STTR grant application forms are PHS-6246-1 for Phase I and 6246-2 for Phase II (the same forms as for the SBIR grant application). The application forms are included in the PHS solicitation documents.

To obtain a copy of the NIH STTR Program Solicitation, contact:

Massachusetts Technological Laboratory, Inc.
13687 Baltimore Ave.
Laurel, MD 20707
301-206-9385
Fax: 301-206-9722

To keep informed about the details of upcoming STTR program solicitations, get on the mailing list for the quarterly SBA pre-solicitation announcement:

Office of Innovation, Research and Technology
U.S. Small Business Administration
409 3d Street, SW (6th Floor)
Washington, DC 20416
202-205-7777

NIH Physician Scientist Award (PSA; K11, K12)

- K11 is an individual award; K12 is a Program award and requires a program director as well as individual sponsors for each candidate.
- Supported by only some of the NIH Institutes
- Restricted to individuals with an M.D. (or equivalent) degree
- Candidates generally should have completed at least one year of postgraduate clinical training by the time the award is made.
- Intended to encourage newly trained clinicians to develop independent research skills and experience in basic science
- The PI does not have to have a well-defined research problem at the time of application.
- A sponsor with extensive research experience in a basic science is required throughout the tenure of the award.
- Provides support for up to 5 years experience in a supervised basic science research setting. Phase I (the first 2 or 3 years) may include didactic study and laboratory experience. Phase II (up to 3 years).
- The candidate and the sponsor are jointly responsible for preparing the research development plan.
- Applicants may not submit other NIH grant applications concurrently but may do so at the end of Phase I.
- Candidates with previous NIH research support (or equivalent) do not qualify.
- Three letters of recommendation are required.

NIH Research Career Re-Entry Program (K17)

- A postdoctoral award that provides support to basic or clinical scientists who are re-entering active careers in science or academic medicine and who show high potential as basic or clinical researchers if enabled to update their skills.
- This was a new program announced in 1993. Watch for more information in the *NIH Guide to Grants and Contracts*, or call the Grants Information Office.

Behavioral Science Track Award For Rapid Transition, NIMH

To facilitate entry of new investigators into behavioral science research. Program will support:
- Preliminary data acquisition or pilot work
- Relatively new or novel research approaches
- Enhancement of the capability of new investigators in behavioral science research

Provides rapid review of and funding decisions about applications.

Application Procedures:
- Grant application must be on form PHS-398. "PAR-94-002, NIMH B/START" must be entered in item 2a on the Face page of the application form. "NIMH Expedited Review" must be typed in the top margin of the Face page.
- The Biographical Sketch must not exceed 1 page.
- Sections 1–4 of the Research Plan must not exceed 5 pages.

Mechanism of Support:
B/START awards will use the NIMH Small Grant (R03) mechanism. Support may be requested for up to 1 year. The total direct costs for the 1 year request may not exceed $25,000. B/START awards are not renewable.

Funds Available:
In FY 1994, between $800,000 and $1,600,000 will be available to fund between 20 and 40 B/START grants. This level of support is dependent on receipt of sufficient applications of high scientific merit. Although this program is provided for in the financial plans of the NIMH, awards are contingent on availability of funds for this purpose.

To Apply:
Submit the signed original and 4 copies to DRG, and simultaneously send a *complete* copy to:

Dr. Salvatore Cianci
Division of Extramural Activities
National Institute of Mental Health
5600 Fishers Lane, Room 9-97
Rockville, MD 20857

Review:
Applications will be reviewed by NIMH Study Sections.
Applicants will be notified in 3–4 months.

Inquiries:
Applicants are strongly encouraged to contact NIMH program staff prior to preparing a B/START application to clarify issues or questions.
    Direct inquiries regarding programmatic issues to:

Hilleary D. Everist, Ph.D.
Division of Neuroscience and Behavioral Science
National Institute of Mental Health
5600 Fishers Lane, Room 11-103

Rockville, MD 20857
301-443-8033
Fax: 301-443-4822
BITNET: EH5@NIHCU

Direct inquiries regarding fiscal matters to:

Diana S. Trunnell
Grants Management Branch
National Institute of Mental Health
5600 Fishers Lane, Room 7C-15
Rockville, MD 20857
301-443-3065
Fax: 301-443-6885

See *NIH Guide for Grants and Contracts*, Vol. 22, No. 36, October 8, 1993, pages 28–31.

NIH human brain project: phase 1 feasibility studies

A broadly based Federal research initiative to encourage and support investigator-initiated basic and clinical neuroscience research and investigator-initiated research on informatics resources that could be used to facilitate neuroscience research. Particular emphasis is on research concerning computer storage and manipulation of neuroscience information, network systems, and associated tools that will give neuroscientists access to the stored information. The networks will also provide electronic channels of communication and collaboration to geographically distant laboratories. To optimize the utility of these technologies to neuroscience researchers, the utilities will be developed in the context of specific neuroscience research. The scientific question being addressed will be considered as important as the technology being developed.

Mechanisms of Support:
Research project grant (R01) and exploratory grant (P20).

"Letter of Intent"
Applicants should submit a "Letter of Intent" by designated receipt dates (call for dates) to:

Michael F. Huerta, Ph.D.
National Institute of Mental Health
5600 Fishers Lane, Room 11-95
Rockville, MD 20857
301-443-3948
Fax: 301-443-4822

The "Letters of Intent" will be distributed to all sponsoring agencies.
For further information and a list of sponsoring agencies, see *NIH Guide for Grants and Contracts*, Vol. 22, No. 13, April 2, 1993, pages 14–18.

H. SOME NSF AWARDS

The NSF programs listed below are available through some or all of the NSF Directorates.

NSF Research Planning Grants (RPG)

One-time, limited awards for preliminary studies and other activities to strengthen the investigator's planning and proposal writing capabilities and to facilitate the development of more competitive NSF research proposals. Directed specifically at increasing the participation of *women and underrepresented minorities* in the nation's research enterprise.

NSF Career Advancement Awards (CAA)

Intended to expand opportunities for researchers to advance their careers. CAAs are appropriate for independent investigators whose careers are still evolving, or for other experienced researchers who are changing research direction or who have had a significant research interruption. Directed specifically at increasing the participation of *women and underrepresented minorities* in the nation's research enterprise.

NSF Research Initiation Awards (RIA)

One-time research grants made by NSF disciplinary programs to provide opportunities to *promising minority investigators* for enhancing their capability as independent investigators. Directed specifically at increasing the participation of underrepresented minorities in the nation's research enterprise.

NSF Research in Undergraduate Institutions (RUI)

Provide support for research and research equipment for faculty in nondoctoral departments in *predominantly undergraduate institutions*. In addition to fulfilling the usual NSF requirements, RUI proposals must also describe the expected impact of the proposed research on the research and training environment of the department.

NSF Research Experiences for Undergraduates (REU)

Provide opportunities for *undergraduate students* to be direct participants in research or related scholarly activities in the sciences, mathematics, and engineering.

NSF Research Opportunity Awards (ROA)

Offer *faculty at institutions with limited research opportunities*, a chance to participate in research under the aegis of NSF investigators at other institutions.

Note: NSF Program officers may be contacted via Internet by appending @nsf.gov after the first initial and last name (for example, Dr. John Ryff would be jryff@nsf.gov) or via BITNET by appending @nsf.

Programs from NSF Division of Graduate Education and Research Development

The NSF programs listed below are available through the Division of Graduate Education and Research Development, Directorate for Education and Human Resources, National Science Foundation:

1. NSF Graduate and Minority Graduate Research Fellowships Program
2. NATO Postdoctoral Fellowships in Science and Engineering
3. NSF Graduate Research Traineeships
4. NATO Advanced Study Summer Institute Travel Grant Program
5. NSF Visiting Professorships for Women
6. NSF Faculty Awards for Women (revised in 1993)
7. NSF Presidential Faculty Fellows Awards
8. NSF-NATO Postdoctoral Fellowships: Outreach to Eastern Europe

Sample Outline
for the Research Plan:
Section C, NIH-RO1

(PHS Form 398; Revised 9/91)

Section C of the grant application includes the Research Plan.

(*Note:* This is not the only possible outline; it is only a sample outline; *your* outline should fit the needs of *your* project—*but must follow NIH instructions.*)

The outline below for an NIH grant application is available on disk from TWC/EA, Box 645, Belmont, MA 02178, for $11 + $3 (P&H). Available on 3.5-inch disks only. Can be formatted for Microsoft Word for the Macintosh, MS-DOS, or text-only. Please specify desired format. Allow 4–6 weeks for delivery.

SPECIFIC INSTRUCTIONS—RESEARCH PLAN

I. Introduction: Only for revisions (3 pages) or supplements (1 page)
  1. *Summary* of substantial additions, deletions, and changes. (Highlight changes by brackets, indents, or change of type style.)
      a. Addition: Page y, ¶x describes ...
      b. Addition: Page v, ¶w describes ...
      c. Deletion: Page x, ¶z has been deleted because ...
      d. Change: Page m, ¶n has been changed to reflect ...
  2. Responses to criticisms in previous Summary Statement
      a. Response to pink sheet ¶x
      b. Response to pink sheet ¶y
  3. Work done since prior version of application was submitted
      a. Set of experiments # 1: completed since prior submission
      b. Set of experiments # 2: begun since prior submission
II. Research Plan: Maximum of 25 pages total for Sections 1–4 of Research Plan
  1. Specific Aims: 1 page
    Broad, long-term objectives; what the research is intended to accomplish; hypotheses to be tested
      a. Specific Aim 1
      b. Specific Aim 2
      c. Specific Aim 3
  2. Background and Significance: 2–3 pages
    You should address each of the 4 issues listed below. Part a. Background, will generally be the longest part of this section, but it is the least important from the per-

spective of the Reviewer's ability to judge your quality as a scientist. Any bright high school student can probably write a good Background section. It takes the knowledge and experience of a good scientist in the field to *evaluate* the existing knowledge!

   a. Background (Cite pertinent references and list them in the bibliography, Section 9: Literature Cited.)

   b. Critical evaluation of existing knowledge

   c. Gaps that this project is intended to fill

   d. Importance of the research: Relate Specific Aims to Broad, long-term objectives and health relevance.

      i. Specific Aim 1 will ... toward the Broad, long-term objectives.

      ii. Specific Aim 2 will ... toward the Broad, long-term objectives.

      iii. Specific Aim 3 will ... toward the Broad, long-term objectives.

3. Progress Report: 6–8 pages

(For competing continuations and supplements)

[*Preliminary studies* : Recommended for *new* applications (in place of Progress Report)]

   a. Beginning and ending *dates* for the period covered since the last competitive review

   b. List of *all personnel*. Give information requested on page 21 of instructions in PHS-398 (Rev. 9/91).

   c. Progress. Summarize previous Specific Aims, give succinct account of progress toward their achievement and importance of findings.

      Include small but readable and well-labeled figures, tables, and copies of photos; provide original full-size photos in the Appendix.

      Cite your own publications in the text, and list them in the appropriate section at the end of the Progress Report or Preliminary Studies.

      In *new applications* a Preliminary Studies section is recommended but not required. It is important to include this section even though it is "optional." Describe preliminary studies pertinent to the application and/or give other information that will help establish your experience and competence to pursue the proposed project.

      (1) Specific Aim 1 (from previous application)

         (a) Summary of Specific Aim 1 (from previous application)

         (b) Progress toward achievement of Specific Aim 1 (from previous application)

         (c) Importance of findings related to achievement of Specific Aim 1 (from previous application)

      (2) Specific Aim 2 (from previous application)

         (a) Summary of Specific Aim 2 (from previous application)

         (b) Progress toward achievement of Specific Aim 2 (from previous application)

         (c) Importance of findings related to achievement of Specific Aim 2 (from previous application)

      (3) Discuss any changes in Specific Aims since the project was last reviewed competitively; provide a rationale for the change.

   d. Publications. Give titles and complete references

      Submit 5 collated sets of *no more than* 10 such items in the Appendix.

New applications: List any pertinent publications and submit 5 collated sets of *no more than* 10 such items in the appendix.

(1) *Published* materials
    (a) Original research reports
        (i) Hokum, J. and Pokum, L., ...1995
        (ii) Hokum, J. and Pokum, L., ...1994
        (iii) Hokum, J. and Pokum, L., ...1993
    (b) Review articles
    (c) Books
    (d) Abstracts
(2) Manuscripts submitted or accepted for publication
    (a) Original research reports
    (b) Review articles
    (c) Books
    (d) Abstracts
(3) Patents
(4) Invention reports
(5) Other printed materials

4. Research Design and Methods: 13–16 pages (the maximum length of Sections 1–4 must not exceed 25 pages)

Cite pertinent references in this section, and include them in the bibliography (Section 9: Literature Cited).

a. Research Design to accomplish Specific Aim 1. If applicable, describe the overall Research Design. Include all pertinent *control experiments*.
b. Procedures (methods) to carry out the Research Design for Specific Aim 1. (Include pertinent *control experiments* for procedures.)
c. Means by which data will be *collected, analyzed,* and *interpreted*
d. For any new methodologies: Explain advantage over existing methodologies.
e. Discuss *potential limitations and difficulties* of proposed procedures.
f. Discuss *alternative approaches* to achieve the aim.

Repeat a. through f. for each Specific Aim. In some proposals it may be more appropriate to discuss some of these items together for 2 or more Specific Aims. The decision should be made on the basis of, first, clarity and, second, brevity.

General procedures (methods) that apply to more than one Research Design should be grouped together under the heading "General procedures (methods)," described once (rather than being repeated) and referred to as necessary.

g. Give tentative sequence or timetable for the studies. (Be brief.)
h. Point out procedures, situations, or materials that may be hazardous to personnel.
    For each case, *specify precautions to be exercised.*

5. *Human Subjects*
6. *Vertebrate animals*
7. *Consultants/Collaborators:* Provide letters and biosketches for each such person; place the letters in this subsection.
8. *Consortium/Contractual agreements:* See NIH instructions.
9. *Literature Cited:* 6 pages maximum. Choose wisely. Use a consistent format. Include titles and make sure references are complete.

APPENDIX III

General Checklist

This checklist was adapted from a list I received from a Federal agency that funds proposals in the social sciences. It was a list of reasons why some proposals at that agency are not funded. I have reworded the statements and made some minor changes and additions to the list.

A. Are the Research Goals Appropriate and Clear?

A1. Is the topic [or purpose(s)] appropriate for support by the granting agency? If in doubt, call or write the agency to ask.

[For an RFP (Request for proposal): Is the topic responsive to the scope of the announcement?]

A2. Are the purposes of the study clear and sufficiently detailed? Are the hypotheses explicit?

A3. Are the research goals worthy of support?

A4. Have the collected data been analyzed fully and appropriately?

A5. Where pertinent, have you included specific end points, applications, or products in the research goals?

B. Is the Study Design Good?

B1. Have you determined that the research proposed has not been done by others? Don't waste your time. Perhaps the study design was tried and judged inadequate by others (insofar as it is possible to assess this). Don't reinvent the wheel!

B2. Is there sufficient attention given to related research by others? Have you cited their work?

B3. Is the study design carefully related to the purposes of the project?

B4. Will the study design provide the data needed to achieve the aims of the project? Will the study yield enough data (cases) to support the analysis?

B5. Is there evidence of coherent direction in the study? (Not just parts thrown together)

B6. Is the proposal well coordinated and clearly related to a central focus?

B7. Is the sampling design appropriate? Have you justified the sample size?

B8. Are the data unbiased? Is there recognition of the problems of bias and ways to correct the bias?

B9. Is the methodology sufficiently detailed?

B10. Have you spelled out:
   a. The major dependent and independent variables?
   b. How the data will be obtained and analyzed?
   c. How the data will be interpreted?

d. Whether the data contain enough information to support the proposed analysis?

B11. If appropriate, have you built into the study design a means and time frame for evaluating progress toward fulfilling the aims of the project?

C. Are Staff, Time, and Budget Appropriate?

C1. Are specific tasks clearly related to personnel, time, and budget?

C2. Is there sufficient time commitment by the principal investigators? (Avoid small allocations of time among a large number of investigators.)

C3. Are the scientific disciplines of the research team (including consultants) appropriate for the topics to be investigated?

D. Is the Overall Presentation Good?

D1. Have you spelled out a specific plan of research rather than expected the Reviewers to trust in your past reputation?

D2. Have you accounted for the possibility that the Reviewers have not read about your past research? That is, is the proposal complete without the Reviewer having to refer to additional materials?

D3. Is there a balanced presentation in the proposal? Does the proposal focus on particular data sets and techniques of analysis without obscuring the overall research goal? Does the proposal relate each specific focus to the overall goal? (Have you started with a problem or topic and looked for data sets that address the issues rather than started with a data set and looked for a research problem that might be appropriate for that data set?)

E. Administrative Detail

E1. Is the budget realistic for the work proposed?

E2. Is the budget justification sufficiently detailed to allow Reviewers to relate each phase and level of the project to the budget?

E3. Have you provided letters that outline willingness to participate and extent of commitment for all consultants, collaborators, and subcontractors?

E4. Have you
a. Filled out and obtained signatures for the cover page? If you wait until the last minute, the appropriate official may be out of town.
b. Entered the appropriate page numbers in the Table of Contents?
c. Made sure the Abstract reflects the contents of the application?
d. Provided the necessary information and forms concerning
i.   Human studies (including gender and minority inclusion)?
ii.   Humane treatment of vertebrate animals?
iii. Other assurances (Inventions and patents, Debarment and suspension, Drug-free workplace, Lobbying, Delinquent Federal debt, Misconduct in science, Civil rights, Handicapped individuals, Sex discrimination, Age discrimination, Recombinant DNA)?
iv.   Personal data on ethnic origin, etc.? (Optional)
v.   Other grant support?
vi.   Resources and Environment (Facilities and Equipment)?

   Include support services and description of work ambiance.
   (Who is available for collaboration and exchange of ideas?)

   vii. Checklist (2 required pages for NIH applications)?
   Have you numbered them as the last 2 pages of the application?

e. Mailed the application in time to be received by the deadline?

f. Provided a *stamped*, self-addressed postcard (to receive acknowledgment of application receipt)?

g. Marked your calendar at 2 weeks after submission to be sure you have received the postcard acknowledging receipt of your application by the agency?

h. Marked your calendar at 6 weeks after submission to be sure you have received your review board assignment?

Sample Budget Justifications

This appendix contains excerpts from Budget Justifications from 2 actual grant applications. The first is part of a sample Budget Justification for a sample budget such as the one shown in Part III of this book, in the section entitled "Administrative and Financial Information." This is followed by the Budget Justification from the proposal for which the Summary Statement is shown in Example B, Appendix V, a proposal that the Reviewers considered to be "an extremely well-written grant proposal." The examples of Budget Justifications shown here are not the only way to write a Budget Justification, but they illustrate a format that I considered effective after listening to about 600 budget discussions (3 meetings per year × 2 years × 100 proposals per meeting = 600!) during the time I was a member of an NIH Study Section.

BUDGET JUSTIFICATION EXAMPLE A

(1) Personnel $145,777

    (a) Dr. Jones, Principal Investigator (salary + fringe) $68,185
Dr. Jones has planned this project, including the specific experiments to be carried out. He will be responsible for managing the project and for analyzing and interpreting the data with the help of Dr. Smith. He and Dr. Smith will jointly develop manuscripts for publication as is warranted. Dr. Jones has specific expertise in ___ . He will spend 100% of his time on this project year round. He has a long track record in the field of ___ .

    (b) Dr. Smith, Investigator (salary + fringe) $39,892

Dr. Smith is an established investigator in the field of ___ and will provide the "hands on" experience with respect to ___ . She will be responsible for carrying out the ___ aspect of the experiments described in the methods section of the proposal. This project cannot be carried out without a person with the expertise and competence of Dr. Smith for successful resolution of the experiments. Dr. Smith has been with the University of ___ for 6 years and has collaborated with Dr. Jones for the last 3 years. They have been a very successful team and have published 11 papers in well-reviewed journals during their collaboration.

        Note that Dr. Smith's salary is based on $45,800 for full time. She has a three-quarter-time appointment at the university during the academic year and plans to devote 75% of her time to this research project. ($3/4 \times 9/12 = 0.56 \times 0.75 = 0.42 \times$

$45,800 = $19,236). During the 3 summer months, she will work full time at the university and devote 100% of her time to this project. ($1.0 \times \frac{3}{12} = 0.25 \times 1.0 = 0.25 \times \$45,800 = \$11,450$). Fringe benefits have been calculated at 30%.

(c) Mr. West, Research Assistant (salary + fringe) $22,100
Mr. West will devote 100% effort to this project on a year-round basis. He has been working with Dr. Jones for the last 9 years and has developed unique expertise in the field of ____ . Mr. West has been a co-author on 15 publications during his time in Dr. Jones's laboratory. His full-time effort is essential for carrying out the experiments on ____ which are an integral part of the total research project.

(d) Technician (To be named, salary + fringe) $15,600
In addition to Mr. West, the research assistant, a medium level technician is essential for carrying out this project. The laboratory currently does not have someone in this category. The intention is to hire a person with a B.A. degree who has extensive experience in carrying out ____ experiments. We will specifically look for a person who has had hands-on experience working with ____ in a system similar to the one in which we propose to work in this project.

(?) Consultant Costs $0
Dr. Northstar, consultant, is a full professor at the University of ____ department of ____ . She is a nationally known expert in ____ and is currently writing a book on this subject. She has agreed to be a consultant at no charge for the ____ part of the project who will advise on ____ and will also provide help with data analysis (see letter in Section 7 of the Research Plan).

(3) Equipment $32,560
(a) Zeiss microscope, model XYZ $29,710
We have been using a microscope that belongs to Dr. M in the department of ____ . Dr. M will be leaving the University of ____ at about the time that this project is scheduled to begin if it is funded. Dr. M will take his microscope with him to the University of ... . Because a good-quality microscope is essential to carrying out this research project, we are requesting money to buy a model XYZ Zeiss microscope.

(b) Diamond knife $2,500
Dr M. will be taking his diamond knife with him when he leaves this department. Therefore, we are requesting $2,500 to purchase a diamond knife for cutting thin sections for these experiments.

(c) Embedding oven $350
We have been using Dr. M's embedding oven. He will take this piece of equipment to the University of ____ . We are therefore requesting $350 to purchase an embedding oven.

(4) Supplies $9,384
(a) Rats (including maintenance) $1,840
For additional details about budget justification, see Example B below.

BUDGET JUSTIFICATION EXAMPLE B

This Budget Justification; is from a grant proposal that reviewers considered to be "an extremely well-written grant proposal." Example B in Appendix V is the Summary Statement for this proposal.

(1) Personnel $ ___

    (a) PI and Collaborating Investigator $___

        Dr. ___ and Dr. ___ have planned this project and will, for the most part, plan the specific experiments to be carried out. We will be entirely responsible for analyzing and interpreting the biochemical data; we will also plan the morphological experiments, but because neither of us have "hands-on" experience in this area, the work will of necessity be done by someone experienced in morphological techniques and the anatomy of the ___.

    (b) Research Associate (To be named) $ ___

        This is the person who will provide the "hands-on" experience and will (with the help of the research assistant) be responsible for carrying out all the morphological aspects of the experiments described in the "Methods" section of the proposal. This project cannot be carried out without a morphologist of this level of competence and someone to help with the more routine aspects of the lengthy experimental work-up. A search cannot be initiated for this individual unless and until funding is obtained. The research associate would be responsible for carrying out and helping to interpret the morphological experiments. This individual would have to be experienced in both light and electron microscopy and be familiar with ___ anatomy in particular. He/she would presumably have had 3 or more years of postdoctoral experience in ___ morphology.

    (c) Research Assistant $ ___

        Mr. X will assist in carrying out both the morphological and biochemical experiments. He is familiar with tissue work-up, sectioning, and photographic techniques and will also be able to assist with handling of animals, as well as the more routine aspects of the biochemical assays. He will be primarily responsible to the Research Associate morphologist, but will also be directly responsible to the PI and Co-investigator in helping to set up certain ___ experiments and run the necessary assays.

(2) Consultant $0

        Dr. ___ at the ___ Hospital, Department of ___ is a known expert in ___ and is currently finishing a chapter on this subject. He has agreed to be a consultant, at no charge, and will also provide ___ material from ___, as they become available (see letter in Section 7 of the Research Plan). In addition, he will help us procure such material from other sources.

(3) Equipment $23,805

    (a) Zeiss microscope $21,605

(b) Diamond knife $2,000

The ___ Morphology Unit at ___ is a well-equipped, but heavily used facility. Most equipment necessary to carry out this project is available through the Unit; however, Dr. ___ the Unit head, has indicated that because of the heavy use required for carrying out this project, a separate light microscope and diamond knife will be essential for our work. Fluorescence optics will be necessary for ... experiments to localize and quantify various ___, e.g., ___ . It is estimated that this microscope will be used substantially on a daily basis by both the Research Associate Morphologist and the research assistant. In addition, it will be used frequently by the PI and Collaborating Investigator to review the results of experiments and discuss the interpretations with the Research Associate morphologist.

(c) Embedding oven $200

Although embedding ovens are available at ___, we have been advised by the Morphology Unit to have our own for the purposes of optimal curing of plastic sections.

(4) Supplies $11,739

(a) Animals $2,687

We consider that a full-time Morphologist with a full-time Research Assistant will be capable of carrying out about 2 experiments (each having 10 to 12 morphological samples and an equivalent number of biochemical samples)/week, for 3 weeks of every month. The 4th week will be used to record and assess the results, including taking and processing photographs. We are thus calculating costs on the basis of 38 weeks for experiments, taking into account 3 weeks vacation time/year.

(i) Eggs $979

We estimate 2-$\frac{1}{2}$ dozen eggs/week at $6/dozen plus $8 delivery charge = $874 at current prices. With 12% inflation by the beginning of the project period, this cost would be $979 for the first year of the project.

(ii) Other Animals $1,708

The second experiment each week will involve bovine ___ half of the time and in vitro experiments in newborn and young rats during the remaining weeks.

- Cow (organ) $1,140

$2/___ × 20 ___ + $20 delivery charge = $60/week × 19 weeks = $1,140.

- Rats (Cost and care) $568

Current price of one litter of rats (newborn) $18.65. We project $20 by the beginning of the project period. One litter/week for 19 weeks = $380. Animal room charge for maintenance of one cage of rats at $188/year/cage = $188. Total for rats and care = $568.

(b) Medium and serum $920

    (i) Medium $570
We estimate a total of 24 chick embryo ____ cultures/ week for the total of morphological and biochemical samples. These samples require 20 ml of medium/ flask, i.e., one 500-ml bottle/week. (Bovine ____ will be maintained in reusable glass flasks and will require only small amounts of medium.) We project $15/ bottle by the beginning of the project period. $15 × 38 weeks = $570.

    (ii) Serum $350
Fetal calf serum, essential for the maintenance of chick embryo ____ in culture, is $29.20/100 ml. We estimate 12 bottles/year. $29.20 × 12 = $350.

(c) Chemicals, glassware, plasticware $1,812
    (i) Chemicals $600
Antibiotics, buffers, assay reagents for biochemical experiments, radioactive precursors for uptake and in- corporation studies, etc. We estimate $600.

    (ii) Plastic flasks $912
We have found X flasks to be optimal for ____ cul- tures. 24 flasks/week at $1/flask for 38 weeks = $912.

    (iii) Counting vials and scintillation fluid $300
We will be as conservative as possible in this area, but the project will require a small number of incorpora- tion and uptake studies. We estimate $300 in this cat- egory.

(d) Microscopy supplies $3,450

    (i) Dissecting instruments $1,000
For example, microdissecting scissors costs approxi- mately $100. We estimate $1000 in this category.

    (ii) Fixatives $1,500
Glutaraldehyde, paraformaldehyde, osmium tetrox- ide, dehydrating agents, embedding compounds, and stains for light microscopy. We estimate $1500.

    (iii) Other supplies $950
This includes grids, grid holders, and stains for elec- tron microscopy and embedding molds, disposable beakers, disposable gloves, slides, cover slips, and vials required for light microscopy.

(e) Photo supplies $2,870

    (i) Black and white film $456
2 rolls/experiment, $3/roll, 2 experiments/week × 38 weeks = $456.

(ii) Color slides $304

1 roll/week × $8/roll for film and processing × 38 weeks = $304

(iii) Paper for printing black and white photos $1,710

We plan to use multigrade resin paper, 50 sheets/experiment (including test sheets). 2 experiments/week = 100 sheets/week. $45/100 sheets ¥ 38 weeks = $1,710.

(iv) Photochemicals $400

For processing black and white film and prints. We estimate $400/year.

(5) Travel $2,550

Because of the nature of the proposed work, which involves ____ as a model of ____, it will be important for the Research Associate to go to both the ____ meeting and the ... meeting. In addition, it will be important for the PI to attend conferences specifically concerned with the latest development on ____ once a year to keep up with both the clinical and research areas related to this disease. In November, 19XX, a _____ symposium (II) took place in _____. Another _____ Symposium is scheduled in early 19XX (see _____ Newsletter, Vol. X, No. Y, page Z, Sept. 19XX)

The total figure for travel is based on $850 for this year's _____ travel budget. (This figure was arrived at by the _____ Committee at ____, calculated on the basis of budget fares and double room occupancy.) Assuming similar costs for the other 2 meetings, in the same geographic area, and allowing a small increment for inflation, we are estimating $2550 in the travel category for the first year.

(6) Other expenses $3,280

(a) Publication costs $1,000

These include drafting, photography, photocopy charges, etc. Publications resulting from this project will of necessity involve numerous photographic plates. The current page charge for half tones, for example, in the Journal of XYZ is $70/page for short papers and $100/page for longer papers. 300 reprints for a 6-page article will cost at least $150.

We estimate at least one major publication/year:

(i) Drafting	$200
(ii) Photographs	$150
(iii) Page charges (6 × $70)	$420
(iv) Reprints (500)	$230
Total	$1000

(b) Users' fee for the Morphology Unit $2,280

Because of increased expenses and decreased funding, the Morphology Unit at ____ has instituted a $3-per-hour "use fee" for all users.

The items included in the users' fee do not cover any supplies requested above; they do include service contracts, and use of available instruments, liquid nitrogen, etc.

The budgeted amount is based on 20 hours of use/week.

(7) Budget for subsequent years

   (a) Each category is increased by 4% per year to account for inflation.

   (b) No additional equipment is requested in years 02 and 03.

   (c) "Other Expenses" is increased by $1000 in year 03 for sharpening the diamond knife.

Sample Summary Statements ("Pink Sheets") and Excerpts of Grant Proposals

This appendix contains excerpts from some sample Summary Statements (edited for reasons of confidentiality) for a number of grant proposals submitted to NIH with a variety of outcomes. For some of the more recent Summary Statements, I have also included (through the kind generosity of the PIs) excerpts of the proposals for which the Summary Statements were generated.

The Summary Statement is prepared by the Scientific Review Administrator of the Study Section and is based on the Reviewers' reports, the Readers' comments, and the discussion of all the Study Section members.[1] (Each application has *at least* a primary and secondary Reviewer and one Reader; sometimes there is also a tertiary Reviewer and additional outside Reviewers or reviews by mail.) I have put in italic type some of the key words and phrases that may help to direct your thinking when you write your grant proposal. As you read the Summary Statements, note this emphasized text and also the dates and the priority scores! Remember that the voting categories and merit descriptors changed in the fall of 1991 and again at the end of 1994. Before 9/91, the 3 voting categories were "Approval," "Disapproval," and "Deferred for additional information."

From 1991 to the end of 1994 there were only two voting categories: "Not Recommended for Further Consideration" (NRFC, informally referred to as "Nerfed") and "Deferred for additional information." The applications that are assigned merit ratings were informally referred to as the "Scored" applications. In September 1994, NIH replaced "NRFC" with "Noncompetitive" (NC) for all R01 and R29 applications reviewed by DRG as of the February 1995 review cycle (see pages 20 ff). However, NC is not considered a voting category. Thus, the only official voting category for these types of applications is "Deferred." The "NRFC" designation is still in use for other types of NIH applications and, according to a reliable NIH source, may possibly be reintroduced in the future (to co-exist with "NC") for review of R01 and R29 applications. Note that NRFC indicates that an application does not have substantial scientific merit. NC, on the other hand, does not mean that an application lacks merit, but rather, that it is not likely to be funded in the current funding climate.

If you study the samples carefully, you will get a good idea of what Reviewers look for in an application. Perhaps, with the help of this book, your Summary Statement will also contain the statement shown in italic at the beginning of the "Critique" in Example B. When you write and edit your proposal, remember that Reviewers are generally very overworked people who are reviewing proposals in their "spare time"—sometimes late at night or on a commuter train. Use good psychology, good organization, and clear presentation to make the Reviewer's job as easy as possible. If your grant proposal is written so that all

---

[1] Beginning in 1994 NIH began "streamlining" peer review. As a result, the nature of the Summary Statement has changed. See Liane Reif-Lehrer, "Science Community Gives Mixed Review To Triage." *The Scientist*, November 28, 1994 pages 1, 8–9 and Liane Reif-Lehrer, *Journal of the National Grantseekers Institute*, Vol. 2, No. 1, 1995.

information needed by the Reviewer is easy to find and unambiguous, s/he is likely to view your proposal more favorably—all other things being equal.

All priority scores and percentiles have been rounded off to preserve the anonymity of the donors of the Summary Statements.

Examples of Reviewers' reports for 2 National Science Foundation (NSF) grant proposals are given in Appendix VIII-B.

TABLE OF CONTENTS FOR APPENDIX V

(SS = Summary Statement)

EXAMPLE A

Excerpts from a Summary Statement for a proposal with a priority score of 180 (very good in 1979). This project was funded for 5 years with the budget reduced as indicated.

SUMMARY STATEMENT

Degree: Ph.D.

Requested Start Date: 04/01/79

Recommendation: Approval

Priority Score: 180

Special Note: No Human Subjects

No Recombinant DNA Research is Involved

Project Year	Direct Costs Requested	Direct Costs Recommended	Previously Recommended	Grant Period
03	113,873	96,117		4/1/79
04	126,253	101,408		4/1/80
05	139,533	107,109		4/1/81
06	155,590	114,406		4/1/82
07	173,518	122,236		4/1/83

RESUME: A *competent* biochemist requests continued support for studies on the _____ as a model system of a _____ tissue and as a system for a study of _____ in the tissue. *The problem is complex but important,* the *program well organized,* and the *principal investigator has demonstrated by his published work in this field that he is capable of conducting this program.* Approval is recommended with some reduction in the budget.

DESCRIPTION: ...

CRITIQUE: This is a long but *well-organized, detailed presentation* of an immensely complex subject. Working with a small group, but *collaborating effectively* with a number of other investigators, the principal investigator has made *reasonable progress* over the past three years *in spite of moving his laboratory* in 1976 and in spite of the complexity of the problem. He is a competent biochemist who *has been able to develop the necessary techniques of cell biology to follow this problem.* The general question of the regulation of _____ and the specific problem of the regulation of the appearance of _____ *are of fundamental importance.* It is of considerable interest to elucidate the role of the _____ and to determine if it is involved in the modification of _____. The specific aims delineated in the application are *highly ambitious* and cover a *wide spectrum of initiatives.* Of particular importance are the problems of the _____ in the _____ and determination of the physiological function of the _____. The *difficulty in achieving the overall objectives of the project are complicated by* the fact that the applicant is studying the control of _____ whose role is not known, whose distribution is only vaguely suspected, and whose induction can be modified by widely differing compounds. *There is also some concern* that the model system _____ is not _____ typical

_____ and that the influence of the _____ environment produces anomalous effects. Nevertheless, the *principal investigator's work has been well received, he has been productive, publishing generally in critically reviewed journals,* and has clearly *demonstrated the intellectual capacity* to attack this most difficult problem. Approval is recommended with a reduced budget.

INVESTIGATOR: _____, Ph.D., received his B.A. at _____ University and his Ph.D. in _____ at the University of _____. He took a three-year postdoctoral at _____, with _____, a well-known scientist, who introduced him into the field of _____. Since _____, he had held appointments in various branches of _____ and is now _____. *He has published some twenty papers* dealing with _____ and their effect upon the _____, and in the case of _____, upon the human. *A number of papers have recently been submitted for publication and are included with this application.*

RESOURCES AND ENVIRONMENT: These are adequate.

BUDGET: The following reductions are recommended.
Personnel: *Delete the Research Assistant* _____ since there *does not appear to be a strong argument* for both a full-time Research Associate and a Research Assistant.

Travel: Allow Domestic and Foreign Travel ($500 and $850 in the first year.)
Reduce travel in future years to $1,000.

EXAMPLE B

Excerpts from a Summary Statement for a well-written grant proposal that does not have sufficient preliminary data to convince the Reviewers of the feasibility of the study.

RESUME: This proposal outlines histological and biochemical studies of the _____ of victims of _____ disease. Effect on high _____ associated with the disease will be studied in animal _____. The *proposal is weakened by the absence of preliminary data* demonstrating the _____ pathology presumed to accompany _____ disease. The _____ *biochemical studies are enthusiastically approved,* but the *morphological studies are discouraged until an expert in* _____ *can be recruited.* Approval is recommended for the requested time and reduced amount.

CRITIQUE: *This is an extremely well-written grant proposal* that suggests a great many *sophisticated biochemical experiments* on *in vivo* and *in vitro* animal models and even some attempts at _____. *All the experimental manipulations hinge on* there actually being pathology of the _____, *which has yet to be demonstrated.* There is said to be _____ in _____ cases, but this may only be a manifestation of the increased _____ that is a symptom of the disease. *There is also no evidence,* cited in this proposal at least, of _____ impairment in the affected patients with _____ syndrome. *Neither has it been demonstrated* that there are definite morphological changes in the _____ itself, _____ which are highly selectively damaged in the _____ appear to be normal in _____, and the only hint of pathology is apparently some _____. No biochemical analyses have been done on affected _____ to see if the elevated _____ levels have affected the _____ cycle, the formation of _____, or _____. *The whole grant proposal is written around the supposition that* the latter _____ systems are affected in _____ tissue in _____ syndrome and that because the _____ is more easily studied under experimental conditions of high _____ than _____ tissue, the _____ is an ideal model for _____ syndrome.

It would seem to be a first priority of the proposed project to thoroughly investigate the human material, both _____ and _____, for details of structural damage and for problems in the _____ systems. *If it can be demonstrated* that either one of these approaches show pathology in the _____, then the animal _____ experiments will certainly be valid and address the question of _____. The *recruitment of a good electron microscopist is essential* for the morphological studies although not crucial to the whole application, for if the biochemical assays indicate a defect, then *the biochemical experiments alone will likely lead to a better understanding* of the role of increased _____ in artificially produced _____ syndrome _____ simply because we need to know more concerning _____ in the vertebrate _____. The *principal investigator is known for the unique contributions from her lab* concerning _____ and _____ *and has developed some impressive in vitro experimental designs.* For example, most recently, *she has been successful* with _____. *We do not doubt her capabilities to produce meaningful results and a strong research program in* _____. On the other hand, Dr. _____'s *expertise in* _____ *studies has not been demonstrated to date,* and there is **some** *concern that this part of the proposal cannot be attempted without a competent electron microscopist.* If the pathology in _____ syndrome or _____ is manifest only as subtle changes in _____, *they might not be unequivocally detected by the anatomical approaches proposed* here. The use of _____ and _____ methods to demonstrate _____ in _____ or in _____ *are interesting approaches, but again no expertise in these areas* *is offered by any member of this grant application.* In sum, the proposal contains *interesting and worthwhile experiments* in the principal investigator's principal area of expertise and are *sure to lead to meaningful information* concerning _____. *However, the research is not necessarily addressing the question of* _____ *syndrome and may not actually be what the title of the application suggests—namely, a model for* _____ *syndrome.* Approval is recommended particularly for the biochemical aspects of the proposal. It would seem most appropriate to *consider support for the work after preliminary experiments by the principal investigator have indicated the presence of clear pathology* in the human _____ material. Current grant supports from the _____ Institute should be sufficient to allow such *pilot studies.*

EXAMPLE C

An example of a Summary Statement for a successful application with a good priority score that was funded for 5 years.

SUMMARY STATEMENT

Review Group: Application Number:

Meeting Date:

Investigator: Ph.D.

Position:

Organization:

City, State:

Project Title:

Recommendation: Approval   Priority Score: 150

Special Note: No Human Subjects

Project Year	Direct Costs Requested	Direct Costs Recommended	Previously Recommended	Grant Period
04	75,188	57,983		7/1/80
05	99,268	78,896		7/1/81
06	112,514	85,871		7/1/82
07	120,701	93,388		7/1/83
08	130,749	101,596		7/1/84

RESUME: A *most capable investigator* requests five years continued support for studies related to _____. Various agents will be tested for their effects on the levels of _____, and effective compounds will be further assessed for the effect on a variety of _____ characteristics related to _____. The *concepts are sound* and the *experiments well planned* using both *in vivo* and *in vitro* approaches. Approval is recommended.

DESCRIPTION: In this application the principal investigator proposes to investigate _____.

CRITIQUE: The *prior* three-year *award* (two-year reporting period) *has been productive.* It was shown that _____. Recent studies using _____ also revealed _____. During this period there were *four publications and two papers in press.* This is an *extremely interesting proposal* and addresses *important problems* of _____. The *applicant is an established investigator* in the fields of _____.

She recently moved her interest into the _____ aspects of the _____. The ten specific *aims listed are straightforward and logical, and all should produce new data* concerning the effect of _____. She bases her expanded studies on _____ responses of the _____ which may be influenced by 1) _____ 2) _____ 3) _____ 4) _____. It is interesting that she addresses the source of the _____. Therefore, it is proposed to conduct studies with _____ and to monitor their _____ compared to controls. It would also be appropriate to monitor _____.

Throughout the application, the principal investigator considers the _____ collectively, and, particularly with the isolation procedures, it appears that after isolation of the _____, levels in the total tissue will be studied without regard to the component layers. It is only in the latter part of the application that the effect of some of these _____ influences in the component layers is considered. It would appear to be advisable to divide the _____ into its components after excision. The *proposed studies on _____ may not be as straightforward as the applicant proposes. It is not clear* whether _____ or _____ will be used. One of the major factors which could affect _____ is _____, a component of the vehicle in _____.

A few suggestions should be noted for improvement of this otherwise excellent project. For comparing the efficacy of a drug, _____ will be used as a control. The _____ *may not be a suitable control,* since _____. The effect of _____ *should be examined.* The assessment of the _____ is reasonable, but the _____ studies under the influence of a number of these compounds *could also be further expanded* to look at _____. Certainly the studies as planned should produce some interesting data on _____. The methodology is relatively standard, save for a change in _____. *A weakness in the proposal is the lack of any indication of the numbers of determinations* for each procedure or drug or *in vivo* treatment regimen. The principal investigator's *prior studies and those reported in the proposal indicate, however, that she is a most careful worker* and that, despite the lack of prescribed numbers, she will produce some interesting and reliable data. Approval is recommended.

INVESTIGATORS: _____, Ph.D., _____ University, 1971, currently _____. Her emphasis has been on _____ research as interfaced with _____ both as related to _____ and to _____. She is *extremely competent and active* in this field.
_____, M.S., _____ University, has experience with _____ and _____.

RESOURCES AND ENVIRONMENT: These are *very good. Collaboration* on biochemical techniques with Drs. _____ and _____ should be useful.

BUDGET: The following reductions are recommended:

Personnel: *Delete the Research Technician.* Adequate assistance is otherwise requested.

Supplies: *Reduce* from _____ to _____, since neither _____ nor assays will be performed each week.

Travel: *Reduce* from $1200 to $600.

EXAMPLE D

A Summary Statement for a proposal with a good priority score that involved a site visit.

SUMMARY STATEMENT

Degree: Ph.D.

Requested Start Date: 09/01/75

Priority Score: 160

Recommendation: Approval

Special Note: Project Site Visit
      Executive Secretary's note

Project Year	Direct Costs Requested	Direct Costs Recommended	Previously Recommended	Grant Period
10	75,511	75,511		9/1/75
11	83,797	83,797		9/1/76
12	91,765	91,765		9/1/77
13	100,576	100,576		9/1/78
14	110,217	110,217		9/1/79

RESUME: *Past performance assures continued excellent productivity in this important study* of _____ in the _____ *and other tissues.* His *budget requests are reasonable and justified,* and the full period of time requested should be allowed. *Consideration should be given in future applications to separating the two areas of investigation covered in this grant.*

PROJECT SITE VISIT: A site visit was held to learn the scope of the applicant's current interests and relative priority of the various aspects of the project. The Reviewers assembled at _____ for a pre-site-visit meeting. By 9:30 Dr. _____ joined the Reviewers for a discussion of the project followed by a tour of the laboratories. After lunch, the Reviewers met to write a report. No separate site-visit report has been written.

DESCRIPTION: The application is concerned with the role of _____.

CRITIQUE: The *strengths of this proposal* lie (a) in the increased background and fundamental knowledge of _____ (*an area much needing investigation*), which will be revealed by the studies, and (b) in that the approach to _____ was developed in the PI's laboratory and the *application is a logical continuation of the work of a leader in this field.* The *weakness* lies in that the *area covered by the application is rather diffuse,* encompassing *too large an area of investigation.* It is recognized that when the applicant applied for a second grant, it was made a supplement to his existing grant, combining two areas. Hence, in the writing of this application an emphasis was placed on the _____ aspect to the detriment of that part of the application concerning the _____ effect on _____. *The application, as written, essentially consists of two separate parts which, in reality, warrant different priorities.*

It is hoped that the _____ screening of _____ will be pursued only until sufficient specificity, or lack of same, is demonstrated in each system and that full, in-depth studies will not be made with each available _____. *It is recommended that this be brought to the attention of the applicant.*

The *aims* of the proposal are *very logical,* progressing from the _____ established over the last five years by this investigator. The chosen approach is also *valid* and most *adequate* to achieve the ends anticipated in the proposal. The procedures are ones which have been utilized in the applicant's laboratory for a number of years and offer *no technical problems.* The *applicant has more than adequately demonstrated his competence* previously with the techniques and methodology. The research will undoubtedly produce new data concerning _____ and will shed new light on this phenomenon; in addition, the *expected data should confirm various hypotheses* concerning the mechanism of _____ and its inhibition or acceleration. The proposed *work has significance* in the area of providing a _____ basis for the understanding of _____ processes in addition to basic knowledge of _____ per se and the understanding of _____ processes in the _____. The proposal may set the groundwork for potential clinical therapeutic application in the treatment of _____ with regard to _____. The _____ and data gathered in the proposed study should cast some light on this problem.

Past progress on the award has been most substantial, with the principal investigator establishing _____ as a real phenomenon. The *contribution made by the applicant is very significant* not only in the _____, but also in other tissues. The applicant's *laboratory is possibly the only one pursuing these studies, and this should be encouraged.*

INVESTIGATOR: The principal investigator has shown himself to be *able, competent and experienced* as evidenced by the *past publications* in a variety of research areas. *He is a leader in the* _____ *field* and is most *familiar with the necessary techniques.* The *senior technician* has also been *associated with the project for several years.*

RESOURCES AND ENVIRONMENT: The facilities and equipment are more than adequate for this study. The environment is entirely appropriate for good interchange of ideas with others, and the *connection with Dr.* _____ *is excellent and beneficial.*

BUDGET: Most *reasonable* and presented at as low a level as conceivably possible. *All items are justified on the basis of the proposal.* The full five years of support are needed in order to achieve the aims of this proposal.

EXECUTIVE SECRETARY'S NOTE: The reviewers recognize that the applicant wrote an all-encompassing application since two previous applications had been combined into one grant. This raised certain *problems in assessing the application,* since some areas of the proposal were considered to have a higher priority than others. The current Reviewers, therefore, wish to express disagreement with the philosophy of blending two diverse areas of interest into one application. This action encourages applicants to submit proposals which attempt to *coalesce different areas of interest, often to the detriment of the application as a whole.*

EXAMPLE E

A Summary Statement for a grant proposal with a poor priority score.

SUMMARY STATEMENT

Degree: Ph.D.

Requested Start Date: 07/01/77

Recommendation: Approval   Priority Score: 360

No Human Subjects

Project Year	Direct Costs Requested	Direct Costs Recommended	Previously Recommended	Grant Period
01	76,971	39,010		7/1/77
02	94,749	48,055		7/1/78
03	96,090			

RESUME: Support is requested for a study of _____. Animals will be used for this study _____. The *aims are worthwhile, the investigator is competent*, but a number of the aspects of the *protocol* are *not well formulated.* Approval for two years is recommended to give the principal investigator the *opportunity to demonstrate the feasibility* of this project, especially the ability to acquire a sufficient number of _____.

CRITIQUE: The *aims* of this project *are important.* The interrelationships of _____ diseases certainly should be investigated, and the use of animal models is a viable approach to this problem. Although the aims are laudable, the *research plan is vague and has weaknesses.* The prior _____ results noted by Dr. _____ are of interest. However, in the appendix article the differences between _____ *are not analyzed* with respect to the degree of _____ or necessity for _____, which could be accounting for these differences. Moreover, the increased _____ are only documented for two patients. Dr. _____ plans to use _____ kits for the measurements of _____. *These are not always ideal,* and he notes that a bioassay also will be used in some cases. His experimental protocol utilizing controls seems adequate, but it is unclear from his description of his procedures how often the various parameters will be measured, at what time intervals, and when the animals will be sacrificed. *Will* the two to three months of initial *observations be sufficient to document* the _____, and, moreover, how long will it take in these animals before _____? It is at this time that these _____ analyses would be most productive _____. He does not approach the interesting problem, based on his own observation, of why the _____ does not reduce _____. *Simply determining the levels of the four parameters and vaguely intimating that _____ will be examined is not a sufficient research plan.*

There is some *concern about aspects of the methodology.* For the _____ experiments, the principal investigator notes that it takes approximately x animals with pooled blood samples to get enough volume to carry out the procedure. If this be the case, *one must question* how many blood samples will be available to prove or disprove the hypothesis. In order to obtain sufficient blood for a single determination of _____, approximately x animals will be required; to determine the _____ activity, y ml of whole blood is required. The need for such levels of animals and blood samples *will complicate the overall experimentation.* It is only planned to measure _____. However, other _____ have an effect on _____, and some of the previous work would indicate that _____ is equally promising. *Certain manipulations should be carried out that are not mentioned.* Certainly, _____ examinations in the _____ would be important and could be correlated to the _____ parameters. Also, efforts to measure _____ might be very illuminating.

Approval is recommended for two years. The *time is reduced because there is some considerable doubt that he will be able to get sufficient numbers* of _____. Two years should be sufficient to *demonstrate the feasibility* of this project.

<u>INVESTIGATORS</u>: _____, Ph.D., is Professor and Director of the Laboratory _____. He has worked extensively in _____. His *bibliography is extensive* in this regard. He is *fully capable* of carrying out the proposed studies.

Dr. _____ is Associate Professor in the College of _____. *His role would be* to handle and study the _____ from which specimens would be taken in the protocol. This would be done under a subcontract to the University of _____. His bibliography includes numerous articles on _____.

Dr. _____, M.D., University of _____, is Associate Professor of _____, _____ University Medical School. *He would supervise* the _____ work proposed for the later years of the study. His bibliography indicates *extensive experience* on topics of _____.

<u>RESOURCES</u> <u>AND</u> <u>ENVIRONMENT</u>: Excellent

<u>BUDGET</u>: For the two years recommended for approval, the following changes in the budget are recommended.
Personnel: *Delete* support for Dr. _____, *since this position is not justified* and does not appear necessary to carry out this project. *Delete* a research assistant. One research assistant on this project should be sufficient. Furthermore, there is a research assistant *on another grant* who probably could be called upon when needed.
Travel: Reduce from _____ to _____.
Other expenses: Reduce from _____ to _____, since this is a feasibility study and there is some question about the availability of _____. If such _____ become available in sufficient number, the amount for this category should be increased.

EXAMPLE F

A Summary Statement for a proposal with a very poor priority score.

SUMMARY STATEMENT

Degree: Ph.D.

Requested Start Date: 12/01/77

Recommendation: Approval   Priority Score: 400

Special Note: No Human Subjects

Project Year	Direct Costs Requested	Direct Costs Recommended	Previously Recommended	Grant Period
01	63,903	37,011		12/1/77
02	70,803	57,138		12/1/78
03	77,000	63,702		12/1/79

RESUME: Although there is a need to establish the role of _____ in _____, and the possible role of _____ in preventing the _____, the principal Investigator *has approached the problem superficially.* Nonetheless, *to encourage the investigator to examine in depth his initial observation* that _____, approval is recommended with a reduction in the budget.

DESCRIPTION: The specific aims of this project are _____.

CRITIQUE: In preliminary studies the principal investigator has observed that _____. He is of the opinion that this system may be _____. He has further observed that _____. There has been *considerable interest recently* in the role of _____. However, *it remains to be clearly established* whether the _____ has the suggested role. In support of the evidence for a role of _____ in the _____ and the beneficial effect of _____ in the treatment of _____, *he cites largely unpublished work* in _____ (p. 10). Reference is also made to a paper presented to the _____ meeting in 1974. *Because of the unpublished nature of this work, it is difficult to evaluate* whether _____ has, in fact, a therapeutic effect.

Nevertheless, there is *clearly a need* for careful investigation to study _____.

The *preliminary evidence supporting the* _____ *is weak and unconvincing.* A claim has been made that _____; *however, the values reported are based on a difference of two large numbers.* In the second assay procedure where _____ was used, _____. This may not be applicable to _____ which contains _____. Also, *it is difficult to see* how in the presence of such large concentrations of _____ will accumulate in _____.

The principal investigator's assessment of the current status of information of the role of _____ in _____ processes is *superficial* and in many places *inexact* (p. 9). In describing the role of _____, he does not mention that _____. *His explanation* of how _____ may occur during _____ *begins with a typographical error (or, possibly* worse, *a misunderstanding of inter-, intra-, and extracellular*), and then proceeds to a *distorted view* of how _____. He rather *one-sidedly* invokes _____ as the cause of _____, when there is abundant evidence from _____ and others that _____. Other *cited literature is given a one-line evaluation slanted toward his own view of things.*

The *application* is, in places, rather *carelessly prepared* and, *occasionally, even incomprehensible.* For example, on page 9, section B, there seems to be a *confusion* between the prefixes inter–, extra–, and intra–. The term _____ is *used incorrectly* on page 11. These should be termed _____. The term _____ is *not appropriate.* In the discussion of his observations that _____ can prevent _____, it is *surprising that he does not discuss the work of* _____, who have shown that _____ have similar effects. With regard to the effect of _____, the mechanism _____ is *not well worked out,* and the _____ involvement *may not be as straightforward as implied* in this application.

On the positive side, there is some need to critically examine the role of _____. Approval is recommended.

INVESTIGATORS: _____, received a Ph.D. _____ from the University of _____ and is currently a Research Associate in the Department of _____, _____ Medical School. He has *fourteen publications listed in his bibliography; two of these are in preparation; some of them are in journals such as Science and J. of* _____.

Dr. _____, Assistant Professor in the Department of _____, is listed on page 2 as Co-investigator on this application, but *no biographical sketch* is provided.

RESOURCES AND ENVIRONMENT: Dr. _____ is apparently moving into a new _____ square foot space this month. *Facilities are probably good.*

BUDGET: The following *reductions* are recommended.
Personnel: *Because of the limited scope, delete* the 100% Research Assistant _____, the _____ Laboratory Assistant _____, and Secretary _____.
Equipment: *Reduce* from _____ to _____.
Supplies: *Reduce* from _____ to _____.
Travel: *Reduce* Domestic Travel from $800 to $600, and *delete* Foreign Travel.

EXAMPLE G

Excerpts from a primary reviewer's report. The Study Section voted to defer this grant application.

Grant Number _____

Name of PI _____

X/X/1977

Title: _____

DESCRIPTION: This is a three-year proposal to study the effects of _____ in _____ tissue, particularly as it relates to certain disease states.

The thesis upon which this proposal is based is that a variety of events leading to _____ damage with impairment of _____ may be related to _____ damage. Apparently, *preliminary work in Dr.* _____ *'s laboratory has indicated* the existence of _____ in a variety of _____ tissues. *However, no data are given.* Dr. _____ *conjectures* that _____ may be caused by destruction mediated by _____ accumulated over the _____ . He bases this on observations by others that _____ level increases in _____, and draws the analogy that an increase of _____ might predispose to _____.

The *specific aims are vague* but relate to refinement of analyses of _____, as well as _____, in the various _____ tissues. The levels of these two _____ will also be measured under a variety of _____ conditions, once baseline levels are established. Levels of _____ and _____ will also be measured. Models of _____ and _____ will be induced, and changes in _____ will be determined. Lastly, some histopathology *is alluded to* (last sentence, paragraph 2, page 11). Experiments will utilize _____ and similar laboratory animals.

CRITIQUE: This proposal is based on *recent interesting findings* about the role of _____ in _____ tissues. *Unfortunately, the proposal is vague,* and *much of the methods section, after the initial description of a variety of published* _____ *assays, is really more of a discussion section than a section on methodology.* In addition, *Dr.* _____ *does not seem to be up to date* on recent developments in this area. He mentions in his background section that no data on _____ or on _____ are yet available in the scientific literature (paragraph x, page y); thus, *he is unaware* of the paper by _____ in the Journal of _____ (19XX), entitled _____. *Nor is a reference given to* the paper by _____, in the October 19XX issue of _____, entitled _____, which addresses itself specifically to this question. Likewise, the *discussion of* _____ *and* _____ *in the methods section refers to "extensive investigation of"* _____, *but only a single reference to a paper by* _____ *is given. No reference is made to* a voluminous amount of work from _____ laboratory on the involvement of _____ in the _____ and its possible involvement in _____. The *proposal has not been well thought out, is sloppily written, and has apparently not been proofread.*

Sentences such as the last one on page 13 of the proposal make no sense at all.

I found it *difficult* in several places *to understand what Dr.* _____ *was trying to say.* For example, he says that _____. The next sentence is _____ (last paragraph, page 14). *It is difficult to decide whether the problem is writing or logic.*

The two-paragraph section on _____ and _____ on page 15 is a discussion of some *vague ideas* on possible involvement of _____ in _____, but *not a single specific experiment is mentioned,* nor is any specific methodology given. The same is true for the methods section entitled _____ on page 16 and the section on _____ on the same page. In the methods section on _____, he proposes three types of experiments, but *no methodology is given,* nor is there any statement of any awareness on his part of how much material is necessary to do a single determination of either _____ or _____. *Are the proposed experiments feasible* without using an inordinately large number of animals? How many _____ are necessary to do a single _____ determination?

There are certainly *some interesting possibilities* in this grant, and there is no question but that there is a great need to study the possible involvement of _____ and _____ in _____. However, I can only *characterize this grant proposal as "FUZZY."*

INVESTIGATOR: _____, M.D., _____ School of Medicine, 19_____, is currently instructor of _____ at School of Medicine in _____. He has an *appreciable bibliography, but a number of the entries are abstracts or talks presented at meetings.* There are *no publications of which he is the sole author.*

RESOURCES AND ENVIRONMENT: These are probably good.

BUDGET: The *budget seems high* for the proposed work, and *no justification* is given for any of the budgetary items.

Dr. _____ *is asking* _____ *for a* _____, *but in the facilities available he says that he already has a* _____.
He is asking for a _____, but there is a _____ available.
He is asking for a _____, but there is *no budget justification* given, and it is not clear to me that he couldn't do with the _____ one instead.
I doubt that he needs $ _____ for _____.
It seems to me that there would be a _____ that he can use until he gets some data.
The *supplies category is awfully high* as well as _____ and _____. The miscellaneous items should be cut to _____.

REVIEWER'S RECOMMENDATION: Either approval with a pretty low degree of enthusiasm or disapproval???

EXAMPLE H

Summary Statement for a grant application that was disapproved.

SUMMARY STATEMENT

Requested Start Date: 1981

Recommendation: Disapproval

Special Note: Human Subjects—Protection Adequate

RESUME: Continued support is requested to _____. *The proposal's technical aspirations constitute both its strength and its weakness.* The method of _____ would provide some technical improvements over the more conventional techniques of _____. However, it is *not apparent that the increased technical sophistication would be justified by the theoretical importance* of the proposed experiments. *Nor is it likely, based on past performance of Dr.* _____ *(the Principal Investigator), that these experiments would reach fruition.* Disapproval is recommended.

CRITIQUE: The salient feature of the proposed *experiments* is that they are *technically difficult and sophisticated* _____. Dr. _____ claims that the accuracy of this technique would be _____. However ingenious this technique of _____ might be, *it would surely take a long time to achieve* prior to the _____ of _____ useful data. However, the technical sophistication of the _____ technique is the only feature of this proposal *which distinguishes it from previously reported investigations* on the effect of _____ on the activity of _____.

Based on past performance, it is unlikely that Dr. _____ *would bring these experiments to a successful conclusion.* It is a regrettable but sobering fact that *since 1971, Dr.* _____ *has appeared as the senior author on only one nontechnical, refereed, full-length paper, and this paper was unrelated to any of the proposed experiments.* In previous reviews, Dr. _____ was forewarned concerning his *lack of productivity,* most recently in 1978. Since that warning, one abstract, _____, has been produced in collaboration with Dr. _____, who spent two years with Dr. _____ as a postdoctoral fellow working on the problem of _____.

A preliminary manuscript received late in the review period did little to assure the reviewers that any of the proposed experiments can be successfully carried out by the Principal Investigator. The sample _____ furnished with this manuscript shows that at least _____ can be measured with more than adequate accuracy with the _____, but _____ is another problem. There is an apparent _____ artifact. Even worse, *the investigator shows a total lack of seasoned judgment* in correlating _____ data with _____. We are told that _____, but no evidence is given _____. A check made in the _____ during _____ would be appropriate. *There is no indication that this investigator has even thought about this procedure.* Even worse, we are told that past interpretations of _____ are incorrect, all based on apparently one _____.

INVESTIGATORS: Dr. _____ is currently a _____. After completing his doctoral dissertation at _____, he took a postdoctoral fellowship with Dr. _____ at the University _____. In 19XX, he moved to his present institution. His work during the past nine years has been characterized by a range of interests: investigations of _____. *His publication record has probably suffered as a consequence of his technical and multifaceted interests.*

EXAMPLES I, J, AND K

On the following pages are 3 consecutive Summary Statements received by the same investigator for 3 consecutive grant applications submitted at 3-year intervals. The first application was for an R23 award; R23 was a predecessor of the FIRST Award (R29). This investigator was a mature researcher who, however, had never been a principal investigator and was also entering a new field of study. All three requests were funded.

EXAMPLE I

SUMMARY STATEMENT
(Privileged Communication)

Application Number: 1 _____ C1

Dual Review: _____

Review Group: _____ STUDY SECTION

Meeting Date: FEB/MARCH 1979

Investigator: _____   Degree: Ph.D.

Position.

Organization: _____

City, State: _____   Request Start Date: 09/01/79

Project Title: Biochemical Aspects of _____

Recommendation: Approval   Priority Score: 180

Special Note: Norm Score: 200

     No Human Subjects

     No Recombinant DNA Research Involved

Project Year	Direct Costs Requested	Direct Costs Recommended	Previously Recommended	Grant Period
01	10,000	10,000		
02	10,000	10,000		
03	10,000	10,000		

RESUME: A well-qualified and experienced biochemist *requests modest funds* to investigate the processes involved in _____. This is a *significant and worthwhile project* that merits enthusiastic support. Approval is recommended for the time and amount requested. However, it *should be conveyed to the investigator that this application, or an expanded version of it, is sufficiently ambitious and wide-ranging to merit full support at a level commensurate with a regular research grant application.*

<u>DESCRIPTION</u>: The overall purpose of the proposed research is the investigation of factors that are involved _____.

Laboratory Animals: _____.

<u>CRITIQUE</u>: Experiments described by the principal investigator are *very ambitious in range.* Several studies involve the use of developing _____ as a means of correlating a particular property with the appearance of _____: 1. Histological studies will be done to determine _____. 2. _____ activity will be monitored so as to follow _____. In addition, _____ will be evaluated. 3. _____ incorporation will be followed with the hope of isolating a specific _____. The first two sets of experiments should be relatively straightforward, whereas the third one requires the ability to isolate _____.

A particularly strong point for this application is the documentation of a number of preliminary results. These appear to be of good quality. For example, one group of results concern _____ studies on _____. Dr. _____ has measured _____. Dr. _____ believes that this may be related to a requirement for _____.

Dr. _____ has also begun an examination of _____. The _____ preparation was obtained by _____. Primary fractionation on _____ showed a number of _____ bands. The pattern was completely different from those of _____. Dr. _____ *appears to be aware of the problem* that _____. However, he has omitted the _____ steps and modified the technique in other ways so that apparently the _____ appears to be good by _____.

In summary, this is a very *ambitious application that is backed up by promising preliminary results. The proposed work is directed to a significant area of* _____ *research.* The principal investigator is *well trained* to carry out many of the areas of research proposed.

<u>INVESTIGATOR</u>: Dr. _____ received his Ph.D. in _____ in 19XX from _____ University, where he worked with Dr. _____ on _____. He took two postdoctorals, one between 19XX and 19XX with Dr. _____. The second, _____ between 19XX and 19XX with Dr. _____, where his work was on _____. He then went to _____ University between 19XX and 19XX, where he carried out studies on _____. Between 19XX and 19XX he was a _____ in the laboratory of Dr. _____ at _____, where his work was mainly on the _____. In 19XX, he joined the _____ as an _____, where he is carrying out research on _____ as well as _____ studies. He also holds a position of _____ at _____.

<u>RESOURCES</u> <u>AND</u> <u>ENVIRONMENT</u>: These appear to be *adequate* for the proposed research.

<u>BUDGET</u>: At $10,000 per year, the maximum for an R23 Award, the *budget is very reasonable.*

EXAMPLE J

SUMMARY STATEMENT
(Privileged Communication)

Application Number: 1 R01 _____-01

Dual Review: _____

Review Group: _____ Review Group

Meeting Date: FEB/MARCH 1982

Investigator: Degree: Ph.D.

Position:

Organization: _____

City, State: _____   Request Start Date: 09/01/82

Project Title: _____

Recommendation: Approval   Priority Score: 170

Special Note: No Human Subjects

Project Year	Direct Costs Requested	Direct Costs Recommended	Previously Recommended	Grant Period
01	76,907	76,907		
02	82,300	82,300		
03	90,510	90,510		

RESUME: Dr. _____ has proposed studies whose goals are the characterization of the components and their functions of the _____. *Several components of these studies seem desirable.* These include characterization of the _____, determination of the presence of _____, and a cross comparison to determine differences in _____ distribution in different _____. Approval is recommended for time and budget with *high enthusiasm.*
DESCRIPTION: ...

CRITIQUE: This is a *carefully organized research plan that follows logically from extensive preliminary data* collected by the principal investigator. The project is a very important one, for little information is now available on the paths for transfer of material between _____ and the functions of the _____. The proposal includes both *projects which will undoubtedly succeed* and provide important information, such as the _____, and more speculative projects on the functions of _____. However, the *more speculative projects are based on substantial preliminary data and are worth pursuing.*

A major potential problem in this research, the *contamination of material from* _____, *is serious. The principal investigator is fully aware of such criticism and has diligently attempted to deal with it. This is a major strength in the proposal.* Nonetheless, *questions remain.* In particular, the separation _____ may require further analysis. The *principal investigator might be encouraged,* insofar as possible, to carry out _____ analysis on the material obtained by the _____ procedure of _____. The alternative mode of preparation of _____ is an important complementary method. This should ensure more complete _____.

<u>INVESTIGATOR</u>: Dr. _____ received his Ph.D. from _____ University in _____ in 19XX. He did postdoctoral work with Dr. _____ at _____ and spent _____ years at _____ with Dr. _____. Dr. _____ was a _____ with _____ at _____ University from 19XX to 19XX. His training ranges from _____ to _____. Dr. _____ has been an _____ at _____ since 19XX. The principal investigator is *very well trained* in _____ techniques and is *well able to carry out the proposed experiments.*

<u>RESOURCES</u> <u>AND</u> <u>ENVIRONMENT</u>: Equipment and laboratory *facilities are very adequate* for the proposed research, and the *scientific environment is excellent.*

<u>BUDGET</u>: The budget is appropriate for the proposed research.

EXAMPLE K

SUMMARY STATEMENT
(Privileged Communication)

Application Number: 2 R01 _____ -04

Dual Review: _____

Review Group: _____ Review Group

Meeting Date: FEB/MARCH 1985

Investigator: _____   Degree: Ph.D.
Organization: _____

City, State: _____   Request Start Date: 09/01/85

Project Title: _____

Recommendation: Approval   Priority Score: 150

Human Subjects: 10—No Human Subjects Involved

Animal Subjects: 30—Animals Involved—No IRG comments or concerns noted

Project Year	Direct Costs Requested	Direct Costs Recommended
04	97,404	97,404
05	115,138	115,138
06	122,840	122,840
07	134,350	134,350
08	144,015	144,015

OUTSIDE OPINION:

RESUME: An experienced research worker requests five years of support to extend his studies on the _____. *The investigator has pioneered work in this area and has made significant contributions to its development.* He proposes to extend studies on the structure and function of the _____ and to determine _____. These studies may assist in understanding the nature of _____. Approval is recommended in time and amount.

DESCRIPTION: ...

CRITIQUE: Because the functions of _____ depend on a supply of _____, it is important to understand how the _____ works. It is logical to assume that the _____. *The present proposal is important* because so little is known about the chemical composition and functions of the _____. Dr. _____ has previously analyzed _____ and characterized some of the _____.

Of various _____, the investigator is particularly interested in _____. His main interest lies in the elucidation of the role of _____. *Experiments are designed to answer several key questions* such as: Can _____? Can _____? Does _____ ? Can

_____? Affirmative answers to these questions are necessary but not sufficient to establish that _____ plays a role in _____. In addition to the *in vitro* experiments, *in vivo* experiments are essential in which _____ of the _____ is quantitatively determined at _____. In view of the *research capacity* of Dr. _____'s laboratory, this project alone would take all his time and efforts. *Overcommitment to diversified problems as stated may not be rewarding in the long run.* His *publication record and progress report* indicate that his expertise and background are strong in _____. The *investigator is therefore encouraged to emphasize* in his approach quantitative aspects of _____.

The investigator seeks to extend his studies of _____ to determine if it can _____. Mimicking the _____ found adjacent to _____ would appear important for this experiment. The investigator also seeks to determine whether _____ may participate in a _____. Drs. _____ and _____ have postulated _____. The investigator should note that this is a quantitatively rare process as measured by Drs. _____ and _____ and *could not expect to be detected by his proposed procedures.* In addition, based upon _____ *it is difficult to imagine how* _____ *could successfully* _____. The *investigator is encouraged to scrutinize his preliminary data with these considerations in mind.*

The investigator will further pursue _____. The use of _____ methods is proposed in order to preserve _____. *However, this method may not remove all traces of* _____, *whose presence could complicate interpretation of the results. Validity of the measurements will depend upon demonstration that such interference is not present.*

The investigator proposes to investigate whether _____ can be _____. It will be necessary to prepare each of the _____, and the *investigator proposes trying new procedures* rather than reproducing the lengthy conventional ones. *For the sake of efficiency it would nevertheless seem more reasonable to use the worked-out published procedures rather than to develop totally new ones for such restricted purposes—purposes which are also somewhat peripheral to the stated central objectives of the research.*

It is proposed to evaluate the mechanism of _____. The _____ *approaches outlined seem straightforward in approach and well designed to elicit the information desired.* It is with the _____ and _____ approaches that *some caution is due.* At least *four other laboratories* and their collaborators seem to be *uniquely capable* in performing studies involving these skills. The *investigator would be well advised to concentrate on those areas to which he can make some unique contributions.*

_____ is suggested to have _____. The investigator proposes to further study its _____ properties by _____ measurements and by _____ followed by _____. Hopefully, this will help in understanding how its _____ is important in its _____ properties. The determination of _____ is proposed via use of _____. *The investigator presents the theory behind the approach but does not appear to be familiar with analogous work which has been published on the* _____ [J. _____ (19XX)]. The _____ *chemistry is far from trivial and is not undertaken lightly.* Considerable experience in _____, the _____ desired by the investigator, has been obtained by the laboratory of _____, and by that of _____. *These investigators may help the applicant evaluate* what kind of commitment would be involved in cost and time of _____ and in amounts of _____ required.

The search for _____ represents a *fruitful approach* to understanding the functions of the _____. This is an area pioneered by the investigator and which is worthy of renewed attention. The investigator proposes the use of novel _____ in order to definitively _____.

The origins of the _____ will be sought using _____. *This would appear to be a difficult problem* to undertake, although the choice of animal seems reasonable based upon techniques available for dealing with the _____. This is to be coupled with investigation of the _____. *Either of these two topics would be sufficiently broad and open-ended to warrant full-scale multi-year studies in themselves. The investigator will certainly need to ask pointed questions and focus narrowly on principal vs. peripheral objectives.*

It is of interest to extend these studies to models of _____, and the investigator proposed use of the _____. *However, at the 1984 _____ meeting, the validity of this model was questioned. The investigator may wish to restrict these studies to the better developed models.*

INVESTIGATOR: Dr. _____ received his B.A. in _____ from _____ College and his Ph.D. in _____ at _____. He received postdoctoral *training in several fine laboratories* and was _____ at _____ from 19XX–19XY. Since that time he has been _____ at _____. *During the last grant period he has published 10 papers with 2 more in press and another submitted for publication.*

RESOURCES AND ENVIRONMENT: These are adequate for performance of the research proposal.

BUDGET: The proposed *budget is reasonable and justified.* Approval is recommended in time and amount.

EXAMPLES L AND M

Example L is the Summary Statement for an application that was approved but *not* funded. It is followed by Example M, the Summary Statement for the *same* investigator's revised application, which *was* funded. Note the change in priority score and percentile rank.

EXAMPLE L

SUMMARY STATEMENT
(Privileged Communication)

Application Number: 2 R01 _____ -07

Dual Review: _____

Review Group: _____ Study Section

Meeting Date: OCT/NOV 1984

Investigator: _____   Degree: Ph.D.

Organization: _____

City, State: Request Start Date: 06/01/85

Project Title: _____

Recommended: Approval   Priority Score: 160
        Percentile: 40.0

Human Subjects: 10—No Human Subjects Involved

Animal Subjects: 10—No Live Vertebrate Animals Involved

Project Year	Direct Costs Requested	Direct Costs Recommended
07	141,687	117,417
08	145,811	124,391
09	155,905	134,485
10	166,707	0
11	178,264	0

ADMINISTRATIVE NOTE:

RESUME: Dr. _____'s *interesting and productive studies* on the _____ will be related to the _____. Future results *may be expected to generate information on key steps* in the regulation of _____, *but the newer directions of research have only been briefly described.* Dr. _____ *is highly qualified* to pursue these studies. To facilitate an early review of the detailed plans for new departures, support is recommended for only three years at this time.

DESCRIPTION: ...

CRITIQUE: This is a *well-written, carefully documented proposal* to continue a productive line of research on an *important subject:* the physical basis of _____ in the _____ of _____. This *research promises to continue to make important progress* in the understanding of _____ in systems containing _____. This application proposes to extend this study to another similar _____, and the *prospects for success appear good.* This is *very timely research,* since previous models for _____ have recently been questioned, resulting in increased attention to possible changes in these _____.

Dr. _____ has been a *leader in the study of* _____ *for the past ten years, and progress in the current period was excellent, resulting in nine papers in refereed journals of high quality.* Previous studies were about evenly divided between studies of _____ and studies of _____ in _____, and the proposed work shifts more emphasis toward the _____ studies and toward studies of _____.

Most of the _____ analysis will be done with _____ previously characterized by Dr. _____. These *experiments are well designed,* and Dr. _____ *discusses clearly* the need to distinguish between changes in _____ and changes in the _____ properties of _____. *Nevertheless, it remains a difficult problem that cannot always be solved and inevitably results in some ambiguity in data interpretation. The problem of the role of* _____ *in* _____ *requires a more global view* of the various _____. Dr. _____ intends to put together all of the _____, but the parameter monitored will in most cases be *restricted to* _____.

A *universal concern* in _____ studies is _____. Dr. _____ states that this can be an advantage, but *his arguments are not convincing.* Comparisons with _____ data will help, but _____ is a very gross measure containing contributions over all the _____.

The project increases the emphasis on _____ measurements to provide _____ information to complement the _____ measurements. This should help provide a more complete picture of the _____ interactions in this system.
In general, it remains to be seen whether _____ are important in _____, so that the proposed increased emphasis on _____ is important.

Proposed studies on _____ *are only briefly sketched,* but the *collaboration with Dr.* _____ *looks promising.* Similarly, the _____ studies in *collaboration with Dr.* _____ *should continue to be interesting.* Proposed studies are similar to those on _____, although these are at a much earlier stage. *This part of the project has become much more interesting recently,* in light of evidence obtained from others that suggest the importance of _____. The importance of _____ was recently described, but *the proposed new work is only briefly alluded to.*

INVESTIGATORS: Dr. _____ obtained his Ph.D. in _____ from the University of _____ in 19XX, did postdoctoral work with _____ at _____ University from 19XX to 19XX, and then joined the Department of _____ at _____, where he is now a _____. He has an *impressive publication record* in the field of _____, particularly in the study of _____. *No one is better qualified than he to carry out the proposed research.*

Dr. _____, Research Associate, obtained his Ph.D. in _____ recently from _____ University. During the past year he has worked directly with Dr. _____ on _____.

<u>BUDGET</u>: The request is one-third higher than the current award; *addition of another staff person is difficult to justify,* and therefore funds for a research assistant ($_____) may be *omitted.* The *price of the* _____ *appears high*—$X,000 should prove adequate. Other categories are appropriate. *The new directions of this project are not described in sufficient detail, and therefore support should be limited to three years at this time.*

<u>ADMINISTRATIVE</u> <u>NOTE</u>: *A parallel application is pending before the* _____ program of the NSF (#_____).

EXAMPLE M

Example M is the Summary Statement for the revised application written in response to the Summary Statement given in Example L. The revised application *was* funded.

SUMMARY STATEMENT
(Privileged Communication)

Application Number: 2 R01 _____ -07A1

Dual:

Review Group: _____ Study Section

Meeting Date: June 1985

Investigator: _____   Degree: Ph.D.

Organization: _____

City, State: _____   Request Start Date: 12/01/85

Project Title: _____

Recommended: Approval   Priority Score: 130
                                                          Percentile: 9.0

Human Subjects: 10—No Human Subjects Involved
Animal Subjects: 10—No Live Vertebrate Animals Involved

Project Year	Direct Costs Requested	Direct Costs Recommended
07A1	146,310	146,310
08	154,762	154,762
09	166,806	166,806
10	179,814	179,814
11	193,863	193,863

ADMINISTRATIVE NOTE:

RESUME: *Dr. _____, a leader in the study of _____, has been highly productive of important contributions.* The work will be extended to _____. *The work is sound and innovative, and the results have broad implications for _____. Continued support is enthusiastically endorsed.*

DESCRIPTION: *This is a revised continuation application. The previous version was highly recommended for approval last fall, but it was not supported.* The ...

CRITIQUE: *Dr. _____ has quite successfully dealt with the earlier questions in the review. New data are cited in the application and provided in additional manuscripts to show that _____ is capable of _____. The evidence also indicates that _____. Dr. _____ also plans to _____, to provide a second _____. This strategy will re-*

quire the difficult use of the _____ which consists of _____. In any investigation which requires the use of _____, the question of _____ introduced by _____ always arises. Dr. _____ *is keenly aware of potential pitfalls and is prepared to deal with them.* A subtle _____ is introduced in the _____; this _____ has been well characterized. It is this _____ that leads to _____. Other new data show that the loss of _____ is related to _____. This _____ is related to the extent of _____. *The arguments are convincing that* the _____ are indeed advantageous.

Previous studies carried out by Dr. _____ and collaborators have *yielded a powerful and clever approach* to investigate the _____. This is based on the unique _____. Dr. _____ *has had remarkable success* in exploiting the _____ that take place _____ . *Ten full papers have been published in refereed journals for work that was carried out in the last three years. Two additional manuscripts are listed as pending. This is a very productive record. The quality of the papers is generally high.*

The present proposal describes *a sharply focused research direction* and shows a *well-planned and carefully thought out project.* Studies currently underway in Dr. _____'s laboratory have emphasized _____, but with a leaning toward _____. The proposed work will have a heavy emphasis on correlation of _____ studies with _____. This *shift of emphasis is both timely and well justified* because sufficient knowledge is now on hand about the behavior of _____.

Evidence is accumulating to suggest that _____. The proposed involvement of _____ is likely to be valid, but its precise role remains to be elucidated. How well the _____ of _____ that was first demonstrated by the applicant, and has since been extensively investigated by him, would fit into the overall scheme *remains to be seen. It is likely that some very interesting information will be forthcoming* from Dr. _____'s laboratory.

The proposed *work specifically related to* _____ *is less well developed, and the potential success in this component is somewhat less certain.*

Some efforts during the next period will be spent on _____. This *represents a new direction* for Dr. _____. *This expansion is logical* because _____. *His collaborator,* Dr. _____, has expertise in the _____ and *will contribute significantly* to the proposed work in which the _____ methodologies successfully used for _____ will be applied to _____. *A significant paper has been published from this collaboration* in which _____.

INVESTIGATORS: Dr. _____ obtained his Ph.D. in _____ from the University of _____ in 19XX, did postdoctoral work with _____ at _____ University from 19XX to 19XY, and then joined the Department of _____ at _____, where he is now a _____. He has an *impressive publication record* in the field of _____, particularly in the study of _____. *No one is better qualified than he to carry out the proposed research.*

Dr. _____, Research Associate, obtained his Ph.D. in _____ recently from _____ University. During the past year he has worked directly with Dr. _____ on _____.

BUDGET: *The request is similar to the previous application but is now thoroughly justified,* and no changes are needed.

ADMINISTRATIVE NOTE: *A parallel proposal is pending before the NSF (#_____).*

EXAMPLE N

This is a Summary Statement for an application that received a very poor priority score and was not funded. This detailed Summary Statement provides particularly good examples of the things reviewers look for when they review an application.

SUMMARY STATEMENT
(Privileged Communication)

Application Number: 1 R01 _____-01

Dual Review: _____

Review Group: _____ Study Section

Meeting Date: FEB/MARCH 1987

Investigator: Degree: Ph.D.

Organization: _____

City, State: Requested Start Date: 07/01/87

Project Title: _____

Priority Score: 420

Percentile: 95.0

Recommended: Approval

Human Subjects: 10—No Human Subjects Involved

Animal Subjects: 30—ANMLS INV.—VERIFIED, NO IRG CONCERNS OR COMMENT

Project Year	Direct Costs Requested	Direct Costs Recommended
01	122,817	88,042
02	130,095	95,320
03	139,313	104,538

RESUME: This _____ study will examine _____ changes in the _____ associated with the disruption of _____ in _____. *The proposal was found conceptually weak. The experimental design lacks in precision, and some experiments are seriously flawed. Despite these weaknesses,* it was felt that the *study may add some new information* on _____. Approval with a modest reduction in budget was therefore recommended.

DESCRIPTION: (*adapted from the investigator's abstract*): The long-term objective of the proposed studies is _____.

CRITIQUE: This is a *well-organized and concisely written* proposal to study _____ changes in the _____ associated with the disruption of _____ in _____ and _____ exposed to _____. The *proposal addresses an interesting question,* i.e., whether the changes in _____ that are observed in _____ during _____ can be correlated with _____. The investigator speculates that the disappearance of _____ may be due to _____. Since some _____ changes in other _____ have been described in the literature, a closer look at _____ in this respect is justified, and the *study can* thus *contribute to the overall picture of* _____. Although the proposed *studies would inevitably come short of establishing* the direct causal relationship between _____ and _____, they *nevertheless may result in interesting observations* which could lead to further exploration of this relationship. The part of the proposal that deals with monitoring _____ represents *a definite strength of the project. These studies have been carefully designed* and will provide a comprehensive picture of the state of the animals in regard to _____. The *observations will not have much independent value or novelty, however, since the* _____ *changes of these parameters have been extensively studied.* Nevertheless, the significance of this part of the proposal is in relationship to _____ studies that will be performed on the same animals.

Another major strength of the proposed research is that the _____ analyses will be performed in animals with clearly defined and monitored deficits. The _____ analyses are relatively simple and take advantage of computerized _____ programs, which are described in detail. *Most of the proposed techniques are feasible and capable of yielding the desired descriptive information.* The investigator is a *well trained* _____ with experiences in both _____ and _____ techniques. *However, he has had only limited experience in* _____. Dr. _____, co-investigator, is an experienced _____ and appears to be *fully competent* to carry out the _____ experiments and _____.

The project has also a number of weaknesses. The described studies represent *a data-gathering search with no underlying hypotheses and little explanation of how the collected data will be interpreted.* Furthermore, there are *no preliminary results* suggesting that _____ may occur. *In the absence of such preliminary data, the entire project may be a futile search which will yield little, if any, new information,* since most of the _____ aspects of the _____ have already been described in _____. There are *several serious concerns* in regard to the _____ part of the proposal. This part *lacks essential details,* and therefore *in several instances, one could only guess what exactly is planned to be studied.* For example, it was *not clear how* _____ in experiment B under Specific Aim 1 are possible from _____ that will be taken at regular intervals. It appears that the *resolution achieved with such a technique is not sufficient to identify* the location and concrete boundaries of _____. It *is not clear* then how the comparisons of _____ and _____ are possible with this technique. In experiment C under Specific Aim 1, number and size of _____ will be determined in three unspecified _____. *What happens if* _____ *is found? What exactly will be measured and how? How will the individual* _____ *be identified?* There is *no description* of these aspects. All this *leaves an impression that very little thought has been given to experimental design.*

There are also *flaws in the design of specific experiments.* Experiment D includes _____ analysis where the investigator plans to study distribution of _____ and examine the possibility of _____ of different _____. As stated, there is *no indication that the investigator has prior experience with* _____ and *whether any of these procedures have already been established in his laboratory. Controls,* _____, *possible problems* that can be encountered in _____, or even the *exact organization* of these experiments are *not discussed, nor are the probable outcome and interpretation of results. A similar criticism* applies to _____, which is *only mentioned briefly.* Further, experiments combining _____ and _____ *cannot be successfully completed using the described procedures.* The purpose of these experiments is to identify _____. The _____ giving rise to the particular _____ will be identified by _____. The _____ *are not described.* It *is probably not possible* to _____. Moreover, it is *not discussed how* the _____ sites *will be controlled, which is of crucial importance* in _____ with its closely situated _____ and functionally diverse _____. *No other* _____ *experiments have been planned.* Therefore, it is *not clear how the goal of this part of the project will be achieved.* In another set of studies the _____ investigator plans to _____. *No details of these experiments are given.* It is mentioned, however, that all results will be _____ using a computer _____. The _____ demonstration of the _____ content within each of these _____ *will also be impossible to obtain from these experiments, since the* _____ used *is not compatible with* _____. This will be done on normal _____ and, as could be guessed, will involve description of _____ and probably some kind of measurement. *What exactly will be achieved in this study and how the results can be related to those in other parts of proposal is not discussed.* The final part of the proposal involves _____ with *unidentified goals, unspecified* _____ and _____.

In summary, *the proposal is incomplete. The essential details are omitted both with regard to the methodology and with respect to how results are to be interpreted.* Moreover, the *proposal is conceptually weak, lacks focus, and logical design of experiments is nonexistent.* Some of the *techniques proposed appear inadequate to achieve the specific aims.* The outcome of other experiments, i.e., _____, can be *compromised by the lack of experience of the investigator in this methodology.*

INVESTIGATORS: _____ is Associate Professor of _____ in the Department of _____ at _____ Medical School. He received a Ph.D. in _____ from _____ in 19XX. *He published 20 original papers and 6 chapters. He has been involved for years in cooperative studies with* Dr. _____ on _____.

Dr. _____ is a Research Associate in the _____ at _____ Medical School. He received a Ph.D. in _____ from the University of _____. He *has co-authored 6 papers and 1 book chapter.*

BUDGET: *Appears somewhat excessive.* Dr. _____'s involvement in the project can be reduced to 50% ($1X,XXX), and the research assistant can be *deleted* ($1X,XXX). Supplies can be *reduced* by $4XXX.

EXAMPLE O

This is the Summary Statement for a proposal that was funded at its third submission. The third submission was written using the advice set forth in a workshop given by Liane Reif-Lehrer—advice that is, to a large extent, set forth in this book.

SUMMARY STATEMENT
(Privileged Communication)

Application Number: 1 R01 _____-01A1

Review Group: _____ Study Section

Meeting Date: June 1987

Investigator: _____   Degree: Ph.D.

Organization: _____

City, State: _____   Request Start Date: 12/01/87

Project Title: _____

Recommended: Approval

Priority Score: 130

Percentile: 4.0

Human Subjects: 10—No Human Subjects Involved

Animal Subjects: 30—ANMLS INV.—VERIFIED, NO IRG CONCERNS OR COMMENT

Project Year	Direct Costs Requested	Direct Costs Recommended
01A1	123,282	123,282
02	127,441	127,441
03	133,324	133,324

RESUME: This is an *excellent proposal* from a *very strong research group.* The research is *highly likely to produce very important data.* The proposal is recommended for approval with *strong enthusiasm.*

DESCRIPTION: (*Adapted from investigator's original abstract.*) This research project deals with the study of _____.

CRITIQUE: This *amended application* was originally submitted as an R01 application. The next submission was expanded and submitted as a FIRST Award application. That application was *reviewed very favorably but did not have a sufficiently high[2] priority score to receive funding.* At that time there were concerns expressed in the review that the investigator may be too senior for the FIRST Award funding mechanisms. In addition, there

---

[2] The reviewer means "good" priority score here, which would be a low number, i.e., a score close to 100.

were some *potential methodological limitation concerns* identified. *This revised application has addressed all of the concerns in the previous review in a satisfactory manner.*

This proposal represents a natural extension of previous studies of this group. The overall goal is to study _____ with special emphasis on dealing with the mechanisms which affect _____. The proposal *outlines a logical series of experiments* dealing with _____. They will use _____, a _____ model of _____ In all cases, _____ will be measured. In addition, _____ will be measured using a _____ The research is *highly significant* in that these will be the first studies measuring _____ and _____ simultaneously. The studies deal with the fundamental mechanisms which govern _____. The *studies will help to develop a novel* _____ *for measuring* _____ using a _____ means. These measurements will then be compared with the _____ method for measuring _____.

The methodology is appropriate for the proposed research, and, in fact, *the unique methodology is a strength of the proposal.* A problem of the previous application was that there was concern about several limitations of the proposed methodology. However, the *investigators have added a substantial amount of text indicating that they are well aware of these limitations and do, in fact, have a great deal of insight into the ways of solving any potential problems that arise. It is now clear that the research will provide a substantial amount of new and important data.*

INVESTIGATORS: Dr. _____ is _____ in _____ at _____. He obtained his Ph.D. degree in _____ from _____. Dr. _____ lists *a number of publications in both the* _____ *and the* _____ *literature.* He is a *well-trained* investigator who is *very likely to successfully accomplish the goals* of the project. Also participating will be Dr. _____, _____ in _____. He is a *well-known and capable* investigator *in this area of research.* Dr. _____ is a _____ in _____. He received an M.D. degree from _____ and has been a _____ in this department since _____. *Other collaborators* include: _____. These collaborators *add important expertise* to the project. Together, this *investigative team is extremely well qualified* to carry out the proposed research.

BUDGET: The budget is appropriate as requested.

EXAMPLE P

A Summary Statement and Structural Outline of a proposal by an investigator who received a MERIT Award (See Glossary for definition of MERIT Award).

SUMMARY STATEMENT
(Privileged Communication)

Application Number: R01

Review Group: _____

Meeting Dates: IRG:__, 1990

        Council: __, 1990

Investigator: _____   Degree: Ph.D.

Organization: _____

City, State: _____   Requested Start Date: x/x/91

Project Title: _____

                                     Percentile: 2.0

Recommended: Approval   Priority Score: 120

Human Subjects: 10—No Human Subjects Involved

Animal Subjects: 10—No Live Vertebrate Animals Involved

Project Year	Direct Costs Requested	Direct Costs Recommended
14	1XX,XXX	
15	XXX,XXX	
16	XXX,XXX	As requested
17	XXX,XXX	
18	2XX,XXX	

RESUME: This is *clearly an outstanding proposal by an investigator who has demonstrated a consistent ability to form incisive hypotheses* about the molecular basis of _____ and to test them rigorously with an effective combination of 3 methods: x, y, z. There is every reason to expect continued outstanding progress in this research.

DESCRIPTION: ...

CRITIQUE: _____ is one of the most important general problems in biology, and system X provides the central model system for this type of process.

Progress in the past five years has been outstanding, resulting in ten journal articles, x book articles, and x abstracts. Several of these are *ground-breaking papers,* such as x & y articles in which Dr. _____ and co-workers have demonstrated that _____, or the _____ paper in which they have shown that _____. Dr. _____ has also demonstrated in his published work that _____. These and other results followed from a *creative and logical series of studies* proposed in the previous application. They establish Dr. _____ as the *current world leader* in _____, and they *promise to shed light* on analogous _____ processes involving other _____.

The *proposed work is described clearly and logically.* Much of the work centers on the production of _____, based on the *already impressive progress* in establishing _____ and obtaining _____. This previous progress, coupled with the *detailed studies* of _____, indicates that Dr. _____ *will almost certainly be successful* in _____. The *rationale* for the selection of _____ *is particularly sharp.* All of the _____ methods described are ones for which Dr. _____ *has already established expertise.*

The proposed _____ *studies of* _____ *are particularly elegant.* A collection of _____ will be _____ and _____ will determine _____ as a function of _____ and other _____ This should permit _____. *The major weakness of this approach is* _____, *which could* _____ *and complicate interpretation.* Dr. _____ *is well aware of this issue* and *aware of the need to* make _____ measurements to assure _____ Perhaps the *proposal could have been strengthened by* plans to _____ The _____ studies will be nicely complemented by _____, *helping to remove much of the ambiguity of interpretation.*

The proposal should perhaps be strengthened further by using _____ in order to _____, instead of just using _____.

INVESTIGATORS: Dr. _____ received the Ph.D. in _____ from _____. His *publication record is moderate in quantity but outstanding* in his fundamental contributions to _____ and _____. He is *extremely well qualified* to continue to direct the proposed research.

Dr. _____, Research Associate, will receive the Ph.D. in _____ from _____ University in 19XX and has recently started working with Dr. _____. His *experience in* _____ *is excellent* and should prepare him well for the proposed research.

BUDGET: The request is *appropriate and well justified.* The increase by more than one-half over the present level is due to the addition of the research associate and the increased need for expensive supplies for the _____ aspects of the project.

EXCERPTS FROM THE PROPOSAL WHICH RESULTED IN A MERIT AWARD AND FOR WHICH THE SUMMARY STATEMENT IS GIVEN ABOVE.

ABSTRACT:
The *long-term objective* of this project is to elucidate the molecular mechanism of _____ and its regulation by _____. The *key questions* that we wish to address are: 1) How is _____? 2) How does _____? Our approach is to determine _____. The specific aims of this application center on _____. The *principal methodologies* that we will employ are _____. *Results from these studies will allow us to* _____. Since _____, *information derived from this work may contribute towards the diagnosis, prevention, and ultimately the cure of* _____.

RESEARCH PLAN
A. Specific Aims:

1) The *long-term objective* of this project is to elucidate the molecular mechanism of _____. The approach is to determine _____, and to study _____. It is hoped that this will _____.

2) The Specific Aims for the forthcoming grant period are as follows:
   a) To detect and characterize _____.
   b) To elucidate the mechanism of _____.
   c) To elucidate the mechanism of _____.

3) The *methodologies* that will be used are as follows:
   a)
   b)
   c)
   d)

B. Background and Significance (Abbreviations are listed on page X.)

It is well established that _____. What remains not fully understood are _____. The key questions are i) How does _____? ii) How does _____?

Mechanism of X: ...

Mechanism of Y: ...

General Background
1)
2)
3)

It seems clear that ...
The work proposed in the specific aims is directed towards the questions raised with respect to _____. In our previous studies we have successfully _____. A *major drawback in these studies* is that _____ and that _____. For the forthcoming grant period, the methodologies for _____ *have been established* in my laboratory precisely for the purpose of _____ Our approach will allow us to _____ and to _____. We should point out that although _____ and _____ have made and will continue to make great strides in elucidating _____, neither technique is as yet viable for the study of _____. We feel that our approach of combining _____ with _____ and _____ *techniques offers unique opportunities for deciphering* _____.

C. Progress Report
   1) *Period:* _____, 1985 to _____, 1990.
   2) *Personnel:* ...
   3) *Previous period's accomplishments:*
      a)
      through
      k)
   4) *Summary of importance:*
      a)
      b)
      c)
      d)

5) *Changes in Specific Aims:*

There will be no change in the overall direction of the project, nor will there be any change in the general approach of _____. A *major addition to our methodology*, however, is the use of _____.

6) *Publications:*
   a) *Journal articles:*
   b) *Book articles:*
   c) *Abstracts:*

D. Experimental Design and Methods

This section was organized as follows:

Outline:
1) Research Designs for SA a:
2) Research Designs for SA b:
3) Research Designs for SA c:
4) Methods
   a)
   through
   h)

This was followed by an 8-page narrative that parallels the above outline. The narrative begins:
1) Major topic A
   a) *X studies.* Our *general strategy is* to _____

   Thus, such *measurements will reveal* whether _____. Depending on whether _____ or _____, *we will be able to deduce* whether _____.

   The measurements will be carried out first in _____ and then in _____. An increase in _____ *can be interpreted as* _____, *although it can be argued that* _____.

   b) *Y studies.* _____ will be labeled with _____ and will then be identified by _____. A finding of _____ *would provide conclusive evidence that* _____.

   c) *Z studies.* For each _____, the _____ will be _____ to measure _____. The measurements will be made in _____ as well as in _____. The *ultimate goal is to* _____.

ABBREVIATIONS:

EXAMPLE Q

Summary Statement for a proposal that was funded on the first revision.

SUMMARY STATEMENT
(Privileged Communication)

Application Number: 1 R01_____01A1

Review Group: _____

Meeting Dates: IRG: 1990

Council: 1990

Investigator: _____   Degree: Ph.D.

Organization: _____

City, State: _____   Requested Start Date: x/x/90

Project Title: _____

Percentile: 13.0

Recommended: Approval   Priority Score: 150

Human Subjects: 10—No Human Subjects Involved

Animal Subjects: 10—No Live Vertebrate Animals Involved

Project Year	Direct Costs Required	Direct Costs Recommended
01A1	1XX,XXX	
02		XXX,XXX
03	XXX,XXX	About 10% less
04	XXX,XXX	than requested
05	1XX,XXX	

RESUME: This is an *exciting proposal* from a *well-qualified and experienced* investigator. The *techniques to be used are state-of-the-art* and *will provide quantitative data rela*ting to the role of _____. Approval is recommended for the time requested and a modest reduction of the budget.

DESCRIPTION: ...

CRITIQUE: This revised application *disputes the criticisms* pertaining to _____ studies that were proposed in the 1988 application but *responds to the reviewer's enthusiasm for the other studies by now concentrating on those aspects that were favorably reviewed.* In addition, *much new preliminary and supporting data and several publications lend considerable strength to the current application.* The *hypotheses to be tested and convincing arguments in support of these hypotheses are clearly and succinctly described.* The *review of the literature is excellent,* and *new ideas are brought* to the _____ research from observations that have been made by others in _____.

Progress in the past two years *is impressive.* Dr. X has co-authored 10 papers documenting her commitment and developing expertise in the use of _____ and _____. Large numbers of _____ have been available to her for previous studies, thus, providing assurance that she will have adequate supplies for the proposed studies. The _____ *techniques* to be utilized to identify and quantitate _____ *are state-of-the-art,* and the *results that can be obtained are beautifully illustrated.*

The major hypothesis to be tested is that _____. The *proposed experiments should provide answers to these important questions. Appropriate controls* and *statistical analysis of the results* will be used. *The investigators are aware of the pitfalls that might be encountered and have plans for dealing with them.* The techniques to be used require meticulous attention to detail, but Dr. X's *ability to apply rigorous standards to her work is apparent in her previous publications and discussion of the proposed research.*

INVESTIGATOR: Dr. X is a _____. She received her Ph.D. in _____. She would devote 100% effort to the proposed research. Dr. Y will *collaborate* with her in proposed studies utilizing _____ measurements of _____ by _____ techniques. He will *make* his _____ *instrument available* for her use.

RESOURCES AND ENVIRONMENT: These are adequate.

BUDGET: This is *an expensive first R01,* but the principal investigator must support 100% of her effort plus that of a research associate. *If* the principal investigator has *not* been *invited* to present data at the _____ conference, consider removing that travel money on year one. *"Other Expenses" are too high* and should be reduced to $X,XXX.

Example R

Summary Statement for a successful competing continuation application by a Principal Investigator who has already received 28 years of continuous funding for the same project.

<u>SUMMARY STATEMENT</u>
(Privileged Communication)

Application Number: 2 R01_____28

Review Group: _____

Meeting Dates: IRG: 1992

                        Council: 1993

Investigator: _____   Degree: Ph.D. equivalent

Organization: _____

City, State: _____   Requested Start Date: x/x/93

Project Title: _____

IRG Action: Priority Score: 170   Percentile: 16.0

Human Subjects: 10—No Human Subjects Involved

Animal Subjects: 30—ANMLS INV.-VERIFIED, NO IRG CONCERNS OR
                           COMMENT

Gender: 60—Not Clinical Research

Minority: 70—Not Clinical Research

Project Year	Direct Costs Required	Direct Costs Recommended	Estimated Total Costs
28	2XX,XXX		3XX,XXX
29	XXX,XXX		XXX,XXX
30	XXX,XXX	As requested	XXX,XXX
31	XXX,XXX		XXX,XXX
32	XXX,XXX		XXX,XXX
TOTAL	1,XXX,XXX		2,XXX,XXX

<u>RESUME</u>: An *experienced scientist* proposes to continue studies of _____ by evaluation of a new _____ that may or may not prove to be less toxic than those that have previously been evaluated. Based on his *excellent track record* and expertise with _____, the *experiments can be expected to provide definitive results*. All the materials to be evaluated *offer promise,* and the results of these studies *could lead to better* _____.

<u>DESCRIPTION</u>: ...

<u>CRITIQUE</u>: This is a competing renewal of a *productive program* that has been in place for 27 years. Dr. X and his collaborators have *made major contributions to our understanding of* _____. In addition, Dr. X, in collaboration with _____, has added to our

understanding of _____. He proposes to continue both lines of investigation using established techniques but without Dr. X or a replacement (*no explanation given*).

This current application has two specific aims. In specific aim one, Dr. X will continue to develop a new _____. The effect and behavior of _____ will first be studied. *No indication is given in the application as to what criteria will be used to determine* _____. It is assumed that the studies will be similar to studies that have been published with other potential _____ by Dr. X. If _____ proves _____, additional studies need to be done in _____ to determine, among other things, if there is an increase in _____.

_____ will also be evaluated as a _____ in a _____ model that has been used successfully in previous experiments. *Preliminary results in x abstracts in 1990 and 1992 support the hypothesis that* _____.

Preliminary experiments supposedly have shown that _____ is adequate (data not given) for _____. Peculiarly, at this point, it is stated that _____ will be evaluated by _____ (*no reference given*).

In a fourth experiment of specific aim 1, the _____ will be determined in _____.

Specific aim 2 is completely unrelated to aim 1 but is an extension of years of previous work. This group *reported* at the _____ meeting this year that _____. They propose to continue these studies by comparing _____. This is a small part of the proposed work.

The *major strengths of this application are the track record of the principal investigator and his expertise in* the development and testing of _____. In addition, *preliminary data support each hypothesis*, and *the results will be of clinical relevance.*

A weakness is failure to review work by others with any of the _____ that will be used or to discuss their mechanisms of action. For example, *why is* _____ *going to be evaluated? What kind of* _____ *is* _____? *Another weakness is only using* _____ to evaluate _____. *It will also be important to do confirmatory experiments in* _____, especially to determine if _____ occur with any of the _____.

<u>INVESTIGATORS</u>: Dr. X is the principal investigator of this application and is listed at *100% commitment*. He has *extensive experience in* _____. He is *extremely well qualified to perform the proposed studies.*

Dr. Y is a _____ investigator who will spend 10% effort on the project, being specifically responsible for _____.

Dr. Z will contribute 20% effort, concentrating on the preparation of the _____.

Dr. V, research fellow, will be joining the group and will be involved in _____.

Dr. Q is a _____ who has experience in _____.

Dr. W is a _____ who will be focusing on _____.

<u>BUDGET</u>: As requested.

EXAMPLES S AND T

Summary Statements for 2 sequential applications for a competing continuation: an initial application for 5 years of support that was not funded and a revised application requesting 4 years of support that was funded for 4 years. Note the change in priority score and percentile rank.

EXAMPLE S

The Summary Statement for the initial application.

SUMMARY STATEMENT
(Privileged Communication)

Application Number: 2 R01_____06

Review Group: _____

| Meeting Dates: | IRG: | Fall 1992 |
| | Council: | 1993 |

Investigator: _____   Degree: Ph.D.

Organization: _____

City, State: _____

Project Title: _____   Requested Start Date: x/x/93

IRG Action: Priority Score: 200   Percentile: 40

Human Subjects: 10—No Human Subjects Involved

Animal Subjects: 30—ANMLS INV.—VERIFIED, NO IRG CONCERNS
                      OR COMMENT

Gender: 60—Not Clinical Research

Minority: 70—Not Clinical Research

Project Year	Direct Costs Required	Direct Costs Recommended	Estimated Total Costs
06	1XX,XXX	1XX,XXX	2XX,XXX
07	XXX,XXX	XXX,XXX	XXX,XXX
08	XXX,XXX	XXX,XXX	XXX,XXX
09	XXX,XXX	————	————
10	XXX,XXX	————	————
TOTAL	8XX,XXX	4XX,XXX	7XX,XXX

<u>RESUME</u>: This application is a request for five years of support to continue a project *funded previously for five years*. It addresses several issues in _____, especially the multiple functions of _____ as a consequence of _____ relationships. The *first four aims are generally well focused*, but the *last two aims are less well justified*. Also there are *concerns*

about the *specificity* of the _____. Finally, *progress during the prior funding period was less than could have been anticipated.* Three years of support are recommended.

DESCRIPTION: ...

CRITIQUE: This proposal *addresses an issue of importance* in _____. It is apparent that adequate definition of _____ must include the characterization of the properties on _____. Selected were several _____ of particular interest in which to carry out these investigations. Aim 1 is to identify _____. The basis for this study is the recent manuscript which shows that _____. It is planned to first confirm that _____ and then identify _____. *It is highly likely that there will be success in the first effort* because *preliminary data* showing the ability to do _____ were provided. More *dubious* is the assumption that _____ is proof for _____. There is certainly an *awareness* that this component is not _____. While the lack of _____ is certainly an argument for _____, it certainly *does not rule out* _____.

The planned *search for* _____ *is limited by* the availability of _____. Planned experiments will look for _____; no _____ will be used; and _____ *will not indicate* _____. Nonetheless, this is a beginning for the study of the complex issue of _____, and the *techniques proposed could provide some answers* even though the *aim is overstated.*

This *aim could also be criticized* on the grounds that *there are many other possible substances that could be studied other than the two that are chosen.* Current trends in _____ are a reminder that *some as yet ill-defined* _____ *could be present as well.*

Aim 2 will address the issue of _____ to see if _____. Following this, combined _____ will be carried out as with _____. Particular attention will be paid to _____. *Techniques for* _____ *were acquired and are now in hand. It* is planned to combine this with _____ , but, again, *only the* _____ *seems adequate* for the task of _____.

In Aim 3, attention will be directed to _____. These _____ have been postulated to _____. _____ *should confirm/refute* the _____ which has been questioned by some. _____ *controls should be performed to assure* that the _____ is not a function of _____.

Aim 4 is to determine whether _____. There are *letters indicating the availability of* _____ for this study, and the *findings should aid in defining the roles* of _____ and _____ relative to _____.

Aim 5 involves a return to a model system of _____. The *approach is limited by the use of* _____ which *will identify some, but not necessarily all,* of the _____. Also the study as described requires that _____. Finally, Aim 6 will examine the _____. These last two aims *are less well justified* than the first four and *could be omitted* from the project.

It must be noted that much of this work requires use of _____ that were frequently prepared _____ from systems and species very different than the ones used in this study. *Interpretation of the results depends on* _____. Although it is clear that there is the knowledge to conduct *appropriate* _____ *controls, it would be reassuring,* when _____ are used in a new system, that _____ be verified by _____. This is *not in-*

cluded in the application and is missing as well from a lot of _____ literature. It is still important to consider whether _____ corresponds to _____. It is *surprising how often this additional level of control provides additional insight into* _____.

Finally, *progress during the preceding five years was much less than could have been anticipated. Only five papers* are listed in the Progress Report. *Two of these papers,* both of which were published, *were* in fact *submitted prior to the previous application.* Of the three remaining papers, one is "in press," a second is "accepted with minor revisions," and *a third is "in preparation."*

INVESTIGATOR(S): Dr. X completed a Ph.D. in _____. *Progress as evidenced by publication related to the project has been relatively poor.* However, during this time, Dr. X has published 3 other papers, not listed in the Progress Report, on _____ in collaboration with Drs. _____ and _____. These circumstances may have limited progress on the proposal under consideration here.

BUDGET: Travel is reduced to $X to allow for one trip to one national meeting. Additional domestic as well as foreign travel are *poorly justified* and *not recommended.* The _____ requested in year 02 is *poorly justified* and *not recommended* (_____). Three years of support are recommended in order *to closely monitor progress.*

EXAMPLE T

The Summary Statement for an application that was funded on the first revision. Example S is the Summary Statement for the initial application (for 5 years of support), which was not funded. The revised application requesting 4 years of support was funded for 4 years. Note the change in priority score and percentile rank between Example S and Example T.

SUMMARY STATEMENT
(Privileged Communication)

Application Number: 2 R01_____06A1

Review Group: _____

Meeting Dates: IRG: Summer 1993

Council: 1993

Investigator: _____   Degree: Ph.D.

Organization: _____

City, State: _____   Requested Start Date: x/x/93

Project Title: _____

IRG Action: Priority Score: 150   Percentile: 9.0

Human Subjects: 10—No Human Subjects Involved

Animal Subjects: 30—ANMLS INV.—VERIFIED, NO IRG CONCERNS OR COMMENT

Gender: 60—Not Clinical Research

Minority: 70—Not Clinical Research

Project Year	Direct Costs Required	Direct Costs Recommended	Estimated Total Costs
06A1	1XX,XXX	As requested	2XX,XXX
07	1XX,XXX	As requested	XXX,XXX
08	1XX,XXX	As requested	XXX,XXX
09	1XX,XXX	As requested	3XX,XXX
TOTAL	7XX,XXX	7XX,XXX	1,1XX,XXX

RESUME: In a *revision* of a competing renewal application, a *well-qualified investigator* requests support to study _____. He plans to use _____ and _____ techniques to study _____. The *proposal addresses very important questions* about _____ with *sophisticated _____ techniques* that can tell us a great deal about _____. The *proposal is well organized, highly focused and well conceived.* In addition, the *PI has demonstrated expertise in all of the required methodology.*

DESCRIPTION: (Adapted from applicant's abstract) ...

CRITIQUE: This is a *revision* of a previous proposal to use a variety of primarily _____ techniques to study _____. *Particular attention will be paid to* the question of how _____. Either these substances are _____ or, alternatively, _____. *The work is important because* it addresses the area of _____. The importance of this lies in the *emerging concept* that _____. The _____ *significance* of these _____ ultimately depends on detailed knowledge both of the mechanisms that control _____ as well as _____. To address some of these issues, the principal investigator *proposes to use a combination* of _____ as well as _____. *This analysis will* _____.

Overall, this is a *much improved proposal for 4 rather than 5 years* as in the original proposal. *As recommended in the prior review, two of the original specific aims have been deleted,* and *some of the criticisms directed at the four remaining specific aims have been addressed.* One concern was that _____. _____ will now be applied routinely to test _____. In addition, _____ will be used *to verify the conclusion* of his prior study that only _____. The *proposal is well organized and highly focused. Data obtained from this work could prove significant* in an attempt to understand the implications of _____.

The principal investigator's modest progress during the prior grant period was criticized in the previous review. This has improved somewhat, since he now has *an additional two papers in press and two more under consideration.* Aside from the numbers, which are admittedly low, *two of the papers on* _____ *are potentially very important* and form the principal background for the current proposal. The principal investigator and collaborators have *made the observation that* _____. The *implications of this finding will be pursued* in specific aims 1 and 2. In addition to work either published or submitted, the principal investigator *has made progress in developing techniques* to _____. Finally, he *has worked with Dr. Y to acquire techniques for* _____. *Success* with the specific aims of the current proposal ultimately *depends on his skill in routine application of these techniques.*

Recent work of the principal investigator *has clearly shown* _____. In specific aim 1, *in response to the criticism* that _____ might not reliably detect _____ and did not rule out _____, the principal investigator *plans to confirm* that _____ by carrying out _____. He will also use _____ techniques to try to relate _____ to _____ and to identify _____. The *PI has extensive experience in these methods;* the _____ to be used *are the most appropriate choices;* and *important findings are anticipated. In response to* concerns about _____, the principal investigator also *plans to utilize* _____ to determine _____. In fact, the principal investigator now *proposes throughout this project to address* _____ *more carefully* using _____ protocols. Although his *approach cannot rule out* the existence of an as yet unidentified _____, it *will add force* to the prior study. While the *PI has not previously used these techniques, he has a letter of assurance from* Dr. _____ *that he will help him with this aspect* of the studies.

Aim 2 seeks to pursue the question of _____ by extending the results and methods of aim 1 to _____. The _____ of choice is the well-known _____. In preparation for these experiments, the *PI has acquired skill in* _____. In addition to studying _____, the principal investigator *should be able to* _____. If successful, *achieving this aim will provide refinement to our understanding of* _____.

Aims 3 and 4 center on another *well-characterized* _____. This _____ is an *excellent choice* for the study of _____. In a recent paper, _____ and _____ have provided *convincing evidence* that _____. The principal investigator plans to determine if _____. As suggested in the prior review, *appropriate* _____ *controls* are added.

In aim 4, as an extension of aim 3, the principal investigator will look at _____. These *studies will be of particular interest with respect to the continuing controversy regarding* the role of _____. It may turn out that _____ will be seen. *This would be an important generalization of the concept* derived from the work on _____.

In summary, this *revision is markedly improved*. It is *clearly written* and *describes a well-reasoned approach to a question of importance* not only for _____ but also throughout _____. *Some of the issues raised by the previous study section remain unresolved;* in particular, the *modest productivity* during the previous study section remains unresolved, as does the *lack of attention to the stated goals of the previous grant. However, the latter does not diminish enthusiasm for the present proposal, since the proposed aims have a much higher priority than the aims in the original application.*

INVESTIGATOR(S): Dr. _____ received a Ph.D. in _____. It is clear that the *principal investigator does exceedingly painstaking work on very important questions.* He is a *skilled researcher who is capable of developing procedures as needed.* He addresses _____ largely through *collaborations. He is an important asset in the field of* _____.

BUDGET: The budget and its *justifications are reasonable*, although it is *not clear why* _____ is mentioned. The *work is technically demanding and requires skilled technical support.* The budget is, therefore, recommended for consideration as requested.

Example U

The Summary Statement for—and structured outline of excerpts of—a grant application that was awarded for the time requested at about 2% below the level recommended for the first year. This is the same investigator whose Summary Statements are given in Examples I, J, and K.

SUMMARY STATEMENT
(Privileged Communication)

Application Number: 2R01_____ -09

Review Group: _____

Meeting Dates:　　IRG:　　　1990

　　　　　　　　　Council:　　1991

Investigator: _____　　　　　　　　　　　　　Degree: Ph.D.

Organization: _____

City, State: _____　　　　　　　　　　　Requested Start Date: x/x/91

Project Title: _____

Percentile: 15.0

Recommended:　　　Approval　　　　　　　　Priority Score: 160

Human Subjects:　　10—No Human Subjects Involved

Animal Subjects:　　30—ANMLS INV.-VERIFIED, NO IRG CONCERNS OR COMMENT

Project Year	Direct Costs Required	Direct Costs Recommended
09	1XX,XXX	
10	XXX,XXX	
11	XXX,XXX	As requested
12	XXX,XXX	
13	2XX,XXX	

RESUME: An *experienced and productive researcher* requests five years of support to extend his studies on _____. The investigator *pioneered work in this area* and *has made significant contributions* to its development. He proposes to extend studies on _____. The *major strength of the proposal is the principal investigator's background and experience* working in this field. The *proposal itself suffers from having too many projects described in a superficial manner. Based primarily on track record,* approval is recommended in time and amount.

DESCRIPTION: ...

CRITIQUE: The long-term objective of the proposed research is to identify and investigate the _____ components of _____ required to maintain _____.

The present *proposal is important* because it will *add to our knowledge* of _____. The *strengths of the proposal* lie in the *experience of the PI* in this field and the *likelihood that he will produce results of value and significance.* The *major weakness* of the proposal *is the "wish-list" approach to experiments* (which the *PI acknowledges* on p. x), resulting in *many experiments that are not well justified* and in *sketchy details about interpretation of results.* In a couple of important instances, the *background literature is not very critically interpreted* and preliminary and/or controversial *data accepted at face value.*

Progress during the last grant period *was excellent* with 17 papers published or in press and another 4 submitted. The work during this period *produced important new information* that *received a great deal of attention.*

In proposed experiments, *new evidence will be sought for* _____. The ability of _____ to _____ will be studied. The *rationale* for these experiments *is presumably* that all of these latter agents can participate in some way in _____. *However,* _____ and _____ are _____. *Why would one expect* _____? Another experiment deals with _____. While _____ must occur during _____, *it is not clear* that _____ can occur directly from _____. *Although the principal investigator may be aware of this problem, he does not communicate it well in the proposal, leaving himself open to the criticism that these experiments are poorly rationalized.*

The principal investigator proposes to study _____. The rationale suggested is that _____. *Why is it easier* to study _____? *What are the advantages?* The _____ has yet to be isolated (although the principal investigator states that this is a simple problem), and _____ is apparently easily obtained by conventional techniques used by the investigator. *The significance of this experiment is not clearly expressed.*

The _____ is straightforward and will be done in *collaboration* with Dr. Y. The applicant has _____ and states that he hopes to obtain another _____ from Dr. Z. He will also examine _____. The principal investigator is reminded that _____ *may have to be taken into account* in these studies. The applicant will investigate the notion that _____. This will be done by _____. This *experiment may be very difficult to interpret.* _____ *conjectures* that _____.

Experiments will also be done on _____. These are *interesting* and *likely to provide some clues* as to the role of these _____ in the _____.

Experiments designed to look at _____ are *insufficiently described.* The principal investigator proposes to measure the amounts of _____ and _____. *How he intends to accomplish this* _____ *is never clarified.*

In summary, this proposal covers a great many aspects of the _____, and the investigator and his associate propose to examine a large number of different, albeit interrelated, factors in _____. *Possible negative findings and alternative approaches are not addressed.* The *experiments and possible interpretations should be presented in more detail.* The *major positive point* to this proposal is that the investigator has a *strong past history of productive research* in this area and has *5 collaborators to assist him in areas in which he is not experienced.* In addition, the *experiments outlined are appropriate,* and the *subject is an interesting and important one. In the future, the PI should be more detailed in presenting experimental methodology and more critical in interpreting experimental results and possible pitfalls.*

INVESTIGATORS: Dr. X received his Ph.D. from _____. He has done *pioneering work* on _____ and is *highly qualified* for the proposed work. The CV's of *6 collaborating investigators* are attached. All of these are appropriate for their assigned roles in the project.

BUDGET: The budget is *generally well justified.*

EXCERPTS FROM THE APPLICATION FOR WHICH THE SUMMARY STATEMENT IS GIVEN ABOVE.

ABSTRACT:

The _____ is _____. Because it is _____, it is in a strategic position to perform several important functions for _____. The _____ is probably involved in _____. Furthermore, some components of the _____ may play _____ roles in _____. The *long-term objective* of the proposed research is to identify and investigate _____ components of this _____ *that may be required to maintain the health of* _____ and to examine how they function.

Our studies continue to focus on _____. The *emphasis has gradually shifted away from* _____ analysis of _____ per se, *towards* examination of _____ interactions. *Specific aims are:* (1) Correlate structure with function for _____. Investigations of _____ will continue. In addition, _____ will be *evaluated as a model for* _____. (2) Continue to study _____ ; these may _____. Search for _____. (3) Determine whether _____. Of particular interest are whether _____ and whether (and how) the _____ (4) Examine _____.

The *methodology* for these projects includes assays (_____, _____, and _____), separation procedures (_____, _____, _____, _____), _____, and _____ techniques.

It is anticipated that the proposed investigation of the _____ will *increase our knowledge of how the health of* _____ is maintained and *provide clues about faulty functioning in disease states.*

BUDGET JUSTIFICATION:

Adjustments for inflation: In all categories, including personnel, I have increased the requested amounts by x% per year. For specific pieces of equipment, I have *added x% per year to current catalog prices.*

Personnel:

The *PI will plan the research, oversee experiments, interpret results, write papers, and take part in many of the experiments* (particularly _____ and preliminary work requiring new methods). The *staff associate* has had *extensive experience* in _____ method development, and will carry out the _____ and _____ experiments. The *research assistant* will perform most of the routine experiments. The *secretary* will answer phone calls and help with correspondence and manuscripts.

The *salaries requested are in accordance with* _____ *guidelines.* My salary will be average for _____ with x years of service in that capacity. Mr. Y's salary reflects a x% increase over current. The secretary's services will be shared with other scientists in _____. *Fringe benefits are currently x% of salaries;* I have used this figure throughout.

Equipment:

First year: The *pH meter* (Fisher _____ model x) and *analytical balance* (_____ model x) are *replacements* for items that have been broken and that, because of funding cuts, I have not been able to replace. *At present we have to use equipment in other labs, at considerable inconvenience.*

Second year: Funds are requested for a good _____ (_____ model x, current price is $ _____). The project on _____ hinges on sensitive, high-resolution _____ analysis of these _____. At present, *the only* _____ *in the building is* from the 1960s; _____ *can no longer get replacements parts* for this instrument, which is very *often nonfunctional and, at best, unreliable.* Furthermore, it is *not possible to use* _____ (which, in the past 10 years, have almost completely replaced _____) with this _____. Therefore, we would like to replace it with a new _____, complete with _____, _____, and _____, data-handling capability.

Third year: A _____ for _____ will be requested for experiments _____. *For preliminary experiments we borrowed* a _____ and attached it to our _____. However, not only would this be *inconvenient for intensive, long-term experiments,* but also it is *not clear how long the* _____*'s owner will be at* _____. I would like to purchase a _____ (present price $x), which is suitable for _____.

Fifth year: Many assays in my lab require a reliable _____. My _____ *Model x* _____ *is 14 years old and is beginning to develop problems.* I expect to have to replace it some time during the next 5 years. I would like to get a _____ Model x (current price $_____).

Supplies:

Tissues and laboratory animals: Many studies will be performed on _____. These are available from _____ at $x per _____ plus $x delivery fee. *We anticipate about* 25 _____ experiments per year, each using about _____. _____ will be required for _____ experiments (_____) and when very _____ preparations are needed (_____). *I anticipate purchasing* 100 _____ per year ($x each, including shipping) and *holding each* _____ *about x weeks* (for _____ experiments). *Care charges are* _____ per day per _____.

Chemicals, etc.: Materials required for _____ are expensive. These include _____ to be used in _____ ($_____ for x), and _____ ($_____ each for _____ for _____ experiments, $_____ each for _____ experiments). _____ for _____ are $ _____ per _____. Each order of _____ costs $_____. Other chemicals to be purchased include _____, _____, and _____.

Travel:

I expect to present papers at _____ every year. In addition, in the first, third, and fifth years I would like to attend the _____ meetings on _____. In the second and fourth years I expect to go to _____ meetings.

Other expenses:

Service contracts include $_____ (first-year estimate) for *preventive maintenance* of my
_____ model _____ and $_____ for my _____ model _____. *Publica-
tion costs include* drafting, photography, page charges, and reprint costs. In addition,
_____ word-processing staff may soon be *charging fees* for their services. We use the
_____ *computers* at _____ for analyzing and graphing data.

A. Specific Aims:

The *overall goal* of the proposed research is to examine _____ for its contributions
towards maintenance of _____ health. Aim 1 expands our functional and structural
study of _____, the only _____ that has been well characterized. Aim 2 examines
_____. Aim 3 deals with possible _____. Aim 4 probes interactions between
_____ and _____.

1. *Heading*: Because of its location and _____, _____ is *hypothesized* to act
    as a _____. We would like to learn more about _____ function and struc-
    ture. *Specifically*, (a) Is _____ capable of _____? Are these _____ spe-
    cific? Are _____ involved? (b) Upon _____, _____ is obtained. What
    is the structure of this _____? Does it _____? Can it serve as a model for
    an _____? (c) What is the function of _____?

2. *Heading*: We have shown that _____. (a) Can these _____ be demon-
    strated by _____ to be normal components of _____? (b) Do they dis-
    play _____? (c) Does the _____ contain _____, such as _____?
    (d) Can roles for _____ be demonstrated in _____?

3. *Heading*: Nothing is known about possible _____ involvement in _____.
    In particular: (a) In spite of _____, levels are maintained in _____. Could
    _____ have a role in _____? Perhaps _____? (b) How do _____?
    (c) Are specific _____ involved in any of these processes? Does _____ act
    as _____? If so, how _____?

4. *Heading*: There are several contributions to _____ health that _____
    could make. Do other _____ components assist _____? *Specifically:* (a)
    The _____ appears to mediate _____. Will experiments conducted on
    _____ material confirm our evidence for _____? (b) Work on models of
    _____ indicate that _____ may be required by _____. Can such a
    factor be found in _____? (c) Similarly, is there any evidence for _____?

B. Background and Significance

B1. *Definition and importance of* _____.
B2. *Structural features of* _____.
B3. *Components of* _____.
B4. _____ *transport through* _____.
B5. Other functions of _____.
B6. *The* _____ *in health and disease.* Malfunctioning of _____ components
     appears to be important in several _____ diseases.

C. Progress Report

Dates and personnel.

This application covers the period x/84– x/90.

Key personnel (Name)	Title	Dates of service	% Effort

Resulting publications and manuscripts:

Publications are listed as *a. through u.*

Papers on _____ (h, o), _____ (l, u), and _____ (s, t) are *included in this list because the methods developed will be useful for the proposed work.* Reprints and preprints are *submitted in the Appendix* for all original articles (not reviews) dealing directly with _____ .

Summary of previous specific aims.

C1.
    a.
    b.
    c.
    d.
C2.
    a.
    b.
C3.
    a.
    b.
    c.
C4.
    a.
    b.
    c.
    d.

Progress for previous Specific Aims.

Progress has been made towards achievement of most of these aims, as will be summarized in the remainder of Section C. The structure and function of _____ received most of the attention, but considerable effort was devoted to _____ and _____ .

Some new methods were useful for several aspects of this work: (1) _____ . (2) _____ . There follows a description of progress for each aim. *Five figures of data from pilot experiments are included.* (3) _____ .

Summary of the importance of the findings.

1.
2.
3.
4.

Changes in specific aims:

Aims 1, 2, and 4 remain constant, with *some changes in emphasis; aim 3 has been changed.*

Aim 1 (_____). *The emphasis was on* _____; *it is now on* _____.

Aim 2 (_____). The previous period established the presence of _____ in the _____. The next period will examine their function and search for _____.

Aim 3 (*old,* _____; *new,* _____). *Many of the prominent* _____ *proved to be contaminants.* The new aim will examine _____.

Aim 4 (_____). _____ will be re-examined. *Emphasis will change from* _____ *to* _____.

D. Experimental Design and Methods

General statement. This description of *experimental strategy and tactics parallels the Specific Aims.* The investigations of _____ components and functions proposed there are explored here; *the numbering system is consistent with these Aims.* However, *there sometimes is overlap of methodology, and cross-referencing is necessary. Each technique will be described for the first experiment that requires its use in a major way. Methods that have been used for publications from this lab, such as* _____, *will be merely mentioned.*

D1. *Heading.* We have found that _____ is the major _____ component of _____ and shows _____, consistent with its being a _____. I will now seek more evidence for this role. We have also shown (Section C1a4) that _____. Part **a** of this section is concerned with further investigations of _____. Parts **b** and **c** are attempts to _____.

D1a. *Heading.* The *rationale for this set of experiments* was given in Sections C1a4, and preliminary data were shown in Figure 1. The method is to _____. *These preliminary results show* that _____. The next step will be to _____.

Then I would like to find out if _____ is specific or whether other _____ would do as well. After that we shall see if _____ affects _____ (since _____, et al. 198x, indicates that _____). For *preliminary experiments,* _____ will be used; if the results are interesting, then the method of _____ et al. (198x) will be used to obtain _____. The *last phase of this experiment is to* determine _____ for this work, both _____ and _____ (as in _____ et al., 198x) will be used.

Similar studies will be done with _____. In this case, *the intent is to see whether* _____. *A very preliminary experiment was conducted* in which _____. *The results were promising;* _____. However, _____ will be required for measurements with sufficient sensitivity for quantitative measurements. This compound will be synthesized from _____ (Company name) by _____. In addition, it may be possible to _____.

_____. Larger amounts of _____ will be required for complete studies. *The procedures to _____ are long and tedious. I have arranged a collaboration with _____ to develop _____.*

A *preliminary experiment*, in which _____, *failed to yield measurable* _____. *One problem might be that* we _____ (_____, 19xx), _____. *This experiment will be repeated, using* _____ *in a controlled manner* (_____, 19xx). If successful _____ is obtained, the _____ will be compared to those for _____ This *should yield information about the mechanism of* _____.

It is also possible that _____ cannot _____. This hypothesis will be examined if altering the method of _____ (see above) does not work.

There are *two additional, high-risk experiments I would like to try, if time permits:* (i) _____ If so, _____ might play a role, since they _____. I would use _____ for the same types of experiments outlined above for _____, to see whether _____ (ii) *One way to tell whether* _____ *is needed for* _____ *is to* _____ *and see if* _____. *This could be done by* _____ (_____, 198x).

D2–D4. Other excerpts from the Methods section (this section included many citations).

This section *proposes experiments to validate* that _____.

However, *to prove that this is the case*, I would like to demonstrate (in a *collaboration* with _____) that _____.

The *methods are sensitive enough that* _____.

I am aware that _____ can be complicated by _____ (_____, 19xx). Dr. _____ (_____, 198x) is *well acquainted with these procedures and complications* and will *collaborate* with me on this project.

The *strategy will be* to see if _____. *If positive results are obtained, we can then try to* _____.

The *first attempt, which proved very promising*, was _____. It remains to be seen whether _____.

There *may be a disease-related aspect to this project.*

It has been hypothesized that _____ (_____, 198x). A *new twist* on possible _____ comes about through the *recent discovery that* _____ (_____, 199x). Therefore, we would like to analyze _____ (see D2b) _____ to see if _____.

The *methods to be used are* those developed by _____ (198x, and later papers from that lab) for analysis of _____. These methods consist of _____. Dr. _____

has had extensive experience with developing and employing _____ *(see his Biosketch), and will perform this aspect of the work.*

Because _____, *we want to determine whether* _____.

These projects carry greater risks and will be abandoned quickly if they are not promising.

We *have good evidence from* _____ *that* _____.

We would like to *get a clearer picture of how* _____.

Timetable

Project	Project Year				
	1	2	3	4	5
D1.*	_____	_____	_____	_____	_____
D2.	_____	_____	_____		
D3.		_____	_____	_____	
D4.				_____	_____

*The name of each project is stated in the table in abbreviated form.

I realize that I have proposed more experiments than can probably be completed by my small laboratory. However, I think I have demonstrated (Section C) that we can handle several projects simultaneously. In addition, I *want the flexibility to be able to drop projects that turn out not to be fruitful,* either *because of technical difficulties* (which may be the case with D4c) *or* because of *negative results* (a possibility with D1c and D2b).

Example V

A Summary Statement for one PI's project for a program project (PPG) application. A structural outline of an excerpt from the PI's section of the PPG application follows the Summary Statement.

The PPG was awarded in 1993. It received an overall priority score of 110 and a percentile score of 0.2. The individual project excerpted (specific aims only) below received a priority score of 100, the best possible score.

SUMMARY STATEMENT

DESCRIPTION: ...

CRITIQUE: Dr. X *has accomplished most of his aims* of the previous five-year funding period to characterize the structure and function of _____, specifically in relation to _____, and the mechanism of action of _____ correlation of _____ with biological activity. *Due to significant budget cuts, he could not achieve his aim of* _____ and _____. These latter studies are now part of the current proposal.

An important accomplishment during the last grant period is _____.

Besides the _____, similar _____ *has been shown to be an important factor in* _____. Dr. X's *isolation of* _____ *is novel and is expected to have a significant role in* _____. Also, considering the fact that this _____ inhibits _____, it is *likely that* _____ *plays a significant role in* the regulation of _____. *Dr. X's discovery of the* _____ *turns this project into an excellent complement to the other three projects* of this program that primarily investigate _____.

This *well-planned project is expected to provide extremely useful information on* _____.

INVESTIGATOR: Dr. X received his Ph.D. in _____ from _____ University in 19xx. He received postdoctoral training at _____. Dr. X *has published extensively on* _____. He is *highly qualified to carry out the proposed research.*

BUDGET: The requested *budget is well justified.*

RECOMMENDATION: Further consideration is *recommended with outstanding priority for five years of support at the requested budget level.*

Structural Outline of an Excerpt from the PI's Section of the PPG Application for which the Summary Statement Is Given Above.

Specific Aims from the grant proposal:

The *overall goal* of this proposal is to study the _____ mechanisms involved in the regulation of _____ during _____.

We *have recently achieved* _____ and *have shown* that _____ We *have also estab-lished* that _____ This raises the possibility that _____. These *results strongly sug-gest* that _____ In the proposed studies the structure and _____ function of _____ and _____ *will be investigated by pursuing the following Specific Aims:* (a) Studies on the mechanism of action of _____. (b) _____ and _____ char-acterization of _____. *Using* _____ *methodology, we plan to* _____ in order *to determine* _____ *and to correlate* the _____ information with mechanistic as-pects of _____. (c) Studies on the _____. The _____ action of _____ will be studied. The effect of _____ on _____ will be *examined by using* _____. The question whether _____ is present in _____ as well as in _____ will be studied. (d) Studies on _____. The association between _____ and _____ *will be investigated* in order *to characterize* the _____ as-sociated with _____. (e) Studies on the _____ and _____ of _____. In parallel, *we will study* _____ *using* _____. (f) Studies to _____ whether _____. If _____, we will further characterize _____. The *results of these stud-ies will hopefully delineate* _____ which we have isolated from _____ and *help us to understand* whether or not _____ also operate in _____ and in other types of _____.

EXAMPLE W

A Summary Statement for a competing continuation application for 5 years of support that was funded with few reservations for the amount requested.

SUMMARY STATEMENT
(Privileged Communication)

Application Number: 2 R01_____12
DUAL: X

Review Group: _____

Meeting Dates: IRG: X/1990
                 Council: X/1990

Investigator: _____   Degree: Ph.D.

Organization: _____

City, State: _____   Requested Start Date: x/x/90

Project Title: _____

                                                            Percentile: 15.0

Recommended: Approval   **Priority Score: 150**

Human Subjects: 10-No Human Subjects Involved

Animal Subjects: 10-No Live Vertebrate Animals Involved

Project Year	Direct Costs Required	Direct Costs Recommended
12	2XX,XXX	
13	XXX,XXX	
14	XXX,XXX	As requested
15	XXX,XXX	
16	2XX,XXX	

RESUME: This *ambitious proposal* to examine in detail the interacting systems in _____ *is a logical extension of the present highly productive effort* by Dr. X and his associates. The applicant's past and *proposed use of* _____ *is unusually rigorous;* he combines a *profound understanding of the theory and practice of* _____ with the *rigorous approach* of the _____ and _____ properties of _____. *Dr. X has established himself as a leading investigator of* _____.

DESCRIPTION: ...

CRITIQUE: This project continues to be aimed at *very significant goals, asking fundamental questions* about _____. *Progress in the past five years has been excellent, with 12 refereed papers, many of which are in first-rate journals. Recent progress is outstanding:* 5 of these papers in the past year. *This project has never been more productive. The* _____ *studies, which rep-*

resent only a small portion of Dr. X's effort, have not been as productive, and it could be suggested that they not be continued at this point. The similarity of _____ in the two _____ suggests a reasonable role for the _____ subproject. However, the latter is at an earlier developmental stage, since _____ problems have not yet been fully worked out, and therefore future progress is less certain.

A variety of *important questions* about the mechanism of _____ *will be addressed through the use of* _____ and _____. An *apparent contradiction is developing* in ideas about the _____. Dr. X has recognized this quandary and will test a number of hypotheses that bear directly on the issue of whether _____ or _____.

Dr. X will continue his examination of _____. Interactions between _____ and _____ will be examined as functions of _____ to reveal a more complete description of _____. *A possible criticism of this work could be the heavy emphasis on* _____. *However, continued emphasis on this topic is justified by the extensive evidence accumulated by Dr. X that* _____.

Dr. X *has planned a careful and thorough approach to answering basic questions about the mechanism of* _____. Of course there is the *usual limitation* of _____ studies, that the _____ may be perturbing the system, *but Dr. X will use several* _____ *to minimize this possibility.* The comparative work on _____ *is less well thought out, but could yield useful results.* The specialization of the _____ in each of these _____ has not yet been rationalized with their _____. Dr. X's studies *will shed light on these issues* and on _____ as well.

Perhaps *the most fundamentally important experiments are* the _____ studies _____. Dr. X plans to _____ and measure the change in _____. Experiments will be conducted in the presence of _____ in order to establish whether _____. The *feasibility of the experiments in the absence of* _____ *has already been established in collaboration with Dr. Y.* _____ *will be more difficult.* Dr. X proposes the use of _____, but *no evidence is yet given to predict the success of this* _____. These experiments *will test whether* the apparent contradiction is a result of the _____ or whether fundamental tenets of _____ need to be rethought.

A *particular strength* of this continuation proposal are the *collaborations*, some of which are *already underway*, which *should extend Dr. X's research into new areas.* The work with Dr. Y on _____ will extend the project from _____ to _____, *a major advance in establishing the* _____ *relevance of the work. Perhaps this new technology for the research could have benefited from more detailed explanation.* The continued *collaboration* with Dr. _____ on _____ *has great potential* for probing the relationships of _____, _____, and _____ in this system.

<u>INVESTIGATORS</u>: Dr. X obtained his Ph.D. in _____. He has an *impressive publication record in the field of* _____, particularly in the study of _____. He is *eminently qualified to carry out the proposed work.*

Dr. A *has been working with Dr. X since 19xx,* and has *8 publications relating directly to the proposed work. He has been instrumental in developing the methods* used in Dr. X's laboratory and is *uniquely qualified* to carry out the _____ experiments. Dr. B holds a Ph.D.

in _____. *He brings to the project expertise in* _____. Dr. C received his Ph.D. in _____. He *has co-authored 9 articles on* _____; his postdoctoral studies with Dr. X *will be supported by the NSF.*

<u>BUDGET</u>: The request represents a continuation of the present level of recommended support and *is wholly appropriate.*

EXAMPLE X

The Summary Statement for an 01A2 application that was *revised 3 times* (4 submissions) but was funded on the second revision (01A2), following a project site visit (PSV). The 01A3 revision was withdrawn after the applicant was informed that the 01A2 application was to be funded.

SUMMARY STATEMENT
(Privileged Communication)

Application Number: 1 R01 _____ 01A2

Review Group: _____

Meeting Dates: IRG: X/1991
                  Council: Y/1991

Investigator: _____   Degree: Ph.D.

Organization: _____

City, State: _____   Requested Start Date: x/x/91

Project Title: _____

Percentile: 21.0
Priority Score: 140

Recommended: Approval
Human Subjects: 10-No Human Subjects Involved
Animal Subjects: 10- No Live Vertebrate Animals Involved
Gender: 60-Not Clinical Research
Minority: 70-Not Clinical Research

Project Year	Direct Costs Required	Direct Costs Recommended
01A2	1XX,XXX	
02	XXX,XXX	As requested
03	1XX,XXX	

PROJECT SITE VISIT MADE.

RESUME: Approval is recommended for this previously deferred revised application to define _____. _____ is a major health problem, and this *outstanding proposal can provide timely and critical information.*

DESCRIPTION: ...

CRITIQUE: The site visit provided new information *not clarified in the grant application.* Dr. X presented an overview of _____. Although it was *difficult to obtain a precise understanding* of how experiments would be conducted, it was clear that Dr. X had a *logical sequence of experiments* in mind to examine the effects _____.

Dr. X will *rigorously describe* _____. Her experience with _____ and her understanding of _____ cause her to concentrate on _____ as the only relevant experimental system. This has *sound justification* because _____.

The PSV members pointed out that *a central issue remained unclear:* How would Dr. X divorce the effects of other _____ components, such as _____, from the effects of _____ itself? It was the consensus that an experimental design in which _____ is the only variable is imperative if meaningful data are to be generated. To accomplish this, Dr. X must have a _____ control that is not _____. Dr. X *presented an acceptable plan* for obtaining this essential component. She *will use three approaches* to try to obtain _____.

While the second approach may be somewhat dubious, the first and third *approaches have merit.* Dr. X also indicated that she would use _____ as a positive control.

Other minor *points of concern* are 1) the apparent lack of quantitation of _____, 2) the heterogeneity of _____, and 3) the absence of attention to _____. More attention should be paid to _____ protocols. However, it was the opinion of the PSV team that *these problems did not seriously detract from the overall quality of the application.*

These studies are based on the hypothesis that _____. *This is, in all, an outstanding proposal.*

INVESTIGATORS: Dr. X received her Ph.D. in _____. She is presently professor of _____. Dr. X lists *numerous publications* in the areas of _____ and _____. She is *competent in* the _____ elements of the proposed research.

BUDGET: The *budget is reasonable for the work described* and is approved in the time and amount requested.

NIH INFORMATION

A. NIH Institutes, Centers, and Divisions

NIH INSTITUTES

2-Letter Code	Acronym	Institute	Telephone Number
CA	NCI	National Cancer Institute	301-496-5583
EY	NEI	National Eye Institute	301-496-5248
HL	NHLBI	National Heart, Lung, and Blood Institute	301-496-4236
AG	NIA	National Institute on Aging	301-496-1752
AA	NIAAA	National Institute on Alcohol Abuse and Alcoholism	301-443-3860
AI	NIAID	National Institute of Allergy and Infectious Diseases	301-496-5717
AR	NIAMS	National Institute of Arthritis, Musculoskeletal and Skin Diseases	301-496-8188
HD	NICHD	National Institute of Child Health and Human Development	301-496-5133
DE	NIDR	National Institute of Dental Research	301-594-7629
DK	NIDDK	National Institute of Diabetes, and Digestive and Kidney Diseases	301-496-3583
DA	NIDA	National Institute on Drug Abuse	301-443-1124
ES	NIEHS	National Institute of Environmental Health Sciences	919-541-1167
GM	NIGMS	National Institute of General Medical Sciences	301-496-7301
MH	NIMH	National Institute of Mental Health	301-443-4513
NS	NINDS	National Institute of Neurological Disorders and Stroke	301-496-5751
NR	NINR	National Institute for Nursing Research	301-496-0207
DC	NIDCD	National Institute of Deafness and Other Communication Disorders	301-496-7243

OTHER NIH FUNDING COMPONENTS

LM	NLM	National Library of Medicine	301-496-6308
HG	NCHGR	National Center for Human Genome Research	301-402-0911
RR	NCRR	National Center for Research Resources	301-594-7938
TW	FIC	John E. Fogarty International Center	301-496-2075

NIH NON-FUNDING COMPONENTS

CC	Warren Grant Magnuson Clinical Center	301-496-2563
DRG	Division of Research Grants	301-594-7248
DCRT	Division of Computer Research and Technology	301-496-6203

B. DRG Review Sections

The Review Sections of the Referral and Review Branch of DRG are administrative group-ings of Initial Review Groups which consist of sub-committees called Study Sections.

REVIEW SECTIONS OF THE REFERRAL AND REVIEW BRANCH OF DRG

Behavioral and Neurosciences Review Section	BHNS
Biological and Physiological Sciences Review Section	BPS
Chemistry and Related Sciences Review Section	CRS
Clinical Sciences Review Section	CLIN
Microbial and Immunological Sciences Review Section	MIS
Technology and Applied Sciences Review Section	TAS

The Heads of the Review Sections of the Referral and Review Branch of DRG are given in Section D3b, below.

C. DRG Study Sections

In spring 1994, DRG reorganized its approximately 100 Study Sections into 19 chartered subject-oriented Initial Review Groups (IRGs), each composed of 3 to 7 sub-committees called Study Sections (see list below). In addition, DRG has 6 Special Emphasis Panels (SEPs), one for each of the 6 DRG review sections (see Figure A1-7). The IRGs, Study Sections, their codes, and the relevant SRA and her/his phone number are listed in an NIH brochure, *DRG Organization and Functions* (July 1993). As this book goes to press, this brochure is being updated to reflect the reorganized DRG structure. The new bro-chure, a part of which is reproduced on page 173, is available from the Grants Informa-tion Office (301-594-7248.) The Scientific Review Administrators and members of the Study Sections are listed in an NIH publication entitled *NIH Advisory Committees: Au-thority, Structure, Functions, Members* which is updated periodically. The last edition was published in April, 1993. NIH is discontinuing publication of a paper edition of this book and making it available only on-line. Appendix 4 in the book *A Guide to NIH Grant Programs,* by Samuel M. Schwartz and Mischa E. Friedman (Oxford University Press, New York, 1992) has a convenient summary of the DRG Study Section assignment areas. The Study Section membership roster is available on-line (see page 352). For up-to-date information about Study Section meeting dates, agendas, and rosters, call the DRG Office of Committee Management, 301-594-7265.

The 19 Initial Review Groups (IRGs) formed by DRG in 1994 showing their component sub-committees (Study Sections) and the DRG Review Section with which they are affiliated are listed below.

Behavioral and Neurosciences Review Section

BIOBEHAVIORAL AND SOCIAL SCIENCES INITIAL REVIEW GROUP

Behavioral Medicine
Biopsychology
Human Development and Aging (subcommittees 1, 2 and 3)
Social Science and Population

NEUROLOGICAL SCIENCES INITIAL REVIEW GROUP

Neurology A
Neurology B (subcommittees 1 and 2)
Neurology C
Neurological Sciences (subcommittees 1 and 2)

SENSORY SCIENCES INITIAL REVIEW GROUP

Sensory Disorders and Language
Hearing Research
Visual Sciences A
Visual Sciences B
Visual Sciences C

BEHAVIORAL AND NEUROSCIENCES SPECIAL EMPHASIS PANEL

Biological and Physiological Sciences Review Section

CELL DEVELOPMENT AND FUNCTION INITIAL REVIEW GROUP

Biological Sciences (subcommittee 2)
Cellular Biology & Physiology (subcommittees 1 and 2)
Molecular Cytology
Human Embryology and Development (subcommittee 2)
International & Cooperative Projects
Molecular Biology

ENDOCRINOLOGY AND REPRODUCTIVE SCIENCES INITIAL REVIEW GROUP

Biochemical Endocrinology
Endocrinology
Human Embryology and Development (subcommittee 1)
Reproductive Biology
Reproductive Endocrinology

GENETIC SCIENCES INITIAL REVIEW GROUP

Biological Sciences (subcommittee 1)
Genetics
Genome
Mammalian Genetics

PATHOPHYSIOLOGICAL SCIENCES INITIAL REVIEW GROUP

Lung Biology and Pathology
Physiology
Respiratory and Applied Physiology
Physiological Sciences

BIOLOGICAL AND PHYSIOLOGICAL SCIENCES SPECIAL EMPHASIS PANEL

Chemistry and Related Sciences Review Section

BIOCHEMICAL SCIENCES INITIAL REVIEW GROUP

Biochemistry
Biomedical Sciences
Medical Biochemistry
Pathobiochemistry
Physiological Chemistry

BIOPHYSICAL AND CHEMICAL SCIENCES INITIAL REVIEW GROUP

Molecular and Cellular Biophysics
Biophysical Chemistry
Metallobiochemistry
Bio-organic & Natural Products Chemistry
Medicinal Chemistry
Physical Biochemistry

ONCOLOGICAL SCIENCES INITIAL REVIEW GROUP

Chemical Pathology
Experimental Therapeutics
Metabolic Pathology
Pathology B
Radiation

CHEMISTRY AND RELATED SCIENCES SPECIAL EMPHASIS PANEL

Clinical Sciences Review Section

CARDIOVASCULAR SCIENCES INITIAL REVIEW GROUP

Cardiovascular
Cardiovascular and Renal
Experimental Cardiovascular Sciences
Hematology (subcommittees 1 and 2)
Pharmacology

HEALTH PROMOTION AND DISEASE PREVENTION INITIAL REVIEW GROUP

Epidemiology & Disease Control (subcommittees 1 and 2)
Nursing Research
Safety and Occupational Health
Toxicology (subcommittees 1 and 2)

MUSCULOSKELETAL AND DENTAL SCIENCES INITIAL REVIEW GROUP

General Medicine A-1
General Medicine B
Oral Biology and Medicine (subcommittees 1 and 2)
Orthopedics and Musculoskeletal

NUTRITIONAL AND METABOLIC SCIENCES INITIAL REVIEW GROUP

Clinical Sciences (subcommittees 1 and 2)
General Medicine A-2
Metabolism
Nutrition

CLINICAL SCIENCES SPECIAL EMPHASIS PANEL

Microbial and Immunological Sciences Review Section

AIDS AND RELATED RESEARCH INITIAL REVIEW GROUP

AIDS and Related Research Subcommittees A through G

IMMUNOLOGICAL SCIENCES INITIAL REVIEW GROUP

Allergy and Immunology
Experimental Immunology
Immunology
Immunological Sciences
Immunology, Virology, and Pathology

INFECTIOUS DISEASES AND MICROBIOLOGY INITIAL REVIEW GROUP

Bacteriology & Mycology (subcommittees 1 and 2)
Experimental Virology
Microbial Physiology & Genetics (subcommittees 1 and 2)
Tropical Medicine & Parasitology
Virology

MICROBIAL AND IMMUNOLOGICAL SCIENCES SPECIAL EMPHASIS PANEL

Technology and Applied Sciences Review Section

TECHNOLOGY AND APPLIED SCIENCES INITIAL REVIEW GROUP

SSS[1] (subcommittees 1 through 9)
SSS-W
SSS-X
SSS-Y
SSS-Z

---

[1] Special Study Section

SURGERY, RADIOLOGY AND BIOENGINEERING INITIAL REVIEW GROUP

Diagnostic Radiology
Surgery, Anesthesiology and Trauma
Surgery and Bioengineering

MULTIDISCIPLINARY SCIENCES SPECIAL EMPHASIS PANEL

DIVISION OF RESEARCH GRANTS STUDY SECTIONS (JULY 1993)

Study Section	Code	SRA	Telephone number† (area code 301)
Adolescent Family Life	AFL	Robert Weller, Ph.D	594-7340
AIDS and Related Research–1	ARRA	Sami A. Mayyasi, Ph.D.	594-7073
AIDS and Related Research–2	ARRB	Gilbert W. Meier, Ph.D.	594-7118
AIDS and Related Research–3	ARRC	*Marcel W. Pons, Ph.D.	594-7210
AIDS and Related Research–4	ARRD	Mohindar S. Poonian, Ph.D.	594-7112
AIDS and Related Research–5	ARRE	Mohindar S. Poonian, Ph.D.	594-7112
AIDS and Related Research–6	ARRF	Gilbert W. Meier, Ph.D.	594-7118
AIDS and Related Research–7	ARRG	Gilbert W. Meier, Ph.D.	594-7118
Allergy and Immunology	ALY	Howard M. Berman, B.S.	594-7234
Bacteriology and Mycology–1	BM1	Timothy Henry, Ph.D.	594-7228
Bacteriology and Mycology–2	BM2	William C. Branche, Jr., Ph.D.	594-7297
Behavioral Medicine	BEM	*Carol Campbell, M.S.	594-7165
Behavioral and Neurosciences–1	BNS1	Luigi Giacometti, Ph.D.	594-7122
Behavioral and Neurosciences–2	BNS2	Luigi Giacometti, Ph.D	594-7122
Biochemical Endocrinology	BCE	Michael Knecht, Ph.D.	594-7247
Biochemistry	BIO	Adolphus P. Toliver, Ph.D.	594-7263
Biological Sciences–1	BIOL1	Richard King, Ph.D.	594-7097
Biological Sciences–2	BIOL2	Camilla Day, Ph.D.	594-7389
Biological Sciences–3	BIOL3	Nancy Pearson, Ph.D.	594-7388
Biomedical Sciences	BIOM	Charles Baker, Ph.D.	594-7170
Bio-organic and Natural Products Chemistry	BNP	Harold Radtke, Ph.D.	594-7212
Biophysical Chemistry	BBCB	John Beisler, Ph.D.	594-7149
Bio-Psychology	BPO	A. Keith Murray, Ph.D.	594-7145
Cardiovascular	CVA	Gordon Johnson, Ph.D.	594-7216
Cardiovascular and Renal	CVB	Anthony Chung, Ph.D.	594-7338
Cellular Biology and Physiology–1	CBY1	*Gerald A. Greenhouse, Ph.D.	594-7385
Cellular Biology and Physiology–2	CBY2	Gerhard Ehrenspeck, Ph.D.	594-7387
Chemical Pathology	CPA	Edmund S. Copeland, Ph.D.	594-7154
Clinical Sciences–1	CLIN1	Josephine Pelham, B.A.	594-7114
Clinical Sciences–2	CLIN2	Josephine Pelham, B.A.	594-7114

†The DRG is scheduled to move to Two Rockledge Centre, Rockledge Drive, Bethesda, MD in early 1995. It is possible that the move will result in new telephone numbers for all DRG offices. Please note that organizational changes in the DRG Review Sections may have caused some discrepancies between this 1993 list and the 1994 list shown in the previous section.
*Referral Officer

Study Section	Code	SRA	Telephone number† (area code 301)
Diagnostic Radiology	RNM	Catharine Wingate, Ph.D.	594-7295
Endocrinology	END	Syed Amir, Ph.D.	594-7229
Epidemiology and Disease Control–1	EDC1	Scott Osborne, Ph.D.	594-7194
Epidemiology and Disease Control–2	EDC2	Horace Stiles, Ph.D.	594-7194
Experimental Cardiovascular Sciences	ECS	Richard A. Peabody, Sr., Ph.D.	594-7344
Experimental Immunology	EI	Calbert Laing, Ph.D.	594-7190
Experimental Therapeutics–1	ET1	Phillip Perkins, Ph.D.	594-7324
Experimental Therapeutics-2	ET2	Marcia Litwack, Ph.D.	594-7366
Experimental Virology	EVR	Garrett V. Keefer, Ph.D.	594-7099
General Medicine A–1	GMA1	Harold Davidson, Ph.D.	594-7313
General Medicine A–2	GMA2	Mushtaq Ahmad Khan, D.V.M., Ph.D.	594-7168
General Medicine B	GMB	Daniel McDonald, Ph.D.	594-7301
Genetics	GEN	David J. Remondini, Ph.D.	594-7202
Genome	GNM	Cheryl Corsaro, Ph.D	594-7336
Hearing Research	HAR	Joseph Kimm, Ph.D	594-7257
Hematology 1	HEM1	Clark K. Lum, Ph.D.	594-7260
Hematology–2	HEM2	Jerrold Fried, Ph.D.	594-7261
Human Development and Aging–1	HUD1	Teresa Levitin, Ph.D.	594-7141
Human Development and Aging–2	HUD2	Peggy D. McCardle, Ph.D.	594-7293
Human Development and Aging–3	HUD3	Anita M. Sostek, Ph.D.	594-7358
Human Embryology and Development–1	HED1	Arthur S. Hoversland, Ph.D.	594-7253
Human Embryology and Development–2	HED2	Arthur S. Hoversland, Ph.D.	594-7253
Immunobiology	IMB	Betty J. Hayden, Ph.D.	594-7310
Immunological Sciences	IMS	Anita Weinblatt, Ph.D.	594-7175
Immunology, Virology and Pathology	IVP	Lynwood Jones Jr., Ph.D.	594-7262
International & Cooperative Projects	ICP	Sandy Warren, D.M.D., M.P.H.	594-7289
Lung Biology and Pathology	LBPA	Anne P. Clark, Ph.D.	594-7115
Mammalian Genetics	MGN	Jerry H. Roberts, Ph.D.	594-7051
Medical Biochemistry	MEDB	Alec Liacouras, Ph.D.	594-7264
Medicinal Chemistry	MCHA	Ronald J. Dubois, Ph.D.	594-7163
Metabolic Pathology	MEP	Marcelina Powers, D.V.M., M.S.	594-7120
Metabolism	MET	Krish Krishnan, Ph.D.	594-7156
Metallobiochemistry	BMT	Edward J. Zapolski, Ph.D.	594-7302
Microbial Physiology and Genetics–1	MBC1	Martin L. Slater, Ph.D.	594-7176
Microbial Physiology and Genetics–2	MBC2	*Gerald Liddel, Ph.D.	594-7167

Study Section	Code	SRA	Telephone number (area code 301)
Molecular Biology	MBY	Robert Su, Ph.D.	594-7320
Molecular and Cellular Biophysics	BBCA	Nancy Lamontagne, Ph.D.	594-7147
Molecular Cytology	CTY	*Ramesh K. Nayak, Ph.D.	594-7169
Neurological Sciences–1	NLS1	Andrew Mariani, Ph.D.	594-7206
Neurological Sciences–2	NLS2	Stephen Gobel, D.D.S.	594-7356
Neurology A	NEUA	Joe Marwah, Ph.D.	594-7158
Neurology B1	NEUB1	Lillian Pubols, Ph.D.	594-7235
Neurology B2	NEUB2	*Herman Teitelbaum, Ph.D.	594-7245
Neurology C	NEUC	Kenneth Neurock, Ph.D.	594-7123
Nursing Research	NURS	Gertrude K. McFarland, D.N.Sc.	594-7080
Nutrition	NTN	Sooja Kim, Ph.D.	594-7174
Oral Biology and Medicine–1	OBM1	Larry Pinkus, Ph.D.	594-7315
Oral Biology and Medicine–2	OBM2	Priscilla Chen, Ph.D.	594-7315
Orthopedics and Musculoskeletal	ORTH	Ileen E. Stewart, M.S.	594-7282
Pathobiochemistry	PBC	Zakir H. Bengali, Ph.D.	594-7317
Pathology A	PTHA	Jaswant S. Bhorjee, Ph.D.	594-7236
Pathology B	PTHB	*Martin Padarathsingh, Ph.D.	594-7192
Pharmacology	PHRA	Joseph A. Kaiser, Ph.D.	594-7241
Physical Biochemistry	PB	*Gopa Rakhit, Ph.D.	594-7166
Physiological Chemistry	PC	Jerry Critz, Ph.D.	594-7322
Physiological Sciences	PSF	*Nicholas Mazarella, Ph.D.	594-7098
Physiology	PHY	Michael Lang, Ph.D.	594-7332
Radiation	RAD	Paul Strudler, Ph.D	594-7152
Reproductive Biology	REB	*Dharam S. Dhindsa, D.V.M., Ph.D.	594-7218
Reproductive Endocrinology	REN	Abubakar A. Shaikh, D.V.M., Ph.D.	594-7368
Respiratory and Applied Physiology	RAP	Everett Sinnett, Ph.D.	594-7220
Safety and Occupational Health	SOH	Gopal Sharma, D.V.M., Ph.D.	594-7130
Sensory Disorders and Language	CMS	Jane Hu, Ph.D.	594-7269
Social Sciences and Population	SSP	Robert Weller, Ph.D.	594-7340
Service Delivery Improvement	SDI	Robert Weller, Ph.D.	594-7340
Surgery, Anesthesiology and Trauma	SAT	Keith L. Kraner, D.V.M.	594-7308
Surgery and Bioengineering	SB	*Paul R. Parakkal, Ph.D.	594-7258
Toxicology–1	TOX1	Alfred Marozzi, Ph.D.	594-7278
Toxicology–2	TOX2	Alfred Marozzi, Ph.D.	594-7278
Tropical Medicine and Parasitology	TMP	Jean Hickman, Ph.D.	594-7078
Virology	VR	Rita Anand, Ph.D.	594-7108
Visual Sciences A	VISA	Anita Suran, Ph.D.	594-7132
Visual Sciences B	VISB	Leonard Jakubczak, Ph.D.	594-7198
Visual Sciences C	VISC	Carole Jelsema, Ph.D.	594-7311

SPECIAL REVIEW SECTION

SSS-1		Eileen W. Bradley, D.Sc.	594-7188
SSS-2		Donald Schneider, Ph.D.	594-7053
SSS-3		Harish C. Chopra, Ph.D.	594-7342
SSS-4		Nabeeh Mourad, Ph.D.	594-7213
SSS-5		*Melvin M. Ketchel, Ph.D.	594-7391

Study Section	Code	SRA	Telephone number (area code 301)
SSS-6	Marjam Behar, Ph.D.		594-7376
SSS-7	Houston Baker, Ph.D.		594-7374
SSS-8	Nadarajen A. Vydelingum, Ph.D.		594-7350
SSS-9	Bill Bunnag, Ph.D.		594-7360
SSS-X	Lee Rosen, Ph.D.		594-7276
SSS-Y	Eugene G. Hayunga, Ph.D.		594-7243
SSS-Z	Richard Panniers, Ph.D.		594-7348
REFERRAL SECTION			
Chief	Patricia Straat, Ph.D.		594-7250
Assistant Chiefs	Julius Currie, Ph.D.		594-7250
	Suzanne Fisher, Ph.D.		594-7250
	Rosemary Morris, Ph.D.		594-7250
Project Control	Jeanne Malcom		594-7224

D. Specific Sources of NIH Information

Note: (1) There are frequent personnel changes at NIH, so the information below may change periodically.[2] Check with the Grants Information Office (301-594-7248) for up-to-date information. (2) Dr. Howard Schachman from the University of California (Berkeley, CA 94702) was chosen in 1994 by NIH Director, Harold Varmus, to be a part-time ombudsman between NIH and the research community. There will also be an ombudsman for clinical researchers but this position was not filled at the time this book went to press.

1. RESEARCH GRANTS POLICY

Dr. Wendy Baldwin	Deputy Director for Extramural Research, Office of the Director	301-496-1096
Dr. George Galasso	Associate Director for Extramural Affairs, Office of the Director	301-496-5356
Mr. Geoffrey Grant	Acting Director, Office of Policy for Extramural Research Administration	301-496-5967
Dr. Carlos Caban	NIH Extramural Programs Management Officer	301-496-2241
Dr. Samuel Joseloff	Chief, Grants Information Office, Division of Research Grants	301-594-7248

2. RESEARCH TRAINING POLICY

Dr. Walter Schaffer	Chief, Research Training and Special Programs Office, Office of the Director	301-496-9743

[2]Many phone numbers in the Westwood Building were changed from 301-496 numbers to 301-594 numbers in 1992.

3. DIVISION OF RESEARCH GRANTS

Dr. Jerome Green*	Director	301-594-7181
Dr. Donald Luecke	Deputy Director	301-594-7251
Dr. Anthony Demsey	Chief, Referral and Review Branch	301-594-7139
Dr. Patricia Straat	Deputy Chief for Referral, Referral and Review Branch	301-594-7250
Ms. Jean Malcolm	Head, Project Control	301-594-7224
Dr. Faye Calhoun	Deputy Chief for Review, Referral and Review Branch	301-594-7139
Dr. Raymond Bahor	Associate Chief, Referral and Review Branch	301-594-7364

The organizational structure of the NIH/DRG is shown in Appendix I-F, Figure A1-7.

a. Receipt and Assignment of Applications

Applications to NIH are received by the Referral Section, Referral and Review Branch, Division of Research Grants. The Referral Section includes the Referral Officers and also a Project Control Unit, which keeps track of applications.

Referral Section, Referral and Review Branch of DRG:

Dr. Patricia Straat	Chief	301-594-7250
Dr. Suzanne Fisher	Special Assistant to the Chief	301-594-7250
Dr. Julius Currie	Assistant Chief	301-594-7250
Dr. Rosemary Morris	Assistant Chief	301-594-7250
Ms. Jean Malcolm	Head, Project Control	301-594-7224

b. Scientific Merit Review of Applications

Review for scientific merit of applications is carried out by Initial Review Groups (IRGs), which are subdivided into Study Sections. Study Sections within DRG are part of the DRG Referral and Review Branch. The Review Sections of the Referral and Review Branch of DRG are administrative groupings of Initial Review Groups and their component Study Sections.

Heads of the Review Sections of the Referral and Review Branch of DRG:

Dr. Samuel Rawlings	Chief, Behavioral and Neurosciences Review Section (BHNS)	301-594-7151

* Dr. Green retired March 1995.

Dr. Donna Dean	Chief, Biological and Physiological Sciences Review Section (BPS)	301-594-7386
Dr. Asher Hyatt	Chief, Chemistry and Related Sciences Review Section (CRS)	301-594-7150
Dr. Jeanne Ketley	Chief, Clinical Sciences Review Section (CLIN)	301-594-7375
Dr. Bruce Maurer	Chief, Microbial and Immunological Sciences Review Section (MIS)	301-594-7093
Dr. Elliott Postow	Chief, Technology and Applied Sciences Review Section (TAS)	301-594-7272

4. AWARDING BUREAUS, INSTITUTES

Associate Directors for Extramural Programs (or Equivalent Positions):

Ms. Barbara Bynum	National Cancer Institute	301-496–5147
Dr. Ronald Geller	National Heart, Lung, and Blood Institute	301-594-7454
Dr. Walter Stolz	National Institute of Arthritis, Diabetes, and Digestive and Kidney Diseases	301-594-7527
Dr. Milton Corn	National Library of Medicine	301-496-4621
Dr. Miriam Kelty	National Institute on Aging	301-496-9374
Dr. John McGowan	National Institute of Allergy and Infectious Diseases	301-496-7291
Dr. Michael Lockshin	National Institute of Arthritis and Musculoskeletal and Skin Diseases	301-496-7495
Dr. Wendy Baldwin	National Institute of Child Health and Human Development	301-496-1848
Dr. Lois Cohen	National Institute of Dental Research	301-594-7638
Dr. Anne Sassaman	National Institute of Environmental Health Sciences	919-541-7723
Dr. Jack McLaughlin	National Eye Institute	301-496-9110

Dr. Sue Shafer	National Institute of General Medical Sciences	301-594-7751
Mr. Ed Donohue	National Institute of Neurological Disorders and Stroke	301-496-9248
Dr. John Dalton	National Institute of Deafness and Other Communication Disorders	301-496-8693
Dr. Judith Vaitukaitis	National Center for Research Resources	301-496-6023
Dr. David Wolff	Fogarty International Center	301-496-1653
Dr. May Lucas	National Institute for Nursing Research	301-496-0523
Dr. Mark Guyer	National Center for Human Genome Research	301-496-0844

Note: Although NIAAA, NIDA, and NIMH became NIH institutes on October 1, 1992, grant applications to these 3 Institutes will continue to be reviewed by Study Sections within these Institutes (rather than DRG Study Sections) until 1996. The NIAAA, NIDA, and NIMH review groups function in a manner similar to those of NIH/DRG.

5. GENERAL INFORMATION

a. Research Involving Human Subjects or Vertebrate Animals

| Dr. Gary Ellis | Director | Office for Protection from Research Risks | 301-496-7005 |
| Dr. John Miller | Deputy Director | Office for Protection from Research Risks | 301-496-7005 |

b. Privacy Act

| Ms. Cheryl Seaman | NIH Privacy Act Officer | 301-496-2832 |

Or contact the appropriate NIH Component Privacy Act Coordinator

c. Freedom of Information Act

| Ms. Joanne Bell | NIH Freedom of Information Act Officer | 301-496-5633 |

Or contact the appropriate NIH Component Freedom of Information Act Coordinator

d. Public Information

| Ms. Anne Thomas | Acting Associate Director for Communication | Office of the Director | 301-496-4461 |

Ms. Anne Thomas   Director, Division   Office of the Director   301-496-5787
of Public Information

e. Publications and Single Copies of Application Kits

Dr. Samuel Joseloff   Chief   Grants Information Office,   301-594-7248
Division of Research Grants

E. NIH: An Agency of the Public Health Service

The Department of Health and Human Services (DHHS) is one of the Executive Departments of the Executive Branch of the U.S. government (Appendix I-F, Figure A1-4). The Public Health Service (PHS) is an agency within the Department of Health and Human Services (DHHS). The organizational structures of DHHS, PHS, and NIH are shown in Appendix I-F, Figures A1-4 through A1-6, respectively.

Department of Health and Human Services (DHHS)
Hubert H. Humphrey Bldg.
200 Independence Ave., S.W.
Washington, DC 20201
202-619-0257

Public Health Service (PHS)
5600 Fishers Lane
Rockville, MD 20857
301-443-2403

Public Health Service
Hubert H. Humphrey Bldg.
200 Independence Ave., S.W.
Washington, DC 20201
202-690-6867

Public Health Service
Office of Research Integrity
301-443-3400

The Public Health Service has 8 agencies:

Agency for Health Care Policy and Research (AHCPR)   301-594-1364
Agency for Toxic Substances and Disease Registry (ATSDR) 404-639-0727
Centers for Disease Control and Prevention (CDC)   404-639-3311
Food and Drug Administration (FDA)   301-443-3170
Health Resources and Services Administration (HRSA)   301-443-2086
Indian Health Service (IHS)   301-443-3593
National Institutes of Health (NIH)   301-496-4000
Substance Abuse and Mental Health Services Administration 1-800-729-6686
   (SAMHSA)   or 301-468-2600

BRIEF COMMENTS ON PROPOSALS SUBMITTED TO THE NATIONAL SCIENCE FOUNDATION

By Bruce E. Trumbo[1]

Professor of Statistics and Mathematics,
California State University, Hayward

Almost all of the general principles and many of the specific suggestions in Dr. Reif-Lehrer's manuscript would apply to the writing of an effective proposal for submission to any agency or foundation. Because the National Science Foundation (NSF) is another major source of support for scientific research, the editors have asked me to discuss briefly some respects in which NSF differs from NIH. I have chosen to emphasize two differences that I think have particular impact on the planning and writing of proposals.

DIFFERENCES IN MISSION

The first important difference between NSF and NIH is that Congress has given them different scientific missions. NSF does not make grants for research mainly oriented toward clinical medicine but does support basic research in almost all scientific fields, such as sociology, physics, biology, economics, psychology, chemistry, mathematics, engineering, and so forth. The foundation also makes grants to support science education, but this discussion is restricted to grants for research projects.

Some projects involving basic scientific research also have potential clinical applications and so may fall within the missions of both agencies. It is no longer permissible to submit the same proposal to both NSF and NIH. If you submit a proposal that was not funded by one agency to the other agency, you must, of course, restructure the text to conform to the appropriate format for the agency to which you are submitting the application. In such cases, each agency gives a separate review to the proposal it receives and cooperates with the other to avoid double funding, or perhaps to arrange joint funding. (If your research may overlap more than one section at NSF, send a single proposal directed to one section and in the cover letter give your suggestions for possible joint review by other sections. The final decision on program assignment is up to NSF.)

---

[1] This chapter was revised by Sherwin S. Lehrer, (Senior Staff Scientist, Boston Biomedical Research Institute; Principal Associate, Department of Neurology, Harvard Medical School; Member of an NSF Review Panel, 1985–1988) for the second edition of *Writing a Successful Grant Application*. The book was further revised for this book by Bruce Trumbo and by Hartmut Wohlrab, Ph.D., Senior Staff Scientist, Boston Biomedical Research Institute, Research Associate, Department of Biological Chemistry and Molecular Pharmacology, Harvard Medical School, and Member of an NSF Review Panel beginning in 1992.

Programs and Proposals

The NSF booklet *Grant Proposal Guide* (NSF 94-2, January 1994) describes the basic procedures for applying for all general research grants. (Most of the proposals to NSF and most of the funds granted by NSF fall into this general or nonselected category.) Because of the varying patterns of research activity across the broad spectrum of scientific work supported by NSF, however, it is not possible to be as specific about the details of how a proposal is handled at NSF as Dr. Reif-Lehrer has been about NIH. A proposal by a mathematician may involve the principal investigator, one graduate student, and use of a computer. A proposal by a group of astronomers or high-energy physicists may involve detailed administrative considerations and scheduled use of a multi-million-dollar facility. Clearly, the details of processing and reviewing proposals must differ from section to section within NSF. It is important for writers of proposals to be aware of deadlines and of any special proposal-writing suggestions of the NSF section that handles their area of science. Most NSF sections distribute such information widely, for example, through the *NSF Bulletin*, in professional journals, to university research offices, and to present grantees. A brief phone call or letter to the appropriate NSF section may help to define the relevance of a particular proposal to a particular program, but remember that NSF program officers are not paid to be consultants in grantsmanship.

In addition to general research grants, NSF supports a variety of cooperative international and exchange programs. NSF also establishes special programs from time to time to meet specific needs—support for a conference in an expanding research area or for a particular kind of instrumentation, for example. Other current NSF programs include Research Opportunities for Women, various instructional and research instrumentation programs, and a number of fellowships.

These programs are announced in brochures that give the details for application. Unfortunately, sometimes the legislative, budgetary, and legal considerations that go into establishing these programs leave little time between formal announcement in a brochure and the deadline for applying. However, the fact that a particular program is under consideration at NSF is generally not a secret from the scientific community it will serve (and which has doubtless been lobbying for it), even though the most specific details are available only in the formal announcement. Moreover, many such programs continue essentially unchanged through several fiscal years. (At a university the spring schedule of classes is not often available the previous summer, but clever students generally find no real surprises in the schedule when it is published.) Thus, the scientist who knows his research needs and capabilities and who pays some attention to trends of NSF support can often consider in advance the general thrust of possible proposals for special program funds. It is important, however, to read carefully the brochure describing a specific program to determine the purposes for which it has been established, the exact eligibility and contractual requirements, and so forth, before deciding to apply. Far-fetched rationalizations that attempt to squeeze a proposal (however sound scientifically) into an ill-fitting mold waste the time of proposers, reviewers, and program officers alike. Remember also that different agencies have different formats for proposal submission. For example, NSF tends to be somewhat less formal than NIH in terms of the Research Plan (except for very strict page limits); but the budget pages are prescribed and are different from those of NIH.[2] In addition, NSF likes to cost-share with the grantee institution.[3] Also, at NSF, indirect costs are included in the total award and are not negotiated separately.

---

[2] This chapter was revised in mid 1993; the new *NSF Grant Proposal Guide*, issued in 1994, has many similarities to the NIH PHS-398 and has more form pages than the previous NSF instructions for grant applications.

[3] Cost-sharing is very important at NSF and is mandated in certain specific NSF programs, especially those involving equipment. Cost sharing should be summarzied on the Budget Form and explained in the Budget Justification. Also, because of tight funding, budgets are generally and significantly cut. Issues of cost-sharing are often discussed with administrators of grantee institutions in the course of budget negotiations.

DIFFERENCES IN METHODS OF PROPOSAL REVIEW

A second major difference between NSF and NIH is the review process. The use of Initial Review Groups by NIH is described in detail in the main manuscript. NSF uses a variety of review procedures, less uniform than the NIH process with its review groups. Some NSF programs arrange panel meetings of Reviewers, typically with the presumption that each panel member has studied the proposals before the panel meeting. Often, panel members or outside Reviewers have submitted written reviews before the panel meets. Thus, the essence of an NSF panel meeting is usually a round-table discussion focusing initially on many individual reactions to each proposal, often with the experts in the field summarizing the proposal first. Sometimes, panels are asked to rank proposals or to sort them into several categories as to merit, but anything approaching the detailed score-keeping approach used at NIH is rare in an NSF panel meeting. Even when NSF Reviewers meet in face-to-face discussions, their interaction is likely to be structured somewhat more loosely than at an NIH Study Section, with each review panel having its own flavor, set by the Program Director.

Many NSF programs use mail reviews. Typically, the program director will initially select several outside Reviewers for a proposal, following guidelines to ensure balance. Reviewers are asked to comment on all aspects of the proposal and to rate it as Excellent, Very Good, Good, Fair, or Poor, where each category is carefully defined by NSF in terms of scientific merit, capability of the investigator, development of human resources (e.g., training graduate students), and the availability of resources. Additional reviews are often sought to reconcile differences in Reviewer reaction or to pursue issues raised by the first round of Reviewers. Based on the relative merit determined by the panel and/or mail reviews, the panel may informally recommend[4] funding or "declination" of the project. For projects recommended for funding, the Program Director attempts to fund as many proposals as possible with the available funds. Often, the panel recommends a revised, smaller budget, consistent with the requirements of the reviewed project, which may then permit funding of more projects.

Copies of Reviewers' comments (but not their names)—and, in some cases, a summary of the panel discussion—are sent to the principal investigator after final action on the proposal has been taken. These comments can be educational for both successful and unsuccessful applicants.

Because the *initial* impression of each panel Reviewer and the *only* impression of a mail Reviewer is the solitary one of a fellow scientist reading the proposal, it can be argued that the NSF review system places a heavy responsibility on the proposer to communicate ideas in a clear and organized way and to document the budget adequately. Some Reviewers will be researchers in the same narrow subfield as the proposer, and others will be viewing the proposal from some scientific distance. It is important for proposal writers to give attention both to explaining exactly what is proposed and to showing its place and importance in the context of the field as a whole.

This latter point takes on added significance when one reflects upon the fact that the program director, who cannot possibly be an expert in the narrow subfield of each proposal he or she handles, selects the Reviewers based largely on information contained in the proposal. Some NSF Programs actively solicit lists of proposed Reviewers from applicants. But an equally important way for a proposer to help ensure that the first round of

---

4   The mandate of the panel/reviewers is to assign a merit descriptor to applications. Although panel members may — and often do — recommend funding or "declination" of a project, the ultimate decision about funding lies with the NSF staff.

Reviewers will provide the balanced body of opinion and evaluation needed for a prompt and fair decision is to make sure that the essence and importance of the proposal are clear and to provide a bibliography that is neither skimpy and skewed towards publications of the PI and her/his colleagues nor padded and expansive.

CONCLUSION

These observations are based on personal experience with NSF as (at different times in the past) applicant, Reviewer, and program director. They have no official status.

One further personal reaction may be in order. I have had a few opportunities to compare the NSF and NIH review processes for essentially identical proposals. In each of these instances the procedural differences mentioned here, while important, were of far less practical significance than the astonishing similarities in results. The same issues were discussed, the same objections offered, the same strengths noted, the same budget items questioned, and the same conclusions reached.

The main manuscript begins with the comment that a good proposal requires, above all else, a good idea. By bad presentation it is possible to obscure a good idea from Reviewers either at NSF or NIH. A routine or mediocre idea will look no better than routine or mediocre when viewed through either pair of spectacles.

More about the National Science Foundation (NSF)

A. General Information

In this Appendix, I have tried to provide readers who may be interested in applying to NSF for funding with some basic information about the grants process at NSF.

Each year, NSF receives more than 40,000 proposals for new or renewed support for research, graduate fellowships, and science and engineering education activities and makes approximately 10,000 new awards.[1] These go mainly to universities, colleges, academic consortia, nonprofit institutions, and small businesses. (Some awards given are very small, such as conference awards.) NSF does not operate laboratories but does support National Research Centers, oceanographic vessels, and Antarctic research stations. The Foundation also aids cooperative research between universities and industry and U.S. participation in international scientific efforts.

The NSF grant application form and instructions for preparation and submission of the application are contained in the NSF *Grant Proposal Guide (GPG)*, NSF 94-2, January, 1994.[2] *The use of the GPG became mandatory on April 4, 1994.*

NSF generally uses *grants* for awards in support of research and education in science and engineering. In cases in which an assistance project requires substantial NSF technical or managerial involvement during the project performance period, NSF uses *cooperative agreements*. While the GPG is generally applicable to both types of assistance awards, cooperative agreements may include different or additional requirements. Contact the relevant Program Officer before preparing an application.

SUMMARY OF MAJOR CHANGES IN THE GPG COMPARED TO GRESE[3]

- Inclusion of a Proposal Forms Kit (a complete package of forms necessary for submission of unsolicited proposals to NSF). The Proposal Forms Kit is available within—or separate from—the GPG. The forms may be duplicated or computer simulated. The new forms listed below have been added to simplify proposal submission and review.

  —Project Summary (NSF Form 1358)
  —Table of Contents (NSF Form 1359)

---

[1] The BIO Directorate award rate in the early 1990s was 15-20% for regular full awards. About 20% of these applications consisted of revised applications.

[2] The GPG replaced *Grants For Research and Education in Science and Engineering* (GRESE), NSF 92-89 (October 1992), in January 1994.

[3] As was the case in the GRESE, the GPG has inconsistencies in the outline form used in the instructions. Do not allow these inconsistencies to deter you from writing a well-organized, consistent proposal with good logical flow. Your proposal will be read by your peers. Write to fulfill their expectations.

—Project Description (NSF Form 1360)
—Bibliography (NSF Form 1361)
—Biographical Sketch (NSF Form 1362)
—Facilities, Equipment and Other Resources (NSF Form 1363)

- Cover Sheet (NSF Form 1207) has added new blocks to indicate proposals from "Beginning Investigators," "Group Proposals," and "Small Grants for Exploratory Research."
- Arrangement for submission of required documentation has been modified.
- A new section, "Conformance with Instructions for Proposal Preparation," has been added.
- *Project Description* has been limited to 15 single-spaced pages, *including* text, visual materials, and *Results From Prior NSF Support* (Progress Report), which can be no more than 5 of the 15 pages.
- Designates that *no* appendix materials may be submitted without prior approval.
- Line item about cost-sharing has been added to the summary proposal budget.
- Percent effort has been dropped in favor of reporting level of effort as "person-months devoted to the project."

For additional information about NSF Grant Application preparation:

- NSF *Grant Proposal Guide.*
- NSF *Grant General Conditions.* Copies may be obtained from Forms and Publications, National Science Foundation, 4201 Wilson Boulevard, Arlington, VA 22230.
- Information about the NSF grant process, proposers, and grantees is available in the NSF *Grant Policy Manual,* NSF 93-213 (see Appendix XI, "Resources").
- Chapter VI of Title 45 of the *Code of Federal Regulations,* a compendium of basic NSF policies and procedures for use by the grantee community and NSF staff. The manual is available only by subscription (GPO Subscription Number: 9380031-500000-6; $21.00 domestic, $26.25 foreign) from the Superintendent of Documents, U.S. Government Printing Office, Washington, DC 20402.
- Watch for NSF announcements in the *NSF Bulletin,* which may also be accessed through STIS (See Appendix XI, "Resources").

INFORMATION ABOUT NSF

- NSF Information Center: 703-306-1234
- NSF Policy Office: 703-306-1241
- NSF Science and Technology Information System (STIS)

NSF/STIS gives electronic access to:

- NSF program announcements and press releases
- NSF *Guide to Programs*
- NSF *Grant Application Guide* (GPG)
- *NSF Bulletin*
- General NSF publications and reports
- NSF organization charts
- The NSF Phone Book
- Abstracts of NSF awards (1989–present)
- NSF vacancy announcements
- Other NSF publications

STIS can be accessed in 5 ways:

1. Documents via e-mail

   Send a message to *stisserv@nsf.gov* (Internet) or *stisserv@NSF* (BITNET). The text of the message should be as follows (the Subject line is ignored):

   get index

   You will receive a list of all the documents of STIS and instructions for retrieving them. Requests for electronic documents should be sent to stisserv, as shown above. Requests for printed publications should be sent to *pubs@nsf.gov* (Internet) or *pubs@NSF* (BITNET).

2. Anonymous FTP

   FTP to *stis.nsf.gov*. Enter *anonymous* for the username and your e-mail address for the password. Retrieve the file index. This contains a list of the files available on STIS and additional instructions.

3. On-Line

   If you are on Internet: Telnet *stis.nsf.gov*.

   At the login prompt, enter *public*.

   If you are dialing in with a modem: Choose 1200, 2400, or 9600 baud, 7-E-1. Dial 703-306-0212 or 703-306-0213. When connected, press Enter. At the login prompt, enter *public*.

4. Direct e-mail

   Send an e-mail message to *stisserv@nsf.gov* (Internet) or *stissserv@NSF* (BITNET). Put the following in the text:

   get stisdirm

   You will receive instructions for this service.

5. Gopher and WAIS

   The NSF Gopher is on port 70 of *stis.nsf.gov*. The WAIS server is also on *stis.nsf.gov*. You can get the *".src"* file from the "Directory of Servers" at *quake.think.com*. For more information, contact your local computer support organization.

For more information about access to STIS, get the STIS flyer (NSF 91-10, rev. 10-25-92) from NSF Forms and Publications Unit, 4201 Wilson Boulevard, Arlington, VA 22230. For an electronic copy of the flyer, send an e-mail message to stisfly@nsf.gov (Internet) or stisfly@NSF (BITNET). Or contact:

e-mail: *stis-request@nsf.gov* (Internet)
        stis-req@NSF (BITNET)
Phone: 703-306-0214 (voice mail)
TDD: 703-306-0090

MAKING CONTACT WITH NSF

Because the scope of projects reviewed by NSF Panels is broader than that of projects reviewed by NIH Review Groups, the details of processing and reviewing proposals differs more from section to section at NSF than at NIH (see Appendix VII in this book). *Before you begin to write* an NSF grant application, you should *get specific information from the NSF division relevant to your proposal* and discuss your project with NSF staff by letter, telephone, or in person. Determine the purpose of the program, the exact eligibility, any contractual requirements, submission deadlines, etc. This is especially important if you are thinking of applying to one of the special programs sponsored by NSF.

WHAT NSF IS LOOKING FOR

The scientific mission of NSF:

- The mission at NSF is to support the most meritorious research, whether basic or applied.
- NSF is interested in the potential of the proposed research to contribute to better understanding or improvement of the quality, distribution, or effectiveness of the nation's scientific and engineering research, science education, and human resource base.
- NSF supports basic research in almost all scientific fields, such as sociology, physics, biology, economics, psychology, chemistry, mathematics, and engineering.

NSF has 7 discipline-based Research Directorates:[4]

Directorate	Acronym	Telephone Number
Biological Sciences	BIO	703-306-1400
Social, Behavioral, and Economic Sciences (this Directorate includes the various international programs)	SBE	703-306-1700
Computer Information Science and Engineering	CISE	703-306-1900
Education and Human Resources	EHR	703-306-1600
Engineering	ENG	703-306-1300
Geosciences	GEO	703-306-1500
Mathematical and Physical Sciences	MPS	703-306-1800

The NSF Directorates are further subdivided into Divisions (see the GPG).

Individuals whose work falls within the mandate of NSF should be aware that NSF has become increasingly interested in matters of the science "Infrastructure." One of the compelling issues involved in science "Infrastructure" relates to maintaining adequate numbers of trainees who will become the scientists of the future and ensuring that such opportunities be equitably open to women, minorities, and handicapped individuals. To this end, NSF has established a number of specific programs targeted to meet the needs of special groups and to further the aspect of the NSF mandate that deals with building the science "Infrastructure." If a potential applicant or the applicant's institution matches the goals of a particular NSF Program, it is important for the applicant to specify this match clearly in the appropriate part of her/his grant application.

---

[4] The NSF Biological, Behavioral, and Social Sciences Directorate (BBS) was split into the Social, Behavioral, and Economic Sciences Directorate (SBE) and the Biological Sciences Directorate (BIO) in 1991–1992.

PREPARING AN NSF APPLICATION

Who may submit

- Scientists
- Engineers
- Science educators
- Graduate students are *not* encouraged to submit research proposals; however, some NSF divisions accept proposals for Doctoral Dissertation Improvement Research grants that are submitted by a faculty member on behalf of the graduate student. Graduate students should arrange to serve as research assistants to faculty members.

Categories of proposers

1. *Universities and colleges.*
2. *Nonprofit, nonacademic institutions* in the United States that are directly associated with educational or research activities.
3. *For-profit organizations*—especially if proposals are for cooperative projects involving universities and the private sector.
4. State and local governments—organizations that broaden the impact, accelerate the pace, and increase the effectiveness of improvements in science, mathematics, and engineering education in both K-12 and post-secondary levels.
5. *Unaffiliated individuals* (i.e., those not affiliated with an institution) *may* apply to NSF for support if they have the capability and use of facilities needed to perform the work and agree to fiscal arrangements that are satisfactory to the NSF Grants Officer. Contact the appropriate program before preparing a proposal for submission. Each NSF activity has its own rules about specific awards.
6. Foreign institutions—only for the U.S. portion of a collaborative effort.
7. Federal agencies are not normally supported; inquire about exceptions.

NSF normally does not support the following categories of work:

- Technical assistance
- Pilot plant efforts
- Research requiring security classification
- The development of products for commercial marketing
- Market research for a particular project or invention
- Bioscience research with disease-related goals including work on the etiology, diagnosis, or treatment of physical or mental disease, abnormality, or malfunction in human beings or animals
- Animal models of such conditions
- Development or testing of drugs or other procedures for the treatment of such conditions

However, research in bioengineering, with diagnosis or treatment-related goals, that applies engineering principles to problems in biology and medicine while advancing engineering knowledge is eligible for support. Bioengineering research to aid people with disabilities is also eligible.

Research proposals *(not proposals for conferences or workshops)* to the Biological Sciences Directorate may not be duplicates of proposals to any other federal agency for simultaneous consideration. The only exceptions to this rule are (1) proposals in which the proposers and program managers at relevant Federal agencies have previously agreed to a joint review and possible joint funding of the proposal and (2) proposals from beginning investigators (beginning investigators are individuals who have not been a principal investigator on a federally funded award with the exception of doctoral dissertations, postdoctoral fellowships, or research planning grants). For proposers who qualify under this exception, processing will be assisted by completing the block entitled "Beginning Investigator" on the "Cover Sheet For Proposal to the National Science Foundation," NSF Form 1207.

NSF application due dates

Regular proposals may be submitted to NSF at any time. However, for programs that use Review Panels, the Panels meet on specific dates, 2 to 3 times per year. (Call the relevant Program Officer to find out about meeting dates.) You may want to aim to get your application to NSF in time to be reviewed at one of these meetings. Some NSF programs set target dates or deadlines for submission. Target dates and deadlines are published in the *NSF Bulletin*, in specific program announcements and solicitations, and on STIS. *It takes about 6 months to process an NSF application.*

1. NSF Program *deadlines:* Unless otherwise stated in announcements or solicitations, proposals postmarked after announced cutoff dates generally will be returned to the proposer.
2. NSF *target dates:* Unless otherwise stated in announcements or solicitations, proposals postmarked after these target dates will be reviewed, although they may miss a particular Panel meeting (which means they may be less than up-to-date by review time!). Call to find out when the panels meet and submit in time to get reviewed at the meeting.
3. NSF programs not listed under "program deadlines" or "target dates" will accept proposals at any time.

THE REVIEW PROCESS AT NSF

- It takes about 6 months to review and process an NSF application.

- Proposals are reviewed by the relevant NSF Program Officer and 3 to 10 other experts in the field of the proposal. Some NSF programs have Review Panels that meet; others rely entirely on mail reviews. Overall, NSF relies much more heavily on mail reviews than NIH does, and NSF Program Officers often seek additional Reviewers by mail to reconcile differences in Reviewer reaction or to pursue issues raised by the first round of Reviewers.

- PIs may suggest qualified Reviewers for their proposals and may also indicate individuals to whom their proposal should *not* be sent for review.

- Recommendations for awards are reviewed further by senior NSF Staff for conformance with NSF policy.

- Additional material, which might affect the outcome of the review, *may not be sent* after proposal submission *except with permission* from the relevant Program Officer.

- NSF may choose not to review an application for a project that is submitted simultaneously to NIH. Call NSF Program Office to inquire.

- Revised proposals must respond to major comments resulting from prior NSF review, or they may be returned without review. However, revised proposals are treated as new and are subject to standard review procedures.

NSF REVIEW CRITERIA

NSF Reviewers assess applications according to 4 established criteria:

1. Research performance competence
   —Capability of the investigator(s) including:
     - Record of past accomplishments
     - Communication of significant findings
     - Sharing of data and other research products
   —Technical soundness of the proposed approach
   —Adequacy of the institutional resources available
2. Intrinsic merit of the research
   Likelihood that the research will:
   —Lead to new discoveries or fundamental advances within its field of science and engineering or
   —Have substantial impact on progress in that field or other scientific and engineering fields
3. Utility or relevance of the research
   Likelihood that the research can contribute to the achievement of a goal that is extrinsic or in addition to that of the research field itself and thereby serve as the basis for new or improved technology or assist in the solution of societal problems.
4. Effect of the research on the infrastructure of science and engineering
   Potential of the proposed research to contribute to better understanding or improvement of the quality, distribution, or effectiveness of the nation's scientific and engineering research, education, and human resources base

The criteria are applied as follows:

- Criteria 1, 2 and 3 apply to and must be addressed in the evaluation of *every* research proposal.
- The relative weight given to criteria 2 and 3 depends on the nature of the proposed research:
   —Criterion 2 (intrinsic merit) is emphasized in the evaluation of *basic research* proposals.
   —Criterion 3 (utility or relevance) is emphasized in the evaluation of *applied research* proposals and certain goal-oriented NSF activities (see the GPG).
   —Criterion 4 is for evaluation of proposals in terms of their potential for improving the scientific and engineering enterprise and its educational activities in ways not covered by the first 3 criteria (see the GPG).

SOME TYPES OF NSF PROPOSALS

Individual grant applications

- Proposal initiated by principal investigator (PI).
- Applicant enters appropriate Program title on application Cover Sheet (NSF Form 1207).

Program title is chosen from list given in the GPG.

- Applications of affiliated individuals are submitted to NSF via their institution.

Group proposals

- Defined as a proposal submitted by 3 or more investigators that combines, into one administrative mechanism, several projects that ordinarily would be funded separately.
- A single individual bears primary responsibility for the administration of the grant.
- Several investigators may be designated as co-principal investigators.
- Group proposals (see the GPG) are subject to different page limits.

Small Grants for Exploratory Research (SGER)

- Intended for small-scale, high-risk exploratory research in the fields of science, engineering, and education. See the GPG for descriptions of exploratory research.
- Require only *one* copy of a 2- to 5-page project description.
- Require brief biosketches only for principal investsigator and co-principal investigator (maximum: 5 significant publications or other research products).
- Maximum award = $50,000; usually for 1 year (maximum of 2 years); nonrenewable.
- Have no submission deadlines.
- Are not subject to peer review; reviewed only by the relevant Program Officer.

Potential applicants for SGER grants should contact the appropriate Program Officer (see the GPG for details).

Specialized equipment grants

See the GPG.

Proposals to the Engineering Directorate

See the GPG.

Proposals involving vertebrate animals

See the GPG.

Accomplishment-Based Renewal (ABR) applications

Provide an alternative choice for dealing with the project description of a renewal application. ABR proposals have *different page limits* and may *not* be submitted for consecutive renewals.
See the GPG for additional information about special programs.

PROPOSAL PRESENTATION

General information to be presented in an NSF application:

1. Objectives and scientific or educational significance of the proposed work
2. Suitability of the methods to be employed

3. Qualifications of the investigator and the grantee organization
4. Effect of the activity on the infrastructure of science, engineering, and education in these areas
5. Amount of funding required and justification
6. Merits of the proposed project
7. Other miscellaneous information and assurances

A grant application to the NSF "should be prepared with the care and thoroughness of a paper submitted for publication" and should provide sufficient information to enable Reviewers to evaluate the proposal in accordance with the 4 NSF merit review criteria.

Order of presentation

NSF requires the parts of the grant application to be presented in a particular order. See the GPG about which forms are optional and which are mandatory.

- Information about PIs/project directors: NSF Form 1225 (original signature copy only)
- Cover Sheet: (NSF Form 1207) Cover Sheet page 1, all copies; Cover Sheet page 2, original copy only. Cover Sheet page 2 contains a variety of certifications. See information about certifications in the GPG.
- List of suggested Reviewers—or Reviewers to whom your application should *not* be sent (original copy only)
- Deviation Authorization (original copy only, if applicable)
- Project Summary (NSF Form 1358)
- Table of Contents (NSF Form 1359)
- Project Description [including Results From Prior NSF Support (Progress Report), if applicable]. Maximum of 15 single-spaced pages (NSF Form 1360).
- Bibliography (NSF Form 1361)
- Biographical Sketches (NSF Form 1362)
- Budget: NSF Form 1030 (cumulative and annual budgets, including subcontract budgets, if any)
- Budget Justification. Maximum of 3 single-spaced pages.
- Current and Pending Support (NSF Form 1239)
- Facilities, Equipment and Other Resources (NSF Form 1363)
- Special information and supplementary documentation
- Appendices (submit only if requested by the program or if specific approval of the relevant Program Officer has been obtained).

Preparing the application for submission

Formatting and type size specifications
Conformance with instructions for proposal preparation is required by NSF and will be strictly enforced unless a deviation (written approval) has been obtained from the cognizant NSF Assistant Director or designee or by the inclusion of specific different requirements in another NSF Announcement or Solicitation. This includes page limits and type size restrictions. Program officers at NSF are now being held accountable for these administrative details. Grant proposals that do not conform to the instructions are being returned without review.

Formatting instructions

- Proposals for grants, cooperative agreements, and contracts submitted to NSF, as well as reports, publications, and correspondence relating to NSF proposals, are required to use the metric system unless impractical or inefficient.
- Use Metric A4 or 8.5" × 11.5" paper.
- Use single-spaced typing or printing.
- Type size must be 10 to 12 points in a clear and readily legible font.
  —For constant spacing, use no more than 12 characters per 2.54 cm.
  —For proportional spacing, use an average of 15 characters per 2.54 cm.
- Margins should be approximately 2.54 cm (= 1 inch) at the top, at the bottom, and on each side.
- Each section of the proposal must be separately paginated and must include both the section and page number on the bottom center of each page (e.g., C-1, C-2). (Note names of Sections[5] in the GPG.)
- The original signed copy of the application should be printed only on one side of each sheet. Additional copies may be printed on both sides.

Preparation for mailing

- Appendix A in the GPG indicates the number of copies of the proposal required by the different NSF Divisions; the number, shown in parentheses, includes the original signed copy.
- Proposals must be stapled in the upper left-hand corner but otherwise unbound.
- Include a *self-addressed, stamped* postcard so that you will get acknowledgment of receipt of your application by NSF. You can also (1) purchase a mailing receipt at the Post Office for about 50 cents or (2) send your proposal by Express Mail or a courier service, which automatically provides a mailing receipt and also ensures prompt delivery. Mailing receipts do not, however, ensure that your application has been received by NSF, so enclosing the postcard and tracking its return are important.
- Proposals should be addressed to

  > **Announcement No.** _____
  > (or, for unsolicited proposals: **NSF Program** _____)
  > National Science Foundation **PPU**
  > 4201 Wilson Boulevard, Room P60
  > Arlington, VA 22230

- The delivery address *must clearly identify the NSF announcement or solicitation number* under which the proposal is being submitted, if applicable. If unsolicited, enter the program to which the proposal should be directed (see list of programs in the GPG).
- If you must mail your proposal in more than 1 package, mark, *on each package*, the *total number of packages.*
- Alternatively, you may submit your application electronically. See information about the EPS Project in the GPG and Appendix I-A of this book, or contact Mr. Jerald Stuck (703-306-1144).

---

[5] There is an ambiguity about the word *Section* as used in the GPG. The GPG uses the word *Section* for the main sections of the GPG denoted by Roman numerals, and also for the subsections denoted by upper case letters. The page numbers, as indicated here, should be designated by the uppercase letter for the subsection, followed by the page number.

AFTER YOU MAIL THE PROPOSAL

- You should receive an acknowledgment of receipt of your application (your post-card) within 2 weeks.
- Subsequently, you will receive the official acknowledgment of receipt from NSF that will show the NSF proposal number and cognizant NSF program to which the proposal has been assigned. Later communications about the proposal should be addressed to the cognizant Program Officer and identified by the proposal number (See the GPG.)
- Send additional supporting materials if appropriate and if you get permission.
- After the review, you will receive verbatim copies of all the Reviewers' reports (*excluding* the names of the Reviewers) and in some cases, a summary of the panel discussion. The Reviewers' reports are usually on the NSF Proposal Evaluation Form shown in Fig. A8-1. You are also entitled to request and obtain certain other "releasable" material in the file about your proposal. You may *not* request information that identifies your Reviewers.
- Notification of award (usually for no more than 3 years) is by letter addressed to your organization. You get a copy.
- If your application is declined, you may request the reasons for the action from the Program Officer. (See the GPG for more information about this and about requesting reconsideration of actions.) Keep in mind that in these times of tight funding, the most common reason for an application not being funded is lack of funds!
- Information about extensions and additional support is given in the GPG.
- NSF encourages communication between principal investigators and Program Officers concerning progress on NSF-supported projects—but not during the time the proposal is under review.

B: Examples of Reviewers' Reports for Two Grant Proposals Submitted to NSF

APPLICATION 1

Two Reviewers' reports for an NSF application (mid 1980s) that was funded.

Reviewer 1

This proposal outlines _____ and _____ studies involving _____ and other _____ on _____ with a view to testing an _____ and a _____ model. The investigator favors the _____ model, and the proposed studies are to be carried out with heavy emphasis on a previously proposed model (ref. X of the bibliography).

*The applicant recognizes the importance of*_____ in the regulation of a number of biological processes and ultimately wishes to relate _____ and the _____ behavior of _____ to its _____ function. It is somewhat puzzling that the framework for the proposed studies is a rather formal one with *little regard to current* _____ *information on* _____ . Thus _____ is referred to as _____ (second paragraph, page _____), and *only passing mention is made of the important recent studies establishing* the _____ of _____ which show it to be a rather _____ with _____ —a _____ quite similar to that recently established for _____ . *No mention is made of*_____ *studies* that have shown that it is possible to distinguish _____ changes within _____ as _____ .

NATIONAL SCIENCE
FOUNDATION

OMB NO: 3145-0060
NSF FORM 1(5/90)

PROPOSAL EVALUATION FORM

PROPOSAL NO.	INSTITUTION	PLEASE RETURN BY
PRINCIPAL INVESTIGATOR	NSF PROGRAM	
TITLE		

Please evaluate this proposal using the criteria presented on the back of this review form.   Continue on additional sheet(s) as necessary.
If appropriate, please include in a separate paragraph, comments on the quality of the prior work described in the 'Results from Prior NSF Support' section.

OVERALL RATING   ☐ EXCELLENT   ☐ VERY GOOD   ☐ GOOD   ☐ FAIR   ☐ POOR

REVIEWER'S SIGNATURE	REVIEWER'S NAME AND ADDRESS (TYPED)
OTHER SUGGESTED REVIEWERS (OPTIONAL)	
PROPOSAL FILE	

Fig. A8-1   NSF Proposal Evaluation Form.

The proposed *studies would have more value if specific experiments had been spelled out* relating the _____ to _____ .

Mention is made of the use of _____ but *no information seems to be provided concerning the value of* such _____ *in interpreting the results again in relation to* _____ changes within the _____ . While the proposed studies involving _____ *may constitute a valuable complement* to studies carried out in various laboratories involving _____ methods, the *lack of correlation with* _____ changes would make the *interpretation of the results difficult.* The use of a model in which distinctions among _____ are not incorporated *may create further difficulties.*

The investigator has had a *broad experience in the field of* _____ . The biographical sketch refers to *over 105 publications.* The list of more recent publications shows continued interest in _____ studies utilizing *sophisticated techniques. The publication record* does not show extensive previous involvement with _____, particularly with respect to the experimental approach.

The budget appears reasonable except that the reduction of travel to $ _____ per year is recommended.

Rating: Good

Reviewer 2

It is rather disconcerting that the PI apparently has an incomplete knowledge of the *wealth of information* that has been derived on _____ (see _____). Using this and the information provided by other investigators, the *PI could greatly increase the effectiveness of his proposed studies by narrowing in on* _____ where significant _____ could be expected. In this regard the suggestion to use _____ would be impossible. Further, the _____ that he proposes to use as _____ *may be difficult to obtain,* and it *might be more effective to use* _____, which has also been shown to dramatically affect _____ . *It detracts from the strength of the proposal that important studies on* _____ *are apparently not recognized.*

The investigator seems *well qualified* to conduct the _____ experiments and to do the necessary _____ to make a contribution to this area, although his *productivity in the last x years has been modest. One does not get a sense of confidence in the investigator's ability to produce* the _____ necessary _____ for the successful completion of these studies. Some *preliminary data would have been very helpful* in this regard.

Understanding the mechanism of _____ is, however, a very *relevant and meritorious area of research. The* proposed *studies should contribute to the efforts of many in this area.*

Rating: Good

APPLICATION 2

Five Reviewers' reports for a 1992 NSF renewal application that was not funded.

Reviewer 1

This *ongoing study* is aimed at _____.

This research program employs _____ to _____. The major emphasis in the proposed work will be on _____ information obtained from _____ measurements. This *methodology has a firm theoretical basis with which the authors are familiar.* Notice is made of the difference of these two methods in terms of _____. This *could prove interesting in terms of* the determination of the variations in _____. *Some of the proposed studies are also of a confirmatory kind in which experiments that previously gave somewhat unexpected results will be repeated with a different* _____ *at a different* _____ *to see if the same conclusions are reached. In the* _____ *field, this is welcome conservatism.*

Overall this looks like a nice proposal.

Overall rating: Between *Good* and *Very Good* (2.5).

Reviewer 2

BRIEF SUMMARY: . . .

EVALUATION:
1. Research performance competence:
   a. Capability of the investigators (recent publications)

   Dr. X is a *highly respected* _____ with *long-standing expertise in* _____. His *involvement with* _____ *is fairly recent, but he has gained the appropriate expertise to carry out the proposed work.* During the first 3 years of NSF funding, Dr. X *has successfully assembled the equipment and initiated studies* on _____ *resulting in one paper accepted in the* _____ Journal. This *represents fairly slow progress.* The *paper*, in which it was shown that _____ , *does establish feasibility of this type of experiment.*

   b. Technical Soundness

   The techniques used _____ appear to be *straightforward, since this approach has been used successfully in a number of other laboratories, and the preliminary data appear to be of high quality.* However, due to Dr. X's relatively recent foray into _____ , a *more detailed discussion of the techniques of data acquisition and analysis in this area would have been helpful.*

   c. Institutional Resources: *good*

2./3. Intrinsic merit of the research/relevance:

   The goals of the research _____ to measure _____ are of *substantial potential significance* for understanding _____. The *research plan is somewhat ambitious,* including a large number of different _____ to be studied. This proposal *needs much more discussion of the procedures* to be followed in labeling, demonstrating site-specificity, exchanging _____ into _____, and demonstrating that _____. *The discussion of specific models to be tested, and how the data will be analyzed to test them, should be sharpened up.*

SUMMARY: This project is a good idea that could provide important data, but progress in the first funding period has been disappointing, and the proposal needs more focus on the _____ needed to validate the data.

Overall Rating: Good/Very Good (where E[6] = top 10%, VG = top ⅓, G = mid ⅓).

Reviewer 3

Dr. X is a *highly respected researcher* who is an *expert in* _____. *Among his past contributions are* the development of _____. This *proposal is technically very sound and has a high probability of success.* The *facilities of the researcher and support personnel are excellent.*

The present proposal is a continuation of the recent work from X's lab. His *primary*

---

[6] E = Excellent, VG = Very Good, G = Good.

goal is to look again at _____. *In the past, Dr. X has failed to find* _____. *Should Dr. X's results be confirmed, this would contradict a long-standing view that* _____ is a prerequisite to _____. The _____ data are model-dependent, whereas the _____ that Dr. X uses is a direct measure of _____. One additional approach to be taken will be _____. This *study also has the potential to clarify* the differences between _____ and _____.

Another study involves determination of _____ in the _____. It is *difficult to see the relationship of this to the rest of the proposal.*

Dr. X also proposes to study _____. He will look for alterations in the _____ resulting from these _____. *One difficulty that may be encountered is* distinguishing _____ from _____. *Both of these* _____ *have been reported in the literature but are not discussed here.* Dr. X did mention the use of _____ in some experiments. This _____ does not _____, so this _____ *may provide unambiguous results.* Similar studies have been done in _____, but these *are not discussed in this proposal.*

Finally, _____ are planned. *Not much detail is given on these experiments* except that techniques are available for quantitating _____.

The studies with _____ and _____ are *very interesting and could help to show* the mechanism by which these agents affect _____. These studies *would have been even more exciting if possible outcomes of these experiments were discussed in terms of a model.* The _____ studies have the potential to be interesting, *but not enough detail is given to judge exactly what will be done.*

Overall Rating: Very Good

Reviewer 4

The *progress report does not show dramatic progress toward resolving* the _____ issues, *but the measurements are excellent*, and *it is clear that this applicant has mastered the use of* the _____ (instrumentation that he took up rather recently).

This applicant has *high competence* in _____ and is *especially knowledgeable about* _____. He *has taken up* _____ *only relatively recently*, but it is obvious from the application that he *is using it more than adequately.* As he says, using _____ has certain advantages worth exploiting. There is *also a disadvantage* in that (without enormous technical difficulties) _____ cannot be measured, thus *forcing the investigator to rely on somewhat uninterpretable* _____ assays. *But I am sure that a seasoned investigator will realize the limitations.*

All the specific tests proposed are logical, feasible, and worth doing. There is a *question* in my mind as to *whether the* _____ *methods are best suited for* detecting _____, but the *applicant seems well aware of this possibility, and it is worth taking a chance on his good sense.* Magnitude of support should be gauged in relation to his other support, as there *must be significant overlap.*

Overall rating: Excellent/Very Good

Reviewer 5

This is an *outstanding proposal.* The *investigators have successfully developed an experimental system, which makes it possible for the first time to study* _____ in an organized _____. They have *demonstrated very convincingly* that the system is *technically sound* and has *excellent potential to yield new, interesting information* as to the mechanism of _____. The proposed *research addresses excellent questions and will fill an important gap* between _____ studies on _____ and _____ studies on _____.

Dr. X is an *accomplished, productive researcher* who *has made critical contributions to our current understanding of* _____. He has *extensive experience in a wide range of* _____ and _____ methodologies, including the theories and practice of the modern _____ techniques. He is *very well-qualified to carry out the proposed studies* in this project.

Productivity during the previous grant period was *very impressive with seven full high quality publications.* Although *only one of the seven was directly related to the project* funded by the NSF, *this is understandable, since* setting up a complicated experimental system such as the one used by the applicant and working out all the technical problems takes a considerable amount of time.

Overall rating: Excellent

C. Sample Outline for an NSF Proposal

The following outline for an NSF grant application is available on disk from TWC/EA, Box 645, Belmont, MA 02178, for $11 + $3 (P&H). Available on 3.5-inch disks only. Can be formatted for Microsoft Word for the Macintosh, MS-DOS, or text-only. Please specify desired format. Allow 4–6 weeks for delivery.

Please do not use the outline provided *instead* of reading the instructions. It is your responsibility to read and meticulously follow the instructions of the granting agency to which you are applying. The information presented here is intended as a guide to, not a substitute for, the original instructions.

Note that some NSF programs operate from more specific program announcements, which may be somewhat different from the general provisions of the GPG. NSF encourages contact with program personnel before proposal preparation to determine (1) whether a formal application is appropriate and (2) requirements that are specific for application to that program.

A grant application to NSF "should be prepared with the care and thoroughness of a paper submitted for publication" and should provide sufficient information to enable Reviewers to evaluate the proposal in accordance with the 4 merit review criteria discussed in Appendix VIII A of this book and in the NSF Grant Proposal Guide:

1. Research performance competence
2. Intrinsic merit of the research
3. Utility or relevance of the research
4. Effect of the research on the infrastructure of science and engineering

Note: In this outline the NSF Grant Proposal Guide NSF 94-2 will be referred to as the GPG.

GENERAL INFORMATION TO BE PRESENTED IN AN NSF PROPOSAL (SEE THE GPG PAGE 1, ITEM A)

- Objectives and scientific or educational significance of the proposed work
- Suitability of the methods to be employed
- Qualifications of the investigator and the grantee organization
- Effect of the activity on the infrastructure of science, engineering, and education in these areas
- Amount of funding required

- Merits of the proposed project
- Other miscellaneous information and assurances

SPECIFIC INFORMATION TO BE PRESENTED IN AN NSF PROPOSAL

Assemble the specific items listed in this outline in the numbered sequence given below. The numbering system in the NSF/GPG is different from that used in this outline.[7] In your grant proposal, use the numbers given by NSF rather than my numbers.

1. *Information about principal investigators/project directors*
   - Use *Form 1225.*
   - Submit a single copy.
   - *Form 1225 must be received* before the proposal is reviewed, but filling in the requested *information is optional,* except for the question concerning information about current or previous research support.
   - If you don't want to give the information, check in the next-to-the-bottom box of each column.
   - Attach Form 1225 on top of the cover page of the copy of your proposal that has the original signatures.
   - Notice that your *name does not appear* on this form.
2. *Cover Sheet* (Referred to as Item 1 in the GPG, page 4)
   - Use NSF Form 1207.
   - Page 1: all copies; page 2: original only.
   - Indicate the specific organizational unit most appropriate to consider your proposal in the appropriate box on the cover sheet.
   - For a list of NSF programs, refer to Appendix A, page 23, of the GPG.
   - If work will be done away from the campus of the submitting organization, indicate the "Name of Performing Organization."
   - For renewals, indicate if this is to be submitted as an *ABR* renewal (see GPG).
   - *Title*
     —Brief and scientifically valid
     —Intelligible to a scientifically literate reader
     —Suitable for use in the public press
     —Subject to editing by NSF
   - Proposed *duration for which support is requested.* Should be consistent with the nature and complexity of the proposed activity. Maximum of 5 years.
   - Indicate *desired start date* for project (see GPG).

     The review process at NSF takes about 6 months. Start dates cannot be guaranteed.

   - *Check* appropriate *boxes* for special conditions:
     —Beginning investigator, etc.
     —Profit-making organization (small business, minority-owned business, woman-owned business)
     —Accomplishment-based renewal (see below).
     —Etc.

---

[7] This is because the NSF GPG simply bullets the sections of the proposal listed on page 3 and then numbers the parts — beginning with "Project Summary" — from "A" to "J" at the top of page 4, but then "Project Summary — Proposal Section A," is labelled Item "2" on page 5! I have numbered the items required in numerical order to give the reader a logical sense of the order of required items.

- *Signature of PI*, page 2 of cover sheet (only one copy).
- *Signature and title of Organizational Officer* having responsibility for government business relation, page 2 of the cover sheet (only one copy).

  Signature certifies compliance with assurances (see GPG).
  Proposals are *incomplete* if endorsement signatures are omitted.
- Various certifications (see GPG):

  The proposer must use the proposal Cover Sheet, page 2, to submit the following required certifications:

  —Drug-Free Workplace: By signing page 2 of the proposal Cover Sheet.
  —Certification for Principal Investigators and Co-Principal Investigators: regarding statements contained in the proposal, authorship and reporting of the research, and scientific conduct of the project.
  —Certification for Authorized Institutional Representative or Individual Applicant: A certification is required to be completed by the authorized institutional representative or individual applicant which certifies that the statements contained in the proposal are true and complete to the best of their knowledge and that the Institution (or Individual) agrees to accept the obligation to comply with award terms and conditions.
  —Debt/Debarment and Suspension: Check the appropriate box on the cover sheet.
  —Certification Regarding Lobbying: See page 2 of the Cover Sheet. This certification is only required when the proposal budget request exceeds $100,000.
  —Profit-making organizations must indicate their status on the cover sheet (see Guidelines in the GPG).

3. Optional: *List of suggested Reviewers*, or Reviewers *not* to include (original copy only).
4. *Deviation Authorization* (original copy only, if applicable). Any deviations from the instructions in the GPG that are mandated by instructions in a Program Announcement or by written approval by an NSF Program Officer.
5. *Project Summary* (Referred to as Item 2, Proposal Section A in the GPG)
   - Use NSF Form 1358.
   - *1-page maximum.*
   - Write the project summary last!
   - Should be a self-contained description of the activity that would result if the proposal is funded. NSF specifies a *Summary* (not an abstract of the proposal).
   - Should be suitable for publication.
   - Put your name, Social Security number (optional), and the project title at the top of the sheet.
   - Write in the third person.
   - Include:
     —Statement of *objectives*.
     —*Methods* to be employed.
     —*Significance* of the proposed activity to the advancement of knowledge.
   - Should be informative to other persons working in same or related fields.
   - Try to *make understandable* to scientifically literate readers.
6. *Table of Contents* (Referred to as Item 3, Proposal Section B in the GPG, page 5)
   - Use NSF Form 1359.
   - Adhere to instructions about font size and formatting specifications as noted at the top of Form 1359.

- Fill in page numbers in the *final* draft of the proposal.
7. *Project description* (Progress Report and Research Plan) (Referred to as Item 4, Proposal Section C in the GPG, page 5)
   - Use NSF Form 1360 for page 1 of proposal (optional)
   - This is the main (science) part of the grant application.
   - *Both new and renewal applications must present preliminary data (feasibility studies) for the project described in the current application if not covered in a Progress Report.*
   - For a renewal application, there are 2 choices for dealing with the project description: *Traditional Renewal or Accomplishment-Based Renewal (ABR)* (See GPG).
     —Traditional Renewal: Written as for a new application.
     —Accomplishment-Based Renewal (ABR): Affects only the project description; all other parts of the application remain the same.
     - Project description (see below) is replaced by no more than 6 *relevant* publications from preceding 3- to 5-year period (two of these may be "in press," see GPG).
     - Include a summary of plans for the proposed project period (*4-page maximum*).
     - Clearly indicate in the proposal and on the Cover Sheet that this is an ABR proposal.
     - *ABR proposals may NOT be submitted for consecutive renewals.*
   - *The project description is limited to 15 single-spaced pages, including* a maximum of 5 pages of "Prior Support from NSF" (Progress Report) *Thirty (30) double-spaced pages are NOT acceptable!* The page limits *include* visual materials, such as charts, graphs, maps, photographs, and other pictorial presentations. Note that Group Proposals, Accomplishment-Based Renewals (ABR), SGER proposals, and certain other types of applications are subject to different page limits (see GPG, page 5).
   - *If* you have good reason to exceed the page limits, discuss your justification for additional pages with the appropriate Program Officer *before* submission.

   Parts of the Project Description
   A. *Results From Prior NSF Support* ("Progress Report"). First part of the project description. *Pertinent only for renewal applications.*
      - This section is required if the principal investigator has received an NSF award in the past 5 years; see the GPG.
      - *Maximum: 5 single-spaced pages.*
      - NSF Form 1360 may be used to submit page 1 of the project description. Photocopies of Form 1360 may be used for continuation pages. Use of this specific form is *not* required.
      - Include in this section:
        1) NSF award number, amount and period of support
        2) Title of project
        3) Summary of results of completed work
           - Number items in the Progress Report to correspond to the numbers of the Specific Aims of the preceding proposal.
           - Summarize the Specific Aims of the preceding application, and give a succinct account of progress (published and unpublished) toward their achievement.
           - Discuss any changes in original Specific Aims.

- Include any contribution to development of human resources in science and engineering.
- Summarize the importance of the findings.

4) List publications resulting from and acknowledging the NSF award.

> Give titles and complete references to all publications, manuscripts accepted for publication, patents, invention reports, and other printed materials that have resulted since the last competitive review. *Clearly distinguish between original papers, reviews and abstracts, etc.: Group them.*

5) Give a brief description of available data, samples, physical collections, and other related research products not described elsewhere.
6) For renewals, describe the relation of completed work to proposed work.
7) For renewals from *academic institutions*, include:
   - Information on human resources development at the post-doctoral, graduate, and undergraduate levels.
   - Identify by name all graduate students who participated in the research.

> Reviewers will be asked to comment on this information.

B. *Research Plan*

Second part of the project description.

Required for *new* proposals and traditional *renewals*.

Be sure to "reference" this section (especially "Background") and other appropriate parts of the project description. The references go into the Bibliography.

Provide a *clear statement of work to be undertaken*. (See page limits discussed above). Include

- *Objectives* (Specific Aims) for the period of the proposed work
  —Describe concisely and realistically:
  - The long-term objectives of the project, and
  - What the specific research described in the application is intended to accomplish, including any hypotheses to be tested or clear specific questions to be answered (no grandiose designs).
  —State objectives (Specific Aims) in form of short, bulleted items, rather than narrative paragraphs, if appropriate.

> "To study the effect of substance X on system Y" is not a good specific aim!

—Understand the difference between

> *Broad, long-term objectives:*

> For example: Develop materials that are superconducting at room temperature. (Hard to quantify progress).

> and

> *Specific Aims:*

> For example: Synthesize and define the conductive properties of glasses with the structure $A_x B_y O_z$. (Something that could be

crossed off a list of *n* items needed to further the broad, long-term objectives).

- *Expected significance*
  Clearly state why the information to be obtained is useful. That is, what can you do with the information after you get it?
  —Relation of the proposed work to the *long-term goals* of the project.

  > State *concisely* the importance of the research by *relating* the Objectives (Specific Aims) to the long-term goals (broad, long-term objectives).

  —Relation of the project to the *present state of knowledge* in the field (background).

  - *Briefly* sketch the background for the proposal
  - Critically *evaluate* existing knowledge.

  —Relation of the work proposed in this application to the *work in progress* by the investigator *under other support.*
  —Relation of the project to *work in progress elsewhere.*

  > Discuss the *gaps* in the present state of knowledge that your research project is intended to fill.

- Outline of the general plan of work (Experimental Design and Methods)
  —Explain the broad design of activities to be undertaken.
  —Give an adequate description of experimental methods and procedures.
  —Distinguish between the overall experimental design (i.e., research design) and the specific methods.
  —Number the items in this section to correspond to the numbers in the "Specific Aims" section.
  —*Do not repeat (but rather refer to)* identical procedures that apply to more than one Specific Aim.
  —Describe and/or reference protocols.
  —For new methods, explain *why* they are *better* than existing methods.
  —Discuss *control experiments.*
  —Explain how the data are to be *collected, analyzed,* and *interpreted.*
  —Discuss potential *difficulties* and *limitations* of the proposed procedures and *alternative approaches* to achieve the aims.
  —Point out procedures, situations or materials that may be *hazardous* to personnel, and describe *precautions* to be exercised.
  —Where appropriate, outline plans for *preservation, documentation, and sharing* of data, samples, physical collections, and other related *products of research.*
  —For proposals that involve use of human subjects, hazardous materials, vertebrate animals, or endangered species, proposals for equipment, or proposals to the Directorate for Engineering, see detailed information in the GPG.
  —Provide a tentative *sequence* or *timetable* for the project. (Be realistic, not exact).
- Collaboration

—Describe any substantial *collaboration* with individuals not referred to in the budget.

—Document each such collaboration with a letter from the collaborator.

—Letters of collaboration should go after the budget pages unless otherwise specified by your Program Officer.

8. *Bibliography* (referred to as Item 5, Proposal Section D in the GPG, page 6)
   - Use NSF Form 1361 (use of form is optional).
   - *Required*
   - No page limit
   - *Provide pertinent* literature references.
   - *Be sure citations are complete (full names of authors, title, and complete reference).*
   - *Citations should be:*
     —Thorough and relevant.
     —Current: Reviewers are interested in how *up to date* you are.
     —Chosen wisely. Your choices tell the Reviewer something about your quality as a scientist!
     —Presented in *consistent format* (all authors, book or journal title, volume number, page numbers, year).
   - Be sure that every citation in the bibliography is referred to in the text.
   - Be sure that every citation in the text is listed in the bibliography.

9. *Biographical sketches* (biosketches) (referred to as Item 6, Proposal Section E in the GPG, page 6)
   - Use NSF Form 1362.
   - See the GPG for definitions of Personnel categories.
   - *Required for all senior personnel.*
   - *Maximum of 2 pages per investigator.*
   - Follow instructions on Form 1362 and in the GPG.

     List postdoctoral training under "Education."

   - Publications (include "in press"); maximum of 10, 5 of which should be closely related to the subject of the project.
   - List of individuals, other than those cited in the publication list, with whom the investigator has collaborated on a project, book, article, report, or paper within the last 48 months. *If none, state "None."*
   - Names of each investigator's own graduate and postdoctoral advisers and advisees.

     The information in the 2 preceding items is used to help identify potential conflicts or bias in the selection of Reviewers.

     For postdoctoral fellows, other professionals, and graduate students (research assistants), include exceptional qualifications that merit consideration in the evaluation of the proposal.

     For Equipment proposals, see GPG.

10. **Budget** (Referred to as Item 7, Proposal Section F in the GPG, page 6)
    - Use NSF Form 1030.
    - Make *1 copy* of Form 1030 *for each year* of support requested and 1 copy for the *cumulative budget*. (Write "Year X" or "Cumulative Budget" at top right.)
    - Photocopy Form 1030 *after* filling in items that remain the same for each bud-

get year but *before* filling in items that change from year to year.

— *Budget categories* (See GPG, page 6):

- *Salaries and wages* (See GPG).

  A.[8] *Senior personnel salaries*

  —NSF funds may not be used to augment total salary or rate of salary during the normal faculty appointment term (except at certain predominantly undergraduate institutions).

  —Summer salary is limited to 2/9 of the regular academic year salary

  —For senior personnel list:
  - Names
  - Number of academic-year, summer, or calendar-year person-months of funding requested

  B. *Other personnel salaries*

  Enter, in the parentheses on Form 1030, the number of individuals in each category.

  —For postdoctoral associates and other professionals:
  - List each position.
  - Specify number of full-time-equivalent person-months.
  - Specify rate of pay.

  —For graduate and undergraduate students, technicians, secretaries, clerical workers, etc., list only:
  - Total number of persons in each category.
  - Total amount of salary per year in each category.

     Salaries must be consistent with the grantee institution's regular practices.

     Tuition remission costs for students: List separately under "Other Direct Costs" or "Fringe Benefits," as appropriate.

  C. *Fringe benefits* (are treated as direct costs)

- *Other Budget Categories*

  D. *Permanent equipment*

  —Defined as greater than $500 acquisition cost and service life of more than 2 years.

  —*General-purpose (e.g., office) equipment is not eligible!*

  —Items costing more than $1,000 must be listed separately.
  - Describe item.
  - Give estimated cost including tax.

  E. *Travel*

  1) Domestic travel (For investigators and consultants).
  - Specify who will travel and give the total number of trips to be taken. Give details in the Budget Justification.
  - Travel must enhance ability to perform the work, plan extensions of the work, disseminate the results of the work.

  2) *Foreign travel* (see GPG, page 7)

  F. *Participant support costs* (see GPG, page 7)

  G. *Other direct costs* (Justify all costs unless obvious.)

  1) *Materials and supplies*
  - Expendable materials and supplies

---

[8] The "A" here and subsequent numbering in this section refer to the line item numbers on Form 1030.

Reference books and periodicals may be charged if they specifically relate to the project.

- Estimated costs
- Justify. (Give more details when costs are more than $500.)

2) *Publication, documentation, and dissemination costs*
   - Cost of preparing reports, including preparation of illustrations
   - Reprints
   - Page charges
   - For additional permissible charges, see the GPG, page 8.

3) *Consultant services*
   - Give the number of days of expected service and daily compensation rate.
   - Compensation may not exceed the maximum rate established by NSF annually.

     Announced in *NSF Bulletin:* Effective 1/10/93 the rate is $443/day exclusive of indirect costs, travel, per diem, etc. For further information call the NSF Division of Grants and Contracts, Policy Office (703-306-1241).

   - Consultant's travel and per diem costs should be listed *separately* under "Travel."

4) *Computer (ADPE) services* (See GPG, page 8)
   - Retrieval of scientific, technical, and educational information
   - Leasing automatic data-processing equipment (ADPE)
   - List purchase of computer hardware and software under equipment, *not here.*
   - For supercomputer access/support, see GPG, page 17.

5) Subcontracts (see GPG, page 8)
   Line G.5 on Form 1030

H. Total direct costs *(line items A through G on Form 1030).*

I. Indirect costs
   —Negotiated between your institution and NSF. Are included in total award, not negotiated separately. (For information, see GPG and/or call the NSF Cost Analysis Unit, 703-306-1244.)
   —Must be computed for your proposal and listed on Form 1030.
   —For details about eligibility and exclusions, see GPG, page 8.

J. Total direct and indirect costs

K. Residual funds
   See GPG, page 9.

L. Amount of this request

M. Cost sharing
   See instructions in GPG, page 9. If appropriate, list on Line Item M, Form 1030. Explain in the budget justification.

   See GPG, pages 9–10, for a partial list of *unallowable* costs.

11. *Budget Justification* (part of Proposal Section F in the GPG)[9]
    - No form. Use additional sheets of paper.
    - *Maximum of 3 pages.*

---

[9] Note that in the next-to-last sentence under the first paragraph of "Budget" in GPG this section is referred to as "Budget Justification," but in the "Instructions for use of Summary Proposal Budget" on the back of Form 1030, Item 1d specifies that the documentation page(s) be titled, "Budget Explanation Page(s)."

- *Identify each item in the Budget Justification by the line item in the Budget (Form 1030)* (i.e., use the line item numbers on the budget page and cumulative budget page to number the corresponding explanation in the Budget Justification section).
- Put your name, Social Security number, and project title on each sheet.
- *Place the "Budget Justification page(s)"* into the grant application *immediately following the Budget pages.*
- Do *not* alter or rearrange cost categories. Follow the order on NSF Form 1030.
- Be *concise* and, if appropriate—and insofar as page limits permit—use an indented format:

— — — — — — — — — — — — — — —

— — — — — — — — —

— — — — —

For example, for line item "G. Other Direct Costs:"

1. MATERIALS AND SUPPLIES: -- $10,856

    Animals -- $7,950

      z Rats -- $xxx

        x/wk for y weeks for the _____ experiments

      x Rabbits -- $yyy

        y/wk for x weeks for the _____ experiments

    Chemicals-- $1,006

      _____ , 3 gm/month for x months at $x/gm . . . $xyz

      _____ , 7 gm/month for y months at $x/gm . . $zzz

    Glassware --- $ 1,900

More extensive sample budget justifications are given in Appendix IV of this book.

- *Document and justify amounts requested in each budget category.*

    A. *Senior personnel*
- List and justify all senior personnel.
- List individually all senior personnel who were grouped under item A6 on the budget page; for each, list requested person-months to be funded and rates of pay.
- Specify what *unique* role each person will play in the execution of the research (i.e., specific functions in project).
- If you must have "To be named," specify qualifications for the individual to be recruited.

    B. *Other personnel*

    Specify the number of individuals in each category in the parentheses on Form 1030.

C. *Fringe benefits*

State that these have been calculated at X%, in accordance with your institutional guidelines.

D. *Permanent equipment*

- Defined as costing more than $500 and having a useful life of more than 2 years.
- Fully justify only items of equipment costing more than $1,000:

  —Describe each item and its function(s).

  —Give estimated cost, including tax. (Provide a formal written estimate from the company; ask the company to include a statement about anticipated price increases by the probable purchase date.)

  —Show that you have obtained the best discount available, for example, call 703-306-1391.

  —Justify the need for each item requested.

  —Be sure that the item is not already available (i.e., check "Equipment" against "Facilities, Equipment and Other Resources"), and justify *particularly well,* equipment requested that is also listed in "Facilities, Equipment and Other Resources." For example, if you say you have five computer terminals, and you asked for another terminal in the budget, explain why 5 are not enough—or what is unique and necessary about the new one you will buy.

E. *Travel*

1) *Domestic* travel (including travel for consultants). See GPG, page 7.

   - Specify who will travel, the purpose (e.g., name of meeting and whether or not traveler will present a paper or poster), and the relation to the proposed project activities.
   - Place
   - Dates
   - Approximate expenses (including per diem)

     —Estimate expenses based on actual meeting places. Find out where meetings will be and how much it costs to get there.

     —Specify that costs are round-trip, jet-economy rates, shared room, etc.

     —Explain how the travel will enhance your ability to perform the project work, plan extensions of it, or disseminate its results.

2) *Foreign* travel

   Give the same information as for domestic travel, but justify why you need to go out of the country, and give more details when costs are substantial.

F. *Participant support costs*

Primarily for grants to support conferences, workshops, or symposia (see GPG, pages 7–8 and page 15 item VB).

G. *Other direct costs*

1) *Materials and supplies*

   - Indicate types required.
   - Estimate costs.

2) *Publication, documentation, and dissemination*

   Specify and justify briefly the costs of sharing research findings, including but not limited to the items below (see GPG for a complete list):

   - Report preparation
   - Reprints
   - Page charges and certain other journal costs
   - Illustrations
   - Documentation, storage, and indexing of data and databases

3) *Consultant services*
- Give name(s) of consultant(s).
- State each consultant's expertise.
- Give each consultant's primary organizational affiliation.
- Specify daily compensation rate (must not exceed maximum rate established by NSF annually).
- Estimate days of service.
- Consultants' travel costs and per diem expenses should be listed separately under "Travel."
- Justify use of consultant(s) by explaining necessity for their expertise for success of the proposed project.

4) *Computer (ADPE) services*
Justify need for:
- Information retrieval
- Leasing of automatic data processing equipment (ADPE)
Note that:
- Costs must be in line with established rates at proposing institution.
- Purchase of computer equipment should be included under "Equipment," *not here.*

5) *Subcontracts (See GPG, page 8.)*
- Include a complete budget.
- Justify details.

H. *Total direct costs (Sum of A through G on Form 1030)*

I. *Indirect costs*
Specify current rate(s) and base(s).
- Use current rate(s) negotiated with the relevant federal negotiating agency.
- For further information, see the GPG, page 8 and/or call NSF.

J–L. *Fill in appropriate numbers*

M. *Cost Sharing*
See instructions in GPG, page 9. If appropriate, list on Budget Line Item M. Explain here.

12. *Current and pending support* (Referred to as Item 8, Proposal Section G in GPG, page 9)
- Use NSF Form 1239.
- List *all* support from *all* sources. See details in GPG, pages 9–10.
- Include the proposed project.
- List all other projects that require a portion of time of the principal investigator or other senior personnel—even if they receive no salary support for it.
- Regardless of the source of support, give person-months of time to be devoted to each project.
- List all proposals under consideration or to be submitted.
- If the project now being submitted was previously funded by a source other than NSF, give particulars requested in Form 1239 for the immediately preceding funding period.
- If the proposal now being submitted to NSF is also being submitted to other possible sponsors, all of them must be listed.
- The NSF *BIO Directorate no longer allows "concurrent submissions" to any other federal agency* except for (1) proposals by beginning investigators and (2) proposals for which the proposer and the agency program managers have previously agreed to review and administer any resulting award as a joint activity. For other directorates, concurrent submission of a proposal to other organizations will not prejudice its review by NSF.

- Give complete, accurate, and unambiguous information.
- Notify the Program Officer if there are changes in support or pending support after proposal submission.

13. *Facilities, Equipment, and Other Resources* (referred to as Item 9, Proposal Section H in GPG, page 10)
    - Use NSF Form 1363.
    - Follow the instructions on the form.
    - Describe only facilities and major items of equipment applicable to the research proposed.
    - Indicate capacity, pertinent capabilities, relative proximity, and extent of availability to the project.
    - Include description of scientific ambiance, including resources available to you that enhance your ability to do research such as seminars, library facilities, and access to relevant colleagues.

14. *Special information and Supplementary Documentation* (Referred to as Item 10, Proposal Section I in GPG, page 10)
    In some cases, information *relevant* to determining the quality of the proposed research must be included in the proposal but is *not considered within the 15-page Project Description or the Budget Justification* and is not considered Appendix material. See GPG, page 10 and/or contact the relevant NSF Program Officer.
    Examples of such special information are:
    - Rationale for performance of project away from main site or campus.
    - Letters of commitment for collaborative arrangements.
    - Description of activities with actual or potential impact on the environment.
    - Rationale for work in foreign countries.
    - For additional examples, see GPG, page 10.

15. *Appendices* (referred to as Item 11, Proposal Section J in GPG, page 11)
    Appendices are not permitted, except where separate guidelines are provided for a specific program or if explicit permission is obtained from the appropriate Program Officer (Authorized Deviation).
    If you have occasion—or get permission—to have an Appendix:
    - Keep Appendix materials to a minimum.
    - *Appended information must not be used to circumvent the page limits of the Project Description!*
    - Label each Appendix item (Name, Social Security number, project title, title of item).
    - Be sure each Appendix item is referred to in the text of the application.
    - Do not number Appendix pages.
    - Provide a list of Appendix items on a separate sheet at the front of each collated Appendix set.
    - *Do NOT mail the Appendix separately.*

CHECKLIST

- A checklist for proposal submission is provided in the GPG, page 29.
- This checklist is *not part of the application form. Do not submit* the checklist with the application; it is provided for your convenience and to ensure that the proposal is complete.
- Use the NSF checklist when planning your proposal and before mailing your application.

D. *The NSF Electronic Proposal Submission (EPS) Project* [10]

(May 5, 1993)

The NSF Electronic Proposal Submission (EPS) project is the initial phase of NSF's transition from paper-based to electronic processing of proposals. The primary goal of this phase is to understand the current and potential problems and barriers at NSF and at submitting institutions. The EPS software, accompanying data entry utilities and procedures provide the capability for principal investigators (PIs) and university administrative staff to enter the NSF proposal forms data, combine them with PI-created documents (including graphics), print the proposal, and transfer the proposal to NSF. The actual submission is via FTP (File Transfer Protocol) followed by faxing the signed cover sheets.

ABOUT THE PROJECT

—The NSF EPS system is designed to facilitate the creating, editing, and printing of the NSF Common Submission (CS). The CS is the file submitted to NSF. It contains all the data and documents that comprise a proposal. (While the EPS system is designed for electronic submission, the software and utilities may be used to create paper proposals. But these must be submitted in the normal manner.)

—The entire proposal must be submitted electronically. Paper sections, for example, paper appendices, are not acceptable. (However, NSF does not accept faxed proposals.)

—The PI-created documents must be in PostScript, a trademark of Adobe Systems Inc.

—The university's Authorized Institutional Representative's (AIR) office must have access to an Internet host computer to submit the CS to NSF.

—Proposals are deemed received when the CS and the faxed signed cover sheets are both received at NSF. NSF produces all required proposal copies and then processes the proposal in the normal manner.

THE ROLE OF THE AUTHORIZED INSTITUTIONAL REPRESENTATIVE (AIR)

The AIR's signature is required on the cover sheet of the proposal. In no case will a proposal be processed until the fax of the signed cover sheets is received by the EPS office. To further ensure that the AIR controls the submission process, the EPS office at NSF assigns to the university AIR a password and account on the EPS host computer for the FTP'ing[11] of the proposal. The AIR, of course, is free to give the password to other university offices and/or individuals and therefore permit them to submit proposals. The details on obtaining the account as well as the submission procedure are in the NSF Science & Technology Information System (STIS) document epsinfo(.ps).

TO OBTAIN EPS DOCUMENTATION AND PROGRAMS

EPS software and documentation are both available on STIS. You may obtain EPS information from STIS via download, anonymous FTP, or e-Mail. The anonymous FTP server is stis.nsf.gov. To obtain information via e-Mail, send to stisserv@nsf.gov (Internet) or

---

[10] This document is taken essentially verbatim from a document about the EPS Project provided by NSF.
[11] Sending the proposal via FTP.

stisserv@NSF (BITNET). The text of the message should be as follows (the Subject line is ignored):

> get <document name>

The names of the available EPS documents and their contents are:

epsflyer(.ps)	Short summary of the EPS project (PostScript Version)
epsinfo(.ps)	General information about the EPS project (PostScript version)
epsprog4	Instructions to obtain the software and documentation for version 4
epsprog4.exe	The version 4 software, files, and documentation in PC-DOS format
epsprog4.trz	The version 4 software, files, and documentation in Unix format
epsprog4.hqx	The version 4 software, files, and documentation in Mac format
epsbin	Instructions to obtain Unix binaries for version 4
epsbin.sun	The version 4 binary for the Sparc platform
epsbin.aix	The version 4 binary for the RS6000 AIX platform
epsbin.nxt	The version 4 binary for the NeXT platform
epsbin.sgi	The version 4 binary for the Silicon Graphics platform
epslist	Instructions to join the EPS e-Mail list
fmsmart	General information about NSF-style Smart Forms

For general information about STIS, send an e-Mail message to stisinfo@nsf.gov (Internet) or stisinfo@NSF (BITNET) or call 703-306-0214/12 and ask for publication NSF 91-10, the "STIS Flyer."

TO CONNECT TO THE INTERNET

Call the National Network Service Center, the support center for the NSFNet, at 617-873-3400 for information and procedures to connect your university to the Internet.

FOR ADDITIONAL ASSISTANCE

E-Mail: eps @nsf.gov (Internet) or eps @NSF (BITNET)
Phone: 202-357-7439; Fax: 202-357-7663; TDD: 703-306-0090

See information about STIS in Appendix VIII-A.

Some Advice for Applying for Foundation Grants

Foundations are private organizations that give grants to individuals and organizations for a broad range of projects. Some have very specific mandates; others have broader missions. For example, many family foundations are dedicated to specific fields or causes; others, such as corporate foundations, are a philanthropic arm of the parent corporation and provide money for a variety of causes. There are over 33,000 private foundations in the United States that provide funding. In 1992 the total amount of money given away by these foundations was about $9.2 million.

The *Foundation Directory* (1993 edition) divides foundations into 4 general types. These are shown in Table A9-1.

Table A9-1 Types of Foundations

Type	Independent	Company-Sponsored	Operating	Community
Characteristics	Independent. Established to support charitable activities.	Legally independent. Close ties to corporation that provides funds.	Uses resources to do research or provide a direct service.	Publicly sponsored. Supports charitable activities in a specific community or region.
Source of funds	Endowment generally derived from single source + limited tax-deductible contributions.	Endowment + contributions from profit-making corporation.	Endowment generally derived from single source + unlimited tax-deductible contributions.	Unlimited tax-deductible contributions from the public.
Grant-making requirements	Broad discretionary giving but may have specific guidelines and give only in specific fields; often limit giving to local area.	Tend to give in fields related to corporate activities or in communities where corporation operates. Usually give more but smaller grants than independent foundations.	Make few, if any, grants. Grants usually related to program of foundation.	Grants limited to charitable organizations in local community.

It is useful to think of granting agencies as specialized venture capital companies. Although a venture capital company is generally looking for investments that are likely to bring large financial returns, such companies will "gamble" money on you only if the staff members think that you and your team have the background—and exhibit the capabilities—to accomplish what you set out to do. Likewise, a granting agency will fund your project only if its staff members foresee that you will further the agency's cause—that is, in some substantive way help the agency meet its goal. Thus, you—the applicant—must aim to "sell" your idea to the potential funding agency by convincing its staff members that your project will succeed and will fulfill the agency's mandate.

Foundations differ widely in "personality" and "style." Thus, in terms of the particulars, there are probably as many application and review procedures for private foundations as the number of such foundations that provide funding. However, the essentials of the kind of information agencies need from applicants are not so different for the different foundations, nor from the large government agencies. Almost every granting agency will want a description of your project (long-term objectives and specific aims) and information about what has already been done in the field (background), especially by you (preliminary studies/progress report), how you will do the project (project design and methods), and about you (biographical sketch), your track record, your team, and what resources or help you have at your disposal (resources and environment). The agency will also want to know how much money you need (budget) and why (budget justification) and who else has been interested in supporting you and/or your project (other support). Thus, if you know how to write a good NIH application and understand the correct way to approach, interpret, and meticulously respond to instructions, you should be able to write a good application to any agency. A few private foundations have "free-form" applications, that is, with no specified format. For such proposals it is useful to ask a relevant staff member at the organization what information is required. Also ask to see past successful proposals. If all else fails, simulate an NIH application or follow the advice in some of the resources listed in Appendix XI in this book.

As with federal funding, the most important factor—and an absolutely essential component in seeking foundation support—is a good idea. Ideally, the idea should be unique but not so "way out" that it is beyond the comprehension of the Reviewer(s). The latter criterion is especially important with foundation proposals. Although some of these organizations have review boards that include technical experts in your subject matter, others may use only a few Reviewers—or even only one Reviewer (sometimes someone from the agency's own staff) who may have an overall grasp of the subject but may not have an in-depth understanding of your project and field of research.

As is also the case with the NIH funding components, another important factor for success in getting funded is a good match between your research idea and the mission or mandate of the funding agency. Like other grant applications, those to foundations take a lot of thought, planning, and hard work. Therefore, it pays to call a potential funding agency—before you begin writing a proposal—to find out whether the agency is really interested in your project and whether it provides funds sufficient to make it worthwhile for you to apply. Subtle preferences in funding are often omitted from printed materials that an organization may provide. Ask to speak to the person in charge of the particular funding (giving) program, and try to get accurate, detailed information about the organization's mandate and application and review procedures. Submitting an application without previously contacting the program officer and discussing your project can lead to an enormous waste of your time.

Finding the right foundation—one that might be interested in your project—requires that you do some homework. Become acquainted with the various Foundation Center publications and foundation indexes and directories. Some of these listings are now available on computer databases, making it easier to search for those that may be a good match for your project. Once you have determined which foundations may be of interest, send for their annual reports, lists of grants they have funded in recent years, and a roster of their board members, indicating their professional backgrounds (the board members sometimes make the final funding decisions). Find out who is the director of the grants program, how much funding is available for the period for which you are applying, what the application process involves, what the eligibility requirements are, when applications are due, and how long the review process takes.

Your institutional Office for Sponsored Research (OSR) may be able to help you. For example, the Harvard University OSR maintains a library of literature about federal and private sponsorship of research; subscribes to SPIN (Sponsored Programs Information Network, a computer database that provides information about federal and nonfederal sponsors/funding agencies); and also publishes a periodic newsletter that lists information about current funding opportunities, many of them excerpted from the *Federal Register, Commerce Business Daily*, etc. Listings are *not* limited to the sciences; they also cover arts and humanities. Your institutional development office may also have information about foundations. It is also important to check with your OSR to determine whether it is cultivating a relationship with a foundation, thereby—in all likelihood—making it "off limits" to individual grant seekers from the same institution.

If you meet the two requirements outlined above—a good idea and a good match—submission of a well-thought-out, focused, clearly presented proposal that is meticulously responsive to the instructions provided by the agency should make you highly competitive for available funding. If at all possible, it is good to find and study a successful proposal to the foundation in question before you plan your own proposal.

Some foundations require a pre-proposal or letter of inquiry prior to submission of a full-length proposal. In some cases the pre-proposals are reviewed and only a percentage of the applicants are invited to submit a full proposal. Some foundations have fairly lengthy and precise instructions for what they require in the pre-proposal or letter of inquiry. However, some foundations do not provide written instructions for proposal preparation. When this is the case, it is generally safe to provide the information required in an NIH or other major agency application kit.

A number of agencies, once they determine that your project is of interest to them, will work with you to develop the written proposal. In any event, when instructions are provided, one of the clues to success is to read the instructions *word for word* and make an extremely detailed outline of what the agency wants, in what form, in what order, and with what page limits. In my experience, people who simply read through the instructions and then write from the major headings in the instructions often overlook and fail to provide some of the major items on which their proposals will be judged. That instructions sometimes have major topics buried in subtle places in the text may seem unlikely until you consider that the individuals who write the instructions are often not schooled in the art of writing instructions. Thus, the responsibility falls to the applicant to decipher, understand, and respond to what the Reviewers need and want to know.

You should also be aware that, in contrast to public institutions, which readily disclose their application review procedures, private foundations are sometimes quite discreet about disclosing information about their review procedures. If you are unable to determine the level of professional sophistication of the potential Reviewer(s), my advice is to assume that you are writing your proposal for an intelligent and educated nonexpert who is familiar with the generalities of the programs funded by the agency but not conversant with the subtle intricacies of the field. If you write a clear, complete proposal with a clear, succinct abstract, avoiding professional jargon and a condescending tone, you should be on target for the majority of foundation Reviewers.

LETTERS OF INQUIRY AND PRE-PROPOSALS

Some funding agencies require you to submit a letter of inquiry before they will send you the instructions for submission of a full proposal. Some of these agencies have very specific instructions about what is to be included in the letter of inquiry; if so, follow the instructions. If there are no specific instructions, consider the advice below.

- Write the letter from the point of view of the opportunity the agency has in supporting your project, *not* how their funding will fill *your* needs.
- Unless there are specific instructions that require you to write a longer letter, be brief. You should be able to summarize the essentials of your project in one page.
- Address the letter to the person responsible for funding.
- Address the mandate of the agency.
- Explain clearly and succinctly what you propose to do and what you hope to accomplish (or enclose a separate summary of the project).
- Discuss the suitability of your project for the agency's mandate.
- Discuss the amount of funding required.
- Include your resume (up-to-date).
- If appropriate, ask for an appointment with the relevant official.

    Subtle funding preferences of an agency, not made explicit in their brochures, can sometimes be clarified during verbal exchanges.

- Be persuasive but not overbearing.

Some agencies require a more formal pre-proposal. These pre-proposals are evaluated, and only a small number of the proposers may be invited to submit a full proposal. Making this "first cut" does not ensure success in getting funded in response to submission of the full proposal.

THE REVIEW PROCESS AT PRIVATE FOUNDATIONS

- Specifics vary; the process may be more informal than at government agencies in some ways, but some aspects are very formalized.
- The review process is often not as codified as at government agencies, and information about review procedures may not be readily available.
- The review committee is often ad hoc, and size varies from a single staff member to a group as large as an NIH Study Section. The review committee may become the advisory committee for the project.
- The foundation may use outside consultants or Reviewers, often by mail.
- The foundation may make a site visit.
- At some foundations, applicants may be asked to come to the foundation to present their project.
- Because there may be considerable interaction between the foundation staff and the grantee in the course of proposal preparation, the review process may be based much more on the project than on the written proposal.
- There may or may not be a rating of the project or proposal.
- If the review committee is composed largely of outside Reviewers, there may be a second level of review by an in-house staff committee.
- The foundation board of directors (which may be composed entirely of businesspeople who may not be specialists in your field of interest) usually votes on the final recommendation of the review committee.

Some Review Criteria at Private Foundations

- Is there a good match between the proposed project and the mandate (mission) of the funding agency?
- Does the applicant meet the guidelines and qualifications of the funding agency (geography, tax status, etc.)?
- Has the applicant conformed to all proposal submission guidelines of the funding agency:
  —Submission deadline
  —Page limits
  —Appropriate print size
  —Complete application with all parts correctly filled out
  —Appropriate appendices provided
  —Assurances/certifications filed and attested to
  —Neat presentation
- Is the project idea innovative and of high quality?
- Does the applicant demonstrate insight into the problem?
- Does the applicant present clear direction for solving the problem?
- Is there evidence of commitment to the project by the PI and the PI's institution as evidenced by:
  —Track record
  —Financial support (e.g., matching funds)
  —Space and personnel commitment
- Is there evidence that the project will continue after funds provided by the funding agency in question run out?
- Is the project concept exportable? That is, is there a likelihood that the project results will be adaptable to other institutions and/or situations?
- Is the material presented accurate?
- Is there a discussion of alternative approaches to the project?
- Is there a reasonable approach to data analysis?
- Is the project presented clearly?
- Does the applicant demonstrate attention to required details?
- Are there well-thought-out plans for periodic, ongoing evaluation of the project?
- Are there well-thought-out plans for dissemination of project results?
- Is the tone of the proposal positive and confident?
  —Does it de-emphasize the PI's need and emphasize the PI's abilities and accomplishments?
  —Is it enthusiastic but not arrogant?
  —Is it optimistic but not unrealistic?

For more information about writing proposals to private foundations, refer to *Tips for Applying to Private Foundations for Grant Money,* by Reif-Lehrer and *Program Planning and Proposal Writing,* by Kiritz, as well as other references provided in Appendix XI, "Resources."

Strategies for Good Written and Oral Presentations

A. Strategies for Good Expository Writing

Strategies for Getting Started

Write for the reader

Always write for the reader rather than for yourself, the writer. Ask yourself, "What does the reader need and/or want to know about this subject?"

Consider the evaluation criteria

Think about the criteria for the evaluation of the grant proposal (or research paper or other document). What are the reviewers (readers) being asked to assess? Thinking about the evaluation criteria will help to clarify the objectives for you. The more measurable the objectives, the easier the evaluation! (Think about having to grade a multiple-choice test compared to one made up of essay questions.)

Make an outline

An outline is like a road map or blueprint, a plan of "*what* you will write" (the ideas). The text is "*how* you write it" (the words and sentences that express the ideas).

Begin to write only after you have made an outline. An outline will save you much time in the long run and will help you to avoid a lot of frustration. Working on the outline often helps to put into focus what additional information you may need to gather.

Many good writers spend 50–60 % of their project time making the outline, 10–20% of the time writing, and 30% of the time revising! *Begin to write only when you are 99.99% happy with your outline.*

To help you make an outline, write down the answers to the following questions for each pertinent section of the grant proposal:

- What is the purpose of this section of the grant proposal?
- What should the scope of this section of the grant proposal be?
- How should I introduce the subject of this section of the grant proposal? (Your first paragraph)
- What are the main ideas to be included in this section of the grant proposal? (Main topics). If you are writing a proposal, use a checklist to be sure you have included all required information.

—What is the best logical sequence for these main ideas/topics?

—If subheadings would help the reader, the main topics can be used to create subheadings.

—The main topics should also be used to generate good informative topic sentences for each paragraph.

> Tell the reader in the first sentence of each paragraph (or at least each major paragraph[1]) what you are going to discuss in that paragraph. Readers who skim may never get any further. They decide whether or not to read the rest of the paragraph on the basis of what you write in your topic sentence.

- What information should go into each paragraph to support the main idea in the paragraph?

  —These will be subtopics for the outline.

  —What is the best logical sequence for these subtopics within the paragraph?

  —Which of the pieces of information requires particular emphasis?

- What illustrations, diagrams, and/or photos are needed, if any, in each paragraph or section?

- Where should each illustration, diagram, or photo be placed for optimal clarity and effectiveness? (Figures should be placed as close as possible to the text that describes them.)

- What is an effective closing paragraph for this section of the grant proposal? A conclusion? A summary? A recommendation? A plan for future directions?

- Which of the topics and subtopics that you wrote down are essential and relevant, and which ones can be omitted or are not important for this section of the grant proposal?

In the first outline, don't force a structure (i.e., I, II, III, A, B, C, etc.) *if you find it hard to do*. Just get main and supporting ideas onto index cards, Post-it notes, or an outline processor. Use key words and phrases (not whole sentences).

After you have all the ideas written down, organize them (an outline processor can help a lot) so that they have good logical flow. Then flesh out the outline so that it includes everything you want to cover in the document.

Add formal structure (I, II, III, A, B, C, etc.) at the end, if at all. This process helps to check whether the various outline levels are equivalent.

Write a first draft

- Use your outline as a guide when you write the first draft.
- Do not interrupt the flow of writing the first draft by stopping to check spelling, references, or other details. Keep a list of items to check and do it later.
- Use easy, short, familiar words, short sentences, and short paragraphs that start with topic sentences.
- In a complex sentence, put the most important phrase first (emphasis).
- Use subheadings to help the reader find his/her way to information easily.
- Use easy-to-read formatting (appropriate amount of white space insofar as page limits allow).
- Write the way you speak, that is, in a direct, not overly formal manner (but no jargon or slang).

---

[1] When long paragraphs are divided into several shorter paragraphs just to provide "white space" for ease of reading, the subordinate paragraphs may not require topic sentences.

Revise the first draft

- Be sure everything you wrote is accurate, clear, and concise.
- Use a checklist to locate common writing problems.
- Give the reader a choice about how much to read by providing:
  —Table of contents
  —Subject line/summary
  —Subheadings
  —Topic sentences that tell what the paragraphs are about
  —Appropriate format
- Don't let your ego get in the way. The less of your document the reader has to read to get the information he/she wants, the better the job you've done.

STRATEGIES FOR ACHIEVING CLARITY AND BREVITY IN YOUR WRITING

Don't make the reader do extra work

Readers of expository prose generally want the maximum information in the minimum number of words.

- Don't use long or complex sentences that have to be reread to be understood.
- Tell the reader up front what you will discuss in that paragraph.
  —Start each paragraph with a good topic sentence.
  —A good topic sentence also provides the reader with a context into which s/he can fit details that you give subsequently.
  —The object of expository writing is to expose; the reviewer should never have to guess what you mean.
  —Remember that busy efficient people who have time only to skim use the first (topic) sentence of each paragraph to decide whether or not to read the rest of that paragraph.
- Don't use big words that the reader may not understand. (Never send your reader to the dictionary.)

  A brilliant scientist does not necessarily have an extensive literary vocabulary.

  Many scientists now come from other countries and may speak only rudimentary or scientific English.

- Don't use jargon.

  Think about a computer specialist talking to a cardiac surgeon! They might not understand each other at all if they spoke in the jargon of their own fields.

- Avoid use of the words *former* and *latter*.

  The reader may have to reread what came before to see what was *former* and what was *latter*. If the reader is not careful or has a poor memory, unfortunate errors may occur. Consider: "Please take care of my son and my cat while I'm away. Be sure the former is in by 11 P.M.; let the latter stay out all night."

Avoid ambiguity caused by misplaced modifiers or other "reference" problems

Not:
On Tuesday, a volumetric flask was brought to the glassware washing room by a technician with a broken neck.
(Who had the broken neck, the volumetric flask or the technician?)

But:
On Tuesday, a volumetric flask with a broken neck was brought to the glass-ware washing room by a technician.

Not:
After spilling the drink, the photomicrographs were ruined.
(How did the photomicrographs manage to spill the drink?)

But:
After the drink was spilled on them, the photomicrographs were ruined.

Not:
The spectrophotometer should be turned off before leaving the laboratory.
(Does the spectrophotometer really leave the laboratory?)

But:
The spectrophotometer should be turned off before you leave the laboratory.

Not:
A fasting urine specimen should be collected.
(Have you ever heard of a urine specimen fasting?)

But:
A urine specimen should be collected after the patient has fasted for x hours.

Avoid ambiguity caused by uncommitted pronouns

Not:
It has been shown that ...
(Who showed ... ?)

But:
Hooper and Cooper (1984) showed that ...

Not:
It is well known that ...
(By whom?)

But:
A survey done by ABC University has indicated that 57% of faculty members at the university know that ...

Not:
We noted that most of the rabbits were sick and all the rats had bald spots. This finding ...
(Which one—or both taken together?)

But:
Taken together, the findings that most of the rabbits were sick and all the rats had bald spots indicated that ...

Avoid ambiguity caused by complex sentences

- Use short, direct, unambiguous sentences
- Avoid long convoluted sentences such as:

> Looking back on it, it is curious that nobody was heard to ask why, since vitamin A has long been known to be very insoluble in aqueous media in general, scientists did not set about looking for a likely carrier protein that might be responsible for transporting vitamin A to its target tissues.[2]

---

2 Adapted from a sentence by Russell Baker, *New York Times*, February 1, 1986, page 27. This sentence may be fine in a piece of creative writing but not in a grant proposal.

Avoid words and phrases that can be interpreted in more than one way

Vague modifiers
Replace vague modifiers that state opinions with quantitative information

> **Not:** *most* or *many*
> **But:** 68–70%

> **Not:** This experiment requires *enormous* numbers of test tubes ...
> **But:** This experiment requires 133 test tubes ...

Vague reference to time or place
Specify time and place rather than using words like *recently* or *here*.

- What will the word *recently*, in an article you publish in 1994, mean to someone who reads the article in 2001?
- What will the word *here*, in an article you wrote in Boston, mean to someone who reads the reprint in China?

Words or phrases that can be interpreted in more than one way

- The phrase "lightly anesthetized animals ..." was used by a PI to indicate that he was treating the animals with great care but was apparently interpreted by a reviewer as implying that the animals were subjected to pain because they were only lightly anesthetized.
- The word "tree" may bring a palm tree to mind for someone who grew up in Hawaii but may bring a fir tree to mind for someone from Maine.
- "If you leave the door with the venetian blind open, the alarm will go off." Does this mean

    > If you leave the door (the one that has a venetian blind on it) open, the alarm will go off?

    > or

    > If you leave the door closed—but leave the venetian blind open, the alarm will go off?

- Here are some amusing examples from *The Lexicon of Intentionally Ambiguous Recommendations (Acronym: LIAR)*, by Prof. Robert Thornton, Economics Department, Lehigh University, Bethlehem, PA 18015:

    > *To recommend a lazy friend:* "In my opinion, you will be very fortunate to get this person to work for you."

    > *To describe a totally inept person:* "I most enthusiastically recommend this candidate with no qualifications whatsoever."

    > *To describe a "difficult" ex-employee:* "I am pleased to say that this person is a former colleague of mine."

    > *To describe a job applicant who is not worth further consideration:* "I urge you to waste no time in making this candidate an offer of employment."

Avoid sentences that don't give substantive information (e.g., circular sentences)

- "X-related complications will be treated according to general institutional guidelines for X-related complications."
- "In these experiments, we found that sterility is very important. Thus, we concluded that sterility is an important factor in these experiments."

Be brief

Use short, simple words

Not:	But:
Contemplate	Think
Endeavor	Try
Equitable	Equal, Fair
Facilitate	Help
Is indicative of	Indicates
Magnitude	Size
Require	Need
Terminate	End
The reader	You
Utilize	Use

Eliminate unnecessary words/phrases

- Extra words waste the reviewer's time—and your space. Save space for more important information—remember the page limitations.
- When you edit your proposal, ask yourself—*for each word:* Is this word really necessary? Does it add anything to the meaning of the sentence?

Not:	But:
Arrived at the conclusion	Concluded
As a matter of fact	Actually
At the present time	Now
At this point in time	Now
Data given in the 3d column are	Data in the 3d column are
Do a study of the effects of x on y	Study the effects of x on y
Due to the fact that	Because
Every single night	Every night
For the purpose of	For, To
Give assistance to	Assist, Help
Have a preference for	Prefer
If you should have any questions, feel free to contact me at XXX	If you have questions, call XXX
In a number of cases	Some, Several
In addition to	Also
In all probability	Probably
In excess of	More than
In order to	To
In the amount of $x	For $x

Not:	**But:**
In the course of	While, During (Note: *while* and *since* generally refer to time.)
In the event that	If
In the majority of instances	Usually (most of)
In the nature of	Like (similar to)
In the near future	Soon
In the neighborhood of	About
In the not too distant future	Soon
In the vicinity of	Near
In view of	Because
In view of the fact that	Because
(Don't use the word *fact* unless it refers to a fact.)	
It is imperative that	Be sure that
It is interesting to note that	Note that, Note:
It is of interest to note that	Note that, Note:
It is possible that the cause of	The cause may be
It would thus appear that	Apparently
Last but not least	Finally, Lastly
Make decisions	Decide
Make decisions about	Decide on
May result in damage	May damage
Must necessarily	Must
Needless to say	(Then why bother to say it?)
On a few occasions	Occasionally
On the assumption that	Assuming that
On the other hand	Or
Prior to	Before
Serve to make approximations	Approximate
Subsequent to	After, Following
Take action	Act
Take into consideration	Consider
The instruments which are located in	The instruments in
The process of extracting the	Extracting the
With regard to	Regarding
With the exception of	Except

Not:	**But:**
Reports were lengthy this year because the page limitations were eliminated from the instructions.	Reports were long this year because there were no page limits.
Please find enclosed, herewith, my new paper which was published in January of this year.	Here is my January 19XX paper.
At the present time we are experiencing precipitation.	It's raining.

Not:	**But:**
One of the members of the group said ...	A group member said ...
There is a new method that helps ...	A new method helps ...
He said the reason the grant was late was because ...	He said the grant was late because ...
It was suggested by the Reviewers that the Principal Investigators include an Appendix to amplify the background section.	The Reviewers suggested the Principal Investigators include an Appendix to amplify the background section.
The reason I am worried is because I think she is writing a very poor grant proposal.	I am worried because I think she is writing a very poor grant proposal.
The Progress Report was in need of additional data.	The Progress Report needed more data.
It is imperative that you fill out the personal data sheet.	You must fill out the personal data sheet.

Avoid redundancy

Don't say the same thing in three different ways out of insecurity. Say it once, and say it right.

In the expressions below, you only need one of the words; for example, "each" or "every" (Not both!) Decide which is the better word in the context in which it is to be used.

- Each and every
- First and foremost
- In this day and age (Consider using "now" instead.)
- One and only

Avoid obvious, trite phrases

You can often *omit:*

Needless to say (Then why bother to say it?)

In summary

In the last analysis

In actual fact (How can a fact not be actual? Is it really a fact?)

The fact of the matter is (Is it really a fact?)

It is apparent that

In my opinion (If you say something, it is usually understood to be your opinion. If you must make clear that something is your opinion, use the shorter expression, "I think.")[3]

Consider omitting unnecessary transition words and phrases such as "In conclusion, ..." (But *keep* transition words that tell the reader that you are "changing direction:" For example, "In contrast, ..." "Nevertheless, ... ")

---

[3] I think, I feel, I believe: If your field is psychology it may be appropriate to say, "I feel." If your field is religion, it may be appropriate to say, "I believe." If your field is science, or you are engaged in a research aspect of your profession, it is generally more appropriate to say, "I think."

Use active voice rather than passive voice when appropriate

Passive voice contains some form of the verb "to be" before the main verb. Therefore, the passive voice form may have extra words.

The active voice is also clearer; it tells you up front who (or what) did (or does or will do) the action of the verb. The passive voice is often used to evade the issue and does not give this information.

To turn a passive voice sentence to an active voice sentence, answer the question—up front—"Who (or what) is doing the action of the verb?"

Passive/passive:

It *was suggested* that the laboratory reports *be revised.* (9 words)

Who did the suggesting?
Who will do the revising?

Note that one can provide the desired information in passive voice, but it makes for an awkward sound:

It *was suggested* by John that the laboratory reports *be revised by Joe.*

Active/passive:

John suggested that the laboratory reports *be revised.* (8 words)
Who will do the revising?

Active/active:

John *suggested* that Joe *revise* the laboratory reports. (8 words)

Note that providing the desired information may make the sentence longer but clearer:

The head of the department suggested that the post-doc revise the laboratory reports. (14 words)

In trying to decide on the best form, the priorities should be accuracy first, clarity second, brevity third, and so forth.

Note that passive voice occurs in all tenses:

Past tense:

Passive voice:	The solutions were mixed.
	The solutions were mixed by John.
Active voice:	John mixed the solutions.

Present tense:

Passive voice:	The solutions are being mixed.
Active voice:	John is mixing the solutions.

Future tense:

Passive voice:	The solutions will be mixed.
Active voice:	John will mix the solutions.

Avoid turning verbs into nouns

Not:
Utilization of marine plant species for food *production* will bring about a *reduction* in food costs and *creation* of cheaper sources of calories. (23 words)

But:
Utilizing (Using) marine plant species to *produce* food will *reduce* food costs and *create* cheaper sources of calories. (17 words)

Avoid unnecessary "ing" words

Not:
They were meeting to ...
He will be going to ...

But:
They met to ...
He will go to ...

Be aware of style

Try to express rather than impress

- Use simple (but not simple-minded or simplistic) words.
- Use short, direct sentences (about 17 to 23 words is a reasonable length), but avoid a choppy first-grader sound by judicious use of transition words (Although, However, Nevertheless, etc.).
- Use short paragraphs that begin with *informative topic sentences.*
- Be quantitative.

    Replace "opinion" modifiers with quantitative modifiers.
    Not: *the majority of* **But:** 88–90%

- Avoid phrases or modifiers that *may* not add to the critical essence of what you want to say:

    Not: Let us concentrate first on the X molecule, which is very large and, therefore, it ...
    But: The X molecule is very large; therefore, it ...

    Not: This interesting observation suggested to us that we should perhaps carefully examine X, which revealed that ...
    But: Careful examination of X revealed that ...

- Let your data and presentation speak for you:

    Not: This *cleverly conceived* experiment ...
    But: This experiment . . . (and then provide a table or figure that makes the reader immediately aware of how cleverly conceived the experiment is.)

- Avoid an undue amount of self-praise:
    —Our *tremendously unique* method for ...
    —Our laboratory is the *best known in the world* for ...
    —We have the *largest collection* of ... in the country.

- Avoid pompous language

Not:
"Nosocomial infection"
"Iatrogenic condition"

But:
"Hospital-acquired infection"
"Physician-induced condition"

One of your Reviewers may not be an M.D.!

Avoiding unnecessary "heavy" medical jargon is especially important if you are a physician researcher proposing a project that involves a lot of basic science. Such a proposal is likely to have at least one Ph.D. Reviewer. Sending this Reviewer on frequent trips to a medical dictionary wastes her/his time! On the other hand, you don't want your M.D. Reviewer to wonder how you got through medical school. Take a reasonable "best-compromise" approach.

Not:
Unless all parties to the plan interface imminently, the project will be rendered inoperative.

But:
Unless everyone cooperates now, the project won't work.
(Negative tone)
or
If everyone cooperates, the project will be successful.
(Positive tone)

Be consistent with respect to:

- Form/format
- Pronoun versus noun to which it refers
- Singular versus plural
- Subject versus object
- Tense

Use parallel construction

Not:
His job consisted of *organization* of new projects, *researching* current projects, *to write* progress reports, and *being available to help* the junior staff.

We couldn't decide between *rental,* leasing, and buying a new spectrophotometer.

But:
His job consisted of *organizing* new projects, *researching* current projects, *writing* progress reports, and *helping* the junior staff.

We couldn't decide between *renting,* leasing, and buying a new spectrophotometer.

Avoid short, choppy sentences
Use, but don't overuse, transition words.

Not: Good expository writing is difficult. It is an important skill to master. It requires much time and effort. It is worth it. Writing is necessary for job advancement. It improves self-image. It provides satisfaction. Everyone should take a good course in business writing.

But: Good expository writing is difficult, but it is an important skill to master. Although it requires much time and effort, it is worth it. Writing is necessary for job advancement. It also improves self-image and provides satisfaction. Everyone should take a good course in business writing.

Avoid excessive multiple modifiers

- The attractive, upgraded, computerized, large, heavy, expensive, recently purchased, spectrophotometer ...
- The computer-based integrated decision support environment ...

Avoid jargon "ize" and "wise" words

Acceptable:	Not acceptable:
The car has been winterized.	The plan has been operationalized.
Clockwise (in the manner of)	Budgetwise (with respect to)

Try not to split infinitives

Not: Be sure *to quickly go* ...
But: Be sure *to go quickly* ...

However, splitting the infinitive sometimes avoids ambiguity or makes for a better flow. Consider the difference in meaning in the following sentences:

She will try *to more than justify* the cost of the computer.
She will try *to justify more than* the cost of the computer.
She will try *more than to justify* the cost of the computer.

The 3 sentences above do not have identical meanings. Position the modifying words "more than" so as to achieve clarity (get the correct meaning).

Don't overstate your case

- Avoid superlatives: Use "best," "most," etc., only if you are *sure* the superlative is correct:

    Not: One of the best ways to purify ... is ...
    (There can be only one *best* way!)

    But: ... is the best way to purify ...

- Avoid useless modifiers:

    "I repeat this experiment every *single* month." (Are there double months—or married months?)

Think about emphasis

Emphasis is important in the context of the psychology of the reader.

- In a sentence, start with the clause you want to stress:

    In the previous project period, three approaches were developed to solve ...

    Three approaches were developed in the previous project period to solve ...

    Three approaches to solve ... were developed in the previous project period.

- Don't begin a paragraph with unimportant words:

    Not: *First let us consider that* rain helps plants grow.
    But: Rain helps plants grow.

Be aware of tone

- Attitude, mood, and tone are sometimes "contagious."
- Be positive.

    Not: I won't be able to finish this project by the end of the first year.
    But: I will be able to finish this project by March of the second year.

- Avoid words that may upset the reader.
  - —Words that are inherently negative, such as: *intolerable, misguided, unfair, wrong, unfortunately*
  - —Words that have negative connotations

Positive or neutral connotation	Negative connotation
Methodical, Meticulous	Fanatical, Nit-picking
Economical, Frugal	Cheap, Chintzy
Uninformed	Ignorant
Firm	Inflexible
Forceful, Persevering	Overbearing, Dogged
Colorful	Gaudy
Problem	Disaster

- Use neutral words to avoid sexual bias.

    The English language is inherently masculine. Don't make it more so. The use of "s/he" and the plural "they" instead of "he or she" are polite and acceptable.

Say	Instead of
Business executive or manager	Businessman or Businesswoman
Chair, Chairperson, or moderator	Chairman
Member of the clergy	Clergyman
Firefighter	Fireman
Supervisor	Foreman
Police Officer	Policeman
Flight attendant	Stewardess or Steward
Human race, humanity, humankind	Mankind
Synthetic	Man-made
Utility hole	Man-hole

    But remember that the main purpose of your proposal is to communicate what you propose to do to the Reviewer. Don't go "overboard." (See *Guide to Nonsexist Language*, which can be purchased from Project on the Status and Education of Women, Association of American Colleges, 1818 R Street, N.W., Washington, DC 20009.)

- Understand where you stand with respect to the reader.
  This issue is important in interaction, correspondence, and collaboration with people from other countries or cultures and at other authority levels.
  - —Cultural differences

United Kingdom	United States
Tendency to be more formal, especially when dealing with older people	Tendency to be quite informal, unless dealing with older people or people from other cultures
Dear Sir:	Dear Bill:
Having been privileged to receive your esteemed patronage in the past, we think you will be interested to know that ...	Because you've been so generous with funding for our project in the past, we thought you'd like to know that ...

—Authority
- If *you* have the authority, say: "*I suggest ...*"
- If you are addressing "the boss," say: "*I would like to suggest ...*"

If you have a question on English language usage, call the National Grammar Hotline. In Massachusetts the hotline is located at Northeastern University (617-373-2512). A free directory (published annually) of Grammar Hotlines in other areas of the U.S. is available. To order the directory, send a self-addressed stamped #10 envelope to:

Ms. Donna Reiss, Director
National Grammar Hotline Directory
Tidewater Community College
Writing Center
1700 College Crescent
Virginia Beach, VA 23456
804-427-7170

B. Strategies for Giving a Good Oral Presentation

Your reputation as a scientist depends a great deal on talks you give at other institutions (seminars) and at professional meetings. The quality of the science is the most important factor. However, the quality of your presentation cannot help but make an impression. Therefore, it is important to learn to give a good talk. In addition, there is a chance that you may get site-visited when you submit a grant application. It is important that you be able to present your project clearly to the site visit committee and convince the members that you have a good project and will be able to carry it out well. Here are some strategies for giving a good talk. Like proposal writing, public speaking is a learnable skill. Like most other learnable skills, it takes a knowledge of the principles and a certain amount of practice to become good at it.

Not all the advice given below pertains to all kinds of talks. For example, a 10-minute talk requires some strategies that are different from those required for a 1-hour talk. Likewise, a formal talk at a professional meeting where the physical setup has been organized for the occasion by experienced personnel requires less attention to details about equipment than a talk you will give in a place where the host (and sometimes the speaker) must arrange things specifically for your talk. Giving a lecture to a class and giving a workshop to a group of adults require somewhat different but related skills.

Before you agree to give a talk, be sure that (1) you have something significant to say about the subject and (2) you can speak about the subject with authority and conviction. Your excitement or boredom about a subject tend to be highly contagious to the audience.

GENERAL CONSIDERATIONS

- Make frequent eye contact with the audience.
- Practice good voice projection.
- Develop an air of confidence (even if you are nervous inside).
- Avoid having the audience be distracted from what you say by what you do or wear.
  - Don't fiddle with things (the microphone cord, your papers, your fingers, etc.); don't scratch your head, etc.
  - Avoid excessive pacing or gesticulation.
  - Be aware of appropriate dress and general appearance; the audience is likely to get distracted by unusual clothes, egg on your tie, a green Mohawk hairdo, or a button missing in an awkward place.

COMBAT NERVOUSNESS

- Know your subject matter.
- Be prepared.
- Get used to giving talks by offering to give them rather than avoiding them.
- Keep in mind that for many people, age and experience take care of nerves.
- Get enough sleep the night before the talk.
- Deep breathing and exercise help some people calm down.

PREPARE FOR YOUR TALK AHEAD OF TIME

Think about preparation time

- The longer the talk, the longer the time to research the topic, make slides, etc.
- The shorter the talk, the longer the time to prepare for the presentation per se. For example, there is no time to be casual in a 10-minute talk. To give a good very brief presentation, you need to memorize or almost memorize—the talk.
  —Give yourself ample time to practice your talk—at least by yourself, preferably in front of one or more experienced colleagues. Ask them to critique both the content and the presentation. Practice good tone and timing; don't drone or race.

Aim to communicate

- Be aware that people come to your talk with different perspectives.
- Consider that different words mean different things to different people.
- Think about connotation versus denotation of words.
- Understand that for communication to occur, what the audience perceives you to have said must match what you intended to say.

How many people will you be speaking to? (How large is the room?)

- Consider the print size on slides.
- Will you need a microphone?
- Would a flip-chart be visible at the back of the room, or do you need an overhead projector?

Call ahead to ensure that you have all the equipment you need for your talk

- Projector (extra projector or lamp housing or at least an extra bulb)
- Does the projector project from behind the screen or onto the front of the screen? (This may make a difference in the direction that you place your slides in the tray!)
- Remote control for the projector
- Screen (what size?)
- Flip-chart/overhead projector (appropriate pens, plastic film on which to write)
- Blackboard, chalk, and erasers or whiteboard, pens, and moist towels
- Pointer (extra batteries; some laser pointers require a lot of energy)
- Microphone
- Lectern or podium
- Glass and water within easy reach of the speaker's table
- If possible, get a sense of the physical facility. (Occasionally at large hotel-based

meetings, you may have to do the best you can with some difficult circumstances, such as simultaneous talks in adjacent rooms divided by a non-sound-proof movable wall!)

PLAN YOUR TALK BASED ON THE NEEDS OF THE AUDIENCE—NOT JUST YOUR NEEDS!

- Focus on what the audience wants and needs to know about the subject in addition to what you want to tell them.
- Have some understanding of the audience's level of expertise in your subject; don't talk down to the audience, and don't talk above their level of understanding.
- Provide an amount of introduction to your subject commensurate with the audience's level of understanding of the subject.
- Don't use jargon that the audience may not understand.
- Don't take leaps of logic when you talk. You know your subject intimately; the audience may not! Aim to keep the audience with you.

Make an outline for your talk

- Keep it simple; stick to one or two main points; educate—don't overwhelm—the audience.

  Don't make an effort to impress the audience; let the quality of the content and presentation speak for itself.

- Have good logical progression.
- Provide appropriate details.
- Prepare good, appropriate visuals. (A picture is worth a thousand words.)
- Give credit to the work of others.

Plan what you will say

- For each point in the outline
- For each visual you show

Prepare a thoughtful attractive handout (lecture outline)

- Bring more than enough copies for the people in the audience—or send the outline ahead to the host and ask her/him to have photocopies made on-site. Providing the audience with a good outline of what you plan to say allows people to pay attention to your talk rather than be distracted by taking notes.
- Include a bibliography in case someone wants additional details.
- Make the preparation time and the extent of the handout commensurate with the occasion and your budget.

THINGS TO DO/CHECK BEFORE THE TALK

- Get to the room early.
- Have a brief script about yourself ready to provide to the host if s/he asks how you wish to be introduced.
- Be prepared to introduce yourself if asked to do so.

- Put your slides in the projector tray, and review *every* slide to be sure it is right side up and frontwards.
- Determine where the switches for the overhead lights and the microphone are located.
- Check to see that everything you need is available.
- Check to see that everything works properly.
- Adjust the microphone volume.
- Distribute the lecture outlines, or leave them in a place where people can pick one up as they enter the room.
- If you are sponsoring the talk, check on refreshments.

THINGS TO CONSIDER BEFORE AND DURING THE TALK

- Speak slowly and clearly.
- Talk to the audience—not at them—and be sensitive to their reactions.

  Good speakers are able to adjust their delivery, if necessary, in response to subtle signals from the audience: facial expressions, body language, interactions between people in the audience. For example, if you observe that someone looks puzzled, you might say (without directly addressing the person in question—which might make her/him feel embarrassed), "Perhaps I could explain that in another way ..."

- Don't read your talk. It's okay to use notes, but make frequent eye contact with the audience. It's even better to use your visuals to remind you of what comes next.
- Be positive. Negative attitudes are contagious.
- Interject humor and illustrative stories when appropriate; it keeps the talk at a human level and helps keep the audience involved.
- Don't insult your audience.
  —Don't put the audience into the position of having to show their ignorance; don't ask, "How many of you don't know ...?" Say: "Some people may not be aware that ...."
  —Don't call on people or embarrass them in any other way.
  —Don't use words that people in the audience may not understand.
  —Don't tell jokes that may hurt people's feelings; e.g., ethnic jokes.
  —When appropriate, translate highly technical material into simpler language.
  —Don't sound pompous or arrogant.
- Try to make your audience feel comfortable enough to ask questions—no matter how ridiculous the questions may seem to you. ("The only stupid questions are the ones you don't ask.") If you embarrass someone who asks a question you may inhibit others from speaking and, thus, are less likely to have a lively discussion about your talk.

WHEN THE TALK BEGINS

- Thank the host for her/his introduction.
- Try to establish rapport with the audience early.
- If the host has not given sufficient background information about you and your work, introduce yourself further before you begin your talk—the audience usually wants to know about your authority to talk to them on the subject in question.

- Tell the audience whether you wish to be interrupted for questions or prefer people to hold questions and comments until the end of the talk.
- Tell the audience what you are going to tell them. Have this information on a slide, or write it on a flip-chart, board, or overhead.
- Present the main part of your talk.
- Be sure that you point to specific things on your slides, and let the pointer rest on the part of the slide you are discussing long enough for everyone to concentrate on it.
- Try to help the audience make connections between what you are telling them and information they already know. People remember things better when they can make such associations; help them. Tie your recent developments to the background work in the field.
- Tell the audience outright and clearly when you are about to make a transition from one topic to another.
- If and when appropriate, try to involve the audience rather than just lecturing at them.
- Periodically, briefly sum up what you have said up to that point: "So at this point we knew (know) that ..."
  —Reinforces what you have already told the audience
  —Helps those who got derailed (mind wandered, fell asleep, etc.) to get back on track
- End your talk with
  —A strong positive closing (perhaps the direction your work will take in the future or some possible long-range benefit of your work to society)
    and
  —A summary: Tell the audience what you have told them and what the "take-home" message is. Have this information on a slide or write it on a flip-chart, board, or overhead.
- Stay on schedule. This includes leaving time for questions.
- Take questions and comments from the audience and, if appropriate, ask for feedback.
  —If your host does not help you choose who gets to ask questions, then it is your job to do so in a fair, orderly manner.
  —Don't let one person monopolize the discussion.
  —Don't get into arguments with the audience. The objective is to discuss and enlighten, not to "win."
  —Don't be afraid to say "I don't know."
  —If appropriate, offer to find out the answer to an unresolved question and call the person who asked the question when you have the answer.
  —If appropriate, offer to remain after the talk and answer additional questions on a one-to-one basis.
- Have business cards and appropriate reprints with you for people who may want to contact you or read about your work in more detail.

APPENDIX XI

RESOURCES

CONTENTS FOR APPENDIX XI: RESOURCES

ABOUT THE RESOURCE APPENDIX

This appendix includes a variety of resources that might be helpful to researchers and proposal writers. Most of the listings are books and programs that came to my attention in the course of my work. Some of the items listed are resources that I have found particularly useful. Some are books or software programs that have been graciously sent to me for examination by publishers and software companies. Others are items that have been recommended by colleagues or about which I have only read.

I am not endorsing or (with a few exceptions) recommending the items listed below. They are not necessarily the only—or best—in their category. The purpose of this appendix is primarily to make you aware of the types of resources that are available to (1) help you work faster and more efficiently, (2) relieve you of tedious chores that can be done by computers, service agencies, etc., and (3) leave you the greatest possible amount of time to do your creative work. I hope you will use the resources in this list as a guide—a means to alert you to the types of resources that exist, should you wish to investigate whether they might be useful for you. Before investing time and money in a book, a software program, or a service, ask colleagues what else is available in a particular category; get recommendations from people whose opinions you truStreet

Keep in mind that technology advances very rapidly. Books and software programs are upgraded frequently, and superb resources of today often succumb to newer and better technologies within a relatively short time. In the computer industry especially (but not uniquely), products often appear and disappear within a few years. You can be left without further support for a product and without appropriate upgrades as system requirements change. The demise of a product is not necessarily a reflection of its quality. Some very useful products have disappeared after only a brief existence, presumably for "market" reasons. It is in your interest to check into the history and stability of a vendor prior to making an expensive purchase. Before using the services of any vendor, investing money to purchase any product, or committing time to learning to use the product, it is important to get advice from colleagues who may be familiar with the product, and/or read reviews of the vendor and the product.

All addresses, phone numbers, and prices, where listed, were verified in summer/fall 1993. Prices given in this Appendix are subject to change without notice. Where included, their purpose is simply to give you some idea of the magnitude of the cost of the product.

Because there may be future editions of this book and because clients and people who attend my workshops sometimes ask me to recommend resources, I would welcome readers' recommendations of items to add to this liStreet In addition, I welcome receiving desk copies of books and Macintosh software from publishers that might be useful for my readers and workshop audiences. Because I am not an IBM user, I would especially appreciate recommendations about DOS and Windows programs that users have found particularly helpful. Between publication of this book and a possible future edition, I will try to list interesting new resources in my workshop outlines or perhaps even as an insert in future printings of the current edition of this book.

BOOKS AND ARTICLES ABOUT GETTING GRANTS AND WRITING GRANT PROPOSALS

Adelstein, S. J., "Preparing A Grant Proposal," *Invest Radiol*, Vol. 22, 1987, pages 250–252.
Bauer, D. R., *The "How To" Grants Manual: Successful Grantseeking Techniques For Obtaining Public and Private Grants,* 2nd ed., American Council on Education, Series on Higher Education, Oryx Press, Phoenix, AZ, 1993.

Burns, M. E., *Proposal Writer's Guide,* Development and Technical Assistance Center, Hartford, CT, 1989. 35 pages. Available from DATA, Inc. Publication Department, 70 Audubon Street, New Haven, CT 06510; 203-772-1345.

Geever, J. C., and McNeill, P., *The Foundation Center's Guide to Proposal Writing,* The Foundation Center, New York, 1993.

Advice on how to create a funding request; how to research, contact, and cultivate potential funders; how to fine-tune each part for different proposals. Includes excerpts from actual grant proposals, including cover letters, project descriptions, and budgets. $29.95 ($4.00 P&H). Available from the Foundation Center, 79 Fifth Avenue, New York, NY 10003-3076; 1-800-424-9836, 212-620-4230; Fax: 212-807-3677.

Gordon, S. L., "Ingredients of a Successful Grant Application to the National Institutes of Health," *J Orthop Res,* Vol. 7, 1989, pages 138–141.

Grantsmanship: Money and How to Get It, 2nd ed, Marquis Academic Media, Marquis Who's Who, Chicago, 1978.

Hill, W. J., *Successful Grantsmanship,* 4th ed., Grant Development Institute, Steamboat Springs, CO, 1980.

Hogan, A. R., "Few Applicants Appeal Denial of Grants," *The Scientist,* Vol. 1, No. 15, June 15, 1987, page 1.

Hoke, F., "Computer Aids Help Find and Manage Research Grants," *The Scientist,* Vol. 8, No. 11, May 30, 1994, page 17.

Kiritz, N. J., and Mundel, J., *Program Planning and Proposal Writing* (Introductory version), The Grantsmanship Center, Los Angeles, CA, 1988.

An 11-page article about writing proposals to foundations. Includes examples of budgets and budget justifications. Available from Associated Grantmakers of Massachusetts, Inc., 294 Washington Street, Suite 840, Boston, MA 02108; 617-426-2606; Fax: 617-426-2849; or Grantsmanship Center, 1125 West 6th Street, 5th Floor, P.O. Box 17220, Los Angeles, CA 90017; 213-482-9860; Fax: 213-482-9863. Expanded version: 48 pages. $4 from L.A. (include $2 for P&H). To register for Grantsmanship Center workshops: 1-800-421-9512.

Krathwohl, D. R., *How to Prepare a Research Proposal: Guidelines for Funding and Dissertations in the Social and Behavioral Sciences,* 3rd ed., 1988. Distributed by Syracuse University Press, 1600 Jamesville Ave., Syracuse, NY 13244-5160; 1-800-365-8929, 315-443-2597.

Kurzig, C. M., *Foundation Fundamentals: A Guide for Grant Seekers,* The Foundation Center, New York, 1981.

Locke, L. F., Spirduso, W. W., and Silverman, S. J., *Proposals That Work: A Guide for Planning Dissertations and Grant Proposals,* 3rd ed., Sage Publications, 1993. Sage Publications, 2455 Teller Rd., Thousand Oaks, CA 91320-2218.

Lucas, Robert A., *The Grants World Inside Out,* University of Illinois Press, Urbana and Chicago, 1992.

A humorous view of the grants world.

Making the Grant Process Work: A Collection of Federal Administration Guidelines

Contains government guidelines; information on cost principles, audits, and indirect cost rates; rules on maintaining a drug-free workplace and nonprocurement debarment and suspension. New Edition, 1993, $73. Capitol Publications, 1101 King Street, P.O. Box 1454, Alexandria, VA 22313-2054; 1-800-221-0425, 703-739-6444.

Margolin, J. B., *The Individual's Guide to Grants,* Plenum Press, New York, 1983.

Detailed guidance on how to identify and approach sponsors, how to write a proposal, and how to follow up if your application is turned down.

Margolin, J. B., *Foundation Fundamentals,* 4th ed., The Foundation Center, New York, 1991.

How to target funding sources and approach sponsors. Has a chapter on corporate grants.

Meader, R., *Guidelines For Preparing Proposals*, 2nd ed., Lewis Publishers, Boca Raton, FL, 1992; $27.00 Available from CRC Press, 2000 Corporate Blvd., Boca Raton, FL 33431; 407-994-0555.

Review of 1st ed.: Harold Waters, Deputy Chief for Referral in the NIH Division of Research Grants (DRG), in *Chemical and Engineering News*, June 3, 1985, page 53.

Ogden, T. E., *Research Proposals: A Guide to Success*, Raven Press, New York, 1991. See also correspondence by D.B. Northrup and the author (T.E. Ogden) in *FASEB Journal*, Vol. 5, 1991, pages 2486-2487.

Pocket Proposal Style Manual: For Writers and Editors of Government Proposals, 2nd ed., Tekne Press, Inc., Chapel Hill, NC, 1989, 65 pages, $12.95. Available from Ross Pipes and Associates, Inc., 400 South Elliott Rd., Chapel Hill, NC 27514, 1-800-326-0781, 919-933-5111.

Reif-Lehrer, L., *Writing a Successful Grant Application*, 2nd ed., Jones and Bartlett Publishers, Boston, MA, 1989.

Reif-Lehrer, L., "Confessions of an NIH Grant Proposal Reviewer," *The Scientist*, Sept. 5, 1988, page 19.

Reif-Lehrer, L., "Going for the Gold: Some Dos and Don'ts for Grant Seekers," *The Scientist*, Apr. 3, 1989, page 15.

This article was reprinted by NIAAA as a brochure to send to potential applicants. A new brochure, updated by Liane Reif-Lehrer in 1994, was issued in November 1994.

Reif-Lehrer, L., "Dissecting and Demystifying an NIH Grant Application," *The Scientist*, Sept. 18, 1989, page 19.

Reif-Lehrer, L., "Increasing Your Odds of a Granted Future," *SCI/GRANTS News*; Oct., 1989, page 5.

Reif-Lehrer, L., "An NIH Site Visit Need Not Provoke a Tension Headache," *The Scientist*, Sept. 17, 1990, page 23.

Reif-Lehrer, L, "Tips for Applying to Private Foundations for Grant Money," *The Scientist*, Sept. 16, 1991, page 20.

Reif-Lehrer, L., "Teaching Good Communication/Proposal-Writing Skills: Overcoming One Deficit of Our Educational System," *Journal of Science Education and Technology*, Vol. 1, No. 3, 1992, pages 211–219.

Schumacher, D., *Get Funded! A Practical Guide for Scholars Seeking Research Support from Business*, Sage Publications, 1992, 304 pages, $39.95 (hardcover); $18.95 (paperback). Available from Sage Publications, Inc., P.O. Box 5084, Thousand Oaks, CA 91320-2218; 805-499-0721; Fax: 805-499-0871.

Schumacher, D., "Getting Grants from Industry Requires Partnership Approach," *The Scientist*, Sept. 14, 1992, page 21.

Schwartz, S. M. and Friedman, M. E., *A Guide to NIH Grant Programs*, Oxford University Press, New York, 1992, 296 pages, $39.95.

See also review by Daniel E. Atkinson, *Science*, Vol. 261, July 23, 1993, pages 498–499.

Small Business Innovation Research Programs: Funding to Finance Your Ideas, 1991, $10. Available from KPMG Peat Marwick, P.O. Box 23331, Newark, NJ 07189; 201-307-7892; Fax: 201-307-8071.

Trumbo, B. E., "How to Get Your First Research Grant," *Statistical Science*, Vol. 4, 1989, pages 121-130.

Emphasis is on applications to NSF.

Wallen, D., *In $earch of Funding*, 1990, $34.95. Available from University of New Mexico, Office of Research Administration, Scholes Hall 102, Albuquerque, NM 87131; 505-277-2256.

> A 30-minute videotape and accompanying booklet about grant-getting strategies, identifying funding sources, writing proposals, etc.

White, V., *Grant Proposals that Succeeded*, Plenum Press, New York, 1983.

White, V. P., *Grants: How to Find Out About Them and What to Do Next*, Plenum Press, New York, 1979.

> Lots of good information, but some of the agencies listed no longer seem to exist.

BOOKS ABOUT WRITING AND EDITING

Cook, C.K., *Line by Line: How To Edit Your Own Writing*, Houghton Mifflin, Boston, 1985.
> 219 pages, indexed. Hardback, $14.95.

Day, R.A., *How to Write and Publish a Scientific Paper*, 3rd ed., Oryx Press, Phoenix, AZ, 1988.
> 211 pages. Paperback. Contains good advice for scientists who write research papers; also contains some marvelous Snoopy cartoons.

Graham, B.F., *Five Fast Steps to Better Writing*, Opus Mundi, Ottawa, Ontario, Canada, 1985.
> 103 pages of writing tips. Paperback, $3.95.

Hawkins, S., and Sorgi, M., *Research: How to Plan, Speak and Write About It*, Springer-Verlag, New York, 1985; 1-800-777-4643.

Manhard, S.J., *The Goof-Proofer*, Collier Books, Macmillan Publishing Co., New York, 1987.
> An 84-page book on common errors in English usage. Paperback.

Ross-Larson, B. *Edit Yourself: A Manual for Everyone Who Works With Words*, W.W. Norton & Co., New York, 1982.
> Lots of useful advice about how to achieve brevity.

Shertzer, M., *The Elements of Grammar*, Collier Books, Macmillan Publishing Co., New York, 1986.

Strunk, W., Jr., and White, E. B. *The Elements of Style*, 3rd ed., Macmillan, New York, 1979.
> A 92-page, indexed book on English usage. A classic. Paperback, $2.95.
>
> Also available on disk from Microlytics, Inc., 2 Tobey Village Office Park, Pittsford, NY, 14534; 716-248-9150; Fax: 716-248-5659. Sales only: 1-800-828-6293.

Thornton, R., *Lexicon Of Intentionally Ambiguous Recommendations (LIAR)*, Meadowbrook, distributed by Simon & Schuster, New York, 1988.
> A 108-page, humorous paperback book about the ambiguities of the English language. Although the humor is of uneven quality, at its best it is very funny—and is a wonderful illustration of English usage to avoid when writing grant proposals. The book is no longer in print, but may still be available from the Lehigh University Bookstore, 215-758-3375, for $4.95 plus shipping.

Tichy, H.J., *Effective Writing for Engineers, Managers, Scientists*, 2nd ed., John Wiley & Sons, New York, 1988.
> See also an excerpt from the book in *The Scientist*, Oct. 31, 1988, page 18.

ARTICLES AND BOOKS THAT MAY BE OF INTEREST TO RESEARCHERS AND GRANT APPLICATION WRITERS

Anderson, C., "NSF's New Random Inspections Draw Fire," *Science*, Vol. 261, July 16, 1993, page 289.

"Conference on Plagiarism," *ASBMB News*, Summer 1993, page 6.

"FASEB Seeks Assistance from Deans, Editors in Getting Credit for NIH," *FASEB Newsletter*, Vol. 26, No. 6, September/October 1993, page 6.

Garfield, E., "Citation Searches Can Be Powerful Tools in Combating Redundant Publication," *The Scientist*, April 19 1993, page 12.

Hawkins, C., and Sorgi, M., *Research: How to Plan, Speak and Write About It*, Springer-Verlag, Berlin, 1985; 1-800-777-4643.

Hoke, F., "Bibliography-Building Software Eases A 'Cruel' Task," *The Scientist*, January 11, 1993, page 18.

Hoke, F., "Scientific Graphing Software Tools Fill Important Niche," *The Scientist*, June 14, 1993, page 18.

Kaufman, R., "Biotech Job Fairs—A New Method of Searching for Research Employment," *The Scientist*, June 14, 1993, page 8.

Mansfield, E., "How Do We Measure What We Get When We 'Buy' Research," *The Scientist*, August 19, 1991, page 11.

Meyer, K. A., "How Well Do Grantsmanship Guides Address the Literature Review?" *SRA Journal*, Vol. 20, No. 3, Winter 1988, pages 29–33.

Reif-Lehrer, L., "Suggestions for Saving Your Time—And Keeping Your Cool," *The Scientist*, Sept. 5, 1988, page 19.

Reif-Lehrer, L., "Using New Science Resources: A Key to Staying Competitive," *The Scientist*, Oct. 30, 1989, page 22.

Reif-Lehrer, L., "For Today's Scientist, Skill in Public Speaking Is Essential," *The Scientist*, May 14, 1990, page 25.

Reif-Lehrer, L., "Promoting Yourself Is Key to Climbing Academic Ladder," *The Scientist*, July 20, 1992, page 20. (See also related letters to the editor: *The Scientist*, Sept. 14, 1992, page 11.)

Reif-Lehrer, L., "Science's Golden Rule: Give Back to the Community," *The Scientist*, Dec. 7, 1992, page 21. (See also Commentary by Eugene Garfield on page 12.)

Reif-Lehrer, L., "Effective Teaching Is a Skill That Researchers Can Learn," *The Scientist*, June 28, 1993, page 20.

Rosovsky, H., *The University: An Owners Manual*, W. W. Norton & Co., New York, 1990.

Survival Skills for Scholars. A series of books by different authors with titles such as *Getting Tenure, Improving Writing Skills*, and *Coping with Faculty Stress*, Sage Publications, 2455 Teller Rd., Thousand Oaks, CA 91320-2218, 1993.

Verba, C., *Graduate Guide to Grants*. $22 + $3 P&H. Available from GSAS, Harvard University, Byerly Hall, 8 Garden Street, Cambridge, MA 02138; 617-495-1814; Fax: 617-495-2928.

> Annual publication of Harvard Graduate School of Arts and Sciences. Designed to assist graduate students in locating grants and fellowships that are applicable to the wide range of fields represented in the arts and sciences.

Verba, C., *Harvard Guide to Postdoctoral Fellowships*. $5 + $3 P&H. Available from GSAS, Harvard University, Byerly Hall, 8 Garden Street, Cambridge, MA 02138; 617-495-1814; Fax: 617-495-2928.

> Annual publication of Harvard Graduate School of Arts and Sciences. For new PhDs and individuals at a relatively early stage of an academic career or independent scholarship career.

Verba, C., *Scholarly Pursuits: A Practical Guide to Academe*, 3rd ed., Harvard University, 1993. $5 +$3 P&H. Available from GSAS, Harvard University, Byerly Hall, 8 Garden Street, Cambridge, MA 02138; 617-495-1814; Fax: 617-495-2928.

> Practical advice on professional development at each juncture on the path to an academic career: applying for fellowships, getting works published, seeking the initial teaching position or postdoctoral fellowship.

Wolpert, L., "Science's Negative Public Image: A Puzzling and Dissatisfying Matter," *The Scientist*, June 14, 1993, page 11.

Yien, C., "Building United States—Asia Scientific Exchange," *Science*, Vol. 262, October 15, 1993, page 367.

ABOUT PEER REVIEW

The first 3 publications listed below are out of print; check the library.

Grants Peer Review: Report to the Director, NIH, Phase I, December, 1976. U.S. Government Printing Office, 1977-241/161/3032.

Decisions by the Director, NIH, on Recommendations of Grants Peer Review Study Team, February 8, 1978.

Opinions on the NIH Grants Peer Review System, Phase II of the Report to the Director, NIH by the NIH Grants Peer Review Study Team, December, 1978. U.S. Government Printing Office: 1979-281–217/3138.

Charrow, R. P., Esq., "The Legal System Confronts Peer Review: Is a Tradition About to Be Breached?" *Journal of NIH Research*, Vol. 5, November, 1993, pages 90–92.

Cohen, J., "Study Sections: Does a Superb System Need a Tune-Up?" *Science*, Vol. 261, September 24, 1993, pages 1678–1679.

GAO (U.S. General Accounting Office) conducted a questionnaire study of Federal peer review systems in 1992. The results of the study were published in June 1994 (GAO/PEMD-94-1). The title is: *Peer Review: Reforms Needed to Ensure Fairness in Federal Agency Grant Selection*. For further information, call Mr. Patrick Grasso, Assistant Director, Program Evaluation and Methodology Division, GAO, 202-512-2900 or Mr. Dan Rodriguez, 202-512-3827; Fax: 202-512-2622.

Green, J.G., Calhoun, F., Nierzwicki, L., Brackett, J. and Meier, P., "Rating Intervals: An Experiment in Peer Review," *FASEB J*, Vol. 3, 1989, pages 1987–1992.

Henley, C., "Peer Review of Research Grant Applications at National Institutes Of Health," *Federation Proceedings*, Vol. 36, 1977, 2066–2068, 2186–2190, 2335–2338.

Marshall, E., "Varmus: The View from Bethesda," *Science*, Vol. 262, November 26, 1993, pages 1364–1366.

McCarthy, P., "Peer Review Comes Under Scrutiny in Biomedicine," *The Scientist*, May 30, 1994, page 1. (About peer review of journal articles.)

"NASA Needs to Improve Peer Review System for Life Sciences Research," *FASEB Newsletter*, Vol. 26, No. 6, September/October, 1993, page 2.

"Peer Review Goes Under the Microscope," Meeting Briefs, *Science*, Vol. 262, October 1, 1993, pages 25–26.

Raloff, J., "Revamping Peer Review: The National Science Foundation Will Allow More Peering into its Reviews," *Science News*, Vol. 137, April 14, 1990, page 234.

Sanders, H. J., "Peer Review: How Well Is It Working?" *Chemical & Engineering News*, March 15, 1982, pages 32–43.

Seiken, J., "Journal Referees Report That Authors Call Many of the Shots," *The Scientist*, August 19,1991, page 18.

Seiken, J., "A Reviewer's Eye View of Evaluation Processes at NIH, NSF," *The Scientist*, March 2, 1992, page 19.

Zurer, P., "NIH Pondering Further Changes in Grant Approval Process," *Chemical & Engineering News*, July 25, 1994, pages 20–21.

FOR WOMEN IN SCIENCE

ASBMB Directory of Women Scientists, 1993–94. Available free from ASBMB Public Affairs Office, 9650 Rockville Pike, Bethesda, MD 20814-3996; 301-530-7147; Fax: 301-571-1824.

Gornick, V., *Women in Science: Portraits from a World in Transition*, Simon & Schuster, New York, 1983.

Holloway, M., "A Lab of Her Own (Trends in the Sociology of Science)," *Scientific American*, Vol. 269, No. 5, November 1993, pages 94–103.

Silverman, E. R., "New NSF Report on Salaries of Ph.D.s Reveals Gender Gaps in All Categories," *The Scientist*, August 19, 1991, page 20.

REFERENCE BOOKS

Authors Guide to Biomedical Journals: Complete Manuscript Submission Instructions for 185 Leading Biomedical Periodicals, Mary Ann Liebert, Inc., 1651 Third Ave., New York, NY 10128; 1-800-654-3237, 212-289-2300; Fax: 212-289-4697.

CD-ROMS in Print: An International Guide to CD-ROMS, Meckler Corp., 11 Ferry Lane, West, Westport, CT, 06880; 1-800-632-5537, 203-226-6967; Fax: 1-800-858-3144. Annual publication.

Chambers Science and Technology Dictionary, P.M.B. Walker, (Ed.), Chambers, New York and Cambridge, England, 1990, ©1987.

Chicago Guide to Preparing Electronic Manuscripts: For Authors and Publishers, University of Chicago Press, Chicago, 1987. $9.95.

Concise Encyclopedia of Biochemistry, Walter de Gruyter, Berlin, New York, 1988.

Directories in Print, Gale Research, Inc., 835 Penobscot Bldg., Detroit, MI 48226; 313-961-2242.
Lists all directories printed in the United States. Updated annually.

Dictionary of Biotechnology, 2nd ed., James Coombs, Stockton Press, 49 West 24 Street, 9th Floor, New York, NY 10010.

Directory of Federal Laboratory & Technology Resources—A Guide to Services, Facilities and Expertise, published by NTIS, Springfield, VA 22161; 703-487-4650. Reference order # PB93-100097. $65 + $3 P&H.
Lists all Federal Laboratory Technology Transfer offices, capabilities of resources, name and phone number of contact person at each facility, etc. Detailed indexes.

Encyclopedia of Associations, Gale Research, Inc., 835 Penobscot Bldg., Detroit, MI 48226; 313-961-2242.
Lists all organizations in the United States. Three volumes. Updated annually.

Gale Directory of Databases, Gale Research, Inc., 835 Penobscot Bldg., Detroit, MI, 48226; 313-961-2242.

International Dictionary of Medicine and Biology, 1986, John Wiley & Sons, Inc., 605 Third Ave., New York, NY, 10158; 212-850-6000.

McGraw-Hill CD-ROM Science and Technical Reference Set, McGraw-Hill Book Company, 11 West 19th Street, New York, NY, 10011; 212-337-5961.
A combination of the *Concise Encyclopedia of Science and Technology* and the *Dictionary of Scientific and Technical Terms.* Lets you look up a term in the dictionary while you are reading an article in the encyclopedia.

Science and Technical Books and Serials in Print, R. R. Bowker, 121 Chanlon Road, New Providence, NJ 07974.
Annual publication.

World of Learning, Europa Publications, Ltd., 18 Bedford Square, London, WC1B 3JN, England.

Lists universities and academic societies all over the world. Annual publication.

ARTICLES AND BOOKS TO HELP YOU ACCESS COMPUTER RESOURCES FOR RESEARCHERS[1]

Dern, D. P., *The Internet Guide for New Users*, McGraw-Hill, 1994, $27.95.

Estrada, S., *Connecting to the Internet*, 1993. O'Reilly & Associates, Inc., 103 Morris Street, Suite A, Sebastopol, CA 95472. $15.95.

Fisher, S., *Riding the Internet Highway*, New Riders Publishing, Carmel, IN, 1993.

Fraase, M., *The Mac Internet Tour Guide: Cruising the Internet the Easy Way*, Ventana Press, 1993, $27.95 with disk. Also available: *The PC Internet Tour Guide and The Windows Internet Tour Guide,* 1994, $24.95 each with disk. 1-800-743-5369.

Gilbert, D., "The Global Library," *Trends in Biochemical Sciences (TIBS)*, Vol. 18, No. 3, March 1993, pages 107–108.

About Internet services for scientists.

Gilster, P., *The Internet Navigator: A New User's Guide to Network Exploration*, John Wiley & Sons, 1993. $24.95.

Internet World Magazine, bimonthly, Meckler Corp, 11 Ferry Lane, West, Westport, CT 06880; 1-800-632-5537, 203-226-6967; Fax: 1-800-858-3144. $4.95/issue.

Kehoe, B., *Zen and the Art of the Internet: A Beginner's Guide to the Internet*, 2nd ed., Prentice-Hall, New York, 1992.

Krol, E., *The Whole Internet User's Guide and Catalog*, 1992, O'Reilly & Associates, Inc., 103 Morris Street, Suite A, Sebastopol, CA 95472.

LaQuey, T., *Internet Companion: A Beginner's Guide To Global Networking*, Addison Wesley, Reading, MA, 1993.

Marine, A., Kirkpatrick, S., and Neou, V. (Eds.), *Internet: Getting Started*, PTR Prentice-Hall, 1993. $28.

Margolis, P. E., *Random House Personal Computer Dictionary*, Random House, New York, 1991. $10.

Paperback, 512 pages, over 1,500 entries.

Smith, R. J., and Gibbs, M., *Navigating the Internet*, Sams Publishing, Carmel, IN, 1993. $24.95.

User's Guide to Gopher at NIH. Available from NIH DCRT Project Control Office, Bldg.12A, Room 3009, Bethesda, MD 20892. July 1993.

24-pages. Explains what NIH Gopher is and how to use it.

NEWSLETTERS AND PERIODICALS

Many of the commercial publications are expensive. Check your library or Office for Sponsored Research/Office for Grants and Contracts.

Many government agencies publish newsletters and other publications that provide insights into the activities of the agency. Many of these publications are free of charge. For example, the Agency for Health Care Policy and Research (AHCPR) publishes a monthly newsletter called *Research Activities*. (References cited in the newsletter can be obtained

---

[1] Some of the references in the list below were taken from an article, "Getting Your Feet Wet in a Sea Called Internet," by L. R. Shannon, *New York Times*, Tuesday, October 26, 1993, page C9.

from the agency or purchased from NTIS.) Many components of NIH publish a large number of information booklets.

ASBMB News
A quarterly publication of the American Society for Biochemistry and Molecular Biology. Sent to members.

ASBMB News, ASBMB Public Affairs Officer, 9650 Rockville Pike, Bethesda, MD 20814-3996; 301-530-7147; Fax: 301-571-1824.

"The Blue Sheet"—Health Policy and Biomedical Research News of the Week
Published by F-D-C Reports, Inc. By subscription ($390/year) from Drug Research Reports, 5550 Friendship Blvd., Suite 1, Chevy Chase, MD 20815-7278; 301-657-9830; Fax: 301-656-3094 (24-hour).

Commerce Business Daily (CBD)
A daily list of U.S. Government procurement invitations, contract awards, subcontracting leads, sales of surplus property, and foreign business opportunities.

By subscription from Superintendent of Documents, U.S. Government Printing Office, Washington, DC 20402. $261/year (1st class mail); $208/year (2nd class mail). 202-512-2303; Fax: 202-512-2168.

CBD Weekly Release is a customized extract of CBD. For an annual subscription cost of $237, you will be provided with all information from the CBD in up to 5 subject categories. Contact United Communications Group, P.O. Box 90608, Washington, DC, 20077-7637; 1-800-929-4824, Ext. 223. This organization also publishes a Federal Contractor's Handbook ($29.95).

Contributions
Issued 6 times/year. A magazine focusing on fund raising, nonprofit management, and marketing. $24/year from Contributions, 634 Commonwealth Ave., Suite 201, Newton Centre, MA 02159; 617-964-2688; Fax: 617-964-4910.

Chronicle of Higher Education
A newspaper for colleges and universities and their faculty members.

Weekly (49 issues/year). $75/year. The Chronicle of Higher Education, 1255 23 Street N.W., Washington, DC 20037, 1-800-842-7817, 202-466-1200; Fax: 202-466-2078.

Chronicle of Philanthropy (The Newspaper of the Non-profit World)
Provides news of corporate and individual giving, foundations, fund raising, taxation, regulation, etc.

22 issues/year. $67.50/year. The Chronicle of Philanthropy, 1255 23 Street N.W., Washington, DC 20037; 1-800-842-7817, 202-466-1200; Fax: 202-466-2078.

FASEB Public Affairs Newsletter
Issued monthly.

Available free to members of FASEB (Federation of American Societies for Experimental Biology), 9650 Rockville Pike, Bethesda, MD 20814; 301-530-7075.

Federal Grants and Contracts Weekly——Project Opportunities in Research, Training and Service
By subscription ($369/year) from Capitol Publications, 1101 King Street, P.O. Box 1454, Alexandria, VA 22313-2054; 1-800-221-0425, 703-739-6444.

Grant Proposal News

Semimonthly (except Jan., July, Aug., and Dec.); $150/year. Available from Grants Administration News Company, P.O. Box 964, Berkeley, CA 94701.

Grantsmanship Center Magazine (formerly the *Whole Nonprofit Catalog*)

Often has valuable articles and listings for grant seekers and fund raisers. Publishes directories of fund-raising software, references, advice articles, etc.

Available free to qualified agencies from the Grantsmanship Center, 1125 West 6th Street, 5th Floor, P.O. Box 17220, Los Angeles, CA 90017; 213-482-9860; Fax: 213-482-9863.

Health Grants and Contracts Weekly –Selected Federal Project Opportunities

By subscription ($349/year) from Capitol Publications, 1101 King Street, P.O. Box 1454, Alexandria, VA 22313-2054; 1-800-221-0425, 703-739-6444.

HLB Newsletter——Reporting on Heart, Lung and Blood Disease Research Program, Policy Development

Published 24 times/year. Nathaniel Polster, editor. By subscription ($296/year) from HLB Newsletter, 821 Delaware Ave. S.W., Washington, DC 20024; 202-488-7533.

The Journal of NIH Research—Life sciences and general biomedical research and news about NIH

Free to principal investigators of *funded* NIH grants. $79.00 (for individuals) for 12 issues/year. 1444 I Street N.W., Suite 1000, Washington, DC 20005; 1-800-878-4644, (202)785-5333; Fax: 202-872-7738.

Medical Research Funding Bulletin

Reports on grants and contracts that are available from federal and private sources in the health field. 36 issues/year. $68/year.

Science Support Center, P.O. Box 7507, FDR Station, New York, NY 10150; Tel/Fax: 212-371-3398.

National Fund Raiser

"How-to" instructions for a variety of fund-raising methods. Geared mostly to development but has occasional articles about grantsmanship. 12 issues/year and working tools/supplements; $95. Includes toll-free consulting hotline.

Barnes Associates, 603 Douglas Blvd., Roseville, CA 95678; 1-800-231-4157, 916-786-7471; Fax: 916-782-2145.

NIH Week. See NIH listings.

NSF Bulletin. See NSF listings.

ORI Newsletter

Published quarterly by Office of Research Integrity (ORI), Public Health Service, Rockwall II Bldg., Suite 700, 5515 Security Lane, Rockville, MD 20852.

Science & Government Report

A science policy newsletter that deals with government activities concerning issues of science, technology, and higher education.

3736 Kanawha Street N.W., Washington, DC 20015; 1-800-522-1970; in Washington, DC: 202-244-4135, 202-785-5054. 20 issues/year, $425.

The Scientist

A newspaper for science professionals. Regular feature articles on research, profession, opinion, tools and technology, listings of "hot papers," career opportunities, scientific software directory, equipment marketplace, etc.

Published by *The Scientist*, Inc., 3600 Market Street, Suite 450, Philadelphia, PA 19104; 1-800-258-6008. By subscription (24 issues/year; $58/year) from *The Scientist*, 5615 W. Cermak Rd., Cicero, IL 60650; 1-800-593-2193; 312-762-2193. Free to members of qualified professional organizations (ask your professional organization).

Now available *free* on-line via Internet (full text, including tables, only; no graphics or photos):

Via FTP:
> Type: **ftp ds.internic.net**
> At name prompt, type: **anonymous**
> At password prompt, type: **your username@internet address**
> At next prompt, type: **cd pub/the-scientist**
>> —If you know the issue date,
>>> at prompt, type: **get the-scientist-yymmdd**
>>>> where, for example, **yymmdd** – 940920 and designates
>>>> September 20, 1994
>> —If you don't know the issue date, you can get a directory listing
>>> at prompt, type: **dir**
> Then, to select issue, type: **the-scientist-yymmdd**
> To end, type: **quit**

Via WAIS:

> Type: **telnet ds.internic.net**
> At login, type: **wais**
> At search prompt, type: **db the-scientist**
> At next search prompt, type: **query_(term/s to be searched)**
> To view a retrieved item, type: **view_(item number to be viewed)**
> To search within the issue retrieved:
>> —To search *forward* in an issue, type: **find_(term/s to be searched)**
>> —To search *backward* in an issue, type: **nfind_(term/s to be searched)**
> To end, type: **quit**
> [The help menu can be accessed at any time by typing **?** or **help?**]

Via GOPHER (on Internic (AT&T) Gopher Server):
If you don't have Gopher software on your PC, you can use AT&T's Gopher. To do this:

> At prompt type: **telnet ds.internic.net**
> At login, type: **Gopher**
> At prompt, "Terminal Type is 'unknown,'"
>> Enter a new value, and then press RETURN, that is:
>>> —if you *know* your terminal type, type: **the number of the terminal**
>>> —if you *do not know* your terminal type, type: **vt100**

In either case, *follow your entry by pressing the return key*

From the ensuing successive menus, choose:

    4. InterNic Directory and Database Services (AT&T)/

        Then choose:

    4. InterNic Database Services (Public Databases)/

        Then choose:

    5. The Scientist - Newsletter

If you have Gopher software on your personal computer:

At prompt, type: **gopher Internic.net 70**

From the ensuing successive menus, choose:

        4. InterNic Directory and Database Services (AT&T)/

Then choose:

        4. InterNic Database Services (Public Databases)/

Then choose:

        5. The Scientist - Newsletter

For further information/help contact: *The Scientist,* 1-800-258-6008.

SciTech Book News

An annotated bibliography of new books in science, technology and medicine. Emphasis is on graduate-level texts, serious scholarly treatises, and professional references.

Published monthly (10 issues/year) by Book News, Inc. $65/year for personal subscriptions.

This company also publishes *Reference and Research Book News* (published 8 times/ year; $58/year for personal subscriptions).

Both of these publications are now available on *Bowker's CD-ROM Books in Print with Book Reviews Plus.* May be available on-line in 1994. Call for information.

Book News, Inc., 5600 N.E. Hassalo Street, Portland, OR 97213; 1-800-853-8231, 503-281-9230; Fax: 503-287-4485.

Washington Fax

A daily (5 times/week) 2-page information service—by fax—that provides news about federal policy that affects research in the life sciences. $690/year. Subscription price includes interactive information service: Subscribers can call for more in-depth information about articles or to ask questions about science policy.

Washington Fax, 572 Elm Street, South Dartmouth, MA 02748; 508-999-6097; Fax: 508-994-9366.

INFORMATION ABOUT NATIONAL INSTITUTES OF HEALTH

NIH Switchboard Operator: 301-496-4000

NIH Grants Information Office: 301-594-7248

NIH Grant Line. An Electronic Bulletin Board Information System that provides access to the *NIH Guide to Grants and Contracts*, DRG Study Section rosters, listings of NIH New Grants and Awards, and other NIH information. For information about the NIH Grant Line, call Dr. John C. James, 301-594-7270.

NIH Grants Administration Information Sources: A pamphlet which includes listings of NIH personnel in central service organizations or awarding units who are responsible for grants administration. Gives their telephone numbers and building and room numbers. Revised annually in AuguStreet Available from the NIH Grants Information Office: 301-594-7248.

NIH Gopher Server, access available over Internet (tunnel to gopher @ helix.nih.gov); for information, send e-mail to Gopher@Gopher.NIH.Gov.[2] For other information about NIH Gopher Server, call Ms. Charlene Osborn, 301-496-4823.
The NIH Gopher Server provides:

1. The *NIH Guide to Grants and Contracts* in a searchable form and generally has the Guide available about a week or more before the printed version.
2. Access to CRISP data, a database of information about all *funded* NIH grants. For information, call Ms. Seu Lain Chen, 301-594-7267.
3. Access to the Johns Hopkins University Gopher Server, which has additional information about grants.

To Obtain PHS-398 Application Forms

Single copy: Grants Information Office (PHS-398), Division of Research Grants (DRG), National Institutes of Health (NIH), Westwood Bldg., Rm. 449, Bethesda, MD 20892; 301-594-7248.

Multiple copies: Office Services Section (PHS-398), Division of Research Grants (DRG), National Institutes of Health (NIH), Westwood Bldg., Rm. 436, Bethesda, MD 20892; 301-594-7378.

NIH-DRG Grants Inquiries On-line

For information about electronic access (via BITNET) to extramural program guidelines that are also available in printed form from the Grants Information Office, call 301-594-7248.

NIH Publications

Unless otherwise noted, NIH publications are available free from the Grants Information Office, Division of Research Grants, National Institutes of Health, Bldg. WW, Room 449, Bethesda, MD 20892, 301-594-7248. Note that the new PHS-398 kit (Rev. 9/94) may contain a list of publications available from the Grants Information Office and a tear-out order form to simplify ordering of publications.

Activity Codes, Organization Codes, and Definitions Used in Extramural Programs

(IMPAC: A Computer-Based Information System of the Extramural Programs at NIH/PHS) Contains Activity Codes and brief descriptions of NIH Extramural Programs. Published September 1992.

Calendar of Meetings and Events

Annual publication that lists meetings sponsored by NIH and by major medical societies and biomedical research associations.
Available from NIH Division of Public Information, 301-496–5787.

---

2 This period is to end the sentence and is *not* part of the e-mail address.

Competency Rosters of NIH Initial Review Groups: Beginning July 1, 1992

Lists IRG members by Study Section and gives each member's area(s) of competence/specialization.

The book is prepared by the Associate Director for Referral and Review and is intended for administrative use only. It is a good companion to *NIH Advisory Committees: Authority, Structure, Functions, Members.*

Director's Chairpersons Meeting: Summary Report (January 17, 1992)

Summary of meeting of Dr. Bernadine Healy with chairpersons of NIH IRGs.

Topics include how to get the best scientists as IRG members, limiting funds to individual investigators, identifying and reviewing innovative research, alternatives to the current peer review process.

DRG: Oganization and Functions

A pamphlet updated in July 1993 that shows the organizational structure of DRG and lists the DRG Study Sections, their IRG code, the relevant Review Section, and the names and phone numbers of the Scientific Review Administrators. It also indicates which SRAs are Referral Officers. This pamphlet will probably be updated in 1994 to reflect the 1994 reorganization of the DRG Referral and Review Branch.

DRG Peer Review Trends: Workload and Actions of DRG Study Sections, 1980–1990

Contains statistical information related to Study Section workload, actions, etc. Compiled by the DRG Information Systems Branch.

Grants Administration Information Sources

Listings of individuals in central service organizations/awarding units who are responsible for administration of NIH extramural programs. Revised April 1992. U.S. Government Printing Office, 1992-622-777/60150.

Information from the NIH on Grants and Contracts, October 1991

A list of books, brochures, periodicals, articles, guidelines, and application forms (many free); explains what each publication is about and where to get it. A new edition is expected in 1994.

Minorities in Extramural Grant Programs: Fiscal Year 1982–1991

An analysis of trends of participation by racial/ethnic groups in competition for NIH Extramural grants over the preceding decade in the form of charts, tables, and text.

Published by the Statistics, Analysis, and Evaluation Section, Information Systems Branch, Division of Research Grants, NIH. U.S. Government Printing Office, 1993—351-597. Will probably be updated biannually.

NIH Healthline

Consumer health information from NIH. Monthly publication of 2-to- 3-page summary articles about 3 to 5 NIH-supported research projects. Gives a sense of projects currently of interest to NIH.

NIH News and Features

(Replaces the previous *News and Features from NIH*)
Published in 2 forms:
A 5-page handout version published 6 times/year.
A 40-page magazine version published 2 times/year.
Articles, in lay language, about research activities at NIH and at some of its grantee

institutions. Published primarily for science writers, reporters, magazine writers, educators, and others who specifically request the publication.

Available free (by written request) from NIH Office of Communications, Public Information Branch, Bldg. 31, Room 2B–10, 9000 Rockville Pike, Bethesda, MD 20892; 301-496-1766; Fax: 301-402-0395.

National Institutes of Health Grants and Awards: NIH Support Mechanisms

Gives an overview, largely in the form of charts, about the programs available at each of the NIH Institutes. October 1990.

National Institutes of Health Organization Handbook

Contains organization charts and brief description of the functions of each of the Institutes, Centers, and Divisions of the NIH. NIH Manual 1123 (spiral bound), June 1993.

Available from the Division of Public Information, OD, NIH, 9000 Rockville Pike, Bldg. 31, Room 2803, Bethesda, MD 20892; 301-496-1766; Fax: 301-402-0395; and from Management Analysis Branch, Division of Management Policy, 301-496-2461.

National Institutes of Health Research Training and Career Development Programs

Lists all *intramural* and *extramural* research training and career development programs at NIH from high school through postdoctoral training. NIH 93-2273, September 1993.

Available from NIH Office of Education, Bldg. 10, Room 1C-129, 9000 Rockville Pike, Bethesda, MD 20892; 301-496-9743.

NIH Almanac

An annual publication that contains pertinent facts about the NIH, including historical data, the mission and organization and major programs of each Institute/Center/Division, biosketches of the Institute Directors, etc.

Available from the Division of Public Information, OD, NIH, 9000 Rockville Pike, Bldg. 31, Room 2803, Bethesda, MD 20892; 301-496-4143.

NIH Data Book 1992

An annual publication that contains financial information about NIH programs and related Federal and national activities. NIH Publication No. 92–1261.

NIH /ADAMHA[3] Extramural Programs: Funding for Research and Research Training

NIH Publication No. 91-33. Latest issue: August 1992. U.S. Government Printing Office, 1992-626-516-60715.

NIH Extramural Trends FY 83–92

An analysis of NIH extramural programs over the preceding decade in the form of charts, tables, and text.

NIH Publication No. 93-3506. Published November 1993. Updated annually by the Information Systems Branch, DRG, NIH.

NIH Guide for Grants and Contracts

Information about new/ongoing NIH programs, changes in policy, workshops, etc.

Published weekly by the Printing and Reproduction Branch, NIH, Room B4BN23, Bldg. 31, Bethesda, MD 20892.

Available free from NIH Guide Distribution Center, National Institutes of Health,

---

[3] The 3 research institutes of ADAMHA became part of NIH as of October 1, 1992.

Room B3BE07, Bldg. 31, Bethesda, MD 20892; 301-496-1789. Also available electronically to institutions via BITNET or INTERNET. Alternative access is through the NIH Grant Line by using a personal computer (data line 301-402-2221). Contact Dr. John James, 301-594-7270, for details, or send an e-mail message to ZNS@NIHCU.[4] Note that there is some possibility that in the future the Guide may be available *only* via electronic access.

NIH Peer Review of Research Grant Applications

This booklet is based on a set of slides prepared by the Referral and Review Branch of DRG. It gives a brief overview of the review process.

Contains a list of NIH information sources with names and phone numbers (the phone numbers are incorrect in the interim edition) and a brief list of references.

Revised February 1992. (An updated interim unbound photocopy edition is available in 1993. It is undated but contains the new voting procedures for Study Sections instituted in 1991 and has data for 1992 grant review but does not have the new telephone numbers for DRG that were assigned in 1992.) As of May 1994, there is still no new edition.

NIH Peer Review Notes

Published before each cycle of scientific review meetings to inform NIH consultants and staff about developments related to DRG and Institute review policies and procedures.

NIH Advisory Committees: Authority, Structure, Functions, Members

Contains descriptions and memberships of the committees advisory to NIH, arranged by Institute, Center, and Division served, and also has information about frequency of meetings and occasional other details. NIH Publication No. 93-10, April 1993. Updated annually. *Will be issued only on-line in the future.* Call 301-594-7265 for information about Internet and Bitnet access to Study Section rosters.

For other questions contact the Committee Management Office, National Institutes of Health (NIH), Bldg. 31, Room 3B-55, Bethesda, MD 20892; 301-496-2123; Fax: 301-496-1567.

---

[4] Note added at press time about the *NIH Guide for Grants and Contracts Electronic Distribution List* (taken from *NIH Guide,* Vol. 23, No. 20, May 27, 1994, pages 1–2. LISTSERV distribution of the NIH Guide:

1. NIHGDE-L is now an open list.

The NIHGDE-L list is now open for subscriptions from individuals. To minimize the possibility of errors, it is best for each person to subscribe him/herself to the list. Subscribing and unsubscribing to/from a list is done via e-mail. BITNET users should send mail to LISTSERV@JHUVM, and Internet users to LISTSERV@JHUVM.HCF.JHU.EDU. To subscribe to the E-Guide list, the text of the mail should be:

SUBSCRIBE NIHGDE-L First-name Last-name

The First & Last names should be in upper & lower case; e.g.:

SUBSCRIBE NIHGDE-L Bill Jones

This will register the e-mail address from which the mail was sent for E-Guide distribution. If you wish to have the E-Guide sent to an address from which mail cannot be sent (e.g., an internal distribution list), send mail to WKJ@NIHCU (BITNET) or WKJ@CU.NIH.GOV (Internet). To remove yourself from this list, send mail to LISTSERV@JHUVM (or LISTSERV@JHUVM.HCF.JHU.EDU) containing as the text: UNSUBSCRIBE NIHGDE-L

2. Table of Contents list established.

Some users who subscribed to the NIHGDE-L list had problems with the volume of mail that was received each week. They would prefer to see a table of contents, and access the NIH Guide files via Gopher when necessary. For that purpose, the NIHTOC-L list has been established at the NIH. It will contain only the table of contents for each week's NIH Guide. It is an open list that one can subscribe to by sending mail to LISTSERV@NIHLIST or LISTSERV@LIST.NIH.GOV (Internet). The mail should contain as text:

SUBSCRIBE NIHTOC-L First-name Last-name

If you do subscribe to the NIHTOC-L list and are already subscribed to the NIHGDE-L list, you will probably want to UNSUBSCRIBE from that list.

INQUIRIES: Myra Brockett, Institutional Affairs Office, National Institutes of Health, Building 1, Room 328, Bethesda, MD 20892; Email: Q2C@NIHCU or Q2C@CU.NIH.GOV

Orientation Handbook for Members of Scientific Review Groups, **November 1983; Interim revision: March 1992.**
Information about the peer review process for members of Study Sections. Has bibliography on peer review.

See also the document reproduced in Appendix I-D-1 of this book entitled *Guide for Assigned Reviewers' Preliminary Comments on Research Grant Applications (R01).*

Preparing a Research Grant Application to the National Institutes of Health
Fifteen selected articles by NIH staff.

May 1987; revised October 1993.

PHS Grants Policy Statement
Department of Health and Human Services (DHHS) Publication No. (OASH) 90-50,000 (Rev. October 1, 1990). A photocopy update, dated 9/1/91, is available.

Small Business Innovation Research (SBIR) Grant Applications
Department of Health and Human Services
Document PHS 93–2 (U.S. Government Printing Office, 1993–717-094/60949)

For information, contact Research Training and Special Programs Office, National Institutes of Health, Bldg. 31, Room 5B44, Bethesda, MD 20892; 301-496-1968.

Women in Extramural Grant Programs: Fiscal Year 1982–1991
An analysis of the success of women in participation/competition for NIH extramural grants over the preceding decade in the form of charts, tables, and text.

Developed by the Statistics, Analysis, and Evaluation Section, Information Systems Branch, DRG, NIH.

National Institutes of Health Grants and Awards: NIH Funding Mechanisms
Gives an overview, largely in the form of charts, about the programs available at each of the NIH Institutes. September 1993.

National Institutes of Health New Grants and Awards
Gives grant numbers, titles, principal investigators, institutions, dollars awarded, etc.

Four quarterly volumes. Arranged by state, city, and institution. Prepared by Information Systems Branch, Division of Research Grants, National Institutes of Health, Bethesda, MD 20892.

No longer available on paper. Available on-line via NIH Bulletin Board.

National Institutes of Health Postdoctoral Research Fellowship Opportunities Catalog
Describes the missions of the Institute and Center programs to which candidates may apply. NIH Publication 91-213. Prepared by National Institutes of Health, Office of Education, Bldg. 10, Room 1C-129, 9000 Rockville Pike, Bethesda, MD 20892; 301-496-2427.

National Institutes of Health RESEARCH Grants (Fiscal year Funds)
Referred to as the "Brown" books. An annual compilation of *National Institutes of Health New grants and awards.* Prepared by Information Systems Branch, Division of Research Grants, National Institutes of Health, Bethesda, MD 20892. No longer available on paper. Will be available via NIH Gopher, probably by 1994.

NIH RFP's Streamlined
For information, see *NIH Guide for Grants and Contracts,* Vol. 22, No. 12, March 26, 1993, page 2, or contact Division of Contracts and Grants, NIH, Bldg. 31, Room 1B19, Bethesda, MD 20892; 301-496-6014.

A large number and variety of NIH Institute-specific publications

Many of these are free, and you can request to be on the mailing liStreet For example, *NIGMS Research Reports* (301-496-7301) is designed to inform readers about what the grantees of the Institute of General Medical Sciences are doing. The publication lists a sampling of recent NIGMS grant awards and gives a brief sketch of 3 or 4 NIGMS-funded research projects that have yielded interesting results. *NIGMS is the only entirely extramural NIH Institute,* but many other Institutes provide a variety of publications that can give you a sense about their research interests and priorities.

INFORMATION ABOUT NATIONAL SCIENCE FOUNDATION

NSF Information Center:	703-306-1234
NSF Graduate Fellowship Program	703-306-1694
NSF Policy Office	703-306-1241

For information about new telephone numbers at NSF in Arlington, VA, send a fax to: "Attention: NSF Information Center, 703-306-0250." Include your fax number. NSF will fax back the new correct telephone numbers.

STIS (NSF Science and Technology Information System) gives electronic access to NSF program announcements, the *NSF Bulletin* and other information about NSF, 703-306-0214. For detailed information, see Appendix VIII-A.

NSF Outreach Service

NSF staff members are available on a limited basis to give orientations about NSF funding opportunities, especially at institutions that are not major recipients of NSF funds. Requests should be made *in writing* to: Mr. Patrick M. Olmert, NSF Outreach Coordinator, External Affairs Section, NSF Office of Legislative and Public Affairs, 4201 Wilson Blvd., Arlington, VA 22230.

NSF Publications

NSF publications are available from NSF Forms and Publications Unit, 4201 Wilson Boulevard, Arlington, VA 22230; 703-306-1130; Fax: 703-644-4278; Voice-mail: 703-306-1128; E-mail: pubs@nsf.gov (Internet); pubs@NSF (BITNET)

Requests must include NSF publication number, title, number of copies needed, your name, and a *complete* mailing address. Publications should be received within 3 weeks after ordering.

Unless otherwise noted, all publications in the list of NSF publications are available free from the NSF Forms and Publications Unit, 4201 Wilson Boulevard, Arlington, VA 22230.

FY 1993 Budget Overview: National Science Foundation

Budgets and budget requests for the individual NSF directorates and funding levels by program.

International Opportunities for Scientists and Engineers (NSF 93-51)

NSF Division of International Programs. U.S. scientists and engineers may request support from international programs for activities in the following broad categories: (1) research collaborations that include cooperative research, joint seminars and workshops, and planning visits to work out details of joint projects and (2) international research experiences for junior scientists that include postdoctoral and junior investigator research fellowships, dissertation enhancement awards, and summer institutes for graduate students.

National Science Foundation Annual Report
Issued annually about midyear. Covers activities of the previous fiscal year.

National Science Foundation (NSF) Bulletin
Issued monthly except July and AuguStreet News about NSF programs, deadlines for grant application submissions, meetings, and sources of additional information.

National Science Foundation: Grant General Conditions
General information about the responsibilities and requirements related to NSF grant programs.

National Science Foundation: Grant Policy Manual
Information about the NSF grant process, proposers, and grantees. Updated periodically. NSF 93-213. Available for $26 from Superintendent of Documents, U.S. Government Printing Office, Washington, DC 20402; 202-783-3238.

National Science Foundation: Grant Proposal Guide (GPG)
Contains application forms and instructions for applying for an NSF grant. Document NSF 94-2.

The *Grant Proposal Guide* (GPG), NSF 94-2, replaced *Grants for Research and Education in Science and Engineering* (GRESE), NSF 92-89 (October 1992), in early 1994.

National Science Foundation: Guide to Programs, Fiscal Year 1994
Document NSF 93–167
Changes in programs listed in the booklet are announced in the *NSF Bulletin*.

NSF's Financial Management Status Report and Five-Year Plan for FYs 1992–1996
NSF 92-103. Out of print.

NSF-INRIA Collaborative Research
Guidelines for special collaborative program with the French National Institute for Research in Computer Science and Applied Mathematics (NSF 93-104). NSF Division of International Programs.

NSF's Research Opportunities for Women Program: An Assessment of the First Three Years
Summary of a study of the effectiveness of the NSF Research Opportunities for Women (ROW) Program. Written by NSF Program Evaluation Staff. NSF 90-13, January 1990.

Program announcements for a variety of programs to enhance training and research opportunities for teachers, undergraduate students, and undergraduate faculty.
For publications about specific programs, call the NSF general information number.

Proposal Review at NSF: Perceptions of Principal Investigators
Report of a survey by NSF's Program Evaluation Staff. NSF Report 88–4, February 1988 (Rev. 4-90).

Publications of the National Science Foundation
A list of publications produced by NSF. Most of them are free. NSF 92-143 (OMB No. 3145-0058).

Report of the Merit Review Task Force (NSF)

Report of a comprehensive examination of the traditional NSF mechanism for making choices about distribution of available funding (the merit review system). Recommendations for changes to the system. NSF 90-113, August 23, 1990.

Small Business Innovation Research (SBIR) Grants—NSF

Program solicitation. Contains eligibility requirements, instructions, and application forms for applying for a Phase I SBIR Award. Also contains research topic descriptions and *a sample of a successful Phase I proposal.* Document NSF 93-18 (OMB No. 3145-0058).

For information, write: ATTN: SBIR, National Science Foundation Forms and Publications Unit.

Recorded information hotline: 1-800-999-7973.

Hotline about national SBIR conferences: 407-791-0720.

Summary of Awards

Each of the Divisions within the NSF Directorates publishes an annual *Summary of Awards.* These booklets also contain information about the disciplinary research programs within the division.

SUPPORT for Research Visits and Postdoctoral Study in Japan, the Former Soviet Union, and Other Countries

NSF supports a variety of programs for training and research in other countries. For publications about specific programs, call the NSF general information number.

Track Record of NSF's Proposal Review

NSF 91-81. Out of print.

INFORMATION ABOUT OTHER GOVERNMENT AGENCIES

Contract Research and Technology Program (Guide to Programs), Office of Naval Research (ONR–1)

The guide describes grants and contracts available through the Office of Naval Research (ONR).

In addition to other programs, ONR has a Biological Sciences Division with programs in Molecular Biology and Cellular Biology; ONR also has a Psychological Sciences Division.

Available from Office of Naval Research, 800 N. Quincy Street, Arlington, VA 22217; Guide: 703-696-4108; Technical Director's Office: 703-696-4517.

Unsolicited Proposal Guide: Air Force Systems Command

For *Research Interest Brochure* and *Proposer's Guide*, write or call Air Force Office of Scientific Research, Bolling Air Force Base, Washington, DC 20332; 202-767-4912. Director's Office: 202-767-5017. Life Sciences Directorate: 202-767-4278.

U.S. Army Research Office Program Guide

For Biosciences Research Program that supports basic research in the biological sciences, exclusive of medical, behavioral, and social science research. No deadlines; review activity is ongoing. Contact: Ms. Shirley R. Tove, Head, Biology Branch, Chemistry and Biological Sciences Division, Army Research Office, P.O. Box 12211, Research Triangle Park, NC 27709-2211; 919-549-4344, 919-549–4214, 919-549-0641; Fax: 919-549-4288.

U.S. Department of Agriculture, Competitive Research Grants Program

For information, write or call Grants Administrative Management, Office of Grants and Program Systems (OGPS), U.S. Department of Agriculture, Aerospace Center, Ag Box 2241, Room 323, 901 D Street S.W., Washington, DC 20250-2241; 202-401-5022. To locate other USDA departments, call USDA Locator: 202-720-8732.

U.S. Department of Energy, Office of Energy Research, Application and Guide for the Special Research Grant Program

Revised periodically; last revised in 1993.

    Available from DOE Contracts and Grants Office, 301-903-5544.

    For other information, write or call U.S. Department of Energy, Office of Energy Research, Washington, DC 20585; 202-586–5430.

    Scientific programs include

Biological Energy	301-353-2873
Chemical Sciences	301-353-5804
Ecological Research	301-353-4208
Health Effects Research	301-353-5468
Human Health and Assessments	301-353-5355

Strategic Environmental Research Defense Program (SERDP)

A federal program set up in 1990 to help solve the defense-related environmental problems of the nation by funding environmental research. A goal of the SERDP is to transfer technology—in both directions—between government agencies and the commercial/private sector (including universities). The program is a joint effort of the Department of Defense, Department of Energy, and the Environmental Protection Agency. To be eligible, projects must be of interest to one of these 3 agencies and must be related to defense needs. National Oceanic and Atmospheric Administration (NOAA) helps to oversee the program. An information packet is available from Dr. Robert Oswald, Ph.D., Director of Research and Development, U.S. Army Corps of Engineers, and Executive Director of SERDP, 202-272-0254.

INFORMATION FOR CLINICIAN RESEARCHERS

Some medical professional organizations give grants and awards. For example, there is a joint American Academy of Family Physicians Foundation (AAFP/F) and American Academy of Family Physicians (AAFP) grant awards program that supports various research projects in family medicine/practice. Most grant awards are for one- to two-year projects for under $20,000. They also administer several smaller awards for Clinical Research by Family Practice Residents/Physicians.

    American Academy of Family Physicians Foundation (AAFP/F), 8880 Ward Parkway, Kansas City, MO 64114-0418; 1-800-274-2237, Ext. 4440.

    Check with your specialty professional organization for possible grants and award programs.

INFORMATION FOR SMALL BUSINESSES

Small Business Innovation Research (SBIR)

See Appendix I-G for details about SBIR program.

U.S. Small Business Administration (SBA)

SBIR Pre-Solicitation Announcement (PSA); published quarterly by SBA (March, June, September, December). Contains information about all the SBIR solicitations scheduled for release during the following 3-month period, as well as for those announced previously that are still open. You can ask to be put on the mailing liStreet

Note: SBA distributes the PSA but not the individual solicitations.

U.S. Small Business Administration
Mail Code: 6470
409 Third Street, S.W. (8th Floor)
Washington, DC 20416
1-800-8-ASK-SBA (1-800-827-5722); 202-205-7777; TDD: 202-205-7333
Fax: 202-205-7064.

SBIR Representatives of the Participating Federal Agencies

DEPARTMENT OF AGRICULTURE
Dr. Charles F. Cleland
Director, SBIR Program
U.S. Department of Agriculture
Room 323, Aerospace Building
901 D Street, S.W.
Washington, DC 20250-2200
202-401-4002

DEPARTMENT OF COMMERCE
Dr. Joseph Bishop
DOC SBIR Program Manager
Suitland Professional Center
SPC, Room 307
Suitland, MD 20233
301-763-4240

Mr. James P. Maruca
Director, Office of Small and Disadvantaged Business Utilization
U.S. Department of Commerce
14th and Constitution Avenue, N.W.
HCHB, Room 6411
Washington, DC 20230
202-482-1472

DEPARTMENT OF DEFENSE
Mr. Robert Wrenn
SBIR Program Manager
OSD/SADBU
U.S. Department of Defense
The Pentagon—Room 2A340
Washington, DC 20301-3061
703-697-1481

DEPARTMENT OF EDUCATION
Mr. John Christensen
SBIR Program Coordinator
U.S. Department of Education
Room 602D
555 New Jersey Avenue, N.W.
Washington, DC 20208
202-219-2065

DEPARTMENT OF ENERGY
Dr. Samuel J. Barish
SBIR Program Manager—ER-16
U.S. Department of Energy
Washington, DC 20585
301-903-3054

DEPARTMENT OF HEALTH AND HUMAN SERVICES
Mr. Verl Zanders
SBIR Program Manager
Office of the Secretary
U.S. Department of Health and Human Services
Washington, DC 20201
202-690-7300

DEPARTMENT OF TRANSPORTATION
Dr. George Kovatch
DOT SBIR Program Director, DTS-22
U.S. Department of Transportation
Research and Special Programs Administration
Volpe National Transportation Systems Center
55 Broadway, Kendall Square
Cambridge, MA 02142-1093
617-494-2051

ENVIRONMENTAL PROTECTION AGENCY
Mr. Donald F. Carey
SBIR Program Manager
Research Grants Staff (RD-675)
Office of Research and Development
Environmental Protection Agency
401 M Street, S.W.
Washington, DC 20460
202-260-7899

NATIONAL AERONAUTICS AND SPACE ADMINISTRATION
Mr. Harry Johnson
Director, SBIR Office—Code CR
National Aeronautics and Space Administration Headquarters
300 E Street, S.W.
Washington, DC 20546-0001
202-358-0691

NATIONAL SCIENCE FOUNDATION
Mr. Roland Tibbetts
Mr. Ritchie Coryell
Mr. Darryl G. Gorman
Mr. Charles Hauer
Dr. Sara Nerlove
SBIR Program Managers
National Science Foundation—V-502
4201 Wilson Boulevard
Arlington, VA 22230
703-306-1391

NUCLEAR REGULATORY COMMISSION
Ms. Marianne M. Riggs
SBIR Program Representative
Program Management, Policy Development and Analysis Staff
U.S. Nuclear Regulatory Commission
Washington, DC 20555
301-415-5822
(*Note:* Although NRC has a Washington, DC address, it has a Rockville, MD telephone number.)

The SBA/SBIR mailing list

The SBA Office of Innovation, Research and Technology of the U.S. Small Business Administration maintains a computerized listing of firms that have requested each issue of the SBA/SBIR Pre-Solicitation Announcement (PSA) when it is published.

To be added to the mailing list, contact:

Office of Innovation, Research and Technology
U.S. Small Business Administration
409 Third Street, S.W. (8th Floor)
Washington, DC 20416
202-205-7777

There is no single mailing list for receiving copies of all of the SBIR Program solicitations. You will receive only a copy of the PSA each quarter. The PSA lists release dates for each SBIR solicitation and about ordering specific program solicitations.

INFORMATION ESPECIALLY FOR NONSCIENTISTS

Kiritz, N. J., and Mundel, J., "*Program Planning and Proposal Writing*," The Grantsmanship Center, Los Angeles, CA, 1988.

An 11-page article about writing proposals; there is also a 48-page version. Published by the Grantsmanship Center (see address under Resource Centers).

Especially good for writing foundation proposals; includes examples of budgets and budget justifications.

Available for $4 (+ $2 P&H) from the Grantsmanship Center or Associated Grantmakers of Massachusetts, Inc. (See addresses under Resource Centers.)

Government agencies that fund programs in nonscience areas

Write to the agencies for information about their programs and for application kits.

U.S. Department of Housing and Urban Development
451 Seventh Street, S.W., Washington, DC 20410

Guidelines for Unsolicited Proposals
Available from HUD User ($4, prepaid)
P.O. Box 6091, Rockville, MD 20850; 1-800-245-2691; 301-251-5154;
Fax: 301-251-5747.

National Endowment for the Arts
Nancy Hanks Center, 1100 Pennsylvania Avenue, N.W., Washington, DC 20506;
202-682-5400.

Dance	202-682-5435
Design Arts	202-682-5437
Expansion Arts	202-682-5443
Folk Arts	202-682-5449
Presenting and Commissioning	202-682-5444
Literature	202-682-5451
Media Arts	202-682-5452
Museums	202-682-5442
Music	202-682-5445
Opera–Musical Theater	202-682-5447
Theater	202-682-5425
Visual Arts	202-682-5448
International (exchanges for artists)	202-682-5422

National Endowment for the Humanities
Division of Research Programs, Room 319, 1100 Pennsylvania Avenue, N.W., Washington, DC 20506; 202-606-8438.

National Foundation for the Improvement of Education
1201 16th Street, N.W., Washington, DC 20036; 202-822-7840; Fax: 202-822-7779.

U.S. Department of Education
Grant Application Control Center, Washington, DC 20202; 202-708-5514.
USDE Locator (to get phone numbers of other departments): 202-708-5366.

Books and periodicals

The following are geared primarily to education and are available from:

Capitol Publications, Inc.
P.O. Box 1453
Alexandria, VA 22313-2053
1-800-327-7203, 1-800-221-0425, 703-739-6444; Fax: 703-739-6517

Catalog of Federal Education Grants (CFEG). An easy-to-use reference service to help you find federal education grants. Indexed in several ways. Monthly updates. $200/year.

Education Grants Alert. The most current federal and private grants available for K–12 programs. Includes deadlines, funding priorities, winning strategies, and proposal-writing techniques plus direct access to an editorial board of funding experts. Weekly. ($299/year).

Education Grantwinners: Models for Effective Proposal Structure and Style. A collection of winning proposals for projects funded by the Education Department, National Endowment for the Humanities and National Science Foundation. $97.

Foundation and Corporate Grants Alert. Information about foundation and corporate funders. Includes current and upcoming funding opportunities, contact persons, amount that will be awarded, purpose, and tips on how to improve your chances of winning. Monthly. ($245/year).

Grants Development Kit. Forms, charts, outlines, checklists, tips, and strategies to streamline the grant-seeking process. $45.

Grants for Schools: How to Find and Win Funds for K–12 Programs. A step-by-step guidebook to help you get started in grant seeking. Includes details on Federal competitive grants and a variety of foundation grants. Sample forms, charts, and logs that you can use plus tips on how to set up a grants development operation, write a better proposal, and manage funded grants. $64.

Grants for Special Education and Rehabilitation: How to Find and Win Funds for Research Training and Services. A guidebook for special educators. Includes details on Federal competitive grants and a variety of foundation grants. New edition, 1993. $63.

Grants Management Kit. Forms, charts, checklists, tips, and strategies to streamline the grant-seeking process (3-ring notebook). $43.

Grantseeker's Guide to Project Evaluation. A step-by-step guide on how to plan and design an evaluation, collect and analyze evaluation data, manage an evaluation, and write a complete report. Contains a glossary of terms, sample evaluation plans, a description of statistical methods, and a bibliography of additional resources. $49.

Models For Success: A Look at Grant-Winning Proposals. A specially chosen collection of winning grant proposals. Includes the original grant program announcements. $95.

Private-Sector Proposals: Models of Winning Structure and Style. Proposals that received funding from a variety of foundations and corporations. Each entry includes the proposal as it was originally submitted to the funder, including description of project needs, activities, budgets, personnel, objectives, evaluation plans, timetables, and partnerships. $69.

Substance Abuse Funding: A Look at Grant-Winning Proposals. A collection of winning proposals. $94.

Writing Grant Proposals That Win. A step-by-step guide on how to assemble a winning grant proposal. $75. A software program based on this book is also available on disk for the Macintosh and for DOS-based PCs. The program helps you organize one or more proposals and a help file walks you through the elements required in the proposal and gives examples. This program is useful for people who write proposals to foundations. $125 for single-user version.

DIRECTORIES OF GRANT SUPPORT

Check at your grants office or at the library; many of the directories listed below are expensive.

Annual Register of Grant Support 1994: A directory of funding sources
Public, corporate, private, and community funding; special-interest grants. Published annually in September of year prior to year in title. $175.

> National Register Publishing Company, Reed Reference Publishing, 121 Chanlon Road, New Providence, NJ 07974; 1-800-521-8110; in NJ: 908-464-6800; Fax: 908-665-6688

ARIS (Academic Research Information System)
Information about Federal government and private funding sources.

> Published in 3 sections: Arts and Humanities, Biomedical Sciences, and Social and Natural Sciences. Each report comes out 8 times/year; the two science reports have supplements that come out about 3 weeks after the main report. Individual subscriptions: Science reports: $110/year; Arts and Humanities: $65/year.
> > Also available on disk (except for the supplements) as text file Word Perfect 5.1:
> > > 5.25-inch disks: Science reports: $140/year; Arts and Humanities: $95/year.
> > > 3.5-inch disks: Science reports: $150/year; Arts and Humanities: $105/year.
> Academic Research Information System, 2940 16th Street, Suite 314, San Francisco, CA 94103; 415-558-8133; Fax: 415-558-8135.

Biomedical Index to Public Health Service Supported Research (BI)
This 2-volume *Biomedical Index to PHS-Supported Research* contains information about all funded NIH grants and about intramural programs of NIH and FDA. It is generated annually directly from the CRISP file. The BI is available from the U.S. Government Printing Office. 202-783-3238. $81.

Catalog of Federal Domestic Assistance (CFDA)
A list of Federal funding opportunities that is indexed by (1) agency program, (2) functional category, and (3) subject.

> Available from Superintendent of Documents, U.S. Government Printing Office, Washington, DC 20402; 202-512-2303; Fax: 202-512-2168. About $40.

Corporate and Foundation Grants 1994
A comprehensive listing of more than 95,000 recent grants to nonprofit organizations in the United States. Grants are listed in 8 subject categories and then by city and state of recipient organization. There is also an alphabetical listing of grantors and application procedures published in 2 volumes by The Taft Group. $155.

> The Taft Group also publishes:

- Numerous other directories (A catalog is available.)
- *Directory of Corporate and Foundation Givers* on CD-ROM will be available in 1994 ($795 for single users)

- *Winning Grant Proposals,* edited by Gordon Jay Frost, 160 pages, 1993. The full texts of more than 12 successful proposals from 1990 to 1992.

The Taft Group, 835 Penobscot Bldg., Detroit, MI 48226; 1-800-877-8238, 313-961-2242; Fax: 313-961-6083.

Directory of Biomedical and Health Care Grants, 8th Edition, 1993
Details on funding programs in health and related fields. $84.50
   Oryx Press, 4041 North Central at Indian School Road, Phoenix, AZ 85012-3397; 1-800-279-6799; Fax: 1-800-279-4663.

Directory of Financial Aids to Women, 1991–1992
Lists more than 1,700 scholarships, fellowships, grants awards, loans, and internships primarily or exclusively for women.
   By Dr. Gail Ann Schlachter, 468 pages, $45. TGC/Reference Service Press, 1100 Industrial Rd., Suite 9, San Carlos, CA 94070; 415-594-0743.

Directory of Grants in the Humanities 1993/94
Lists Federal sources, such as the National Endowment for the Humanities, state government programs, university-sponsored programs, and corporate or foundation funding sources, such as the Carnegie Corporation of New York. Includes a comprehensive subject index and a program category index. $84.50.
   Oryx Press, 4041 North Central at Indian School Road, Phoenix, AZ 85012-3397; 1-800-279-6799; Fax: 1-800-279-4663.

Directory of Research Grants 1994
Lists Federal, state, and private funding sources, and Federal funding programs such as the National Science Foundation and the National Endowment for the Arts. Also includes state government programs and private foundation and corporate funding sources. $135.
   Oryx Press, 4041 North Central at Indian School Road, Phoenix, AZ 85012-3397; 1-800-279-6799; Fax: 1-800-279-4663.

Federal Register
Published each weekday. Lists all Federal grant opportunities and program deadlines, U.S. government notices, public regulations, etc.
   By subscription from Superintendent of Documents, U.S. Government Printing Office, Washington, DC 20402; 202-512-2303; Fax: 202-512-2168.
   For new subscriptions only: Superintendent of Documents, P.O. Box 371954, Pittsburgh, PA 15250-7954.
   $375/year (paper, *Federal Register* only); $353/year (microfiche); $415/year (*Federal Register* + monthly index + monthly list of Code of Federal Regulations Sections Affected).

Federal Research Report
Weekly report on Federal grants and contracts available to research institutions. $214.50/year.
   Business Publishers, Inc., 951 Pershing Dr., Silver Spring, MD 20910-4464; 301-587-6300; Fax: 301-585-9075.

Foundation Directory and Supplement
The Foundation Center, 79 5th Ave., New York, NY 10003-3076.

Published annually. Lists foundations with assets over $2 million that distribute $200,000 or more in grants annually. The supplement is published 6 months after the directory.

See other publications of the Foundation Center under the listing for the Foundation Center in this Appendix.

Foundation 1000

1993/1994 Edition. Data on the 1000 largest foundations in the United States. Type of projects supported, key personnel, application guidelines, and current program interests. $225. The Foundation Center, 79 Fifth Avenue, New York, NY 10003-3076; 1-800-424-9836, 212-620-4230; Fax: 212-807-3677.

Funding for Anthropological Research

Identifies funding sources for anthropological research and activities. Includes government agencies, private and corporate foundations, associations and organizations, institutes and centers, museums, libraries, and professional societies. Information about grants, awards, scholarships. $74.50.

Oryx Press, 4041 North Central at Indian School Road, Phoenix, AZ 85012-3397; 1-800-279-6799; Fax: 1-800-279-4663.

Public Health Service: Profile of Financial Assistance Programs

A compendium of PHS programs compiled from the *Catalog of Federal Domestic Assistance*. Describes PHS programs by agency. OASH-92-002.

Available from the Office of Management, PHS, 301-443-1874.

Smith Funding Report

Quarterly guide to research project grant opportunities offered by private and corporate foundations for educational and health institutions. $195/year.

Smith Funding Report, Inc. 76 Oneil Circle, Monroe, NY 10950-3210.

Sources of Federal Funding for Biological Research

Primarily for environmental research. Includes parasitology, agriculture, etc. Published in 1983 (remaindered at $5); new edition due out in 1994 or 1995. May be available on disk by 1995.

Association of Systematics Collection, 730 11th Street, N.W., 3rd Floor, Washington, DC 20001; 202-347-2850; Fax: 202-347-0072.

DIRECTORIES ABOUT AVAILABLE SUPPORT PUBLISHED BY THE FOUNDATION CENTER

The Foundation Center, 79 Fifth Avenue, New York, NY 10003-3076; 1-800-424-9836, 212-620-4230; Fax: 212-807-3677.

Arts Funding: A Report on Foundation and Corporate Grantmaking Trends, 1993

Directory of Japanese Giving

Foundation Giving: Yearbook of Facts and Figures on Private, Corporate, and Community Foundations, 1993

Foundation Grants to Individuals, 8th Edition

Guide to Funding for International and Foreign Programs, 1992

Guide to U.S. Foundations, Their Trustees, Officers and Donors

Japanese Corporate Connection: A Guide for Fundraisers

National Guide to Funding for Elementary and Secondary Education, 2nd Edition, 1993

National Guide to Funding for the Environment and Animal Welfare, 1992

National Guide to Funding for Women and Girls, 2nd Edition, 1993–94

National Guide to Funding in Arts and Culture, 2nd Edition, 1992

National Guide to Funding in Health, 3rd Edition, 1993

National Guide to Funding in Higher Education, 2nd Edition, 1992

The Foundation Grants Index

Who Gets Grants/Who Gives Grants: Nonprofit Organizations and the Foundation Grants They Received, First Edition, 1993

The Foundation Center also publishes numerous other specialized grant guides for particular subjects/fields, including several education grant guides targeted to particular levels of education.

For a catalog of Foundation Center publications, call: 1-800-424-9836.

For information on computer access to the Foundation Center's databases through DIALOG, call DIALOG at 1-800-334-2564. To learn more about which on-line utilities provide "gateway" access or for free materials to help you search Foundation Center files, call the Foundation Center's On-line Support Staff at 212-620-4230.

DIRECTORIES ABOUT FUNDRAISING FROM CORPORATIONS

Corporate Directory
Profile of 10,000 public companies; contains 7 indexes (alphabetical listing, geographic by state, officers and directors, etc.)
Annual publication; $360/year. Also available on CD-ROM, $595.
Walker's Western Research, 1650 Borel Place, Suite 130, San Mateo, CA 94402, 1-800-258-5737, 415-341-1110; Fax: 415-341-2351.

Corporate 500: The Directory of Corporate Philanthropy
Annual publication. The Public Management Institute, 358 Brannan Street, San Francisco, CA; 415-896-1900.

Corporate Foundation Profiles
7th Edition. Information on 247 U.S. corporate foundations that give at least $1.25 million annually. Provides grant maker's name, address, contact person, and purpose. Gives limitations and application guidelines. $195. The Foundation Center, 79 Fifth Avenue, New York, NY 10003-3076; 1-800-424-9836, 212-620-4230; Fax: 212-807-3677.

Corporate Philanthropy Report
Essential information for development professionals. Reviews critical issues that influence corporate philanthropy. Published monthly, except September and January. $200/year ($165/year for nonprofit organizations). Capitol Publications, Inc., P.O. Box 1453, Alexandria, VA 22313-2053; 1-800-327-7203, 1-800-221-0425, 703-739-6444; Fax: 703-739-6517. Also available from The Foundation Center, 79 Fifth Avenue, New York, NY 10003-3076; 1-800-424-9836, 212-620-4230; Fax: 212-807-3677.

National Directory of Corporate Giving
3rd Edition. Information on over 2300 corporate philanthropy programs. $195. The Foundation Center, 79 Fifth Avenue, New York, NY 10003-3076; 1-800-424-9836, 212-620-4230; Fax: 212-807-3677.

The Yellow Books

Published by Monitor Publishing Company, 104 Fifth Avenue, 2nd Floor, New York, N.Y. 10011; 212-627-4140; Fax: 212-645-0931.

Associations Yellow Book
Who's Who at the Leading U.S. Trade and Professional Associations
Has 7 indexes including: Master Association Index, Individual's Name Index, Acronym Index, Geographic Index. Published semiannually; $165/year.

Corporate Yellow Book
Who's Who at the Leading U.S. Companies
Lists names, titles, addresses, and telephone numbers of corporate leaders and concise descriptions of each company's business for over 1000 companies. Quarterly; $215/year.

Federal Regional Yellow Book
Who's Who in the Federal Government's Departments, Agencies, Courts, Military Installations and Service Academies outside of Washington, DC.
Published semiannually; $165/year.

Federal Yellow Book
Quarterly; $215/year.

International Corporate Yellow Book
Quarterly; $215/year.

News Media Yellow Book of Washington and New York
Who's Who Among Reporters, Writers, Editors and Producers in the Nation's Government and Business Capitals.
Published semiannually; $165/year.

COMPUTERIZED RESOURCES (SOFTWARE AND ON-LINE) FOR FUNDING INFORMATION

See also:
- Franklin Hoke, "Computer Aids Help Find and Manage Research Grants," *The Scientist,* May 30, 1994, pages 17-18.

- *Online Access*

  A periodical for personal computer users interested in learning about on-line services, commercial databases, etc. Covers a broad range of topics. Each issue contains feature articles about the on-line industry. Monthly publication. $19.50/year.

  Chicago Fine Print, Inc., 920 N. Franklin Street, Suite 203, Chicago, IL 60610-3119; 312-573-1700; Fax: 312-573-0520.

CRISP (Computer Retrieval of Information on Scientific Projects)

A database, managed by NIH/DRG, containing information about all *funded* NIH grants and about intramural programs of NIH and FDA. For certain large grant programs the individual subprojects are identified as independent records. For extramural programs the abstracts furnished by the PIs are entered into the file; for intramural programs the annual report abstracts are used; for contracts, project officers prepare abstracts. Ten to 20 indexing terms are also assigned to each project by technical information specialists from the Research Documentation Section. The indexing terms are taken from the regularly updated, computerized *CRISP Thesaurus*. The 2-volume *Biomedical Index to PHS-Supported Research* (BI) is generated annually directly from CRISP.

For searches/information, contact:

Research Documentation Section
Information Systems Branch
DRG/NIH
Westwood Bldg., Room 148
Bethesda, MD 20892
301-594-7267

CRISP is accessible via BRS (1-800-955-0906) and DIALOG (1-800-334-2564) and is also available on-line via NIH Gopher Server.

CRISP is also available on CD-ROM (updated quarterly) for DOS and Windows and may be available for Macintosh in the future. The CD-ROM was prepared by the DRG Information Systems Branch and has powerful text searching capabilities. Annual subscription rate $93; single copy $24. Orders: 202-783-3238; Fax: 202-512-2250, or mail: Superintendent of Documents, P.O. Box 371954, Pittsburgh, PA 15250-7954.

A toxicology subset of CRISP is available via the MEDLARS TOXLINE.

Federal Assistance Program Retrieval System (FAPRS)

For locating federal funding sources.

Check with the grants office at your institution.

For information, write or call Federal Program Information Branch, Budget Review Division, Office of Management and Budget (OMB), 6001 New Executive Office Bldg., Washington, DC 20503; 202-395-3112, 202-395-3000.

Federal Information Exchange (FEDIX)

An on-line database retrieval system for information about Federal research and educational opportunities, including grants. The service, intended to be a link between the Federal government and academia, is operated by a private company, Federal Information Exchange, Inc., but is financially supported by a coalition of Federal agencies.

The service is free and can be accessed directly via modem (1-800-232-4879; within Maryland, 301-258-0953) or via the Internet.

For information and a free User Guide, call 301-975-0103, fax to 301-975-0109, or write to FEDIX, 555 Quince Orchard Road, Suite 200, Gaithersburg, MD 20878.

Government Information Services
Maintains a database of both federal and private funding sources.

Fee for service.

For information, write or call Government Information Services, 4301 North Fairfax Dr., Suite 875, Arlington, VA 22203; 1-800-876-0226, 703-528-1082; Fax: 703-528-6060.

Grants Database
Provides instant access to thousands of grants programs. A comprehensive source of current information on grants offered by government, corporate, and private funding sources. Available through the Dialog and Orbit on-line systems. For subscription information, contact Dialog: 1-800-334-2564 (1-800-3DIALOG) or Orbit: 1-800-456-7248 (customer service), 1-800-955-0906 (sales).

Oryx Press, 4041 North Central at Indian School Road, Phoenix, AZ 85012-3397; 1-800-279-6799; Fax: 1-800-279-4663.

Grants Subject Authority Guide: A paperback guide to *The Grants Database.* A thesaurus of the grants subject indexing system; lets grant seekers formulate their search strategies before accessing *The Grants Database,* thus saving time on-line. $29.50.

Capitol Publications, 1101 King Street, P.O. Box 1454, Alexandria, VA 22312-2054; 1-800-221-0425, 703-739-6444.

Grants Search CFDA
An easy-to-use software program and user manual that allows you to search the Catalog of Federal Domestic Assistance (CFDA) by choosing your own key words. The search will provide you with the number of programs that match your key words and let you see the entire program description and eligibility requirements immediately. $375. Capitol Publications, 1101 King Street, P. O. Box 1454, Alexandria, VA 22313-2054; 1-800-221-0425, 703-739-6444.

Sponsored Programs Information Network (SPIN)
A computerized database for locating funding sources (federal, nonfederal, corporate) that assists faculty and administrators (at institutions of higher education, teaching/research hospitals, and research institutes) in identification of external support for research, education, development, etc., projects. Sponsors are national and regional in scope and are *not limited to science/medicine/technology.*

Check with the grants office at your institution; it may subscribe and provide searches free to members of your institution. The subscription price depends on whether the system is updated biweekly, monthly, or quarterly. Ask your grants office how up-to-date its system is kept.

For information, write or call Sponsored Programs Information Network, InfoEd, Inc., 453 New Karner Road, Albany, NY 12205; 1-800-727-6427, 518-464-0691; Fax: 518-464-0695; Internet: office@infoed.org.

RESOURCE CENTERS FOR FUNDING INFORMATION

The Office for Sponsored Research (OSR) or Office for Grants and Contracts at your institution.

At many universities the OSR (1) publishes a monthly bulletin or newsletter, (2) maintains lists of granting agencies, and (3) lists small grants given by the university.

Academic Research Information System, Inc. (ARIS)
Information about government and other sources of grants and contracts in science, social science, and arts and humanities.

For information and prices, write or call Academic Research Information System, Inc. (ARIS), Redstone Bldg., 2940 16th Street, Suite 314, San Francisco, CA 94103; 415-558-8133.

Associated Grantmakers of Massachusetts (AGM), Inc.
A resource center for philanthropy; the research library has a reference collection of publications and other information on foundation and corporate grant making and nonprofit management including Massachusetts grant makers, national foundations, corporate giving, IRS 990-PF forms, journals, newsletters, fund raising manuals, and proposal-writing guides. Associated Grantmakers has orientation sessions for first-time users (by appointment). In 1994, AGM is exploring the possibility of computerizing some of its resources.

For information, write or call Associated Grantmakers of Massachusetts (AGM), Inc., 294 Washington Street, Suite 840, Boston, MA 02108; 617-426-2606; Fax: 617-426-2849.

The Grantsmanship Center
The Grantsmanship Center, 1125 West 6th Street, 5th Floor, P.O. Box 17220, Los Angeles, CA 90017; 213-482-9860.

Publishes a funding newsletter, the *The Grantsmanship Center Magazine* (formerly the *Whole Nonprofit Catalog*), available free to qualified agencies. The Grantsmanship Center also sells books and reprints of articles related to proposal writing and fund raising and sponsors workshops on writing grant proposals; to register, write or call The Grantsmanship Center, 1125 West 6th Street, 5th Floor, P.O. Box 17220, Los Angeles, CA 90017; 213-482-9860, 1-800-421-9512.

OTHER RESOURCES

Workshops on proposal writing and related topics

Tech-Write Consultants/Erimon Associates
On site half-day, one-day, and multiday workshops: "How To Write A Good Grant Application." Can be geared to scientists or to a more general audience. Tuition depends on group size and length of workshop. A workshop outline is provided.

Rates for 1994: Half-day workshop: $75/person (minimum of 20 people) plus cost of materials, travel expenses, and per diem for speaker. Discounts for groups of over 100 people. (Grant Proposal-Writing Workshop may be available on videocassette in the future.)

Also available:

- Workshops on business writing
- Workshops on time management
- Consultation with individuals about proposal writing, business writing, and other expository writing
- Coaching for oral presentations

Workshop Leader: Liane Reif-Lehrer, Ph.D.
For complete syllabus, rates and references, contact:

Tech-Write Consultants/Erimon Associates
Box 645, Belmont, MA 02178
617-863-1117; Fax: 617-674-0436

Capitol Publications
Sponsors periodic workshops on various aspects of grantsmanship.

Capitol Publications, Inc.
P.O. Box 1453
Alexandria, VA 22313-2053
1-800-327-7203, 1-800-221-0425; 703-739-6444; Fax: 703-739-6517

David Bauer Associates
Seminars and other resources for proposal writers

Great Plains National (GPN) produces a set of 10 videotapes: *Winning Grants: A Systematic Approach for Higher Education* (David Bauer), $1,995. Available from the American Council on Education, Videocassette Services, Box 80669, Lincoln, NE 68501; 1-800-228-4630.

David Bauer Associates
2604 Elmwood Ave., Suite 248
Rochester, NY 14618
1-800-836-0732

Federal Grants and Assistance Training Catalog

Management Concepts Incorporated
1964 Gallows Rd.
Vienna, VA 22182
703-790-9595; Fax: 703-790-1371

Get Funded!
Practical workshops for faculty and other academic leaders seeking grants and gifts from business and industry.

Lecture/slide presentations, professional workshops, individualized consultation.

Basic principles, benefits of industrial support, differences between federal and corporate grants processes, the partnership concept, and many other relevant topics. A workbook is provided.

Workshop Leader: Dorin Schumacher, Ph.D., author of *Get Funded! A Practical Guide for Scholars Seeking Research Support from Business*, Sage Publications, 1992.

Dorin Schumacher, Ph.D.
P.O. Box 2758
West Lafayette, IN 47906
317-497-2383; Fax: 317-497-2967

Grantsmanship Center Training Program
5-day workshops; pre-scheduled series in major cities or on-site.
Tuition $495/person.

The Grantsmanship Center
650 S. Spring Street, Suite 507
P.O. Box 6210
Los Angeles, CA 90014
1-800-421-9512 (not for CA, HI, or AK), 312-689-9222

NIH Workshops

Various topics such as grants administration, human subjects protection, and care of vertebrate animals.

Watch the *NIH Guide for Grants and Contracts* for announcements.

NIH also frequently sponsors seminars at major scientific meetings. The talks are given by NIH staff members and are generally about topics related to grants and funding at NIH.

For workshops on human subjects protection call Ms. Darlene Marie Ross, OPRR, NIH, Bldg. 31, Rm. 5B63, Bethesda, MD 20892; 301-496-8101. For workshops on animal welfare education, call Ms. Roberta Sonneborn, OPRR, NIH, Bldg. 31, Rm. 5B63, Bethesda, MD 20892; 301-496-7163. For workshops on other subjects, contact the Grants Information Office, 301-594-7248.

SBIR Conferences

Periodic conferences to help familiarize potential applicants with the SBIR Program are held in major cities. It is also an opportunity for small business personnel to meet representatives of large corporations. Topics include:[5]

> Starting and financing the small high-tech firm
> Understanding government accounting requirements
> Creating and managing a joint venture
> Negotiating an SBIR contract
> Marketing techniques for small high-tech firms
> Planning for government audits
> Developing effective high-tech business plans
> Understanding federal procurement regulations
> Patents and nondisclosure agreements
> Financing via SBIR Phase III commitments
> International market opportunities
> SBIR proposal preparation
> U.S. and foreign licensing
> Seeking venture capital
> Finding corporate partners and closing the deal

For information about the conferences, contact Department of Defense/National Science Foundation, National SBIR Conferences (NSBIR), 1201 East Abington Drive, Suite 400, Alexandria, VA 22314. Conferences are run by Foresight Science and Technology, Inc., 6064 Okeechobee Blvd., P.O. Box 170569, West Palm Beach, FL 33417. There is a hotline to call for further information: 407-791-0720; Fax: 407-791-0098.

Service facilities for science researchers and other resources that may enhance efficiency and productivity

Organizations that provide a variety of products or high-quality services (often for a fee) can be an important resource for scientists, especially those who work in settings where these resources are not readily available within the scientists' own institutions. Anything that frees your time to do research—which only you can do—is probably a bargain. (See Liane Reif-Lehrer, "Using New Science Resources: A Key to Staying Competitive," *The Scientist*, Oct. 30, 1989, page 22, but be aware that the information about *specific* resources in that article is outdated.) The number of fee-for-service resource agencies has increased greatly in recent years. In addition, some instrumentation companies will let

---

[5] The topics in this list are from the 1993–94 SBIR conference announcement.

you come and run your own samples on an instrument that you are thinking of purchasing and will train you to use the instrument if you purchase it.

In addition to commercial service facilities for science researchers, there are many government-supported (NIH, NSF, DOE, etc.) resources. Some of the government-supported facilities are located on the premises of private institutions. The Biomedical Research Technology Program (BRTP, NIH/NCRR) puts out an annual report of centers funded by NCRR. This report can be obtained from BRTP, NIH/NCRR, 5333 Westbard Ave., Rm. 8A15, Bethesda, MD 20816; 301-594-7934.

The agencies listed below are examples of the types of resources available and are intended to start readers on a search to find resources for their own specific needs.

American Type Culture Collection (ATTC)

Stores and dispenses cultures. Provides cell lines, DNA products, bacteria, yeasts, and viruses. Accepts and requests biological materials from scientists. Catalogs of products are available on hardcopy or on disk. Also sells an index of uses and applications of the biological materials distributed by ATCC, publishes a free quarterly newsletter, and sponsors workshops about a variety of research techniques. Investigators can access ATTC strain data via 3 on-line services, including the BIOSIS Life Science Network. Sponsored visiting scientists may use ATTC facilities.

> ATTC
> 12301 Parklawn Drive
> Rockville, MD 20852
> 301-881-2600; Fax: 301-231-5826
> Sales:1-800-638-6597
> Information about workshops: 301-231-5566; Fax: 301-770-1805
> ATTC/NIH On-line: 1-800-647-4710, 301-881-4909

BioAlmanac

A protein information reference library (database) on a disk. Includes information such as molecular weights on SDS gels, isoelectric points, subunits, and other standard reference information, all with full citations.

Requires CD-ROM drive. Available for DOS; will run under Windows. May be available for the Macintosh in the future. Free demo disk available.

Blue Lightning Data and Software, Inc., Paoli Technology Enterprise Center, 19 E. Central Ave., Paoli, PA 19301; 1-800-447-3769; Fax: 215-695-9388.

Single release, $350; Single release + 1-year subscription (4 updates), $999.

Digital Imaging

The companies listed below supply equipment for digital imaging.[6] Digital imaging is useful for microscopy but is also replacing photography for certain other types of information storage and analysis such as slides for presentations, densitometry of bands on gels, and DNA sequence analysis on gels.

> Carl Zeiss, Inc.
> 1 Zeiss Drive
> Thornwood, NY 10594
> 1-800-233-2343
> Fax: 914-681-7446

---

[6] All but one of the listings in this category were taken from the article, "Digital Imaging In Microscopy Offers Greater Control, More Options," by Franklin Hoke, *The Scientist*, November 1, 1993, page 19.

Eastman Kodak Co.
Advanced Imaging Technology Group
901 Elmgrove Rd.
Mail code: 35405
Rochester, NY 14653-5405
1-800-242-2424
Fax: 716-726-9868

Image Systems, Inc.
8835 Columbia 100 Parkway, Suite A
Columbia, MD 21045
410-995-0748
Fax: 410-995-1335

JEOL USA, Inc.
11 Dearborn Road
P.O. Box 6043
Peabody, MA 01961-6043
508-535-5900
Fax: 508-536-2205

Leica, Inc.
111 Deer Lake Road
Deerfield, IL 60015
1-800-248-0123
Fax: 708-405-0147

Nikon, Inc.
1300 Walt Whitman Road
Melville, NY 11747-3064
1-800-526-4566
Fax: 516-547-0299

Olympus America, Inc.
Precision Instruments Division
4 Nevada Drive
Lake Success, NY 11042
1-800-446-5967
Fax: 516-222-7920

Photometrics
3440 East Britannia Drive
Tucson, AR 85706
602-889-9933
Fax: 602-573-1944

Center for Fluorescence Spectroscopy (CFS)

Provides state-of-the-art fluorescence spectroscopy services (time domain and frequency domain fluorescence instrumentation) and sponsors courses on various aspects of fluorescence spectroscopy. Staff members are available to assist users with experimental design, data acquisition, and analysis. Computers are available for on-site analysis. A dial-in phone line enables off-site analyses.

Susan M. Rhinehart
Center for Fluorescence Spectroscopy
Department of Biological Chemistry
University of Maryland School of Medicine
660 West Redwood Street
Baltimore, MD 21201-1596
410-328-8409; Fax: 410-328-8408/8297

GenBank

An NIH database of all known nucleotide and protein sequences including supporting bibliographic and biological information. As of October 1993, GenBank contained over 157 million nucleotide bases from some 143 thousand different sequences. Entries include concise description of sequence, scientific name, and taxonomy of the source organism, table of features specifying coding regions, other sites of biological significance, and protein translations for coding regions. Has been run since October 1992, by the National Center for Biotechnology Information (NCBI), part of NIH National Library of Medicine (NLM). Los Alamos National Laboratory (LANL) has participated in GenBank since 1982 as a contractor with responsibility for data entry and maintenance. International collaboration with the EMBL Data Library in Heidelberg, Germany, and the LDNA Data Bank of Japan (DDBJ) in Mishima provides shared collection and exchange of sequence information.

GenBank data are available on CD-ROM through a subscription service with the U.S. Government Printing Office, 202-783-3238; Fax: 202-512-2233. Order forms are included in each issue of *NCBI News*, a free publication (6 issues/year) available from NCBI. Retrieval software is available for the Macintosh and Windows. Can also be accessed via Internet. GenBank extracts data from relevant journals, but researchers can submit data directly to the database.

GenBank
National Center for Biotechnology Information
Bldg. 38A, Rm. 8S-803
8600 Rockville Pike
Bethesda, MD 20894
301-496-2475; Fax: 301-480-7241

E-mail addresses:

- General information about NCBI and services: info@ncbi.nlm.nih.gov
- Submission of sequence data to GenBank: gb-sub@ncbi.nlm.nih.gov
- Revisions to GenBank entries and notification
  of release of "hold until published" entries: update@ncbi.nlm.nih.gov

Human Genetic Mutant Cell Repository

Establishes, characterizes, and stores cell lines from people with genetic disorders and from seemingly normal individuals as controls. Also stores other cell lines for gene mapping and other studies. Provides cultures and purified DNA from selected cell lines, together with detailed background information to qualified investigators for a fee. Maintains a database on cell lines. Database includes clinical information and a bibliography of publications citing cell line use. Funded by NIGMS.

Coriell Cell Repositories (CCR) also house the Aging Cell Repository, funded by NIA, and the National Cell Repository, funded by NIMH. In addition, CCR, in partnership with the National Disease Research Interchange (NDRI) and the Juvenile Diabetes Foundation International, created the Human Biological Data Interchange (HBDI) Cell Repository, which focuses on juvenile diabetes. In 1993, CCR began operation of a Cell Repository funded by the American Diabetes Association, whose focus is on adult-onset diabetes.

> Coriell Cell Repositories (CCR)
> Coriell Institute for Medical Research
> 401 Haddon Ave.
> Camden, NJ 08103
> 609-757-4836, 609-757-9697; Fax: 609-757-9737
> To place orders: 1-800-752-3805

Laboratory for Fluorescence Dynamics (LFD)

An R&D and service facility funded by NIH.

Develops hardware, software, and applications for measurement of time-resolved fluorescence in biological samples. Maintains and upgrades (about twice a year) a software package, *Globals Unlimited,* for analysis of fluorescence and anisotropy data. This software has an open architecture that allows users to add on their own applications.

Maintains state-of-the-art laboratory for scientists who bring samples or do their experiments at the laboratory. No charge for use of services by academic researchers.

> Laboratory for Fluorescence Dynamics
> University of Illinois at Urbana-Champaign
> Department of Physics
> 126 Loomis Laboratory
> 1110 West Green Street
> Urbana, IL 61801
> 217-244-5620; Fax: 217-244-7187

Liver Tissue Procurement and Distribution System (LTPADS)

NIH service contract to obtain portions of resected pathologic human liver from transplants from regional centers for distribution to scientific investigators throughout the United States. Liver is prepared according to the investigator's specifications. Requests could, for example, include a particular metabolic disorder or disease entity or the general process of cirrhosis. A limited supply of "normal" liver specimens may be requested, but the waiting time is much longer than for pathologic liver specimens.

For information and proposal forms, contact:

> Harvey L. Sharp, M.D.
> Principal Investigator, LTPADS
> c/o Elizabeth Webster
> Box 279 UMHC
> University of Minnesota Hospitals
> Minneapolis, MN 55455
> 612-624-1133; Fax: 612-624-2682

See *NIH Guide for Grants and Contracts,* Vol. 21, No. 42, November 20, 1992, pages 1–2.

National Cancer Institute (NCI) Resource List

The National Cancer Institute maintains an annually updated list of biological, epidemiological, chemical, and other resource centers for researchers involved in cancer-related research. The resource centers are listed below by category. The printed list of resource centers and periodic updates are available from:

Program Director of Research Resources
Biological Carcinogenesis Branch
Division of Cancer Etiology
National Cancer Institute
NIH
Bethesda, MD 20892
301-496-9740; Fax: 301-496-2025

Cell Culture Identification Service
Isozyme analysis, immunofluorescence, and karyotypic analysis (chromosome banding)

Dr. Joseph Kaplan
Children's Hospital of Michigan
3901 Beaubien Boulevard
Detroit, MI 48201
313-745-5570

> Cite Contract #N01-CP-33063.
> Inquire about costs.

Antisera/Antibodies

- Goat antisera against avian, bovine, feline, murine, and primate intact viruses and viral proteins
- Antibodies to immunoglobulins for a number of species
- Preimmune sera available for some virus antisera

> Alice K. Robison, Ph.D.
> BCB Repository
> Quality Biotech, Inc.
> 1667 Davis Street
> Camden, NJ 08104
> 609-966-8000; Fax: 609-342-8078

> > Cite Contract #N01-CP-15665.
> > Costs: $75.00/5 ml (antisera)
> >   25.00/5 ml (preimmune sera)
> >   65.00/100 ml (immunoglobulins)
> >   (frozen material)

Viruses produced in vivo and in vitro
Avian, feline, murine, and primate

Alice K. Robison, Ph.D.
BCB Repository
Quality Biotech, Inc.
1667 Davis Street
Camden, NJ 08104
609-966-8000; Fax: 609-342-8078

> Cite Contract #N01-CP-15665.
> Inquire about costs.

Monoclonal antibodies/blocking peptides

- Monoclonal antibodies with specificities for synthetic peptides representing the amino acid sequences of the left end, right end, and active site of oncogene products of avian and mammalian retroviruses
- Blocking peptides
- Cell lines producing the monoclonal antibodies

> Alice K. Robison, Ph.D.
> BCB Repository
> Quality Biotech, Inc.
> 1667 Davis Street
> Camden, NJ 08104
> 609-966-8000; Fax: 609-342-8078
>> Cite Contract #N01-CP-15665.
>> Costs (not including Shipping and Handling):
>> Peptides: $25.00/mg
>> Ascites fluid: $45.00/ml
>> Cell culture: $100.00/culture

Human sera

From donors with:

- Various malignancies (including nasopharyngeal carcinoma)
- Nonmalignant disorders
- Normal individuals

> Program Director, Research Resources
> Biological Carcinogenesis Branch, DCE, NCI, NIH
> Executive Plaza North, Room 540
> Bethesda, MD 20892
> 301-496-1951; Fax: 301-496-2025

Costs: Shipping and handling charges only.

Histologic slides of rodent tumors

From the Division of Cancer Etiology's Registry of Experimental Cancers: 16 study sets containing histologic slides of spontaneous and induced rodent tumors (rats, mice, etc.) with accompanying syllabi.

> Registry of Experimental Cancers
> National Cancer Institute, NIH
> Building 41, Room D311
> Bethesda, MD 20892

Costs: Available for up to two months at no charge to cancer investigators worldwide.

Chemical Carcinogenesis Research Information System (CCRIS)

- Maintained by NCI.

- Available on-line through the NLM Toxicology Data Network (TOXNET) system.
- Contains evaluated data and information in the broad areas of chemistry, toxicology, and hazardous waste: carcinogens, mutagens, tumor promoters, cocarcinogens, metabolites of carcinogens, and carcinogen inhibitors.
- Information is derived from published review articles, ongoing current awareness survey of primary literature, NCI/NTP's short- and long-term bioassay studies, the IARC Monographs on the Evaluation of Carcinogenic Risk of Chemicals to Man, and special studies and reports.

> Dr. Thomas P. Cameron
> Office of the Director
> Division of Cancer Etiology
> National Cancer Institute
> Executive Plaza North, Room 712
> Bethesda, MD 20892
> 301-496-1625

Inquire about costs.

Survey of Compounds Which Have Been Tested for Carcinogenic Activity, PHS-149, 1987–1988 and 1989–1990

Publication prepared under contract to NCI.

> Dr. Thomas P. Cameron
> Office of the Director
> Division of Cancer Etiology
> National Cancer Institute
> Executive Plaza North, Room 712
> Bethesda, MD 20892
> 301-496-1625

Inquire about costs.

Longitudinal database on biological and human health outcomes from halogenated biphenyl exposure (Michigan Long Term PBB Study)

- A study of 4000 participants from rural farms in Michigan, by the Michigan Department of Public Health, dealing with accidental exposure (through consumption of contaminated farm animals and food products) to polybrominated biphenyls (PBBs).
- Cohort enrolled and characterized in 1975–1976.
- Database contains demographic, health history, medical condition, reproductive history, blood and tissue analyses, and chemical/environmental exposure information, major life events: birth, death, cancer and major illnesses.
- Supported by the National Cancer Institute, National Institute of Environmental Health Sciences, Centers for Disease Control and Prevention, and the Food and Drug Administration.
- Updated annually.
- Database is available for collaborative research investigating biological and human health outcomes from halogenated biphenyl exposure.

> Dr. Harold E. B. Humphrey
> Michigan Department of Public Health
> Division of Health Risk Assessment
> 3423 North Logan, P.O. Box 30195
> Lansing, MI 48909
> 517-335-8350

Costs: Free to qualified investigators

The Tumor Virus Epidemiology Repository (TVER)

- Contains sera and other biological samples from more than 13,000 patients and controls obtained in 12 countries
- Established primarily to support collaborative research on the role of Epstein-Barr virus (EBV) in Burkitt's lymphoma and related diseases
- Sera characterized for human herpes virus 6 (HHV) antibodies are also available.
- The TVER collection is available for new collaborative studies and some independent research.
- The most extensive collections are serum samples from patients with Burkitt's lymphoma.

> Dr. Paul H. Levine
> Viral Epidemiology Branch
> DCE, NCI, NIH
> Executive Plaza North, Room 434
> Bethesda, MD 20892
> 301-496-8115

Costs: Free to collaborating investigators. Others: dependent on processing time.

Veterinary Medical Data Program

- Animal Morbidity/Mortality Survey of Colleges of Veterinary Medicine in North America
- A registry of veterinary medical information about animals seen at collaborating veterinary teaching facilities; 3 million hospital episodes have been abstracted and computerized in a standardized record format.
- Disease information is coded using the scheme of the Standard Nomenclature of Veterinary Disease and Operations.
- Maintained by the National Cancer Institute
- Computer tapes available on request

> Dr. Howard M. Hayes
> Environmental Epidemiology Branch
> EPB, DCE, NCI, NIH
> Executive Plaza North, Room 443
> Bethesda, MD 20892
> 301-496-1691

Inquire about costs.

Human fibroblast cultures from individuals at high risk of cancer

- Cultures from selected members of cancer-prone families and some normal family members

- Collection is historical with unknown viability and contamination status.
- Catalog of cell lines is not available.
- Follow-up on many individuals is not available.
- Information requests should include potential use of cultures.

> Chief, Genetic Epidemiology Branch
> DCE, NCI, NIH
> Executive Plaza North, Room 439
> Bethesda, MD 20892
> 301-496-4375

Costs: Free to collaborating investigators. Others: $70/cell line.

Repository of biological specimens from homosexual men

- Developed by National Institute of Allergy and Infectious Diseases and National Cancer Institute
- Specimens were collected through cooperative agreements with 5 major U.S. universities for studies of the natural history of AIDS.
- Information about applying for collaborative use of these specimens is available from the NIAID Project Officer or the NCI Co-Project Officer.

> Chief, Epidemiology Branch
> AIDS Program, NIAID
> CDC Bldg., Room 240
> National Institutes of Health
> Bethesda, MD 20892
> or
> Chief
> Extramural Programs Branch, EBP
> Division of Cancer Etiology, NCI
> Executive Plaza North, Room 535
> Bethesda, MD 20892

Observed versus Expected (O/E) Software System

- Developed by the Epidemiology and Biostatistics Program of the National Cancer Institute
- The Observed versus Expected (O/E) Software System calculates:
  —the number of observed events (e.g. cancer cases or deaths) in a study group at risk
  —the number of expected events in a study group based on the rate of occurrence in some standard or referent population
  —the ratio of observed to expected events
  —the significance of this ratio
  The system is user friendly and capable of executing a series of calculations by different variables such as age, time group, date of exposure, age at date of exposure, duration of exposure, year relative to entry, and cause of event.
- The O/E System provides tables by race, sex, and user-defined variables; allows user-defined latency intervals, and accepts standard or user-prepared rates.
- O/E is written in COBOL and is exportable to most mainframes.

Ruth Wolfson
Epidemiology and Biostatistics Program, DCE, NCI, NIH
Executive Plaza North, Room 443
Bethesda, MD 20892
301-496-1691

Costs: Free to investigators interested in epidemiologic research.

Occupational Mortality Analysis Software System

- Developed by the Epidemiology and Biostatistics Program of the National Cancer Institute.
- Software calculates proportionate mortality ratios, proportionate cancer mortality ratios, or mortality odds ratios using occupational information on the death certificates from 24 states for 1984–1989.
- Data were assembled through a collaborative effort involving the National Center for Health Statistics, the National Institute for Occupational Safety and Health, and NCI.
- The program is user friendly and allows analysis of data by (1) occupation, industry, or occupational/industry combinations; (2) age group; (3) states or geographic regions; (4) race groups (black and white); (5) sex, and (6) underlying causes of death.
- Program is written in Wylbur Command Procedures and is exportable to most mainframes.

Program information:

Mustafa Dosemeci, Ph.D.
Occupational Studies Section
EBP, DCE, NCI, NIH
Executive Plaza North, Room 418
Bethesda, MD 20892
301-496-9093; Fax: 301-402-1819

Questions about nature and source of the occupational mortality data:

Jeff Maurer, M.S.
Mortality Statistics Branch
Division of Vital Statistics, NCHS
6525 Belcrest Rd., Room 840
Hyattsville, MD 20782
301-436-8884; Fax: 301-436-7066

Costs: Free to investigators interested in occupational epidemiologic research.

Computer-aided occupational and industrial code searching program (CODESEARCH)

- Developed by the Epidemiology and Biostatistics Program of the National Cancer Institute (NCI)
- CODESEARCH allows the code assigner to select appropriate codes from existing classification systems for job or industrial titles from work histories of the study subjects.
- The program is user friendly and allows searches from 4 occupational classification systems:

—1977 Standard Occupational Classification Manual (SOC)
—1980 SOC
—1970 Bureau of Census Occupational Classification System (BOCOC)
—1980 BOCOC

and 4 industrial classification systems:

—1972 Standard Industrial Classification System (SIC)
—1987 SIC
—1970 Bureau of Census Industrial Classification System (BOCIC)
—1980 (BOCIC)

- Program is written using PC-Clipper software and is exportable to most 486 PCs.

> Mustafa Dosemeci, Ph.D.
> Occupational Studies Section
> EBP, DCE, NCI, NIH
> Executive Plaza North, Room 418
> Bethesda, MD 20892
> 301-496-9093; Fax: 301-402-1819

Costs: Free to investigators interested in assignment of occupational and industrial titles from work history data.

Resources related to smoke and smoke condensate components

- Chemical data base on smoke and smoke condensate components
- A contractor with experience in the development of analytical methods for the determination of constituents of cigarette smoke and cigarette smoke condensates and of specialty instrumentation for inhalation toxicology is available to assist qualified investigators with particular interest in human and animal model exposure to environmental and sidestream smoke.
- Analytical support for the collection, separation, and elucidation of environmental carcinogens including combustion and smoking-related exposures

> Harold E. Seifried, Ph.D.
> Chemical and Physical Carcinogenesis Branch, DCE, NCI
> Executive Plaza North, Room 700
> Bethesda, MD 20892
> 301-496-5471; Fax: 301-496-1040

Inquire about costs.

Chemical Carcinogen Reference Standard Repository

- Reference quantities of over 750 compounds including dilute aqueous standards of PAH deoxyguanosine-3'-monophosphates for Randerath ^{32}P post labeling assays, fecapentaenes, food mutagens, polynuclear aromatic hydrocarbons (PAH), PAH metabolites, radiolabeled PAH metabolites, nitrogen heterocycles, nitrosamines/nitrosamides, aromatic amines, aromatic amine metabolites, azo/azoxy aromatics, inorganics, nitroaromatics, pesticides, pharmaceuticals, natural products, dyes, dioxins, and chlorinated aliphatics. A number of radiolabeled PAH metabolites and nitrosamines are also available.
- Data sheets provided with compounds include chemical and physical properties, analytical data, hazards, storage, and handling information.
- Catalog available upon request.

Manager, NCI Chemical Carcinogen Repository
Midwest Research Institute
425 Volker Boulevard
Kansas City, MO 64110
816-753-7600, Ext. 523; Fax: 816-753-3664

Manager, NCI Radiolabeled Chemical Repository
CHEMSYN Science Laboratories
13605 W. 96th Terrace
Lexena, KS 66215
913-541-0525; Fax: 913-888-3582

Costs: Subject to chemical class code and quantity.

National Cell Culture Center

National Center for Research Resources (NCRR), NIH

A resource facility that provides large-scale mammalian cell culture services to researchers throughout the United States and Canada. The Cell Culture Center can provide:

- 10 to 30 liters of mammalian cells in suspension or monolayer cultures on a weekly basis
- 0.5 to 100 grams of monoclonal antibodies
- Large-quantity production on nonhybridoma cell secreted proteins. (Quantities vary depending on individual cell lines.)

A request form can be obtained from the Cell Culture Center and must contain a description of the relevant research project. Following approval of the request by the Cell Culture Center's Scientific Advisory Board, the applicant's cell line is sent to the Center and grown to the requested amount. Researchers are charged only for consumable materials and a portion of the labor costs required for each project.

Programmatic inquiries:

Louise E. Ramm, Ph.D.
Biological Models and Materials Research Program
NCRR
Westwood Building, Room 8A07
Bethesda, MD 20892
301-402-0630

Applications and resource inquiries:

Dr. Mark Hirshel
Director, National Cell Culture Center
8500 Evergreen Boulevard
Minneapolis, MN 55433
1-800-325-1112

See *NIH Guide for Grants and Contracts,* Vol. 22, No. 5, February 5, 1993, Part I, pages 1–2.

National Disease Research Interchange (NDRI)

A center for the procurement, preservation, and distribution of normal and diseased human tissues and organs available for biomedical researchers. NDRI provides 165 different types of human tissue procured from autopsies, eye banks, surgical procedures, and organ retrieval programs and tailors the procurement and preservation to the researcher's scientific protocol. Donor information accompanies all distributed tissue samples. To obtain human tissue for research, investigators must submit a formal brief application for specific types of tissue. Requests are reviewed by a committee of advisors for scientific merit and feasibility. Once approved, a procurement proposal is developed with the investigator for each specific tissue, outlining the constraints with regard to donor criteria, tissue size, processing needs, and time/delivery limitations. Investigators may request to have tissue delivered fresh with or without tissue culture media, frozen, or fixed. A modest service fee is paid by the investigator. NDRI is supported by a cooperative agreement award from the Biological Models and Materials Research Program, National Center for Research Resources, NIH.

National Disease Research Interchange
2401 Walnut Street, Suite 408
Philadelphia, PA 19103
1-800-222-NDRI (6374), 215-557-7361; Fax: 215-557-7154

See *NIH Guide for Grants and Contracts,* Vol. 22, No. 17, April 30, 1993, page 4.

National Resource for Transgenic Animals

The NIH National Center for Research Resources announced (*NIH Guide for Grants and Contracts,* Vol. 22, No. 13, April 2, 1993, pages 6–8) availability of an RFA to establish National Resource(s) for Transgenic Animals. Watch for the possible establishment of such a resource in the future.

Inquiries: 301-594-7933

Pittsburgh Supercomputing Center (PSC)

Funded by NSF. NSF gives grants to people to use the supercomputers. Potential users must apply to NSF or to PSC. Can be accessed by corporate users for fee-for-service.

PSC
4400 Fifth Avenue
Pittsburgh, PA 15213
1-800-221-1641 (Inside PA: 1-800-222-9310, 412-268-4960); Fax: 412-268-5832

Protein Data Bank

An international repository for the results of macromolecular structural studies of proteins, tRNAs, polynucleotides, viruses, and polysaccharides. Three classes of information are collected, stored, and distributed: atomic coordinates, structure factor-phase data, and NMR experimental data. Also available: bibliographic entries for macromolecular structures for which coordinates are not yet available. Protein Data Bank is funded by the NSF, NIH, and DOE and is located at Brookhaven National Laboratory.

Protein Data Bank
Chemistry Department
Brookhaven National Laboratory
P.O. Box 5000
Upton, NY 11973-5000
516-282-3629; Fax: 516-282-5751

Access is also available via Internet using Anonymous FTP: pdb.pdb.bnl.gov

Protein Information Resource (PIR)

Maintains a government-funded database (the PIR-International Protein Sequence Database) that contains over 60,000 protein sequences and associated information. Available quarterly on tapes and CD-ROM. Also available on-line. Call about information and prices.

National Biomedical Research Foundation (NBRF)
c/o Georgetown University Medical Center
3900 Reservoir Road., N.W.
Washington, DC 20007
202-687-2121; Fax: 202-687-1662

National Facility for Analytical Ultracentrifugation
Provides:

- Instrument and software engineering
- Collaborative research and service for protein characterization
- Training for scientists, technicians, and students from both industrial and university laboratories

Also sponsors conferences and workshops to catalyze the exchange of technology and expertise.

National Facility for Analytical Ultracentrifugation
Biotechnology Center
University of Connecticut
Storrs, CT 06269-3125
203-486-4462/5011

Learning about new products and technology

Biotechnology Directory 1994 by J. Coombs and Y.R. Alston
Products, companies, research, and organizations.
  Annual. $240.

Stockton Press
49 W. 24th Street, 9th Floor
New York, NY 10010
1-800-221-2123 or call collect to 212-673-4400; Fax: 212-673-9842

1994 GEN Guide to Biotechnology Companies
Genetic Engineering News: a compendium of 7 guides. Provide data on biotechnology companies, bioprocess engineering firms, peptide companies and peptide instrumentation firms, law firms with expertise in biotechnology, venture capitalists that fund biotechnology, recruiters specializing in biotechnology, and biotechnology consultants. Updated annually.
  Available as a book or on 3.5-inch computer disk.

Mary Ann Liebert, Inc.
1651 Third Ave.
New York, NY 10128
1-800-654-3237, 212-289-2300; Fax: 212-289-4697

Biotech Visions
Training video for biotechnology: an overview of DNA-cloning techniques intended primarily for training technicians in the laboratory. Also useful for teaching high school level students and as a refresher for more advanced students and professionals. The 2-volume (90 minute) training video is $89.99 with a 30-day money back guarantee.

RESOURCES **387**

The company responds only to queries sent by mail.

Biotech Visions
P.O. Box 5331
Boston Turnpike Station
Shrewsbury, MA 01545
1-800-536-2246 (sales only); Fax: 1-508-764-1503

Taped Technologies
Produce videotapes of scientific procedures for training laboratory personnel.

Taped Technologies
P.O. Box 384, Logan, UT 84321
801-753-6911; Fax: 801-752-5616

Federal Quality Institute (FQI)
Established in 1988 to promote and facilitate the implementation of quality management throughout the Federal government. Offers a variety of services such as technical assistance, training, publications, and an electronic bulletin board. Publishes an annual catalog of management documents and a database user's guide.
Information Center: 202-376-3753

Magazines that introduce new products and commercial techniques
These magazines are largely supported via advertisements. They are useful for keeping up with new methods and instrumentation via the ads and articles that discuss new techniques and products. They are *usually available free to researchers in the field.*

American Laboratory	$195/year
American Biotechnology Laboratory	$128/year
American Clinical Laboratory	$190/year
American Environmental Laboratory	$145/year

International Scientific Communications
30 Controls Drive
Box 870
Shelton, CT 06484-0870
203-926-9300; Fax: 203-926-9310

BioTechniques
Monthly publication about new and improved techniques in biotechnology. Complimentary to bioresearch scientists.
Eaton Publishing also runs BioTechNet, which is an international network for life scientists and permits access to Internet. Call about fees for using BioTechNet.

Eaton Publishing
154 E. Central Street
Natick, MA 01760-5414
508-655-8282; Fax: 508-655-9910

Scientific Computing and Automation
Monthly. $60/year. Free to qualified individuals.

Gordon Publications, Inc.
301 Gibraltar Drive, Box 650
Morris Plains, NJ 07950-0650
201-292-5100; Fax: 201-898-9281

Places that provide used or inventory-excess equipment

Boston Computer Exchange (BoCoEx)

A broker for computer hardware and software. Makes no sales; stocks no inventory. Based on the premise that computers that have become obsolete for some users often have capabilities far in excess of the needs of other users.

Prospective sellers list their equipment with BoCoEx, which adds the listing to a database carried by four on-line computer information services and by the UPI wire service. The list is also published in *PC Week, Computer World,* and other magazines and newspapers and is available by subscription directly from BoCoEx.

Prospective buyers can respond directly to offerings in the BoCoEx listing or can submit a "buy order" for a specific type of equipment. In the latter case, BoCoEx will conduct a search to find the requested material. BoCoEx deals with individuals, universities, and commercial organizations.

It is a good idea to do some market research before dealing with BoCoEx so that you know when you see a good deal. Service contracts are available for some items.

Boston Computer Exchange Corporation
Box 1177
Boston, MA 02103
1-800-262-6399, 617-542-4414; Fax: 617-542-8849

National Association for the Exchange of Industrial Resources (NAEIR)

Accepts donations of *new* excess-inventory items such as laboratory equipment and supplies, medical items, office supplies, computer software, safety equipment, electronic components, etc. from manufacturers and distributes them to educational institutions that are tax exempt under IRS section 501(c)(3).

Catalog (5 times/year) lists available items.

Fees: $50 initiation fee, $595/year membership fee, plus $39.50 per order for shipping & handling

NAEIR
560 McClure Street, P.O. Box 8076
Galesburg, IL 61402
1-800-562-0955, 309-343-0704; Fax: 309-343-0862

Used Energy-Related Laboratory Equipment (ERLE) Grant Program

Open to any institution of higher education.

Search available items via a catalog or electronic listing.

ERLE list usually includes about 300 to 500 items, ranging from simple laboratory devices to costly instruments, and includes computers and computer peripherals.

To receive an item, the requesting organization must first file a claim for a specific item and then complete an application that justifies the equipment grant. Catalog subscription costs $91/year (12 issues) from GPO, 202-783-3328. Open 7 days/week, 24 hours/day. General information:

Program Manager
ERLE Program
U.S. Department of Energy (DOE)
Office of University and Science Education, ET-31
1000 Independence Avenue, S.W.
Washington, DC 20585
202-586-8947; Fax: 202-586-0019

For a complimentary copy of catalog call 202-586-8947
Can also be accessed via computer and modem or Internet: 1-800-783-3349
Help line: 301-975-0103
Telnet: Fedix.Fie.com

Equipment Marketplace
At the back of each issue of *The Scientist,* published twice a month.

The Scientist, Inc.
3600 Market Street, Suite 450
Philadelphia, PA 19104
1-800-258-6008

On–line science and technology information systems

Many agencies now provide data on-line for access by researchers from their personal or mainframe computers. There are many such resources, some of them specializing in particular areas of interest; for example, there are Gopher Servers that specialize in biosciences (Biogophers). Some of the resources available at Biogophers include:[7]

- Gene and protein sequence databanks (GenBank, EMBL, PIR, etc.)
- Protein structural coordinate databank (Brookhaven PDB)
- *Arabidopsis, Caenorhabditis elegans, Drosophila,* microbial, and human genome databases
- Public software for the biosciences (IUBio archive)
- Biology (BioSci) network news archive
- NIH, NSF, and other funding agency information
- Medical informatics
- American Physiological Society information
- Biology systematics, taxonomy, organismal and ecology data
- Library catalogs around the world

Listed below are examples of some on-line resources; for additional information, see the Gale Directory of Databases, Gale Research, Inc. Detroit, MI, 1993. Another good resource is the annual database issue of *Nucleic Acids Research,* a journal published by Oxford University Press. The 1993 database issue was Volume 21, July 1, 1993. See also:

Online Access
A periodical for personal computer users interested in learning about on-line services, commercial databases, etc. Covers a broad range of topics. Each issue contains feature articles about the on-line industry. Monthly publication. ($19.50/year.)

Chicago Fine Print, Inc., 920 N. Franklin Street, Suite 203, Chicago, IL 60610-3119; 312-573-1700; Fax: 312-573-0520.

Biosis
Abstracting and indexing service for the life sciences. Indexes over half a million references annually from nearly 7000 international serials. BIOSIS produces several databases including:

- *Biological Abstracts* (paper)
- *Biological Abstracts/RRM* (reports, reviews, and meetings) (paper)
- *BIOSIS Previews* (on-line)

---

[7] The following bulleted list is taken from D. Gilbert, "The Global Library" (about Internet services for scientists), *Trends in Biochemical Sciences* (TIBS), Vol. 18, No. 3, March 1993, pages 107–108.

A combination of the other two abstract services provided on-line. Also available on CD-ROM.

BIOSIS, 2100 Arch Street, Philadelphia, PA 19103-1399; 1-800-523-4806, 215-547-4800; Fax: 215-587-2016.

BRS (BRS On-line Products)
(Formerly: Bibliographic Retrieval Service)

Specializes in medical, biomedical, and pharmaceutical information.
Bibliographic citations and abstracts. Full texts available on some databases.

- After Dark: Discount for searching at off-peak times
- Colleague (for physicians): menu-driven
- BRS/Search: command-driven

Prices vary according to service.

InfoPro Technologies, Inc., 8000 West Park Drive, McLean, VA 22102; Customer Service: 1-800-289-4277; Sales: 1-800-955-0906.

Medline
Index to articles in over 3200 journals.

Check at your institutional library, or call BRS/Colleague: 212-247-7770; Cambridge Scientific AbStreet: 301-951-1400; DIALOG: 1-800-334-2564, 415-858-3742; EBSCO: 213-530-7533; Horizon: 213-479-4966; On-line Research: 212-408-3311; Silver Platter: 617-239-0306.

For information about obtaining matching funds for students and hospital house staff, call PaperChase, Beth Israel Hospital, Boston: 1-800-722-2075.

NIH Research Resources Database
The National Institutes of Health (NIH) Research Resources subfile (NIHRES) of the DIRLINE (Directory of Information Resources On-line) database is available on the National Library of Medicine's (NLM) computer and includes biomedical resources (supported by NIH funds) that are available to researchers throughout the country. These include materials, substances, organisms, databases, and equipment, which may be valuable to other scientists, electron microscopy facilities, primate colonies, specialized laboratories, and cell culture collections. The NIHRES files provide information about the availability of these research resources to the scientific community. The Institutes, Centers, and Divisions (ICDs) of NIH, including the National Center for Research Resources (NCRR), have contributed information about these valuable resources to the DIRLINE database. DIRLINE and the NIHRES component may be accessed by a variety of terminals or microcomputers connected to NLM's computer facility. Connection is established via direct telephone line, the TELNET, TYMNET or CompuServe nationwide telecommunications networks, or the Internet. DIRLINE is also available using GRATEFUL MED, NLM's user-friendly software for IBM-compatible PCs or Macintosh computers. This software, available for $29.95 through NTIS, allows novice users to access the NLM system and the NIHRES subfile of DIRLINE to easily obtain the information they need. For further information about DIRLINE access, contact the MEDLARS Management Section of NLM at 1-800-638-8480.

See *NIH Guide for Grants and Contracts,* Vol. 22, No. 21, June 11, 1993, page 2.

STN International
An on-line scientific and technical information network of more than 160 on-line databases that allow scientists to retrieve:

- Up-to-date information about the latest developments in biomedicine and bioscience
- Information on a wide variety of scientific and technical topics, including biology, bioengineering, pharmaceuticals, biochemistry, environmental health, agricultural science, and food technology, as well as many other subject areas
- Retrospective information about specific fields of interest
- Chemical structures
- Numerical information
- Full-text literature files
- Traditional bibliographic databases

STN also offers software tutorials, workshops, and a newsletter.

STN International, The Scientific and Technical Information Network
c/o Chemical Abstracts Service (CAS)
A Division of the American Chemical Society
2540 Olentangy River Road
P.O. Box 3012
Columbus, Ohio 43210-0012
Switchboard: 614-447-3600; General Fax: 614-447-3713
Help Desk: 1-800-848-6533, 614-447-3698
Customer Service: 1-800-753-4227, 614-447-3731; Fax: 614-447-3751

There is a $25 fee to obtain a log-in I.D. number; other costs vary depending on the database being searched.

Other sources of technology search and/or document and information services

Federal Depository Library Program
Close to 1400 Depository Libraries throughout the United States contain information from the federal government on subjects ranging from agriculture to zoology. *Access is free.* To locate the Depository Library nearest to you, write to:

Federal Depository Library Program
Office of the Public Printer
Washington, DC 20401
202-512-0146, 202-512-1014

Regional Medical Libraries
Information retrieval services are available via Regional Medical Libraries and academic and health science libraries throughout the United States through a network supported by the National Library of Medicine. A list of Regional Medical Libraries and information about network services may be obtained from the Public Information Office, National Library of Medicine, Bethesda, MD 20894; 301-496-6308.

Keyword Thesaurus
Keyword Thesaurus (5th edition). A classification system containing terms and codes used by NSF, NASA, NIH, DOD, ONR, Federal Aviation Administration, and Air Force Office of Scientific Research to help identify areas of interest for Federal funding of research and other sponsored programs. Available for purchase on disk or paper from Rodman and Associates, 555 Quince Orchard Rd., Suite 200, Gaithersburg, MD 20878; 301-963-5226.

Agency for Health Care Policy and Research (AHCPR) "Instant Fax" Automated Retrieval System

To obtain documents and publications from AHCPR, such as *AHCPR Research Activities*, quick reference guides for clinicians, patient's guides developed by AHCPR-sponsored clinical practice guideline panels, grant announcements, and press releases. Instant Fax is a fully automated fax-on-demand system providing 24-hour service, 7 days a week. There is no charge for the service other than the telephone call from your fax machine to the Instant Fax computer at AHCPR headquarters in Rockville, Maryland. To use AHCPR Instant Fax, you need access to a fax machine with a telephone handset. The system can currently process 4 calls at a time. Ultimately, it will be able to handle 20. The list of publications is updated periodically.

For questions about AHCPR Instant Fax, call 301-227-8364, Ext. 159.

Hard copies of AHCPR publications are available; call 1-800-358-9295 for a catalog or to order publications.

To use AHCPR Instant Fax:

To receive a current contents list:

1. Dial 301-227-0800 on a fax machine.
2. At the prompt from the AHCPR Instant Fax voice, press 1.
3. Follow the prompts given by the AHCPR Instant Fax voice to complete the transaction.

To order a fax of a publication:

1. Select the 6-digit publication number from the AHCPR Instant Fax contents list
2. On your fax machine, dial 301-227-0800.
3. At the prompt from the AHCPR Instant Fax voice, enter the 6-digit publication number, then press the # key. If you make a mistake, press zero to start over.
4. To confirm the transaction, the AHCPR Instant Fax voice will repeat the publication number you selected. Press 1 to verify the selection; press zero to cancel the requeStreet
5. When the AHCPR Instant Fax voice prompts you, press the "Start/Copy" or "Receive" button on your fax machine and hang up the telephone.

See *AHCPR Research Activities*, March 1993, pages 8–9.

Other organizations that provide search and/or document services

Some of the information in this subsection is taken from page 17 of PHS 93-2, *Omnibus Solicitation of the Public Health Service for Small Business Innovation Research (SBIR) Grant and Cooperative Agreement Applications*, U.S. Government Printing Office, 1993-717-094/60949, and page 13 of NSF 93-18, *NSF Small Business Innovation Research (SBIR) Program Solicitation*, OMB No. 3145-0058.

Aerospace Research Applications Center
611 North Capitol Ave.
Indianapolis, IN 46204
317-262-5003

Kerr Industrial Applications Center
Southeastern Oklahoma State University
Durant, OK 74701
405-924-6822

NASA/Florida State Technology Applications Center
State University System of Florida
500 Weil Hall
Gainesville, FL 32611
904-392-6626

NASA Industrial Applications Center
University of Pittsburgh
701 LIS Building
Pittsburgh, PA 15260
412-624-5211

NASA/UK Technology Applications Programs
University of Kentucky
109 Kinkead Hall
Lexington, KY 40506
606-257-6322

National Technical Information Service
5285 Port Royal Road
Springfield, VA 22161
703 487-4600

NERAC (Northeast Research Applications Center)
Tolland, CT 06084
203-872-7000

NSF Research Reports
Capital Systems Group, Inc.
1803 Research Boulevard
Rockville, MD 20850
301-216-1168

National Technology Transfer Center (NTTC)
Wheeling Jesuit College
316 Washington Avenue
Wheeling, WV 26003
1-800-678-6882, 304-243-2455; Fax: 304-243-2463
    An information center congressionally funded through NASA. The mission of
NTTC is to put people in contact with researchers in the 17 federal laboratories/
facilities. The services are free. In 1993, NTTC had over 700 laboratories/facilities in
their database. NTTC also provides:

- Toll-free hotline ("Business Gold") to Federal technology information 1-800-
  678-6882 (1-800-678-NTTC). Available 24 hours a day, 7 days a week; there
  are no connect or usage charges. Most information on the system is free and
  can be downloaded to users' computers.
- An electronic bulletin board (Send information to add to the bulletin board
  via Fax: 304-243-2539)
- A newsletter: *Technology Touchstone*
- NTTC minority institution Technology Apprenticeship Program (TAP) designed

to encourage minority participation in U.S. technology transfer. Chairperson: Joseph Allen, Director of Training and Economic Development at NTTC.
- Customized seminars and short courses on the technology transfer process
- Curriculum development
- Needs assessment/evaluation of programs
- *Funds for strategic partnering*

There are also *6 regional Technology Transfer Centers in the United States.* The regional centers deal with research in the private sector as well as with government laboratories/facilities. Dialing 1-800-472-6785 will automatically route your call to the center nearest to the geographical area from which you are calling.

Great Lakes Industrial Technology Center
Dr. J. W. Ray, Director
25000 Great Northern Corporate Center, Suite 260
Cleveland, OH 44070-5310
216-734-0094; Fax: 216-734-0686

Mid-Continent Industrial Technology Center
Mr. G. Sera, Director
Texas A&M University System
College Station, TX 77843-3401
1-800-548-1546, 409-845-8762; Fax: 409-845-3559

Center for Technology Commercialization
Dr. Wm. Gasco, Director
Massachusetts Technology Park
100 North Drive
Westborough, MA 01581
508-870-0042; Fax: 508-366-0101

Mid-Atlantic Technology Applications Center
Ms. L. S. Hummel, Director
University of Pittsburgh
823 William Pitt Union
Pittsburgh, PA 15260
1-800-257-2725, 412-648-7000; Fax: 412-648-7003

Southern Technology Applications Center
Mr. J. R. Thornton, Director
University of Florida, College of Engineering
Box 24, One Progress Boulevard
Alachua, FL 32615
1-800-225-0308; in Florida: 1-800-354-4832, 904-462-3913; Fax: 904-462-3898

Far West Regional Technology Transfer Center
Robert L. Stark, Director
University of Southern California
3716 South Hope Street, Suite 200
Los Angeles, CA 90007-4344
1-800-872-7477, in California: 1-800-642-2872, 213-743-6132; Fax: 213-746-9043

National Technical Information Service (NTIS)
U.S. Department of Commerce
Springfield, VA 22161
1-800-553-6847, 703-487-4600; TDD: 703-487-4053
Fax: 703-321-8547, 703-321-9038
To identify a title for sale: 703-487-4780
NTIS On-line Searching Help Desk: 703-487-4640
For help with NTIS QuikSERVICE: 703-487-4788

   NTIS collects and disseminates the broad scientific, technical engineering, and business information that is produced with Federal support but not peer reviewed or published in journals; e.g., information on Federal Research In Progress is stored on the (FEDRIP) Database, which NTIS manages. The abstracts, title of the project, the grantee institution, the principal investigator/program director, and amount of the award for all NIH-funded research grant applications are sent to NTIS via the PHS CRISP subfile, which is added to the FEDRIP Database, where it is merged with data from 11 government sources.
   Information collected by NTIS is available to the public from DIALOG and Knowledge Express (both, electronic access; *fee for service*); NERAC, Inc. (Batch Searching and SDI services *for a fee*); Federal Depository Libraries.
   NTIS issues monthly update tapes to commercial/university sources.
   NTIS charges for its services.
   NTIS Publications available free of charge:

- CD-ROMs and optical discs available from NTIS
- *FEDRIP Database on DIALOG: A Search Guide*
- *FedWorld:* an NTIS pilot project to allow computer users to access Federal information systems electronically
- *Handbook of NTIS Services for Federal Agencies*
- *NTIS Alerts:* Twice-monthly summaries of the newest government research, technologies, and studies of value to your work. A catalog of topics, order codes, and prices
- *NTIS Catalog of Products and Services*
- NTIS collection of videotapes
- *NTIS Database on BRS: A Search Guide*
- *NTIS Database on ORBIT: A Search Guide*
- *NTIS Database on STN: A Search Guide*
- *NTIS On-line Alert*
- NTIS software products
- NTIS subject category descriptions
- Published search master catalog: Selected bibliographies of scientific, technical, and engineering information. (Published searches are annotated bibliographies that summarize completed research from the U.S. Government and worldwide sources.)
- *Selected Research in Microfiche* (SRIM)
- U.S. Government software for microcomputers

Miscellaneous other information

Meeting abstracts on-line or on disk

Some professional societies now provide abstracts for their annual meetings either on-line or on disk. For example, FASEB (Federation of American Societies for Experimental Biology) provides a free (other than for telephone charges) on-line service that lets you search by key words, phrases, authors, and/or institutional affiliation; the screen displays the abstract and session numbers but not the abstract. The Biophysical Society provides similar information on disk together with a program that allows you to choose the talks you want to go to and then prints out a schedule for you, indicating conflicts.

Journals on CD-ROM or with ancillary information on disk

Some journals are now available on CD-ROM, e.g., *Protein Science*, published by Cambridge University Press. This allows readers to search articles and use text portions for keeping personal notes on new developments in the field.

Protein Science also comes with a Mac or DOS diskette containing abstracts, references and certain data sets for all the papers in the journal issue.

More journals are likely to provide CD-ROM alternatives and/or ancillary diskettes in the future. Watch for announcements.

IMPAC (Information for Management, Planning, Analysis, and Coordination)

A computer-based information system for extramural programs of NIH/PHS; maintains, for example, statistical information about grant applications and funding. Information, 301-496-7400.

Chemical and Biochemical Supply Companies

A number of chemical and biochemical supply companies sell books relevant to their products and the needs of their customers.

SOFTWARE

Watch for computer software programs that may be of help (1) in your research, (2) for writing grant proposals and research papers, (3) for managing grant and laboratory budgets, (4) for keeping up with the literature, (5) for managing and saving your time, and (6) for other research-related matters. Watch also for optical character recognition programs, which can save typing time by allowing you to word-process text that has been scanned into the computer. Several such programs are already available. Another new technology, now in its infancy, that may emerge in the next few years is computer voice recognition, which enables the computer to type spoken messages.

Be aware that some companies have toll-free 800 numbers but do not publish them. If you ask for the 800 number and the company has one, it will usually give it to you, especially if it perceives that you will become a customer.

There are many more useful programs available than those listed here, and new programs to meet a variety of specific needs emerge every few months. As stated at the beginning of this appendix, I am not endorsing or—in most instances—even recommending the software programs listed below. I am only calling these resources to your attention should you wish to investigate whether they might be useful for you. The programs listed here are not necessarily the only—or the best—programs in their category. I have included in this list, programs (1) that I use, (2) about which I have heard good things from colleagues, and (3) that I have read about and perceived as being of possible interest to the readers of this book. I have also been pleased to examine and—if I deemed them appropriate—listed programs for which software developers sent me copies for consideration. It will be obvious from the listing that I am a Macintosh user, and therefore the list is heavily weighted on the side of Macintosh programs. I am always happy to entertain suggestions from readers (especially DOS and Windows users), which I will add to this list should there be a future revision of this book.

Word processing programs, other than those specifically dedicated to scientific writing, are not included; they are too numerous to mention, and I assume that by now most readers have access to a general word processor. (See the article by C. D. Potter, "Word Processors Keeping Pace with Scientists' Needs," *The Scientist*, September 20, 1993, page 17.) Spelling checkers are now generally included in word-processing programs and are thus also not included unless they are specifically useful for writing research reports. Some word-processing programs now also include grammar checkers, but I have listed some grammar checking resources that may be useful. I have assumed that most readers who need spreadsheets have already settled on a program that meets their needs.

Before purchasing any software program, be sure to determine the system requirements, including the amount of RAM and storage memory required—not just to mount the program, but also to run it effectively. It is also wise to ask about possible incompatibility with software that you already have. Also be aware that most software programs, even for the Macintosh, have become increasingly complex and generally require at least some up-front learning time.[8] Before you spend the time, be sure that (1) you have chosen the program best suited to your needs and (2) the time saved in the long-run will have been worth the time invested in learning how to use the program.

The programs listed below are arranged by category for their primary function, but some are multifunctional. The addresses and phone numbers listed below are correct as of summer 1993. Prices given below were obtained in summer 1993 and are included only as a rough guide. All prices are subject to change without notice. Many software programs can be purchased at substantial discounts from the list price at local stores or mail-order houses. Many vendors offer site licenses for institutions with multiple users. Also be aware that companies occasionally offer *competitive upgrades* at very substantial savings. That is, a company will sell you a complete new program for an upgrade price if you can prove ownership of a similar program made by another software company. Check catalogs of software distributors for announcements of *competitive upgrades*.

Here are a few mail-order houses that may be useful for purchasing software and computer accessories:

Diskette Connection	1-800-654-4058
Diskette Gazette	1-800-222-6032
In California:	408-262-6660
Mac Connection	1-800-800-2222
	1-800-800-0002
Tiger Software (Mac and IBM)	1-800-666-2562
Inmac (PC)	1-800-547-5444
Mac Zone	1-800-248-0800
Mac Warehouse	1-800-255-6227

Resources for finding out about new software for researchers, university educators, and proposal writers

The Scientist: "Scientific Software Directory"
Professional journals
Exhibits at national scientific conferences
Computer magazines: *MacWorld, MacUser, PC Magazine, Byte,* etc.

---

[8] The problem is exacerbated because the quality of the documentation (user manual) often is not up to the quality of the program.

ACS Software

A division of the American Chemical Society. Catalog lists software programs for chemists and other scientists (for IBM-compatible and Macintosh computers). ACS Software, 1155 16th Street N.W., Washington, DC 20036; ACS Distribution Office, Dept. 190, P.O. Box 57136, West End Station, Washington, DC 20037; 1-800-227-5558, 202-872-4363; Fax: 202-872-6067.

Biotechnology Software

A bimonthly journal that provides comprehensive coverage and reviews of software to assist bioscientists in the choice and use of computers and computer software. $95/year. Mary Ann Liebert, Inc., 1651 Third Ave., New York, NY 10128; 1-800-654-3237, 212-289-2300; Fax: 212-289-4697.

Europa Scientific Software Corporation (es²c)

Catalog lists scientific software programs for IBM-compatible and Macintosh computers. Programs address the needs of researchers in all scientific disciplines. Customers of es²c receive unlimited toll-free technical support. The company gives discounts to academic institutions. Europa Scientific Software Corporation (es²c), 14 Clinton Drive, Hollis, NH 03049-6595; 1-800-522-4440, 603-595-7415; Fax: 603-889-2168.

Macintosh Product Registry

A quarterly periodical. Redgate Communications, 660 Beachland Blvd. Vero Beach, FL 32963; 407-231-6904 ($15/issue). Also available on CD-ROM.

Trinity Software

College-level tutorials and simulation programs for chemistry and some research and productivity enhancement software for chemists/biochemists. Trinity Software, P.O. Box 960, Campton, NH 03223; 1-800-352-1282, 603-726-4641; Fax: 603-726-3781.

Alpha Media

Software programs related to medicine: Anatomy, medical art and instruments, graphics, medical dictionaries, etc. Free catalog available. Alpha Media, 4501 Glencoe Avenue, Ground Floor, Marina Del Rey, CA 90292-6372; 1-800-832-1000.

Image Analysis Software[9]

All the programs listed in this category are for "Windows."

Optimas

> 170 West Dayton, Suite 204
> Edmonds, WA 98020
> 1-800-635-7226; Fax: 206-775-3640

Global Lab Image

> Data Translation Inc.
> 100 Locke Dr.
> Marlboro, MA 01752
> 508-481-3700; Fax: 508-481-8620

---

[9] All programs listed in this section are taken from the article by Franklin Hoke, "Image Analysis Under Windows: New Tools for Biologists," *The Scientist*, May 17, 1993, page 19.

Mocha
  Jandel Scientific
  2951 Kerner Blvd.
  San Rafael, CA 94901
  415-453-6700; Fax: 415-453-7769

Image-Pro Plus
  Media Cybernetics Inc.
  8484 Georgia Ave.
  Silver Spring, MD 20910
  301-495-3305; Fax: 301-495-5964

Scientific graphing/plotting and statistics software

See also, Franklin Hoke, "Scientific Graphing Software Tools Fill Important Niche," *The Scientist*, June 14, 1993, pages 18–19. For a review of statistical software for Macintosh computers, see *Macworld Magazine*, October 1993, pages 81 and 116–121.

PROPHET Software

NIH, National Center for Research Resources (NCRR)

The Biomedical Research Technology Program, NCRR, has available a 1993 release of its low-cost PROPHET information management, analysis, and visualization package. With a vastly improved graphical user interface, you can choose commands from pull-down menus, provide information through dialog boxes tailored for each task, and readily invoke a variety of analysis tools. The new graphical interface is a dynamic window environment with full color, multiple fonts, and multiobject screen management. PROPHET runs on powerful networked workstations, and its graphical interface provides easy access to the system's extensive capabilities.

The PROPHET software package is fully documented, engineered, and supported by scientific software professionals. PROPHET has the following features:

- Spreadsheet-style data entry and organization
- Clinical study data management
- Statistical and mathematical modeling
- Detailed two-dimensional graphs (scatterplots, histograms, bar graphs, and boxplots)
- Biological simulation and modeling
- Molecular modeling and display
- Nucleic acid and protein sequence manipulation, analysis, and display
- Developing custom applications via a high-level programming language and debugger
- Interfaces to Ingres, SAS, GenBank, and PIR Protein Sequence Database
- On-line system with integrated text and graphics
- Hotline and electronic mail support

PROPHET is available on UNIX and ULTRIX workstations with Motif, OpenLook, and DECwindows windowing systems. These workstations include Sun-4, SPARCstation, and DECstation 5000. Additional ports and continuing enhancements are planned.

For further information, contact:

Dr. Richard DuBois
Biomedical Research Technology Program
NCRR

Westwood Building, Room 8A-15
Bethesda, MD 20892
301-594-7934

See *NIH Guide for Grants and Contracts*, Vol. 22, No. 25, July 16, 1993, pages 2–3.

Macintosh Programs

CA-Cricket Graph III
Graphing software. Macintosh, $89.

Computer Associates International
One Computer Associates Plaza
Islandia, NY 11788-7000
1-800-225-5224, 516-342-5224

KaleidaGraph
Data analysis and graphics application. Macintosh, $249.
Synergy Software
2457 Perkiomen Ave.
Reading, PA 19606
215-779-0522

Also available from es²c, 1-800-522-4440.

StatView
Data analysis and graphing software. Mac, $595.

Abacus Concepts
1918 Bonita Ave.
Berkeley, CA 94704
510-540-1949

MS-DOS/Windows Programs[10]

Axum
MS-DOS, $495.

TriMetrix, Inc.
444 N.E. Ravenna Blvd., Suite 210
Seattle, WA 98115
206-527-1801; Fax: 206-522-9159

CoPlot
MS-DOS, $159.

CoHort Software
P.O. Box 1149
Berkeley, CA 94701
510-524-9878; Fax: 510-524-9199

---

[10] Most of the programs listed below are taken from the article by Franklin Hoke, "Scientific Graphing Software Tools Fill Important Niche," *The Scientist*, June 14, 1993, page 18.

Fig. P
MS-DOS Windows, $499. Free demo disk available.

Biosoft also publishes a periodic newsletter, *Biosoft News*, which describes various educational and simulation software products carried by the company.

BIOSOFT
P.O. Box 10938
Ferguson, MO 63135-9913
314-524-8029; Fax: 314-524-8129

Graftool (MS-DOS) and *Standard Graphics* (Windows)

Graftool (MS-DOS), $495. Standard Graphics (Windows), $495

3-D Visions
2780 Skypark Drive
Torrance, CA 90505
310-325-1339; Fax: 310-325-1505

InPlot

Scientific graphics. DOS only, $395. Windows version available in 1994. (See review in *Laboratory Microcomputer*, July 1991.)

GraphPad
10855 Sorrento Valley Road, Suite 203
San Diego, CA 92121
1-800-388-4723, 619-457-3909; Fax: 619-457-8141

InStat

Biostatistics. DOS and Macintosh, $95. (See reviews in *Macworld Magazine,* November 1993 and *Personal Computers and Hospital Pharmacists,* September 1992.)

GraphPad
10855 Sorrento Valley Road, Suite 203
San Diego, CA 92121
1-800-388-4723, 619-457-3909; Fax: 619-457-8141

Origin

Windows, $495.

MicroCal Software, Inc.
1 Roundhouse Plaza
Northampton, MA 01060
800-969-7720, 413-586-2013; Fax: 413-585-0126

Also available from es²c, 1-800-522-4440.

PlotIt

MS-DOS, $495; Windows, $595.

Scientific Programming Enterprises
P.O. Box 669
Haslett, MI 48840
517-339-9859; Fax: 517-339-4376

Sigma Plot
MS-DOS, $495.

> Jandel Scientific
> 2591 Kerner Blvd.
> San Rafael, CA 94901
> 415-453-6700; Fax: 415-453-7769
>
> Also available from ACS Software, 1-800-227-5558.

Especially for clinician researchers

PC!INFO
A database management package for storage, retrieval, and analysis of medical (or other) research data. The program can mathematically manipulate, statistically analyze, and graphically display data. Tailored to the needs of *clinician researchers* who track their patients and collect and analyze longitudinal data. MS-DOS only. Demo disk available for $50; complete package, $995.

> Retriever Data Systems
> 1102 33rd Ave. South
> Seattle, WA 98144
> 206-324–2203

Modeling, simulation, design software

There are many computer programs that are useful for teaching, simulating laboratory experiments and for molecular modeling in various science fields. They run the gamut from relatively low-cost individual user programs to very expensive software intended primarily for institutional (shared) use. It is often difficult to find a single program that has all the features you would like. Clearly, the more powerful (and usually more expensive) programs tend to have more—and more powerful—features.

Alchemy III
Interactive 3D molecular visualization and analysis program. Includes an extensive fragment library and supports structure import from over 90 databases. Features include a variety of display styles, built-in virtual trackball for easy structure rotation, energy minimization, molecular fitting and analysis, and a two-way interchange with the MM2 program. DOS and Windows, $795; Macintosh, $950.

> Tripos Associates, Inc.
> 1699 South Hanley Street
> Street Louis, MO 63144-2913
> 314-647-1099
>
> Also available from es²c, 1-800-522-4440 and ACS Software, 1-800-227-5558.

Cambridge Scientific Computing (CSC) software for chemists (for the Macintosh)

- *CSC ChemDraw and CSC ChemDraw Plus*
  2D chemical structure and reaction mechanism drawing package. Includes a wide range of bond tools, predefined templates, arrows and orbitals, and general-.purpose drawing and text tools. The Plus version adds coloring and user-defined template capabilities. ChemDraw, $495; ChemDraw Plus, $795.

- *CSC Chem3D and CSC Chem3D Plus*

  3D molecular modeling program. User can create models using the built-in tools and substructure library, or import them from a variety of sources. Program performs energy and molecular dynamic calculations and displays interatomic distances and angles. The Plus version adds coloring and more advanced minimization techniques. CSC Chem3D, $495; CSC Chem3D Plus, $795.

- *CSC ChemFinder*

  Database for managing chemical compound information, integrating 2D structure, 3D modeling, and other information in a simple graphical spreadsheet format. $495.

- *CSC ChemOffice and CSC ChemOffice Plus*

  Integrated 2D, 3D, and database package including CSC ChemDraw, CSC Chem3D, and CSC ChemFinder (CSC ChemOffice Plus includes CSC ChemDraw Plus and CSC Chem3D Plus). CSC ChemOffice, $995; CSC ChemOffice Plus, $1,595.

  > Cambridge Scientific Computing
  > 875 Massachusetts Avenue
  > Cambridge, MA 02139
  > 1-800-950-3023, 617-491-6862; Fax: 491-8208

  Also available from es²c, 1-800-522-4440 and ACS Software, 1-800-227 5558.

Design-Ease

Software for design of experiments. Sets up and analyzes two-level factorials that identify the critical factors for improvement of products and processes. Menu-driven. Graphics for analyses. DOS, $395. Macintosh version expected in 1994.

> Stat-Ease, Inc.
> Hennepin Square, Suite 191
> 2021 East Hennepin Avenue
> Minneapolis, MN 55413-2723
> 1-800-325-9829, 612-378-9449; Fax: 612-378-2152

Also available from es²c, 1-800-522-4440.

Design-Expert

Software that provides 3D response surface optimization for process variables and mixture components. Menu-driven. Mouse support. DOS, $795. Macintosh version expected in 1994.

> Stat-Ease, Inc.
> Hennepin Square, Suite 191
> 2021 East Hennepin Avenue
> Minneapolis, MN 55413-2723
> 1-800-325-9829, 612-378-9449; Fax: 612-378-2152

Also available from es²c, 1-800-522-4440.

Desktop Molecular Modeller

For IBM PC. Version 3.0 due in 1994.

Permits construction, manipulation, and calculation of molecular structures. 2700 atom limit. Energy minimization algorithm, valence checks, etc. Menu-driven.

Main program, $495. Modules on biochemistry, organic chemistry, inorganic chemistry, $95 each.

Oxford Electronic Publishing
Oxford University Press
200 Madison Avenue
New York, NY 10016
1-800-334-4249, 212-679-7300, Ext. 7370; Fax: 212-725-2972

Gene Construction Kit

DNA manipulation, design, and drawing tool. Automatically tracks construct history and produces publication quality output; allows graphical manipulation of DNA sequences while tracking ends. DNA can be displayed as a sequence or graphic; multiple constructs can be viewed and manipulated simultaneously. Macintosh. Free demo disk available.

Textco, Inc.
27 Gilson Road
West Lebanon, NH 03784
Tel/Fax: 603-643-1471

Knowledge Revolution (Software for Physicists)

- *Interactive Physics*
  Educational physics simulation program with animation. Macintosh and Windows. $399.

- *Working Model*
  Professional engineering applications with animation. For Macintosh and Windows. $995 ($495 for educational use).
  Demo disks and a video demo available for both programs.

  Knowledge Revolution
  15 Brush Place
  San Francisco, CA 94103
  1-800-766-6615, 415-553-8153; Fax: 415-553-8012

MacImdad

Molecular modeling package specifically designed for modeling complex biological macromolecules; includes, in compressed form, all of the protein and nucleic acid structures in the Brookhaven Protein Data Bank. Supports multiple visualization styles and conformations and creates animated displays of sequence frames. Macintosh, $3,000.

Molecular Applications Group
445 Sherman Avenue
Palo Alto, CA
415-473-3030

Also available from es²c, 1-800-522-4440.

Nanovision

Molecular graphics for the Macintosh; displays molecular models in a variety of styles (models up to 32,000 atoms). Built-in periodic table. Cut and paste structures into word-processing programs. List price, $295; Academic price, $264; ACS member price, $245.

ACS Software
American Chemical Society
1155 16th Street, N.W.,
Washington, DC 20036
1-800-227-5558, 202-872-4363; Fax: 202-872-6067

Swivel 3D Professional

Allows user to do 3D modeling and animation. Can be used, for example, to simulate mechanical models including anatomical structures. Macintosh, $695.

MacroMedia
600 Townsend Street
San Francisco, CA 94103
415-252-2000; Fax: 415-626-0554
Product literature: 1-800-945-4061, 1-800-326-2128
Orders: 1-800-457-1774

Sequence and other analyses

Intelligenetics

DNA and protein sequencing software analysis program. DOS and Macintosh (about $3,000) and several mainframe computers ($4,000 to $15,000).

Intelligenetics, Inc.
700 East El Camino Real,
Mountain View, CA 94040
1-800-876-9994, 415-962-7300; Fax: 415-962-7302.

MassSpec

Graphics-based mass spectrum analyzer. Once a suspected structure has been drawn using the built-in tools, the program generates a database of fragments resulting from 1-, 2-, and 3-bond cleavages. These fragments and corresponding mass numbers can then be compared to the observed peaks in a mass spectrum for structure verification. DOS and Macintosh, $125.

Trinity Software
P.O. Box 960
Campton, NH 03223
1-800-352-1282, 603-726-4641; Fax: 603-726-3781

Also available from es²c, 1-800-522-4440.

Oligo

Oligonucleotide primer and hybridization probe optimization program. Searches DNA or RNA sequences and automatically selects optimal Polymerase Chain Reaction (PCR) primers based on Tm, dimer/hairpin formation tendencies, internal stability, and many other factors. DOS and Macintosh, $800.

National Biosciences
3650 Annapolis Lane, North
Plymouth, MN 55447
612-550-2012

Also available from es²c, 1-800-522-4440.

Software and other aids for making slides/transparencies for presentations[11]

Making slides

3M Company
1-800-328-1371

Provides free professional advice for creating visual aids/graphics.

3M also maintains a service called the Meeting Management Institute. It is a resource library of articles about studies of effective presentations and media management. For information, contact Ms. Susan Putman, 3M Meeting Management Institute, 3M Center Bldg., A145-5N-01, 6801 River Place Boulevard, Austin, TX 78726-9000; 512-984-7119.

DigiGraphics (formerly National Slide Discounters)

P.O. Box 196
Ivy, VA 22945
1-800-765-8859, 804-971-6698; Fax: 1-800-765-6172, 804-979-8409

Make slides (from your graphic/text) with a 24-hour turn-around time, if necessary. Will make slides from a fax! Also make computer-generated slides from some of the popular computer software presentation programs for IBM compatibles and Macintosh. $2.50 to $5.00 per slide. I have been using this company to make slides for my workshops for about 3 years and have found it to be particularly efficient, courteous, and responsive to my needs.

Using digitalized images on disks instead of slides

See Franklin Hoke, "Digital Imaging in Microscopy Offers Greater Control, More Options," *The Scientist*, November 1, 1993, page 19. See also "Digital Imaging" in this Appendix.

Books about preparing presentations

Brody, Marjorie and Kent, Shawn, *Power Business Presentations: How to Connect With Your Audience and Sell Your Ideas*, John Wiley & Sons, New York; 1-800-225-5945. $12.95.

Leech, Thomas, *How to Prepare, Stage and Deliver Winning Presentations*, AMACOM Books, 1-800-538-4761. $27.95.

Peoples, David, *Presentations Plus*, 2nd ed., John Wiley & Sons, New York, 1-800-225-5945. $14.95.

Kodak Corporation has 2 publications about presentations: *Presenting Yourself* (S-60; $14.95) and *Slides: Planning and Producing Slide Programs* (S-30; $17.95); 716-724-2783.

Presentation software programs

Before investing in a presentation program, be sure the service bureau you use to make your slides supports that program.

Aldus Persuasion

Aldus Corporation
411 First Avenue South
Seattle, WA 98104-2871
1-800-627-8880, 206-622-5500

---

[11] Some of the information in this section is taken from an article by Melissa Wahl, "How to Become a Master at Show and Tell," *Executive Female*, May/June 1993, pages 61–62.

ClarisImpact

Claris Corp.
5201 Patrick Henry Drive
Santa Clara, CA 95052
1-800-628-2100

Corel Draw

Corel Corp.
1600 Carling Avenue
Ottawa, Ontario, Canada
K1Z 8R7
613-728-8200

DeltaGraph Professional

DeltaPoint, Inc.
2 Harris Court, Suite B1
Monterey, CA 93940
408-648-4000

Freelance Graphics

Lotus Development Corporation
55 Cambridge Parkway
Cambridge, MA 02142
617-577-8500

Harvard Graphics

Has a free advice line for registered users.

Software Publishing Company
3165 Kifer Road
P.O. Box 54983
Santa Clara, CA 95051
408-986-8000

MORE

See section on Writing Aids.

PowerPoint

Microsoft Corporation
One Microsoft Way,
Redmond, WA 98052-6399
1-800-426-9400; Fax: 206-936-7329

Writing aids

Outline Processors

If you write without making an outline first, you are probably wasting a lot of time in the long run. Outline processors are very useful tools for making outlines. Some word-processing programs, such as Microsoft Word, have built-in outline processors. Outline processor features vary. Get the program that best suits your work habits.

Dyno Notepad

An easy-to use outline processor with a number of additional features. Dyno Notepad is an upgrade from a program previously called "ACTA" (formerly published by Symmetry Software Corporation). Windows and Macintosh, $60.

> Portfolio Software
> 1 Millet Street
> P.O. Box 1010
> Richmond, VT 05447-1010
> 1-800-434-0066, 802-434-4000; Fax: 802-434-7000

Inspiration

An outline processor that allows you to work in a standard outline mode or a graphic/diagram mode and switch easily back and forth between the two modes with a single keystroke. The special feature of this program is the ability to use "free-form" diagrams for brainstorming. Good for those who don't like the constraints of a formal outline. Macintosh, $145. Available for Windows in 1994.

> Inspiration Software, Inc.
> P.O. Box 1629
> Portland, OR 97207
> 503-245-9011; Fax: 503-246-4292

MORE

Outline processor with graphing and presentation capabilities. Allows you to to work in standard outline form, bullet charts, or tree-chart diagrams and easily switch between these forms. A versatile program with many graphic display options. Symantec Corp. *plans no upgrades of this program and may not provide support in the future. Check before you buy.* Macintosh, $395.

> Symantec Corp.
> 175 West Broadway
> Eugene, OR 97401
> 1-800-441-7234;1-800-222-2616, 503-345-3322; Fax: 503-334-7473

Fax product information retrieval system: 1-800-554-4403, choose option #1 and dial in your fax number. "MORE" is document # 140.

Scientific word processors/typesetters

Classic Textures

Typesetting program for technical publishing. Macintosh, $695.

> Blue Sky Research
> 534 SW 3rd
> Portland, OR 97204
> 503-222-9571

> Also available from es²c, 1-800-522-4440.

T³

Word processor for technical/multi–lingual writing. Handles mathematical equations and complex chemical formulas including multi–ring organic structures. DOS, $495. Demo disk available for $60.

TCI Software Research, Inc.
1190–B Foster Road
Las Cruces, NM 88001
1-800-874–2383; 505-522-4600

Also available from es²c, 1-800-522-4440 and ACS Software, 1-800-227-5558.

MathType

Equation editor. Uses point and click techniques. More than 275 math symbols and templates and a customizable palette. Automatically formats equations as you type. Can be cut and pasted into other applications. Macintosh and Windows, $199.

Design Science
6475B East Pacific Coast Highway, Suite 392
Long Beach, CA 90803
310-433-0685

Also available from es²c, 1-800-522-4440 and ACS Software, 1-800-227-5558.

Scientific Word

Scientific document processor with equation editor. Windows, $595.

TCI Software Research, Inc.
1190–B Foster Road
Las Cruces, NM 88001
1-800-874-2383; 505-522-4600

Also available from es²c, 1-800-522-4440.

Dictionaries, thesauruses, and subject-specific spell checkers

American Heritage Dictionary, 3rd Edition

A dictionary that is available on your hard disk. Comes in both Standard and Deluxe versions.
Standard version: DOS, Windows, and Macintosh, $59.95.
Deluxe version: Includes *Roget's Thesaurus*. Comes on 18 (800K) disks! DOS, Windows, or Macintosh, $129. The Deluxe version is also available on CD-ROM with voice (it pronounces the words), $59.95.

Softkey International
450 Franklin Road, Suite 100
Marietta, GA 30067
1-800-277-5609; Fax: 404-427-1150

Dorland's Medical Speller

Works only with Word Perfect (DOS and Windows), $89.

Word Perfect, The Novelle Applications Group
1555 N. Technology Way
Orem, UT 84057-2399
1-800-321-4566, 801-321-4566; Fax: 801-228-5377

Oxford Science Shelf

• *Oxford Concise Science Dictionary*
  7,500 entries: biology, chemistry, physics, earth sciences, astronomy, mathematics,

etc. Appendices include the periodic table, fundamental constants, etc. Allows users to automatically convert Standard International units to nonstandard units.
- *Oxford Dictionary for Scientific Writers and Editors*
  Similar to the *Oxford Dictionary for Writers and Editors* (also available electronically). Provides scientists, science writers, and science publishers with a clear and concise style guide for use in the preparation of scientific material for publication.
- *Oxford Dictionary of Computing*
  4,500 terms: programming, computer organization and architecture, software and hardware developments, networking, and information technology. DOS (3.5-inch and 5.25-inch disks), Windows, and Macintosh, $129.

Electronic Publishing
Oxford University Press
200 Madison Avenue
New York, NY 10022
1-800-334-4249, 212-679-7300, Ext. 7371 or 7127; Fax: 212-725-2972

SciWords
Spell checker with regular dictionary plus 75,000 scientific and technical terms.
Works with Word Perfect (DOS, Windows, Macintosh) and Microsoft Word (Windows, Macintosh), $75.

Word Perfect, The Novelle Applications Group
1555 N. Technology Way
Orem, UT 84057-2399
1-800-321-4566, 801-321-4566; Fax: 801-228-5377

Also available from es^{2}c, 1-800-522-4440 and ACS Software, 1-800-227-5558.

Stedman's 25 Plus Medical and Pharmaceutical Spell Checker
A medical and pharmaceutical spell checker. Contains 170,000 medical words and 30,000 pharmaceutical words. Works with Microsoft Word (Windows and Macintosh) and Word Perfect (Windows, DOS, and Macintosh), $99.

Word Perfect, The Novelle Applications Group
1555 N. Technology Way
Orem, UT 84057-2399
1-800-321-4566, 801-321-4566; Fax: 801-228-5377

Stedman's Medical Dictionary on Disk
A medical dictionary with 100,000 medical definitions based on *Stedman's Medical Dictionary*. Can be used with any character-based word processor for DOS, Windows, or Macintosh, $129.

Word Perfect, The Novelle Applications Group
1555 N. Technology Way
Orem, UT 84057-2399
1-800-321-4566, 801-321-4566; Fax: 801-228-5377

Word Finder Plus (Version 5.01)
Electronic thesaurus for Macintosh and Windows. Easy to use. Permits automatic replacement of alternative word. Very handy for those who do a lot of writing. $29.95.

Microlytics, Inc.
2 Tobey Village Office Park
Pittsford, NY 14534
716-248-9150; Fax: 716-248-5659. Sales only: 1-800-828-6293

Document comparison software

Docucomp II

Allows you to compare 2 versions of a document. The program highlights what is different between the 2 documents and also provides a summary report of the differences. *A great tool if you have to submit a revised grant application!* Mac version, $179; DOS version, $199.95. Network version available.

Mastersoft, Inc.
8737 East Via de Commercio
Scottsdale, AZ 85258
1-800-624-6107

Grammar checkers

Correct Grammar

A grammar checker for style and punctuation. DOS, Windows, $49.95; Macintosh, $79.95.

Softkey International
450 Franklin Road, Suite 100
Marietta, GA 30067
1-800-227-5609; Fax: 404-427-1150

Correct Writing

A reference guide for improving writing skills. Gives rules for capitalization, correct punctuation, hyphenation, etc. Provides guidelines for formatting bibliographies, indexes, etc. Gives frequently used signs, symbols, and abbreviations. The rules are a combination of various writing conventions, including those of the U.S. Government Printing Office. Macintosh, $29. Can be used as a stand-alone application or as a desk accessory.

Softkey International
450 Franklin Road, Suite 100
Marietta, GA 30067
1-800-227-5609; Fax: 404-427-1150

Grammatik, Version 5.0

A grammar checker for style and punctuation. Works with Word, Word Perfect, Lotus AMI PRO. DOS, Windows, and Macintosh, $99.

Word Perfect, The Novelle Applications Group
1555 N. Technology Way
Orem, UT 84057-2399
1-800-321-4566, 801-321-4566; Fax: 801-228-5377

Groupware

Groupware is group-authoring software. Although the hidden text and annotation features of some word-processing programs such as Microsoft Word can be used for reviewer's comments on documents generated by an author, these programs do not provide the convenience or trail of edits and documentation provided by the dedicated groupware programs.

Mark Up

A disk-based program that can also be used on networks. Lets you create an image of a document that can be annotated on disk by multiple reviewers/editors. Readers can zoom-in on or enlarge text. The annotations of the readers show their "signatures," so you can identify who made which comment. The readers cannot change the original document, but the author can merge any of the suggested edits with the original document. Macintosh, $122.

> Mainstay
> Funsoft Corp.
> 591-A Constitution Ave.
> Camarillo, CA 93012
> 805-991-6540; Fax: 805-484-9428

Lotus Notes

Lotus Development Corporation has a program called Lotus Notes that serves a group-authoring function but also has many other sophisticated features. However, *Lotus Notes* is based on a client-server relationship and requires networking capabilities; all participating parties must own the workstation software ($495 each), and one person must also own the server software ($495). The server software is available only for OS2; the workstation software is also available for the Macintosh. A demo disk is available.

> Lotus Development Corporation
> 55 Cambridge Parkway
> Cambridge, MA 02142
> 1-800-346-1305, 617-577-8500

Writing resumes

Resume Kit

Nine professionally designed resume layouts targeted at disciplines such as engineering, high tech, and academia allow up to five entries for general/business experience. All fonts, margins, tabs, and spacing are preset but can be modified. Has a spell checker, an automatic mail merge function linked to a contact database for fast mailing, an appointment manager with on-screen calendar, and a contact manager that reminds you when it's time for call-backs. DOS only (Macintosh version discontinued), $29.99

> Softkey International
> 450 Franklin Road, Suite 100
> Marietta, GA 30067
> 1-800-227-5609 (Sales); Fax: 404-427-1150

PFS: Resume and Job-Search Pro

A selection of resume formats. The program has scalable fonts, extensive Houghton Mifflin Thesaurus, and global spell checking. Up to 15 10-line entries available under general/business experience. Allows you to generate personalized mailings with the contact database, using mail merge feature. On-screen appointment manager. DOS and Windows, $79.

Softkey International
450 Franklin Road, Suite 100
Marietta, GA 30067
1-800-227-5609 (Sales); Fax: 404-427-1150

Page layout (desktop publishing)

Sophisticated word-processing programs such as Microsoft Word now allow a reasonable amount of page formatting, for example, columns and tables. However, for real page layout a dedicated page layout program is necessary. These programs allow you to lay out a page including text and graphics that simulates the traditional paste-up but with many shortcut features. For example, you can wrap text around graphics, rotate text, etc.

PageMaker 5.0

PageMaker is one of the premier programs of its type. Although the several page layout programs with which I have had contact require a significant amount of learning time to use the full potential of the programs, PageMaker is reasonably easy to use and can be used at various levels of sophistication. The program requires 15 meg of disk space! Macintosh, $895. Windows version available. For additional information see the review in *MacWorld Magazine*, November 1993, page 48.

PageMaker
Aldus Corporation
411 First Avenue South
Seattle, WA 98104-2871
1-800-627-8880; Fax: 206-489-3446
Customer support: 206-628-2320
Technical support for the Macintosh: 206-628-4501; for Windows: 206-628-4531

Drawing programs

Canvas

For creating graphics for presentations, technical illustrations, etc. Allows for resizing, precision text handling, graduated color fills, and more.
Available for Macintosh and Windows, $259.

Deneba Software
7400 S.W. 87th Avenue
Miami, FL 33173
305-596-5644; Fax: 305-273-9069

ClarisDraw

ClarisDraw is the successor to MacDraw software and has 75 new features compared to MacDraw Pro. ClarisDraw integrates drawing, painting, and presentation capabilities, allowing users to create technical drawings, slides, flyers, etc. The program has extensive, predefined chart style options and a library of 3,400 clip-art selections. It also permits editing of scanned images, precise placement of graphic elements, and advanced text handling such as automatic alignment. Permits direct importing of multiple text and graphics and exporting to desktop publishing programs. Supports full color and gray scale. Also supports QuickTime, allowing you to put graphics in motion. Requires hard disk and 2 to 4 meg of RAM, depending on the system. Macintosh and Windows, $399.

Claris Corp. will continue to support MacDraw II and MacDraw Pro through the end of 1994. Upgrades from MacDraw II and MacDraw Pro to ClarisDraw are available.

Claris Corp.
5201 Patrick Henry Drive
Santa Clara, CA 95052-8168
1-800-544-8554, 408-727-9054
Tech support: 408-727-9054
Fax answer line: 1-800-800-8954

Help with other languages (software and other)

Software Language Programs

Berlitz Interpreter

Essentially an on-screen bidirectional language dictionary. Lets you type in a word and get the translation on screen (English, German, French, Spanish, Italian). Macintosh, DOS, and Windows, $34.95.

Microlytics, Inc.
2 Tobey Village Office Park
Pittsford, NY 14534
716-248-9150; Fax: 716-248-5659
Sales only: 1-800-828-6293

Globalink Power Translator

Foreign language translation software for DOS, Macintosh, Windows, and UNIX. Automated translations in Spanish, French, German, Chinese, or Russian to/from English. Allows you, for example, to scan an article from a foreign language journal into your computer and translate the file into English or translate an English article into another language. Translation speed is about 20,000 words/hour. Can achieve up to 90% accurate, idiomatically correct, full sentence translations with use of industry-specific subject dictionaries. User can buy specialized, industry-specific subject dictionaries, ready-made from Globalink, or can build their own subject dictionaries. Single-word and semantic unit dictionaries (Spanish, French, German, English, Chinese, Russian) are built into the software. Network compatible.

Two programs available:

Power Translator	*Power Translator Professional*
• Accepts only ASCII files	• Accepts formatted files like Word Perfect
• Can use only built-in general dictionary	• Can use specialized dictionaries available from Globalink or created by user
• Does not permit on-screen editing	• Permits on-screen editing and gives thesaurus choices
• DOS, $149; Windows, $249;	• DOS, Windows, OS/2, $795;
• Also available from es²c, 1-800-522-440	Macintosh, $595. and UNIX, $2,995 (UNIX program includes all subject dictionaries).

See review of translation software in *BYTE Magazine*, January 1993 (McGraw-Hill).

Subject dictionaries currently available: law, business, computers, etc. Chemical, pharmaceutical, and medical should be available by 1994. Not all subject dictionaries are available in all languages.

Spanish chemical dictionary $89
Russian business dictionary $89
German computer dictionary $89
And more

Globalink, Inc.
9302 Lee Highway, 12th Floor
Fairfax, VA 22031-1208
1-800-255-5660, 703-273-5600; Fax: 703-273-3866

Language Assistant Series

Bidirectional translation software package (French, German, Italian, Spanish). Available for DOS and Windows. Will translate an entire document with or without user interaction. $99.95/language.

Microtac Software
4655 Cass Street, Suite #214
San Diego, CA 92109
1-800-366-4170, 619-272-5700; Fax: 619-272-9734

Transparent Language

A unique way to learn or brush up on a language. Learn by reading foreign language stories on-screen. If you click on any word, the translation of the word and the phrase in which the word appears are shown on-screen. Allows user to create personal word lists and review notes. Audiocassettes available to give you correct pronunciation.

Available in 1993 for French, German, Spanish, Italian, and Latin. Available in the future for Russian. Macintosh or IBM-compatible software. The basic program is often available on special offers for about $70. Prices of additional stories vary with length: about $15 to $30; matching audiocassette, about $10.

Transparent Language, Inc.
22 Proctor Hill Road
P.O. Box 575
Hollis, NH 03049-9961
1-800-752-1767, 603-465-2230; Fax: 603-465-2779

Other Language Programs For DOS

Selective Software, caters mostly to the DOS user. They carry an interesting selection of language programs, including one that apparently does translations.

Selective Software
3004 Mission Street
Santa Cruz, CA 95060
1-800-423-3556; Fax: 615-867-5318

Nonsoftware Language Resources

American Translators Association
79 West Monroe Street
Chicago, IL 60603
312-236-3366
Japanese Language Division: 312-779-3009

Canada Institute for Scientific and Technical Information (CISTI)

Depository of publications translated by individuals at Canadian universities, businesses, government departments, etc. CISTI may acquire the U.S. Library of Congress NTC collections in the future. Provides photocopies of translated documents for a fee. In 1993, the fee for non-Canadian clients was $14 (Canadian) per 10 pages. (Services and prices were under review in fall 1993.)

> Canada Institute for Scientific and Technical Information (CISTI)
> Document Delivery Department
> Building, M-55
> National Research Council, Canada
> Ottawa, Ontario, Canada K1A OS2
> 613-993-9251; Fax: 613-952-8243

Japanese Technical Translators (JTT)

Translate Japanese and major European language (not Russian) documents from or into English. Prices depend on the character count of the document.

> JTT
> 959 Reed Avenue
> Sunnyvale, CA 94086
> 1-800-858-9215, 408-739-9215; Fax: 408-720-9416

Joint Publication Research Service (JPRS)

JPRS is an agency of the U.S. government that translates documents for the U.S. Government. Documents come from newspapers, journals, speeches, and broadcasts and are managed by University Microfilms International.

Mostly science/technology/engineering but also some political science, economics, etc.

Documents are classified into the following categories: Africa, Asia, East and West Europe, Latin America, and Near EaStreet

Monthly index (on paper) of documents translated by JPRS + an annual cumulative index (on microfiche), $855/year. Documents listed in the index can be purchased on microfiche for $25/document.

> University Microfilms International (UMI)
> 300 North Zeeb Road
> Ann Arbor, MI 48106-1346
> 1-800-233-6901; 313-761-4700; Fax: 313-973-1540

National Translations Center (NCT)

The Library of Congress Translations Center for patents and papers relating to scientific and technical research was *closed in September 1993 because of lack of funding. Translations of items prior to 1989 are still available from the Photo-duplication Service, 202-707-5650.*

Programs that enhance your learning, teaching, and research capabilities

Keyboard Publishing Software

This company has combined software and video capabilities to produce some exciting computer-based learning/teaching/research tools. Whole textbooks are provided on computer disks, thus giving users the ability to search, create outlines, and keep a stack of "index cards" for study and review of information. The programs also have "bookmark" and "annotation" features. Many programs are available for both Macintosh and Windows. Programs available in 1993 include:

The Merck Manual (16th edition)
Histology Video Review
Medical Microbiology (J. Sherris, 2nd edition) and Microbiology Quizbank
Pharmacology TextStack (T. Theoharidis, Little Brown) and Quizbank
Robbins Pathologic Basis of Disease
Animated Dissections for Anatomy for Medicine (ADAM); an interactive program that lets the user view body tissues through 40 layers and functions as an "electronic cadaver."

Some of the Keyboard Publishing programs require large amounts of RAM and disk storage space. Call Keyboard Publishing for computer requirements and prices.

Keyboard Publishing
482 Norristown Road, Suite 111
Blue Bell, PA 19422-9801
1-800-945-4551, 215-832-0945; Fax: 215-832-0948
Via Internet: KEYBOARDPUBL@APPLELINK.APPLE.COM

Programs to help increase your efficiency and time management

Keeping up with the literature

Annual Reviews Preprints and Reprints
Provide published and not-yet published Annual Review articles and articles from any source, cited in any Annual Review.

Articles cost $13.50 regardless of length. Price includes shipping by 1st class postage.

Annual Reviews publishes an Annual Review of Annual Reviews, which lists upcoming publications. For information, call Annual Reviews: 1-800-523-8635, 415-493-4400, Ext. 1.

Annual Reviews Preprints and Reprints (ARPR)
P.O. Box 990
Burlingame, CA 94011-0990
1-800-347-8007; 415-259-5017
Fax: 1-800-347-8008; 415-259-5018

Cambridge Information Group
Multimedia publishers of abstract and index databases. Publish a large number of print journals and microfiche. Provide digests of worldwide scientific research. Have a document delivery service. *Databases are also available on CD-ROM, on magnetic tape, and on-line. Cambridge Scientific Abstracts* catalog is available.

Publications include:	Frequency of Publication	Price per year
EIS Digest of Environmental Impact Statements	Bimonthly	$525
Health & Safety Sciences Abstracts	Quarterly	$645
BioEngineering Abstracts	Monthly	$535

Computer & Information Systems Abstracts	Monthly	$1,265
Cambridge Biotechnology/BioEngineering Research		
Abstracts (set of 4 titles):	——	$895
Medical & Pharmaceutical Biotechnology Abstracts	Bimonthly	$215
Agricultural & Environmental Biotechnology Abstracts	Bimonthly	$215
ASFA Marine Biotechnology Abstracts	Quarterly	$215
BioEngineering Abstracts	Monthly	$535
Human Genome Abstracts	Bimonthly	$215
Conference Papers Index with Annual Index (expanded)	Bimonthly	$995

Back volumes are available from Journal Sales and Marketing Department; call for prices and availability.

Cambridge Information Group
7200 Wisconsin Avenue, Suite 601
Bethesda, MD 20814
1-800-843-7751, 301-961-6700/6750; Fax: 301-961-6720

Citation Indexes (Specialty Citation Indexes) on CD-ROM

Rapid access to full bibliographic data, cited references, and *abstracts* for article published in your field.

On Compact Disc. Bimonthly updates.

Editions available: *Biochemistry & Biophysics, Biotechnology, Biomedical Engineering, Chemistry, Neuroscience, Materials Science.* Each subscription includes back years to 1991 except for *Biochemistry & Biophysics,* which goes back only to 1992. Each edition $1,950/year except *Neuroscience,* $1,450 and *Materials Science,* $975.

Institute for Scientific Information (ISI)
3501 Market Street
Philadelphia, PA 19104
1-800-336-4474, Ext. 1483, 215-386-0100
Fax: 215-386-6362

Current Contents on Disk

A disk version of Current Contents. Bibliographic data on articles contained in journals allow you to browse, search, retrieve, download, and print entries. Lets you create custom search files that run your profile search on each disk. Searches key words from author's key words and from article bibliography. Available without or with abstracts.

The *Genuine Article* function generates an order for an article via ISI document delivery service. One keystroke displays ordering information.

The *Request-a-Print* function lets you order a reprint of an article from the author on *ISI Request-A-Print* printer-ready form.

Available on DOS (5.25-inch or 3.5-inch disks) or Macintosh.

Some editions of Current Contents will be available on CD-ROM in 1994.

Current Contents on disk is also available for the disciplines listed:

Discipline	Without Abstracts	With Abstracts
Life Sciences J-1200 Series (1200 journals covered)	$615	$1033
Life Sciences J-600 Series (600 journals covered)	$445	N/A
Agriculture, Biology & Environmental Sciences	$457	$803
Physical, Chemical & Earth Sciences	$457	$803
Clinical Medicine	$457	$803

| Engineering, Technology & Applied Sciences | $457 | N/A |
| Social & Behavioral Sciences | $457 | N/A |

Current Contents is also available for Arts and Humanities, but only on paper.

The *Genuine Article:* About $10 per 10 pages or less; about $3 per additional 10 pages. Delivery by Fax or Federal Express for a fee (call for specifics).

Institute for Scientific Information (ISI)
3501 Market Street
Philadelphia, PA 19104-9981
1-800-336-4474, 215-386-0100; Fax: 215-386-2911

Current Science

Books and journals that review the current literature in specific subject areas.

On paper:
- *Current Biology, Current Drugs, Current Medicine, Current Science, Science Press.* Monthly or bimonthly journals that report on new developments in the specific field.
- *Current Opinion.* Available in Biotechnology, Cell Biology, Genetics and Development, Immunology, Neurobiology, Structural Biology, and others. Monthly or bimonthly. Brief review articles (about 5 pages) with bibliographies, written by active researchers.
- *Macromolecular Structures.* Annual publication. Gives details of structural work reported during the preceding year, including X-ray, NMR, and other data.

On computer disk:
- BIObase: Bibliographic information in Biotechnology, Cell Biology, Genetics and Development, Immunology, Neurobiology, and Structural Biology. Includes comments by experts in the relevant area. Information can be printed or exported to other programs. Yearly subscriptions ($330 for personal use) include updates every 2 months. Available for Macintosh, DOS, and Windows. Free demo disk available.
- MEDbase: Similar to BIObase. Available in 20 areas of medicine. Yearly subscriptions ($330 for personal use) include updates every 2 months. Available for Macintosh, DOS, and Windows. Free demo disk available.

A 133-page catalog is available.

Current Science Group
20 N Third Street
Philadelphia, PA 19106
1-800-552-5866, 215-574-2266; Fax: 215-574-2270

PaperChase

An on-line service that searches Medline, Health Planning and Administration, AIDS-Line, and CancerLit. User can print or download references or abstracts and also order photocopies of articles.

PaperChase is owned by Beth Israel Hospital in Boston. Connection charge is $23/hour plus printing charges. There is no monthly minimum, no subscription fee, and no sign-up charge.

PaperChase
350 Longwood Ave.
Boston, MA 02115
1-800-722-2075, 617-278-3900; Fax: 617-277-9792
Available on Internet: Telnet to pch.bih.harvard.edu

Reference Update

Current Awareness Service covering more than 1300 biomedical and scientific journals. Annual subscription options include Basic, Deluxe, and Deluxe with Abstracts. Subscriptions updated weekly. Available via disk, modem, or Internet. Reference Update allows automatic export to Reference Manager. DOS and Macintosh (52 issues), $399–$999.

Research Information Systems, Inc.
2355 Camino Vida Roble
Camino Corporate Center
Carlsbad, CA 92009-1572
1-800-722-1227, 619-438-5526; Fax: 619-438-5573

Managing bibliographies

See also: (1) Franklin Hoke, "Bibliography-Building Software Eases A Cruel Task." *The Scientist*, January 11, 1993, page 18. (The Software Directory on page 31 of that same issue of *The Scientist* lists 39 database and bibliographic software suppliers and 8 on-line services.) (2) Franklin Hoke, "Making the Online Connection with Bibliographic-Database Software," *The Scientist*, June 27, 1994.

EndNote, EndNote Plus, EndLink

A reference database and tool for creating and managing bibliographies. Stores up to 32,000 references. Has space for abstracts.

Works as a desk accessory (Macintosh) with Microsoft Word and several other word processors. Can be installed as a "hot key" in Word Perfect on the PC. Latest version is accessible from within Microsoft Word. Automatically reformats bibliographic entries to style required by different journals.

EndNote Plus also has quick searches by any field, a case-sensitive search option, a sort feature, a find duplicates feature, and the program handles journal abbreviations.

EndLink translates bibliographic references from on-line services into EndNote database records. Call Niles to determine database compatibility.

See review in *MacWorld Magazine*, September 1992.

Macintosh and DOS, EndNote, $149; EndNote Plus, $249; EndLink, $99. Windows version expected in 1994.

Niles and Associates, Inc.
800 Jones Street
Berkeley, CA 94710
1-800-554-3049, 510-559-8592; Fax: 510-559-8683

EndNote Plus and EndLink are also available from es²c, 1-800-522-4440.

Papyrus

Reference management and bibliography generation program. Stores up to 2 million references, provides instant searching of database by any combination of fields, and imports references from most CD-ROM and on-line databases. Works together with most word processors (DOS and Windows-based) to automatically retrieve citations and assemble a bibliography according to any format style. DOS, $99.

Research Software Design
2718 Kelly Street
Portland, OR 97201
503-796-1368

Also available from es²c, 1-800-522-4440.

Reference Manager

Bibliographic database management software program, available in three modules:

Reference Manager Special Edition. Unlimited number of databases; limited to 400 references per database. Can work with optional modules listed below. DOS, Macintosh, and Windows, $79.

Reference Manager Professional. The basic program lets you add references, search and retrieve, generate bibliographies, choose 3 journal formats, or customize your own, etc. DOS, Macintosh, $299; Windows, $349.

Optional modules:

Journal formats. Optional module containing more than 100 journal formats. DOS, Macintosh, and Windows, $59.

Capture. Lets you automatically import references with abstracts from more than 120 electronic database sources. DOS, Macintosh, $99; Windows, $149.

Splicer. Lets you use Reference Manager from within a word processor. DOS, Macintosh, $99. Windows, included with basic program at no extra charge.

Complete package (*Reference Manager Professional* + all optional modules), all platforms, $499.

Research Information Systems, Inc.
2355 Camino Vida Roble
Camino Corporate Center
Carlsbad, CA 92009-1572
1-800-722-1227, 619-438-5526; Fax: 619-438-5573

Managing grant budgets

See also: Franklin Hoke, "Computer Aids Help Find and Manage Research Grants," *The Scientist,* May 30, 1994, pages 17-18.

Grant Accountant

Accounting software program to track expenditures charged to various grants. Provides reports on the status of all accounts. Designed specifically for academic departments. Can be customized to match the requisition forms of any institution. Each expenditure can be allocated to any number of grants or categories within the grant. DOS only, $495.

Research Information Systems, Inc.
2355 Camino Vida Roble
Camino Corporate Center
Carlsbad, CA 92009-1572
1-800-722-1227, 619-438-5526; Fax: 619-438-5573

Grant Manager

Grant fund accounting and ordering. Targeted to university-based grant recipients. DOS and Macintosh, $425.

Niles and Associates, Inc.
800 Jones Street
Berkeley, CA 94710
1-800-554-3049, 510-559-8592; Fax: 510-559-8683

Managing laboratories

HyperLab

Integrated laboratory management system for "data basing" and tracking chemical, restriction enzyme, lab supply, and other inventories. Also performs routine scientific computations (radiation decay, buffer prep, unit conversions) and contains word-processing functions for automating notebook entries and generating orders. DOS, $219.

> SEEG Scientific
> 28 South Main Street, #246
> Randolph, MA 02368
> 617-961-7334; Fax: 671-843-0321

> Also available from es²c, 1-800-522-4440.

InTend

Laboratory organization software. Calculates buffer ingredients, keeps track of protocols, etc. DOS only, $195.

> GraphPad
> 10855 Sorrento Valley Road, Suite 203
> San Diego, CA 92121
> 1-800-388-4723, 619-457-3909; Fax: 619-457-8141

> Also available from es²c, 1-800-522-4440.

Information retrieval, labeling programs, and address lists

Super QuickDEX

I have been using QuickDEX for about 9 years and would have a hard time managing without it or a similar program. QuickDEX is a Macintosh desk accessory, which means that it can be called up while other programs are running. You can get very rapid access to stored information by searching for any string of information. Great for replacing most of those little notes that you can never find. I even use it to jot down where I have filed things I might otherwise hunt for. Super QuickDEX has a new multiple-keyword search feature and other features for merging information, formatting envelopes, etc. Macintosh, $89.95.

See the review of personal contact managers, including QuickDEX II 2.3, in *Computer Currents*, June 1992, page 33, and the review of Super QuickDEX in *MacWorld*, February 1993. Also, watch for an additional product, *Infogenie* (to be released at the end of 1994) which will provide a choice of "field" and "no-field" entries.

> Casady & Greene, Inc.
> 22734 Portola Drive
> Salinas, CA 93908-1119
> 1-800-359-4920 (sales only), 408-484-9228; Fax: 408-484-9218

Dynodex

An address book for the Macintosh. Allows you to print addresses to envelopes, rotary cards, labels, double-sided address books, and pages for personal organizers. Will do mail-merge. Allows you to synchronize data between two files. Windows, $59.95; Macintosh, $69.

> Portfolio Software
> 1 Millet Street
> P.O. Box 1010
> Richmond, VT 05477-1010
> 1-800-434-0066, 802-434-4000; Fax: 802-431-7000

Now Contact

A labeling program and contact/address manager. *Now Contact* is a synthesis and upgrade of two programs, FastLabel and FastEnvelope, formerly published by Vertical Solutions, which has now merged with Now Software. *Now Contact* allows you to easily print all sorts of labels (address labels, diskette labels, name badges, rolodex cards, etc.) and envelopes, manage address lists, create address books, and keep track of phone calls, letters, and other documents. Requires System 7, 2 MB RAM, a hard disk, and MacPlus or higher. Macintosh, $99.

Now Software, Inc.
921 SW Washington Street, Suite 500
Portland, OR 97205-9940
1-800-237-2078, 503-274-2800; Fax: 503-274-0670

Calendar, alarm, and scheduling programs

I can't imagine how I managed all those years before the advent of reminder programs. I find them indispensable. While you are engrossed in writing a grant application, these programs remind you that it's time to change the buffer for a dialysis or that a seminar is about to begin—or that you have a dentist appointment, or that it's been 6 weeks since you submitted your proposal and you should have received your Study Section assignment. The calendar function lets you schedule months (even years) ahead. Many other useful features. Specifics differ from program to program. Before you invest in one of these programs, talk to colleagues to get a sense of what features are important to different people, and then try to assess what's important to you.

See the review about desktop calendars by Franklin N. Tessler, a radiologist and *MacWorld* contributing editor, in *MacWorld Magazine*, July 1993, pages 104–109.

ACT!

A contact manager with field-oriented rolodex, activity scheduler, pop-up reminder, mail-merge, and report generator. The program contains a full-function word processor with spell checker, comprehensive report generating and mailing list capabilities, and an automated telephone dialer that keeps date and time records of interactions with people you contact. Many other features. Macintosh, $250; Windows, $399; DOS, $399.

Symantec Corp.
175 West Broadway
Eugene, OR 97401
1-800-441-7234, 1-800-222-2616, 503-345-3322; Fax: 503-334-7473

Fax for product information retrieval system: 1-800-554-4403, choose option #1 and punch in your fax number. Document # 500 is a list of all the Symantec products about which you can get faxed information. ACT! for DOS is #160, ACT! for Windows is #170, ACT! for Macintosh is #180, ACT! Network version is #185.

Claris Organizer

A calendar program, alarm program, contact manager, and notes program integrated into a complete personal information manager program, Has "drag and drop" technology.

Claris Corp.
5201 Patrick Henry Drive
Santa Clara, CA 95052-8168
1-800-544-8554, 408-727-9054
Tech support: 408-727-9054
Fax answer line: 1-800-800-8954

Easy Alarms

Calendar, reminder, and to-do list for the Macintosh, $35.

> Lets you view 1 month at a time. Has a search feature.

> Nisus Software
> 107 S. Cedros Avenue
> Solana Beach, CA 92075
> 1-800-922-2993, 619-481-1477; Fax: 619-481-6154

First Things First and First Things First Proactive

A to-do list with reminders; Proactive is an outlining program integrated with a calendar program. Macintosh, $39.95 (Proactive, $75)

> Visionary Software
> 1820 S.W. Vermont Street, Suite A
> Portland, OR 97219
> 1-800-877-1832, 503-246-6200; Fax: 503-452-1198

Now Up-To-Date 2.0

Reminder control panel enables you to add and edit calendar events without launching the program; fully customizable display; plentiful keyboard shortcuts. Allows you to create multiple categories for group-related events. Program integrates with Now Contact. Macintosh, $99.

> Now Software, Inc.
> 319 S.W. Washington, 11th floor
> Portland, OR 97204
> 1-800-237-3611,503-274-2800; Fax: 503-274-0670

Smart Alarms 7 and Appointments 7 with MacList

Time management tools for the Macintosh. The alarm program and diary work together to remind you of tasks and appointments. Reminders pop-up while other applications are running, but you can specify when—or during which applications—you prefer not to be disturbed. The appointment calendar has a search feature. The alarm program does not. Note that older versions of Smart Alarms appear to be incompatible with the Radius Pivot monitor.

Smart Schedules

Essentially an electronic Daytimer; keeps track of appointments, meetings, to-do lists, and notes. Also includes an alarm program.

Both "Smart" programs available from:

> Jam Software
> P.O. Box 4036-0898
> Meriden, CT 06450-0898
> 203-630-0055; Fax: 203-686-1900
> Technical support: 415-663-1006

COMPUTER RESOURCES FOR GRANTS ADMINISTRATORS

(Many of the resources listed below are expensive and are primarily intended for sponsored program administration offices.)

Computer-Based Teaching Programs

Proposal preparation and review, research administration, fiscal management of funded projects, ethical issues in research and science, commercializing research, etc.

Sylvan Lake Associates, P.O. Box 3262, South Padre Island, TX 78597; Tel/Fax: 210-761-2589.

Fund Accounting Management Expert (FAME)

A PC-based information system for financial management and research administration.

Medical Business Systems (MBS), 6680 Beta Drive, Cleveland, Ohio 44143, 1-800-682-2479, 216-461-7650; Fax: 216-461-7038.

KPMG Peat Marwick Grants Management Systems

Software applications for management of research space and sponsored projects information; especially geared to budgetary matters.

KPMG Peat Marwick Grants Management Systems, 2001 M Street, N.W., Washington, DC 20036; 202-467-3000.

Research Administration Management Systems (RAMS)

Software for research administration. Includes faculty and personnel profiles, proposal and award reporting, regulatory compliance, project accounting, and budgetary reports.

Research and Management Systems, Inc., 555 Quince Orchard Road, Suite 200, Gaithersburg, MD 20878; 301-963-5226; Fax: 301-975-0109.

Space-Aid

A Windows and Macintosh program for tracking research space information. Maintains research space requirements for grant proposals, including availability and percent use by project, etc.

Integrated Solutions, 1761 Stewart Avenue, New Hyde Park, NY 11040; 516-437-2456; Fax: 516-358-9474.

Sponsored Programs Administrative Systems (SPAS)

A computerized data management system for sponsored programs administration. Includes a comprehensive approach to collecting and reporting information about grant applications, faculty grant profiles, human subject protocols, etc. Put out by the same company that developed SPIN.

InfoEd, Inc., 453 New Karner Road, Albany, NY 12205; 1-800-727-6427, 518-464-0691; Fax: 518-464-0695.

MISCELLANEOUS RESOURCES

Professional journals

Check the various professional journals for information about the latest developments not just in your field but also for developments in instrumentation, software, etc. and about jobs, career advice, special interest groups, etc. Don't limit yourself to the journals in your own field; be sure to peruse the general journals as well. Some of the journals have special topic issues; for example, *Science* publishes a supplement entitled *Guide to Scientific Products, Instruments and Services*, a careers issue, and an issue that focuses on issues of importance to women scientists. The American Chemical Society publishes a manual of commercially available chemicals called *Chemcyclopedia*.

Professional organization newsletters

Many professional organization newsletters have useful information about the funding situation, upcoming professional meetings, conferences and courses, career and job opportunities, new products, etc.

Professional meetings

Meetings often sponsor (1) exhibits where you can find out about new products, and new books and (2) ancillary workshops about funding matters, grantsmanship, new techniques, etc.

Science News

Concise overview of all fields of science. Published weekly except the last week of December, $39.50/year.

> Science News Service, Inc.
> 1719 N Street, N.W.
> Washington, DC 20036-2888
> 202-785-2255; Fax: 202-785-1243
> Subscriptions: 1-800-247-2160
> Customer Service: 1-800-347-6969

Scientific American

Articles about all aspects of science. A good way to keep up with developments outside your own field. Published monthly. $36/year.

A new journal, *Scientific American, Science & Medicine*, was launched in Spring 1994. $59/year.

> Scientific American
> 415 Madison Avenue
> New York, NY 10017-1111
> 1-800-333-1199; Fax: 212-355-0408

Tuesday *New York Times* Science Section

News about recent developments in science, written in lay language.

Numerous "Health Newsletters"

Many of these are published by major universities and medical schools.

Some examples are *Harvard Health Letter, Johns Hopkins Medical Letter: Health After 50, Tufts University Diet and Nutrition Letter*, and *University of California at Berkeley Wellness Letter*. Articles in lay language about health issues, new drugs, preventive medicine, etc. An interesting indication of health issues that concern the public and health researchers— and thus, perhaps the seeds of some high-relevance research project.

SOME USEFUL ADDRESSES AND TELEPHONE NUMBERS

General

American Association for the Advancement of Science (AAAS)
1333 H Street, N.W.
Washington, DC 20005
202-326-6448

American Association of University Women (AAUW)
1111 16th Street, N.W.
Washington, DC 20036
202-785-7700

Dedicated to educational equity for women, this organization has an Educational Foundation, which provides assistance in the form of grants and fellowships to graduate students and women trying to re-enter the workforce.

American Library Association
50 East Huron Street
Chicago IL 60611
1-800-545-2433; 312-944-6780

This organization can be a resource with regard to issues of literacy, intellectual freedom, and information services. For example, in 1993, the American Library Association worked with a group of scientists to launch a national program to try to interest children of middle-school age in science.

The American Library Association also publishes 2 journals:

1) *Choice*, a journal for academic libraries.
Executive Editor: Ms. Pat Sabosik, 203-347-6933
Publish book reviews for acquisition librarians at academic libraries, e.g., *A Guide to NIH Grant Programs* by Samuel M. Schwartz and Mischa E. Friedman was reviewed in *Choice*.

2) *Booklist*
Executive Editor: Mr. John Morr, 1-800-545-2433
Reviews books to help acquisitions librarians with purchasing decisions.

For more information about the American Library Association, call Ms. Patricia Martin, at 1-800-545-2433, Ext. 5045; Fax: 312- 280-3224.

ASBMB Mentoring Program
Sandra Bonetti
Chemistry Dept.
University of Southern Colorado
2200 Bonforte Boulevard
Pueblo, CO 81001-4901
719-549-2526; Fax: 719-549-2732

This program is sponsored by the ASBMB Subcommittee on Equal Opportunities for Women and aims to match potential mentors with those who need counseling.

ASBMB Symposia Office
9650 Rockville Pike
Bethesda, MD 20814-3998
301-530-7010; Fax: 301-530-7014

Association of American Colleges
1818 R Street, N.W.
Washington, DC 20009
202-387-3760; Fax: 202-265-9532

Association of American Medical Colleges (AAMC)
2450 N Street, N.W.
Washington, DC 20037
202-828-0400; Fax: 202-785-5027

Association of American Universities
One Dupont Circle, N.W., Suite 730
Washington, DC 20036
202-466-5030

Association of Independent Research Institutes (AIRI)
Dana-Farber Cancer Institute
44 Binney Street
Boston, MA 02115
617-632-3606; Fax: 617-632-3608

Center for Advanced Training in Cell and Molecular Biology
Dr. Roland M. Nardone, Director
The Catholic University of America
620 Michigan Avenue, N.E.
Washington, DC 20064
202-319-6161; Fax: 202-319-4467

> This center also administers the Discovery Center for Cell and Molecular Biology, an NIH-funded training center for students and teachers.

Cold Spring Harbor Laboratory (CSHL)
P.O. Box 100
Cold Spring Harbor, NY 11724
516-367-8397

Council of Biology Editors
111 East Wacker Drive
Chicago, IL 60601
312-616-0800

Council on Foundations
1828 L Street, N.W., Suite 300
Washington, DC 20036
202-466-6512; Fax: 202-785-3926

> An association of grant-making foundations and corporations. Has programs and services for members including a variety of publications about foundation philanthropy. A free catalog is available.

Electronic Federal Bulletin Board

> GPO Office of Electronic Information Dissemination Services
> 202-512-1526; Fax: 202-512-1262

- Self-service access to government information in electronic form at reasonable rates.
- Direct ordering capabilities for all U.S. Government Printing Office sales items through the free e-mail service.

- Retrieval of new product announcements, subject bibliographies, and other free bulletins.
- Telephone support.
- Free user's manual and file documentation.
- Federal Bulletin Board software offers:
  —Electronic file transfer: More than 2500 files from Federal agencies including DOE, DOS, EPA, and the Supreme Court. Browse file lists, review descriptions, and transfer selected files to your own computer.
  —e-mail: Allows users to place electronic orders for all GPO products and to communicate directly with the systems operator.
  —Special Interest Group (SIG) Bulletins

FASEB Summer Research Conference Office
Ms. Adele F. Hewitt, Conference Coordinator
9650 Rockville Pike
Bethesda, MD 20814-3998
301-530-7094; Fax: 301-571-0650

Conferences are at 3 locations:

- Vermont Academy, Saxtons River, VT 05154
  Contact: Ms. Adele F. Hewitt, 301-530-7094; Fax: 301-571-0650
- Copper Mountain Resorts, Copper Mountain, CO 80443
  Contact: Ms. Jackie Spangler, 301-530-7093; Fax: 301-571-0650
- University of California, Santa Cruz, CA 95064
  Contact: Mr. Ken Vienot, 301-530-7095; Fax: 571-0650

Federal Depository Library Program
Office of the Public Printer
Washington, DC 20401

Access is free. Write for address of nearest library. Information about subjects from agriculture to zoology.

Fogarty International Center
NIH
Bldg. 31, Room B2C32
Bethesda, MD 20892
301-496-2515

Funds traveling fellowships and a variety of international programs.

Gordon Research Conferences
Gordon Research Center
University of Rhode Island
Kingston, RI 02881-0801
401-783-4011/3372; Fax: 401-783-7644

June–August address:
Gordon Research Conferences
Colby-Sawyer College
New London, NH 03257
603-526-2870; Fax: 603-526-4717

The Interface Group
300 First Avenue
Needham, MA 02194
617-449-6600

Specializes in trade shows such as COMDEX, the largest computer industry trade show in the United States, and ALEX (Analytical Laboratory Exposition and Conference). The ALEX show combines exhibits of new research equipment and lectures and tutorials on lab management. (See article by E. R. Silverman, "Contest Demonstrates That Inventing Has Its Rewards," *The Scientist*, October 4, 1993, page 9.)

International Agency for Research on Cancer (IARC)
(Centre International de Recherche sur le Cancer)
150 Cours Albert Thomas
F-69372 Lyon, Cedex 08
France
7 27 38485; Fax: 7 27 38575

The cancer research arm of the World Health Organization (WHO). Fosters international collaborative research on cancer. Organizes workshops, symposia, training courses, and conferences. Compiles statistics about various aspects of cancer epidemiology, research, etc.

International Council of Scientific Unions (ICSU)
51 Boulevard des Montmorency
75016 Paris, France
1 45 25 0329; Fax: 1 42 88 9431

ICSU's mission is to encourage scientific activity (especially in natural science) for the good of humankind. ICSU initiates and coordinates international research projects and acts as a forum for the exchange of ideas, communication of scientific information, and development of standards in methodology, nomenclature, and units.

Jackson Laboratory
600 Main Street
Bar Harbor, ME 04609
207-288-3371

Keystone Symposia (Keystone, Colorado)
Drawer 1630
Silverthorne, CO 80498
303-262-1230; Fax: 303-262-1525

Library of Congress
101 Independence Avenue, S.E.
Washington, DC 20540-0001
Main Number: 202-707-5000
Public Affairs: 202-707-2905

- Science and Technical Division (give reference service by phone), 202-707-6401.
- Photoduplication Service (provides hard-to-get references and translations of patents and papers relating to scientific and technical research from before 1989), 202-707-5650.

- The bibliographic database of all holdings of the Library of Congress are available via Internet; for information, call 202-707-6401.
- Has its own Gopher system ("LC Marvel") to provide easy access to library resources. Users can access the Library of Congress on-line catalog system and get a variety of information via a menu of options. Access to the LC Marvel gopher is free: marvel.loc.gov, port 70.

MEDLARS Management Service Desk
1-800-638-8480

Also provides information about Medline.

National Council of University Research Administrators (NCURA)
One Dupont Circle, N.W., Suite 220
Washington, DC 20036
202-466-3894; Fax: 202-223-5573

National Health Council
1730 M Street, N.W., Suite 500
Washington, DC 20036-4505
202-785-3913

Among other activities, the National Health Council distributes printed materials about health careers and related subjects.

National Inventors Hall of Fame
c/o Ms. Rose Heintz
National Invention Center
80 West Bowery Street, Suite 201
Akron, Ohio 44308
1-800-968-4332, 216-762-4463; Fax: 216-762-6313

Sponsor an annual contest for college and university students to promote the ability to do scientific problem solving. (See article by E. R. Silverman, "Contest Demonstrates That Inventing Has Its Rewards," *The Scientist*, October 4, 1993, page 20.)

NATO (North Atlantic Treaty Organization)
Division of Scientific and Environmental Affairs
1110 Brussels, Belgium
02-728-41-11; Fax: 02-728-41-17

Responsible for promoting and administering:

- Scientific exchange programs between member countries
- Research fellowships
- Advanced study institutes
- Advanced research workshop programs
- Special programs of support for the scientific and technological development of less advanced member countries

For information, contact:

Dr. Jean-Marie Cadiou
Assistant Secretary General/NATO

Netlib
>   e-mail: **netlib@ornl.gov** and type: **Send index**

>   A software warehouse established with an NSF grant. Netlib provides scientists with information in various disciplines, including documents, data sets, a collection of software for solving problems that are ubiquitous in science, and information about scientific conferences. There are programs for linear equations and for network computing. The service is free, open 24 hours a day, has over 20,000 items on its menu, and is apparently unique for its quality assurance.

Office of Laboratory Animal Research (OLAR)
OD/NIH
Bethesda, MD 20892
301-402-1058

>   An NIH office within the Office for Extramural Research, OD, which deals with more general (nonregulatory) aspects of animal research, for example, correspondence related to the pros and cons of using animals in research.

Research ! America
1522 King Street
Alexandria, VA 22314
1-800-366-2873, 703-739-2577; Fax: 703-739-2372

>   A not-for profit organization devoted to increasing public awareness of and support for medical research. Its primary goals include building a strong citizen advocacy base, making medical research a higher medical priority, and stimulating interest in health-related careers.

Research Administrators Certification Council
c/o Professional Testing Corporation
1211 Avenue of the Americas, 15th Floor
New York, NY 10036
212-852-0400; Fax: 212-852-0414

Society of Research Administrators (SRA)
500 N. Michigan Avenue, Suite 1400
Chicago, IL 60611
312-661-1700; Fax: 312-661-0769

Serono Symposia USA
100 Longwater Circle
Norwell, MA 02061
1-800-283-8088; 617-982-9000; Fax: 617-982-9481

>   The educational, not-for-profit division of Serono Laboratories. The goal of Serono Symposia USA is to promote scientific and clinical education for scientists, physicians, nurses, pharmacists, and patients. Serono Symposia sponsors international scientific symposia, postgraduate courses, seminars, lectureships, independent study offerings, course syllabi, abstract books, symposium proceedings, slide lecture series, videotapes, and educational brochures. They are accredited by the Accreditation Council for Continuing Medical Education.

Third World Academy of Sciences
c/o International Center for Theoretical Physics
P.O. Box 586
Strada Costieras 11
Miramare
I-34100 Trieste, Italy
39-40-2240-1; Fax: 39-40-224-163, 39-40-224-559
e-mail:BITNET: twas@itsictp

> Fosters research and contacts for scientists for third world development. Sponsors international and regional meetings, workshops, and symposia in developing countries. Provides travel grants to bring in participants from other third world countries and principal speakers from other countries. Awards prizes, research grants, and fellowships to third world scientists. Publishes a quarterly newsletter, biannual conference proceedings, and a yearbook.

University Microfilms International (UMI)
300 North Zeeb Road
Ann Arbor, MI 48106-1346
1-800-233–6901, 313-761-4700; Fax: 313-973-1540

Woods Hole Marine Biological Laboratory (MBL)
Woods Hole, MA 02543
508-548-5123

> Sponsors courses, workshops, and seminars on various subjects for scientists who want to learn new techniques or learn about new fields.

U.S. Government Printing Office
732 North Capitol Street, N.W.
Washington, DC 20401
202-512-0000; Fax: 202-512-2250 (For publication information)

Government books

General interest

Index to the United States Patent Classification System, December 1992
An alphabetical listing of subject headings, cross-referencing indicia numbers to specific classes and subclasses in the patent classification system. S/N 903-006-00026-9. $15.

General Information Concerning Patents: A Brief Introduction to Patent Matters
Describes what a patent is, tells what items can be patented, and provides a general description of patent laws and the function of the U.S. Patent and Trademark Office. Includes blank patent application forms, lists the necessary filing and maintenance fees. S/N 003-004-00661-7. $2.25.

Health and Human Services Telephone Directory
S/N 017-000-00258-9. $14.

National Institutes of Health Telephone Directory
S/N 017-040-00518-1. $43.

For traveling scientists

Health Information for International Travel, 1992
Compiled by the Centers for Disease Control and Prevention. Advises travelers about health risks they might encounter overseas. Gives information on preventive measures, immunization requirements, and recommendations. S/N 017-023-00190-6. $6.

World Fact Book, 1992
Profiles geography, people, government, economy, communications, and defense of over 200 countries. Includes maps and illustrations. S/N 041-015-00172-8. $29.

The books listed above can be purchased from:

> U.S. Government Books
> Superintendent of Documents
> P.O. Box 371954
> Pittsburgh, PA 15250-7954
>
> or
>
> P.O. Box 37000
> Washington, DC 20013-7000
>
> A free catalog of books on agriculture, business, energy, health, space, etc. is available.

To receive shipments by other than regular mail:	202-783-3238
For nonsubscription inquiries:	202-512-2457
For subscription inquiries:	202-512-2303
To fax orders:	202-512-2250

U.S. government bookstores
For a *Guide to Government Publications (Subject Bibliography Index),* write to Superintendent of Documents and ask for SB-599.

> Superintendent of Documents
> U.S. Government Printing Office
> Washington, DC 20402
> 202-783-3238

There are about 12,000 titles in the U.S. Government Printing Office (GPO) inventory. The GPO operates U.S. government bookstores around the United States. All the bookstores accept VISA, Mastercard, and Superintendent of Documents deposit account orders. All stores are open Monday through Friday with the exception of Kansas City, which is open 7 days a week. The addresses, telephone, and fax numbers for the regional bookstores are given below:

Atlanta, Georgia
First Union Plaza
999 Peachtree Street, N.E.
Suite 120
Atlanta, GA 30309-3964
404-347-1900; Fax: 404-347-1897

Birmingham, Alabama
O'Neill Building
2021 Third Avenue, North
Birmingham, AL 35203
205-731-1056; Fax: 205-731-3444

Boston, Massachusetts
Thomas P. O'Neill Building
Room 169
10 Causeway Street
Boston, MA 02222
617-720-4180; Fax: 617-720-5753

Chicago, Illinois
One Congress Center
401 South State Street, Suite 124
Chicago, IL 60605
312-353-5133; Fax: 312-353-1590

Cleveland, Ohio
Room 1653, Federal Building
1240 East Ninth Street
Cleveland, OH 44199
216-522-4922; Fax: 216-522-4714

Columbus, Ohio
Room 207, Federal Building
200 North High Street
Columbus, OH 43215
614-469-6956; Fax: 614-469-5374

Dallas, Texas
Room 1C50, Federal Building
1100 Commerce Street
Dallas, TX 75242
214-767-0076; Fax: 214-767-3239

Denver, Colorado
Room 117, Federal Building
1961 Stout Street
Denver, CO 80294
303-844-3964; Fax: 303-844-4000

Detroit, Michigan
Suite 160, Federal Building
477 Michigan Avenue
Detroit, MI 48226
313-226-7816; Fax: 313-226-4698

Houston, Texas
Texas Crude Building
801 Travis Street, Suite 120
Houston, TX 77002
713-228-1187; Fax: 713-228-1186

Jacksonville, Florida
100 West Bay Street, Suite 100
Jacksonville, FL 32202
904-353-0569; Fax: 904-353-1280

Kansas City, Missouri
120 Bannister Mall
5600 East Bannister Road
Kansas City, MO 64137
816-765-2256; Fax: 816-767-8233

Laurel, Maryland
U.S. Government Printing Office
Warehouse Sales Outlet
8660 Cherry Lane
Laurel, MD 20707
301-953-7974, 301-792-0262; Fax: 301-498-9107

Los Angeles, California
ARCO Plaza, C-Level
505 South Flower Street
Los Angeles, CA 90071
213-239-9844; Fax: 213-239-9848

Milwaukee, Wisconsin
Room 190, Federal Building
517 East Wisconsin Avenue
Milwaukee, WI 53202
414-297-1304; Fax: 414-297-1300

New York, New York
Room 110, Federal Building
26 Federal Plaza
New York, NY 10278
212-264-3825; Fax: 212-264-9318

Philadelphia, Pennsylvania
Robert Morris Building
100 North 17th Street
Philadelphia, PA 19103
215-597-0677; Fax: 215-597-4548

Pittsburgh, Pennsylvania
Room 118, Federal Building
1000 Liberty Avenue
Pittsburgh, PA 15222
412-644-2721; Fax: 412-644-4547

Portland, Oregon
1305 S.W. First Avenue
Portland, OR 97201-5801
503-221-6217; Fax: 503-225-0563

Pueblo, Colorado
Northwest Banks Building
201 West 8th Street
Pueblo, CO 81003
719-544-3142; Fax: 719-544-6719

San Francisco, California
Room 1023, Federal Building
450 Golden Gate Avenue
San Francisco, CA 94102
415-252-5334; Fax: 415-252-5339

Seattle, Washington
Room 194, Federal Building
915 Second Avenue
Seattle, WA 98174
206-553-4270; Fax: 206-553-6717

Washington, DC
U.S Government Printing Office
710 North Capitol Street, N.W.
Washington, DC 20401
202-512-0132; Fax: 202-512-1355
and
1510 H Street, N.W.
Washington, DC 20005
202-653-5075; Fax: 202-376-5055

INFORMATION ABOUT JOBS[12]

NSF Vacancy Hotline
Lists current job vacancies at NSF.
1-800-628-1487; in Arlington, VA, 703-306-0080; TDD: 703-306-0090

Career Connection
299 West Hillcrest Drive, Suite 106
Thousand Oaks, CA 91360
1-800-967-0020; 805-374-8777

Life Science Associates
2100 Embarcadero, Suite 101
Oakland, CA 94606
510-436-3976

The Lendman Group
5500 Greenwich Road
Virginia Beach, VA 23462
804-473-2480

The Job Seeker
Rt. 2, Box 16
Warrens, WI 54666
608-378-4290; Fax: 608-378-4290

[12] The middle 3 listings in this category were taken from Ron Kaufman, "Biotech Job Fairs—A New Method of Searching for Research Employment," *The Scientist*, June 14, 1993, page 8.

Lists vacancies in the environmental and natural resource professions nationwide. Published twice/month. 6 issues/$19.50; 12 issues/$36; 24 issues/$60. Listings are free for employers.

Job listings in many professional journals.

For example, *Academic Physician and Scientist*, a collaborative publication with the Association of American Medical Colleges (AAMC), bills itself as "The comprehensive single source for positions in academic medicine." Subscriptions to *Academic Physician and Scientist* are free to academic physicians and scientists. *Academic Physician and Scientist,* 907 Embarcadero, Suite 4, El Dorado Hills, CA 95762; 916-939-4242; Fax: 916-939-4249.

See also the 2 resume writing software products from Softkey International listed above under "Software."

Glossary

AAMC Association of American Medical Colleges

AAUW American Association of University Women

Abstract A brief description of a project, consisting of a concise summary of each major section of—in the case of a grant application—the proposal's research plan. The abstract should be both an accurate summary of and an appropriate introduction to the final draft of the proposal. It should concisely describe the broad, long-term objectives of the proposal, the specific aims, the health-relatedness or other relevance of the project, and the research design and methods. In an NIH grant application the "Abstract" is referred to as "Description" in the NIH Instructions and goes on NIH Form, page 2 in the PHS-398 packet.

Academic Research Enhancement Award See: NIH Academic Research Enhancement Award.

Actions on applications See: Study Section Actions on applications.

Activity code A 3-character (letters/digits) code assigned by the NIH to identify special groupings of support mechanisms. For example, R01 indicates an individual research grant. General categories include research grants, contracts, training grants, fellowships, and cooperative agreements.

ADAMHA Alcohol, Drug Abuse and Mental Health Administration. This former agency was a component of the PHS that included 3 Institutes that became part of NIH in 1992: National Institute on Alcohol Abuse and Alcoholism (NIAAA), National Institute on Drug Abuse (NIDA), and National Institute of Mental Health (NIMH). The remaining ADAMHA agencies became the Substance Abuse and Mental Health Services Administration (SAMHSA), one of the components of the PHS.

Administrative Note An addendum to an NIH Summary Statement about aspects of an application other than scientific or technical merit that the SRA or the Study Section members consider sufficiently important to bring to the attention of the Institute or Council.

ADPE Automatic data processing equipment.

Advisory Council The advisory body of the potential awarding component (Institute, Center, or other unit) that carries out the second level of the NIH dual review system. Each NIH funding component has an Advisory Council or Board composed of 12 or more members, both scientists and nonscientists. Applications in the top two thirds of the "scored application stack" and their Summary Statements are forwarded to the appropriate Institute (or other funding component) Council for further review and possible recommendation for funding. (Watch for some possible changes in fall 1994 in the number and types of grant applications sent to the Council.) The Council evaluates applications against program priorities and relevance and makes recommendations—but no decisions—about funding to the Institute staff. Like a Study Section, the Council is only advisory. Funding decisions are made by Institute staff.

AGAS See: Automated Grant Application System (NIH).

Agency See: Funding agency.

AHCPR   Agency for Health Care Policy and Research, a component of the PHS.

AIDS   Acquired Immune Deficiency Syndrome.

AIR   See: Authorized Institutional Representative's office (NSF).

AIRI   Association of Independent Research Institutes.

Amended application   See: Revised application.

Anonymous FTP   A File Transfer Protocol (computers, on-line, networking).

Applicant   At NIH the term "Applicant" technically refers to the principal investigator's institution during the application and review process. After funding has been awarded, the institution becomes the "grantee." In common parlance, Applicant often refers to the person submitting a grant application.

Applicant interview   Another name for a reverse site visit.

Application   A written request to a funding agency for support of a specific project. Strictly speaking, at NIH an application that is funded results in a grant, whereas a proposal that is funded results in a contract.

Application for Supplement   A request for additional funds for a project. At NIH the request can be for the current operating year or for any future year previously recommended for funding. Requests may not extend beyond the limit of the funded project period. An application for a supplement may be noncompeting (administrative) or competing. If the application is funded, the grant is referred to as a Supplemental grant or simply a Supplement.

Application kit   The packet of information provided by a potential funding agency, that contains the instructions and, in some cases, forms necessary for submission of an application for funding. At NIH the PHS-398 booklet contains the instructions and application forms for several different types of grants.

Appropriations   Limitations on funds authorized by an act of Congress that permits federal agencies to incur obligations and make payments out of the Treasury for specified purposes during specified time periods.

Approved   A former voting category for actions taken on grant applications at NIH Study Section meetings. This voting category was discontinued in 1991. See: Voting categories.

AREA Grant/AREA Award   See: NIH Academic Research Enhancement Award.

ARPA   Advanced Research Projects Agency, a component of DOD.

ASCII   American Standard Code for Information Interchange. A code used by computers to represent text. Using ASCII makes it possible for computers to read text entered in other computers. ASCII code represents letters by numbers; for example, A is 65, B is 66, Z is 90, a is 97, b is 98, c is 99, z is 122, ? is 63, etc.

Assurance of compliance   Refers to assurances (e.g., Civil Rights Act, Affirmative Action rulings, protection of human subjects, humane treatment of animals, etc.) that applicant institutions must file before they can qualify for funding from government agencies.

ATSDR   Agency for Toxic Substances and Disease Registry, an agency of the PHS.

Authorized Institutional Representative's Office (AIR)   The university office authorized to submit a grant application via NSF Electronic Proposal Submission (EPS). The office must have access to an Internet host computer to submit the Common Submission (CS) to NSF.

Automated Grant Application System (AGAS)   An NIH system that enables preparation of grant applications in an electronic medium. AGAS is a free-standing personal computer-based program (DOS and Macintosh versions) that guides the user through the entry of all the required application data and then formats the data for transmission to NIH. It is a form-independent system that treats the application as a set of data, not a set of Form pages. The program contains context-sensitive help, extensive error-trapping procedures that prevent submission of incomplete applications, and electronic sign-off via a confidential code. The transmission of applications is possible (i.e., authorized) only via the grants office (or other relevant office) at the applicant organization. Development of the AGAS software is the first part of a long-range project known as the NIH Electronic Grant Application Development Project (EGAD Project), which is intended to enhance the efficiency, accuracy, and effectiveness of the extramural program activities of the PHS at both the applicant and federal levels. As this book goes to press, NIH has decided to seek commercial developers for the AGAS software. See: Electronic Grant Application Development Project.

Award   Funds that have been obligated by an NIH funding component (or other funding agency) for a particular project.

Awarding component   See: Funding component.

Background and Significance   The section of an NIH grant application in which there is a brief description of the background for a proposal, generally including a critical evaluation of the existing knowledge, and statements about the importance of the research, the gaps in the field of study/work that the project is intended to fill, and the relationship of the specific aims to the broad, long-term objectives of the proposal. Many grant applications contain some variant of a Background section. The Background section usually contains citations to the works of others in the field. The references cited are listed in the bibliography. (In an NIH application the bibliography is called "Literature Cited.")

BBS   Bulletin Board System (computers).

BHNS   Behavioral and Neurosciences Review Section (One of 6 Review Sections in the NIH/DRG Referral and Review Branch).

BI   Biomedical Index to Public Health Service Supported Research. A 2-volume index that contains information about all funded NIH grants and about intramural programs of NIH and FDA. It is generated annually directly from the CRISP file and is available from the U.S. Government Printing Office.

Bibliographic Retrieval Service (BRS)   A vendor of computer database information, derived from a number of sources and made available for on-line searching by the vendor. BRS is used by many scientists to access Medline for searching the scientific literature. BRS accesses information not only about medicine and the life sciences, but also about physical and applied science, education, business, social sciences, humanities, and other disciplines.

Biogophers   Gopher Servers on computers that specialize in biosciences. See, for example, "NIH Gopher Server."

Biographical sketches   A required component of many grant applications that consists of information about the background and accomplishments of key personnel on a project. Information usually includes education (through postdoctoral training), research and professional experience (previous employment), honors, memberships in federal government public advisory committees, and a list of publications. In an NIH application kit a specific form is provided.

Bioinformatics   The field of biological computing.

Biomedical Research Support Grant (BRS) (S07)   An NCRR program also referred to as BRSG. This award was initially intended to strengthen, balance, and stabilize PHS-supported biomedical and behavioral research programs at qualifying institutions through flexible funds, awarded on a formula basis, that permitted grantee institutions to respond quickly and effectively to emerging needs and opportunities, to enhance creativity and innovation, to support pilot studies, and to improve research resources, both physical and human. Because of decreased funding in recent years, this program was limited for 1992 to 100 grants of $50,000 each, awarded on a competitive basis. Because there were no appropriations for the program for 1993 and

1994, NCRR has not solicited applications for the award. However, the NCRR/BRS Program remains active; future awards will depend on future appropriations.

Biosketches   See: Biographical sketches.

BITNET   One of the largest Wide Area Networks (WANs), used extensively by universities. BITNET has gateways (connections) to many other networks, including Internet.

BNL   Brookhaven National Laboratory.

BOCIC   Bureau of Census Industrial Classification System.

BOCOC   Bureau of Census Occupational Classification System.

BoCoEx   Boston Computer Exchange. A broker for computer hardware and software.

BPS   Biological and Physiological Sciences Review Section (One of the 6 Review Sections in the NIH/DRG Referral and Review Branch).

BRDPI   Biomedical Research and Development Price Index (generally referred to as the "Bird-Pie"). The BRDPI is developed for the NIH to measure changes in the prices of items and services required for its research and development activities. The BRDPI is used to find constant dollar amounts from current dollar figures.

Broad, long-term objective(s)   The ultimate goal(s) of the work proposed in a grant application. The Broad, long-term objectives are generally not achievable within one or two project periods but are what the PI is striving to achieve in the long run. This is in contrast to the Specific Aims, which are generally intended to be achievable within one or two project periods.

BRS   See: Bibliographic Retrieval Service.

BRS/BRSG   See: Biomedical Research Support Grant (NIH/NCRR).

BRTP   Biomedical Research Technology Program (NIH/NCRR).

Budget for total project period   This is the part of a grant application in which the PI delineates costs for all years of a project and accounts for annual raises and other predictable changes in the budget such as new expenses that may arise in later years of the project: repairs, replacements, beginning new experiments that require new supplies, additional personnel, etc. (In the NIH application this information goes on the top part of Form page 5.)

Budget justification   The section of the application in which the PI explains why the funds listed in the budget pages are being requested. (In the NIH application this information goes on the bottom part of Form page 5 and continuation pages.)

Carryover   An NIH grant application, not recommended for funding at a given Council meeting, that had a priority score close to the payline score and is held over for possible funding before the end of the fiscal year if funds become available.

CBD   *Commerce Business Daily.*

CCRIS   Chemical Carcinogenesis Research Information System (NCI).

CDC   Centers for Disease Control and Prevention, a component of the PHS. Although the Centers for Disease Control was renamed Centers for Disease Control and Prevention on October 29, 1992, it was decided to retain the original acronym, CDC. CDC is based in Atlanta, Georgia.

Center Core Grant   A grant awarded by NIH to support shared resources and facilities for categorical research by a number of investigators from different disciplines who provide a multidisciplinary approach to a joint research effort—or from the same discipline who focus on a common research problem. The Core Grant is integrated with the center's component projects or program projects but is funded independently from them.

CFDA   Catalog of Federal Domestic Assistance. A list of federal funding opportunities. The catalog is available from Superintendent of Documents, U.S. Government Printing Office, Washington, DC 20402.

CFR   See: Code of Federal Regulations.

Chairperson of Study Section   A scientist member of an NIH Study Section selected by the SRA to moderate the discussion of the scientific merit of the applications during the Study Section meeting.

Chartered review groups   NIH Initial Review Groups that have been officially and legally established. Some chartered review groups are divided into subcommittees called Study Sections.

Checklist   Generally a list of items or information required to complete a grant application. In an NIH application the checklist refers specifically to the 2 Form pages in the application kit that are required as the last 2 pages of the application. The NIH checklist deals with assurances and certifications, program income, and indirect costs.

CLIN   Clinical Sciences Review Section (One of the 6 Review Sections in the NIH/DRG Referral and Review Branch).

Code of Federal Regulations (CFR)   A codification of current general rules and permanent rules that have been published in the *Federal Register*. Regulations are grouped by subject categories in some 200 volumes, organized into 50 titles representing broad areas subject to regulatory action. Updated annually.

Co-investigator   An investigator listed in a grant application who bears equal responsibility with the PI for the work proposed. Although this term is used frequently within the community of scientists, it is not officially recognized by NIH. NIH prefers the use of the terms "Collaborating Investigator" or simply "Investigator."

Competing continuation   At NIH, an application for continuation of a project beyond the currently funded project period. A competing continuation application requires peer review.

Computer network   See: Network.

Computer Retrieval of Information on Scientific Projects (CRISP)   A database containing information about all *funded* NIH grants and about intramural programs of NIH and FDA. CRISP is available on-line via NIH Gopher Server. (Compare IMPAC, which contains PHS application and award information.)

Consortium   A group of 2 or more organizations that enter into a contractual arrangement to work together on a project. A written interorganizational agreement that ensures compliance by all the organizations with pertinent Federal regulations and policies must be provided to the potential funding agency.

Continuation application   See: Noncompeting continuation.

Contract   An instrument to procure (purchase) research—usually applied research. Work required is spelled out by the funding agency, which generally exercises more control—including stricter financial accountability—over the recipient than in the case of a grant. A contract, like a grant, is a type of award.

Cooperative Agreement   A type of NIH or NSF award. At NIH a Cooperative Agreement is identical to a grant except that there is substantial programmatic involvement by the sponsoring agency. U01 is a Research *Project* Cooperative Agreement, U19 is a Research *Program* Cooperative Agreement, U43 and U44 are Phase I and II, respectively, for *SBIR* Cooperative Agreements.

Cost sharing   The sharing of the costs of a project by 2 or more organizations, often a funding agency and the PI's institution. Some funding agencies give preference to institutions that will cost-share the project.

Council   See: Advisory Council.

CPI or cpi   Characters per inch (refers to type size).

CPO   Division of Contracts, Policy and Oversight (NSF).

CRISP   See: Computer Retrieval of Information on Scientific Projects.

CRS   Chemistry and Related Sciences Review Section (One of the 6 Review Sections in the NIH/DRG Referral and Review Branch).

CS   See: NSF Common Submission.

CSHL   Cold Spring Harbor Laboratory.

Cumulative Budget   In an NSF grant application, the budget for the entire proposed project period.

Cycle   At NIH this refers to a grant review period. There are 3 review periods per year for R01 applications.

Cycle receipt dates   The deadline for submission of an NIH grant application to be reviewed during that review cycle.

DAI   Dissertation Abstracts International (a subsidiary of University Microfilms International).

DARPA   Defense Advanced Research Projects Agency.

DAW   See: Division of Animal Welfare (NIH).

DCE   Division of Cancer Etiology (NCI).

DCRT   Division of Computer Research and Technology (NIH).

Deferral   The NIH Study Section action of deferring an application for additional information—to be obtained usually by mail but sometimes by a project site visit or reverse site visit.

Deferred   See: Deferred for additional information.

Deferred for additional information   One of the voting categories used at an NIH Study Section meeting. The deferral mechanism is used when a basically good grant application is missing readily definable information that the Study Section members think they can obtain by mail or—in some cases—via a project site visit. A deferred application is usually reviewed again at the next Study Section meeting.

Department of Health and Human Services (DHHS)   A presidential cabinet department which consists of 5 components: Public Health Service (PHS), Office of Human Development Services, Health Care Financing Administration, Social Security Administration, and Family Support Administration. NIH is, in turn, a component of the PHS.

Detailed budget for first 12 months   A detailed listing of the funds needed to carry out the research proposed in a grant application. Includes cost of personnel (salaries + fringe benefits), consultants, equipment, supplies, travel, patient care costs, alterations and renovations, consortium/contractual arrangements, and a variety of other expenses.

DGA   Division of Grants and Agreements (NSF).

DGC   Division of Grants and Contracts (NSF).

DHHS   See: Department of Health and Human Services.

DIALOG   An electronic service through which one can access information (e.g., abstracts of all funded NIH research grant applications) collected and stored by the National Technical Information Service (NTIS).

Direct costs   Costs readily identified as necessary to carry out a project, e.g., salaries, fringe benefits, equipment, supplies, project-related travel, and publication costs. Direct costs are requested by the grantee and are subject to approval by the grantor.

DIRLINE   The Directory of Information Resources on-line database available on the National Library of Medicine's (NLM) computer.

Disapproved   A former voting category for actions taken on grant applications by NIH Study Sections. This voting category was discontinued in 1991. See: Voting categories.

Discretionary funds   Money that has *not* been earmarked for specific items and can be allotted at the discretion of an administrator. That is, it is a nonbudgeted award with no categorical breakdown of how the funds are to be spent. The Biomedical Research

Support Grant funds (S07), although "on hold" in 1993, are discretionary funds. Not to be confused with the term "discretionary grant."

Discretionary grants   According to Congressional parlance, discretionary grants are those for which discretion is allowed the awarding office (e.g., the 21 funding components of NIH) to determine the type of activity to support (e.g., research, training, etc.) and the level of support (amount of funding). Compare "mandatory grants."

Division of Animal Welfare (DAW)   A division of the NIH Office for Protection from Research Risks (OPRR). DAW administers the PHS Policy on Humane Care and Use of Laboratory Animals via a multifaceted approach that includes (1) review and approval of (a) assurances and (b) reports from institutions certifying that required internal semiannual inspections of animal facilities and evaluation of programs have been conducted, (2) review of research protocols by IACUCs, (3) requirements for prompt reporting of serious noncompliance, (4) evaluations of allegations of noncompliance, (5) conduct of special reviews or site visits at selected institutions, and (6) a nationwide education program about appropriate treatment of laboratory animals.

Division of Human Subject Protections (DHSP)   The division of the NIH Office for Protection from Research Risks (OPRR) that administers the DHHS regulations (45CFR46) for protection of human subjects.

Division of Research Grants (DRG)   A division of NIH that sets up Study Sections (both standing and, when necessary, ad hoc) to review applications for research grants (R01), Research Career Development Awards (RCDA), First Awards (R29), Academic Research Enhancement (AREA) Awards (R15), and fellowships (NRSA). Most grant applications submitted to various agencies of the Public Health Service (PHS) must be submitted through the Referral Section of the NIH/DRG. This includes applications intended not only for the NIH, but also for the Food and Drug Administration (FDA), Agency for Health Care Policy and Research (AHCPR), Health Resources and Services Administration (HRSA), and Centers for Disease Control and Prevention (CDC). DRG is not part of any NIH Institute. It is a separate body of the NIH that answers to the Director of NIH and is advisory to the Institutes.

DOA   Department of Agriculture.

DOC   Department of Commerce.

DOD   Department of Defense.

DOE   Department of Energy.

DOEd   Department of Education.

DOS   Department of State.

DOT   Department of Transportation.

DRG   See: Division of Research Grants.

Dual peer review system   The two-tiered review system used at the NIH. The first level of review is by a Scientific Review Group (SRG), constituted by scientific discipline or biomedical topic. The SRG is called an Initial Review Group (IRG) when pertaining to grant applications (as opposed to contracts). The IRGs are divided into subcommittees called Study Sections. The second level of review is by the Advisory Council or Board of the potential awarding component (Institute, Center, or other unit).

Earliest possible start date   The review process at NIH takes about 9 months. It is important to enter the correct starting date (according to the table in the PHS-398 instructions) on the Face page in the item "Dates of the entire proposed project period." For example, if an application is submitted for the Feb. 1 deadline (new R01 or R29 application), the starting date would be Dec. 1.

EBP   Epidemiology and Biostatistics Program (NCI).

EGAD Project   See: Electronic Grant Application Development Project.

Electronic Grant Application Development (EGAD) Project　A long-range project being developed at NIH by the Division of Computer Research and Technology (DCRT) in conjunction with the Division of Research Grants (DRG) to facilitate the processing of all types of grant applications. The project is intended to enhance the efficiency, accuracy, and effectiveness of the extramural program activities of the PHS at both the applicant and federal levels. Ultimately, Reviewers' reports, Summary Statements, award notices, etc. will also be created and sent via electronic medium. The first step of the EGAD Project was to develop software called the Automated Grant Application System (AGAS) that enables preparation of grant applications in an electronic medium. As this book goes to press, commercial developers are being sought to continue and complete development of the software. See: Automated Grant Application System.

EPS Project　See: NSF Electronic Proposal Submission (EPS) Project.

Expository writing　A style of writing that serves to elucidate or interpret, expose, expound, or set forth. It is generally the form used to write grant applications, scholarly articles, etc.

Extramural research　Usually refers to research funded by NIH but carried out outside of NIH.

FDA　Food and Drug Administration, a component of the PHS.

Federal Depository Libraries　Libraries that contain federal information. There are some 1400 such libraries across the United States. They contain information from the federal government on subjects ranging from agriculture to zoology. Many of them are housed in existing state or law libraries. These libraries must provide *free* public access to the Federal Depository Library materials even if the library that houses the Federal Depository collection is a nonpublic library. Much of the information collected by the National Technical Information Service (NTIS) is available in Federal Depository Libraries, but many of the collections tend to be incomplete compared to the information available on the NTIS FEDRIP Database. (See: NTIS.)

Federal Depository Library Program　A program providing free access to the close to 1400 Depository Libraries throughout the United States that contain information from the federal government on subjects ranging from agriculture to zoology. See: Federal Depository Libraries.

Federal Quality Institute (FQI)　Established in 1988 to promote and facilitate the implementation of quality management throughout the federal government. Offers a variety of services such as technical assistance, training, publications, and an electronic bulletin board.

Federal Research In Progress (FEDRIP) Database　A database managed by the National Technical Information Service (NTIS) on which is stored the broad scientific, technical, engineering, and business information that is produced with federal support but not peer reviewed or published in journals (the so-called "grey literature").

FEDRIP　See: Federal Research In Progress Database.

FEDRIP Search Guide　A guide to the FEDRIP Database, available free from NTIS.

Fellowships　Limited grants that support continuing or advanced education of researchers or other scholars. At NIH, fellowship awards do not require Council review.

FFRDC　Federally Funded Research & Development (R&D) Center.

FIC　Fogarty International Center, one of the non-Institute funding components at NIH.

First author　The first author is the one whose name appears first in the byline of a publication. The general understanding is that the first author did the major part of the work. The senior author, whose name often appears last on the byline, is often the director of the research group, who may or may not have done any work on the project and whose name may have been added simply as a courtesy.

FIRST Award   See: NIH FIRST Award.

Fiscal year (FY)   The fiscal year at NIH goes from October 1 to September 30. Data about Study Section actions are compiled primarily by fiscal year of Study Section meeting.

Fixed fee   At NIH, any amount of funding in excess of allowable direct and indirect costs. Commercial grantors normally provide grantees with direct costs, indirect costs, and a negotiated fixed fee. The fixed fee, generally a percentage of the sum of the direct costs and the indirect costs, is a profit to the grantee, that is, it is money provided over and above the allowable amount necessary for the project. Although DHHS normally prohibits issue of funds over and above those required to do a project, an exception has been dictated in the case of the SBIR and STTR programs. In accordance with the SBA Policy Directives, the SBIR and STTR Programs are required to provide a reasonable fee, consistent with normal profit margins, to the small business recipients of SBIR and STTR grants. The fixed fee provided by NIH under contracts is approximately 7%. For grants the applicant organization may propose a fixed fee in the budget.

FOI   See: Freedom of Information Act.

Foundations   Private organizations that give grants to individuals or organizations for a broad range of projects. Some have very specific mandates; others have broader missions. For example, many family foundations are dedicated to specific fields or causes; other foundations, such as corporate foundations, are a philanthropic arm of the parent corporation and provide money for a variety of endeavors. There are over 33,000 private foundations in the United States that provide funding. In 1992 the total amount of money given away by these foundations was about $9.2 million.

FQI   See: Federal Quality Institute.

Freedom of Information Act (FOI)   A law that requires the release of certain information about grants that have been awarded. Information is given on request, irrespective of the intended use of the information. For information about the types of information that are generally available and *not* available for release, see page 35 of the NIH Instructions (PHS-398, Rev. 9/91). Final determination about information release is made by NIH. The principal investigator/program director of the grant in question is consulted and informed about any such release of information.

FTE   Full-time equivalent (personnel budget).

FTP   See: Anonymous FTP.

Funding agency   An organization that awards funding, generally in response to an application.

Funding component   A term used at NIH for the Institutes and Centers that fund projects. In 1993 there were 21 funding components at NIH, including 17 Institutes [counting the National Institute for Nursing Research which was the National Center for Nursing Research (NINR) until June 10, 1993, and the 3 Institutes that were transferred from ADAMHA in 1992], the National Library of Medicine, the National Center for Human Genome Research, the National Center for Research Resources, and the John E. Fogarty International Center. There are also 3 non-funding components among the 24 NIH Institutes/Centers/Divisions: Division of Research Grants, Warren Grant Magnuson Clinical Center, and Division of Computer Research and Technology.

FY   See: Fiscal year.

Gantt chart   A chart that depicts progress in relation to time, often used in planning and tracking a project.

GAO   General Accounting Office. A separate agency of the U.S. government that is an investigative arm of the Congress. The GAO examines government programs for efficiency and effectiveness of expenditures. For example, in 1992–1993 the GAO conducted a study of federal peer review systems.

Gateway   A combination of hardware and software that links two different types of computer networks.

Gigabyte   1,024 megabytes = 1.073 billion (2 to the 30th power) bytes (computer). Abbreviation is G or GB.

GNP   Gross national product.

Gopher Server   See: NIH Gopher Server.

GPO   Government Printing Office

Grant   A form of sponsorship for a project, the ideas for which generally originate with, and are designed and carried out by, the applicant. The project may be education, research, a performance, creation of a work of art, construction of a housing development or other community improvement, organization of a conference, travel with a purpose, acquisition of equipment, etc. The grant may cover part or all of the expenses associated with the project. It may cover only direct operating costs, or it may also cover indirect (overhead) costs. A funding agency, for example, NIH, acts as the "patron" and provides financial assistance. Although people often make statements such as "my grant is due," or "I have to write a grant," they are actually referring to the application. The grant is the award they get if their application is successful. Strictly speaking, at NIH a successful application is funded as a grant whereas a proposal that is funded results in a contract.

Grant Line   See: NIH Grant Line.

Grantee   Technically, refers to the principal investigator's institution once funding has been awarded; in common parlance, *grantee* may refer to the PI.

Grantee institution   Technically, this statement is redundant in NIH parlance because only an institution can be a grantee. However, this expression is often used loosely to refer to an institution that has received funding.

Granting Agency   See: Funding agency.

Grants Assistant   See: Grants Technical Assistant.

Grants Technical Assistant (GTA)   Maintains the organization of the Study Section office at NIH and assists the SRA with many of her/his required duties.

Grateful Med   NLM's user-friendly software for IBM-compatible PCs or Macintosh computers that allows novice users to access the NLM computer system including the NIHRES (NIH Research Resources) subfile of the NIH DIRLINE (Directory of Information Resources On-line).

Grey literature   Scientific, technical, engineering, and business information, produced with federal support but not peer reviewed or published in journals.

GTA   See: Grants Technical Assistant.

Health-relatedness   The relationship between a research project and its ultimate potential for improving the health of the public. The health-relatedness is, in a sense, a statement of how well the research described in an application matches the mission of an agency interested in health care; for example, the mission at NIH is "to improve the health of the nation."

HHMI   Howard Hughes Medical Institute.

High Risk/Innovative Research Identification   An attempt, as of the fall 1993 NIH/DRG Study Section meetings, to identify High Risk/Innovative [also called "high risk/high impact" (HR/HI)] research proposals and document this status in the Summary Statement critique so that these applications may be considered for funding even though they may be somewhat beyond the normal funding payline. A tracking system to monitor and assess the results of this new procedure is being developed. The proposed change came into DRG-wide use in 1994.

HR/HI   High Risk/High Impact Research. See: High Risk/Innovative Research.

Human studies   Research, as defined in DHHS regulations (45CFR46), that involves direct interaction or intervention with *living* persons, including acquisition or recording of private information, except as waived or exempted by the DHHS regulations. Human studies research requires *prior* assurance to OPRR of compliance with DHHS regulations and certification of IRB review and approval. The DHHS regulations for protection of human subjects extend to the use of human organs, tissues (e.g., biopsy specimens, tissues which have been surgically removed for medical reasons, etc.), and body fluids, as well as graphic, written, or recorded information (e.g., data collected from patient chart records), if any of the aforementioned are derived from individually identifiable human subjects. Certain studies involving human subjects (e.g., surveys in which the investigator does not record any identifiers or sensitive information) are exempt from the DHHS regulations. A list of exemptions and more detail about the DHHS regulations are given in the PHS-398 instructions. The use of autopsy material is governed by state and local law and is not directly regulated by DHHS regulations (45CFR46) for the protection of human subjects. IRB approval from an appropriate IRB is required to receive an NIH award, but not to apply for an award. The Division of Human Subject Protections (DHSP) of the NIH Office for Protection from Research Risks (OPRR) administers the DHHS regulations (45CFR46) for protection of human subjects.

Hypothesis   A hypothesis is defined as "A proposition tentatively assumed in order to draw out its logical or empirical consequences and so test its accord with facts that are known or may be determined," *(Webster's Third New International Dictionary)*. Simply placing the phrase, "The hypothesis is ..." before a string of words does not make the statement a hypothesis. A hypothesis generally states a problem in a form that can be tested and also generally predicts a possible outcome. For a more extensive discussion of the nature of a hypothesis, see pages 23–29 in the book by Locke et al., cited in Appendix XI.

IACUC   See: Institutional Animal Care and Use Committee.

IARC   International Agency for Research on Cancer (Lyon, France).

ICDs   Institutes/Centers/Divisions; components of NIH.

ICSU   International Council of Scientific Unions.

IHS   Indian Health Service, a component of the PHS.

IMPAC   Information for Management, Planning, Analysis, and Coordination. A computer-based information system for many *extramural* programs of NIH/PHS. IMPAC contains application *and* award information, in contrast to CRISP, which contains information only on funded research.

Indirect costs   An award component provided by some funding agencies to help defray expenses incurred by the grantee (the PI's institution) in providing support services that are usually shared by other projects, such as administrative expenses, plant operation and maintenance (library, rest rooms, cafeteria, electricity and other utilities, security, institutional store, parking facility, etc.). The indirect costs are usually based on a percentage of total direct costs—or in some cases a percentage of salaries and wages—previously negotiated between the grantee institution and the grantor.

Informatics   See: Bioinformatics.

Institute   A funding component of NIH. In 1993 there were 21 funding components at NIH, including 17 Institutes [counting the National Institute for Nursing Research, which was the National Center for Nursing Research (NINR) until June 10, 1993, and the 3 Institutes (NIAAA, NIDA, NIMH) that were transferred from ADAMHA in 1992], the National Library of Medicine, the National Center for Human Genome Research, the National Center for Research Resources, and the John E. Fogarty International Center. There are also 3 nonfunding components among the 24 NIH

Institutes/Centers/Divisions: Division of Research Grants, Warren Grant Magnuson Clinical Center, and Division of Computer Research and Technology.

Institution   Technically refers to the organization that applies to a funding agency for funding.

Institutional Animal Care and Use Committee (IACUC)   A committee at the PI's institution that reviews projects that involve the use of vertebrate animals. At NIH a grant recipient may not begin work on a project that involves use of vertebrate animals until a verification of the date of IACUC approval has been submitted to the NIH awarding component.

Institutional grants office   An office at a grantee institution that is in charge of administering the funds granted to the institution. Such offices are often called the Office of Grants and Contracts or the Office for Sponsored Research but are commonly referred to simply as the "Grants Office."

Institutional Review Board (IRB)   A committee, set up at a grantee institution, that reviews requests by PIs for permission to do research that involves human studies.

Intent to apply   See: Letter of Intent.

Interactive Research Project Grants (IRPGs)   Investigator-Initiated Interactive Research Project Grants. An NIH program announced in April 1993 to encourage stronger collaboration among research scientists. The program involves coordinated submission of research project grant applications to support formal collaborative relationships between investigators whose research shares a common theme and common objectives.

Internet   A high-speed computer network for interchange of information, data, images, and mail between computer sites. In some sense, Internet may be considered to be like a postal service for electronic communications. Internet began about 2 decades ago as a Department of Defense (DOD) network called ARPAnet. Internet offers a wide range of services such as electronic mail (e-mail), bulletin boards, and file transfer. Some computers can access Internet directly, whereas others must be connected via an access system. The Internet links more than 770,000 computers in the United States that reach over 100 other countries and some 15 million people and is expected to reach some 45 million computers by 1995. The Internet is not actually a single network, but rather an interconnection of over 7,000 smaller networks. (Much of this information was taken from the *Boston Computer Society Magazine*, October 1993, page S-4.) For information about getting connected to Internet, contact your local university public information office, or call 1-800-444-4345 and choose option #3. For more information, see references in Appendix XI.

Intramural research   Often refers to research done at NIH.

Investigator   One of the key personnel in a project who shares in the planning and execution of the project. The principal investigator (PI) is the individual who assumes the responsibility for carrying out the work or research described in the grant application and is the person who normally communicates with the funding agency, writes noncompeting and competing continuation applications, etc.

IRB   See: Institutional Review Board.

IRG   Initial Review Group. See: SRG and Study Section.

IRPG   See: Interactive Research Project Grants.

K11/K12   See: NIH Physician Scientist Award.

K17   See: Research Career Re-entry Program.

Key personnel   At NIH the individuals at the applicant's institution or elsewhere, including the PI, collaborating investigators, individuals in training, and support staff who will participate in the scientific execution of a project (whether or not salaries are requested for these people in the application).

Keyword Thesaurus   A classification system containing terms and codes used by NSF, NASA, NIH, DOD, ONR, the Federal Aviation Administration, and the Air Force Office of Scientific Research to help identify areas of interest for federal funding of research and other sponsored programs.

Knowledge Express   An electronic service through which one can access information (e.g., abstracts of all funded NIH research grant applications) collected and stored by National Technical Information Service (NTIS).

LAN(s)   Local Area Network(s). See Network.

LANL   Los Alamos National Laboratory.

LC Marvel   Library of Congress Gopher System. Provides free and easy on-line access to the library resources.

Letter of inquiry   A letter required by some funding agencies before the agency will send an applicant the instructions for submission of a full proposal. Some agencies have very specific instructions about what is to be included in the letter of inquiry.

Letter of intent   A statement—required of PIs at some institutions—that alerts the institution that the investigator intends to apply for a specified amount of funds at a particular funding agency within a specified time period. This statement of intention gives the investigator's institution a chance to (1) consider whether it is willing and able to administer the grant if it were funded and (2) keep an investigator from applying for a grant that does not provide overhead and that would create a so-called overhead-deficit at the institution.

Level of support   Amount of funding.

Literature cited   In an NIH application, the bibliography of references cited throughout the application but usually arising primarily from the Background and Significance section and the Research Design and Methods section.

Mandate (mission)   The goal of a funding agency or the problem that an agency has set itself, as a goal, to solve. Some agencies seek to achieve their goal(s) partly—or entirely—by providing grants in response to applications from researchers and/or other scholars. For example, the mission of NIH is "to improve the health of the people of the United States by increasing our understanding of the processes underlying human health and by acquiring new knowledge to help prevent, detect, diagnose, and treat disease." Some granting agencies change their missions from time to time.

Mandatory grants   In Congressional parlance, mandatory grants are those for which Congress appropriates certain funds to specific recipients and prescribes a formula that determines the amount of funding. Compare "discretionary grants."

MARC Awards   See: Minority Access to Research Careers.

Marvel   See: LC Marvel.

MBS   Minority Biomedical Support grants.

MEDLARS   Medical Literature Analysis and Retrieval System. A computer database produced by the National Library of Medicine.

MEDLINE   One of the databases within the MEDLARS System.

MERIT Award   Method to Extend Research in Time Award (R37) (NIH). Investigators may not apply for MERIT Awards. Established investigators who have a good "track record" and who receive priority scores in the 20th percentile or better on a new or competing continuation application for an individual R01 grant in an area of research that is of special importance or promise may be nominated for a Merit Award. Nomination is by program staff or members of the cognizant national Advisory Council/Board from the potential funding Institute/component. Such nomination is generally made and considered at the Council meeting following the Study Section meeting at which the investigator's application was assigned a priority score. Merit

Awards are generally given for 8 to 10 years, inclusive of the years of support recommended for funding in the submitted application.

Merit Descriptors   The descriptive words used by reviewers at NIH Study Section meetings to describe each of the ranges of Scientific Merit Ratings:

Numerical Rating Range	Corresponding Merit Descriptor
1.0–1.5	Outstanding
1.5–2.0	Excellent
2.0–2.5	Very good
2.5–3.5	Good
3.5–5.0	Acceptable

Merit Rating   See: Scientific Merit Rating.

Methods   The specific techniques/experiments to be used in the context of the research design of a grant application to achieve a specific aim or group of specific aims.

Minority Access to Research Careers (MARC)   Fellowship and training grant mechanisms at NIH aimed at increasing the number of well-trained minority scientists in health-related areas.

MIS   Microbial and Immunological Sciences Review Section (One of the 6 Review Sections in the NIH/DRG Referral and Review Branch).

Mission   See: Mandate.

MPO   Misconduct Policy Officer (NIH).

MSTP   Medical Scientist Training Program.

NAEIR   National Association for the Exchange of Industrial Resources. Accepts donations of *new* excess-inventory items such as laboratory equipment and supplies, medical items, office supplies, computer software, safety equipment, electronic components, etc. from manufacturers and distributes them to educational institutions that are tax exempt under IRS section 501(c)(3).

NAS   National Academy of Sciences.

NASA   National Aeronautics and Space Administration.

National Technical Information Service (NTIS)   A component of the U.S. Department of Commerce. The primary mission of NTIS is to collect and disseminate to the public the broad scientific, technical engineering, and business information that is produced with federal support but not peer reviewed or published in journals (the so-called "grey literature"). NTIS stores the information on the Federal Research In Progress (FEDRIP) Database, which NTIS manages. NTIS issues a monthly update tape to various commercial and university sources. NTIS is self-supporting and charges for its services. Information collected by NTIS is available to the public from (1) DIALOG and Knowledge Express (both via electronic access; fee for service), (2) NERAC, Inc. (batch searching and SDI services for a fee), and (3) Federal Depository Libraries. The abstract, the title of the project, the grantee institution, the principal investigator/program director, and the amount of the award for all NIH-funded research grant applications are sent to NTIS via the PHS CRISP subfile, which is added to the FEDRIP Database, where it is merged with data from 11 government sources.

National Technology Transfer Center (NTTC)   An information center congressionally funded through NASA, with headquarters at Wheeling Jesuit College, Wheeling, WV. The mission of NTTC is to put people in contact with researchers in the 17 federal laboratories/facilities. The services are free. In 1993, NTTC had over 700 laboratories/facilities in their database. There are also 6 regional Technology Transfer Centers in the United States. The regional centers deal with research in the private sector as well as with government laboratories/facilities.

NBS   National Bureau of Standards.

NC   See: Noncompetitive.

NCBI   National Center for Biotechnical Information (part of NLM, NIH).

NCHS   National Center for Health Statistics.

NCRR   National Center for Research Resources (NIH).

NCURA   National Council of University Research Administrators.

Nerf, Nerfed, Nerfing   See: Not Recommended for Further Consideration.

Network   A group of computers that are connected in such a way that they can share information. There are (1) Local Area Networks (LANs), for example, within an office, a building, or a college complex, and (2) Wide Area Networks (WANs), which connect computers worldwide. Internet is a WAN. Networks have Servers and clients. The Servers are the machines (computers) that the clients log onto (e.g., Gopher Server or WAIS Server). The clients are the machines (computers) that log onto the Servers (computers). The Servers can be personal computers (e.g., in a local office network) but are more often fairly powerful computers. There are also peer-to-peer networks that function without Servers (e.g., 2 Macintosh computers that talk to each other). Macintosh computers have built-in file-sharing capabilities that permit these computers to network with each other directly.

New grant application   An application about a new project—at NIH, one that has not received prior NIH funding. It may be from a new PI or from a PI who has previously received funding for a different project. When you read statistics about funding success rates, the category of "New grant applications" generally does not distinguish between grants to new and previously funded PIs.

NIH Academic Research Enhancement (AREA) Award (R15)   An NIH award intended to stimulate research in educational institutions that award degrees to a significant number of potential research scientists but that have in the past not been major recipients of NIH awards. AREA grants may be used for pilot research projects and feasibility studies; development, testing and refinement of research techniques; secondary analysis of available data sets, or other similar discrete research projects that would help to demonstrate research capability by the PI. Eligible applicant institutions include all health professional schools and other academic institutions that offer baccalaureate or advanced degrees in the sciences related to health, *except* those that have received research grants and/or cooperative agreements from NIH (including NIAAA, NIDA, and NIMH) in excess of $2 million per year (direct costs + indirect costs) in 4 or more years during the period FY 1986–FY 1992.

NIH FIRST Award (R29)   A nonrenewable NIH award that provides newly independent investigators with research support that enables them to initiate their own research programs and demonstrate the merit of their own research projects. The award is intended as a transition to more traditional forms of support such as R01 grants. Principal investigators on R29 applications must be less than 5 years past postdoctoral training and must never have been a PI on a regular NIH research grant. The FIRST Award provides funds, not to exceed $350,000 (in direct costs) for 5 years; direct costs may not exceed $100,000 in any budget year.

NIH Gopher Server   An on-line source (available over Internet) that provides access to (1) the *NIH Guide to Grants and Contracts* in a searchable form, (2) CRISP data, a database of information about all NIH-funded grants, and (3) the Johns Hopkins University Gopher Server, which has additional information about grants. See also: WAIS Server.

NIH Grant Line   An electronic bulletin board information system. The Grant Line provides access to *NIH Guide to Grants and Contracts*, NIH/DRG Study Section rosters, listings of NIH New Grants and Awards, NIH extramural program guidelines, the organizational section of the NIH telephone directory (the extramural green pages), and other NIH information.

NIH Guide for Grants and Contracts   A newsletter published weekly by the NIH Printing and Reproduction Branch and available free from NIH Guide Distribution Center. Electronic access is available via computer through the NIH Grant Line or NIH Gopher Server.

NIH Institute program staff   The individuals at the NIH Institutes (or other funding components) who develop program initiatives, provide guidance and assistance to applicants, interpret program policy and guidelines for reviewers, attend Study Section meetings as program resource persons, present Study Section recommendations to the Council, discuss review questions with applicants, make award decisions, monitor research progress during an award period, and evaluate programs.

NIH Physician Scientist Award (PSA) (K11, K12)   An NIH award, restricted to individuals with an M.D. (or equivalent) degree, intended to encourage newly trained clinicians to develop independent research skills and experience in basic science. Candidates generally should have completed at least one year of postgraduate clinical training by the time the award is made. The PI does not have to have a well-defined research problem at the time of application, but a sponsor with extensive research experience in a basic science is required throughout the tenure of the award, which may be for up to 5 years of support.

NIH Reviewers Reserve (NRR)   A pool of Reviewers who can be summoned to serve on an NIH Study Section on an ad hoc basis. Reviewers from the NRR may vote like regular Reviewers. NRR members serve terms of up to 4 years.

NIH Small Grants Programs (R03)   An NIH program that provides nonrenewable funding of a maximum of $50,000 in direct costs for 1 to 2 years for pilot studies, tentative ideas, or high-risk projects that are not yet ready for the R01 mechanism of funding. Some NIH Institutes/funding components have an expedited review procedure for the Small Grants Program. At some NIH Institutes the Small Grants Program requires different page limits—even though the PHS-398 is used to apply.

NIH/OD   Office of the Director of NIH.

NIHRES   The Research Resources subfile of the NIH DIRLINE (Directory of Information Resources On-line) database available on the National Library of Medicine (NLM) computer.

NLM   National Library of Medicine, one of the non-Institute funding components of NIH.

NOAA   National Oceanic and Atmospheric Administration.

No-cost extension   An extension of time given to allow the PI to finish a project during a set time after the end of the original project period. Generally no additional costs are provided. At NIH, such extensions are called noncompeting extensions, minimal further support is sometimes provided via administrative action.

NOFA   Notice of Funding Available. Similar to an RFP.

Noncompeting continuation grant application   At NIH a request for a year of additional support for an existing (previously awarded) grant. A noncompeting continuation grant application is not subject to peer review but is administratively reviewed by the funding component staff and receives an award based on prior award commitments.

Noncompeting extension   See: No-cost extension.

Noncompetitive (NC)   A designation for a grant application under review. Use of this designation was adopted by NIH DRG for review of all R01 and R29 grant applications as of the February 1995 review cycle. To be proposed as Noncompetitive, an application must be judged NC by at least 2 assigned reviewers/readers, but an application can be recalled for full review by even a single Study Section member at any time before or during the Study Section meeting. In contrast to the voting category,

"Not recommended for further consideration" (NRFC—in use at DRG since 1991), which indicates that an application does not have substantial scientific merit, NC implies nothing about the quality of the application; it simply means that the application is not likely to be funded.

Non-funding components of NIH Components of NIH that do not provide funding. There are 3 non-funding components among the 24 NIH Institutes/Centers/Divisions: Division of Research Grants, Warren Grant Magnuson Clinical Center, and Division of Computer Research and Technology.

Not Recommended for Further Consideration (NRFC, Nerf) One of the actions reviewers can recommend for a grant application during or following the Study Section discussion of the application. The voting category "Not Recommended for Further Consideration" means that the "proposed research is not significant and not substantial; or gravely hazardous or unethical procedures are involved; or no funds can be recommended, such as a supplement deemed to be unnecessary." No merit rating is assigned. The NRFC category was introduced in 1991. As of of 1995, it is not being used in review of R01 and R29 applications, but this may change.

NRC Nuclear Regulatory Commission.

NRFC See: Not Recommended for Further Consideration.

NRR See: NIH Reviewers Reserve.

NRSA National Research Service Award. These NIH awards are for researchers in training. The individual awards (F31, F32) are commonly referred to as fellowships. The institutional grants (T32), commonly referred to as training grants, provide research training in specified health-related areas to individuals within an institutional training program. Both awards have the acronym NRSA.

NSB National Science Board (the governing body of NSF).

NSF Common Submission (CS) The file submitted to NSF via the NSF Electronic Proposal Submission Project (EPS). It contains all the data and documents that comprise an NSF grant proposal.

NSF Electronic Proposal Submission (EPS) Project The initial phase of NSF's transition from paper-based to electronic processing of proposals. The ultimate goal is to use electronic communications technology for the relevant aspects of the proposal submission, review, and award processes. NSF and NIH are coordinating the NSF EPS Project and the NIH EGAD Project so that electronic submission will be similar for both agencies. Moreover, NSF has designed its software so that it will be able to be used in the preparation of a grant application to any agency.

NSF National Science Foundation.

NTIS See: National Technical Information Service.

NTP National Toxicology Program (NIEHS).

NTTC See: National Technology Transfer Center.

Numerical rating See: Scientific Merit Rating.

OASH Office of the Assistant Secretary of Health (PHS).

Obligations At NIH, the amounts of money that will have to be paid for awards made, orders placed, services received, etc. for both intramural and extramural activities.

OCR Optical character recognition. The ability of a computer to recognize scanned characters. OCR software permits one to word process text after the text has been scanned into a computer or faxed to a computer from a fax machine.

OD See: NIH/OD.

Office for Protection from Research Risks (OPRR) A component of the NIH Office of Extramural Research, which is, in turn, under the Office of the Director (OD). OPRR is composed of the Division of Human Subject Protections (DHSP) and the Division of Animal Welfare (DAW), which are both regulatory divisions.

Office for Sponsored Research (OSR)   See: Institutional grants office.

OLAR   Office of Laboratory Animal Research (NIH). An office within the Office for Extramural Research, OD, which deals with more general (nonregulatory) aspects of animal research. For example, OLAR deals with correspondence received by NIH concerning the pros and cons of using animals in research.

OMB   Office of Management and Budget.

ONR   Office of Naval Research, a component of the DOD.

OPERA   Office of Policy for Extramural Research Administration (NIH).

OPRR   See: Office for Protection from Research Risks.

ORDA   Office of Recombinant DNA Activities, Division of Science Policy, Office of Science Policy and Legislation, NIH/OD.

ORI   Office of Research Integrity (PHS).

OSI   Office of Scientific Integrity (NIH).

OSR   See: Office for Sponsored Research.

OSTP   Office of Science and Technology Policy.

Other support   A report, in a grant application, of *all* active or pending sources of support for a PI, whether related to the project described in the application in question or not. (At NIH and NSF, forms on which to submit this information are provided in the application kit.)

Outline processors   Software programs that facilitate creation of an outline. The software provides boxes for topics, subtopics, etc., allows for easy vertical or horizontal movement of topic boxes, permits rapid contraction and expansion of topic families, and provides numerous options for formatting and labeling of the outline. See Appendix XI.

Overhead   See: Indirect costs.

Overhead deficit   The difference between the amount of overhead required to actually support a project and the amount of overhead (indirect costs) received for the project from a funding agency. If there are insufficient funds to support the overhead costs of a project, an institution must either take the money from its endowment or raise the money from private donors (development activity), investment income, fees collected from commercial grantors, etc. Because some institutions have no means to acquire the "missing" funds, they may not allow an investigator to apply for a grant that does not provide adequate overhead.

P01   See: Program Project Grant (NIH).

P30   See: Center Core Grant (NIH).

Panel   See: Review panel.

Payline   At NIH, the percentile level up to which grant applications are funded in a given funding cycle. The payline is often also referred to as the "cutoff."

Percentile rank   At NIH the percent of reviewed applications that have scores equal to or better than that of a particular application (within the Study Section in which the application was reviewed) during a 1-year period. If an application is ranked in the 11th percentile, it means that 11% of grants reviewed in the past 3 meetings (the third being the meeting at which the application in question was reviewed) of the relevant Study Section had priority scores equal to or better than that of the application in question.

Percentiles   At NIH the percentiles represent the relative position or rank of each priority score (along a 100.0 percentile band) among the scores assigned by a particular Study Section. Percentiles are calculated against a reference base of research grant applications reviewed by a chartered review group at 3 consecutive meetings. All applications reviewed, whether given a priority rating or "Not Recommended for Further Consideration," or designated Noncompetitive, are included in the calculation of percentiles. The percentile ranks are used to guide the Councils and Institutes in making funding decisions.

Personal data form   A form in the grant application kit, for both NIH and NSF, that is used to collect statistical data about the age, sex, race, and ethnic origin of applicants. The form, which must be submitted but not necessarily filled in, is *not* part of the review process.

PHS   See: Public Health Service.

Physician Scientist Award (PSA)   See: NIH Physician Scientist Award.

PI   See: Principal Investigator.

"Pink Sheets"   See: Summary Statement.

P.L.   Public Law.

Point   A unit of type size; 72 points = 1 inch.

PPG   See: Program Project Grant (NIH).

Pre-application   See: Pre-proposal.

Preliminary studies   A part of a new grant application in which the PI describes work or experiments already performed and data gathered to support the validity of the approach put forward in the application. Preliminary studies help to establish the experience of a new investigator and her/his competence to pursue a proposed project.

Pre-proposal   A brief proposal required by some funding agencies to allow the agency to select the most promising projects for a final competition for funding. A pre-proposal is usually more formal than a letter of inquiry. Generally, pre-proposals are evaluated by the agency, and only a small number of the applicants are invited to submit a full proposal. Making this "first cut" does not ensure success in getting funded in response to submission of the full proposal.

Pre-reviewers   A term used in this book to mean colleagues and other individuals who read and critique a grant application before it is finalized for submission to the relevant funding agency.

PRF   See: Public Reference File.

Primary Reviewers   The Reviewers who have been assigned to review specific grant applications in-depth and are responsible for thoroughly evaluating—in writing (at NIH, according to a set of guidelines provided by DRG)—the scientific merits of these applications. NIH Reviewers must sign a certification of no conflict of interest.

Primary Reviewer's Reports   The report about a grant application undergoing peer review that the primary (i.e., primary and secondary) Reviewers are required to write for an NIH Study Section meeting. The report assesses the grant application with respect to scientific and technical significance of the proposed research, originality, adequacy of the methods, qualifications and experience ("track record")—or potential (for a new applicant)—of the PI and staff, the suitability of the facilities, resources, and scientific ambiance, the appropriateness of the budget, the appropriateness of the requested time, and other factors including assurances and certifications.

Principal Investigator (PI)   The person who has conceived—and accepts the primary responsibility for—the project described in a grant application. Note that the correct term is princi*pal* investigator—not princi*ple* investigator.

Priority score   At NIH the score derived from the merit rating scores assigned by the members of the Study Section. The priority score = 100 × average of merit rating scores for the application. The priority scores are used to calculate percentile rankings.

Privacy Act   A law that permits Principal Investigators/Program Directors to request copies of records pertaining to their grant applications from the NIH component responsible for funding decisions. Established procedures permit the Principal Investigators/Program Directors to request correction of inaccurate records. NIH will amend such records if the agency concurs that the records are incorrect.

Private foundations   See: Foundations.

Program Project Grant (P01)   A grant awarded by NIH to a qualified institution on behalf of a principal investigator for the support of a broadly based, often multidisciplinary, long-term research program with a particular major objective or theme. A Program Project involves the organized efforts of groups of investigators who conduct research projects related to the overall program objective. The grant usually provides support for the projects and for certain shared resources that are necessary for the total research effort.

Program staff   The individuals at a funding agency who are in charge of developing and/or administering program initiatives. See also: NIH Institute program staff.

Progress Report   A part of a renewal grant application in which the PI summarizes the specific aims of the preceding application and provides an account of progress (published and unpublished) made toward their achievement. The Progress Report lends credibility to what the PI proposed in the original application and helps Reviewers assess whether the PI did a good job during the preceding project period.

Project period   The period of time for which funding is provided in response to a grant application.

Project site visit (PSV)   See: Site visit.

Proposal   A term often used interchangeably with the term "application." Also commonly used to refer to the part of a grant application in which the proposed project is described, for example, the research plan in an NIH application, whereas the "application" tends to refer to the completed packet of information submitted to the funding agency. Strictly speaking, at NIH an application that is funded results in a grant for the PI, whereas a proposal that is funded results in a contract for the PI.

PSA   See: Physician Scientist Award (NIH).

PSA   Pre-Solicitation Announcement (e.g., for SBIR).

PSV   Project site visit. See: Site visit.

Public Health Service (PHS)   A component of the Department of Health and Human Services (DHHS). PHS consists of OASH and 8 component agencies: Agency for Health Care Policy and Research (AHCPR), Agency for Toxic Substances and Disease Registry (ATSDR), Centers for Disease Control and Prevention (CDC), Food and Drug Administration (FDA), Health Resources and Services Administration (HRSA), Indian Health Service (IHS), National Institutes of Health (NIH), Substance Abuse and Mental Health Services Administration (SAMHSA).

Public Reference File (PRF)   A list of all U.S. government documents that are for sale by the U.S. Government Printing Office. The PRF is available at libraries on microfiche but tends to be outdated. However, U.S. government bookstores can access an up-to-date on-line version of the PRF.

R&D   Research and development.

R03   See: NIH Small Grants Programs.

R01   Research Project Grant (NIH).

R15   See: NIH Academic Research Enhancement Award.

R21   Pilot projects or feasibility studies (NIH).

R29   See: NIH FIRST Award.

R43/R44   See: Small Business Innovation Research Grant.

RAM   Random access memory (computer). RAM is the main (working) memory used to run programs on a computer. RAM memory is volatile and is lost when the power is turned off. Do not confuse RAM [about 1 to 20 megs (megabytes) on a Macintosh computer] with storage space on a hard disk [perhaps between 40 megs to 1 gigabyte (= 1,024 megs)]. The amount of RAM determines how many programs you can use (have open) simultaneously. The storage space determines how many files you can have (save) on the hard disk.

Rationale   An explanation of the underlying reason (justification) for proposing or doing a project or using a particular approach to solving a problem. Note that "ratio-nale" is different from "significance." The latter has more to do with the possible con-sequences of the project or problem.

RCDA (K04)   Research Career Development Award (NIH).

Readers (Discussants)   Members of an NIH Study Section who are assigned to read spe-cific grant applications in-depth. Like primary Reviewers, Readers must be very knowledgeable about the grant applications that they have been assigned and are ex-pected to participate actively in the discussion of the application at the Study Section meeting. But, unlike the primary Reviewers, the Readers are not required to prepare a written report about the grant application.

Rebuttal   A rebuttal is a response by a PI to a Summary Statement that the PI finds to be erroneous or flawed in some way. A PI who wishes to write a rebuttal regarding an application submitted to NIH should contact an appropriate program staff member at the assigned Institute or other funding component for information about proce-dures to seek redress of her/his concerns. Detailed information about communicat-ing concerns about the review of an application is available from the NIH Grants Information Office, Division of Research Grants. A letter of rebuttal should be con-structive and written in a positive tone, regardless of the problem.

Referral and Review Branch (RRB)   A component of the NIH/DRG that consists of the Referral Section and 6 Review Sections: Behavioral and Neurosciences Review Section (BHNS), Biological and Physiological Sciences Review Section (BPS), Chemistry and Related Sciences Review Section (CRS), Clinical Sciences Review Section (CLIN), Microbial and Immunological Sciences Review Section (MIS), and Technology and Applied Sciences Review Section (TAS). The Referral Section in-cludes the Referral Officers and also a Project Control Unit, which keeps track of applications. The Review Sections are administrative groupings of Initial Review Groups (IRGs) composed of sub-committees called Study Sections.

Referral Officers   The Referral Officers at NIH, usually experienced SRAs, are respon-sible for assigning grant applications to specific Study Sections for review.

Renewal   See: Competing continuation.

Research Career Re-Entry Program (K17)   An NIH postdoctoral award that provides support to basic or clinical scientists who are re-entering active careers in science or academic medicine and who show high potential as basic or clinical researchers if enabled to update their skills.

Research Design   The general approach to be used to achieve a Specific Aim or group of Specific Aims. (Note that the "Research Design" explains "how," whereas the "ra-tionale" explains "why.") Carrying out the Research Design generally involves the use of one or more specific methods or protocols.

Research Plan   The main (science) part of a grant application. The Research Plan almost always consists of some variation of the parts listed below:
- Specific Aims = What you intend to do.
- Background and Significance = What has already been done in the field. Why the work is important.
- Preliminary Studies or Progress Report = What *you* have done already on this project.
- Research Design and Methods = How you will fulfill the aims. How you will do the work.

Request for Application (RFA)   A formal announcement describing an NIH Institute (or other funding agency) initiative in a well-defined scientific (or other) area that invites anyone in the field to submit a grant application for a one-time competition for a specific amount of set-aside funds to be used for a specific number of awards. At NIH, an RFA would be a request to submit an application for a grant. Cf: RFP.

Request for Proposal (RFP)   An invitation by a funding agency to submit a proposal. At NIH an RFP would be a request to submit a proposal for a contract. Cf: RFA.

Reverse site visit   At NIH a type of site visit whereby the PI and certain key members of the research team come to the Study Section meeting to provide additional information to the Study Section members. Also referred to as an "applicant interview."

Review panel   A group of people, usually, but not necessarily, experts in a particular field, that reviews proposals for a funding agency such as NSF. Similar to an NIH Study Section.

Reviewers Reserve   See: NIH Reviewers Reserve.

Reviewer's workload   The number of grant applications a Reviewer has to review plus the number of additional applications s/he has to read for a particular Study Section meeting.

Revision   See: Revised application.

RFA   See: Request for Application.

RFP   See: Request for Proposal.

ROM   Read only memory (computer). Memory in a computer on which data has been prerecorded. ROM cannot be removed or changed; it can only be read. ROM is preserved even when the power is turned off. ROM is used in computers to store, for example, the start-up program.

ROW   Research Opportunities for Women Program (NSF).

RRB   See: Referral and Review Branch.

SAMHSA   Substance Abuse and Mental Health Services Administration. SAMHSA is one of the 8 component agencies of the PHS and is essentially what used to be called ADAMHA, minus the 3 Institutes—NIAAA, NIDA, NIMH—that became part of NIH in 1992.

SBA   Small Business Administration.

SBIR Grant   See: Small Business Innovation Research Grant.

Science and Technology Information System (STIS)   An NSF electronic information system. The *NSF Bulletin* is available on STIS, as is new information about NSF such as new NSF telephone numbers following the NSF move from Washington DC, to Arlington, Virginia, at the end of 1993. STIS also has NSF program announcements, information about available NSF publications, etc.

Scientific Merit Rating   The numerical score assigned to each scored application by each voting member of the Study Section. Scores are 1.0 (best) to 5.0 (worst); scoring is in increments of 0.1. These scores reflect the personal evaluation by the members of the Study Section of the scientific merit of the research proposed in an application. The numerical scores are individually recorded by secret ballot. The research proposed in scored applications is considered to be significant and substantial. The recommendation to assign a numerical score may be for the time and amount requested or for an adjusted time and amount. After the Study Section meeting, the numerical scores for each application are averaged and multiplied by 100 to generate a priority score. Percentile ranks are then calculated for these priority scores. The priority scores and percentile rankings are the primary, but not the only, determinants upon which funding decisions are based. [Funding decisions are also influenced by the Council and are also based on program considerations (program relevance and priorities) and availability of funds.]

Scientific Review Administrator (SRA)   The SRA is a federal employee, usually a Ph.D. or M.D. level scientist, who is in charge of a Study Section. The SRA nominates Study Section members, selects the chairperson for the Study Section, manages the administrative aspects of the Study Section meeting, and prepares Summary Statements ("Pink Sheets").

Scientific Review Group (SRG)   Performs the initial scientific merit review of grant applications and contract proposals. An SRG is referred to as an Initial Review Group (IRG) when pertaining to grant applications (as opposed to contracts). In 1994 the NIH DRG was reorganized into 19 IRGs, each of which consists of sub-committees called Study Sections. In 1994 there are about 100 Study Sections.

SDI Selected dissemination of information.

Senior author The senior author on a publication is often the director of a research group, who may or may not have done any work on the project and whose name may have been added as the last author simply as a courtesy. Be aware of the distinction between the first author and the senior author. The general understanding is that the first author did the major part of the work.

SEP See: Special Emphasis Panel (NIH).

SERDP See: Strategic Environmental Research Defense Program.

Server Computer Server. See: Network.

SGER See: Small Grants for Exploratory Research (NSF).

Shannon Award (R55) James A. Shannon Director's Award. A limited NIH award to investigators to (1) further develop, test, and refine research techniques, (2) perform secondary analysis of available data sets, (3) test the feasibility of innovative and creative approaches, and (4) conduct other discrete projects that can demonstrate the research capability of the PI and lend additional weight to the PI's meritorious but unfunded grant application. These awards cannot be applied for; they are given, at the discretion of the director of NIH, for promising grant applications that just missed the payline. The number of awards varies, depending in part on the funds budgeted to the OD/NIH. These awards may or may not be continued by Dr. Harold Varmus, the new director of NIH, who was appointed in November 1993.

SIC Standard Industrial Classification System.

SIG Special Interest Group (e.g., in computer bulletin boards).

Significance The section of a grant application in which the PI explains why the work is worth doing.

Site visit A visit by a committee of Reviewers and Administrators to a PI's laboratory to get additional information about a project that was not adequately described in a grant application or when information needed to make a recommendation about an application can be obtained only at the proposed research or training site. Recommended at an NIH Study Section or Council meeting in conjunction with a deferral action. Often used when an application involves complex coordination of individuals or institutions; for example, Program Project Grants, Training Grants, etc. In the past, most Program Project Grants were site-visited. This tendency may change as a result of economic pressures because site visits are costly. See also: Reverse site visit.

Site visit team Typically, the site-visit team (for an NIH R01 application) is composed of 3 or more members of the Study Section and, when necessary, ad hoc consultants who are experts in critical aspects of the proposed work. Representatives from the potential awarding Institute also attend the site visit as observers. The site-visit team reports its findings and recommendations back to the Study Section in time for its next meeting.

Small business See: Small business concern.

Small business concern A small business concern is defined by the federal government as one that has 500 or fewer employees and is at least 51% owned by U.S. citizens or lawfully admitted resident aliens.

Small Business Innovation Research (SBIR) Grant A 3-phase program of grants for small businesses (500 or fewer employees) to evaluate or establish the technical merit and feasibility of research and development ideas that may ultimately lead to a commercial product or service and commercial application of the research. Grants are

awarded by federal government agencies with research or R&D budgets in excess of $100 million to support cutting-edge research and development on the nation's most pressing scientific and engineering problems. Awards are made in fields spanning the entire spectrum of federal research and development; for example, advanced composite materials, agriculture, aquaculture, avionics, bioremediation, education, energy, environmental monitoring, manufacturing process control, medical devices, navigation, optical computing, parallel processing software, space propulsion systems, transportation. The SBIR grants, which are administered under the overall guidance of the SBA, are intended to (1) stimulate technological innovation, (2) use small businesses to meet federal research and development needs, (3) increase private sector commercialization of innovations derived from federal research and development, and (4) foster and encourage participation by women and minority and disadvantaged persons in technological innovation. In 1993, 11 agencies participated: DOA, DOC, DOD, DOEd, DOE, DHHS, DOT, EPA, NASA, NSF, and NRC. The agencies involved in the SBIR Program have discretion in the administration and funding levels of awards. Phase I and II: federally funded; Phase III (to pursue commercial application of R&D supported by Federal funds in Phase I and II) is generally supported by non-Federal funds. For *NIH* 1993 *receipt* dates: Phase I awards were: up to $75,000 (for direct plus indirect costs) plus a fixed fee for 6 months; Phase II awards were: normally up to $500,000 (for direct plus indirect costs) plus a fixed fee for 2 years. For NIH:
SBIR GRANTS: Phase I: R43; Phase II: R44
SBIR CONTRACTS: Phase I: N43; Phase II: N44
SBIR COOPERATIVE AGREEMENTS: Phase I: U43   Phase II: U44

Small Business Technology Transfer Program (STTR)   Awards for small businesses (500 or fewer employees) that are involved in cutting-edge research and development on the nation's most pressing scientific and engineering problems in fields spanning the entire spectrum of federal research and development. Grants are awarded by federal government agencies with research or R&D budgets in excess of $1 billion. Funding is derived from fixed percentages of each participating agency's R&D budget. As of FY 1994, 5 agencies are participating: DOD, DOE, DHHS, NASA, and NSF. The agencies involved in the STTR program have discretion in the administration and funding levels of awards. The STTR awards are administered under the overall policy guidance of the SBA and are designed for partnerships between small businesses and research centers at universities and private research institutions. The STTR Program is a pilot program scheduled to begin in FY 1994. It has 3 phases, similar to the SBIR Program. Award levels and period of support: Phase I: up to $100,000 (direct costs plus indirect costs plus a negotiated fixed fee) for 1 year. Phase II: generally up to $500,000 (direct costs plus indirect costs plus a negotiated fixed fee) for 2 years. Phase III is intended for pursuit by the small business, generally using non-federal funds, of the commercialization of the results of the research or R&D funded in Phases I and II.
STTR GRANTS: Phase I: R41; Phase II: R42.

Small Grants for Exploratory Research (SGER)   Nonrenewable awards of $50,000 (usually for 1 year; maximum of 2 years) made by NSF for small-scale, high-risk exploratory research. Only a brief application is required, there is no submission deadline, and applications are not subject to peer review but are reviewed only by the relevant NSF Program Officer.

Small Grants Programs   See: NIH Small Grants Programs.

Snap-out mailers   Computer-generated forms used by NIH to send certain information about a grant application to the PI. One snap-out mailer, the Referral Notification

Assignment, is sent to the PI about 6 to 8 weeks after submission of an application. It shows the serial number assigned to the application, the Study Section assignment, the dates of review by the Study Section and by the Council, the name and phone number of the SRA, and the potential funding Institute assignment. A second snap-out mailer showing the priority score and percentile rank is sent to the PI within 2 weeks after the Study Section meeting.

SOC   *Standard Occupational Classification Manual.*

Special Emphasis Panel (SEP)   At NIH, a special Review Group that is permanently chartered but does not have a standing membership; thus, every time the SEP meets, it has a different ad hoc group of Reviewers.

Specific Aims   A concise description, often in outline form, of what the specific research described in an application is intended to accomplish. The Specific Aims are preferably, but not necessarily, stated as hypotheses to be tested or specific questions to be asked and answered.

SPIN   See: Sponsored Programs Information Network.

Split vote   A split vote refers to the situation at an NIH Study Section meeting whereby the members do not agree on a voting category for a particular grant application. If there are 2 or more dissenting members, they are required to write a Minority Report explaining their reasons for dissenting. If only one member of the Study Section gives a dissenting vote, a Minority Report is optional. In this case the SRA may designate whether such a report must be written. If the SRA does not request a Minority Report, the dissenting member has the option of writing one.

Sponsored Programs Information Network (SPIN)   One of a number of computerized lists (databases) of available funding. See Appendix XI.

SRA   See: Scientific Review Administrator.

SRA   Society of Research Administrators.

SRB   Scientific Review Branch; an obsolete name for the NIH/DRG Referral and Review Branch (RRB).

SRG   See: Scientific Review Group.

STIS   See: Science and Technology Information System (NSF).

STN   Scientific and Technical Information Network.

Strategic Environmental Research Defense Program (SERDP)   A federal program set up in 1990 for funding environmental research in which universities and the private sector can participate. The SERDP program is a joint effort of DOD, DOE, and the EPA. To be eligible, projects must be of interest to one of these 3 agencies and must be related to defense needs. NOAA helps to oversee the program.

STTR   Small Business Technology Transfer Research. See: Small Business Technology Transfer Program.

Study Section (IRG/SRG)   At NIH, an advisory group of about 14–20 members, all scientists, that is constituted by scientific discipline or biomedical topic and provides initial scientific review of grant applications. DRG Study Sections meet 3 times a year, usually for 2 to 3 days at a time, and review about 40 to 120 applications. The Study Section members assign numerical ratings to grant applications and make budget recommendations but no funding decisions. The Study Section provides the first level of review in the NIH dual review system. NIH funding components also maintain Study Sections to review RFAs, and certain other types of grant applications.

Study Section actions on applications   Actions taken on R01 and R29 applications by an NIH Study Section: (1) Designated "Noncompetitive" (NC), (2) deferred for additional information or a site visit, (3) assigned a Scientific Merit Rating. After the Study Section meeting, the grant applications—except as noted below—are sent to the Council/Board of the assigned Institute/Center to be considered for recommendation for possible funding. Applications that are deferred for additional information or designated NC are not sent to the Council/Board. However, the Council may request to see any application reviewed by the Study Section whether scored or not scored. See also: Voting categories, Noncompetitive, and Triage.

Subcontract   A contract between the primary contractor/applicant and one or more other organizations or individuals to obtain goods and/or services to carry out the objectives of the primary contractor/applicant.

Success rate   At NIH, the success rate is the number of competing project grants awarded as a percentage of the sum of the number of applications reviewed and the number of funded carryovers. For practical purposes this is approximately equal to 100 times the number of grants awarded divided by the number of grant applications reviewed.

Summary Statement   At NIH, the report written by the SRA for each reviewed application after the Study Section meeting. It may be only a combination of the primary reviewer's reports, or it may also include comments made by the Readers and other members of the Study Section during the discussion of the application. The Summary Statement, which is sent to the PI about 6 to 8 weeks after the Study Section meeting, shows the priority score and percentile rank for the application and indicates the time and amount of funding recommended by the Study Section. In the past the Summary Statement was commonly referred to as the "Pink Sheets" because it was printed on pink paper. Since 1992, the Summary Statement has been printed on white paper but continues to be referred to informally as the "Pink Sheets." As of 1995, DRG Summary Statements consist only of the individual reviewers' critiques and for applications designated "NC," no longer contain the previously characteristic descriptions of the project. Reviewers are expected to modify their written critiques during the review of an application, for example, removing a criticism that was deemed to be invalid following group discussion. SRAs will write summaries of the Study Section discussion (including budget recommendations, if appropriate) only for applications that receive full review at a Study Section meeting. Applications designated NC are not discussed at the meeting and, therefore, do not include such a summary.

Supplement   See: Application for Supplement.

TAS   Technology and Applied Sciences Review Section (One of 6 Review Sections in the NIH/DRG Referral and Review Branch).

TDD   Telecommunication device for the deaf. The initials *TDD* sometimes precede phone numbers in NIH, NSF, and other funding agency publications, indicating that the device is available on the telephone with that number.

Topic sentence   The first and introductory sentence of a paragraph. Topic sentences are especially important in the type of expository writing used in grant proposals. The topic sentence tells the reader what type of information is to be expected in that paragraph. Well-written, informative topic sentences help busy readers who must rapidly scan long documents to decide which paragraphs they can skip over. When long paragraphs are broken into two or more paragraphs to avoid presenting the reader with a large block of uninterrupted print, the continuation paragraphs may not need topic sentences.

Total cost   The sum of the direct and indirect costs of a project.

TOXNET   NLM Toxicology Data Network.

Track record   The reputation and quality of work of the applicant and her/his team.

Triage   A procedure whereby grant applications, deemed by reviewers to be Noncompetitive (NC) under current funding levels, are *not* discussed at Study Section meetings. NIH already uses triage for specific types of proposals, for example, RFAs. In February

1994 the NIH Division of Research Grants (DRG) began a study of the efficacy of triage for investigator-initiated applications (R01 and R29) reviewed by DRG Study Sections. Triage is intended to streamline the peer review process and decrease the grant review workload for reviewers, SRAs, and members of Advisory Councils. Triage was adopted DRG-wide in September 1994.

TVER   Tumor Virus Epidemiology Repository (DCE/NCI).

U01   Research *Project* Cooperative Agreement (NIH).

U19   Research *Program* Cooperative Agreement (NIH).

U43/U44   *SBIR* Cooperative Agreements for Phases I and II, respectively.

UMI   University Microfilms International.

Unaffiliated individual   An individual who is not officially connected with an institution as an employee, staff member, or faculty member. Many funding agencies do not give funds to unaffiliated individuals, but some do. The National Science Foundation (NSF) is one example of the latter.

Unsolicited proposal   A grant application or proposal that is submitted to an agency at the discretion of the PI but is not in response to a particular RFA or RFP.

USAID   United States Agency for International Development. Administers U.S. foreign assistance programs in the developing countries of the world, including the former Soviet Union. The agency interests include energy, the environment, nutrition, health care, agriculture, and natural resources.

Voting categories   "Not Recommended for Further Consideration" (NRFC = "Nerfed") and "Deferred for Additional Information" are the 2 official voting categories at NIH Study Section meetings in 1994. Scoring, that is, assigning a Scientific Merit Rating, is the action taken by the reviewers on applications that are not relegated to one of the 2 voting categories, but scoring an application is not considered by NIH to be an official voting category. (The voting categories "Approved" and "Disapproved" were discontinued at the end of 1991.) The voting category NRFC was discontinued in 1994 for use on R01 and R29 applications, and replaced by the designation "Noncompetitive" (NC). NRFC continues to be used for review of other types of NIH grant applications and may, in the future, be re-introduced for review of R01 and R29 applications, probably in conjunction with "NC." See Triage and Noncompetitive.

WAIS Server   Wide Area Information Service Server. A network of a large number of computers running software that gives access to information by keywords. The Server is accessible from personal computers (PCs and Macs). Some of the same computers may be in both the WAIS and Gopher Server networks. See also: Gopher Server.

WAN(s)   Wide Area Network(s). See Network.

WHO   World Health Organization

Workload   See: Reviewer's workload.

Index